THE OCEANIC LANGUAGES

THE OCEANIC LANGUAGES

THEIR GRAMMATICAL STRUCTURE, VOCABULARY, AND ORIGIN

BY

D. MACDONALD, D. D.

OF THE NEW HEBRIDES MISSION,
MEMBER OF THE SOCIETE D' ETHNOGRAPHIE, PARIS

GYAN

Published by

Gyan Publishing House
5, Ansari Road
Daryaganj, New Delhi-110002
Phone: 011-47034999, 9811692060
E-mail: books@gyanbooks.com

Distribution Network
gyanbooks.com
India, USA, Canada, UK, Australia, France

ISBN : 978-81-212-4483-1 (PB)
First Published, 1907

2nd Impression 2020

Printed at: Gyan Press, Delhi.

The Oceanic Languages
Author: D. Macdonald, D. D.

THE OCEANIC LANGUAGES

THEIR GRAMMATICAL STRUCTURE, VOCABULARY, AND ORIGIN

BY D. MACDONALD, D.D.

OF THE NEW HEBRIDES MISSION.
MEMBER OF THE SOCIÉTÉ D'ETHNOGRAPHIE, PARIS.

HENRY FROWDE
LONDON, EDINBURGH, GLASGOW, NEW YORK
AND TORONTO
1907

PREFACE

THIS work contains a Grammar and complete Dictionary of the language of Efate, New Hebrides, which is a typical specimen of the Oceanic languages which are spoken by fifty millions, or one-thirtieth, of the human race in islands of the Indian and Pacific Oceans, extending over two hundred degrees of longitude.

It contains also a Comparative Grammar, and, to a sufficient extent, a Comparative Vocabulary of these languages, together with the evidence of their Arabian origin; thus adding these fifty millions to those previously known as Semitic speakers, as, one hundred years ago, the many millions (now 219,725,509) in India were, by similar evidence, added to those previously known as Aryan (European) speakers.

It is a unique unveiling of the linguistic, mental, religious and moral life, social organization, and pre-historic antecedents of the existing Oceanic 'savages', or 'primitive' man.

To those engaged in the study of man, Anthropologists and Ethnologists, more especially to students of Linguistic science, Orientalists, and Semitic scholars, the work should prove a welcome, and even, it may be said, an indispensable aid. To all living and working among these fifty millions of people, missionaries, Government officials, and commercial men, it should be of practical use as helping to that thorough knowledge of the speech and character of the natives which means the power of dealing sympathetically and wisely with them to the advantage of all concerned. This last consideration, the author specially commends to the various Governments that now have possessions, and so have taken up 'the white man's burden' in Oceania—France, Germany, Holland, United States of America, as well as our own United Kingdom and her great self-governing Dependencies in Australasia.

The work should be very valuable among other things as a basis for further investigations all over the Oceanic World.

D. MACDONALD.

LONDON,
Oct. 31, 1907.

CONTENTS

INTRODUCTION

How the present writer was led to take up and prosecute for the last thirty-five years the studies of which the following work is the result may be briefly stated. Sent from Melbourne as a missionary of the Presbyterian Church of Victoria to the New Hebrides, and settled at Havannah Harbour, Efate, in the year 1872, it became his duty to study and acquire the speech of the natives, and to get a thorough knowledge of their mental life, religion and social organization. As these people, like the other New Hebrideans, were cannibal savages, without a written language, and inclined to be unfriendly, this was found to be no easy task. When, in the first years, they were suspicious and would give no help, or decreed a boycott as they sometimes did, there was still one resource open. One could study other Island languages reduced to writing by previous missionaries, and known to be of the same stock, as, e. g. the Aneityumese or Fijian or other Melanesian dialect; the Polynesian, as the Samoan, Maori, and Hawaiian; and going still further afield, the Malayan, and the Malagasy: and it was found that all these threw great light upon the Efatese, and that the Efatese, once, after long years, acquired so that one could think in it, and speak and write it as if it were one's native tongue, threw great light upon them. But still there was something wanting for a complete and satisfactory knowledge. These far-extended Oceanic languages, sprung from the abysm of prehistoric time, were manifestly and admittedly of one stock or origin. What then was that origin? The answer to this question is included in the following pages from which may be seen how great a light it throws upon the grammar and structure, and vocabulary of the Efatese, and of each and all of the other Oceanic languages.

In the sketch-map of the Indian and Pacific Oceans the red tint is not intended to show an exact boundary in Formosa, nor to indicate any view as to the language of the Maldives: and the white spot on the east end of New Guinea is merely to indicate that in that quarter there is apparently some non-Oceanic linguistic element. In the map of the New Hebrides the dotted line is not an exact boundary in Epi. It should be observed that the New Hebrideans are all Melanesian speakers with the exception of a few people on the east of Mai, and those of the villages of Meli and Fila, and of the islets of Futuna and Aniwa, who are Polynesian speakers. All the Efatese speakers have now embraced Christianity. The Efatese New Testament was printed in Melbourne by the British and Foreign Bible Society in 1889, and the Nguna-Efate Old Testament is now being printed by the same great society in London. Other translations of the whole or of part of the Scriptures have been printed in twenty-six different languages or dialects from Aneityum to Santo. Efate is to be the seat of government under the new Anglo-French Convention respecting the New Hebrides. Commercially and linguistically as well as geographically (see the map), it is the central island of the group, and no better standpoint could be chosen from which to study the languages in the other islands that extend from it southwards and northwards. And perhaps no better could be chosen from which to make such a study of the languages of the whole Oceanic family—Melanesian, Polynesian, Malayan, and Malagasy—

than that of which the result is set forth as briefly as possible in the following pages.

The Efatese, with the other New Hebrideans, are a truly primitive people, typical cannibal savages. These people, in accordance with the geographical position of the group, at the end of a long chain of islands extending from the Malay Archipelago, have for ages been completely isolated, cut off from the civilized world, and thus have lived out their linguistic, religious, and social life. The Polynesians, whose dialects are less numerous and differentiated, are more recent comers into the Pacific than the Melanesians. The Malayans and Malagasy, especially the former, have always been more in touch with the civilized world. Of the considerable number of Sanskrit words introduced into the Malayan, probably about the beginning of the Christian era, not a trace is to be found in the Efatese. And of the Mongol element of blood in Malaysia, not a trace is discoverable among the Efatese people. If it be asked in what millennium B. C. the forefathers of the Oceanic-speaking race passed from the Semitic area (see the map) into and settled in the Oceanic world, the question must remain unanswered till Orientalists who are experts in the history of the development of the Semitic race within that area can give the necessary information. Meantime two facts can be given from the Oceanic side which may help towards the settlement of the question. The one is that at the time of that migration the Semitic languages had already attained to their fullest peculiar inflectional development: see, for instance, in Chap. III. *d*, and in the Dictionary and Index, the words **mataku**, to fear; **tili**, or **tuli**, to tell; and **toko**, to sit, abide, in Efate (Melanesian), Samoan (Polynesian), Malay, and Malagasy. This is certain, though the Semitic speech of these migrants may even then already have passed through a subsequent development towards becoming a vulgar dialect or patois. The other is that at the time that oversea migration took place, southwards and eastwards, to Madagascar and Malaysia, the Semites were sufficiently advanced to have ocean-going commerce and vessels capable of making long sea voyages. The names by which those early voyagers called, for instance, their vessels, masts, and oars, and by which their descendants, the Efatese (Mel.), Tahitians (Po.), Malays, and Malagasy, still call them, are the names by which they were first called in Arabia and by which they are called there to this day: see the Dictionary under the words **rarua**, **seme**, **tere**, **uose**, and **balu-sa**, and the Index for these words. These ancient navigators also had all the same name for 'sail', for which see **lai**, Dictionary and Index.

Probably among primitive peoples no better standpoint could be chosen than Efate from which to make a study of the religion and social organization of existing savages. In connexion with what here follows may be consulted two papers by the present writer read before the anthropological section of the Australasian Association for the Advancement of Science, the one (consisting of answers to a list of questions) entitled 'Efate, New Hebrides', at the Hobart Session, 1892, the other 'The Mythology of the Efatese', at the Sydney Session, 1898. The Efatese cannibal savages were a very religious people. Their deities were spirits, some of unknown origin as **uota**,[1] who was known and worshipped by all the Efatese, and **li raḅa** (goddess of famine), worshipped and known only by some of them. All the deities of this kind were represented by stones or rocks—as in early Arabia—which we may call their idols, and known by the general names **fatutabu** and **atatabu**. The spirits whose origin was known were the

[1] See this word in other connexions on pp. xi, xiii, and see the Dictionary and Index.

spirits of their ancestors, or deceased men, and properly called **atamate**. See also **atua** and **suḅe**. Names of acts of worship are **fira, taro-s**, to pray; **ta bituatua**, to speak (one's wishes) while making an offering; **taumafa**, to invoke while making an offering or sacrifice; **bisa taumafa**, to vow to make an offering or sacrifice; **bali**, to fast: see also **naleouan, belaki, tamate, mala** (Tahiti **marae**). The religious authority in every community was called **natamole tabu**: see **tabu** (English *taboo*), prohibited, then sacred, consecrated, holy. He was as the prophet or seer or holy man of early Arabia. See also **arifon**, and **koro, kita, lume**. A 'familiar spirit' was in some places called **tobu**. There were evil spirits greatly feared; see, e.g. **libo, subua, suru-oli**. For the names of the spirits who examine every soul immediately after death at the entrance of Hades, and inflict dreadful punishment on those found wanting, see **seritau, maseasi, faus**, and especially **māki** (for the same in Arabia). For the names of Hades or the Under-world, see **maġaḅoaḅoa** and the six words following it, and **bokas, ebua, buariri, liboki, rales**, and **tūk**. See all the preceding and following words in thick type in both Dictionary and Index.

As to social organization the Efatese people lived in small communities called **launa**, each occupying a certain territory or district. Each **launa** was independent, and comprised (n)**afiti**, slaves; (n)**atatoko**, native-born freemen; (**na**)**manaki**, sojourners (admitted from other **launa**); and the civil and religious heads, (**na**)**uota**, and **natamole tabu**. Underlying this was a certain organization according to which every one of the people of every **launa**, without exception, belonged by birth to one or other of certain kins. Such kins are found among savages elsewhere, and called by Mr. Andrew Lang 'totem kins'.[1] In Efate these

[1] *Social Origins*, by Andrew Lang, and *Primal Law*, by J. J. Atkinson, 1903.

kins are (1) by descent in the female line, that is, each person born belongs to the kin of the mother, and the whole kin is necessarily descended from one original mother, and comprised at first only her and the children she had borne; and (2) with exogamy,[1] that is, intermarriage between males and females of the same kin is prohibited as incestuous. Each kin has a totem name, the name of some plant or animal: thus in Efate we have, for example, the **naui** (yam) kin, the **naniu** (coco-nut) kin, the **namkatu** (a kind of yam) kin, the **uit** (a certain fish) kin, the **karau** (a shellfish) kin. The word for kin is **felak** (also **kainaġa**, and **mitarau**); thus **nafelak naui**, the yam kin, and so with all the other kins. Now the word **felak**[2] (see **ḅala**) points back to the original mother (**ḅila**) of the kin consisting at first of her and her children; **kainaġa** to the time when the kin consisted of her and her children all living and *eating* together; and **mitarau** to the fact that the kin or kindred *branched* out from one source. As marriage was at first rightly prohibited as incestuous between the direct male and female children of the original mother, so, and this is strange to us, the prohibition has remained binding for the same reason ever since upon all males and females however remotely descended from her *in the female line.* Thus we have the totem kin with descent in the female line and exogamy. As to how these kins originally got their totem names, the personal name of the original mother, e.g. of the **naui** kin, most probably was **li naui**, and so with all the other kins. Among the Efatese there was nothing religious about these totem names, or the plants and animals denoted by them: and this is in accordance

[1] *Social Origins*, &c., p. 159, &c.

[2] As in Early Arabia; see *Kinship and Marriage in Early Arabia*, by W. Robertson Smith, new ed., 1903, pp. 37 sqq., 175.

with the statement of Mr. Andrew Lang that 'totems [in other parts of the world] probably in origin had nothing really religious about them'.[1]

Along with and underlying the totem kin, which excluded the husband and father, was the Family which included him as its head. As marriage was by purchase of the wife, she called her husband **uota**,[2] lord, **ana uota**, her lord. If a man purchased additional wives, they were called **ruḅa**, and he was of course the **uota**, lord and owner of every one of them. But for the most part monogamy prevailed among the Efatese, the family consisting of husband and wife, or father and mother, with their children. This among the Efatese savages was the normal family, one man and one woman united in marriage, with their children. Polygamy, though not prohibited, was abnormal, and therefore one great, perhaps the greatest, cause of the incessant feuds and bloodshed among these savages. In the normal family, marriage between certain members of it who were necessarily of different totem kins—and therefore inter-marriageable by the totem kin rule—was, and has ever continued, prohibited as incestuous; and this idea of incest prohibited by religious sanction, first in the family and then also in the totem kin, cannot be otherwise accounted for than as having existed from the beginning owing to the constitution of man as distinct from that of not-man, or brute. For the names or terms of family relationship see **uota**, **ġuruni**; **ab'** or **afa**, or **tema**, **tama**; **ḅile**, or **ḅila**, **raita**, **ere**, **susu**; **natu**, **nati**, **nani**, **nai** (see **ani**); **tai**, **ḅalu**, **kore**, or **ġore**; **atena**, **tobu**; **àlo**, maternal uncle; **ṁo**, **buruma**; **taku**, **tauien**, or **tawien**, and **tua**,

[1] Op. cit., p. 136.

[2] For this same word so used in ancient Arabia, see Robertson Smith, op. cit., pp. 92 sq.

&c. The word m̄o denotes father-in-law, mother-in-law, and son-in-law. For the words which denote how a mother-in-law avoided and concealed herself from her son-in-law, see **lako, ġuku**: when she happened to find herself where he could see her, she crouched, covering her face and bosom until she got beyond the reach of his vision. This could not have been due to the totem kin, and must have been due to the normal, or primitive family: for by the totem kin rule mother-in-law and son-in-law were inter-marriageable as being necessarily of different totem kins; and the rule that such a union was deemed so incestuous as to be impossible must therefore have arisen, not with the totem-kin, but prior to it, in the normal or primitive family.

First, then, there was the normal or primitive family. After that arose polygamy, and the wife and mother's totem kin—a kind of guild from which the husband and father was excluded, but by which he neither was nor could be excluded from his natural kin or blood relationship with his children. This is contrary to Mr. McLennan's primitive promiscuity hypothesis,[1] which Professor Robertson Smith in his work, above cited, has laboured, with much learning, but with conspicuous unsuccess, to apply in the Semitic field.

In the Efatese verbs in the following work, except in the Index, the formative ending **t** is preceded by a hyphen, thus, e.g. p. 218, **luku-ti**, and **luku-taki**, and in every such case the final **i** of the former and **ki** of the latter are the transitive particles, and the words might have been written **luku-t i, luku-ta ki**; see Chap. IV, and for the phonetic variations of the -t Chap. II. The **na** after substantives, as,

[1] For one criticism of which see *The Primitive Family in its Origin and Development*, by C. N. Starcke, 2nd ed., 1896. International Scientific Series.

e. g. **aru na**, p. 110, is the nominal suffix (genitive) pronoun third person; and the same **na** (or **a**, or **n**, or **nia**, or **sa**) after verbs, e. g. **mesau na**, p. 241, **banako sa**, **banak ia**, **bunako n**, p. 129, is the verbal suffix (acc.) pronoun third person: see Chap. V.

This introduction must not be concluded without expressing thanks to the Government of the Commonwealth of Australia for defraying the expense of the publication of the present work.

NOTE.—On p. 9, h′(hw) should be ḳ′(ḳw); and omit **balo-ni** from third line from foot of p. 18.

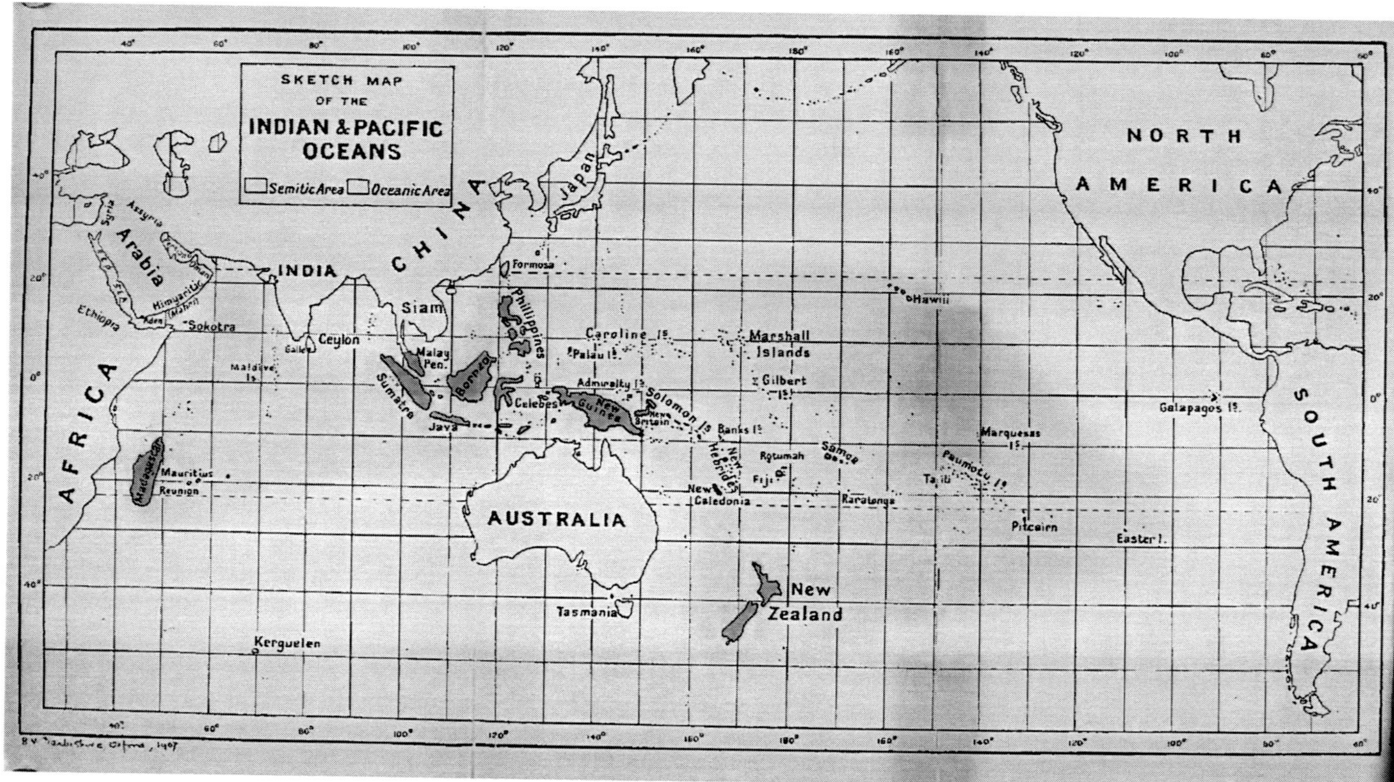
SKETCH MAP
OF THE
INDIAN & PACIFIC
OCEANS
Semitic Area
Oceanic Area
AFRICA
Arabia
Syria
Assyria
Ethiopia
Aden
Sokotra
Himyaritic
INDIA
Ceylon
Galle
Maldive Is.
CHINA
Siam
Malay Pen.
Sumatra
Java
Borneo
Celebes
Philippines
Formosa
Japan
Caroline Is.
Palau Is.
Marshall Islands
Gilbert Is.
Admiralty Is.
New Guinea
New Britain
Solomon Is.
Banks Is.
New Hebrides
New Caledonia
Rotumah
Fiji
Samoa
Raratonga
Tahiti
Paumotu Is.
Marquesas Is.
Pitcairn
Easter I.
Hawaii
Galapagos Is.
AUSTRALIA
Tasmania
New Zealand
Madagascar
Mauritius
Reunion
Kerguelen
NORTH AMERICA
SOUTH AMERICA

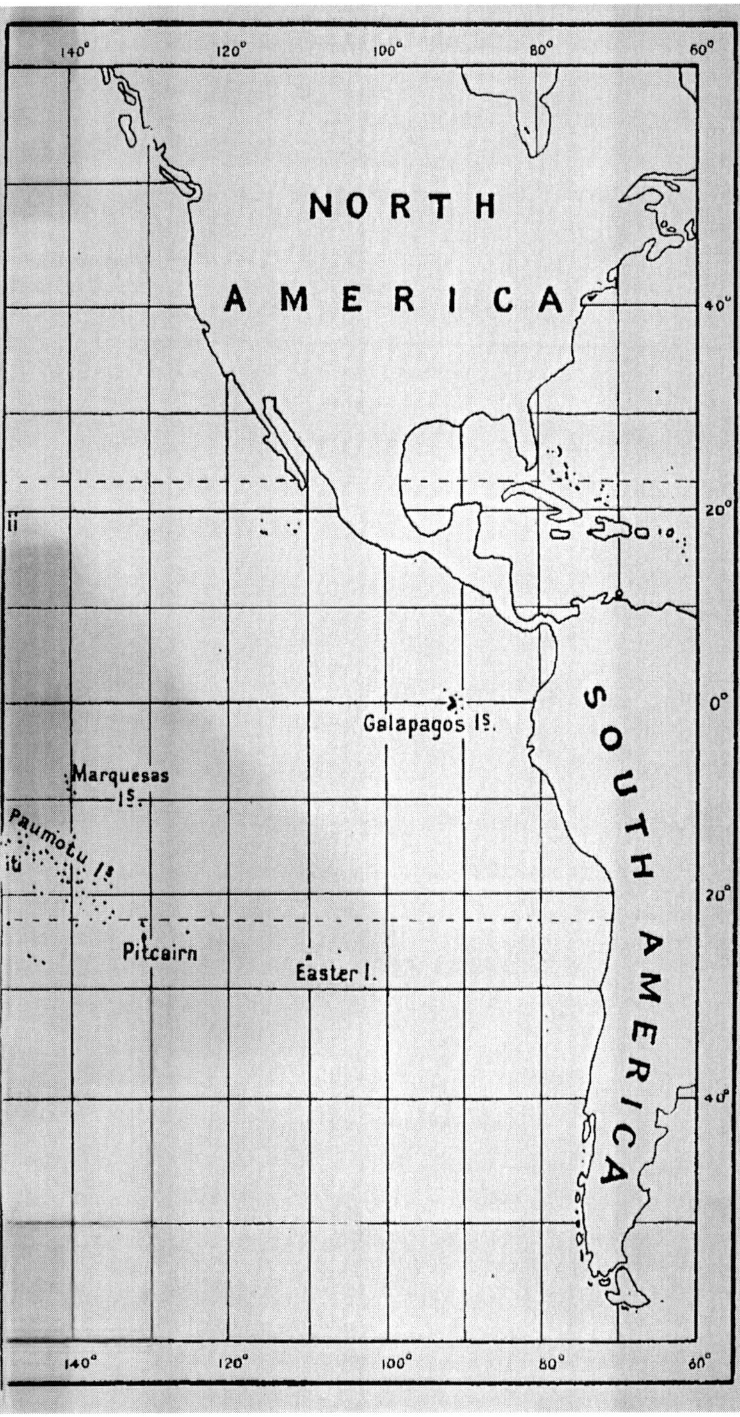

140°
120°
100°
80°
60°
NORTH
AMERICA
40°
20°
0°
Galapagos Is.
Marquesas Is.
Paumotu Is
Pitcairn
Easter I.
SOUTH AMERICA
20°
40°
140°
120°
100°
80°
60°

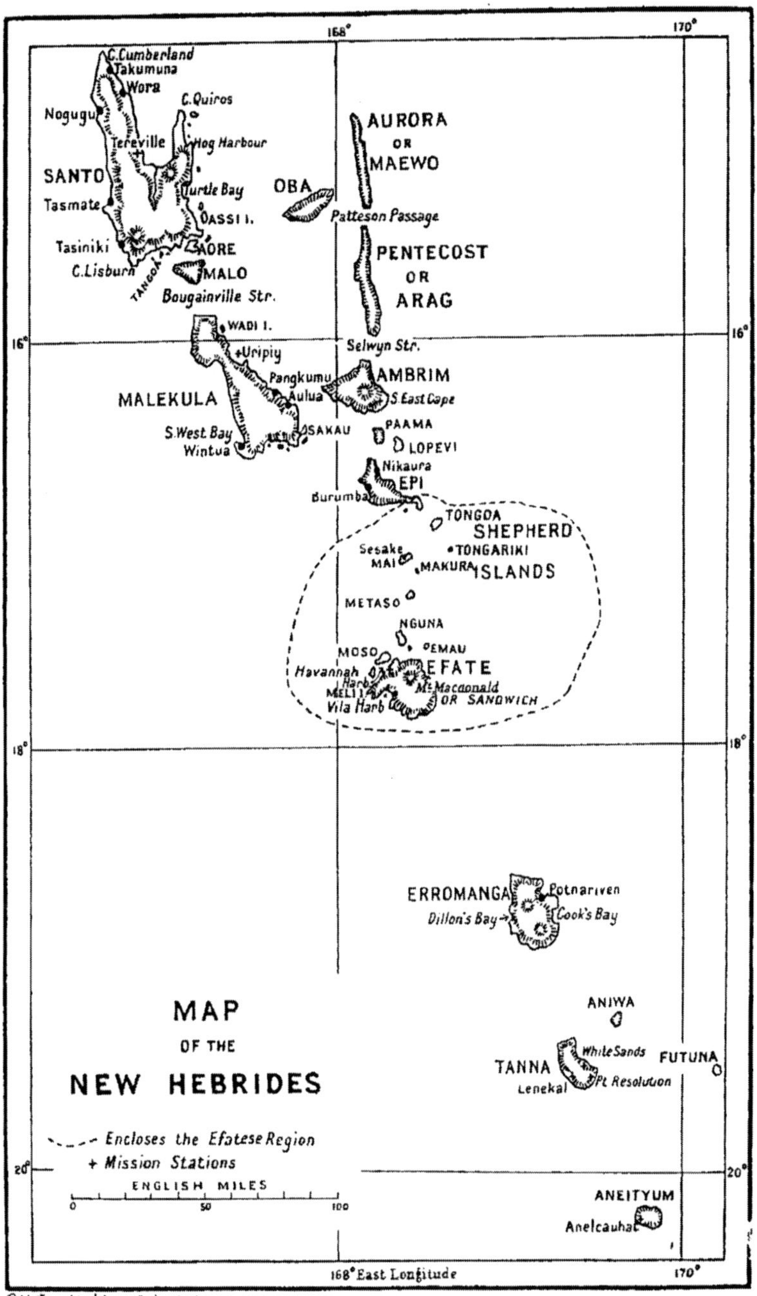

B.V. Darbishire, Oxford, 1907.

OCEANIC LANGUAGES

CHAPTER I

THE PROBLEM

DURING the past century linguistic science has endeavoured to solve the problem of the Asiatic (whether Indo-European, Turanian, or Semitic) relationship of the Oceanic family of languages. Some may question whether our knowledge of the Oceanic languages is as yet sufficiently advanced to permit of the final solution of the problem as to their continental relationship, as it certainly was not in the days of the attempted solutions of it by Bopp[1], in the year 1841, and by Max Müller[2] in the year 1854. If Bopp were living now it is probable that, with our present knowledge of the Oceanic, he would heartily agree with the verdict of linguistic science which has been given against his theory of the relationship of the Malayo-Polynesian languages through the Sanskrit to the Indo-European; and the same may be said of Max Müller and his theory of their relationship through the Thai of Siam to the Turanian. However that may be, the verdict of linguistic science has been decisively given against both of these theories. In the days when they were put forth our knowledge of the Oceanic, then called the Malayo-Polynesian, was too limited. Since then great advances have been made. The multitudinous languages of the Western Pacific—the Melanesian at that time little known, and erroneously supposed to be radically diverse from each other, and from the 'Malayo-Polynesian'—are now well known, and have proved to be closely inter-related, and, while

[1] *Über die Verwandtschaft der Malayisch-Polynesischen Sprachen mit den Indisch-Europäischen*, von Franz Bopp, Berlin, 1841.

[2] In Bunsen's *Christianity and Mankind*.

not derived from, yet radically connected with, the Malayan and the Polynesian, as Gabelentz[1] pointed out as far back as the year 1860. These three groups of languages and dialects—the Malayan, the Polynesian, and the Melanesian—naming them in the order in which they have successively become known, are, as Friedrich Müller has shown,[2] members or branches of the Oceanic, which is as perfectly well defined a family of languages as is the Semitic or the Indo-European. The Oceanic is, as its name indicates, insular. Its habitat, which we may call Oceania, stretches from Madagascar, off the east coast of Africa, across the Indian Ocean to the Malay Archipelago, and on through the Pacific Ocean to Easter Island. On the north it has invaded from the island world, and settled upon only the south-eastern extremity of the Asiatic Continent, hence called the Malay Peninsula. On the south it has not reached the Australian Continent, though closely approaching it in New Guinea. The Islanders who speak Oceanic number about fifty millions, or one-thirtieth of the human race.

To say that the Oceanic languages are a perfectly well-defined family, is to say that they are all sprung from one mother-tongue—the Oceanic mother-tongue; and to establish the Asiatic relationship of the Oceanic is to establish that that mother-tongue was originally carried by its speakers from the Asiatic Continent into the Island world. The question as to whether the Asiatic relationship of the Oceanic can be established is a purely linguistic question, which can only be answered from a due investigation of the available linguistic data. Three great Continents, Asia, Africa, and America, or, counting Australia, four, border on the Island world. It may be held as certain that the relationship of the Oceanic, whatever

[1] H. C. von der Gabelentz, *Die Melanesischen Sprachen nach ihrem grammatischen Bau und ihrer Verwandtschaft unter sich und mit den Malaiisch-Polynesischen Sprachen*, Vol. I, Leipzig, 1861, Vol. II, 1873. Compare the more recent work of the Rev. Dr. Codrington on *The Melanesian Languages*.

[2] Friedrich Müller, *Reise der Fregatte Novara*, Wien, 1867: *Grundriss der Sprachwissenschaft*, Wien, 1882, and following years.

it is, is not African, American, or Australian. Madagascar is near the African coast, but the Malagasy, which belongs to the Malayan or Tagalan branch of the Oceanic, is not related to the African languages. Easter Island approaches nearest, though not very near, to America; but its language, which belongs to the Polynesian branch, is not related to the American languages. And the Melanesian branch, which approaches Australia, is not related to the Australian languages. The pre-historic geological history of the globe, whether as known or merely conjectured, throws no light on the problem of the relationship of the Oceanic. Were it proved, for example, than tens, or hundreds of thousands, or millions of years ago there had been a great continent in Oceania, of which the existing islands are the unsubmerged peaks, or were it proved that such had never been, in either case the Oceanic problem inviting the solution of linguistic science all through the nineteenth century, and now at the beginning of the twentieth still inviting it, would remain exactly the same, wholly unaffected by that proof. Nor would that proof throw any light on what we may call the apparent discrepancy of race and language in Oceania. It would still remain to be accounted for exactly as before. The Oceanic speakers, that is the Oceanic people or race, are a mixed race, not pure white, not pure black, not pure yellow, but, as De Quatrefages has observed,[1] a mixture of all three. Nevertheless, the Oceanic speakers, however the Caucasian, the Negro, or the Mongol physique may be more in evidence in any particular part, constitute mentally, socially, and religiously, as well as linguistically, one great, though much diversified, race or people, just as the languages, though multitudinously diversified, constitute one great family. Though the cases are not exactly parallel, yet in North America at the present time we see Caucasian, Negro, and Mongol all speaking the same language—English, and we know that that language was not originally a Negro, or a Mongol, but an Indo-European tongue. If we could conceive

[1] A. De Quatrefages, *The Human Species*, 3rd Ed., London, 1883.

of some future time at which every other means of knowing this had been swept away, the Indo-European speakers of North America having been fused into one mixed diversified race, linguistic science alone would still be able to prove it. Be that as it may, other means than those of linguistic science do not exist by which to ascertain conclusively the relationship of the Oceanic mother-tongue.

As a matter of fact three parts of the Asiatic Continent have been fixed upon as being, the one or the other of them, the starting-point from which the Oceanic race immigrated into the Island world, over which they gradually spread—the south-eastern or Indo-Chinese Peninsula, the south-central or Indian Peninsula, and the south-western or Arabian Peninsula. If we were to confine ourselves, apart from linguistic science, to the question of the possibility of the race having spread over the whole Oceanic world from any one of these points, we might choose one or other of these three, but there would be no certain proof of the correctness of our choice. The fact that the Negro element in the Oceanic race is older than the Mongol—a fact indicated by its greater predominance in the extremities of Oceania, as well as in the interior and more inaccessible parts of the larger islands—is against the Indo-Chinese Peninsula as the starting-point of the race. In like manner the indications are that the race did not come from the Indian Peninsula into Oceania, but that after it was there Indian civilization came upon it in comparatively recent times, or about the beginning of the Christian era, confining itself mainly, if not wholly, to Java and neighbourhood, where its architectural and other relics still remain. The Indian modifications of the Oceanic alphabetic characters in the Malay Archipelago are such relics. Fundamentally these characters are not Indian, but Phoenician, altogether independently of the Indian, and of a more ancient type of Phoenician than the Indian.[1] No modern alphabets preserve the ancient Phoenician type so markedly as these Oceanic alphabets, and they are therefore

[1] See *Oceania: Linguistic and Anthropological*, London, 1889.

to be regarded as of the highest antiquity. This favours as the starting-point of the Oceanic race the south-western peninsula of Asia, which was, according to Herodotus, the original home of the Phoenicians, from whence they colonized the Tyrian-Sidonian coast of the Mediterranean. And with this the following considerations all agree. From whatever point the Oceanic race migrated into the Island world, they did so in sea-going vessels, and we may reasonably infer that before doing so they were habitually in possession of such vessels, or were a sea-going, commercial people, as for the most part they are to-day. Now in the ancient world, long before the rise of Greece or Rome, it was in the waters of the southern seas alone that ocean-going commerce was begun and carried on for ages by the human race, and that not by the people of the Indian or the Indo-Chinese, but by those of the Arabian Peninsula. It was here that the commercial fleets of Solomon, manned by Phoenicians, made the first long sea-going voyages recorded by history, whether they went, as some think, to the east coast of Africa, or, as others hold with more probability, to India, or as Josephus, than whom there is no weightier historical authority on the subject, says, to the Malay Peninsula. What the Phoenicians of Tyre and Sidon were later on in the Mediterranean, that their ancestors and cousins were then and had been in earlier times in the southern seas of the Island world.[1] In the Arabian Peninsula running out into those seas, and contiguous to Africa, there was, in ancient times, a great commercial empire. Then and to this day in the existing descendants of that long since fallen empire,[2] which colonized the neighbouring Abyssinia, there is, and we may reasonably infer there always was from the earliest times, a large negro element of blood. If we suppose that the Oceanic race originally, in ancient times, migrated from that

[1] See Sir J. Emerson Tennent's *Ceylon*, 5th Ed., London, 1860, Vol. I, Part V, Chap. II, pp. 553-4, &c.

[2] On this 'vieux monde disparu', see Renan, *Histoire des Langues Sémitiques*.

peninsular empire or from among that people, along the east coast of Africa to Madagascar, and along the south coast of Asia to the Malay Archipelago, this fully accounts for the negro element of blood in the race, as we now find it, manifestly an older element in it than the Indian or the Mongol. And as, when modern history lifts the veil from Malaysia, we find the existing or Mohammedan civilization of the Arabian peninsula there, newly introduced and predominating, so there is reason to think that that was only a later wave of immigration and influence from the mother-land of the Oceanic race.

But plausible as all this is it is not till we take into account the linguistic data that we get upon the solid ground of certainty. And first of all it is to be observed that though there was a negro element of blood in the race, due to intermixture, the race itself, as its language proves, was not negro. What that race was can only be determined from its language, and what that mother-language was is to be learned from an examination of its descendants and representatives, the spoken Oceanic languages and dialects of the present day. If the race came from the Arabian Peninsula, the Semitic motherland, sprung from the people of the commercial empire that existed there, then their language was Semitic. For the Phoenicians, the people of that ancient South Arabian empire and of their Abyssinian colony, and their descendants now in Abyssinia and Arabia, all are Semitic speakers. If the race came from the Indian Peninsula one might suppose with Bopp that the language was Indo-European; if from the Indo-Chinese Peninsula, with Max Müller that it was Scythian or Turanian. The problem thus, as is clear, can only be solved linguistically. And the praiseworthy efforts of Bopp and Müller to solve it are valuable if only as having led to the certainty that the Oceanic mother-tongue was neither Indo-European nor Turanian. Their attempts failed because made on insufficient data, and their methods were for the same reason inadequate. One great branch of the Oceanic, the Melanesian, with all the light it throws upon the subject, was to them unknown. They trusted mainly if not wholly on the comparison of words, chiefly the pronouns and numerals, in which there is always great liability to error, and which apart from comparison of grammar and structure can never be conclusive. As to the pronouns, for instance, Bopp, and Max Müller following him, chose to regard the Malay *Kita, Kami,* we, and *Kamu,* ye, as composed of an article *ki,* or *ka,* and the pronouns *ta, mi, mu.* This enabled Bopp to compare the latter with the Indo-European pronouns, and Max Müller, it should be added, to compare them with equal probability or improbability with the Turanian; and by this method the Oceanic pronouns might just as well be compared with any others whatsoever. The fact is, as the Melanesian clearly shows, that this *ki,* or *ka,* is not an article at all, and that this comparison of Bopp, and also that of Müller, founded on the notion that it is, is illegitimate and futile. And again, as to the Malay numerals, *dalapan,* 8, and *salapan, sambilan,* or *sambalan,* 9, Bopp, and Max Müller following him, chose to regard them as compound words, and the prefixed *da* as the numeral 2, and *sa,* 1, *dalapan,* thus signifying 'two taken (from ten)', and *sambilan* 'one taken (from ten)', or as Müller phrases it 'ten minus two', and 'ten minus one'. In this way Bopp for his part makes these words, though not Indo-European numerals, yet to fall in with his Indo-European theory, while Müller, on the other hand, finds in them, while admitting that the Oceanic numerals are not those of the Thai of Siam, a feature 'peculiarly Turanian'. But unfortunately for both contentions these are not compound words at all, but simple primitive numeral words with the first syllable reduplicated in the well-known Oceanic manner: thus *dalapan* is analogous to the Tagalan *dalaua,* 2, found in other dialects as *dalua, darua,* &c., the common unreduplicated form of the word being *rua,* or *lua*; and *sa* of *salapan,* 9, by transposition *sambilan,* is similarly accounted for.

NOTE

In the following pages certain works are referred to thus:—

C.G.S.L. *Comparative Grammar of the Semitic Languages.* By W. Wright, LL.D., Professor of Arabic, University of Cambridge, 1890.

Von Maltzan. For the studies on the Mahri dialect of South Arabia by this writer, see *Z.D.M.G.*, xxv, xxvii.

M.L. *The Melanesian Languages.* By the Rev. R. H. Codrington, D.D. Oxford, at the Clarendon Press, 1885.

Ray's List of New Hebrides Words. (For this see *Journal of the Royal Society of N. S. Wales*, 1893.) By Sidney H. Ray, London. This paper is valuable and contains (1) Introduction, (2) Classified list of Languages, (3) Comparative Vocabulary, and (4) Notes on the Vocabulary.

S.S.S. *South Sea Languages. A series of Studies on the Languages of the New Hebrides and other South Sea Islands*, Vol. II. Tangoan-Santo, Malo, Malekula, Epi (Baki and Bierian), Tanna, and Futuna, Melbourne, 1891. Vol. I. *Three New Hebrides Languages*: Efate, Eromanga, Santo. Melbourne, 1889. These two works edited by the present writer, were printed at the expense of the Trustees of the Public Library, Museums, and National Gallery of Victoria. They are sometimes referred to as Vols. I and II of this series, the present volume being the third and completing one.

The abbreviated titles of other works referred to, do not require any explanation, except *L.*, which stands for Latham's *Comparative Philology*, and *W.*, which stands for Wallace's *Malay Archipelago*, list of words at end.

CHAPTER II

PHONOLOGY

1. The twenty-two letters of the Semitic alphabet, numbered as in Syriac and Hebrew, are represented thus :—

	(*a*)	(*b*)	(*c*)
1.	’, a soft, guttural breathing		
2.	**b**, **b** and **v**		
3.	**g**, **g** and **gh**		**g′** (**gw**)
4.	**d**, **d** and **dh** (as *th* in ‘this’)	**ḍ**	
5.	**h**		**h′** (**hw**)
6.	**w**, **v** and **w**		
7.	**z**		
8.	**ḥ**, a stronger **h**	**ḥ′**	**ḥ″** (**ḥw**)
9.	**ṭ**, a palatal **t**	**ṭ′**	
10.	**y**		
11.	**k**, **k** and as 8		**k′** (**kw**)
12.	**l**		
13.	**m**		
14.	**n**		
15.	**s**		
16.	‘, related to ’ and **ḥ**, **r** grasséyé, **gh**, **ng** (which we represent by **ġ**)	‘‘	
17.	**p**, **p** and **f**		
18.	**ṣ**, **ts**	**ṣ′**	
19.	**ḳ**, a throat *k*, related to ’		
20.	**r**		
21.	**s′** (originally *sh*), **sh**, and **s**		
22.	**t**, **th** and **t**	**t′**	

To the original twenty-two letters, Arabic has added the six modified letters of column (*b*); Ethiopic the four of column (*c*).

2. The letters **b, g, d, k, p, t** had each two sounds, as in Heb. and Arm., the unaspirated as in English, and the aspirated **v** (**bh**), **gh**, **dh**, **kh** (like **ḥ**), **f** (**ph**), and **th**. These letters when aspirated readily passed into **h** and disappeared.[1] In Assy. **m** had the sounds of **m** and **v** (aspirated **b**), and when pronounced **v** readily disappeared: on the other hand, **w** (**v**) might be pronounced **m**. In Arb. **ḍ**, **ṭ′**, **t′**, **ṣ′** are aspirated **d**, **ṭ**, **t**, **ṣ**.

3. In all the Semitic dialects the weak or vowel letters **'**, **h**, **w**, **y** are 'quiescents', that is, readily lose their consonant power and disappear: in addition to these, in Assy. the letters **ḥ**, **ʿ**, and **ʿʿ** are weak or vowel letters, or quiescents, all being pronounced as **'**, or spiritus lenis, **ḥ′**, however, having the sound of **ḥ**. As to the similar confounding and disappearing of **'**, **h**, **ḥ** (**ḥ′**), **ʿ**, (**ʿʿ**) in other Semitic dialects, see *C.G.S.L.*, pp. 49–50; and as to **w** and **y**, pp. 69–74.

4. Dialectically, one or more of the original sounds may be dropped: thus in Assy., as just noted, the sounds of **h**, **ḥ**, **ʿ**, and (if they were original) the aspirated sounds of **b, g, d, k, p, t**. In Assy. No. 17 is pronounced only **p**, in Arb. and Eth. only **f**; in Assy. and Eth. No. 21 only **s**, the original **sh** sound having been dropped. On the other hand, new sounds may be dialectically developed out of, or substituted for, the original, as in Eth. **g′**, **h′**, **ḥ″**, **k′** (if they were not original); Arb. **j** (sometimes to **s′**, **s**) for **g**; Arb. and Arm. **ty** or **ch**, also Amh. **tsh**, or **ts′**, for **k**; Arb. **dzh**, or **dz**, or **ch**, for **ḳ**[2]; Amh. **ty**, or **ch**, and **dy**, or **j**, for **t** and **d**.[3] The ordinary sound of **ḳ** throughout Arabia now is **g**, its original sound having been dropped.

5. Gutturals: **'**, **h**, **ḥ** (**ḥ′**), **ʿ**, (**ʿʿ**), (**h′**, **ḥ″**, **g′**, **k′**), **g**, **k**, **ḳ**, **y**.
Dentals: **d** (**ḍ**), **z**, **ṭ** (**ṭ′**), **l**, **n**, **s**, **ṣ** (**ṣ′**), **r**, **s′**, **t**, **t′**.
Labials: **b**, **p**, **m**, **v**, **f**, **w**.

a. For obvious reasons letters of the same class readily interchange, gutturals with gutturals, dentals with dentals,

[1] *C.G.S.L.*, p. 54. [2] *C.G.S.L.*, pp. 51–2. [3] p. 55.

labials with labials. For examples, see especially Gesenius, *H. Lex.*, first article under each letter; Dillmann, *Eth. Gr.*; *C.G.S.L.*; and for Assy., the Grammars of Sayce and Delitzsch; and for the Mahri, Von Maltzan. As to the gutturals, **g** aspirated is pronounced like **‘‘**, **k** aspirated like ḥ, and ḳ in parts of Syria, Egypt, and Abyssinia like **’**, as is noted in *C.G.S.L.*

b. Interchange of letters of one class with those of another. Gutturals and Dentals: **g** and j (s′, s); **k** and **ty** or **ch**, and **ts**; ḳ and **dz**, or **ch**: see § 4. The change **k** to **t** is seen, e.g., in the Semitic personal pronoun of the first person: for ḥ to **r**, l, and **‘‘** to **rh**, see Von Maltzan. So **‘** to **r** is noted by Gesenius.

c. Dental with Guttural. The change of **t** to **k** is seen in the Semitic pronoun of the second person, and that of **s** (**s′**) to **h**, and **’**, in that of the third person, and in the Causative preformative; and that of **t** to **h**, and **’**, in the Semitic feminine and abstract formative ending. See *C.G.S.L.*, pp. 61–4, for ṣ, ṣ′, to **‘**, **’**, ḳ, and ḥ, and **g**.

d. Guttural and Labial: **y** and **w**; **’** and **w**: *C.G.S.L.* See *Eth. Gr.*, pp. 47, 98, for **k** (ḥ) and **f**, or vice versa, **ko** to **fo**, demonstrative particle. The **kw** sounds in Ethiopic are combinations of Guttural and Labial.

e. Labial and Guttural: Assy. **m** (probably through **ng**) and **g**: Delitzsch. **B** and **h**, Amh. *ba* to *ha*, preposition; Mahri *boriq* to *horiq*, ‘lightning.’

f. Dental and Labial: Arb. **t′** and **f**: *C.G.S.L.*, p. 66.

g. Labial and Dental: in all the Semitic dialects **m** and **n** are often interchanged, as in the plural ending of nouns and pronouns, the mimation—nunation, and the radical letters of words.

6. Letters which readily fall away or disappear are the quiescents, § 4; the aspirated **b**, **g**, **d**, **k**, **p**, **t**, and **m** pronounced **v**, § 2: **v** and **f** pass into **w**, **d** and **t** into **h**, **g** and **k** into **‘** and ḥ or **h**, ḳ into **’**, § 5 *a*; and so disappear: *C.G.S.L.* (as to **d** and **t**, p. 54). **S**, changed to **h**, readily disappears as in the Causa-

tive preformative, and the third personal pronoun; Mahri *itit*, 6, ستة; *homo*, 5, خمسة; *ibet*, 7, سبعة; *hiriq*, 'steal,' سرق. As to **t**, Mahri *iset*, Sokotra *saah*, 9, تِسْعَة.

7. Words whose initial radical was one of the weak letters, or quiescents, § 3, were apt to drop the first syllable, as ידע, 'to know,' דע, דעה, 'knowledge'; אחד, واحد, חד, 'one'; הלך (ילך), 'to go,' לכה, לך, 'go,' Assy. *halak*, 'to go,' *laku*, 'a going.'

On the other hand, a syllable consisting of ', the prosthetic ', with a vowel was often prefixed to a word to make the pronunciation easier: *C.G.S.L.*, pp. 93–4.

8. The Vowels[1]: **a**, **e**, **i**, **o**, **u**, as in Italian.

U, and **u**, or **ui**, as in Scotch *gude*, *guid*, **y**, in Egypt, yclept, syntax, **i** as in sin, **e**, **o**, and **ī**.

A, and **ĕ**, **i**, **o**, **u**; Assy. *-anu*, and *-inu*, Arb. *-an*, H. *-on*.

I, and **e**.

The diphthongs: **ai** (**ay**), and **ē**, **ī**, **a**; **au** (**aw**), and **ō**, **u**, **a**.

9. The Oceanic sounds: the vowels **a**, **e**, **i**, **o**, **u**, as in Italian: in Efatese **ă** is often pronounced like **ĕ**, **ĭ**, or **ŭ**; thus *banatu*, or *banotu*, is often pronounced *bĭnotĕ*, which might as well be written *bĭnotĭ*. The long sounds of a, e, i, u, as in father, fate, feet, moon, are very different. Hence the verbal pronoun of the third person is written by one i, by another **e**, and, as we shall see, represents an original **u** or **y**: compare English *do*, *did* (A.S. *dyde*), Scotch *di*, or *dae*. The diphthongs are ai, sometimes written ei, and **au**: ai passes into ē, or i, or **a**, as in *i bai*, or *i bi seĭ?* 'he is who?' *I mai*, or *i bē*, 'he comes'; *i bai*, or *i ba se*, or *i bē sab?* 'he goes or comes (from) where?' So **au** passes into **o**, **a**, or **u**, as *ġaut*, and *ġat*; and in *kabu*, *kobu*, *kubu*, the **a**, **o**, and **u** are all for original **au**.

Consonants, and mode of representing them.

' is not represented, thus To. *laa*, 'the sun' (not written *la'a*).

b, in the Efatese of this work (and To.), represents both **b** and **p**, and when aspirated becomes **f** which represents both **v** and **f**:

[1] *C.G.S.L.*, Chh. V and IX.

in some Ef. dialects, however, **b**, **p**, **v**, and **f** are all written. In Mg. and My. **b** as in English.

d, in Mg., My., Tanna, Ml., as in English; not in our Ef., but in Ef. dialect, and sometimes pronounced **nd**.

h, as in Semitic, not in our Ef., but in Ef. dialect, Mg., Tanna, Ml., &c.

w, in our Ef. written **u** as French **ou** in 'oui' (wi), written **w** in Ef. dialect.

z, as in Semitic, Tanna, Mare, Mg.

ḥ, as in Semitic, in Mare, Tanna, Ml., Futuna.

ṭ, **tr**, Mg., Ef.

y, written **i** in our Ef., but is written **y** in An., Tanna, Ml., My.

k, **l**, **m**, **n**, **s**, **r**, **t**, as in Semitic.

ʻ. This represents various guttural sounds from **g** (**gh**) to **ʼ**. It has been called 'the Melanesian **g**', and, says Dr. Codrington (who writes it **g**), "has been written **g** (hard), **r**, **ġg**, **gh**, **rh**, and **k** . . . Bishop Patteson was struck by its resemblance to the Arabic Ghain (**ʻʻ**), and Professor Max Müller's description of the Heb. *ain* (**ʻ**) as 'a vibration of the fissura laryngea, approaching sometimes to a trill, nearly equivalent to German **g** in *tage*,' closely suits it".[1]

p, in My., Mg., Tanna, Ml.

ṣ, as in Semitic, in Ef. dialect, Santo, Mg. (written **ts**).

s′, as in Semitic, in Fut., Mare; and in Mg. **s** before **i** becomes **s′**.

The different Oceanic dialects have variously dropped or modified some of these sounds. As to the latter, those, **ch**, My.; **j**, An. (**ch** in 'rich'); and **j**, My., &c., modifications, as in Arb., and Amh., of dentals, are not in Efatese: but the sounds represented by **ġ**, **ḅ**, and **ṁ**, which must now be noticed, are. The sounds of **ḅ** and **ṁ** are not in all the Melanesian dialects, though perhaps in most of them from the New Hebrides to New Guinea. For the New Hebrides, see Vol. II of this

[1] *M.L.*, pp. 204–5.

series, and Ray's list of New Hebrides words; for the Sol. Islands, *M.L.*, Ch. IV; and for Motu (*N.G.*), Law's Dictionary.

The nasalized guttural **ġ** is pronounced like **ng** in 'singing'. It is absent from Tahitian, but is in all the other Po. dialects except Hawaiian in which its place is taken by **n**, and Marquesan in which, according to Tregear,[1] its place is taken by **k**. Ordinarily in Efatese it is a modification of **k**, sometimes of **n**, more rarely of **m**.

Ḅ: the guttural-labial sound symbolized by **ḅ** is that symbolized by **q** in *M.L.* by Dr. Codrington, and in Motu by Laws. In Efatese it is impossible to say sometimes whether the sound is **kw** (like **qu** in English) or **bw**, or **kb**. It is a half-guttural, half-labial sound, and originally a modified guttural like the **kw** sound in Eth. and Amh. But now it sometimes represents not only an original guttural, but an original labial. It is a bridge between the two classes like the Latin QV, a guttural followed by a labial semivowel forming a transition from guttural to labial; thus:[2]

Sanskrit *kis*,	Lat. *quis*,	Oscan *pis*.
,, *çatvar*,	,, *quattuor*,	Umbrian *petur*.
	,, *quisque*,	Gr. *πέμπε*.
Latin *cocus*,	,, *coquo*,	Lat. *popina*.
,, *secundus*,	,, *sequor*,	Gr. *ἕπομαι*.

ṁ: This sound is like **ġm** (**ġw**), or **mw**. It is a nasalized, guttural-labial sound varying between the two classes. It is originally a modification of **ḅ** (**kw**), just as **ġ** is of **k**: **kw** became **ġw**, which passed into **ġm** and **mw**, then **m**, exactly as **kw** passed into **kb**, **bw**, then **b**. Then sometimes an original **b** was pronounced **ḅ**, and an original **m** was pronounced **ṁ**, apparently just as the speaker pleased. In the Efatese New Testament **m** and **ṁ** are both written **m**, but **ḅ** (when distinguished) is written **p**.

'In the Banks Islands the suffixed form of the second per-

[1] *Maori Comparative Dictionary*, Introd.
[2] Smith's *Latin Grammar*.

sonal pronoun (singular) is generally **m**, or **ṁa**, but in Merlav and Ureparapara it has become **ġ**, and in Maewo **ġa'**,[1] Efatese **ma**, dialect **ṁa**. Neither **ġ**, **ṁ**, nor **m** is the original sound in this word: it is **k** which passes into **ġ**, that into **ṁ**, that finally into **m**: in Efatese the word is actually found in all these forms. But in Mota *iṁa*, Ef. *suṁa*, and *suma*, 'house,' Fiji *riġa*, and Ef. dialect *lima*, 'hand,' both the **ṁ** and **ġ** represent an original **m**. The same work states the view that **ġ** in some cases is a change from **k**, but generally from **n**. In Efatese, however, the contrary of this is the fact. A glance at the Dictionary (*infra*) proves that nearly all the words beginning with **k** are pronounced also with **ġ** (often indifferently by the same speaker), and represent words first radical guttural. Only in some cases in Efatese **ġ** represents original **n**, and in other and fewer cases original **m**.

Usually those who have reduced the Island dialects to writing have acted on the right principle of expressing one sound by one character, and if all had used the same character for the same sound nothing would need to be said. But as this is not the case, and to use the same character for entirely different sounds would in the present work be confusing and apt to mislead, such characters have to be as far as possible transcribed into the alphabet above given. Thus the Fijian **c** = **th** in 'the', and the An. **d** = **th** in 'thin', is here **t'**.

New Hebrides **c** = **g** (hard) is here **g**.

The Fijian **q** = **ġk** is here **ġ'**, and **ġg** is **ġ''**.

New Hebrides, Sol. Islands, and Motu **q** is here **ḅ**.

Maori, My., and Mg. **ng** is here **ġ**, as is also New Hebrides, Polynesian, and Fiji **g** (= **ng**).

Mg. and New Hebrides **ts** is here **ṣ**.

" " **tr** is here **ṭ**.

'The Melanesian **g**' (in *M.L.*) is here **ʿ**.

The sound of **ch** in '**loch**' is here **ḥ**.

The Mg. **o** = **u** is here **u**.

The Mg. **y** = **i** (as in 'county') is here **i**.

[1] *M.L.*, p. 214.

My. **j** = English j, and My. **ch** = English **ch** in 'church': in the New Hebrides **j** generally represents the latter, and in the Sol. Islands dialects sometimes the latter, sometimes the former.

The Mg. **j** = **dz**, and is a heavier **z**.

10. Dropping of letters: see §§ 2, 6. Letters aspirated and their disappearance. In Efatese b, i.e. **b** and **p**, is aspirated as in § 2, and then is apt in the same way to disappear. **B** aspirated is **f**, and this passes into **w** and then disappears, as *bora, borauora, mauora,* then *maora.* **M**, as in §§ 2, 6, is sometimes pronounced **f** (**v** or **f**), as *num, nuf,* then *nu* (*nuw*), 'to be ended': this accounts for the disappearance of the original final **m** in this word in Mg. and My. also (see *bunu,* 'to make an end of'), and for the fact that some words in Oceanic have **v**, **f**, or **w** for the original **m**, as Arb., Eth., *mai,* 'water,' Tah., Ef., *vai, fai,* Efate also after the article *n-oai,* for *na-wai,* and *n-ai.* موز, ሙዝ, 'banana,' Fut. *fuji,* My. *pisaģ,* Ef. *ūtĭ, aṣĭ,* dialect *vih* (for *vis*), Mg. *unti,* id.; Ef. *ūnoi,* dialect *mani,* 'male.' In Efatese **m** is often pronounced **f** (**v** or **f**), as *matuna, fatuna,* 'somewhat'; *matoko, fatoko,* 'to abide'; cf. Mg. *mati, fati,* 'dead, corpse.' Thus initial, medial, and final **m** sometimes disappears; final **m** also sometimes as in § 6.

For original **m**, see (Dictionary, *infra*) *katau, ģisa* (*kiha, ģia*), *ra* (*ṭa*), *taot* (*tawot*), *rakum* and *rakua, ūna.*

For original **b**, see *rarua, kusue, borau, kolau, roa* (*roua,* or *rowa,* 'to turn'), *rau, kasau, koau* (and *kabu*), *ātĕ* ('liver'), *masoi* (An. *moijeuv,* Tan. *mahau*), *ui* (*uwi*), *barab* (also, *barau, baram, baraf,* 'long'), *karau* (also *karab* and *karam*), *au* (and *abu*), *rau* (and *raf*), *tau,* 'time, season, year.' For **f**, see *surata* (*suuara, suara*), *uose, ģalau, balu-sa, uolau, matautau, siuo* (*siwo, sua*), *kai* (and *kaf*), *malūs* (and *malifus*).

So according to §§ 2, 6, **g** and **k** disappear, as also does **k** according to § 5.

For original **g**, see *lau* ('sea'), *buto* ('navel'), *lība, fāra.*

For original **k**, see *to* (and *toko*), *borau* (My. *prahu, prau*), *abura* (and *kabuer*), *bau-si,* (Mg. *fehi-zi*). Mg. often has **h** for

k in the prefixed form-particle My. *ka*, Mg. *ha*, Ef. *baka*, and *faka*, Mg. *maha*, and *faha*. How original **k** passes into h and disappears, is seen in the first personal pronoun, My. *aku*, Mg. *ahu*, Sam. *a'u*, Maori *au*, Ef. *k-inau*, An. *a-iñak*, Epi. *naǵ'u*, Ml. *k-inaǵ'*, Kisa *yahu*, Bu. *iyak*, Tanna *iyah*, *iau*, *yak*, Ero. *yau*, Mahri *ho*, 'I': so Assyrian *nini*, Hebrew *anu*, 'we': cf. the other Semitic dialects. According to Crauford, **k** 'by most of the Malay tribes, but not by all, is not sounded when it ends a word, or at most, only as a weak aspirate ... even as a medial letter **k** is elided by some tribes aiming at softness of pronunciation'. The initial **k** of the suffixed second personal pronoun plural disappears thus, Ef. *kama*, and suffix *mu*, My. *kamu*, and *mu*: in Ef. dialects we have this pronoun (separate), after the demonstrative particle *ni*, with the **k** elided, thus, *nikam*, *nëem*, *nem*, *nimu*, 'ye.'

For original **ḳ**, see *buil* (*bulo*, 'early, morning'), *usi* (and *kusi*), *mataku* (and *matau*), *àso* ('bow'), *aso* ('burn,' An. *gas*).

So according to §§ 2, 6, **d** and **t** disappear.

For original **d**, see *fau* (My. *baharu*), *soko*, *kuli* (My.ʳ *kulit*, Mg. *hudiṭa*), *bia* (My. *piät*, Mg. *afi*, and *zafi*), *naḅe* (dialect *mbat*), and the numeral word for 'one'.

For original **t** radical, see *tolu* (so M. Syrian *ṭela*), 'three,' and compare Arb. *t'ali*, 'third.'

For original **t** servile, see *mi-saki* (My. *sakit*), *ma-taku* (Mg. *tahuṭa*): in *misaki*, 'to be sick,' and *mataku*, 'to fear,' the servile **t** is dropped according to §§ 2, 6: see *C.G.S.L.*, where cited there. Final **t** in Malay is in familiar discourse usually softened into a vowel or the aspirate, as *sakit* into *sakih*, *takut* into *takuh*.

As to servile **-t** in Efatese the rule is that when, as in the Semitic dialects, it has no suffix attached to it, it disappears, but when it has it reappears, as *bulu*, *buluti*; *fafano*, *balosi*; and third radical dental is often treated in the same way, as *ala*, *alati*; *amo*, *amosi*; *kamu*, *kamuti*, &c.

11. The quiescents: see § 3. These, as may easily be seen by looking in the Index (*infra*), under the various letters, have usually, not always, lost their consonant power or disappeared, even when they are the first radicals of words, much more of course when second or third radicals. The first radical quiescent has usually either (*a*) lost its consonant power, its vowel only remaining, or (*b*), as in § 7, both it and its vowel have disappeared, or (*c*) it has passed into another sound.

(*a*) For examples of this as to ʼ, see *amau*,[1] *afaru*, *āfa*, *alat*, *kani*;

as to **h**, *abu*, *baġobaġo*, *atu*, *oro*;

as to **w**, *amosi*, *aseli*, *āso*, *atāta*;

as to **ḥ**, and **ḥ′**, *èlo*, *alo* ('to wave'), *ālo* ('uncle'), *asi*;

as to **y**, *aru*, *atai*, *atu*, *uḅa*;

as to ʻ and ʻʻ, *àfiti*, *àliàlia*, *ànu*, *àfina*, *ūta*, *àni*, *ara*; Tahiti *ahuru*, 'ten.'

(*b*) For examples of this as to ʼ, see *fatu*, *roġo*, *safi*, *seli*, *sere*, *teru*; *sikai*, 'one.'

as to **h**, *ta* ('to chop, cut'), *mu*, *bosa*, *teratera*, *rifu*;

as to **w**, *tao*, *kot*, *sieġ*, *taki*, *kita*;

as to **ḥ**, *bei*, *bau* (*bau-s*), *sike*, *turu* (*toro*), *sēs*;

[No such example as to **ḥ′** occurs, see Index under **ḥ′**.]

as to **y**, *būsa*, *tae* (d. for *atai*), *ḅia*, *ma-turu*, *ma* (*susa*);

as to ʻ and ʻʻ, *bea*, *ḅila*, *taoti* (*tàwoti*), *fata* (*uota*), *tefi*, *lasi*, *moru*, *fasu*, *musu*, *sila* (*sol*); Rotti *hulu*, Samoan *fulu*, 'ten.' [Note. Examples of (*b*) are common in reduplicated words as *lolo* (*alo-fi*, also *loa-si*, and *lo-fi*), *momoa*, *bāb*, and *abāb* (*āb*), &c.]

(*c*) For examples of this as to ʼ, see (*ē*), *he*, *fei*, *sei*, interrogative pronoun; *tama*, *taliġa*, *ḅinu* ('to weave'), *bati*, *ġisa*, (*kiha*), *kurunĭ*;

as to **h**, *abu*, *libu*;

as to **ḥ**, and **ḥ′**, *kabu*, *suma* (*hima*, *ema*, *uma*), *lima* ('five'), *laso*, *rakum*, *uis* (*wis*, *ḅis*); *sikai*, *tesa*, 'one';

as to **w**, *boroa*, *bani* (*banu-s*), *ḅalu*, *balo-ni*, *muui* (*mau*), *kan* (*kano*, *kanoka*), *malat* (*malat*), *maraġ* (*burei*), *atĕlaġ* ('moon');

as to **y**, *faru* (*aru*, 'hand'), *uba* and *kuba* ('day');

[1] For these words in other Oceanic dialects, see *infra*, the Dictionary, and for the same in the Semitic dialects, see the Index.

as to ' and '', *uili* (*uli*, *oli*), *kari* ('boy'), *kasu* (*kuu*, 'tree'), *uisi* (*ḅisi*), *ḅaġo*) (*maġo*), *fili*, *bulo* (*buġo*), *ḅinu* ('to whistle'), *m̈ata*, *m̈ota*, *mita* (*mata*, 'eye'), *m̈ala* (*mala*); Maori *ġahuru*, Vila and Meli (Po. Ef.) *ġafuru*, *nofuru*, 'ten.'

Modern English, it may be here observed, has dropped the guttural sounds of the Anglo-Saxon, which are still preserved in other dialects as Scotch and German: cf. *lauch*, Germ. *lach-en*, and *laugh* (*laf*); *eneuch*, Germ. *genug*, A.S. *genoh*, *genog*, and *enough* (*enŭf*), *enow*; A.S. *hoh*, and *hough* (*hok*). So with Efatese as compared with some other New Hebrides and Oceanic dialects. In such examples in English we see not only the sometimes complete dropping, or quiescence, of the ancient gutturals, but also sometimes the passing of them into letters of another class, as here **h**, **ḥ**, **g**, into **f**, **w**, **k**, which now represent them. Such changes in English have taken place in the past, and we know that they have from the comparison of the present English with the other Indo-European ancient and modern dialects. It is exactly so with Efatese or other modern Oceanic dialects. The strong Semitic ancient guttural sounds ', **h**, **ḥ**, ', **ḥ'**, '', **y**, when in past times they were being dropped, either completely disappeared, or passed into other letters, as we have just seen. In My. *initial* **h** (written) is no longer sounded as *hutan*, Ef. *uta*, in which word the **h** represents an original ע, غ: here we see the process of softening the ancient harsher guttural sound in operation as it were.

12. Dialectically one or more of the original consonant sounds may be dropped, as in § 4. In Tahitian all the gutturals have been softened to ', or lost, and **s** is always, **f** often, represented by **h**. In most of the Polynesian dialects all the sibilants have been softened to **h**, and Raratongan has lost even this **h**. Hawaiian has lost all the dentals, and softened **s** and **f** to **h**. Raratongan has lost both **f** and **h**, and also **s**. Tongan, like Arabic, has lost **p**; Malay, like Assyrian, **f**; and Malay **v** Malagasy **w**. Malay and Efatese have lost **z**, and,

like Assyrian and Ethiopic, s′. In Efatese the sibilants have been reduced to s (which in one dialect is softened to h), the dentals practically to t, and the gutturals to k (ġ, ḅ, ṁ); though the sounds of d, g, h are heard dialectically. In the New Hebrides dialects the original Semitic guttural sounds have been well preserved: Futunese shows that Polynesian, and Tanna, Malekula, &c., that Efatese originally had them. The change of k, g, and t to j (ch and j), not in Efatese, is seen, e.g. in Aneityumese (as in Arabic), as in akai*ja*, in*ta*, 'we and thou'; ai*jaua*, *gaua*, 'ye'; *moijeuv*, 'star,' j for original k, is in Ef. *masoi*, Santo *maṣoi*. So the s in Mg. *sufina*, 'ear,' is for original ḳ (قُوفٌ), through j (or ch), as in § 4, My. *kupiġ*, and *chupiġ*, Lampong *chiupiġ*, Batta *tshoppiġ* (*chopiġ*). In Efatese *oili f* ('enter'), q. v. My. *juluk*, also *salat*, or *salap*, Mg. *juluka* (i. e. *dzulu-ka*), the My. j, Mg. dz, Ef. and My. s, all represent the original d, د. The same change of d to j and s is seen in the word for 'one', Ef. *tesa*, Gaudalcanar *kesa*, New Caledonia (Latham), *tat*, *tedja*, i. e. *teja*.

In Ef. k, ġ (sometimes ġ′) according to rule represent (My. and Mg. k, g, and) the Semitic k, g, ḳ, see Index under these letters.

In Ef. the guttural-labial ḅ, ṁ, sometimes represent the guttural quiescents, § 11 c.

In Ef. t (sometimes pronounced ṭ, dialectically ṣ, d) according to rule represents (My. t, d, Mg. t, ṭ, ṣ, d, and) the Semitic t, t′, ṭ, ṭ′, ṣ, ṣ′, d, ḍ, under which letters see Index.

In Ef. s according to rule represents (Mg. and Tanna s, and z, Mare s, s′, and z, Fut. s, s′, and) the Semitic s, s′, z, under which letters see Index.

The Semitic ṣ is represented in Ef. by t or s. See Index under the letter ṣ.

In Ef. l, r, n according to rule represent the Semitic l, r, n, under which letters see Index.

In Ef. b (=b and p), f (=v and f) represent (Mg., Tanna, Malekula, &c., b, p, v, f, and) the Semitic b (v), p (f); and m the Semitic m: see Index under the letters b, p, m.

In Ef. **w** (u) in a few words represents the Semitic **w**: see Index under the letter **w**, and for the rest § 11.

13. In the Oceanic dialects, as in § 5 *a*, letters belonging to the same class, gutturals, dentals, or labials, readily interchange. For instance, original **k**, **g**, **ḳ**, gutturals:

(*a*)	dig	skin	rub	gape, wonder
	k	**g**	**ḳ**	
Ef.	*kili, ġili, ġ'ili*	*kuli*	*kasi, ġasi, ġ'asi*	*maka, maġa*
My.	*gali*	*kulit*	*gisi-k, kisi-k*	*ġaġa, maġa*
Mg.	*hadi*	*hudiṭa*	*kasu-ka*	*ġaġa*
Sam.	*'eli*	*'ili*	*'asi*	*maġa*
Ha.	*eli*	*ili*		

(*b*) Dentals: **t** to **n**, *tuma-ni* and *noba-ni*; *tobu* and *nobu*; *binote* and *binen*. The change of the Semitic formative **-t** to **n** is frequent, and found in all the Oceanic dialects, thus, *bātĕ*, 'four,' N. Guinea (Ray) *bani*, Motu *hani*; *kofu* and *kafu-ti*, Fiji *kovu-ta* and *kovu-na*, My. *kapu-ġ*; *tuku*, Fi. *tuku-t'a*, Sam. *tuu-na*; Mahri *iti-t* (ستة), Mg. *eni-na*, 'six'; Syriac *m-istuta*, Mg. *m-inuna*, Ef. *m-inuġi*, Sam. *inu*, 'drink.' In Madagascar some tribes use **-ṭa** (dialect **-ṣa**), and **-na** interchangeably.

T, **s**: *afiti* and *afisi*; *ta, sa, ti, di, ṣi*, 'not'; *tesa, sikai, siki-tik* (redup.), 'one'; *mita*, Sam. and My. *mata*, Mg. *masu*, 'eye.' The change of the Semitic formative **-t** to **s** (Mg. **s**, and **z**, and dialect **ṣ**) is frequent, and in all the Oceanic dialects, thus *bātĕ*, 'four,' Epi *vāsĕ*; *taġi-si*, My. *taġi-s*, Fi. *taġi-t'a*; *lifu, ma-lifu-s*, Mg. *lefi-ṭa*, My. *lapi-t, lapi-s*, Fi. *lova-t'a*, Sam. *lava-si*, 'to bend'; *bunu-ti*, dialect *bunu-ṣi*, Mg. *funu-si*. In Madagascar, Hova **-ṭa** is in Betsileo dialect **-ṣa**.

T, **r**, **l**: *tiu* and *riu*; *tutu* and *lulu*; *bātĕ*, 'four,' Epi *vērĭ*, Segaar (N.G.) *fal*. The Semitic formative **-t** becomes **r**, **l**, thus, *soka, soka-ta ki, soka-ri*, Tongan *hoko, hoko-ta ki*; *sumi-li*, My. and Java *sumba-t, sumpa-t, sumpa-l, sampa-l*, My. *tampi-na*, Tong. *umo-ji*; *tami-si, sabe-li*, My. *simpu-l*; *roġo, ṭoġo, toġo, doġo, roġo-sa*

NOTE.—Wherever the name of the language is not given, the word is Efatese, and to be found with its meaning in the Dictionary, *infra*.

ki, Fi. *roġo-t'a*, My. *daġa-r*, Mg. *re*, *reni*, *reni-s*, 'to hear'; *kasi*, My. *goso-t*, *kisi-l*, 'rub.' Mg. -ṭa with suffix attached to it becomes t or r, as *ma-taku*, Mg. *tahuṭa*, *hatahurana* (My. *katakutan*); Ef. *mi-tiri*, Mg. *sura-ṭa*, *suratana*, My. *tuli-s*, *tulisan*. The Semitic formative t- is sometimes changed to r-, *ta-usi* and *ra-usi*: so Fi. *ra-* and *ta-* are the same.

Original n to t, s: *ma-nifi*, My. *nipi-s*, *tipi-s*; *mita*, 'eye'; *fatu*, 'stone'; *iġita*, An. *inta*, Mg. *isika*, pronoun inclusive, 'we and thou'; *na* and *sa*, *n*, *s*, pronoun third person, verbal suffix; the same pronoun separate, Ef. *inia*, My. *iña* (*iya*), Mg. *izi*, *isi*; the n of the 'nunation' sometimes becomes s, as Savu *natun*, My. *ratus*, 'hundred.' For this word see Index under letter ꝺ.

n to r: *namu*, 'mosquito,' Tah. *namu* and *ramu*.

s to n: *isuma* and *inuma*.

s to r: *mesau*, *muri*, 'to desire.'

r to s (z): *muri*, 'send back, return,' and *busi*; *ġori*, *ġusu*, 'nose'; *karo*, 'naked,' Mg. *harihari*, and *hazihazi*.

r to t: *-ra* and *-ta*, pronoun suffixed third person plural; *roua* and *toua* (*roa*, *toa*), 'to fall.' When initial r is reduplicated it is usually pronounced t, thus, *roba*, *toroba*; *riġi*, *tiriġi*; *rafi*, *terafi*: in such cases the original letter may be r or t (d).

r to n: *mare* and *mane*, 'man, male'; *manu*, Mg. *vuruna*, My. *buruġ*, 'bird.'

r to l: *roko* and *loko*.

l to n: *tulum* and *tinom*.

In some cases the change may not be direct from the original, but secondary, or through intermediate change or changes: thus, original

l to s, &c.: Arb. *la*, H. *le*, &c., 'not,' we find as *ti*, *di*, *ri*, *sa*, *ṣi*, *ta*, *ni*, Sam. *le*, Maori *te*, My. *ta*, Mg. *ṣi*; and so the article, Arb. *al*, *l-*, we find as *na*, *nĭ*, *in*, *n-*, Sam. *le*, Maori *te*, East Mai *re*, Mg. *nĭ*, Fi. *na* (and *a*). Of these, ṣ and s are from the original l, through t. Tanna *kimia*, *kimyaha*, *kumiar*, Ef. *-akamus*, Fi. *kemuni*, Ml. P. *hamdi*, 'ye': here h, r, s, n, and d are all for original l, which in *kimia* is elided, and is still l in Eromangan *yoril*, 'they.' See Ch. V, I, &c.

So s to l: this may be through t or r (compare the change of s to l in Assyrian before a dental, and of ṣ′ to l[1] in Mahri), as in the word for 'man,' Ef. *ata*, Epi *ata*-mani, Epi *su*-mano, Tanna *yeru*-man, Santo *la*-mani: the letter here represented by t, r, s, l is in this word in Arm. s′ and t, Arb. s, t′, t, Eth. s, Heb. s′. In the words for 'two,' 'three,' and 'eight,' the original initial Semitic letter is s′, s, or t, t′: Epi *chua* (*jua*), and *lua*, Ef. *tua*, and *rua*, and *dua*, and *ṭua*, My. *duwa*, Mg. *rua*, Sam. *lua*, 'two'; Amb. *sul*, Ef. *ṭolu*, *tolu*, and *rolu*, 'three'; My. *lapan* (reduplicated, *dalapan*), 'eight.'

(*c*) Labials: b and m, as *boğ*, and *moğ*; *bunuti*, and *munuti*; *bai*, *mai*, 'to come';

b and w, as *bon* and *uon*; *bora*, and *borauora*;

b and f, as *bano*, *fano*; *bami*, *nafamian*: *be*, *fe*, 'to come';

f and w, *fai*, *uai*, 'water';

m and f, *ma-tuna*, and *fa-tuna*, 'somewhat': this *ma* is the Semitic interrogative and indefinite *ma*, sometimes changed in Assy. to *va*, Himyaritic to *ba*, as in Ef. in the same word, *ma-toko*, it is also *ba-toko*, and *fa-toko*. The m of this word in the interrogative is in Ef. f, Mg. v, My. p; and prefixed, as in the Semitic dialects, in the indefinite sense, to verbs and verbal nouns, it is in Mg. m and f (*ma-*, *fa-*, *mpa-*, *maha-*, *fa-ha-*, *mpaha-*), My. m and b, and p, Ef. b and f, also m (as in *matoko*), Sam. m and f (as in *mata'u*, Ef. *mataku*, and *fa'a-*, Ef. *baka-*, *faka-*, Mg. *maha-*).

m and ṁ, b and ḅ, and vice versa, interchange.

w and b, as *ualu* and *balu*.

w and ḅ, *ualu* and *ḅalu*.

For original initial w, see the Oceanic word for 'moon', *atilağ*, Mg. *vulana*, &c.

For original initial m, see the Oceanic words for 'male', *marĭ*, *manĭ*, *man*, &c., and 'female', *fafine*, &c.

14. Interchange of letters of one class with those of another, as in § 5, *b*, *c*, *d*, *e*, *f*, *g*.

[1] See the Oceanic word for 'sun,' *elo*, Tong. *laa*, &c.

(*a*) Gutturals and Dentals, as in § 5 *b* : Ef. *fila*, Bu. *bilak*, My. *kilat*, Mg. *halaṭa*, 'lightning'; قُرْقْ, My. *kupiġ* and *chupiġ*, Mg. *sufina*, 'ear'; Lobo (N.G.) *komakoma*, Timbora *kiġkoġ*, Mg. *kintana*, My. *bintaġ*, *wintaġ*, *lintaġ*, Chamori *putiun*, Haw. *hoku*, San Christoval (Fagani) *figu*, Marq. *hetu*, *fetu*, Maori *whetu*, Motu *hisiu*, Oba *visiu*, Santo *vitui*, *maṣoi*, Ef. *masoi*, An. *moijeuv*, كَوْكَبْ, Mahri *kabkob*, &c., 'star.' K to n (through ġ), Batta (Sumatra) *aka*, Tanna *ik*, Ero. *ka*, My. and Ef. *aġ*, Ef. dialect ke-*iġa* and ke-*ina* (Mg. *anau*, *ana*-reu), pronoun second person singular. Ef. *kumu* and *akam*, My. *kamu*, Tanna *ituma* and *kimia*, pronoun second person plural. An. ni-*kma* and ni-*jma*, 'hand'; *seik* and *seij*, 'three.' Ef. *kabu*, Ml. *kambu*, Epi *sembi*, Motu *lahi*, Rotuma *rahi*, 'fire': for other examples, see § 11 *c*.

(*b*) Dental and Guttural, as in § 5 *c* : Ef. *sikai*, *siki-tik*, Cayagan *tadai*, Sumatra *sada*, N. Caledonia *tat*, *chika*, 'one.' The Hawaiians wholly confound dental with guttural, t being always pronounced and written k. (In Samoan the increasing tendency is to pronounce t as ʻ.) Thus Maori *ta-ġata* is in Haw. *ka-naka*, Fi. *ta-mata*, Ef. *ta-mole*, 'man.' In the personal pronouns we have Ef. *iġita*, Mg. *isika*, 'we and thou.' How n may become k (or h), through ġ, is seen in this same word, thus *iġita* (for *inita*, Mota *inina*) in one Ef. dialect is *akit*, My. *kita*, Gaudalcanar *ihita* (suffixed Ef. -*nita*, *ġita*, Mg. -*ṣika*), and in the first person exclusive also, 'we and they,' the same n becomes k (or h), through ġ, and is sometimes elided, thus, Ef. k-*inami*, (Santo *anam*), Ef. dialect *aġami*, Aurora *ikami*, *kami*, My. *kami*, Ysabel (Gao) *iʻami*, *ʻai*, Mg. *ahai* (suffixed Mg. -*nai*, Ef. *nami* and -*ġami*) Ulawa *ami*, Motu *ai*; Ef. *au*, dialect *u*, dialect *pu*, *mu*, verbal pronoun, for *nami* as Ulawa *ami*, Motu *ai*, Motu verbal pronoun *a*; Mg. *vatana*, My. *badaġ*, Ef. *batako*, 'body.' And thus the n of the Semitic formative suffix *an*, ـَانْ, in Mg. *ana*, My. *an*, Ef. *an*, or *ana*, is n in Haw., ġ in Maori, Sam., &c., k in Marquesan. In Ef. itself we have *ran*, *raġ*, *rak*, 'time'; and in Maori *raġi* and *raki*, Ef. *laġi*, Haw. *lani*, 'heaven, sky.' So the n of the 'nunation' may become ġ, k as Mg. *ulun*, My. *oraġ*, Ulu (Sumatra) *orak*, 'man'; and Ef. *tasi*,

Ceram *taisin*, and *tasok*, My. *tasik*, 'sea.' Not only **n**, but **l** and **r**[1] may become **ġ**, **k**, **h**, thus the **l** or **r** of the Oceanic numeral 'three' (*tolu*, *tilu*, *selu*, *tir*, &c.) is **g**, and **k**, in My. *tiga*, An. *seik*; Ef. *taliġa*, An. *tikġa*, 'ear.' Ef. *tasila* is in Ef. dialects *tasiġa*, and *aheka*; and *bulo-ni* is in a neighbouring village *buġo-ni*. Malo *tura* is in Epi *taka*, Ef. *taku*, 'the back.' The formative prefix in My. *tar* is in Tagala *taga*; and that in My. *bar* is in Tagala *mag*, Mg. *maha*, Ef. *baka*, or *faka*, Tah. *faa*, or *haa*, Maori *whaka*, the original Semitic being *mata-*. The formative prefix *ta*, תַּ, تَ, may pass into *ka*, *ha* (and then into *a*, as in Ef. dialect *aheka* = *tasila*, as just noted), thus Ef. *tabara*, Maori *tawera*, and *hawera*, 'burned.' This prefix (*ta*) in My. and Ef. is often *ka*, Mg. *ha*, as Ero. *devat-uġi*, Ef. *kafate*, or *kefate* (so with all the numerals), My. *kaampat*, 'fourth,' Mg. *hefarana*, 'four days.'

So the Semitic formative suffix (collective, abstract, feminine) **t**, ת, ة, often becomes **k** (or **h**) in Mg. and My., thus My. *goso-t*, *goso-k*, Mg. *kasu-ka*, Ef. *kasi*, 'to rub.' Mg. *puṣiṭa*, *puṣika*. Ef. *busa i*, 'to smash.' This ending also changes through **k**, or, as in the Semitic dialects, directly, to **h**, and disappears (see *supra*): My. *garu*, *garu-t*, *garo-k*, Ef. *karo*, *karu-ti*, 'to scrape'; Mg. *tapa-ka*, Ef. *tefi*, 'to cut.' But always in such Mg. words the *-ka*, when another suffix (*-ana*) is attached to it, becomes **h** (or **f**, see *infra* under section *c*), as *tapa-ka*, *tapa-hina* (not *tapa-kina*), 'cut off.' This suffix, **-t**, is seen in the Oceanic numeral 'four', as Ef. *bātĕ*, Mota *vat*, Uea *vak*, Pentecost *piët*, N.G. (*L.*, p. 332) *fiak*. The same change of **t** to **k** is seen in the Oceanic word for 'three', which is in Ef. *tolu*, Mare *tini*, but in Lifu *koni*, Uea *kun*.

(*c*) Guttural and Labial, as in § 5: Ef. *kui* and *bui*, *kusu* (dialect *kihi* = *kisi*) and *usi*, *bisi*; Ef. *kau*, My. *gawa* and *bawa*: Ef. *fila*, 'lightning,' Bu. *bilak*, My. *kilat* (also *kilap*, as just noted).

[1] F. Müller, *G. der Sprachw.*, My. §, p. 92, and fol., notes the change of **r** to **g**, **k**, **h**. Among the Malays the **r** is gutturally pronounced, like **r** grasséyé, Northumbrian **r**, in some places. So the Semitic **r** has a guttural tendency.

In Mg. the formative suffix *ka*, with another suffix attached to it, becomes sometimes **h**, sometimes **f**, sometimes either one or the other (e.g. *hirika*, *hirihana*, or *hirifana*, 'bored'), as, *huhuka*, *huhufana* (not *huhukana*), Ef. *kūku*, *ġuku*, *ġukuta*, 'bent,' 'curved.' Ef. dialect *turuk*, as in Arb., but *turubi-si*, as in Eth.: see Dillmann for this change in this and other words, e.g. *Eth. Gr.*, p. 47. **K**, through **ġ**, to **ṁ**, **m**, Ef. **k**, **ko**, **ġo**, **ṁa**, **ma**, Tanna **k**, **m**, suffixed pronoun second person singular: for this **k**, **ġ**, to **n**, see supra, § 14 *a*. In the reduplicated word for 'star' the first **k** has become **f**, **v**, **w**, **b**, **m**, and **p** (**wh**, and **h**), and **l**, the second **k** appears as **g**, **j**, **s**, **ş**, **h**, see § 14 *a*.

(*d*) Labial and Guttural, as in § 5 *e*: see Dillmann, where just cited for this change. Ef. *bisi*, Mg. *fusiṭa* and *kusiṭa*, 'to rub.' Ef. *fila*, 'lightning,' My. *kilat* and *kilap*. Ef. *salub̦e* and *saluke*, 'to be ignorant.' Both Ef. **b̦** and **ṁ** represent sometimes original gutturals as *kuli*, *b̦ili*, and sometimes have passed into pure **b** or **m**; and sometimes represent, as in *salub̦e*, *saluke*, original labials, and sometimes have passed into pure gutturals: that is, these sounds are bridges, which may be crossed either way, between the two classes, gutturals and labials. They are half-guttural, half-labial sounds.

Ef. *fila*, 'lightning,' Bu. *bilak*, Mg. *halaṭa*, Mahri *boriq*, and *horiq*. The change of **f** to **h**, Ef. *ban* or *fan* (I have heard this in d. as *han*), An. *pan* (*apan*), and *han*, 'to go'; Tah. *faa* or *haa*, (Ef. *baka* or *faka*), formative prefix.

M to **ġ** and **k**: compare Assyrian **m** to **g**. Ef. *lumi*, and *luġi*, to swell ('rise up,' of the skin); cognate word *laġi*, My. *laġit*, Mg. *laniṭa*, Haw. *lani*, Maori *raġi*, dialect *raki*, 'the sky, heaven, above': in both of these cognate words, *luġi* (*lumi*), and *laġi*, the original letter is **m**. The change of original **m** to **ġ** is seen also in the word for 'wind', Bugis *lōma*, Maori ma-*taġi*, Fi. *t'agi*, Ef. *laġi*, which see. For the change of **k**, through **ġ**, to **m**, see (*c*).

(*e*) Dental and Labial, as in § 5 *f*. My. *lakat* and *lakap*, Ef. *liku*, *likut*, q.v., 'to adhere': the **t** in this word is the formative ending above mentioned as sometimes passing into k, h, and f. When it occurs in Mg. as ṭa, the ṭ on the addition to it of the other ending (*ana*) passes into t, r, or f, as Ef. *liko, likot*, Mg. *rekiṭa* (or *raikiṭa*), *rekitana*; Ef. *mataku*, Mg. *tahuṭa, hatahurana*, My. *takut, takutan*, 'fear'; Mg. *taraṭa, tarafina* (not *taratina*), Sam. *tilof-ia*, Fi. *tiro, tirova*, Maori *tiro, tirohaġa* (= Mg. *tarafana*), Ef. *tiro*, 'to look, gaze, peep, spy.' The original dental (t) of this ending, retained in one dialect, may have passed into and be retained only as a labial in another, as Mg. *iliṭa*, or *idiṭa, idirana*, 'to enter,' Sam. *ulu, uluf-ia*, Ef. reduplicated *alialia, ululia*, 'entered (by a spirit), possessed'; My. *salat*, and *salap*, Ef. *sili, silif*, 'to enter, insert.' When the t of this ending has changed to n in Mg., this n, on the addition to it of the ending *ana*, often changes to m, as *minuna*, 'to drink,' *minumana* (not *minunana*), My. *minum*, Ef. *minu, minuġ*, Sam. *inu, inumaġa*=My. *minuman*, Mg. *minumana*, Ef. *minuġiana* (the i after the ġ will be explained below): so Mg. *eni-na*, Mg. *ana-m*, 'six'; original initial s in this word sometimes has become f, as Ceram *wonen*, Ml. *won*, Tah. *fene*; so second radical s in the word for 'ten', *fulu, puluh*, and that for 'nine', My. *salapan* (red.), Makassar *jalatien* (red.). In Santo m and n are often used indifferently by different speakers, or even by the same speaker (Vol. II of this series, p. 1). Thus we have Santo *kanim* = Fi. *kemuni*, 'ye,' pronoun second person plural, and Ef. *komàm* and *kinàmi*, 'we and they'; My. *nipis* and *mipis*, Ef. *ma-nifi*, 'thin.' In Rotuma t is very often pronounced f, as *fa*, for *ta*, 'man'; *maf*, for *mat*, 'eye'; *folu*, for *tolu*, 'three,' and so forth.

(*f*) Labial and Dental, as in § 5 *g*. In Santo owing to the confusion, noticed under (*e*), between n and m, we often have n for original m, as *lina* for *lima*, 'five.' In South Santo (Vol. II of this series, p. 1) there is a sound, represented by t, which is described as tp, or a sound between the two. It is a half t half p sound. On the opposite coast of Malekula there is a sound which makes the same confusion between f (or v) and t′. One hears what is at once labial and dental, just as in ḅ and ṁ what is at once guttural and labial: Santo *vate*, and *t'ate*, N. Guinea (*L.* 332) *fiak*, and *tiak*, 'four'; Malekula *ambitu*, and *wontit*, Mysol (*W.*) *fit*, and *tit*, N. Guinea *fik*, *tik*, and *sik*, Java *pitu*, My. *tujoh*, Mg. *fitu*, and (dialect in Sir Joseph Banks) *titu*, 'seven,' Mahri *ibet* (for *sibet*, Assy. *sibit*); Ef. *fanua*, Santo *vanua*, and *t'anua*, 'house, country'; Ef. *fafine*, Malekula *vavine*, and *t'at'ine*, 'woman'; My. *bulan*, Mg. *vulana*, Bu. *ulöģ*, Timuri *fulan*, and *tulan*, Ef. *atĭlagĭ*, *atlaģ* (prosthetic *a*), (Port Praslin *kalan*, Duke of York *kalaģ*, see (*d*) above), Santo *wula*, Fi. *vula*, N. Caledonia *malog*, An. *mohog*, Rotti *bulak*, Sumatra *bulen*, *bulet*, *bula*, Mahri *wareḥ*, *woret*, *eret*, *haret*, *worat*, *wurut*, *wurit*, *airit'*, Tigre *werha*, Sokotra *irah*, 'moon': see Index s. v. ወርኅ (יֶרַח, יְרַח)—not in Arabic.

15. Letters which readily fall away or disappear, as in § 6. For the aspirated **b** (=**b** and **p**), that is, **f** (=**v** and **f**), and **m** (when pronounced **f** which readily passes into **w** and disappears), and for **k** and **t**, see above.

S has sometimes disappeared as (ستة), Mahri *itet*, Mg. *enina*, 'six'; *minuği*, *minuna* (ܡܫܩܐ), 'drink'; Causative prefix *a*, Arb. *a*; pronoun third person, Tanna *in*, Ef. *iğa*, *inĭa*, My. *iña*, Assy. *sunu*, *sina*, הֵמָּה, הֵנָּה, &c.; سبعة, Mahri *ibet*, Mg. Sam. *fitu*, Java *pitu*, 'seven'; خمسة, Mahri *homo*, Marquesan *hima*, Ef. *lima*, Mg. *limi*, and *dimi*, Maori *rima*, Epi *yima*, *sima*, &c., 'five'; سرق, Mahri *hiriq*, Ef. *binak*, *finak*, 'to steal.' In the word for 'five' it is the final **s** that has disappeared.

T initial has disappeared in (تسعة) Mahri *iset*, Sokotra *sa'ah*, M. Syr. *icha* (*itsha*), (Sula *tasia*) Bouru *eshia*, *chia*, *siwa*, Batta *siah*, Santo *siwa*, Mg. *sivi*, Tong. *hiva*, Maori *iwa*, 'nine'; ثمان (Sumatra *lapan*) Savu *panu*, Easter Island *varu*, Mg., Sam. *valu*, Maori *waru*, Carolines *wan*, *wal*, Santo *walu*, *ālu*, Malekula *wal*, *ālu*, Oba *ḅalu*, 'eight.'

L, Ef. *malūs*, *mūūs*; سفل, 'to descend,' Ef. *siwo*, *suwa*, Tong. *hifo*, Sam. *ifo*, An. *asuol* (*asuwol*).

R, Ef. verb. pron. *ru*, and *ĕu*: the **r** here is for original **n** (**m**)[1]:

[1] As in Tanna, verb. pron., r-, thus *even*, to go, *in reven*, he goes, for *in neven*, and so with all verbs. So Ef. *ru ban*, they go, is for *nu ban*, Dual *rā ban*,

Tanna *ilar*, *ilia* (*inira*), אלה, Eth., Amh. *elu*, *ela*, Arb. *ila*, &c. (see Index under the letter א for this). This Semitic personal demonstrative plural pronoun is usually appended in Oceanic to the second and third personal pronouns plural, thus, third person, Ef. *inĭa* (now singular, but originally plural), My. *iña*, Mg. *izi*, *isi* (plural and singular), Ef. *inira*, Mg. *izareu* (for *inareu*), Eromanga *irora* (for *inora*), *yoril* (for *yonil*), Tanna *iraha* (for *inara*), dialects of Tannese *ilar*, *ilat*, *ilah*, *iria*, *ilia*, Fut. (Po.) ak-*iria*, Tong. ki-*nau*, 'they,' lit. (*na-u*), 'they—those.' Second person: Mg. *anareu*, Tanna *kimiaha*, dialects *kumiar*, *kimia*, *itumat*, Malekula dialect *kamito*, Ef. dialect *akamus*, Fi. *kemuni*, 'ye,' or 'you,' literally 'you—those.' أَرْبَعَة, Amh. *arut*, at Arkeeko *ubah*, Sula *riha*, Tagala *apat*, My. *ampat*, Mg. *efaṭa*, Acheen (Sumatra) *baat*, Ef. *bātĕ*, 'four.' 'Fruit,' Aramaic *pĕrah*, *pīra*, Mg. *vua*, My. *buwah*, Ef. *boĭia*, *ua* (*wa*).

N: see the word for 'man' under א, and נ, in Index. Ef. *ani*, or *an* or *a*, 'to abide'; *nani*, and *nai*, or *nei*, 'child,' *bano*, *ban*, and *ba*, 'to go'; Ef. *inau*, Tanna *iau*, &c., 'I'; Arb. *t'ina*, Assy. *sina*, M. Syr. *ṭera*, Mahri *t'aro*, Sokotra *tera*, Celebes *dia*, My. *dua*, Ef. *rua*, *tua*, Mg. *rua*, &c., 'two.' Formative prefix *i*-, for -*in*, Ifal for Infal. So the formative suffix -*na* becomes sometimes -*a*, in Polynesian, and -*ina* in Mg. is both -*ina* and *ia* in Polynesian. The preposition *ni* is often *i* as in Fi., Ef., &c.

The final *a* of the word *t'ina*, *rua*, &c., 'two,' is the *a* of the Semitic dual ending.

Initial **n** of triliterals, as in Heb. and Arm., often disappears: see Index under the letter נ for examples, as *bisa*, 'speak,' *kat*, 'bite,' *sakĭ*, 'ascend,' *buka*, 'swell,' &c. Ef. and Fi. *ni*, and *i*, the preposition, in Arb. لِ. Final **n** also sometimes falls away, as in *karo*, 'throat, gullet,' *sobe*, 'nape of neck.'

M, as we have seen, may disappear whether initial, medial, or final. The **m**, in Arm. and Assy. changed to **n**, of the second and third personal pronouns plural, was apt to fall

they two go, both *ru*, and *rā*, being for *nu*, *nā*, originally *mu*, *mā*, A. *humu*, Dual *humā*.

away, Arb. *antumu*, *antum*, and *antu*, Amh. *antu*, dialect of Syria *anku*, أَنْكُ, and so My. *kamu*, *kau*, and *aǵ'au*, Mg. *anau*, Ef. *kumu*, *akam*, *eǵū*, (suffix, Ef., My. *-mu*, Ef. dialect *kama*), Arb. *tum*, *kum*, Heb. *tem*, *kem*, Tigri *kum*, Eth. *kemu*, Amh. *hu*, Ef. d. *ǵu*, Arb. *tu*, Heb. *tu*, Syriac *tun*, Mandaitic *tun*, *tu*. So in the third person plural, thus Talmudic *in-ho*, *in-he*, for *in-hon*, *in-hen*; M. Syriac *an-i*, in which all that is left of the original pronoun, in Assy. *sunu*, *sina*, Arb. *humu*, *hunna*, Heb. *hem*, *hema*, &c., is *i*, the *an-* or *in-* being demonstrative prefixes. The M. Syr. suffix of this pronoun sometimes retains its n but is usually without it simply as *ē*. In the Semitic dialects generally, however, this pronoun whether separate or suffixed retains its m or n: so also in the Oceanic dialects especially in the suffixed form, thus in My. it is *ĩña*, or *iya*, suffixed *ña*, Mg. *izi*, *isi*, *ia*, *i*, suffixed *ni*, Sam. *ia* (and *na*), suffixed *na*, Ef. *iña*, *iǵa*, *na-i*, suffixed *na*, *ña*, and *mia*. In My. *ma-rika*, 'they,' the *ma* is probably this pronoun, like the *ǵa*, in Ef. *ǵa-ra*, and *za* (for *na*), in Mg. *iza-reu*, and *ini* in Ef. and Santo *ini-ra*, 'they.' This pronoun occurs also as the last part of the combination of the pronouns of the first and third persons called the 'exclusive', 'we and they,' Ef. *kina-mi*, dialect *aǵam*, Santo *ana-m*, My. *ka-mi*, Mg. *aha-i*, suffixed Santo *na-m*, Ef. *na-mi*, Mg. *na-i*.

16. (*a*) Dropping of initial syllables of words first radical weak, or quiescent, and on the other hand, (*b*) adding an initial syllable to words with ʾ (Aleph prosthetic) to lighten the pronunciation, as in § 7.

(*a*) For instance, the three Semitic words given as examples of this in § 7 appear thus in Oceanic, Ef. *atai*, and *tae*, 'to know'; חד, Sumatra *sada*, Gaudalcanar *kesa*, Epi *saka*, Ef. *sika-i*, *tesa*, Sam. *tasi*, N. Caledonia *tat*, &c., 'one'; and Assy. *laku*, Fi. *lako*, 'to proceed,' 'going.'

(*b*) For example إِسْم, 'name,' Ef. *ǵisà*, Malo *isa*, Santo *kiṣa*, Fi. *yat'a*; ፀሐይ, 'sun,' see Index—Ef. *elo*, *alo*, *ali*, My. *ari*, Mg. *andru*, all show this prosthetic syllable, the sound represented by θ, ض, being difficult. So Ef. *atmate*, for *temate*, *atelaki*, for *telaki*; and *atlaġ* or *atĕlaġ* (the moon).

In Efate the first syllable of, for example, *bati*, 'teeth,' is of a different kind: for which see Index under the letter ש. Thus 'teeth' is in Santo *uṣu*, and *peti*, Su. *isi*, Madura *waja*, Celebes *ġisi*, Savu *ġutu*, Gilolo *ġedi*, &c.; and 'head,' in Mahri *here*, *haroh*, *hare* (final s dropped), is in Celebes *urie*, *ulu*, Amboyna *uruka*, (Mg. *luha*), *ulura*, Ceram. *yuli*, Sunda *pulu*, Lampong *uluh*, My. *ulu*, Maori *uru*. As the Index shows, the additional initial syllable in these words for 'teeth' (and 'head'), is that of the Semitic 'broken plural', or rather collective singular. As such 'broken plurals' have almost entirely replaced in Arabic the old or 'sound' plurals, so the latter have almost completely disappeared from the Oceanic dialects.

17. We give here a few specimens showing the letter changes in the words for 'man,' 'male,' 'woman' ('female'), 'sun,' 'day,' 'bone,' and 'child,' &c.

(*a*) نَاس, نَاتْ, אֱנָשָׁא, إِسَانْ, Assy. *yasi*, &c., 'man,' 'human being.' This is the word of which the following forms are given in Max Müller's *Science of Language*, p. 262, *oraġ*, *raġ*, *oran*, *olan*, *lan*, *ala*, *la*, *na*, *da*, *ra*. Ef. *nătă*, *ata*, *ita*, *ta*, and see below under (*d*), and (*e*).

(*b*) مَرْءٌ, (מָרְאָ), 'man, male, vir,' (*c*) مَرْأَة, إِمْرَأَة, 'woman, female.'

(*b*) Ef. Malo, and Oba *mera*, Ef. *mare*, *manĭ*, and *mā*, Ysabel *mara*, and *mane*, and *mae*, Batta *morah*, Satawal *mar*, and *mal*: Reduplicated,

Bima *monemone*, Ml. *banman*, Motu *maruana*, Bali *muwani*, Carolines (Mortlock), *muan*, Ceram *manowai*, Ef. *anoai*, *anöi*, Gilolo *anow*.

The Mg. and My. word for 'male' is quite different, *lahi*, and *laki*, ذَكَر, إِدْكَا.

(*c*) My. *bini*, N. Guinea *bin*, *pine*, Bu. *bai*, Bauro *wai*, Ef. *bite*, dialect *matu*: Reduplicated,

My. *parampuan*, Java *parawan*, *prawan*, Tanna *pilaven*, *pitan*, *bran.* Other Oceanic forms are *mawina, vaivine, faifid, fafine,* Mg. *vavi,* Motu *haine,* Ef. dialect *fafine.* The final **n** is for š, the Semitic feminine ending.

(*d*) Combination of (*a*) and (*b*) signifying 'male', 'husband':

Ef.	*ata-manĭ*	Tanna	*yeru-man*
	ita-mani		*eru-man*
Epi	*eru-măne*	Ml.	*ulu-man*
	ata-mane	Santo	*la-mani*
	su-mano		*le-man*
Ml.	*asa-maġ'*	Fi.	*ata-ġane*
		Tong. & Sam.	*ta-ane, ta-ni*

(*e*) Combination of (*a*) and (*c*) signifying 'woman', 'female,' 'wife':

Ero.	*asi-ven*	Santa Maria	*ta-wa*		
	yare-vin	Fi.	*yale-wa*	S. Cris.	*ura-o*
	li-van		*ale-wa*	Epi	*si-ra*
	ahi-ven		*le-wa*		*ti-ra*
Santo	*le-vina*	Ef.	*la-i*		
D. of Y.	*ta-buan*		or *le-i*		
Mota	*ta-vini*	Vanua Lava	*re-ḅe*	N.G.	*si-ne*
Ml.	*ra-bin*		*re-ene*		*s'i-ne*
Satawal	*ra-bout*		*dre-ne*		
		Ef.	*kuru-ni*	N.G.	*kura-ni*
			or *ġuru-ni*		
			kuru-i		
			or *ġuru-i*		
		Santo	*'ara-i*		
			'aṣa-i		

(*f*) Feminine of (*a*) signifying 'woman':

H. *'is's'ah,* Ch. *'ita,* S. *'atto,* A. *'unt'a.* Ef. *lai, le, li,* Fi. *adi, di,* Mota *iro, ro.* But Ef. *lai* may be *la-i,* see under (*e*).

(*g*) Sun (also day, and daylight), and §§ 13 *b,* 16 *b.* See Index under ፀሐይ 'sun,' Tigre and Amharic *ṣai,* Epi (South-East *ndae* (*dai*), Tarawan *tai,* Cajeli *lehei,* Amblaw *laei,* Meli *rea,* Sulu Islands *lea,* Mota *loa,* Tongan *läa,* Samoan *la,* Maori *ra,*

Lifa *t'o*, *t'u*, Mare *du*, Aurora *aloa*, Efate *elo*, *alo*, *ali*, Mg. *andru*, *anru*, My. *ari*, Lobo *orah* and *oruk*, Mafoor *ori*, Vaturaġa *aso*, Florida *aho*, Fiji *siġa*, San Cristoval *sina*, Motu *dina*, Aneityum *t'iġ*, &c.

(*h*) Bone, v. § 10, and Index under عظم, plural עֲצָמוֹת, Mahri *'aṭaiṭ*, *at'ăt'* (the m dropped), Efate *täot*, or *tawot*, Mg. *täulana* (note the nunation), Guaham *tolan*, Lampong *tulan*, My. *tulaġ*. In this word Efatese has the original plural (feminine) ending t, which the others change to l.

(*i*) Child, father, mother: see Dict. s.v. *ani* (for *nani*). The initial radical (v. Index) is found as w, y, and ' (ا). It is a in My. *anak*, Ml. *anatu-n*, Mg. *anaka*, k in Ef. *kanoa*, *kanoka*, My. *kanak*, and z in Mg. *zanaka*, dropped in Ef. *nati*, *nani*, in which the middle radical l is represented by n, and in *reita n* by r, as in Mg. *reni*, An. and Ml. *risi*, but by l in Pa. *lati*, Fila *leta*, Celebes *leyto*. The third radical d is represented by t, as in Ef. *natu na*, by n, as in *nani na*, by k in Mg. and My. *anaka*, Ef. *kanoka*, and elided in Ef. *nai na*, *kanoa*, Mg. *rai*, Ef. *ere*, Ceram. *ina*, Epi *la*, Ef. *reita*. Fila *leta*, &c.[1]

For the places in the foregoing where the letter changes in the numerals, and certain other much-used words (sun, moon, star, stone, fire, fruit, lightning, wind, heaven, water, ear, man (person), man (male), woman, eye, fruit) are explained, see Ch. VI; and for the same in the personal pronouns, Ch. V. In the foregoing are also explained the words for head, year, sea, navel, name, teeth, bone, skin, house, tree, canoe (ship), and many other nouns, verbs, and particles too numerous to mention here.

[1] See Index.

CHAPTER III

TRILITERALISM AND INTERNAL VOWEL CHANGE

It is now to be shown that the Oceanic primitive language had like each of its sister dialects, Arabic, Assyrian, &c., its share of the common stock of purely and exclusively Semitic triliteral words (nouns and verbs) with the purely Semitic common method of word formation or inflexion by internal vowel change, and external additions (prefixed, infixed, suffixed), and its share also of the limited common stock of purely Semitic particles. This, if it can be shown, will be admitted to be conclusive. The particles will be dealt with subsequently.

The ancient Semitic finite verb, with its perfect and imperfect, was simply a verbal noun[1] joined in a certain way with the personal pronouns, and with it or from it other and numerous verbal nouns[2] were formed by vowel change and external formative additions. The ancient finite verb with its perfect and imperfect so formed is no longer found in the existing broken down Oceanic languages, though as analytic substitutes for it we have as the finite verb for instance in Efatese 'the verbal pronoun' joined with these verbal nouns after the fashion of the Imperfect, as *a bano* I (am, or was) going=I go (or I went), and in Malagasy the 'pronominal adjunctive' joined with these verbal nouns, after that of the perfect, as *tiaku* my loving=I loved, or, I love. The verbal nouns that were formed with or from that of the ancient finite verb were numerous, and in them we have the ground-

[1] *C.G.S.L.*, pp. 164 and 178.

[2] Ibid., p. 195, and Wright's *Arb. Gr.*, I. §§ 195, 196.

forms of the modern Oceanic verb. We may compare here the following Arabic forms:—

1. فَعْلٌ *fa'l* (fa'l*u*, or fa'l*o*, fa'l*i*, fa'l*a*[1]; in the rest I shall not give these final vowels, but the reader should bear them in mind).

2. فِعْلٌ *fi'l.*
3. فُعْلٌ *fu'l.*
4. فَعْلَةٌ *fa'lat.*
5. فِعْلَةٌ *fi'lat.*
6. فُعْلَةٌ *fu'lat.*
7. فَعَلٌ *fa'al.*
8. فَعَالٌ *fa'āl.*
9. فَعَلَةٌ *fa'alat.*
10. فَعَالَةٌ *fa'ālat.*
11. فِعَلٌ *fi'al.*
12. فِعَالٌ *fi'āl.*
13. فِعَالَةٌ *fi'alat.*
14. فُعَلٌ *fu'al.*
15. *fu'āl.*
16. *fu'ālat.*
17. *fa'il.*
18. *fa'īl.*
19. *fa'ilat.*
20. *fa'īlat.*
21. *fa'ūl.*
22. *fi'ūlat* (Heb.).
23. *fu'ūl.*
24. *maf'al.*
25. *maf'il.*
26. *maf'ilat.*
27. *maf'ul.*
28. *maf'ulat.*
29. *maf'alat.*
30. *fu'ulat.*

&c.[2]

Of these forms 1–6 are the commonest in Oceanic. The difference from the Arabic form is mainly in the last vowel of 1–3 (this last vowel is not written in the above as explained) and in the last two vowels of 4–6 (the last being this same unwritten terminal) there being for the final *u*, or *o*, when it is not elided, sometimes *a*, or *i*, and for the *a* before the *-t*, often *u*, or *o*, as in other Semitic languages. We now proceed to compare the Oceanic triliteral words with Arabic, Assyrian, &c.,

[1] In Arabic as in the Semitic mother-tongue every noun ended with one of these italicized vowels, *u*, or *o* (nominative); *i* (genitive); *a* (accusative). Generally the other Semitic languages, and the modern Oceanic use these final vowels indiscriminately, without case signification.

[2] For these and other forms, see Wright's *Arb. Gr.*, Vol. I. §§ 196–219, &c.

just as, for instance, we compare, say Assyrian or Himyaritic words with Arabic, Hebrew, Syriac, or Ethiopic.

Take for example Efate *lifai*, to bend round; *malibai*, bent (the final *i*, transitive particle, is explained below); *lofa*, a thing bent; *lofai*, to bend; *malofa*, bent; *kalofa*, or *kolofa*, bent; *lufa* (Samoan *lavalava*), a wrapper round the loins; Samoan *lofa*, to crouch; *lofata'ina*, to cause to crouch; *lave*, *lavelave* (Arabic *lafelafa*, to wrap round, &c.), to entangle; *lavelavea*, to be entangled; (for *-a*, and *-ta'ina*, see below). Fiji *love*, *lovet'a* (Samoan *lavasi*), to coil, fold, to bend; *kalove*, bent; *salove*, flexible; Malay *lipat*, *lampit*, *lapit*, *lampis*, *lapis*, a fold, to fold, plait; Malagasy *lefiṭa*, also *lufiṭa*, folded, bent, plaited; Arabic *laffa*, to be involved, intertwined, to wrap up, wrap round (oneself, as clothing), to fold, *luff*, *liff*, *luffat*, *liffat*, involved, intertwined, &c.; *loffa*, *loffat*, coil of turban, winding of road. In this example the above given six commonest forms of the modern Oceanic verb (or noun), the ancient verbal noun, are seen, viz.:—

1. *lave*.	3. *lofa*, *love*, *lufa*.	5. *lipat*.
2. *lifa*.	4. *lampit*, *lavasi*.	6. *lovet'a*.

The inference is irresistible that in the Oceanic primitive or mother-tongue this word was triliteral, and had the vowel changes peculiar to the Semitic languages most fully preserved in the ancient Arabic; and that as a triliteral word with the middle radical doubled it underwent the usual contractions, set forth in all Semitic grammars, of such words, as is plainly seen by comparing with the Arabic. These forms, originally verbal nouns and still often used as such, formed from the ancient finite verb, as *lipat*, a fold, *lofa*, a thing bent, or bending, have become ground-forms of the modern verb, as *lipat*, *lipatkan*,[1] to fold; *lofai*,[1] to bend; from which again are formed by external additions modern verbal nouns, and derived verb forms. Thus we have *lipatan*, a fold; *lofaian*, a bending or being bent; *lavelavea*, entangled or entangling; *malibai*, bent; and the derived verb forms (see below):[2]—

[1] For *kan* and *i*, transitive particles, see below on the Particles. [2] Ch. IV.

Safal, Fiji *salove*, flexible.

Mafal, Malay *malipat*, to fold, plait; Efate *malifus*, bent, flexed.

Mifal, Malagasy *milefiṭa*, folded.

Tafal, Fiji *kalove*, Efate *kalofa*, bent.

Manfal, Malagasy *mandefiṭa*, to fold, bend.

Matafal, Samoan *fa'alave*, to take a turn of a rope as round a pin.[1]

It is not proposed to give here these modern verbal nouns, and derived verb forms for the following words, but they may easily be found in the dictionaries.

As is seen in this example the vowels of the ground-forms of the Oceanic verb are retained in the modern derived forms and verbal nouns. It is in the ground-forms therefore that we find the proof of the part played in the ancient language (the primitive Oceanic) by internal vowel change.

To show that this is a fair specimen of modern Oceanic words, that it is not exceptional but only one out of the mass and of a piece with the rest, would prove conclusively that the Oceanic primitive or mother-tongue had like each of the sister dialects, Arabic, Assyrian, &c., its share of the purely and exclusively common stock of Semitic triliteral words with the purely Semitic common method of word-formation or inflexion by internal vowel change and external additions. This then is what we have now to endeavour to show, and we may begin with words belonging to the same special class as this, viz.:—

(*a*) Triliterals with the Second Radical Doubled.

The figures refer to the above given verbal noun forms 1–30. Efate 1 *tabu*, Maori *tapu*, prohibited; Arabic (*dabba*, to prohibit) 1 *dabbu*, a prohibiting, or being prohibited.

Efate 1 *malo*, Malay 4 *malas*, disgusted, loathe, unwilling, averse. Arabic (*malla*, to loathe, be disgusted, unwilling, averse) 1 *mallo*, 4 *mallat*.

[1] For these prefixes, see below on the Formative prefixes.

Efate 1 *tefa*; Fiji 4 *tuva*, to put in a series, range troops in order of battle. Arabic *ṣaffa*, to set or place in order in a series, to arrange the line of battle, 1 *ṣaff*.

Efate 1 *kari*, *karo*, to scratch, scrape, shave, seize, grasp; *karo*, the throat, gullet; *kārĭ*, a plane; Malay *garu*, to rake; Efate 3 *ġura*, to rake; Malagasy 3 *kuri*, to scrape; Efate 6 *ġurasi*, to gnaw; Efate 4 *karaka*, *karati*, *karisi*, *karafi*, *karuti*; Malay *garit*, *garis*, *garut*, *garok*, *garap*, *karut*, *karok*; Malagasy *haraṭa*, to shave; Arabic (*garra*, to drag, snatch, sweep, seize; Hebrew, *garar*, to scrape, sweep, saw); Arabic 1 *garr*: 4 *garrat*; 6 *gurrat*; Hebrew *garon*, the throat, gullet.

Efate 1 *kalu*; 3 *kulu*, a covering, as of cloth or a mat, to cover oneself with such; 4 *kaluti*; 6 *kuluti*, to cover with such, to clasp one round so as to hold him; *kel*, *kelel*, *kelu*, *kelakela*, turn round; Malagasy 6 *hudina*, *hudidina*, and *herina*, Malay *guliġ*, *guluġ*, *goliġ*; 5 *giliġ*, *kaliliġ*, to roll, to turn round; Arabic (*galla*, to cover, &c., Hebrew *galal*, to roll) 1 *gallu*; 3 *gullu*, a covering; Hebrew *gilgal*, a wheel, a whirlwind, compare the analogous Malagasy *hudinkudina*, turned repeatedly; كَرَّ, كَرْكَرَ, ከረረ, تَكَرْكَرَ to turn round, revolve, Ef. *kel*, *kelet*, *kelakela*, *kelekelet*.[1]

Efate 3 *kusi*, and, with *k* elided, *usi*, to follow, to track, to narrate; Malay 6 *usir*, to pursue; Arabic *ḳaṣṣa*, to track, to narrate.

Efate 3 *soka*, to leap, go swiftly, be inflamed with anger, to spear, inivit *mulierem*; Samoan *soso'a*, Tongan *hoka*, to spear, pierce; Arabic *zaḥḥa*, to leap, to go with vehemence, to burn with rage, inivit *mulierem*, to project, to throw.

Malagasy 4 *haraka*, scorched, dried up, parched; Malay *gariġ*, *kriġ*; Efate 1 *kara*, dry; Arabic *ḥarra*; Hebrew *ḥarar*, to be hot, burned, dried up.

Malagasy 1 *tani*, Efate *taġi*, to sound, clank, tinkle, hum,

[1] In this paragraph there are two cognate words (for which see *kel*, *kalu*, in Dictionary), the one beginning with g, the other with k, both second radical, l or r, doubled. The doubled letter is seen in *hudidina*, *kaliliġ*, and the reduplicated form Arb. *karakara*, *karakarat*, Eth. *an-k'ark'ara*, is seen in Ef. *kelakela*, *kelekelet*.

wail; Malay 4 *taǵis*, (Efate, Samoan) *taǵisi*; Arabic *ṭanna*, to tinkle, clank, ring, hum.

Efate 3 *kofu*, to wrap up, enclose, to clothe; Tongan, *kofu*; Samoan *ō'ofu*, to put on a garment; Efate 4 *kafuti*, to wrap up, enclose; Efate *kofu*; Samoan *'ofu'ofu*; Fiji 6 *kovuna*, to envelop in leaves food gathered into a mass to be cooked in the oven; Efate *kofukofua* (*-a*), bent so as to be concave, so Maori *kohu*, *kokohu*; Efate *k* elided, 3 *ofa*, 1 *aba*, to whirl round, so Tahiti *ohu*, which also denotes to bend downwards, to stoop; Hawaiian *ohuohu*, heavy; Efate 1 *kabu* (dialect *koau*), the native food ('pudding') gathered into a mass wrapped in leaves and cooked in the oven, the principal daily food of the natives, so Arabic *kobba*, *kabab*, '*kibby*,' the national dish of the Arabs gathered into a round mass and cooked in the oven. Arabic *kabba*, to roll up into a ball, to make into balls food for cooking; to invert, to stoop, to be heavy; *kabakaba*, to be wrapped up, enveloped, to wrap up or envelop oneself (in one's garment); Ethiopic *kabab*, to whirl round.

Efate 1 *saru*, Malay *saru*, Efate 21 *saruru*, to sound, resound, roar; Arabic (*ṣarra* to make a noise, sound, roar) 1 *ṣarru*; 18 *ṣariru*.

Efate 1 *kaf* bent; Maori *kapu*, curly, the hollow of the hand; Efate *kafīkāfī*, a native basket, to put the hand into such a basket to feel for and take out something; Arabic *kaffa*, to take something stealthily between the fingers; Hebrew *kafaf*, to bend; *kaf*, the hollow of the hand, a hollow vessel; and as to the form compare with *kafĕkāfĕ* Arabic *kafĕkafa*.

Efate 1 *kasi*, to rub; Samoan *'asi*; Malay 6 *gosot*, *gosok*, 5 *gisik*, *kisil*; Malagasy 4 *kasuka*, to rub; Arabic (*ḳas's'a*, to rub) *ḳas's'u*.

Efate 1 *raka*, 24 *maraka*, to desire, will, be willing, desirous of; Syriac *rag*, to desire, will (this in Arabic would be *ragga*), 2 *rega*, desire, will.

Efate 1 *sila*, *silasila*, to sound, crackle, rattle (as thunder); Samoan fai-*tilitili*; Maori whai-*tiri*, thunder; Maori *tiri*, to crackle: Arabic *ṣalla*, *ṣalāṣala*, to sound, crackle, crack, as thunder.

Efate 1 *kala, kalakala*, Malagasy 2 *keli*, or *heli*, little; 5 *kelez*, in imperative passive *kelezu*, verbal noun *kelezina*; *kelezu* is for *kelezi* of which the *u*=*i* in the other Oceanic languages, and written *i* in *kelezina*; 23 *kululi* very small; *heliheli* (and *kedikedi*) to move to and fro; Efate *makalakala*, to move about quickly (as ants). Arabic (*ḳalla*, Hebrew *ḳalal*, to be little) 1 *ḳallu*, *ḳalli*, *ḳalla*, 5 *ḳillat*; Hebrew *ḳilḳel* (pilpel); Arabic *ḳalĕḳala*, to move to and fro.[1]

Efate 2 *siba*, 3 *suba* (*masiba*, a fragment, broken); Fiji *sove*, to break; Malagasy 6 *sumbina*, fragment, broken; Hebrew, Chaldee *s'abab* (this in Arabic would be *s'abba*). to break, Chaldee *s'ibba*, a fragment.

Efate 3 *sumi*, 6 *sumili*; Malay *sumpat, sumbat, sumpal*, 1 *sampal*; Malagasy *tampina*, to plug, stop an aperture; Arabic *ṣamma*, to plug, stop an aperture.

(*b*) Triliterals with the Middle Radical *w* and *y*.

Efate 1 *mate*; Samoan *mati*; Malay *mati*; Malagasy (*fati*, a corpse) *mati*, to die, be dead; Malagasy 4 *matesa*; Mangarevan *mater* in *materaġa*. Arabic *māta*, to die, be dead, 1 (*mawt*) *mat*.

Efate 1 *masi*, to shave; Arabic *māsa*, to shave, 1 (*maws*) *mas*.

Efate 1 *laġa*, 4 *laġat*, to raise; Samoan 1 *laġa*; Maori *raġa*, to raise, Efate *laġi*, up, above, the sky, heaven; Maori *raġi*; Malay 4 *laġit*; Malagasy *laniṭa* id.; Maori 3 *ruġa*, the top, upper part, upwards, on high; Samoan *luġa*; Hawaiian *luna*, id.; Hebrew *ram* (in Arabic this would be *rama*), to be high, to raise; *rum*, height, elevation; *ramah, ramat*, Ethiopic *rama*, a high place, third heaven (Ethiopic).

Efate 3 *soro, sore, suru*; Malagasy 6 *suduka, sudika*, to tell lies, to deceive; Arabic *zāra*, to tell lies, 3 *zuru* or *zoro*.

Efate 25 *mitiri, miṣiri*; Malay 6 *tulis*; Malagasy *suraṭa*, *suriṭa*, to make figures, draw, paint, write; Arabic *ṣāra*, to form, make figures, draw, paint, 6 *ṣurat*.

[1] In the foregoing the uncontracted form appears in some cases, as in My. *kaliliġ*, Mg. *hudidina*, Ef. *saruru*, Mg. *kululi*.

Efate 3 *suru*; Malagasy 4 *saruna*; Malay 6 *suruk*, to conceal; Ethiopic, *sawara* (this in Arabic would be *sāra*), to cover, conceal.

Efate 1 *tani*, 3 *tuni*, 4 *tanumi*, *tanumaki*; Malay *tanam*; Samoan, *tanumia*, *tanuma'ki*, to cover with earth, soil; Arabic *ṭāna*, to cover with earth, clay, soil.

Efate 1 *tiri*, sometimes pronounced *riri*; Maori *rere*; Samoan *lele*, to fly; Arabic *ṭāra*, to fly; 1 *ṭayr* or *ṭair*.

Efate 1 *afa ki*; Malagasy 4 *afina*, to conceal, bury; Efate 3 *ofa ki*; Samoan *ufi*, 6 *ufita'i*, *ufitia*, to cover, conceal; Efate 3 *uwi*; Samoan *ufi*; Malay *ubi*; Malagasy *uvi*, the yam (so called as being a root buried in the ground, or covered with earth); Arabic "*āba*, to be concealed, to conceal, to bury; 1 "*ayb*; 4 "*aybat* (cf. "*ayab*, roots).

Mota 2 *esu*; Polynesian 3 *ora*, *ola*; Malay 6 *urip*; Java 5 *idup*; Efate 25 *mairi*; Malagasy 26 *veluna*; Efate 27 *mauri*, dialect *mole*; Fiji *bula*; Tanna 28 *murif*, *murep*, life, to live; Arabic '*ās'a*, to live; 5 *ēs'at*; 26 *maīs'at*; 25 *maīs'*.

From the examples of verbs middle radical *w* and *y* it is clear from comparison with the Arabic that in the ancient Oceanic such words underwent the regular contractions set forth in Semitic grammars.

(c) Triliterals with ', *h*, *ḥ* (and *ḥ'*), and ' (and ") Middle Radical.

In the Oceanic languages these verbs are contracted like those with *w* and *y*. In Assyrian Sayce (*Assyr. Gr.*) classes verbs middle radical *w*, *y*, ', ', *h* altogether as concave or quiescent verbs. In the Semitic languages in the course of their analytic development these consonants tend to become all alike quiescent, as for instance in Mandean. In Assyrian, according to Delitzsch (*Assyr. Gr.*), ', *h*, *ḥ* (and *ḥ'*), ' (and ") were all pronounced alike as ', or spiritus lenis, that is, have lost their consonant power, *ḥ'*, however, being pronounced like Arabic *ḥ*: the modern Oceanic as distinctly compares in this with the

Assyrian, as it does in the verbal noun forms with the Arabic. It is certain, however, that all these consonants were not always so pronounced, or quiescent, in ancient Oceanic. That they have become so especially when the middle radical of verbs is to be explained not only from their natural tendency to quiesce, but also from the fact that in the verbal noun forms 1–6, which are the common ground-forms of the Oceanic verb, the middle radical always lost its vowel. However it may be explained the fact is certain, as a few examples will show.

Efate 3 *bolo* or *folo*; Fiji 1 *vala*, to do, to act; Efate 6 *bolosi*; Fiji 4 *valata*; Arabic *fa'ala*, to do, to act; 1 *fa'l*; 4 *fa'lat*.

Efate 3 *sulu*, a torch, to light by a torch, to scorch with flame; Samoan *sulu*, a torch, to light by a torch; Malay 6 *suluh*, a torch; Malagasy 3 *sulu*; 2 *silu*; 5 *siluvana*, to light by a torch; Arabic *s'a'ala*, to kindle a fire, light a torch; 6 *s'u'lat* flame.

Efate 3 *soro*, to burn, flame (of fire, of rage); Maori *toro*; Efate 6 *sorofi*, to burn, to flame with rage; Fiji, *t'oroǵa*, to scorch; Arabic *sa'ara*, to kindle a fire, to rage; 3 *su'ru* or *so'ro*, flame of fire, flame of rage.

Efate *bara*, to burn, be burned, kindle; 21 *bauri*, *bauria*, to kindle a fire in the oven; Samoan 1 *vela*; 4 *velasia*; Maori *wera*; Tahiti *vera*, to burn, to heat, to be cooked; Hebrew *ba'ar*, to kindle, burn, be burned; Arabic 1 would be *ba'r*; 21 *ba'ur*.

Efate 1 *taǵi*, 2 *tine*, to carry sail (a canoe); *mitaǵa*, *miten*, to be laden, heavy; 12 *tiana*, or *tiena*, laden, gravid; Malagasy 1 *entana*, burden; Malay 4 *taǵgung*, to bear, carry; Syriac *ṭ'en*, to bear, be laden, *ṭ'ana*, burden; *ṭ'ina*, laden, gravid.

Efate 12 *miala* or *miela*, to be red; Samoan 1 *melo*; Malagasy *mena*, red; Malay *mera*, red, reddish-brown, bay; Arabic *ma''ara* (4), to yield red milk mixed with blood; *ma''ir*, red; *ma''ar*, reddish.

Efate 1 *lami*, to eat; Samoan *lamu*, to chew; Hebrew *laḥam*, to eat; Arabic 1 would be *laḥm*.

Malekula 3 *roso*; 6 *rosovi*; Efate 3 *loso*, to wash; Arabi *raḥaṣa*, to wash; 3 (would be) *roḥṣo*.

Efate 3 *rumi*; Fiji *loma*; Samoan *alofa*, to compassionate, to love; Fiji 6 *lomana*; Samoan (in) *alofagia, fealofani*; Maori (in) *arohatia*; Fiji *loma*, the heart, the inner parts, midst or inside of a thing; Arabic *raḥima*; Hebrew *raḥam*, to compassionate, to love; Arabic 3 *ruḥm* or *roḥm*; Hebrew *reḥem*, the inner parts.

Efate 2 *sila*, to peel, shave off; Malagasy 5 *silaṭa, silaka*; Arabic *saḥ'ala*, to peel, shave off.

Efate 2 *simu*, 3 *tunu*, to heat, be hot, inflamed; Malagasy, Malay, Samoan, Fiji *tunu*; Malagasy 4 *tanina, tanika*; Fiji 6 *vakatununa*; Arabic *saḥ'ana*, to heat, be hot, inflamed; 3 *suḥnu* and *ṣuḥ'nu*; 6 *suḥ'nat*, 4 *sahnat*.

Efate 3 *bono*, to be shut, closed, secret; 6 *bonoti, bunuti, monoti, munuti*, to shut, close, stop, cover, conceal; Maori 1 *pani*, to shut; Hawaiian *pani*, to shut, conceal; Tahiti 3 *puni*, to be enclosed, to hide; *tapuni*, to hide; Mangaiian *puni*, to hide; Tongan *buni*, closed, shut; *tabuni*, to shut, to close up; Samoan 6 *punita'i, punitia*, to stop with, to be shut up; and *moniti*, to stop, cork, plug; Malay 3 *buni*, hidden, to hide (and Sanfal form as in Amharic), *sambuni*, hidden, concealed, secret; Java 6 *buntu*, closed up, shut; Efate *bumuta*, mute, silent (English 'shut up' = silent); Hebrew *baham* or *bahan*, to shut, to cover; Arabic *bahama*, to shut, close, be covered, hid, mute, silent.

Efate 1 *safa, sefa*, to pant, to hasten; 3 *sofa*, phthisis (panting), to pant (to have phthisis) to hasten; Malagasy 1 *sefu*, asthma, *sefusefu*, or *sevusevu*, hurry, haste, breathless; 4 *sevuka*, in haste, bustling; Hebrew *s'a'af*, to pant, to hasten.

Efate 1 *bami* or *fami*, to eat; Tahiti *hamu*, gluttonous, to go to a feast whenever one occurs, to be burdensome to others by eating their food; Hawaiian *hamu*, to eat fragments of food; Maori *hamu*, feeding on fragments; Tongan *hamu*, to eat one kind of food only; Mangarevan *amu*, to eat with the mouth, not using the hands; Hebrew, Ethiopic *pa'am, fa'ama*; Arabic *fa'ama*, to have the mouth full of food, to swallow down.

(*d*) Triliterals with the Third Radical: ', *w*, *y* (*i*), *h*, *ḥ* (and *ḥ'*), ' (and '').

Efate 2 *siko*, to look at; Malagasy *zaha*; Hebrew *sakah*; Chaldee *sĕka*, to look at.

Efate 23 *tubu*, to swell; *tobu* a tumour; *tumbu, tuma*, will; Polynesian 23 *tupu, tubu*; Malagasy *tumbu*, to spring forth, grow, increase; Malay 24 *tumbuh*; Samoan *tupu'* and *tupul*, in *tupu'aga, tupula'i*; Hebrew *ṣabah*, to come forth, to swell, to will; Aramaic *ṣeba*, to will; *ṣebu*, will; Arabic *ṣaba'a* and *ṣabu'a*, to come forth, rise, spring up, project; 23 *ṣubu, ṣubut*.

Efate 2 *kili*; Maori 1 *kari, keri*; Malay *gali*; Malagasy *hadi*; Fiji *kali*, 4 *kalia, kaliva*, to dig; Arabic *karu* (third radical *w*); Ethiopic *karaya* (third radical *y*); Hebrew *karah* (third radical *h*); Aramaic *kĕra* (third radical '), to dig; Arabic 1 *karw*; Ethiopic 4 *keryat*.

Efate, Fiji, *tatalai*, to warm oneself at the fire; Arabic *ṣala*, 1 *ṣaly*, (5) *taṣala*(*y*), to feel the heat of fire, to warm oneself at the fire.

Samoan *talotalo*; Tahiti *tarotaro*, to pray; 4 *talosia*; Efate *tarotaro*; 4 *tarosi*, to pray; Arabic *ṣala*; Ethiopic *ṣalaya*, to pray; 4 *ṣalot*.

Efate 2 *tili*; 3 *tuli*; Malay *tutur*; Samoan 1 *tala*; Malagasy 3 *turi*, to narrate, tell; Malay 6 *turut*, to follow; Arabic *tala*, to follow, to recite, secondary root from *wala*(*y*) (8).

Efate 3 *toko*, (shortened) *to*, *matoko*, to sit, rest upon, stay; Malay *duduk, totok*; Fiji 2 *tiko*; Efate 6 *tokora*; Fiji 5 *tikora*; Malagasy 6 *tuaṭa, tuiṭa, tueṭa*; Arabic *taka*, to rest upon, support oneself upon, sit, recline. This is a secondary root from Arabic *waka* (8) i.e. *'ttaka* to rest upon, sit (Luke xiv. 8, Arabic Version).

Efate 1 *taku, mataku*; Samoan *mata'u*; Malay 4 *takut*; Malagasy *tahuṭa*; Samoan *mata'utia*, fear, to fear; Arabic *taḳa*, (Hebrew *taḳe*), to fear. This is a secondary root from Arabic *waḳa*(*y*) (8) i.e. *'ttaḳa*, to fear (to guard oneself being afraid).

Efate 1 *karai*, to dislike, be averse from, hate; Malay 2 *gili*; Malagasy 1 *hala*; Arabic *kariha*, to dislike, abhor; 1 *karh*.

Malay 4 *s'akit*; Ilocan *masakit*; Efate 1 *masaki*; Tongan *mahaki*; Maori, Rarotongan *maki*; Samoan *ma'i*; Hawaiian *mai*, sickness, to be ill; Arabic *s'aka*, to be sick, have a disease; 1 *s'aka(y)*, 4 *s'akat*.

Efate 1 *maru*, to rub, to joke; Maori 2 *miri*, to rub; Arabic *maraḥ'a*, to rub or anoint with oil, to joke; 1 *marḥ'*.

Samoan 18 *malie*, well, agreeable, right, proper, good; Maori, Mangarevan *marie*; Efate *malei* or *milei*, good, well; Arabic *maluḥa*, to be elegant, beautiful; 18 *mali(y)ḥ*, *maliḥ*, beautiful, good, fit, proper.

Efate 3 *boka* or *buka*, to strike, to reprehend; Malagasy *puka*; Malay 6 *pukul*, to strike; Efate *bukati*; Arabic *baka'u*, to strike, to reprehend; 3 (would be) *buk'*, and 6 *buk'at*.

Efate 23 *roko*, also *loko*, *loku*, and *luku*, and 1 *laku*, to bow, stoop; Samoan *lolo'u*, to bend, curve; Fiji *roko*, a bowing form or posture, curved; 24 *rokota*, to bend a bow; *rokova*, bow to, pay respect to; *rokoroko*, reverence, respect; Efate 4 *lakosa*; 24 *lukuta*; Mangarevan *rokuroku*, a final prayer when the torches are thrown down and extinguished at a funeral; Arabic *raka'a*, to bow, stoop, as from old age, or in prayer; 23 *ruku'*; 4 *rak'at*.

Efate 23 *bulu*, *bule*, complete, the whole; Tongan *fuli*, all; Malay *bulah*, the whole; Arabic *bala"a*, to complete, to go through to the end; 23 *bulu"*.

(*e*) Triliterals with the First Radical *v* (*w*), *y* (*i*), ', *h*, *ḥ* (and *ḥ'*), ' (and ").

Efate 21 *amosi*, *mosi*, *musi*; Maori *muhu*, to rub; Arabic *wamasa*, to rub; 21 (would be) *wamus*.

Efate 8 *bara*; Malay *palu*; Malagasy *veli*; Efate *barati*; Malagasy *velez-*, to beat; Arabic *wabala*, to beat.

Efate 8 *atai*, *tai*, to know; Malay *tau*; Hebrew *yada'*, to know; *da'at*, *de'a*.

Efate 7 *buli*, to abstain, fast; Malagasy *fadi*; Arabic *'abala*, to abstain, fast.

Efate 8 *kani*, to eat; Fiji *kana*; Malay 24 *makan*; Malagasy (transposed for *mahana*), *humana*; 20 *hinana*; 10 *hanina*, to eat; Arabic *'akala*, to eat; 8 *'akāl*; 24 *ma'kal*; Hebrew 20 *'ăkilat*.

Efate 21 *roġo*, dialect, *doġo*; Maori *roġo*, to hear, to smell; Samoan *loġo*; Malay 10 *daġar*; Malagasy *renes-*; Efate 22 *roġosa* ki; Samoan *loġoloġosa 'i*; Efate *roġoroġo* ki, to proclaim, to report; Arabic *'aḍana*, to hear, to smell, to proclaim; 10 *'aḍanat*; 21–22 (would be) *'aḍon*, *'aḍonat*.

Samoan 1 *efu*, dust, to become dust, dust-coloured; Malay *abu*; Tongan *efu*, dust, ashes; Efate *abu*, dust, ashes; *abuabu*, to fly in the air (dust); Arabic *habu*, to fly in the air (dust); 1 (would be) *habw*; 4 *habwat*, dust, colour of dust.

Efate 1 *ta*, to chop, cut, to speak, or utter quickly (as it were to make a chopping noise); Fiji, Samoan *ta*; Efate, Samoan 7 or 8 *tata*; Malay 9 or 10 *tatah*; Malagasy *tatana*; Fiji 4 *taya*, *tala-ka*, *tava-ka*; Arabic *haḍḍa*, to cut, to cut quickly, to chop, to utter speech quickly; 1 *haḍḍa*; 7 *haḍaḍ*; 8 *haḍāḍ*; 4 (would be) *haḍḍat*, and 9 *haḍaḍat*.

Efate 21 *loai*, to rub, smear; 22 *alofi* and *lofi*, also *loasi*, *loari*, and doubled *loloasi*, to rub, to smear or paint the face with a cosmetic or paint; Malay *lulut* and *lulur*, to cleanse the skin by friction and cosmetics, to rub the skin with cosmetics, to smear; Arabic *ḥala'a*, to rub, to smear; 21 *ḥalowa* or *ḥaluw*; 22 (would be) *ḥalowat*.

Efate 1 *elo*, to be sweet, pleasant; Hawaiian 3 *olu*; Arabic *ḥala'*, to be sweet, pleasant, agreeable; 1 *ḥalw*; 3 *ḥolw*.

Efate 23 *ulu*, to grow up, produce leaves, or foliage; *ulu*, a leaf; (doubled) *lulu*, to go up, be high; Hawaiian *ulu*, *uluulu*, to grow up, lift up; Arabic *'ala'*, to go up, be high; Hebrew *'alah*, to go up, sprout forth, grow up; *'aleh*, a leaf; Arabic 13 *'ilawat*, the head; 23 *'uluw*.

Samoan 3 *ulu*, 6 *uluf* (in *ulufia*, Hawaiian *uluhia*, Malagasy 5 *idiṭa* and *iliṭa*, to enter, go in; Arabic *"alla*, to enter, go in);

Chaldee *'alal* (this should have been placed above under verbs with middle radical doubled).

Efate 18 *liko*; 21 *luko* or *luku*, a rope, to adhere or be fastened to; 20 *likoti*; 22 *lukuti*, to fasten, make fast to; Malay 10 *lakat* and *lakap*, to adhere; *lukatkan*, to fasten; Malagasy *raikiṭa*, *rekiṭa*; Arabic *'aliḳa*, to adhere, to fasten to; 1 *'alaḳ*, a rope; 18 *'aliḳ*, 20 *'aliḳat*, 10 *'alaḳat*, 21 *'aluḳ*.

Efate 21 *bulu* or *fulu*, any sticky substance used to cover with as paint, to cover as with a poultice, paint, oil; Samoan *pulu*; Tahiti *puru*; Fiji *bulu*, an external application or thing that covers, to cover with earth or external application, to repair or expiate (cover) an injury, a peace offering, or thing offered as a reparation for an injury; 22 *buluta*; Efate *buluti*; Samoan *puluti*, *puluta'i*; Samoan *fulu*, Futuna *fufuru*, Tahiti *huru*, Efate (dialect) 18 *fili*, Malay *bulu*, Malagasy *vulu*, hair (also down, feathers, wool); Samoan *fulufulua*, Malagasy *vuluina*, hairy; Arabic *"afara*, to cover, to cover and imbue (as the hair with a tincture), to be hairy, shaggy, to forgive; 18 *"afir*, hair; 21 *"afuru*.

(*f*) Triliterals Doubly Weak, that is with two of the above Weak Letters or Quiescents.

Samoan 3 *nofo*, to sit, dwell, live with, remain; Maori-Tahiti *noho*; Efate *no*; Samoan 6 *nohoa*; Mangarevan *nohoka*; Tahiti *nohoraa*, a seat; Paumotan *nohohaġa*, *nohoraġa*, abode, dwelling-place; Hebrew *navah*, to sit, to dwell (also *na'ah*); *navat*, a seat, a habitation.

Efate 1 *leo*, *le*, *lo*, to see; Samoan *leo*; Fiji *rai*; Fiji 4 *rait'a*; Malay *liat*, *kaliat*; Malagasy *hiraṭa*, *hiraṣa*; Efate (dialects) *losi*, *lek*, *lumi*, *libisi*, to see; Arabic *raa*; Hebrew *raah*; Ethiopic *ray*, to see; Arabic 1 *ra'i*; Hebrew *reoh*; Ethiopic *rai*; Arabic 4 *ra't*, *rayat*; Hebrew *reot* or *revot*; Arabic 6 *ruvyat*.

Efate *ba*, *bai*, *be*, *mai*, to come, to enter; Marquesan *memai*, to come; Efate and Polynesian *mai*, hither, towards the speaker; Efate dialect *bē*; Efate 4 *basi*, enter upon, go upon; Fiji *vat'a*; Ethiopic *bawi'*, to come, to enter; Hebrew *bā*, to come, to enter; Arabic *ba'a*, to enter, &c.; Ethiopic 4 *ba't*.

Efate *nēt*, dialect *notu* (Mosin *nat*, Vaturanga *atu* and *tatu*, outwards), to go outwards (opposite of *mai* or *bē*, preceding word) *atu* or *aṣ* in *banotu*, *banaṣ*; Maori *whanatu*; Polynesian *atu*, away, away from, outwards; Ethiopic *waṣa*; Hebrew *yaṣa*; Assyrian *aṣu*, to go out, or outwards; Hebrew *yaṣo* (infinitive or verbal noun = *atu*) and 4 *ṣe't*; Ethiopic *ṣa't* (= *tatu*) and by change of *ṣ* to *n*, *nēt*, *notu*, as Fiji *yani*=*yaṣo*; *ani*=*atu*.

These two Semitic words are the opposites of each other, the one denoting 'exitus, egressus, *sive*, exeundi actus', the other (*ba*, *bawi*) 'introitus', as Ludolf, *Lex. Eth.*, observes s. v. *ṣa't*.

Efate *bano-mai* or *bano-mai*, to come; *banaṣ*, i. e. *ban aṣ*, to go; Maori *whanatu*; Efate *bano*, to go; Maori *whano*, to verge towards, to go on, proceeding towards; Hebrew *panah*, to turn, to turn oneself, to turn the back, to turn in order to go anywhere. Thus *banotu*, *whanatu*=to turn, going away, or outwards, and *bano-mai*, *bano-bē*=to turn coming, to come.

So Fiji *lako-mai*=to proceed coming; *lako-yani*, to proceed outwards, away; *lako*, Malay *laku*, to proceed; Hebrew *halak*; Assyrian *halak*; Assyrian 7 *laku*.

For Maori *haere* in *haere atu*, *haere mai*, see below.

(*g*) Triliterals with the Weak or 'Fleeting' Letter *n* the First Radical.

The Oceanic in dropping this *n* compares with the Hebrew and Aramaic, and not with the Arabic.

Efate 7 *saki*, to ascend, go up; Tongan *haki*; Samoan *a'i*; Hawaiian *ae*; Maori *ake*; Aramaic *nĕsaḳ*, to ascend, go up; Imperative (showing the dropping of the *n*) *saḳ*.

Efate 7 *bīsa* or *basa*, to speak; Tagala *basa*; Fiji 21 *vosa*; 22 *vosata ka*, to speak about; Efate *visura ki*, to converse, talk; Arabic *nabasa* and *nabaṣa*, to speak, talk.

Efate 21 *buka*, a swell, ground swell, to swell, be puffed up, then to have the belly swollen with food; Maori *puku*; Malagasy *vuki*; 22 *vukis-*; Malay 7 *bakat*; Efate 22 *bukutu*; Malay *bukit*; Malagasy *vuhiṭa* or *vuhiṣa*, a rise, a hill; Malagasy *vua-vuhiṭa*, swelled, bulged; *vuhirana*, made to bulge; *vuhirina* (*buhiṭa*), made convex, protuberant: so *buhina*, from 21 *buhi*, an inflated and puffed-up aspect; Arabic *nafaḥ'a*, to inflate, be inflated, to swell.

Efate 8 *kat*, a bite, to bite; Fiji *kata*, to bite; Raratongan *kati*, to bite (doubled), *katikati*, to bite; Malay *gigit*; Malagasy *hehiṭa*, *kaikiṭa*; Aramaic *nĕkat*, to bite.

(*h*) Triliterals with the Three Radicals Strong.

Efate 8 *samat*, *samit*; 15 *sumat*, to beat, whip, chasten, hastening, being quick; Fiji 21 *samuta*, to beat; Malay 8 *chamati*, *chamiti*, a whip or scourge; Hebrew *s'amaṭ*, *s'amaṣ*, to smite, thrust; Arabic *samaṣa*, to strike, to thrust, to urge on a beast violently; *sumaṣ*, hastening, being quick.

Efate 2 *siuo*; 3 *suwa*, to descend, downward, be low; Fiji *sobu*; Samoan 2 *ifo*; Tongan *hifo*; Tahiti *iho*; Aneityumese *asuol*, (*asuwol*); Arabic سَفُلَ, to be low, to descend.

Efate 21 *kamut*, to nip, take with the hand, seize, grasp firmly; Fiji *g'amuta*; Hebrew *ḳamaṣ*, to take with the hand; *ḳamaṭ*, to hold fast with the hand, to seize firmly.

Efate 11 *bilisi*, dialect 14 *bolisi*, to spread out; Malagasy *velaṭa*; Samoan 14 *folas* (in *folasia*); Arabic *faras'a*, to spread out.

Efate 23 *fulusi*, *bulo ki*, &c., to turn; Samoan *fulis* (in *fulisia*); Tongan *fulihi*; Maori *huri*, to turn, turn over; Tahiti *huri*, to roll; Hebrew *falas'*, to roll, revolve (turn).

Efate 12 *siuer* (*siwar*), to walk, proceed, journey; 15 *suwara*, 3 *sur*, 6 *surata*; Samoan 7 *savali*, to walk, proceed; *savalivali* (Pe'al'al[1] form), to walk about; Maori *haere*, *haerere*; Hawaiian

[1] Hebrew and Aramaic.

huele, hele; Moriori *here*; Arabic *safara*, to journey, go, proceed; 7 *safar*, 12 *sifar*, 6 *sufrat*.

These examples sufficiently show that the above Oceanic word first given *lave, lapit, lifa, lipat, love, lovet'a*, is not exceptional, but only one out of the mass and of a piece with the rest, and this conclusively establishes that the Oceanic primitive or mother-tongue had like each of its sister dialects, Arabic, Assyrian, &c., its share of the common stock of purely and exclusively Semitic triliteral words (nouns and verbs) with the purely Semitic common method of word-formation or inflexion by internal vowel change and external additions.

Passive Participle of the First Form 'kal'.

Like the Arabic مَفْعُول are Efate *masua*, مَمْزُوع, مَمْزُوعَة, bald; Efate *matūki* (*taki*), Mg. *matùki*, مَوْثُوق, trusted, firm, steadfast, brave; Ef. مَعْذُور, *matùlŭ*, swollen; and *malārĕ*, or *milate*, Tahiti *mariri*, Samoan *maalili*, Maori *makariri*, Malo *magariri*, مَقْرُور (*maḳrùrŭ*, or *ma'rùrŭ*), cold, 'frigore affectus.'

On the other hand the form فَعُول, which is used for the passive participle in Hebrew, seems to appear in *bārua*; Hebrew *pāru'a*, free from, made naked, devoid of. In such a word as *kasua*, hard, strong, the *-a* may be the feminine ending *-ta* with the *t* elided as in Modern Syriac, or it may be the participle *kasu* (Efate dialect), intensified by the adjective ending *-a*, for which see below.

Active Participle of First Form 'kal'.

In this, in Arabic and Hebrew the vowel of the first syllable of the verb is made long: so Efate *kĭlĭ*, to dig; *kāli*, كَارِ, a digging-stick, a thing for digging; so *sur*, *lāġa*, and analogously *tīla, lēt, lōfa, lūma, nīfi, ōri, sēru, sīko, tūnu, sōro*, &c.

An example of form 15 is seen in the Oceanic word for 'pig', Polynesian *puaka, pua'a, puaa*; Fiji *vuaka*; Efate *uak*, *uaġo* (قَاق, and قَاق, see Index), 15 فُوَاق, and فُوَاق.

An example of the original 'nomen actionis' of the Arabic Conjugation II, form فِعّالْ is seen in Efate *rëàkï*, to strain, a strainer (*colum*), رَاقَ (see Index), رَوَّقَ, to strain; *n.a.*, رِوّاقْ; رَاوُوقْ, a strainer (*colum*).

Remark on Ch. III. It is easy to see from the above, how the ancient triliterals came to be pronounced in the Oceanic dialects, as they prevailingly are, as bisyllabic words with the accent on the first syllable.

CHAPTER IV

INFLEXIONAL OR WORD-FORMING ADDITIONS; PREFIXES, INFIXES, SUFFIXES

Prefixes.

The Semitic inflexional verb-form or 'conjugation' prefixes were three, the causative, the reflexive or reciprocal, and the reflexive; alone or with the pronominal particle *m* prefixed to them. These were:—

1. Causative—Arabic, Ethiopic, Aramaic, *a*, originally *s'a*, *sa* (*ta*, *ti*); Hebrew *hi*; Himyaritic *sa*, and *ha*. *S* to *t*, *h*, and elided.

2. Reflexive or reciprocal—Arabic, Ethiopic, Assyrian, Hebrew *n*, *in*, *i*. *N* elided.

3. Reflexive—Arabic, Assyrian, Hebrew, &c., *ta*, *it*, *it'*.

These three were combined thus:—

4. Causative-reflexive, or simply causative, or transitive (1 and 2). Ethiopic, Amharic *an*; Himyaritic *han*; also Amharic *asan* (for *san*).

5. Causative-reflexive, simply causative, or reflexive, middle (1 and 3). Tigre, Amharic, Ethiopic, Himyaritic, Arabic, *ata*, *ista* (for *sata*), *asta* (for *sata*), *sat'a*, *hat'a*, or *hat'*.

6. Reflexive-passive, or reciprocal-reflexive (2 and 3). Assyrian, Himyaritic *nit'*, *inta*, *itta*.

7. Reflexive-passive (3 and 4). Ethiopic, Amharic *tan*. Also Assyrian (2 and 7), *ittan*, *intan*.

The infinitives and participles of these often had the pronominal particle *m* prefixed, and then with this *m* prefixed were sometimes used for the finite verb. Thus we have *ma* Syriac (Maphel), causative, for the simple *a* (Aphel) of 1. In modern Syriac this has become almost the sole form of the causative. The *m*, whether prefixed to 1, 2, 3, 4, 5, 6 or 7, makes no difference in the signification.

8. Reflexive-passive (3 and 1). Syriac *et'ma*.

9. Apart from these three prefixes, this *m*, or *ma*, was sometimes alone prefixed to infinitives, and to passive participles of the ground-form. Thus in Mahri (modern Himyaritic) the common passive participle is expressed through *m*, which replaces many lost inner passives. See Von Maltzan on the Mahri in *Z.D.M.G.*, Vol. XXVII. This passive form is frequent also in Oceanic, as Efate *baku*, to pluck out, *mafaku*, plucked out; *basu*, to snap off, *mafasu*, snapped off; *bua*, to cleave, *mafua*, cleft; *koto*, to break, *makoto*, broken.

In comparing the Oceanic forms, here following, of the above-given three inflexional prefixes, it is to be observed that the *m* (phonetically varied to *b*, *p*, *v*, *f*) is sometimes separably, sometimes (as in the Syriac Maphel) inseparably, attached to them. Thus we have number for number:—

1. Causative.—Efate *sa*; Tahiti *ta*; Malagasy *a*, *ma*; Dayak *ma*; Bugis, Makassar *pa*; Efate *ba*, *fa*; Mota *va*; Lifu, Mare *a*.

2. Reciprocal, or reflexive.—Dayak *in*, *i*; Tagala *i*; Malagasy *i*, *mi*; Efate *bi*, *fi*; Samoan *fe*; Fiji *vei*.

3. Reflexive.—Makassar, Dayak, Fiji, Efate, &c., *ta*; Malay, Java, Fiji, Efate, &c., *ka* (*t* to *k*); Malagasy, Dayak *ha* (*k*, or *t* to *h*); Fiji (and Ef.) *ra* (*t* to *r*).

And, as above, these three are combined thus:—

4. Causative, transitive (1 and 2).—Malagasy *an*, *man*; Malay, Tagala, Dayak, &c., *man*; Malay, Malagasy *san*. The *n* is often changed for euphony to *ŋ*, *m*, &c. See the grammars.

5. Causative-reflexive, causative, reflexive (1 and 3). Malagasy *aha*, *maha*; Tagala *mag*, *maka*; Makassar *paka*; Efate *baka*, *faka*; Fiji *vaka*; Maori *whaka*; Samoan *faa*; Malay *bar*.

6. Reflexive (2 and 3).—Malagasy *iha*, *miha*.

7. Reflexive of 4 (3 and 4).—Dayak *tan* (Malay, Malagasy *tan*); the *n* changed for euphony, as in 4; also *kan*, Malagasy *kan*. Also (2 and 7), Malagasy *itan*, and *mitan*.

8. Reflexive, or passive of 1 (3 and 1).—Malagasy *tafa*; Dayak *tapa*; Efate *taba*; Oba *tama*; Mota *tava*.

9. Passive participle, or infinitive, of ground-form. See under 9 above. Frequent in Oceanic, Malagasy, Tagala, Samoa, Efate, Solomon Islands, &c.

To these must be added:—

10. Reflexive-passive of 5. Malay *tar*, formed from (*b*)*ar*, as *tan* from *an*, (*m*)*an*.

Other combinations in Oceanic of these inflexional prefixes need not here be noticed, as:—

11. Reciprocal.—Malagasy *ifa* (2 and 1), *ifan* (2 and 4). In Malagasy there are many other combinations of these three particles which need not be noticed here.

Infixes.

These inflexional particles are also found 'infixed' by transposition, as the one numbered 2, giving a reflexive-passive sense, in Java, and in a few words in Malagasy: it is found infixed in Arabic after the second radical of quadriliterals. In Himyaritic and Assyrian *ta* (3) was infixed, and in Assyrian *tan* (3 and 2). In Malagasy *m* is found infixed in a few words. In this case, as in that of the *n* of number 2, the prefix becomes, as in the Semitic languages, by transposition, an infix.

Examples. For the Malayan and Pacific Islands generally see F. Müller, *Grundriss d. Sprachwissenschaft*, and for Dayak, *Grammatik der Dayakschen Sprache*, by Frederik Müller, 1858. For the letter changes of these formative particles see above, Ch. II.

Prefixes.

1. (*a*) Safal, (*b*) Tafal, (*c*) Afal, (*d*) Mafal.

(*a*) Ef. *sarafi*, *saḡaluḡalu*; (*b*) Tahiti *ma*, clean, *tama*, to cleanse; (*c*) Mare *waruma* (Mg. *veluna*, Ef. *moli*, *mauri*), to live, *awaruma*, to make to live; (*d*) Mg. *tahuṭa*, fear, *matahuṭa*, and (in past and future tenses) *atahuṭa*, to fear; Ef. *baḡani*, Fi. *vakani*, to feed, cause to eat, *kani*, to eat; Ef. *marafi*, see *sarafi*, and compare Syriac Afal and Safal of this word.

2. Ifal, Mifal (Nifal, Infal, Ifal). Ef. *fiatu, fimeri, fimuri, bialo, biauli*; Sam. *alofa*, love, *fealofani*, to love one another; Dayak *pukul*, beat, *mamukul*, to beat, *imukul*, to be beaten; Mg. (*m*)*ilahaṭa*, to arrange oneself, to be arranged, from *lahaṭa*; *telu*, three, *mitelu*, to three itself, to be divided into three.

3. Tafal. Ef. *taḅaro, taḅelu, taḅare, taḅara, takel, tatalai, takusi, tausi*, and *rausi*; Eromangan *devat*, Tanna *kuvas*, four, Ef. *kefate*, and *kafat*, fourth; and so with all the numerals.

4. Manfal, Anfal, Sanfal. Mg. *mameluna* (i. e. *manveluna*), *ameluna*, My. *maǵidupi* (*man-idupi*) (and with same meaning 5, Ef. *bakamauri*, Fi. *vakubula*, Sam. *faaola*), to make to live, save. Mg. *hudina* (*herina*) (Ef. *keleti, kelu*), turning round, *saǵudina* (*san-hudina*), a top (spinning, whirling round); My. *buni, sambuñi* (*san-buni*), to conceal, concealed, Ef. *bou, bonoti, bunuti*.

5. Matafal, Atafal. As seen in 4, *baka-*, in Ef., &c., may as to meaning be the same as *man-* in Mg. and My., as is easily explained etymologically, the final particles, in 2 and 3, being both reflexive. Fi. *vakamatea*, Mg. *mahafati*, Tah. *haamati* (My. *mamati*, for *man-mate*, 4, with same meaning), to make die, kill; Ef. *mate*, die, dead. Here it may be observed once for all that formative particles etymologically identical are not necessarily wholly identical in use either in the Semitic or Oceanic dialects. Thus My. *bar-* is the same etymologically as Ef. *baka-*, but not in use: one of the uses of Fi. *vaka-*, not in Ef., is the same as that of My. *bar-*, e.g. My. *barumah* (*bar-rumah, rumah*, house); Fi. *vakavale* (*vale*, house), to have a house; literally, make for, or to oneself a house.

6. Itafal (Intafal, Nithpael). Mg. *fana* (Ef. *bani*), warm, (*m*)*ihafana*, to grow warm; Ef. *rausi*, to follow, *birausi*, to keep on following, follow one another; *toli*, to go before (put behind), *bitoli*, to go before one another (as in a race). See *usi* and *liu*.

7. Tanfal, Itanfal. Mg. *undrika, tanundrika*, (*m*)*itanundrika*, stoop; *laṣaka, tandaṣaka*, (*m*)*itandaṣaka*, fall, sink. So *kan-*, as *usa*, cowardly, *kanusa*, a confirmed coward.

8. ('Etmafal') Tamafal. Ef. *laǵa*. (Mafal) *balaǵati*, to raise; *tubalaǵa*, raised.

9. See above under 9. On 1, 2, 3, 5, 8, 9 in the Melanesian dialects generally, see *M.L.*, pp. 183–9.

For the added initial syllable of the 'broken plurals', see above § 16 (*b*), Ch. II.

Infixes.

(*n*) Mg. *tapaka*, cut off, *tinapaka*, to be cut off, Ef. *tefi*; Java *rayah*, to plunder, *rinayah*, to be plundered: (*m*) Mg. *tani* (Ef. *taği*), and *tumani*, to wail, cry; and compare My. *makan*, Mg. *humana*, Ef. *kani*, to eat. Cousins, *Mg. Dict.*, p. xvii, notes also *ar*, as *ṣapaka*, *ṣarapaka*, which may be the infixed *t*, as in the Arabic eighth conjugation, and Himyaritic 'Patal'.

Ef. *kala*, Mg. *keli*, small: then Mg. *kineli*=Arabic seventh conjugation, Hebrew Nifal of the verb قل, קָלַל.

Suffixes.

In the Semitic languages we have—

1. *t*, forming abstracts and feminines: in all the dialects the *t* is sometimes elided leaving vowel only, as *a*, *i*, *e*.

2. *an*, Assyrian also *in*, Ethiopic also *na*, forming abstracts from verbs, and adjectives from nouns, and intensive adjectives from other adjectives and participles. The *n* is sometimes elided in Hebrew, leaving only vowel *o* for *a*.

3. *tan* (1 + 2), abstracts and adjectives (participles).

4. *awi*, *ai*, *a*, *i*, adjectives from nouns, and intensive adjectives from other adjectives or participles.

5. *iyyat*, *iat*, *it*, *ut*, *ot* (4 + 1), feminine adjectives and abstracts.

6. *ani* (2 + 4), adjectives.

These are found in the Oceanic dialects thus:—

1. Ef. *barua*, and *barbaruta*, fat; *bunuta*, silent (shut up); *bulubulut(a)*, sticky (like plaster or paint); Fi. *drega*, glue, *dreğadreğata*, gluey, sticky: these are really abstract verbal nouns used in the passive sense, from *bono*, shut, *bono-* or *bunuti*, to shut, and *bulu*, plaster, *buluti*, to plaster, Fiji *dreğata*, to glue. This formative ending forms abstract or verbal nouns which sometimes are thus used as passive verbs or adjectives,

but which very often are used as active verbs usually with the transitive particles *-i* or *-ki*, My. *-i* and *-kan*: see below. The *t* or *ta* with the *t* elided is usually *a*, but sometimes *i* or *e*, as in Ef. *sikai*, one; *lai*, mulier, donna, lady; *tokai*, *sukai*.

2. Ef. *arǐfon*, a wise man, a diviner, عَرْفَان, *'arǐfan*, sciens, from *'arafa*, to know, to divine. Ef. *oraorana* and *oroa*, *ḅilana*, or *ḅilena*, and *ḅila*, *teltela*, and *telatelana*; *ra*, branch, *rana* branchy; Mg. *kankana*, worm, *kankanina*, affected with worms (see Index under ק), (Sam. *ane*, *anea*, *aneanea*, has *-a*); *lela*, tongue, *lelana*, talkative; *kiri*, obstinacy, *kirina*, obstinate; *vulu*, hair, *vuluina*, hairy, Sam. *fulufulua*, has *-a*. Usually this ending forms abstract nouns or participles from verbs, or verbal nouns used as verbs; see below. In Ulawa, San Cristoval, and Pentecost the ordinals are formed by *-na*, as *ruana*, second, from *rua*, 2, &c.

3. Ef. *barbaruta* and *barbarutena*, fat; Mg. *uzaṭa*, Ef. *ua*, sinew, *uzatina*, sinewy; *uliṭa*, worm, *ulerina*, wormy (Fi. *uloulo*, *ulouloa*, has *-a*); *sumaṭa*, beard, *sumarina*, bearded; *taùlana*, bone, *taulànina*, bony; Sam. *ola*, life, *olataga*, salvation, a saviour. Usually this ending forms abstract nouns from verbs, as My. *takut*, Mg. *tahuṭa*, abstract nouns (1), which are again used as verbs (compare such secondary roots as שָׁחַת from שׁוּחַ, נָחַת from נוּחַ), from which abstracts or nomina verbi are formed by the ending *an*, as *takutan*, *hatahurana*. The nomina verbi of these verbs, or of verbs without the *-t*, or of verbs with the *-t* alone, may be used, like the Semitic nomina verbi, in both an active and a passive sense, and in the latter case they are like participles or verbal adjectives: thus Ef. *fami*, to eat, *famian*, an eating, or to be eaten, eatable; *bulu*, *buluti*, to plaster, *bulubuluta*, to be sticky, as plaster, *bulutian*, a plastering, or to be plastered. Ef. *tagi*, to wail, *tagian*, a wailing; *tagisi*, to bewail, *tagisian*, a bewailing, or to be bewailed. In Ef. these nomina verbi formed by *-an* cannot be used as verbs, but only either as verbal nouns, thus *nabulutian ni nasuma*, the plastering of the house; or in the passive sense as verbal adjectives, thus *nasuma bulutian*, a

house to be plastered; *nafinağa famian*, food eatable, food to be eaten; *tea tağisian*, a thing or person to be bewailed. To every verb in the Ef. language with or without the *-t* this formative ending, *-an*, may be attached.

The *i* before this ending *an*, as e.g. in *tağisian*, is the transitive particle seen in My. and Ef. *tağisi*, to bewail, suffixed to the verb, but in My. it is never retained in the verbal noun which in this case is *tağisan*, never as it is in Ef. *tağisian*; and so in all cases.

4. (*i*) Aurora and Mota *moai*, first; Ef. *bea*, dialect *bei*, Sam. *mua*, (Aurora *vagaruai*, second). This word in Amharic *fataña*, first, has a more complex ending, according to Prätorius *an*, *i*, and *a* (*ani* as in 6).

(*a*) Cf. *tano*, earth, soil; *tanoa*, earthy, soiled; *oroa*, *sama*, *koa*, *lebalebā*, *lasoa*, *balea*, *sulia*, *fitta*, *ulua*, *koria*; Sam. *fulu*, hair, *fulufulua*, hairy; *nifo*, teeth, *nifoa*, having teeth; *'eli*, rust, *'elea*, rusty; Fi. *dravu*, ashes, *dravudravua*, ashy.

5. Ef. *turiai*, young man, ذُرِّيَّة, same meaning; *tuai*, عَادِيَّة; *munuai*, from *munu* (*bunuti*); (*lebalebā*) *lebalebàra*, (*bağbağoa*) *bağbağōra*, (*milesia*) *milesira*.

6. Eromangan *sainği*, *durunği*, *deselunği*, *devatunği*, first, second, third, fourth, from *sai*, *duru*, *desel*, *devat*, 1, 2, 3, 4; Florida *ruani*, *toluni*, second, third; Gaudalcanar *kehani*, first. So in Ysabel (Bugotu and Gao), the ordinals are formed by *-ni*; Mg. *luhani*, first, head-man, chief, from *luha*, head, Hebrew *ris'oni* (and *ris'on*).

In Polynesian and Melanesian there are two well-known prepositions,[1] Efate *i*, and *ki*; Maori *i*, and *ki*; Samoan *i*, and *'i*; (Fi. *i*, and *ka*, combined *ki*). These, often used as transitive prepositions immediately after the verb connecting it with its object, have come sometimes to be suffixed to the verb and treated as if a part of it; and to this compound verb, as to the simple verb, *-ana* or *-a* is suffixed. Thus from Samoan *nofo*, Efate *no*, to sit, dwell, we have *nofoi*, and *noi*, and from

[1] For these see below on the Particles.

these again *nofoia*, and *noiana*. And so in Polynesian when *-ana* is found as *-na*, as Efate *uta*; Maori *uta*; Efate *utai*, to put freight in a canoe, whence *utaiana*; Maori *utaina*. And so with *ki*, as Efate *lua*, Tongan *lua*, to vomit; then Efate *luaki*, or *lua ki*, Maori *ruaki*, *whakaruaki*, whence *luakiana*, *whakaruakina*. Malay for *i*, and *ki*, has *i*, and *kan*, as (*daulu*, first), *daului*, to anticipate, *daulukan*, to go before, to place before. Thus Ef. and My. *tağisi*; Ef. *tağisian*; My. *tağisan*. Malagasy never has *kan*, or *ki*, thus suffixed, but only *i*, thus Efate (*bunu*, Malagasy *vunu*), *bunui*, to kill, Malagasy *vunui*[1], whence *bunuiana*, or *bunueana*, and *vunuina* (for *vunuiana*); and Efate *so*, Malagasy *anṣu*, to call, then *soi*, *anṣui*[1], whence *soiana*, *anṣuina*.

The suffixes to the primary verb then are:—

TABLE I.

MALAGASY	MALAY	SAMOAN	EFATE
ṭa	t	ta, and a	t, *or* ta, *or* a
ana, *na*	*an*	*na*, or *a*	*ana*, *an*
i	i	i	i
	kan	ʻi	ki
ina		*ina*, or *ia*	*iana*
		Maori *kina*, or *kia*	*kiana*

On these suffixes it is to be observed that the rule is that:—

1. *-ana*, *-ta*, or *-a*, form abstract verbal nouns.

2. *-ana*, but not *-ta*, forms adjectives from nouns.

3. *-ana*, or *na*, or *a*, but not *-ta*, in Malagasy and in Polynesian forms the passives. The passives in Samoan thus

[1] Griffith's *Malagasy Grammar*, pp. 125, 127. Compare the use of this *i* in Fiji, Hazlewood's *Fiji Grammar*, pp. 32–9; thus *rait'i*, passive, 'to be seen,' except before proper nouns and personal pronouns, when it is transitive like the same word in My. *liati*, to see. When the verb with the transitive particle *-i* is used in a passive sense we have the passive of a transitive verb.

formed—for they all end in this *-na*, or *-a*, as *-a*, *-na*, *-ia*, *-ina*, *-tia*, &c.—are actives when 'the pronoun precedes' (Pratt), that is they are passives or actives according to the construction of the sentence.

4. When *-ta*, or *-a*, and *-ana* (*-na*, *-a*), are combined, *-ana* is suffixed to the *-ta*, or *-a*, as in *-tana* (see below), or *-āna* (as in *mataku-a*, *mataku-āna*).

5. When *-ana* (*-na*, *-a*) is combined with the transitive particles *i*, and *ki*, it follows or is suffixed to them, as *-ina*, *-ia*, *-kina*, *-iana*, *-kiana*.

6. When *-t*, or *-ta*, or *-a*, is combined with these transitive particles they follow or are suffixed to it, as *-ti*, *-taki*, *-aki*.

7. Thus while the verbal noun, formed from the primary verb by *-ana*, or *-na*, or *-a*, and that by *-ta*, or *-a*, are both used also as verbs, it is only usually the latter that becomes the basis of a secondary verb, taking, like the primary verb, the suffixes *-ana* (*-na*); the transitive particles *-i*, *-ki*, and *-iana* (*-ina*), *-ia*, *-kia*, *-kiana* (*-kina*), as we are now more fully to see.

How large a part these transitive particles with the formative suffixes *t*, *an*, *tan*, play in the Oceanic dialects may now be shown.

The *-t*, or *-ta*, has undergone various phonetic changes: see above. Thus when the word with it stands independently in the Malagasy Dictionary, it is *-ṭa* (dialect *ṣa*), *-ka*, or *-na*; *-ta* being pronounced *ṭa*, or *ṣa*, and also *-ka* (*t* to *k*), and *-na* (*t* to *n*). But when in grammatical construction, *-ṭa* is pronounced *-ta*, *-ra*, or *-fa*; *-ka* is pronounced *-ha*, or *-fa*; and *-na* is pronounced *-na*, or *-ma*.[1] In addition to these phonetic variants of *-ta*, there are *-sa*, and along with it *-za*, and along with *-fa*, *-va*. The *-ta*, with these phonetic variations is found in the other three Oceanic languages, Ef., My., and Sam., though of course in them *-sa*, and *-za*, are simply *-sa*, while *-fa*, and *-va*, in Malay are simply *-p*, and in Samoan and Efate *-fa*—but *-fa* in Efate is

[1] Parker's *Malagasy Grammar*, p. 19.

pronounced sometimes *-fa*, and sometimes *-va*: again *-na* (for *ta*) is often in them found pronounced *-ġa*—and in Samoan of course, *-ra* is always pronounced *-la*. In Samoan and Efate *-ta* is also found with the consonant elided, as *-a*[1] (Fiji *-wa*, *-ya*, *-a* —the others occur in Fiji as *-ta*, *t'a* (Efate *-sa*), *-ra*, *-na*, *-ġa*, *-ma*, *-ka*, *-va*[2]). With independent words in the dictionary, as those with *-ṭa*, *-ka*, *-na*, in Malagasy, we have it in Samoan as *-ta*, *-ġa*, *-la*, *-a*, the prevailing form being *ġa*, as *fuata*, fruitage, also *fuaġa*, from *fua*: *tula* (Maori *tuġa*), a perch, a standing-place, from *tu*, to stand; *nofoa*, a seat, from *nofo*, to sit: and in other Polynesian dialects we have it as *-na* (Hawaiian), *-ka* (Marquesan); *-a* (Tahiti). As *ṭa*, *-ka*, *-na* in Malagasy, so in Samoan and Polynesian *-ta*, *ġa*, *-a*, may phonetically change when the word is in construction, thus:—

[The letter that is pronounced variously is italicized.]

-ta, or *ġa*, may vary to '*a*, fua*t*a, or fua*ġ*a' fua*t*aġa, fua'aġa.

-ġa to *-ta*, *-'a*, as *ola*, to live, ola*ġ*a, ola*t*aġa, ola'aġa.

.ġa to *-ma*, as *tanu*, to bury, tanu*ġ*a, tanu*m*aġa.

-ġa to *-sa*, as *leo*, to watch, leoleo*ġ*a, leoleo*s*a'i.

-ġa to *-n(a)*, as *alofa*, to love, alofa*ġ*a, fealofa*n*i, alofa*ġ*ia, Maori aroha*t*ia.

-ġa to *-ra*, as Mangarevan *mate*, to die, mate*ġ*a, mate*r*aġa.

ġa to *-la*, '*a*, as *tupu*, to increase, grow, tupu*ġa*, tupu*l*aġa. tupu'aġa.

-ġa to *-a*, as *tuu*, to leave, &c., tuu*ġ*a, tuu*a*ġa.

-ġa to *-ra*, as *tu*, to stand, { *tula*, *tulaġa* (Samoan). / tu*ġ*a, tu*r*aġa (Maori).

-a to *ra*, as Tahiti *fanau*, to be born, fanau*a*, fanau*r*aa.

-t to *-f*, as Sam. *una*, to pinch, una*t*ia, and una*f*ia.

In Malay we have *-t* with all its variants in the dictionary with independent words, and also, but not as a rule, in Efate. In Efate the rule is, as in Malagasy and Samoan, that all the variants of *-ta* appear only in construction.

[1] So in Mod. Syr., see *C.G.S.L.*, p. 54.

[2] Hazlewood's *Fijian Grammar*, p. 32.

Thus we have:—

TABLE II.

MALAGASY	MALAY	SAMOAN	EFATE	FIJI
ṭa, ta	t	ta	ta	ta
ka, ha	k	ʻa	ka	ka
na	n, ġ	na, ġa	na, ġa	na, ġa
fa	p	fa	fa	va
va				
sa	s	sa	sa	t′a
za				
ra	r, l	la	ra, la	ra, la
ma	m	ma	ma	ma
		a	a	a, wa, ya

These Malagasy forms of this suffix, as also those below in Table IV, are used in, e.g. what Griffiths (*Grammar*, pp. 134, &c.) calls the 'Pronominal Adjunctive Conjugation', as *surataku*, I write, in which word *-ta* is the formative suffix of the secondary verb, and *ku* the suffixed pronoun first person singular nominative.

TABLE III.

MALAGASY	MALAY	SAMOAN	EFATE
tana	tan	taġa	tana, tan
rana	ran	laġa, Tah. *raa*	rana
fana	pan	faġa	fana
vana			
hana	kan	ʻaġa	kana
nana	nan, ġan	naġa	ġana
mana	man	maġa	
sana	san	saġa	sana
zana		aġa	ana

Here the Samoan *ġ* is for *n*, but the My. and Ef. *ġ* (in *-ġana*) for *t*, as in Table II. And as in Table II the *-ta* becomes sometimes in Sam. and Ef., and always in Tahiti, *-a*; so the Sam. *-ġa* (in *-laġa*, &c.) for *na* is always in Tahiti *-a* (as in *-raa*) by elision of the *n*, as in Table VI Sam. and Maori (and Tahiti) *-ia* is for *-ina* by the same elision.

With *-i*, Table IV.

Malagasy	Malay	Samoan	Efate
ti	ti	ti	ti
ri	ri	li	ri
fi	pi	fi	fi
vi			
hi	ki		
ni	ni, ġi	ni, ġi	ni, ġi
mi	mi	mi	mi
si	si	si	si
zi			

For these Malagasy suffixes in IV see remark under Table II. The Samoan are found thus with the reciprocal verb, as fealo-fa*ni*, to love one another. The Efate forms are very common as *buluti*, to cover with *bulu*, and from every such verb in Efatese you have the form in Table VI by suffixing *-ana*. The form seen in *buluti*, apart from the reciprocal, is not unknown in Polynesian, e. g. Samoan *puluti* (=Efate *buluti*), whence form of Table VI as *pulutia*. But often in Samoan we find the form like *pulutia*, while that like *puluti* is no longer found, or found only in the reciprocal, or in cognate dialects.

With *ki*, or *kan*, we have Table V.

Malagasy	Malay	Samoan	Efate	Fiji
[wanting]	-tkan	-ta'i	-taki	taka
	-rkan	-la'i	-raki	raka, laka
	-pkan	-fa'i	-faki	vaka
	-kkan			kaka
	-nkan, ġkan	-na'i, ġa'i	-naki, ġaki	naka
	-mkan	-ma'i	-maki	maka
	-skan	-sa'i	-saki	t'aka
		-a'i	-aki	waka, yaka

In Samoan this form, like the previous, is found with the reciprocal verb, as *felamata'i*, to watch for one another, and also independently of it, as *logologosa'i*, to report. In Efate and Malay it is found in this latter way, as Efate *rogosaki*, to listen, or hearken to, Malay *liatkan*, to see.

With *-iana*, we have Table VI.

MALAGASY	MALAY	SAMOAN	EFATE
tina	[wanting]	tia	tiana
rina		lia	riana
fina		fia	fiana
vina		whina (Maori)	
hina		kia (Maori)	
nina		nia, gia	niana, giana
mina		mia	miana
sina		sia	siana
zina			

As Mg. *tahuta*, *ampi-tahurina*, Sam. *mata'u*, *mata'utia*, being frightened (Ef. *mataku*, *matakua*, fear, Table II): here the Polynesian *-ia* is for Po. and Mg. *-ina*, Ef. *-iana*, by elision of the *n* (but the Ef. *-a* is for *-ta*, by elision of the *t*).

Finally, with *-kiana*, we have Table VII.

MALAGASY	MALAY	SAMOAN	EFATE
[wanting]	[wanting]	-ta'ina	-takiana
		-la'ina	-rakiana
		-fa'iga	-fakiana
			-nakiana
			-makiana
		-sa'ina	-sakiana
		-a'ina	-akiana

As Samoan *tuputupula'ina*, to increase, from *tupu*, to grow, whence also are the forms *tupula'i* (V), *tupuga* (II), *tupu'aga*, and *tupulaga* (III), *tupua* (I).

Here let it be observed that all these suffixes are not found with every verb, and that a form wanting in one language may be found in another, e.g. it may be thus with (1) the basis (Table II) of the secondary verb wanting in Samoan *folo* (Maori *horo*), to swallow, but found in Maori *horoġa*.

(2) Some derived form of the secondary verb as Maori *horomi* (Table IV), to swallow, wanting in Samoan, while both have (Table VI) *foloġia*, *horomia*, and Samoan *folomaġa* (Table III), Maori *horomaġa*.

(3) Some derived form of the primary verb (Table I) as Maori *whakahoroa* wanting in Samoan.

(4) In one language in the case of a particular verb the secondary form may be wanting, in another the primary form may be wanting, while in a third we may find both the secondary and primary forms of it, as e.g. in the case of the verb 'to fear', Efate *mataku*, primary only, Malay *takut*, Malagasy *tahuta*, secondary only, Samoan *mata'u*, *mata'utia*, both primary and secondary.

(5) The -*a* of Tables I, II, and VI, whether for -*ta* or for -*na*, is distinct from the ending -*a*, No. 4, pp. 56 and 58, given above.

Ef. examples. Both the primary and the secondary verb with the transitive particles, *i* and *ki*, are transitive, and sometimes with *ki* (so My. *kan*), causative : in this way we have in the Oceanic dialects analytic substitutes for ancient intensives, or causatives. Thus Ef. *roġo*, to hear, *roġi*, v. tr., to hear, *roġoroġoki*, to proclaim, make to be heard : in the last case the reduplication is intensive. Then from these we have *na roġoan*, a report, thing heard ; *na roġian*, a hearing ; *na roġoroġokian*, a proclaiming.

With -*a*, for -*ta*, *mitiri*, to write, *na mitiria*, a writing, so *mataku*, *matakua* ; *tabu*, *tabua* ; *tanue*, *tanua* ; *misaki*, *misakia* ; *milate*, *milatea* ; *tiro*, *tiroa* ; *maieto*, *maietoa* ; *moru*, deep, *na morua*, the deep.

TABLE II.

bunuta	malifus
karaka	tokora (Mg. toeṭa)
talifa	matakua

TABLE III.

bunutān	talifàn	matakuān
karakān	malifusān	

TABLE IV.

buluti	silifi	tanumi
sokari	atuġi, buluni	balosi

TABLE V.

sokataki (soka)	atumaki (atu, atuġi)
tokoraki (toko)	roġosaki (roġo)
silifaki (sili)	toroaki (toro)
tokonaki (toko)	

TABLE VI.

bulutian	silifian	tanumian
sokarian	atuġian, bulunian	balosian

TABLE VII.

sokatakian	tokonakian	roġosakian
tokorakian	atumakian	toroakian
silifakian		

Compare Fi. *keli, kelia, kelivaka*; Sam. *nofo, nofoa, nofoa'i.*

In Madagascar, 'Some tribes,' says Richardson, 'use them (*-ṭa*, *-ka*, and *-na*) interchangeably.' In the Hova dialect itself, as Parker has observed, they are interchangeable in certain words, thus *silaṭa* and *silaka*, Ef. *sila*, chipping off; Mg. *tanina* (also *kanina*) and *tanika*, and *tunu*, roasting, &c. For *-n*, *-ġ* occurs in dialects. Malagasy examples:—*taraṭa*, *tarafina*, ps.p. (Sa. *titotilo*, to spy, *tilofia*, ps.); *unuṭa*, *unutana*, or *unurana*, ps.p. (Sa. *una*, to pinch, pluck off, *unatia* or *unafia*, ps.); *hirika*, *hirihana*, or *hirifana*, ps.p., bored; *minuna* (drink), *minumina*; *andrasana* or *andrazana*, ps.p., being watched; *tandrina*, *tandrinana*, or *tandrimana*, p.p., being taken care of.

Malay examples:—*lulut*, *lulur* (Ef. *loai*, to stroke, paint; *lolo*, *loasi*, or *loari*); *lapit*, *lapis* (Ef. *lifai*, *malifus*, to bend, bent); *lakat*, *lakap* (Ef. *liko*, *likoti*, fasten, &c.); *garut*, *garok* (Ef. *karu*, *karuti*, to scrape); *gosot*, *gosok*, rub (Ef. *kasi*; Mg. *kasuka*, *kusuka*); *tambat*, *tambaġ*, to bind, fasten; *guliġ*, to roll (Mg. *hudina*); *minum*, to drink (Mg. *minuna*).

Efate examples:—As in Mg., My., Sa., and Fi., so in Ef., the *t* may have more than one phonetic form with the same word as *keleti*, *kelufaki* (*kelu*); *sokari*, *sokataki* (*soka*, to join on to); *karuti*, *karisi*, *karafi*, *karaka* (*karo*, *kari*, scratch); (dialects) *balosi*, *baloni*, *buluni*, *buluġi* (*bafano*, wash the hands), Sa. *fufulu*, Fi. *vuluvulu*; *atuġi*, *atumaki* (*atu*, break, smite, &c.), *munuġi* (dialect *munuma*, *munu*, to drink).

In Fiji, words with *-t* are usually transitive verbs, equivalent to Ef. with *-ti*. Fiji examples:—*kovuta*, *kovuna* (*kovu*, wrapper); *tura*, to place (Sa. *tula*, n.; Maori *tuġa*), (*tu*, to stand); *tutaka*, to defend (from *tura*); *rait'a*, to look at (*rai*, to look, seeing); *vakaraitaka*, to show (from *rait'a*); *volia*, to buy (*voli*, barter); *volitaka*, to sell (from *volia*); *vuruya*, to crumble (*vuruvuru*, crumb); *vurutaka*, to crumble (from *vuruya*); *vosaka*, to speak to (*vosa*, speak, speech); *vosataka*, to speak of (from *vosaka*); *roġot'a*, to hear, tr. (*roġo*, to hear, intr.); *roġotaka*, cause to be heard (from *roġot'a*); *roġovaki*, to be spread abroad, of a report (*roġotaka*); *rokota*, to bend, bow (*roko*, a bowing, bent); *rokova*, to bow to (*roko*, *v* for *t*); *t'oroġa*, to singe, scorch (Ef. *soro*, to blaze, burn); *t'orokaka*, to singe, scorch (from *t'oroġa*); *unuma*, to drink (Mg. *minuna*; My. *minum*).

Of the two non-inflexional suffixed particles, really transitive prepositions, *i* is for (*ni*, *ri*), *li*. And *li* is the Semitic preposition in Arb. *li*, of the same meaning, and, what is particularly to the point, of similar use in Arb. after verbal nouns. In Arb., 'the verb may govern either (*a*) the *accusative* of a noun, or (*b*) *a preposition with the genitive* of a noun, which takes the place of the accusative, and gives a greater precision and accuracy to the expression. This government is not restricted to the finite tenses of the verb, but extends to the nomen verbi or actionis, the nomina agentis and patientis, and other verbal substantives and adjectives, whenever and so far as these different kinds of nouns contain somewhat of the conception or nature of the verb.' 'The nomen actionis (with the others above-named) often takes its objective complement not in the *accusative*, but in the genitive with *li*, in which case this preposition is used as an outward exponent of the relation between the nomen verbi and its object. Hence the Arab grammarians rightly call it . . . *the lam* (*li*) *that strengthens the regent* (the nomen actionis or the verbal power which it possesses; for since the verbal force which dwells in the nomen actionis is less than that in the finite verb, the language helps the former to exercise its influence upon the object by annexing to it a preposition expressing the direction of the action towards the object.' It is added, 'This use of *li* to designate the objective complement is common in Ch. and Syriac, rare in Heb. and Eth.'[1] No words could better describe the function of this transitive preposition, whether, as originally, not suffixed, or suffixed as in Tables IV and VI. The other is the Semitic particle *ki*, or *ka*, which was used, like *li*, in Southern Arabic, or Himyaritic, 'as the sign of the accusative, and even of the dative . . . or more exactly, perhaps, of the accusative alone.[2]

See *M.L.*, pp. 137–40, for the following examples:—

-*a*, Mota *matea* (*mate*), death; Maori *matiga*, death; Ef. *matigo*, the grave (place of death).

-*va*, Fagani *ma'eva*, death.

-*he*, Saa *maurihe* (*mauri*), life; Java *urip*, Tanna *murif*.

[1] Wright's *Arabic Grammar*, II, §§ 1, 21, 29.

[2] Halévy, *Études Sabéennes*.

-ra, Mota *togora* (*toga*, Ef. *toko*), behaviour (way of abiding). Ef. *tokora*, a place (place of abiding).

The following word shows many of the changes this ending undergoes:—

كِفَّة, a net (fishing), Ef. dialects *kubena*, *kubeġa*, Sam. *'upeġa*, Tah. *upea*, Maori *kupeġa*, Marquesan *upeka*, Haw. *upena*, Tongan *kubeġa*, a net (fishing): see Index كَفّ.

Plural Endings.

Ancient Semitic masculine in *-m*: see below on the personal pronouns.

Ancient Semitic feminine in *-t*: see Ef. *taot*, and Index under ע.

Dual Ending.

See *rua*, two; Mod. Syriac *tera*, &c., and the verbal pronoun forms of the personal pronouns, *infra*, for the ancient Semitic dual ending *-a* in Oceanic.

Reduplicated Forms.

1. Falfal (Pilpel).

Ef. *kalăkala*, قَرْقَرَ, to laugh.

Ef. *kofŭkofu-a* (*kofu*), A. *kabĕkaba*, Sam. *'ofu'ofu*.

Ef. *kalăkala*, A. *ḳalĭḳala*, H. *ḳelḳel*, Mg. *heliheli*, and *kedikedi*, very small, and of rapid motion, moving about, Ef. *ma-kalăkala*.

Ef. *kelakela* (*kel*) and *kelekelet* (Mg. *hudinkudina*), A. *karĕkara*, and كَرْكَرَة.

Ef. *kafĭkafe* (*kaf*), A. *kafĕkafa*, Maori *kapukapu*.

Ef. *silasila* (*sila*), A. *ṣalaṣala*, Sam. fai-*tilitili* (Ef. *fai*, thunder). In Ef. it is the radical part of the word which is reduplicated, not the formative prefixes or suffixes, thus, *baro*, *taḅaro*, *taḅaro-ḅaro* (see Tafalfal form *infra*), and so *bulu*, *bulubulut*, *bulut*; so *kelekelet*, A. *karekarat*, &c. An exception to this rule is Ef. *mitiri*, *mitimitiri*, the *mi* having come to be regarded as radical.

The Falfal form is frequent in Ef. and other Oceanic dialects.

2. Fafal (Assyrian 'Papel').

Ef. *kakasi* (*kasi*).

Ef. *kakat* (*kati*), My. *gigit*, Mg. *kaikiṭa*.

Ef. *tuturu* (*turu*, *turuturu*, A. *s'alla*, *s'alĕs'ala*); Fi. *tuturu*; Sam. *tutulu*, to drip.

My. *duduk*, Java *totok*, Ef. *toko*, and *to*, to sit, *tokora*, Mg. *toeṭa*. This form is also frequent.

3. Pe'al'al (Hebrew and Aramaic).

Sam. *savalivali*, to keep on walking (*savali*, to walk, Ef. *siuer*, *suuara*). Ef. uses, instead of this, form 2 in this word, *sisiuer*.

4. Sam. *savavali*, another form of *savali*, to walk: compare perhaps חֲצוֹצֵר, the one word of this form in Hebrew, and the original form of the Arabic twelfth conjugation, for which see *C.G.S.L.*, pp. 220–1.

The Falfal and Fafal forms may be said to have partly taken in the later Oceanic dialects, as Ef., the place of the ancient Intensive forms, in Arabic the second conjugation, in Hebrew Piel, but it is easy to show that such forms as these latter (the Intensive forms) belonged to the Oceanic mother-tongue. Thus:

(Arabic 2 and 5.)

Ef. *rèàkĕ*, to strain, and رَوَّقَ, رِوَاقٌ: see above, and Index. And the fifth conjugation or form of the Arabic, which is the reflexive of the second, is seen in

Ef. *ḅaro*, *taḅaro*, to be heedless, refractory, فرع, تَفَرَّعَ.

borai, to split, *tabare* (*tabarre*), to be split, فَرَى, تَفَرِّ.

tatalai, to warm oneself, صَلَى, تَصَلَّى.

tōli (*liu*), to go before (put behind), وَلَى, تَوَلِّ.

talumi, to swallow, لهِم, تَلَهَّم.

See also *tafakka*, *tafaǧka*, *taǧelĭ* (dialect *takel*), *takusi*, &c.

Such Tafalfal forms as *taḅaroḅaro*, *takelkel*, *tabarebare* are also ancient, as

Ef. *rere*, or *rerea*, *tarere*, ܐܬܪܥܪܥ (רָעַע), to break (as breakers rushing on the shore).

(Arabic 1 and 8.)

So the reflexive of the simple or unaugmented verb, Arabic first conjugation, Hebrew Kal, is seen in Ef. *kari*, to hasten, *takari*, كَارَ, (originally) تَقَارَ, 8[1]: and that this form thoroughly belonged to the Oceanic mother-tongue, see above (Ch. III. *d*), the secondary verbs *tuli*, *ma-taku*, and *toko*, for which see also Index under letter ה.

(Arabic 3 and 6.)

The form in the Arabic third conjugation, H. Poël, being simply a lengthening of the first vowel was apt to become unrecognizable in the analytic Oceanic dialects, but appears in Ef. *sīuer* (*sīwer*, *sūwara*), to make a journey, to walk; Sam. *sāvali* (سَفَرَ, Sam. *savali*), سَافَرَ, 3, n.a., سِفَارٌ, Sam. *sāvali*, Ef. *sīuèr*. We have perhaps the reflexive of this, as in Arabic 6, in Ef. *naboa*, or *nabo* (for *taboa*), dialect *tamo*, from *boa*, to be odorous, diffuse odour, or fragrance, فَاحَ (and فَاغَ), 6, n.a., تَفَاوُحٌ.

[1] *C.G.S.L.*, pp. 207–9.

CHAPTER V

PRONOUNS AND PARTICLES

See Dillmann, *Grammatik der Aethiopischen Sprache*, §§ 62–5, and 146, fol.; and *C.G.S.L.*, Ch. VI.

1. The Demonstratives: this, that, here, there.

In the Semitic languages, as Dillman has pointed out, these are *ta*, by letter change *da*, *ḍa*, *za*, *sa*, *ha*, *a*;
na or *an*;
la, or *al*;
ka, *ko*, by letter change *fo*, *po*;
i.

In Oceanic these occur thus:—

Ef. *sĕ*; Ethiopic *zĕ*; Tigre *iz-*; Merlav *se*, Samoan *sia*, *sena*, *senci*.

Ef. *setu*, and *sentu*; My. *situ*; Mg. *izatu*; Ethiopic *zentu*, *zati*.

My. and Mg. *itu*; Aramaic *ide*, *idek*.

Ef. *na*, *ne*, *in*; Sam. *nei*, *na*; My. and Mg. *ini*; Assyrian *annu*, *anna*, *anni*; Heb. *hen*, *hineh*.

Ef. *sin*, *sana*; Sam. *senei*, *sena*; My. *sini*; Mg. *izani*; Aramaic *den* and *zen*; Eth. *zentu*.

Ef. *eru*, *eri*, *ri*, *ra* (see Index under letter ל); Vanua Lava *le*, *lo*; Sam. *la*; Maori *ra*; Mg. *iri*; Aramaic *harka*, *halka*; Assy. *ullu*, *ulli*, *ulla*.

The Article, originally the demonstrative *l*, is in Arabic *al*, *l-*, *a*; Heb. *ha*; in Ef. *in*, *ne*, *na*, and sometimes *a* (very rarely *l-*, *t-*); Mg. *ni*; Sam. *le*; East Mai *re*; Maori *te*; Tong. *he*; Fi. *na*, *a*. In Ef. the article is written prefixed to nouns, and is used prefixed to other demonstratives thus:—

With *s*, *nis* (הלזה); with *n*, *nin*; Sam. *lenei*, *lena*, *lela*; with *t*, *netu*; Santo *natu*; with *k*, *naga*; Santo *nakai*.

The Semitic plural demonstrative, 'these, those,' is formed from the demonstrative *l*, and is in Ethiopic *elu*, *ela*; Heb. *eleh*; Arb. *ilā*, *ulai*; Amharic *ĕla*, &c.; Mg. *re*, in *ireu*, *ireni*, *iretu*, &c., plurals of *iu*, *ini*, *itu*; so Florida *raeni*, these, plural of *eni*, this, exactly as Amharic *elazia*, those; *elayah*, these; plurals of *zia*, *yeh*, that, this; and so also Arabic *dol*, *dola*, plural of *de*, this; Vanua Lava *ter*, *tar*, plural of *te*, *ta*, this. In Amharic it is used also combined as a pluralizing word with the personal pronoun, as *ant*, thou; *elant*, ye: this is frequent in Oceanic, to mark that the personal pronoun (originally plural but now used also for singular) is used in the plural sense only, as Mg. *izi*, they, also he, but *izareu*, they; so Ef. *nara*, *inira*; Santo *inira*, they; *nai*, *inĭa*, being now used for singular 'he'. In Amharic *ĕlā* is used also to form the plurals of Interrogative pronouns (see for this in Oceanic below, on the Interrogatives), and also as an article before proper nouns forming a kind of honorific plural, or plural majestatis:[1] thus also Mg. *ra*, the honorific and personal[2] article.

Ef. *ke*; Mota *ike*; Maori *ko*; My. *ika*, *iki*, *iku*; Assy. *aga*; Aramaic (*ha*) *ik*, *hak*; Arb. *hak* (*hadak*); Amh. *yĭh* (for *yik*); Heb. *ko*; Aramaic *ka*.

This Semitic *k* is used before other demonstratives as an article, thus, before the above *s*, Assy. *agasu*; Ef. *kis*; Banks Islands (Gaua) *kose*; Volow *iges*; Bugis *kotu*. Thus also it is used prefixed to the above *n*, Ef. *kin*; Java *kone*, *kono*; Maori *konei*, *kona*; Assyrian *agannu*. This *k* is also suffixed to other demonstratives, Aramaic *dek*; Arb. *daka*; Santa Cruz *deka*; Sunda *diyak*; Santo *ituga*; and to this again the *n* is added, Aramaic *diken*; Vanua Lava *tigen*.

[1] Prätorius, *Die Amharische Sprache*.

[2] Richardson's *Mg. Dict.*, p. xlix.

The *f*, or *p*, for this *k* (see above), *fo*, or *po*, for *ko*, *ka*, is used exactly as the *k* in Ef., thus *kin*, *ke*, dialects (*ban*, *bon*), *uana*, *uane*, *uin*, *ua*, *uo* (i.e. *wa*, *wo*), *uone*; so *kis*, dialects *uis*, *uase*, *uose*; Celebes (Holontalo) *bo*, *wo*, *botia*, *wotia*.

The demonstrative *i* is seen prefixed in some of the above examples, as in My. *itu*, Aramaic *ide*. In Ef. *i* alone in one dialect denotes 'this'.

The Semitic *ha*, or *a*, is prefixed to other demonstratives as may be seen in the above: when suffixed it points to a distance, thus Amharic *yĭh*, this (for *zĭk*), *zia* (*ziha*), that; Harari *yi*, this, *ya*, that; Ef. *uane*; Tongan *ne*, this; Ef. *uana*; Tongan *na*, that; Aramaic *ai*, this; *aia*, that.

1 *a*. Demonstratives prefixed to the Personal Pronouns.

The demonstrative syllable *an* (*in*, *en*) was so prefixed in all the Semitic languages: in Mahri it has been dropped now from all [1] except the 1st plural. But it is still found generally all over Oceania,[2] Ef. *k-ĭnau*, *aġo* or *naġo*, *niġa*, I, thou, he (see Index).

Another is *k-*, Ef. dialect *ki* (verbal pronoun, 3rd person, used interchangeably with *i*), Pentecost *kea* (pl. *kera*), Gurague (a modern Eth. dialect) *kua*, *kia*, Fi. and Po. *ko*, as in *koia*, *kŏya*, pronoun, 3rd person. This is seen in Himyaritic *k-*, Eth. *kia-*, prefixed to the personal pronouns, usually in the emphatic sense and in the accusative, as *kiaka*, thyself, as for thee, thee thyself. As may be seen in *C.G.S.L.*, in the later Semitic dialects this was used also in the nominative, and became in Arb. *iya*, Tigre *i*. This *i* is common in the Melanesian dialects and in Mg., as e.g. in Tigre *ika*, Tanna *ik*, thou.

Another is *ha*, *a*, Melanesian and Polynesian *a*, Gaudalcanar *aia*, i.e. *a-ia*; so e.g. in Aramaic *ai*, *aia*, for *ha-hi*, *ha-hia*.

[1] *Z.D.M.G.*, XXV.

[2] For a long list of the personal pronouns, v. *M.L.*, p. 112 fol., and Ray's list of New Hebrides words, and see *S.S.S.*, I and II.

The Personal Article *i*: Melanesian (not in Ef.) *ia*, *i*, Mg. *i*, is connected with the third personal pronoun; compare *C.G.S.L.*, p. 182. For Mg. *ra*, see above.

2. The Personal Pronouns.

For these see Index under the letters א and ה, and the above chapter on Phonology, places specified *infra*. Here we may observe—

(1) That the loss in the Oceanic dialects of the distinction of gender in the 2nd and 3rd persons has taken place in the same way in Mod. Syriac[1] in the 2nd and 3rd persons plural, and in Mahri[2] in the 2nd singular.

(2) As to the use of the 2nd plural for the singular in some dialects, as in My. and Mg. (*not* in Ef. and many others), we see an approach to the same thing in the use of Amharic *antu* (you) for the singular, as in English 'you' is commonly used for 'thou'. As to the 3rd personal pronoun, the ancient plural of which is now used in the Oceanic dialects also for the singular, e. g. in My. and Mg., or for the singular mainly, e. g. in Ef., &c., the 3rd plural is used by way of politeness in speaking of a distinguished individual in Amharic and Efatese; and in Mod. Syriac[3] the 3rd plural is often used also for the singular.

(3) This made it necessary to distinguish the word when used in the plural sense alone, and this was done by using it in a different or less contracted form, or more commonly by attaching to it the ancient plural demonstrative (for which see above, and Index under the letter א, أُلَى, &c.), or in some dialects *tou*, or *tolu*, three, thus Ef. and Santo *inĭa*, *inira*, Mg. *izi*, *izareu*, Tanna *in*, *iraha* (for *inara*), dialects (Tanna) *ilar*, *ilat*, *ilia*, *iria*, Futuna (Polynesian) *ak-irea*, all for *inara*, or *inala*, Sam. *latou* (for *na-tou*), Ef. (verbal pronoun) *iru*, *ru*, for *inu*, *nu*

[1] Stoddart's *Mod. Syrian Grammar*, p. 22. [2] *Z.D.M.G.*, XXV, p. 200.
[3] Stoddart, p. 39.

(dialect *ĭū*), 3rd person plural; and *au* for *anu*, or *amu*, for *na-nu*, or *na-mu*, dialects *mu*, *pu*, *u*, 1st person pl. 'exclusive'.

(4) As to the so-called 'exclusive' and 'inclusive', Ef. *inămi*, or *niġămi* (*ninămi*), 'we and they,' and *ninita*, *niġita*, *iġita*, 'we and thou,' it is to be observed (*a*) that according to the native way of speaking the conjunction 'and' is left out in such expressions, thus in Ef. 'thou and John' is 'kumu John', literally 'ye John' (not 'thou John'); and 'he and John' is 'nara John', literally 'they John' (not 'he John'); and so 'I and thou' is 'we thou', *nini-ta*, *iġi-ta*, and 'I and they' is 'we they', *niġa-mi*, *ina-mi*, or *niġi-mi*, *ini-mi*, probably for *nina-umi*, *ina-imi*, or *nin-umi* (the *i* or *u* as in Scotch *gude*); and (*b*) the order of the words in such expressions is different from that in English, in which we say 'you and I,' 'they and we,' and the same as in Arabic, in which the 1st personal pronoun is put first.[1]

(5) The Oceanic mother-tongue formed the plurals of the personal pronouns like the other Semitic languages, and in the 2nd and 3rd, by the ending *m* (as in nouns), with the same interchange, and occasional elision, of *m* and *n*; and the Dual of the 2nd and 3rd as in Arabic by the ending *ā* (see the Ef. verbal pronouns and Index).

(6) These pronouns played the same large grammatical part in the Oceanic as in the other Semitic languages, as separate, prefixed (nom.), and suffixed (to nouns and prepositions, genitive; to verbs, accusative; and to verbs, nominative).

In the Semitic languages the suffixed pronouns were all originally of one form and without the demonstrative prefixed syllable *an*, except 1st person plural and the verbal suffix 1st sing., which retained the *n-*, and except that the *k* of the 1st person interchanged with *t*, and the *t* of the 2nd person with *k*, from the very first. Thus we have the verbal suffix (acc.) in—

[1] Caussin de Percival, *Grammaire Arabe Vulgaire*, § 223.

			Nominal Suffix (gen.)	
	ETH.	EF.	ETH.	EF.
Sing.				
1.	ni (for naku)	nau, au (for naku)	i (for ku)	ġu, dialect k, Santo u
2.	ka	k, ko	ka	ma[1] (for ka through ġa)
3.		(pl. for sing., *n*, *na*)		(pl. for sing.)
Pl.				
1.	na	na (in *na*-mi, *ni*-ta)	na	na (as before)
2.	kemu	mu for kumu (d. kama)	kemu	mu (as before)
3.	homu, omu Arm. hun, hon H. am, amo	n, na, ana	homu Arm. hon	n, na, ana

The verbal suffix in Ef. (and most other Melanesian languages) though *written* separate is really, and as pronounced, a suffix, and should have been written, as the nominal suffix is, suffixed. By prefixing the *an* to these we have the separate pronoun, Heb. *ani*, Assy. *anaku*, Ef. *anu*, *k-inau*, &c., 'I,' and so with the others (see above Ch. II on Phonology, and Index). The nominal suffix with slight phonetic variations here and there is found throughout the Oceanic dialects, and in the mother-tongue was undoubtedly as truly and unmistakably Semitic as in Arabic or Ethiopic. Now, the nominative suffix with the verb in Mg., (a substitute for the ancient perfect), is not used with the verb in most of the Oceanic dialects (and neither the verbal pronoun nor the verbal suffix, on the other hand, is now used in Mg. as it is in Ef.), and is identical with the above, thus:—

Sing.		MALAGASY.	ETHIOPIC.
	1.	ku	ku
	2.	nau (for kau, for kamu), pl. for sing.	ka
	3.	(pl. for sing.) ni	

[1] Aurora *ġa*, Tanna *k* and *m*, Ero. *ka* and *ma*.

Pl.	MALAGASY.	ETHIOPIC.
1.	na (in na-i)	na
2.	na-reu (for *ka*-reu, v. sing.)	kemu
3.	ni (as nominal suffix)	

The verbal pronoun (nom.) in Ef. (and many other Melanesian dialects) is never used except immediately *before* the verb, and any word with which it is used is a verb. Thus we have a substitute for the ancient imperfect which prefixed short forms of the pronoun to the verb.

	EF.	ARB.	EF.	ARB.	EF.	ARB.
Sing.			*Pl.*		*Dual.*	
1.	a	a	*a*-u (*a* for *na*[1])	na		
2.	ku (d. *ko*)	ta	ku, tu	tum, tu	tā	tumā
3.	i	i	iru, ru (for inu, nu)		irā, rā (for inā, imā)	humā

In the singular these Ef. short pronouns strikingly resemble the ancient in every way, but no such resemblance was possible in the plural and dual, which were not so prefixed in the ancient languages except in the 1st plural. The 2nd and 3rd had the same prefixed forms as the singular, and denoted the plural by suffixed particles. The Ef. plural and dual of the 2nd and 3rd persons are simply the short forms of the ancient short pronouns 2nd and 3rd plural and dual as used in the perfect. Here we give an Ef. verb with these verbal pronouns.

bano, 'to go.'

Singular.

1. a bano, I go.
2. ku bano, thou goest.
3. i bano, he goes.

[1] *au* for *na-mu*, see *supra*.

Plural.

1. Exc. a-u (dialects u, bu, mu) bano, we, they go.
1. Inc. tu[1] bano, (we) you go.
2. ku bano, you go.
3. {dialect, iu bano / ru bano} they go.

Dual.

1. Exc. a-rā[2] bano, we they-two go.
1. Inc. tā[3] bano, (we) you-two go.
2. ko rā bano, you they-two go.
3. rā bano, they-two go.

There are only two duals in these, *rā* in the 1st and 2nd being the *rā* of the 3rd, for *nā* (orig. *mā*), they two, Arb. *humā*, and *tā*, ye two, Arb. *tumā*.

For the New Hebrides dialects, see *S.S.S.*, Vols. I and II. For other Melanesian dialects, *M.L.* For the Mg., Richardson's *Mg. Dictionary*, p. xliv fol., and Griffith's *Mg. Grammar*. For Aneityumese, Dr. Inglis's *An. Grammar and Dictionary*.

For the letter changes in the Personal Pronouns, see above, Ch. II, §§ 9, 10, 13 *b*, 14 *a*, *b*, *c*, *e*, 15.

1st person.

II, § 10, separate, sing. and pl.

§ 13 *b*, 'Inclusive,' and § 14 *b*, and § 12. The final syllable is the pronoun of the 2nd person.

§ 14 *b*, *e*, 'Exclusive,' suffix § 15 *m*. The final syllable is the pronoun of the 3rd person.

'Exclusive,' verbal pron., § 14 *b*.

2nd person.

II, § 9, and § 14 *c* (suffix); separate, sing. and pl., § 14 *a*; plural, § 10, and § 15 (*m*), separate and suffix.

And final syllable of 'Inclusive'.

[1] *tu* is for *na-tu*, in Aneityumese *inta*. See Inglis's *An. Grammar and Dictionary*.

[2] The *a* in *ara*, as the *a* in *au*, is for *na*, we.

[3] *tā* for *na-ta*, as *tu* for *na-tu*, note 1.

3rd person.

II, § 13 *b* (suffix), and separate, § 15 (*n*) and (*m*), separate and suffix, and verbal pron.

Verbal pronoun, pl. and dual, § 15, R.

And final syllable of 'Exclusive'.

3. The Relative Pronouns.

These are in origin demonstratives, *C.G.S.L.*, p. 116 fol.

Aramaic *di*, *dĕ*, Eth. *za*, Assy. *sa*, Tahiti *te*, Ef. *te*, *tea*, Tanna *si*, Santo *se*, Mg. *izai*. Ef. *te* is used as in Aramaic as a conjunction, 'that,' 'because,' and also very often in the sense of 'that which,' 'what,' 'he who,' 'they who,' as *te ku tilia i uia*, 'what you say is good,' literally, 'that you say it, is good,' 'that which you say is good.' The demonstratives *nane*, *nag*, or *naga* are commonly used as relatives in Ef.

As in Arb. and Heb. the article is sometimes used as a relative. In Samoan the relative is *lē*, with which we may compare the Modern Arabic *ellī*, Maltese *lī*.

4. The Interrogative Pronouns.

See *C.G.S.L.*, p. 120 fol.

a. أَيّ *ayy*, Eth. *áy*, Heb. *ē*, Aramaic *ē*, *hē*, also *ā*, who, which, what, where?

b. 'Another interrogative pronoun in the Semitic languages is that which is characterized by the letter *m*. Its oldest forms appear to me to be *man* for the masculine, and *mant* for the *fem.*; but in practice *man* is used as the interrogative for persons of both sexes, "who?" whilst *mant* is employed in speaking of things, "what?"'[1] Himyaritic usually changes the *m* into *b* (or *v*), and Mahri *mon* is used of all genders and numbers. The *n* is dropped in the Heb. *mi*, who? and the *nt* in the Arb., Heb., and Arm. *ma*, what?

c. These two, (1) and (2), are combined in Arabic thus, أَيْمَا, Modern *ama*, what? which?

aa. The initial letter of (1), see Phonology, in Ef. has either

[1] *C.G.S.L.*, *loc. cit.*

lost its consonant power as in *ē*, or changed it as in *hē*, *sēĭ*, *fēĭ*, who? Polynesian *vai*, *wai*, *hai*, *ai*, Melanesian *hai*, *hei*, *t'ei*, *tei*, *sei*, *si*, *re*, Mg. *i-za*, who?

bb. My. *mana*, who, what, which, where? Lifu *mene*, what? Epi *va-i*, what? Eromangan *me*, Tanna dialect *ba*, who? Torres Islands (Lo) *va*, what? And with the demonstrative suffixed, as in Arb. *made*, what? we have Ef. dialects *uase*, *fite*, *feha*, Carolines (Strong's Island) *meta*, what? Ef. *uai*, *bai*, *uan*, *ue*, *mbe*, Polynesian *fea*, &c., where?

cc. That is (1) and (2), Ef. *safa*, *sefa*, *hefa*, contracted *să*, Ysabel, &c., *hava*, Fi. *t'ava*, &c., what? which? My. *apa*, Mg. *zuvi* and *uvi* (who? which?), Polynesian *aha*, *aa*, *ă*, what?

d. These pronouns are also as in Arabic, &c., used indefinitely, thus (1) Ef. *sei*, who? also some, any, some one, any one (see Dict. under the word *seġa-*, i.e. *se ġa-*); (2) Po. *mena*, *mea*, anything, something, &c.; and (3) Ef. *sefa*, what? also something, somehow or other, &c.; My. *apa*, Mg. *zavaṭa*; Ef. *matun* or *fatun*; Mod. Syriac *mudi*, for *maden*, *C.G.S.L.*, p. 125.

In Ef. the *ma*, or *ba*, of (*b*) and (*bb*) is suffixed in an indefinite sense to the negative adverb, as it is in Assyrian, thus, *ta*, or *ti*, not, also *tama*, or *tiba*, as *i ta bano*, or *i tama bano*, or *i tiba bano*, he did not go. It is also used, exactly as in Arabic, after nouns and personal pronouns.

This *m*, or *ma*, plays a very large part in the Oceanic dialects, as in all the Semitic languages, prefixed to participles and verbal nouns, and in Ef. may sometimes be used or not as the speaker pleases, thus we can say *i toko*, or *i matoko*, *batoko*, or *fatoko*, he sat, or abode. But usually it has become inseparably prefixed as in the verb-form prefixes *ba-*, *baka-*. In Mg., however, where it is prefixed in the present or indefinite tense, it is dropped in the past and future tenses: see below on the Tense particles.

5. The Interrogative Adverbs.

Generally, in Ef. the above pronouns may be used in the sense of 'where?' 'what (place)?'

With the particle of comparison, كَ, כְּ, as, prefixed to the pronoun in *a*, *aa*, we have a word signifying *quot*, how many? thus كَأَىّ (see Index), *ġisa*, *ġiha*, *his*, *fisa*, *firi*, *pira*, *hia*, *fia*, &c., how many? and used indefinitely, *tot*, so many. In Tanna 'how many?' is *küva* or *keva*, H. כַּמָּה literally, 'as what?'

With the same particle of comparison suffixed to it and the demonstrative *t*, Arm. *d*, prefixed, we have in Ef. a word, *taka*, Arm. *daka* (see Index), and the same with the demonstrative *n* suffixed, Ef. *takana*, Aramaic *dakana*, how? and used indefinitely, 'so,' 'thus.'

With the final conjunction كَىْ, (כִּי) prefixed to the pronoun in (*b*) we have كَيْمَهْ, Ef. *kua* (*kuwa*), or *gua*, Epi *kava-i*, that what? for what purpose? why? Wright's *Arabic Grammar*, I. 351. So with *cc* in Ef., *kasafa* and *kasā*, having exactly the same meaning in one dialect as *kua* in another.

6. Particle of Comparison.

This, as we have seen in dealing with the interrogative adverbs signifying 'how many?' and 'how?' is in Arabic *ka*, Hebrew *kĕ*, as. In Ef. it is *ka* or *kĕ*, as. Prefixed to the demonstrative *da*, *de*, *di*, it is in Arb. *kada* or *kade* (Arm. *kedi*), Java *kadi*, Ef. *kĭte* or *kĭta*, as; literally, 'as this.'

7. Particle of Negation (Negative Adverb).

Arabic *la*, Hebrew *le*, *la*, *lo*, Samoan *lē*, Maori *tē*, Paama *re*, Efate *ti*, *ta*, *di*, *ṣi*, Malay *ta*, Malagasy *ṣi*, not.

The same prefixed to a verb substantive, Aramaic *ata*, *ita*, is: Aramaic *lata*, Mandaitic *laita*, *lata*, Malay *tada*, *tiada*, Malagasy *ṣiadri*, is not, no; and the same with the verb substantive *ka*, Arabic *kana* with the *n* dropped, Malay *tadak* [1], or with the verb substantive *ka*, is, alone; Mandaitic (and Talmudic) *laka*, *lika*, Samoan *le'ai* (*lekai*), Ef. *tika*, *nika*, *ṣika*, *ṣia*, Malagasy *ṣia*, Malay *tak*, is not, no; and with the *l* of the negative elided

[1] On this compound and these Semitic words, see Nöldeke, *Mandäische Grammatik*.

Ethiopic *ako* (so Nöldeke), Tongan *ikai*, is not, no. As already said, the Ef. *tama*, *tab*, or *tiba*, not, is the negative adverb with the *m* of the interrogative pronoun used indefinitely suffixed to it as it is in Assyrian: it is never used in Ef. except immediately before the verb.

8. Particles of Mood.

(1) كَيْ, (כִּי), that, in order that, to, ut: in Ef. this is *ka*, or *k-*, or *ġa*, Malagasy *ka* and *hu*, or *h-*, Malekula *ġ'a*, *ga*, Florida *ġ'a*, *k-*, Raratongan *ka*, Tongan *ke*.

(2) فَ, *fa*, that, so that, in order that, &c.; Ef. *ba* and *b-*, Motu (N.G.) *ba*, Fiji, Maori, and Ysabel (Gao) *me*, Malagasy *fa*, Futuna *pe*, Tanna *pa*, Aneityum *pu* or *mu*, Malekula (*S.S.S.*, p. 42 fol.) *ba*, *b-*.

(3) דִּי, דְּ, H, *di*, *dĕ*, *za*, that, so that, in order that, quod, ut, Merlav, Mota *si*, Lakona *sa*, Mosin *ta*, Vaturaġa *ti*, Lo *te*. For Ef. *te*, see above on the Relative Pronoun, to which it is here to be added that in the sense of a final conjunction, 'that,' it is used with (1). Thus, *taġa* or *tak fano*, that I go, I may go, let me go, I will go, &c. In this Ef. *tak* there are three particles, the *t* of (3); *a*, I, the verbal pronoun; and *k* of (1); and it is to be observed, once for all, that these particles of mood (1), (2), and (3), by which what we call the Imperative, Concessive, Subjunctive, Conditional, and Infinitive are expressed, are also used as particles of the future tense: see below on the Particles of Tense.

In Ef. the ancient order, particle—verbal pronoun—verb, is yet used thus, *ka fano*, *k-* (1)—verbal pronoun (*a*)—verb, 'that I go,' 'to go,' 'I will go,' &c.; so 3rd person singular, *ke fano*, *k-*, *e* (so Florida *ke=k-*, *e*), *fano*, that he go, &c., and 2nd sing. *ba fano*, go (imperative), *b-* (2), *a* verbal pronoun 2nd sing. (for *ka*), and verb, literally, 'that thou go.' Generally in Ef. (1) is used, but in one dialect (2) is used instead of (1) throughout in the same sense. And another order, viz. verbal pronoun—particle—verb, has become the usual order in most dialects, thus instead of *ka fano*, *ke fano* we have *aġa fano*, *iġa fano*, in exactly the same sense, but, literally, 'I to go,' 'he to go.' This variation in Ef. of the order of the three elements of the expression in no way varies the sense, and seems to be purely for euphony, and it is for the same reason that in Ef. and many other Melanesian dialects the verbal pronoun of the 2nd person singular has dropped its consonant and retained only its vowel.

In Malekula (*S.S.S.*, p. 42 fol.) the particle in (2) is used thus (imperative, infinitive, and future):—

	Ml.	Ef.	Florida.	Ef.
Sing.	*To sit.*		*To speak.*	
1.	ba tok	ka tok	ku bosa	ka bisa
2.	bo tok	ba tok	ko bosa	ba fisa
3.	bi tok	ke tok	ke bosa	ko bisa
Sing.	Ef. (dialect)			
1.	aġa tok			aġa bisa
2.	kuġa tok			kuġa bisa
3.	iġa tok			iġa bisa

The particles (1) and (2) are also used thus in Ef.—(1) *i kani kai buka*; Mg. *nihinana izi ka vuki*, he ate (so) that (or, and then, or thereupon) he was satiated. Here Ef. *kai* is *ka* (as in Mg.) with the verbal pronoun *i*.

So (2) Ef. *i kani bo buka*, exactly the same meaning, and *bo* (*o* the ancient 3rd pers. pron.) is used exactly as the Arabic *fa*, see Wright's *Arabic Grammar*, II, § 140. Also in such expressions this particle may be left out, exactly as in the later Arabic usage, thus *i kani buka*. 'He spoke saying', or 'he spoke and said', is in Ef. either *i bisa bo tuli* or *i bisa tuli*. The latter mode of expression is *exceedingly* frequent in Ef., one verb following another, and this is the explanation of it. Here we may note the peculiar Semitic idiom to express 'again' before the verb.

9. 'Again.' This is expressed in Hebrew by שׁוּב (Arm. תּוּב), 'to turn,' 'return,' and in Syriac by ܗܦܟ, 'to turn.' The former of these verbs is used in exactly the same way in Ef.

(see Index), and the latter in Polynesian, Aniwa *foke* (Sam. *fo'i*; Maori *hoki*; Tongan *foki*, to turn). Thus Ef. *roa* (*rowa*, for *rova*), to turn, *i ro bano*, he again went, literally, he 'turned went', or 'he returned went'; and with the prefixed *me*, *i mero bano*, which again is often, the *r* elided, *i mo bano*. In one dialect it is *i mer lĕr bano*, he again went, literally, 'he turned returned went' (*lĕr*, dialect for *liliu*, q. v.). In Aniwa *foke*, as in Syriac, is thus used, see Index for ܗܦܟ, and Uhleman's *Syriac Grammar*, § 82. In Hebrew and Syriac the conjunction is sometimes left out, as always in Ef., in this characteristic expression.

10. Particles of Tense.

The Present Tense.

(*a*) The present or indefinite tense particle is in Ef. *mo* (which in different dialects becomes *bo*, *fo*, *uo*, and even *o*), Mg. *m*-; Malekula *m*-; Lifu *me*; Santo, Oba *mo*; Pentecost *ma*, *me*, &c. In Ef. this particle is, according to its origin, for which see the Interrogative pronouns used indefinitely, Semitic *ma* (compare Hebrew, also *mo*), rather, as in all the Semitic languages, a participle or verbal noun prefix than a tense particle. That this is what it is even in Mg., where it has most the appearance of being a tense particle, is certain: see Richardson's *Mg. Dict.*, p. xxxv, and what has been shown above on the Formative Prefixes. In Mg. it is dropped in the past and future tenses, but in Ef. it is *not* dropped in the future tense, and the indefinite tense is used for both present and past, with, or without (as is the rule) tense particle. On this Semitic *m*, as a similar kind of tense or participial particle, see Isenberg's *Amharic Grammar*, p. 73.

The Future Tense.

(*b*) The particle for this in Mg. is the above (1) in § 8: see Particles of Mood. This is *hu*, or *h*-, alone, in Mg., and the same in Ef. *k*-, or *ga*, but prefixed to (*a*), thus *ka fo bano*, I will or shall go; *ke fo bano*, he will or shall go; and in Ef. with

(2) in § 8, *b-*, or *ba*, as *ba fo bano*, thou shalt go; *iba mo bano*, he will or shall go; in another dialect, *iġa uo bano*, he will or shall go; *aġa uo bano*, I will or shall go. For Florida with *k-*, alone, and Malekula, with (2) *b-* alone, Aneityum *pu* or *mu* alone, Santo *pa* alone, see under Particles of Mood. In Polynesian, Raratongan, we have *ka* (imperative and) future: see Buzacott's *Raratongan Grammar* (1851), pp. 26–8.

Particle of Mood (3) is also, as well as (1) and (2), used as a particle of the future tense, but not in Ef., thus Tanna *te*, or *t-*; Banks Islands *ta*, *t-*; Sam., and Tongan *te*.

The Past Tense.

(*c*) The particle of the past tense is in Mg. *nu*, *n-*; Tanna *n*; Samoan and Tongan *na*. This is, so far as we can judge, the demonstrative *n* (see above); compare the use of this demonstrative with the participle for the finite verb, present, past, or future, in the ancient languages: Gesenius, *Heb. Dict.*, s.v. הֵנָּה. In Fiji *na* is the particle of the present, or future; Aurora *n*, *ni*, future; Pentecost *n*, *nu*, past and present, &c.

Ef. dialect *ka* (past); Fi. *ka* (past, sometimes present), is probably the *ka* in Ef. *tika* (v. Particle of negation), i.e. the verb substantive in Arabic *kana*, and is used like *ḳa* in Mandaitic which according to Nöldeke, is for קאם, whence קאי, קא, קי. Example קאתא, er kommt; Ef. *i ka mai*, he came. In Modern Syriac *ka*, or *ga*.

11. Prepositions.

(1) لِ, ለ, לְ, *li*, *la*, *le*, Tigre *nĕ*, *nĭ*, Gurague *ya*, Tanna *la*, *ya*, Holontalo (Celebes) *li*, Bugis *ri*, My. *di*, *i*, Mg. *ani*, Aneityum *an*, Tagala, Battak *ni*, Ef., Fi., &c., *ni*, *i*, Polynesian *i*; Ef., with suffix pronoun, *na*, *a*, Polynesian *a*, Mg. *a*, Fi. *ne*, *no*; to, of, for; sign of genitive, dative, accusative.

(2) Himyaritic *ka*[1], Amharic *ka*, My. *ka*, Fi. *ka*, Ef. *ki*, *ġi*, Maori *ki*, Sam. *'i*, *o*, Mare *ko*, *o*, Mg. *hu*; Ef., with suffix pronoun, *ka*, *ġa*, *ki*, Fi. *ke*, Po. *o*, to, of, for, by, with, from; sign of accusative, genitive, dative, ablative.

[1] Halévy, *Études Sabéennes*, p. 92 fol.

(3) بِ, በ, בְּ, *bi*, *ba*, *be*, Amharic *ba*, *ha*, Tigre *abĕ*, *a*, Mg. *ami*, Aurora *mi*, Motlav, *Volow b-*, Merlav *be*, Aneityum *va*, *va-i*, Fi. *ve-i*, Ef. *be-i*, *ma*, *mi*, My. *pa-da*, Hawaiian *ma*, Eromangan *bu*, *pi* (*S.S.S.*, I, p. 79); Tanna with suffix pronoun *va*, *fa*, *fu*, *pa*, and consonant elided, Ef. *a*, or *e*, or *i*, Epi *a*, and Ef. after verbs in the sense of 'by' or 'with' (instrumental), 'from,' 'because of,' &c., the suffix pronoun of the 3rd person after it being always *sa*, *s* (for *na*, *n*); Po, *e*, sign of ablative, 'by,' &c.; on, in, at, by, with (instrumental), by (in swearing, Haw. *ma*), &c.; sign of dative, genitive, ablative.

(4) مَعْ (עִם), *ma*, Ef. *ma*, *me*, Melanesian and Polynesian generally *ma*, *me*, Mg. *ama-na*, with, together with; with suffix pronoun in Arabic and many Melanesian dialects, sign of genitive. As to the difference between (1), (3), and (4) in Arabic with the (genitive) suffix pronoun, see C. de Percival, *Gr. Arab. Vulg.*, §§ 279–83. What is *to* or *for* (1) a person, and so (2); what is *in* or *on* (3) a person; and what is *with* or *beside* (4) a person; is, 'his,' or for him.

(5) إِلَى, אֶל־, *ila*, *ele*, Aneityum, Tanna, Eromanga *ira*, Malekula (Maskelynes) *ila*, to, towards.

(5 *a*) عِنْدَ, عُنْدَ, near by, beside, Ef. *uta*, near by, beside.

(6) (2+1) Epi *kin*, dialect *kari*, Mg. *hu ani*, for, My. *akan*, *kan*, to, for; sign of accusative, Malekula *hini*, *gini*, Vaturaġa *kone*; Ef. with suffix pronoun *kana*, *kini*, Epi, *kana*, *kona*, to, for.

(7) (2+3) Fi. *kive-i*, My. *kapa-da*. The *da* in My. *pada* is the demonstrative *da*, *d*, and is used suffixed to this preposition without changing its meaning exactly in the same way in Mod. Syriac, *bud*, *but*, Stoddart, *Gr.*, p. 143; with suffix pronoun, Tanna *kafa*, *kapa*, Ef., Epi *kia*.

(8) (3+2) My. *baki*, *bagi*, Ef. *baki*, Epi *beki*, to; Fagani *fagi*, with; Merlav *mug*, *mugu*, Ef. *magi*, contracted *mā*, Mota *mo*, Po. *mo*, for (dative).

(9) (3+1) Epi *bani*, to, Florida, Vaturaġa *vani*, to, for; Ef. *mani*, *mini*, contracted *mā*, Po. *mā*, for (dative).

Prepositions with the Article as a Relative, or other Relative Pronoun prefixed, as שֶׁל, דִיל, ዘበ, *s'el*, *dil*, *zaba*. Thus with the Article we have :—

(10) (1) Ef. *ani*, *ana*, Erom. *ari*, Sam. *la* (for *le-a*);

(11) (2) Ef. *naġi*, *niġ*, *aġi*, *aġa*, Epi *neki*, Sam. *lo* (for *le-o*);

(12) (1+2) Ef. *anaġa*.

The Article has sometimes become inseparably attached to the preposition as perhaps in Mg. *ani* [1], *ami*, and certainly in Ef. dialect *naġi*, *niġ*, the meaning and use being the same as that of the simple preposition.

With the Relative Pronoun we have :—

(13) (1) Eromangan *sore*, Epi *seni*, Sam. *sā*, שֶׁל.

(14) (2) Samoan *sō*.

(15) (3) Tanna *sava*, *soi*, Epi *sia*, ዘበ.

(16) Sometimes the Relative alone is the sign of the genitive, as Assyrian *sa*, Ethiopic *za*, Aramaic *di*, *dĕ*, Malekula, Epi, Tanna *sa* (*S.S.S.*, II, pp. 38, 89, 123).

For the uses of the prepositions, which vary somewhat both in each of the ancient and in each of the Oceanic dialects, the Grammars must be consulted: see the Grammars in *S.S.S.*, I and II, and those in *M.L.*, and Gabelentz's *Die Melanesischen Sprachen*, Vol. I (1863), especially Ch. XII, and Vol. II (1873). Here we shall give examples of their use with the suffixed pronoun, and it will be sufficient to give that of the 3rd person only (for the other persons see above on the suffixed Personal Pronouns).

(1) Ef. *ana*, Sam. *ana*, Mg. *azi* (for *ani*), Fi. *nena*, *nona*, Tanna *lan*, Ethiopic *lomu*, *lon*.

Fi. *a nena*, Ef. (10) *anena*, *anana*.

Sam. *lana* (for *le-ana*).

(2) Ef. *kana*, *kakana*, Tanna *kun*, M. Syriac *kahun*, *kai*.

Fi. *kena*, Sam. *ona*.

Fi. *a kena*, Ef. (11) *aġana*.

Sam. *lona* (for *le-ona*).

[1] But the *a-* in Mg. *ani*, *ami*, may be *a* prosthetic. Cf. Tigre *abĕ*, for *be*, (3).

(3) Tanna *fun*, Pentecost *bena*, Eromangan *buhni*, *pini*, Heb. *bam*, Eth. *bomu*, *bon*, Mg. *amini*, Pentecost *abena*.

(4) Epi *mano*, Fi. *mena*, Mota *man*, Ambrym *mena*, Arb. *mahum*, *mahun*.

(5) Eromangan *iran*, Malekula *elan*, Arb. *ilahum*, *ilahun*.

(5 *a*) Ef. *utana*, Arb. *'undahum*, *'undahun*.

(6) Ef. *kanana*, *kinin*, Epi *konana*, *kanana*, M. Syriac *ḳalahun*, *ḳalai*.

(7) Tanna *kafun*, Ef. and Epi *kiana* (possessive, with certain nouns), My. *kapadaña*.

(8) Merlav *nugun*; Mota *mon*; Po. *mona*, for (dative).

(9) Ef. *manena*, dialect *māsa* (for *mana*); Po. *māna*, for (dative).

(10) See (1).

(11) See (2).

(12) Ef. *anaǵana*, same meaning as (2).

(13) Samoan *sāna*, same meaning as שֶׁל־; Eromangan *soruǵ*, my, *sorum*, thy, *soremi*, your.

(14) Samoan *sona*, possessive.

(15) Tanna *savani*; Epi *siana*; Eth. *zabomu*, *zabon*.

Conjunctions.

For the Ef. *ǵo*, and; *ko*, or; and *be*, if, see the Dictionary, and for the final conjunctions *ba*, and *ǵa*, or *ka*, see *supra*, § 8. 1, 2. The preposition *me*, or *ma*, with, is used also as a conjunction, and for this and *temate*, a conjunction used only with numerals, see the Dictionary.

CHAPTER VI

SUMMARY. ARABIA THE MOTHERLAND OF THE OCEANIC LANGUAGES

The Article.

See II, § 13 *b*. It is written prefixed in Ef. as in Arb. and Heb.; and is often mistaken by voyagers in Melanesia, collecting from the natives lists of words, for a radical part of the word. It is written separate in Mg. and Polynesian. There is no article in My. as in Syriac.

The Noun.

Number. The ancient 'sound plurals' with ending *m*, or *n*, have disappeared except in the personal pronouns, and been replaced, as largely in Arabic, by the 'broken plurals': see II, § 16 *b*. These 'broken plurals', originally singulars with a collective signification, may take the verb either in the singular or the plural, that is, the verb with the verbal pronoun singular or plural in Ef., thus *nata i bano*, a man goes; *nata ru bano*, men go. The plural may also be denoted in Ef. by a pluralizing adjective after the noun, as, *natamole laba*, many men; *natamole rafalu*, some men, &c. For an example of the ancient plural (feminine) in *-t*: see Ch. II, the word *täot.*

The Dual. See II, § 15 (*n*), and the Personal Pronouns in Ch. V. In Ef. it is seen in the Verbal Pronoun, that is, the short pronoun, expressing person and number, by which the verb is conjugated. It is thus in Ef. retained more fully than in Hebrew, Aramaic, and Ethiopic.

Gender. This is expressed by the words for 'male' and 'female' in Ch. II. Traces of the ancient feminine ending *-t* are still retained in the word for 'female', also in *sikai*, one, and *lai*, woman, lady. For this ending *-t* forming abstract nouns, throughout the Oceanic, see Chs. III and IV, and for its phonetic variations Ch. II.

Case. The ancient terminations in Arabic *-u*, *-a*, *-i*, nominative, accusative, genitive, are now used in Ef., as in Hebrew, &c., without case signification. The expression of the genitive by the 'construct state' is still, however, found throughout the Oceanic, as in all the Semitic dialects, thus Ef. *mitana*; My. *matañа*; Mg. *masuni*, his (or their) eye; Ef. *mita nata*, eye of a person; My. *mata ari*, Mg. *masu andru*, eye of day. The genitive and other oblique cases are also expressed by the prepositions, q.v., in Ch. V.

The letter changes that have occurred in the Oceanic nouns for the following English words, have been explained in Ch. II, viz.:—

sun, 13 *b*, 16 *b*.	heaven, 14 *d*.
moon, 14 *f*.	water, 10, 13 *c*.
star, 12, 14 *a*, *c*.	ear, 14 *a*, *b*, 11 *c*.
stone, 13 *b*.	man, person, 14 *b*, 17.
fire, 14 *a*.	male (*vir*), 14 *c*, 17.
fruit, 15, R.	woman, female, 14 *c*, 17.
lightning, 14 *a*, *c*, *d*.	eye, 13 *b*, 11 *c*.
wind, 14 *d*.	

Many other words are similarly explained in the same chapter, q.v.

It would be easy to give here a long list of words, nouns, and verbs, which have suffered very little phonetic change as compared with these, and the numeral words, and pronouns, but this is not necessary, and may be done by any one from the materials in the following Dictionary, and Index.

The Nunation. For this see II, 13 *b*, 14 *b*. It is seen in

My. *kubiġ*; Mg. *sufina*, ear, أُذُن; in (Ef. *täot*), My. *tulaġ*, Mg. *täulana*, bone, and in the words for 'hundred' and 'thousand,' &c. On this final *n* in the Semitic languages, see *C.G.S.L.*, Ch. VII. It is frequent in My. and Mg., not so in Ef., and not so in Hebrew, Aramaic, &c.

The Numerals. The letter changes in these are explained in Ch. II (see the places indicated):—

1.	11 *b*, *c*, 12, 13 *b*, 14 *b*.	7.	14 *f*, 15.
2.	13 *b*, 15 (*n*).	8.	14 *b*, 15.
3.	13 *b*, 14 *b*.	9.	14 *e*, 15.
4.	13 *b*, 14 *b*, *f*.	10.	11 *a*, *b*, *c*, 14 *e*.
5.	15.	100.	13 *b*, v. Index under letter מ.
6.	13 *b*, 14 *e*, 15.	1000.	v. Index under letter א.

On these we may remark that 1 occurs both in the ancient masculine, Mg. *isaka*, and feminine form, Ef. *sikai*; and 4, 6, and 7, manifestly with the ancient feminine and abstract ending -*t*, throughout the Oceanic.

These twelve Oceanic numerals are the ancient Semitic numerals, but some of them have been lost from certain dialects. Thus, e.g. only the first five are now found in Ef., and in Ambrym the first five, and that for 'ten'. In Santo you find all the twelve in one village, and only the first five in a neighbouring village. In such cases as the latter the natives have found it easier than to remember the second five to substitute for them combinations of the first five thus: 5+1, for 6; 5+2, for 7; 5+3, for 8; 5+4, for 9; 2 of 5, for 10. These combinations in Ef. are *la-tesa*, 6, *larua*, 7, *latolu*, 8, *lifiti*, 9, *rualima*, 10, *latesa* being for *lima tesa*, &c., and *rualima*, two of five, for 10. And Ef. having lost or forgotten the ancient words for 100 and 1000, has substituted for them other words, *bunti* and *manu*.

The Adjective.

For the adjective formative endings, see Ch. IV. In Ef. the adjective follows the noun, and every adjective may be used, with the verbal pronoun, as a verb: thus *fatu kasua*, a hard stone, *fatu i kasua* (the) stone is hard. By adding the formative ending *-an* to an adjective (as to a verb) an abstract noun is formed, thus *nakasuān*, the being hard or strong, hardness, strength.

The Pronouns.

For these, Personal (Separate, Suffix, and Verbal), Relative, Demonstrative, Interrogative, Indefinite, see Ch. V, and for the letter changes in them Ch. II. (As to the Personal Pronouns the places where they are treated in Ch. II are pointed out in Ch. V.)

The conjugation (person and number) of the Ef. verb by means of the verbal pronoun is a real and natural substitute for the conjugation of the ancient verb. As in the ancient languages the verbal pronoun includes or implies in it the verb substantive.

The Verb.

This, as in the ancient languages, is a verbal noun (see Ch. III), thus Arabic *a-mata*, Ef. *a mati*, I (am or was) dying, or dead, rather than, I die, I died. In Ef. from every verb may be formed a verbal noun by the formative ending *-an*, which, if the verb is transitive, may be used in both an active and a passive sense, see Ch. IV, and see the same for the verbal noun formative ending *-t*, with all its phonetic variations as explained in Ch. II. Also the verb forming prefixes (and infixes) are set forth in Ch. IV, and their phonetic variations explained in Ch. II. For the verb forms or 'conjugations', see Ch. IV.

The Adverb.

An adjective may be used adverbially with a verb, thus *i sefa*, he hastens, *i sefa kasua*, he hastens strongly; and with an adjective thus, *uia*, good, *uia biḅilena*, greatly good.

For the interrogative adverbs signifying quot? and how? in

indefinite sense tot, and so, thus; and for 'as', and the negative adverb, see Ch. V.

For the Conjunctions and Prepositions, see Ch. V.

When we say that Arabia is the motherland of the Island family of languages this does not mean that the primitive Oceanic tongue, of which the multitudinous dialects of Oceania as at present spoken are the analytic or simplified descendants—as English is of Anglo-Saxon, or the Romance dialects of Latin—was derived from Arabic; but that Arabia is the motherland of the primitive Oceanic, as it is of the Ethiopic, Amharic, and Tigre, and of the Assyrian, Phoenician, Hebrew, and Aramaic. See *C.G.S.L.*, Chs. I and II. If it had more in common with Arabic than with any other Semitic language, that is because Arabic has more than any other preserved the features of the primitive Semitic tongue, the common mother of all of them. The primitive Oceanic must be regarded, not as a descendant of, but as a sister to the Arabic, Himyaritic, Ethiopic, Assyrian, Phoenician, Hebrew, and Aramaic, and the Ef., Samoan, Mg., Malay, &c., as cousins to the Mahri, Amharic, Tigre, Mandaitic, Modern Syriac, and vulgar Arabic dialects, due allowance being made for the fact that these latter have been always more or less under the conserving influence of the surrounding Semitic literature and civilization, from which the Island dialects have been for ages completely cut off, as well as completely isolated from each other. The word for 'sun' in Oceanic, Ef. *elo*, Tong. *läa*, Tarawan *tai*, is not the common word for 'sun' in Arabic, &c., but it is the common word in Ethiopic, Amharic, and Tigre, *ṣahai*, *ṣai*: but this proves, not that it was derived from Ethiopic, but only that it was derived from the same source as the Ethiopic. The Ethiopic and Oceanic word for 'moon', also in Mahri, Hebrew, and Aramaic, is not in Arabic. The common word for 'fruit', Ef. *ua*, in Oceanic, Ethiopic, Hebrew, and Arm., is not in Arabic. On the other hand, such common Oceanic words, as in Ef. *toko*, sit, dwell, *ma-taku*, fear, are in Arabic (v. Ch. III), and not in Ethiopic, though traces of them appear in Hebrew.

The word *sarafi* (Ef.), q. v., and the common Pacific Island word in Ef. *saki*, q. v., are in Aramaic, not in Ethiopic or Arabic. The word for 'star' is universal in the Semitic and Oceanic dialects, see Ch. II. In a number of dialects springing from the same original inflected tongue it is usual that one may drop one word or inflection, another another. The same is seen in comparing one Island dialect with another. Each dialect has its peculiarities, while nevertheless all have much in common, and this is true whether we compare the Arabic, Ethiopic, &c., with each other; or the Ef., Mg., &c., with each other; or the latter with the former, as shown in Chs. II, III, IV, and V, and as will further appear in what follows.

LIST OF ABBREVIATIONS

a., adjective.
ad., adverb.
art., article.
c., with.
c. art., with the article.
cg., cgg., cognate, cognates.
conj., conjunction.
cf., compare.
d., dd., dialect, dialects.
d. syn. c., dialect synonymous with.
dem., demonstrative.
den., denominative.
der., derivation.
i.q., the same as.
imp., imperative.
inf., infinitive.
inter., interrogative.
interj., interjection.
mid., middle voice.
n. a., nomen actionis (infinitive).
n. ag., nomen agentis (active participle).
n. p., nomen patientis (passive participle).
nom.suf., nominal suffix.
num., numeral.
opp., opposite, opposed.
part., participle.
pers.pron., personal pronoun.
pl., plural.
pref., preformative.
prep., preposition.
prob., probably.
pron., pronoun.
ps., passive.

q. v., which see.
redup., reduplicate.
s., substantive.
s.v., under the word (sub voce).
sing., singular.
syn., synonymous.
syn.c., synonymous with.
t., transitive.
v., vide.
v., verb.
v.c., verb causative form.
v. i., verb intransitive.
v. r., verb reflexive, or reciprocal.
v. t., verb transitive.
verb. suf., verbal suffix.
voc., vocative.

A., Arabic.
Am., Ambrym.
Amh., Amharic.
An., Aneityum.
Arm., Aramaic.
Assy., Assyrian.
Bu., Bugis.
Ch., Chaldee.
E., Ethiopic.
E. Mai, East Mai.
Ef., Efate.
Er., Eromanga.
Fi., Fiji.
Fut., Futuna.
H., Hebrew.
Ha., Hawaiian.
Ja., Java.
Ma., Maori.
Mg., Malagasy.

Ml., Malekula.
Ml. A., Malekula Aulua.
Ml. P., Malekula Pangkumu.
Ml. U., Malekula Uripiv.
Mod. A., Modern Arabic.
Mod. S., Modern Syriac.
My., Malay.
Pa., Paama.
S., Syriac.
Sa., Samoan.
Soc., Socotra.
T., Tigre.
Ta., Tanna.
TaSa., Tangoan Santo.
Tah., Tahiti.
To., Tonga.

Ct., Catafago's Dictionary of Mod. A.
Freytag, Freytag's Arabic Lexicon.
Ges., Gesenius's Dictionary of Hebrew.
Nm., Newman's Dictionary of Mod. A.
St., Stoddart's Grammar of Mod. S.
After an Arabic verb 1, 2, 3, 4, 5, &c., denote its different forms, and (1), (2), (3), &c., its different meanings.
After a Hebrew verb Pi. denotes Piel, Pu. Pual, Hi. Hiphil, Ni. Niphal.

THE OCEANIC LANGUAGES

THEIR MATERIAL, OR VOCABULARY, SET FORTH
IN A COMPLETE

DICTIONARY, COMPARATIVE & ETYMOLOGICAL,

OF ONE OF THEM, THE

LANGUAGE OF EFATE

(NEW HEBRIDES)

A, verbal pron., I: d. **ni,** q.v.

A, v., contraction of **ani,** q.v., to be, or dwell in.

A, prep., see Ch. V. 11, 1, sometimes **e,** or **i,** in, at, to, of. Used prefixed to nouns, as **ataku, etaku,** or **itaku,** at the back, behind; and to the suffixed pronoun of the possessive, as **agu,** my, **ana,** his, dialect **enea,** or **inea,** his, **inu,** my. [The same is found in Mg. *ahi*, my, *azi*, his, and in Sa. *ana*, his.]

A, art., or dem., prefixed to certain words, as to some nouns, and prepositions, **ani,** of, **aki,** or **aġi,** of; and to verbs, **nikam,** d. **aġau,** that which nips, or grasps. [Fi. *a*, an article, prefixed also to prepositions, as *a nei*, *a kei*, denoting the possessive case as in Efatese. The Fi. *a* is a form of the article *na*, and the Efate *a*, being the same as the Fi., must in that case be a form of the common article *na* (*ni*, *ne*, &c.), q.v. *Aġi* (*a ġi*) of, in Efate in one dialect is *naġ* or *naġi* (*na ġi*), of, and the above *nikam*, in another dialect, is *aġau*. The same article is found in Ma. and To. as *a*. In Fi. and Ef., prefixed to possessive prepositions, it has somewhat of the force of a relative pronoun.] H. **ha,** for **hal**; A. **l-, al, a,** sometimes **hal,** art., used also sometimes as a relative pronoun prefixed to verbs and prepositions.

A, interj., O! lo! [Ha. *a*, Tah. *a*, lo! o!] Arm. **ha,** this, as an interjection, lo! H. **hō,** A. **ha, a.**

Āb, s., d. voc., father. [Ma. *pa*, My. *pa*, *pak*, Mg. *aba*.] A. **āb,** H. **āb,** Ch. **aba,** father.

Aba, v. See **ofa.**

Abab, s., father. [Ma. *papa*, My. *bapa*, *bapak*, Mg. *baba*.] See **āb, bāb.** Redupl. of **āb.**

Abu, v., to heal, get well (a

sore), d. **au**, id., d. **mau**, to get well, recover from sickness. [Sa. *mafu*, to heal up, Ma. *mahu*, Mangaian *mau*, heal, Ha. *maha*, be convalescent, Mg. *miafa*, to recover from sickness.] A. ʿ**afa**, 3, 4, restore to health.

Abu, s., ashes, also **afu**, **au**. See following word.

Abuabu, v. redupl., to be dusty, to fly in the air (dust), also **afuafu**, id.; **tano afu**, **tano abu**, **tano au**, ashes; **libu**, v., to be ashy, ash-coloured, dirty, or covered with ashes, as in mourning for the dead, hence **malibu**, v., to be a mourner thus, especially for a deceased husband or wife, and hence **malibu**, s., a widow or widower, that is, one so mourning: **libu**, v., is also found (Bau d.) as **lifu**, **lifulifu**; **mafu**, s., a thick vapour like dust; uncleanness (ritual), which makes the sight dim. [Sa. *efu*, s., *efuefu*, s., dust, *efu*, v., to become dust, *efu*, a., reddish-brown, To. *efu*, s., dust, ashes, *efuia*, a., dusty, covered with ashes, Sa. *lefu*, a., s., *lefulefu*, s., ashes, Ma. *nehu*, s., dust, *nehunehu*, a., dusky, *whakanehu*, v., reduce to powder, Ha. *lelehu*, To. *nenefu*, dimness or weakness of sight, My. *abu*, s., Ja. *awu*, s., dust, ashes, My. *dabu*, *labu*, id., *kalabu*, v., a., ashy, ash-coloured, also *klabu*, Ja. *kluwu*, Mg. *vuvuka*, s., dust, ashes, *mamavuka*, v., to dust, sprinkle with dust, *mavu*, a., brown, *manavu*, v., despise, blacken, sully, *mavuana*, a., unadhesive (applied to mortar), Fi. *dravu*, s., ashes, *dravudravua*, a., ashy, of the colour of ashes, poor, hence *vakadravudravua-taka*, v., to make poor.] A. **haba** (**habu**), v., rise, float in the air (*dust*), become like dust, *de carbone igne extincto*, die, 4, raise or excite dust, **habwat**, dust, colour of dust, Ct. **habut**, dust, dust mixed with ashes, a thick vapour like dust, Nm. **hebwa**, fine dust, powder, **mutahabbi**, weak in sight.

Abuera, and **abura**, s., d. for **kabuer**, q. v.

Āfa (**āva**), s., father, **an afa** his father. See **āb**, d. voc. **afa**.

Āfa, v., swim (*man* or *animal*), d. **ofa**;

Āfā i, v. t., carry (him, or it), d. **ofē**. The first meaning seems not connected with the second, to a European, but a native connects them thus: a man **afa natas**, swims or floats on the sea, the sea **afa natamole** bears or carries the man; so a man **afa ki nakasu**, swims holding a floating stick, but if he gets on to the stick and lets it float him ashore the stick is said to **afa i** carry him. The sea or the stick carries him thus, hence **afa**, v. t., denotes carry a man on one's back, then to carry anything on the back: and as a man so carried clasps with his arms the carrier round the chest, the head of an axe is said to **afa** its handle, and as one carrying a basket on his back holds the string of it over his shoulder, so a man drawing a log by a string thus over his shoulder is said to **afa** it, and a tug steamer is said to **afa** or tow a ship. A dog **afa** a piece of meat, carrying it off firmly held by its teeth, and a man **afa** a pipe or a twig, i.e. carries it held by his teeth. A messenger **afa**, carries his message, a horse its rider, and a warrior **afa**, carries, i.e. leads his troop; also a person **afa naroğitesan**, bears a disease or infirmity or trouble (see **bāfa**);

Afāfa, v. redupl., dd. **ofaofa, ofafa.** [My. *apuğ*, s., a float, *ampuğ*, a., buoyant, *kambağ*, v., to float. Sa. *opeope*, to float, Ha. *ope*, bundle up to carry away, Epi *mava*, d. *mia*, to swim.] A. **'āma**, swim (*man*), go (*camel*), 2, dispose in sheaves or bundles: Nm. float, swim. **'Amat**, a bundle, a float, or raft, for carrying things across water. In this A. word there is the idea of connecting together (as things in a bundle, &c.). In **afai**, carry him, as a floating stick carries a man in the water, or a horse carries him on land, the transitive preposition **i**=**bi** (**afai** = **'āma** bi), gives the verb its transitive force, make to swim, to go, i.e. carry.

Āfa ki, v. t., and **ōfa ki**, to bury, **Maka tāfaki** *, pr. n., name of the person who buried the first men who died in the beginning of the world, according to native story; cf. **safaki**. [Sa. *ufi*, v., cover, conceal, ps. *ufitia*, with instrumental particle *ufita'i*, *ufi*, s., a cover, *ufi*, s., the yam, Efate *ui*, or *uui*, (pronounced *uwi*), the yam, Mg. *afina*, *vu afina*, is concealed, *miafina*, to conceal oneself, *manafina*, to conceal, to bury.] A. **"āba**, be concealed, 2 to conceal, to bury, 5 be absent. See egg. s. v. **bei**, infra. **"Ayāb'**, roots (so called because buried in the ground or covered with earth), Sa. **ufi**, Ef. **uwi**, Ja., My. **uwi**, **ubi**, Mg, **uvi**, yams.

Afaru na, s., d. **ofari**, wing, wings. [Ero. *evlok*, Tidore *filafila*, Torres Islands *perperi*, wing.] H. **'abar**, Hi. to soar, mount upwards in flight, **'eber**, and **'evrah**, wing feather (with which birds soar).

Āf i, v. t., to be near to, d. **ōf i**, A. **wahafa**, to approach, draw near to.

Afin i, v. t., **afan i**, **afen i**, also dd.,

Afis i, and **afit i**, to put or carry under the arm or arms, held between the arm and

* NOTE.—Tafa-ki, and Safa-ki, lit., burying, is of the Ancient Tafal or Safal, i. e. Causative Form.

the side; to cover with its wings, as a bird its young, clasping between the wing and the side. **Afini na**, s., armpit, axilla, and d. **afili na**, id., also the groin. [My. *kâpet, mângâpet*, carry under the arm, Sa. *afisi*, carry under the arm.] A. **"abana**, 8, sub axilla posuit, 1, 3, plait, **ma"bin'**, groin, armpit.

Afiti, s., a slave. This word occurs with the article as **nàfiti**. [My. *beta*, Ja. *patik*, a slave.] H. **'ebed**, Ch. **'abad**, a slave. See **bati**, v.

Afo, s. See **foġa**, and **nafo**.

Afuafu. See **abuabu**.

Aġau, d. **nikam**, s., **a**, or **ni**, art., and **kam**, or **ġau**, nippers, tongs: from the verb **kamu**, q.v. [Fi. *ai qamu*, id., My. *aġkub*, forceps, nippers, pincers.] See **kamu**, **kamut**.

Aġa, for **anka**, art., a., and prep. **ka**, literally that or the to, or that which to; a particle prefixed to the nom. suf. pron., forming a poss. pron. Without the art. it is pronounced **ka**, q.v. See **kaġu**, &c., for meaning.

Aġana, poss. pron., 3 sing.; **aġa, na**. See **kana, kakana, kanana**, and for meaning and use see under **kiana**. Fi. **a kena**.

Aġama, poss. pron., 2 sing.; **aġa, ma**. See **kama**.

Aġaġu, poss. pron., 1 sing.; **aġa, gu**. See **kaġu**.

Aġ'ġami, poss. pron., 1 pl., excl.; **aġa, ġami**. **Kaġamî**.

Aġaġita, poss. pron., 1 pl., incl.; **aġa, ġita**. **Kaġita**.

Aġamu, poss. pron., 2 pl.; **aġa, mu**. **Kamu**.

Aġara, poss. pron., 3 pl.; **aġa, ra**. **Kara**.

Aġam, pron., 2 pl., you, ye; dd. **iġam, niġami, niġkam** (ġk for ġ), **akam, eġū**, the pers. pron. 2 pers. pl., which in one dialect is **kumu**, in another is **kami**, q.v.

Āġ, pron., 2 sing., you, thou; dd. **nāġo, nīġo, nēġo**. See **k, ko, ku, ki**.

Aġi, or **aki**, particle consisting of the art. **a**, and prep. **ġi** (for **ki**, q.v.) to, of; dd. **niġ'**, **naġ, niġi**, or **niġki**, in which the art. is **na**, or **ni**. **Aġi** is often equivalent to **ani**, q.v., but not always: **ani**, or **ini** sometimes means 'of' nearly in the sense of 'from', as **rarua ini sē?** a canoe of (from) what place? which cannot be expressed by **rarua aġi sē?** See the preps. **ki** and **ni**. **Aġi** is often equivalent to the simple prep. **ġi**, or **ki**, but sometimes it means the, the (thing), that which, of, the art. having the force of a relative pronoun.

Āġiēġi, s., c. art. **nagiegi**, the air, breeze: **lagi**.

Aġinaġo, poss. pron., 2 sing., thy, of thee; **aġi, naġo**.

Aġinai, poss. pron., 3 sing., his, her, of him; **aġi, nai**.

Aġinami, poss. pron., 1 pl.

excl., our and theirs, of us and them ; **aġi, nami.**

Aġinara, poss. pron., 3 pl., their, of them ; **aġi, nara.**

Aġinau, poss. pron., 1 sing., my, of me ; **aġi, nau.**

Aġita, poss. pron., a, prep., and nom. suf. **ġita,** ; a, ġita. [Sa. *a tatou,* Mg. *anṣika.*]

Aġo, pron., 2 sing., you, thou ; **aġ, nāġo,** in dd.

Aġu, poss. pron., 1 sing., my ; **a,** prep., and **ġu.** [Sa. *a'u.* Ma. *aku,* Mg. *ahi,* my.]

Aġumu, poss. pron., 2 pl., your ; **a, kumu.**

Aheka, d., **tasila,** d. **tasiġa** ; **sila ia.**

Ais, or **eis,** ad., here, d. **ieta** ; **a,** or **e,** or **i,** prep., and **is,** see **sa, se, s,** this, here ; d. **esas,** q.v. [Mg. *ati, eti, atu, etu,* Ta. *yesa.* My., without prep., *sini, sika,* and with preps. *di* and *ka, disini, kasini.*] H. **zeh,** without prep., here, properly this, Ef. **se,** this, here, E. **zĕya,** here. Also H. **bazeh,** E. **bazya,** c. prep. **ba,** with which is to be compared, Ha. **ma** in **manei,** here, and also generally. The prep. **a, e,** or **i** was also similarly used. See examples of this under the word **iġin,** infra.

Ai, s., c. art. **nai,** water, d. for **nifai,** q.v.

Aia (=d. **āo**), that's it; **a,** dem., and **ia,** 3 pers. pron.

Aîme, s., c. art. **naime,** a stream: preceding word, **ai,** and **me,** q.v.

Aka, a., d. **koa,** and **koakoa,** a., stringy, fibrous, as a yam when cooked (bad to eat); **akoa na,** or **ako ana,** root, its root, lit. and fig. ; **aka,** a relative, family connection (considered as root or offshoot from), **aka na,** d. **ek, eka na** ; in one place **ek** or **eka** denotes great grandfather, and great grandmother (which in another place is denoted by **tai la,** or **tai,** q.v.), in another place **aka** denotes mother (used by a child addressing its mother), d. **iak** (i, art.), **mama** ; **aka na,** or **uaka na (waka na),** fissure, inside of fissure, as of the mouth, of a canoe (hold), of a bag or basket, or of anything; **kaka naniu,** the fibrous substance like coarse cloth that grows round the top of the stem of the cocoanut tree (**naniu**); **makaka,** to be ragged or fissured, as cloth ; **mako,** or **maka,** offspring, in pr. nn. as **mako naru,** &c. ; **taumako,** the wild yam growing on the hills, so called because **koa** or fibrous. **Koa** has the a. ending **a.** [To. *aka,* Fi. *waka,* My. *akar,* Mg. *faka,* root, Ma. long and thin roots, *akaaka,* fibrous roots, *kaka,* a fibre or hair, a garment, a kind of net, Ha. *aa niu*=Ef. *kaka naniu,* also roots (small), offspring, a pocket, a bag, a coarse kind of cloth, Sa. *aa,* fibres of a root, family connection. Mg.

kaki, *ikaki* (*i* art., cf. Ef. *aka*, *iak*), father, papa, Tah. *aa*, root, sieve, &c., *aaa*, the stringy substance in any kind of food or vegetable, native cloth that is not well worked.] A. 'aḳḳa, n.a. 'aḳaḳ, to be split, fissured, 'aḳḳo, a fissure, 'aḳiḳaṭ', a bag (pera viatoria, Ha. aa), also like 'aḳiḳo and 'iḳḳaṭ', hairs of a foetus; 'awaḳo, small shoots sprouting from the upper part of a palm, 'iḳḳano, shoots sprouting from the roots of palms and vines, 'aḳḳa, 4, to send forth such shoots from the roots (*palms or vines*), Mg. **faka**, root, caus. verb **mamaka**, to send forth roots, and My. **akar**, roots of a plant, scandent plant, parts of a plant that climb.

Akam, d.; you; pers. pron., 2 pl. See **kumu**.

Akamus, preceding word, with dem. suffixed. See Ch. II. 13 *b*.

Akē, interj. See **ako**, **ako ri**. [Mg. *akai !*] **A**, interj., and **ke**, q.v.

Akē ri, interj., **akē**, or **aki**, and **ri**, as in **ako ri**, q.v.

Aki, prep., i.q., **aġi**, q.v.

Akit, d., pron., 1 pl., incl., we and you. [My. *kita*, Tag. *kita*, Fut. *akitea*, An. *akaija*.] See **nininta**.

Akoa na, or **ako ana**, s., root. See **aka**.

Ako, interj. For ri, dem. particle, used also as an expletive, and **la**, ad., see these words.

Ako ri la, interj.

Ako ri, interj. **Ako** expresses surprise, wonder, admiration, also mourning, commiseration. **A**, interj., and **ko**, q.v.

Āl, d., syn. with **ēlo**, d. **āli**, the sun. See **ali**.

Alat ia, v. t. (and let, q.v.) to press together, nip as with scissors, or with the teeth, press between two things drawn together, to press, urge, persist, be importunate with, to grasp. The final consonant is often dropped;

Ala, s., c. art. **nāla**, a basket or purse the edges of whose mouth can be closed by being drawn or pressed together, women's carrying basket;

Alati, s., scissors, nippers, clippers;

Alaterabati, also **alati bati ore**, to gnash the teeth, lit., press the teeth together creaking. See **bati** and **ore**;

Ala ġoro ki, v. t., press, urge. See **ġoro**;

Alāla, a., compressing. [Mg. *lasiṭa*, *mandasiṭa*, to pinch.] H. **Laḥaṣ**, to press, squeeze, **'alaṣ**, to urge, S. **'elaṣ**, coegit, arctavit, A. **laḥiṣ**, angustus, arctus (drawn, pressed together).

Alalu, i.q. **elalo**, q.v. See **alo na**.

Alau, s.; **a**, prep., and **lau**, sea; also **elau**, d. **elà**, the sea, on the sea, seawards. [Malo *a lau*, Epi *lau*, My. *laut*, Ja.

lahut, lot, Tag. *dagat,* Marshall Islands *lojet,* the sea, My. *lauti,* v., and *malaut,* v., to put to sea, be at sea in a boat or ship.] A. **logg'**, and **loggaṭ**, or **lojjaṭ**, middle and depth of the sea, ocean, **lajja**, or **lagga**, 8, the sea was wide and deep, or such a sea was sailed over, 2, he entered the vast and deep sea.

Alekabu, c. art., **talekabu**, d. for **arekabu**.

Ali, s., c. art., **nāli,** leaf. leaves: **ulua.**

Āli, s., day (d. **ali**, sun, d. **ali**, light, see **lina**). **Sera ali**, every day, **toko ali**, stay at home during the day, not going to work. Usually this word is doubled, as,

Aliati, s., day. [An. *at'iat*]. And,

Aliati, v. to day, to dawn, to lighten as the dawn. See **al, alo, elo**, the sun, also **meta ni al, meta ni elo**, the sun, lit., eye, i.e., source of day or light. [Mg. *andru,* Malo *alo,* My. *ari, hari,* Sa. *la,* Ma. *ra,* day, Sa. *la,* To. *laa,* Ma. *ra,* My. *mata-ari,* Mg. *masu-andru,* the sun.] For this word see Ch. II. 17, above.

Āl i, v. t., for **ġal i**, or **kal i**, q.v.

Ali, and **alia**, s., place, part, **alia n**, its place or part, d. **male n**, or **mile n**; **luān**, that place, there, for **alia uan, li bān**, d. **lo bōn**, there (**li** for **alia**); **mala**, and **malo**, a place, a part, **malo**, time, i.e., a part of time, as **malo ni aliati**, a part of the day, **malo uan**, that time, or that place, **malo**, trunk of the body, or of a tree, **mala, malala**, an open place or plain, also the village dancing and public worship ground, **malmal**, redup., a small place or part; **mālu, malumalu**, to be bare, clear, as a piece of ground, to be bare, devoid of hair, as the face, **malamala**, naked. [Fi. *mala,* a part, Sa. *malae,* the open space where public meetings are held, Tah. *marae,* the sacred place formerly used for worship, *marae,* a., cleared, as a garden, or a place of worship, Ma. *marae,* enclosed space in front of a house, a yard, *maramara,* a small piece.] A. **'ariya**, to be naked, **'arā'**, **'arā'**, **'araṭ**, an open place, tract, part, **mo'rai**, and **mo'rat'**, naked part of the body not covered with clothing, H. **'arah**, to be naked, **'arah**, a naked or bare place, **ma'ar**, a naked space, void space, **ma'ărah**, a naked place, i.e. a plain or field devoid of trees, **'A. mo'arrai**, naked, bare.

Āliāli, v. i. (doubled), to delay, be slow, and **taliali**, id., intensive. [Cf. Ha. *alia,* v., to wait.] A. **āla** (**alu**), and, 2, **alla'**, and, 5, to delay, be slow.

Alialia, v. i., or a., insane. to be insane; connected with this is **ululia,** inspired, possessed, or entered by a deity (**natemate**) or demon, and, therefore, as a matter of course, out of one's senses. **Alialia** is not used in some places where **ululia** (for **ululuia**) is used in both senses; this latter word is also pronounced **luluia,** and **lulia.** It is a reduplicate and has the ending **ia,** and literally means entered (i.e. by a spirit), possessed. [Sa. *ului-tino,* enter the body, possess (as by an *aitu*), *ulu,* to enter, and *tino,* body, Ha. *uluia,* and *uluhia,* to be inspired, possessed by a spirit, *ulu,* to have spiritual possession, good or bad, *ulala,* insane, out of one's senses, Tah. *uru,* to be inspired, *uruhia,* inspired. This last word corresponds to Sa. *ulufia,* which simply means entered, being the passive of *ulu,* to enter. Corresponding to Sa. *ulu,* to enter, is Mg. *idiṭa,* or *iliṭa,* to enter, and with this latter is connected the reduplicate *adala,* insane, senseless, a lunatic, a fool (cf. Ha. *ulala*). Ef. *lāla,* an idiot, senseless person, fool, may belong here also, and cf. Fi. *lialia,* foolish, crazy, an idiot.] Ch. **'alal,** to enter. S. id., **'al,** he entered, imp., **'ul,** enter, A. **''alla,** he entered.

Note.—The A. is followed by prep. **fi,** the S. by **b** and also **l** (A. **li**): the first of these preps. is used in Mg. (**ami**), as in Jno. xiii. 27, Satan **nidiṭa amini,** entered into him; and the second (**ani,** sometimes contracted to **an** and **a**), as in Lu. xxii. 3, and often: in Sa. we have the last in the **i** of **ulufia,** **i** of Ha. **uluhia,** and in the **i** of **ulu-i-tino,** and of Ha. **uluia,** and Ef. **luluia,** &c. This is the verb constantly used in S., Mg., and Sa., to denote the entering into a man of a spirit. The Ef. and Fi. use another and synonymous verb, Ef. **sili,** to enter, Fi. **t'uru,** id., which is used also in A. to express this idea: for the A. verb corresponding to **sili, t'uru,** see **sili,** infra.

Alo, s., d., the sun. See **ali.**

Alo-fi, v., wave (with a circular and rolling motion) to him, beckon to by so waving the hand, or a branch of a tree; **alof,** and prep. **i**: **bialo,** v. r., wave often, or wave to each other, **alo-alo,** wave repeatedly, **tālo,** go round, avoid, turn round, **taloalo,** keep going round (as on a zigzag or crooked path), turn round. See next word.

Alo n, or **alu n,** s., belly, abdomen, the front, before, d. **al' naru na,** belly, i.e., palm (or front) of his hand; reduplicate **lalo n,** or **lalu n,** id., **elalo,** before (**e,** prep., and **lalo,** front). [Fi. *yalova,* Ml. P. *oruvi,* Ml. U, *oluve,*

TaSa. *lobe* or *love*, Malo *alovi*, to beckon, To. *talu*, to beckon, Sa. *alo*, to fan, *talo*, to fan, to beckon, to wave a piece of *tutuġa* over the dead, begging him to take calamities and diseases with him, *alofi*, to sit in a circle, *alofilima*, palm of hand (i.e., front or belly of hand), Sa. *alo*, belly, under side, Ma. *aro*, face, front, Ha. *alo*, belly, face, Ma. *arohi*, to look for, *arohirohi*, to turn round and round, Ha. *aloalo*, to turn this way and that, *alo*, to elude, to oppose (face, front), to swim (wave hands), double (as a cape, i.e., go round).] A. **ḥala,** to turn round, twist about, desire, look at, turn the eyes or face towards; **ḥiyalo,** the *front* of a thing, Ef. **ālo,** the front (as of the hand, or body), reduplicate with prep. e, **elalo,** at the front, as opposed to **etaku,** (see **taku**), at the back; **ḥayalo,** shadow, image of a man in a mirror, spirit, Fi. **yalo,** id. The Ef. f, Ma. **h,** is the Semitic servile t of the n. a. For this see Ch. II. and Ch. III.

Al' (naru) (for **alo naru**), d., palm (front) of the hand. [Ml. P. *aro*, Malo *lolo*.]

Alo ana, s., maternal uncle; vocative (reduplicate) **lolo** cf. **abab, mama**). [In Ef. dd. syn. **auaua, bau.** Malo **taura** (ta art.), maternal uncle.] A. **ḥ'alo,** maternal uncle.

Aloara, a.; formative ending **ara** or **ra**; and

Aloaloara, a., redupl., ornamented, painted (as cloth). See **alo-fi, loa-ri.** [A different word is Sa. *ilaila*, a., spotted, marked, *ila*, s., a mother's mark, a mark in the skin, To. *ila*, a mole or mark in the skin. A. **ḥ'alo,** pl. **ḥ'īlān,** mole or mark in the skin, **aḥ'yalo,** a., having such marks in the skin, spotted, marked.]

Alo-fi v., rub on (to) it, paint. See **loa, loa-ri a, loa-si,** and **lo-fi.** A. **ḥalā, ḥalū,** or **ḥalō,** rub, smear, paint, adorn.

Ālikas, s., c. art. **nālikas,** for **na uli nakasu,** leaf or leaves of trees. See **uli,** and **kasu.**

Ālsēr, s., c. art. **nālsēr,** dried or withered cocoanut leaves, so called because jagged: from **nal** for **na uli,** leaves, and **sere,** jagged, hairy.

Alu na, s., for **alo na,** q.v.

Āma, poss. pron., 2 sing. thy: **a** prep., and nom. suf. **ma.** [Sa. *au*, Mg. *anau*, thy.]

Amau, a., true: in **loamau,** q.v., **lo,** a thing, and **amau,** also **mau, mori, mauri,** true. H. **aman.** See **mau.**

Amos i, v., to carry on the shoulder, to bear, to carry. Often the final s is dropped; hence

Amo, v., to carry, to put a load on the shoulder; and

Amo-taki, d., id.; and

Amo-rua, am'rua (**rua,** two),

to carry two (burdens), one on each end of a stick (as a Chinaman carries two baskets); the word also occurs in **tak'amo**, d. **takiamo**, to carry a burden on only one end of such a stick; and

Amoamo, c. art. **namoamo**, s., a burden, lit., that which is carried. [Sa. *amo*, v., to carry on the shoulders, *amoġa*, s., a burden, Ma. *amo*, *amohia*, Ha. *amo*, to carry a burden on the shoulder, to carry.] H. **'amas**, bear, carry, especially lift up a load and put it on a beast.

Amo, s., c. art. **namo na**, the lungs, but also

Am' kanoa, the heart, and

Am' insat, the lungs (see **kanoa, insat**); and

Am' molu, the spleen. [Fut. *ama*, Sa. *mama*, the lungs, To. *mama*, id., Ha. *akemama*, the lungs, from *ake*, liver, and *mama*.] In To., Sa., Fut., and Ha., *mama* (a reduplicate) means light, to be light (opp. of heavy), but this is not the stem to which the word *mama* denoting the lungs belongs, and does not occur at all in Ef., though the Ef. *amo* is manifestly the same as Fut. *ama*, and Sa. (reduplicate) *mama*, the lungs. For analogues of *akemama*, see under the word **ate**, the liver. In Ef. **uateam**, q.v., the kidneys, is **ua ate am'**, lit., fruit of the liver (or inside) of the belly (**am'**, the belly): **uateau** (d. **uateaf**), is d. for **uateam'**, and **balau**, q.v. (for **balam'**), the common Ef. for inside, is lit. the hollow of the **am'** (**amo**), i.e., belly. See following—

Amo, s., c. art. **namo**, the soft forming kernel of a young cocoanut: so called like the internal parts of man or animal from the softness and smoothness:

Amoamo, v. i., a., reduplicate, to be soft and smooth, as the forming kernel of a young cocoanut, or the intestines or viscera, or any smooth or polished surface: d. **momoa**. [Sa. *mama*, a., clean (i.e., smooth), Tah. clean, not soiled or polluted, To. and Ma. *ma*, clean. white.] A. **ma'y'**, pl. **ām'a'**, intestinum; also, a level place between two rugged places (Ef. **na momo**, or **na amo'mo**, a smooth and level place between the rocks in a reef), **ma'a**, 4. to have dates ripe or ripening (*a palm*), **ma'w'**, dates on the tree, ripe or growing ripe, **ma'i**, soft. smooth (*of food*), **ma''y'** softness of skin, H. **me'eh**, only in pl. **me'im** or **m'ey** intestines, the belly, then the bosom, heart: cg. is A. **maha**, to gleam with whiteness, to gild, whence **mahw'**, new soft dates. Gesenius gives the radical meaning as 'flowing down, softness', see H. **ma'ah**.

Amo'mo, or **am'mo**, c. art. **namomo**, or **nam'mo**; see s. preceding word: d. **momo**.

Amorĭ. See **mori**.

Amos i, v. t., to rub, to rub in order to make smooth: **mos i**, **mus i**. A. **wamasa**, to rub (a thing), to rub (a thing) that it may be smooth.

Amu, poss. pron., 2 pl., your: **a**, prep., and nom. suf. **mu**.

Ana, form of pers. pron., 3 sing., he, she, preserved in **aneana**: other forms **nai**, **enea** (**inia**), **ġā**.

Ana, poss. pron., 3 sing., his, her, its: **a**, prep., and **na**, nom. suf. [Sa. *ana*, id., Mg. *azi*.]

Anaġaġu, **anaġama**, **anaġana**, **anaġaġita**, **anaġami**, **anaġamu**, **anaġara** (or **anaġata**), poss. prons., syn. c. **aġaġu**, **aġama**, &c., q. v. See Ch. V.

Anaġa, in these words, is the art. a, and preps. **na**, and **ġa** (for **ka**). With **anaġaġu** (for **anakaku**), cf. Mg. d. **anakahi**, id.

Anai, poss. pron., 3 sing., his, her, its: **a**, prep., and **nai**.

Anāna, poss. pron., 3 sing., his, her, its, d. for **aneana**, q.v.

Anĕana, poss. pron., 3 sing., of him, his, her, its: **anĕ** or **anī**, q.v., prep., and **ana**, a form of the pers. pron. 3 sing., orig. pl.

Anekabu, c. art. **nanekabu**, d. for **arekabu**.

Anekama, c. art. **nanekama**, d. for **arekabu**.

Anekabu, c. art. **tanekabu**, d. for **arekabu**.

Anēna, d. for **aneana**.

Anēra, for **anĕara**, often pronounced **anēta**, **anĕata**, d. **arĕara**, poss. pron., 3 pl., of them, their; prep. **anī**, and **ara**, pers. pron., 3 pl.

Anēta, d. for **anēra**.

Anĭ, prep., particle consisting of the art. **a** and prep. **nĭ**, q.v., and often used for the simple prep. **ni**, of, belonging to (genitive prep.), for (dative, rare, this is usually expressed by **magi**, d. syn. **nag'**, or **nig'**, q.v.): generally synonymous with **aġi**, q.v. for a difference.

Anĭġami; d. syn. c. **aġinami**; poss. pron. 1 pl. excl., of us—them (of us and them): **anĭ**, prep., and **ġami** (for **nami**), pers. pron. 1 pl. excl. See **nami**, **kinami**.

Aniġita; d. **aninita**, q.v.; poss. pron. 1 pl. incl., of us—you (of us and you): **ani**, prep., and **ġita** (for **nīta**). See **ninita**, **nita**.

Animu; d., syn. c. **aġumu**; poss. pron. 2 pl., of you, your: **a**, prep., and **nimu** (for **nikamu**), d. **nikam**, pers. pron. 2 pl., d. **niëm**.

Aninita, d. obsolete, syn. c. **aniġita**: **ani**, prep., and **nita**, pers. pron. 1 pl. incl. See **ninita**, **nita**.

Anĭ, v., usually pronounced **enĭ**, d. **onĭ**, contracted to **an**, en, a, o ; c. preformative m' or ma, it is, mān, mā, bān, (and mbān), bā, dd. bon, bēn, bao, baon, maon; to abide, to be, as i ani, or, i an suma, he abides or is at home (in the house), i man, or, i ma tafa, he is on the hill, i man, or, i ma rarua, it is in the ship or canoe, i ma, or, i an til ia, bat ia, he abides (continues), or is telling it, doing it.

Note 1.—The verb an may be thus used before any verb, like toko (contracted to), to sit, dwell, be, with which it is nearly synonymous. But an tano, *lies* or *is* on the ground, toko tano, or to atano, *sits* on the ground, tu tano, *stands* on the ground. Both tu and toko are used before other verbs like an, and toko til ia, tu til ia, like an til ia, denote to abide, continue, or be telling it. Another verb, tau, q.v., is used in the same way before other verbs, as i tau til ia, bat ia, he abides, or is constantly, habitually, or addictedly, or repeatedly, telling, doing it. So Fi. dau, which is the same word. These verbs thus used before other verbs express continuance, intensity, repetition.

Note 2.—The preformative m', ma' (mĕ, mĭ) is used with toko, tu, and tau, as well as with anĭ, an, as matoko (or mato), dd. batoko, fatoko (vatoko), matu, batu, fatu (vatu), mĭtau or mĕtau: with this preformative these verbs have much the same meaning as without it; they have the same meaning with the added idea of continuance. [Mg. *munina*, dwell, reside, inhabit, *unenana*, *funenana* (a dwelling), *mpunina* (dweller).] A. (4) "aniya, to dwell, abide (8) to be, ma"na', dwelling, cf. H. ʻun, to rest, to dwell, maʻon, a dwelling.

(Ani na), nani na, s., child, son or daughter, dd. nati, natu. [My. *anak*, Mg. *anaka*, Ml. d. *anati*, id., My. *kanak* (see *kanao*, *kano*, infra), Mg. *zanaka*, id.] A. wald', walad', walid', E. waldĕ, Amh. wandĕ, T. wadĕ, H. yalid, one born, child, son, from the verb H. yalad, A. walada, to bring forth, bear (*a mother*), to beget (*a father*), A. walid', parent, genitor, father, walidat' mother, genitrix (Nm. wêlid, wêlida, Ct. walidah). My. bâranak (Makassar, ma-ana), to bear a child, bring forth any offspring, have children, be a parent, Sa. fānau (cf. A., 4) to bring forth, fananau, fanafanau, fanaua (ps.), fānau, s., offspring, children, fanauġa, s., offspring, child-bearing.

Note.—The word nani, or nati, natu, son or daughter, probably represents an original masculine (and so that denoting father, A. **walid**, Ml. and Santo **tata**, Santo d. **tai**, Mg. **rai**), but the word belonging to this stem denoting mother, the ancient feminine (**wêlida**, **walidah**). This is in Ef. d. **raite na**, or **reita na**, mother, d. **ere na** (for **era na**), Ta. **iti**, d. **rih**, Am. **rahi**, An. **risi**, Ml. **risi**, d. **are**, Epi d. **la**, Pa. **lati**, Fila **lēta**, Celebes **leyto**, Ef. **kiliti**, q.v. : Ef. voc. **tete**, also in Epi mother, in one d. **la**, in another is **kaine**, i.e. **ka**, art., and **ine** (for **ina**) mother, and this latter is the prevailing form of this word in the Malay Archipelago (see Wallace's list), Amboyna, Ceram, &c., **ina**, Mg. **reni**, and **ineni**, (Ta. d. **nana**). Celebes **undo**, Bu. **indok**, **ina**, My. **indu**, J. **iduġ** ; also Ysabel **ido**, San Cristoval **ina**, Mare **nene**, Duke of York **na**. On these letter changes see Ch. II, above.

Ānoĭ, or **ānuĭ**, d. **ānoai** (**ānowai**), s., c. art. **nānoĭ**, or **nānuĭ**, vir, husband, male: **m** has been elided from the beginning of this word as in **noai**, d. **nai**, d. **nifai** (**nivai**), q.v., water; d. **mane** (**mwāne**), **ma'an** (**mo'an**), male. See **mani**, and Ch. II, 17.

Anu, d., pers. pron. 1 sing., I. See **kinau**.

Ānu na, s. c. art., **nanu na**, his, her, its shadow, **i bi ān' fūr**, it is an empty appearance, mere shadow (worthless). [Epi *ununo*, Malo *unu*, Ml. d. *nunu*, id.] And,

Ān', s., a rope, c. art. **nān'**. These two meanings are also found in the A. A. **'anna**, n. a. **'annu**, **'ananu**, **'ununu**, to present itself, to appear, 2, to hold with a rein ; **'ānu**, a long rope, **'ananu** and **'inanu**, adparitio *rei*, **'ananu**, clouds, H. **'anan**, a cloud : A. **'a'nan'**, demon nature, **ma'nun** and **magnun**, possessed by a demon or spirit.

NOTE.—The radical meaning of **'anan**, is to cover, and cognate are **kanan**, and **ganan** ; A. **ganna**, to cover, to be dark (of the night), to be possessed by a demon and insane, **ginnu**, darkness of night, also demons, spirits, or every kind of them (this is the jin of the 'Arabian Nights'), **ḥin**, a kind of demons, **ginniyyu**, a demon or spirit, **ganunu**, genii. In Ef., d., **unu**, ghost, d. **inini**, spirit, soul, Ml. P. **oni**, **noni n**, his soul, or his shadow, Epi d. **anunu**, soul or spirit, Epi (Baki) **unu**, c. art. **niunu**, soul or spirit, **ununo**, shadow ; and Ml. **oni**, Malo **unu**, one's likeness in water, or in a looking glass. So Ef. **ate**, q.v., denotes the soul, a spirit, one's shadow, and one's likeness in water, or in a looking-glass.

Ao (or **au**), v., d., to bark (as

a dog). See **bakau.** [Sa. *ou*, id.]

Äo, ad., yes. [Ma. *au*.] See **äu.**

Ara, form of pers. pron. 3 pl., preserved in **areara**: other forms **nāra, niġara** (**ġara**). **enera, kiniara.** See Ch. V.

Ara, s., a fence: c. art. **nāra**, d. **nār**: see **koro**, c. art. **nakoro**, id. (ara has the initial **k** elided), **Nār fāt**, d. for **nakoro fatu**, a stone fence.

Ara i, v. t., seek, **ara ika**, search, look for fish, come seeking, **ba ara**, go or come seeking, **ti ara**, press after seeking. [Fi. *qara*, v. t., seek, *qaqara*, *qaraqara*, *vakasaqara*.] S. **ḥar**, to see, look (for).

Araara, or **arāra**, v., reduplicate of **ara**, to join to, join together, connect with, **arāra naui**, attach the yam vines to stakes, **arāra nia**, connect it, **arara ni ora naui ki nakau**, connect or attach the yam vine to the stake: **arāra ki nalo na**, agree to his voice (judgement, opinion, &c.), lit. join on to it, syn. **sokari nalona.** A. **ʻarā**, 3, to join together one thing to another.

Arān, or **orān**, d. **arain**, d. **oraone** (redup.), d. **on**, d. **uen**, s., c. art. **nārān**, &c., sand. In **on**, and **uen** (**wen**), the radical r is changed to n. [Sa., Ma., Tah., To., Ha., *one*, and *oneone*, sand; *oneonea* (*a*, a. ending), sandy.] A. **ḥorr'**, or **ḥorron**, sand, from **ḥarra**, to be hot.

Arai, d., dem. pron., this, that. For the final **ai**, see **uai.** [Ha. *la*, Ma. *ra*, there, Fut. *ra*, that, Mg. *irua*, that, there, *eri*, *ari*, there.] S. **hal**, H. **halah**, there, connected with the dem. H. **hal**, A. **al**, the art.; Ch. **alu, aru**, Ch. and Talmud **harē, are**, dem., lo! there! Of this dem. syllable **al, hal, ar, har**, Gesenius remarks—'It is hard to say which form is the more ancient and primitive;' it is seen also in Arm. **harka, halkah**, here, H. **elleh**, &c., these, those, and in Ef. **aroġ**, (d.), **eri, erik, eru**, q.v. See Ch. V.

Areara, d., for **aneara, anēra**, q.v.; the prep. **anĭ**, or **anĕ**, is **arĕ**, in this word, orig. **ale**, art. **a**, and prep.

Arekabu na, s., c. art. **narekabu**, the liver. See **ate.**

Arĭfōn, s., c. art. **narĭfōn**, diviner, magician. A. **ʻarrafon**, a diviner, from **ʻarafa**, to know, divine, 2, make known, **ʻarĕfān**, one who knows.

Āri, v. t., to plane, scrape off, rub off. [Sa. *oro*, id.] S. **graʻ**, to scrape off, shave, H. **garaʻ.**

Aroġ, d., dem. pron., this. See **arai** and **erik.** The final **ġ**, as in **naġ, naġa**, dem.

Āru na, s., c. art. **nāru na**, hand, arm; fore-foot of a quadruped: **nāru**, arms, i.e., weapons of war, war; **i bi aru uia,** he is industrious, lit. a good hand, **i bi aru sa,** he is handless, lazy, lit. a bad hand. [New Guinea. dd. *uadu, dei,* Ml. P. *fera,* Ml. A. *verua.*] H. **yad,** hand, S. id., A. **yadu** (and **yaddu**), dual, **yadān;** also, **'adu,** dual **'adān,** hand, arm; fore-foot of a quadruped.

Asa, or **isa,** prep. **a,** or **i,** and **sa,** suffix pronouns 3rd person. d. syn. **kina,** prep. **ki,** and s. p. **na,** Fi. **kina,** with, by, on, at, from, because of, him or it. For this prep., see Ch. V, Prepositions, 3.

Asa, ad., the day after tomorrow. See **uāsa.**

Asèlĭ na, s., a friend. [Ml. U. *sele n,* Bu. *sölao,* id.] A. **waṣīl',** intimate friend, from **waṣala,** to join, be joined.

Ās ia, d. **uas ia,** v. t., cut, cut out, as **asi naniu,** cut out the kernel of a cocoanut (to make a water vessel of it), **asi** (**lua namena na**), cut (out his tongue), **asi intàlĕ,** cut the roots of taro (while it is in the water, to pull it out of the ground): hence **maseasi,** q.v. A. **ḥ'adda,** fidit, sulcavit, and

Āsĭ na, s., c. art. **nāsĭ na,** the part of the face bearded, jaw, jawbone, chin. [Malo *ase,* TaSa. *ese,* chin, Ml. P. *fese,* chin, *ese,* cheek.] The radical idea is that of *cutting, sharp, tearing.* A. **ḥ'add',** mala, gena; and

Āsĭ ta bunu, jaw cutting dead; and

Asĭ taġeli, crooked jaw: these expressions denote, the latter crooked talk, the former talk calculated for and resulting in the death of one hated. See **ta, bunu, taġeli.**

Āso, v. i., to burn, be burning (*a fire*), be kindled, to be burnt or scorched (as one's skin, or food in being cooked). [Fi. *qesa, qesaqesa,* a., burnt or scorched, as in cooking. Sa. *'a'asa,* To. *kakaha,* An. *egesgas,* a., burned, *agas,* or *gas,* to burn; hot, burning.] A. **waḳada,** n. a. **waḳdo.** H. **yaḳad,** S. **iḳad,** to burn, be burning, be kindled.

Āso, s., a kind of crab, the robber crab.

Āso, or **āsu,** s., c. art. **nāso,** or **nāsu,** a bow (for shooting arrows). [Aurora *usu,* Paama *hisu,* Ml. P. *vus,* Ml. U. *vis,* Amblaw *busu,* My. *busor,* Saparua *husu,* id.] A. **ḳawsu,** or **ḳāsu,** id. So called from being curved.

Asoara, s., the rainbow. Cloth brilliantly variegated with different coloured bands or stripes is called **na kalu asoara,** a phrase in which the word is an adjective. Also a stone fence constructed of three rows or bands of stone is described as **asoara.** See Index, A. **zabara.**

Asolat, see **soli.**

Asua, v. i., to smoke, c. t. prep., **asuè nia,** to smoke on to it, or him: c. art. it is s., **naasua na**, the smoke of it, its smoke. [Mg. *etuna*, s., smoke, *manetuna*, v., to smoke, My. *asâp* (probably this word lit. means smoke of fire, *api*) *bârâsap*, to smoke, Malo *asu*, s., *mo asuasu*, v., TaSa. *asu*, s., *m'asu*, v., Ml. P. *ese*, s., *mi es*, v., Ml. A. *nahamp basua*, s., lit. the fire smokes, *basua*, v., Sa. *asu*, s., *asua*, and *asuina*, v. ps.] H. **'as'en,** to smoke, **'as'an,** smoke, A. **'at'ana,** 1, 2, 4, to smoke.

Āt, or **āṣ,** c. art. **nat,** q.v., banana.

Ata (or **nata**), s., c. art. nata, d. **na eta** for **na ata,** a man, a person; one, some one; **nata nata,** every one. See **atamole, atemate, ata na, atam̄anī.** [Motlav *et*, Ureparapara *at*, man. See below, Note 2.] A. **nat',** for **nas',** which is the commonly used plural ('pluralis fractus', a collective or abstract, or singular with a collective meaning), of **'insan',** man, male or female, a human being, also umbra hominis (the older plural is **'unas',** with which corresponds H. **'enos',** Arm. **'anas'a,** a man, men), and denotes men, also genii, demons.

Note 1.—A. **'insan,** for which there is also **'īsan,** corresponds to H. **'īs'on,** which is formed from **'īs'** by the ending **on,** and denotes, when followed by the word eye, 'little man of the eye, i.e. pupil in which as in a glass a little image of a man is seen' (Ges.); the **A.** denotes in addition to the meanings given above 'the little image appearing in the pupil of the eye': A. **'insan** is from the root **'ans** and H. **'is',** vir, **'is'ah,** woman, from **'ins',** **'ins'ah,** hence the pl. of **'is'ah** is **nas'im,** corresponding to A. **nisā',** **niswaṭ,** and **niswan,** women. The words **'is',** vir, **is'ah,** woman (and their equivalents in the cognate languages), must be carefully distinguished from that given above under **ata** (or **nata**) denoting 'a human being' whether male or female, though they all belong to the same root or stem.

Note 2.—According to the above, the **t** in **ata,** like that in A. **nat',** represents an original **s** as in **nas'.** In Ef. dd. this **t** is sometimes pronounced nearly as **r,** and **ṣ.** In other New Hebrides dialects this consonant is found as **t, s, r, l;** thus corresponding to Efate **ata-m̄ani,** male (vir), are An. **ata-maiġ,** Fut. **ta-ne** (for **ta-ane**), Ta. **yeruman,** Epi dd. **ata-mani, sumano,** Ml. U. **oro-man,** TaSa. **la-mani.** My. **oraġ,** Mg. **uluna** belong here, and =**ata.** Note 3. See Ch. II, 17.

Ata na, s., c. art. **nata na** (or **nate na**), his spirit, his soul; his shadow; his image (in water or a glass). This is the same word as the preceding, but in this use has the nom. suf. [Sa. *ata*, a spirit, a shadow, Fut. *ata*, a ghost, shadow, image (as in water), picture or likeness, Fila *tano ata*, his soul, Ha. *aka*, the shadow of a person, figure, outline, or likeness.] See preceding word.

Ata i, or **atai,** v. t., to know, d. **tai,** q.v.

Atakasua, a., jealous; suspicious: from **ata** (soul), and **kasua,** q.v.

Atălàġĭ, s., usually written **atelaġi,** d. **atlaġ,** the moon. See Ch. II. 14 *f.*

Atamauri, or **atemauri,** s., the spirit of a living man that has gone out of him during sleep and been seen by someone. This word occurs in one dialect and is composed of **ata,** the soul, and **mauri,** q.v., to live.

Atamate, or **atemate,** s., c. art. **natemate,** spirit of one dead, ghost, spirits of the dead, demons, good or bad spirits, supernatural beings, objects of worship, gods (gen. name). The word is composed of **ata** (above), and **mate,** q.v., to die, be dead, a. dead. [Ml. P. *demej*, Epi dd. *atamate*, *simaro*, Ta. *yeramis*, Ml. A. *temes*, An. *natmas*, id.] The primary meaning of **natemate** seems to be 'dead man': thus a corpse may be called **natemate,** and **natemate** sometimes denotes 'the dead' in a collective sense.

Atamole, s., c. art. **natamole,** man, male or female, a human being, same as **ata,** or **nata,** with the addition of **mole,** q.v., to live, a. living. **Natamole** lit. denotes 'living man'. [Mg. *ulumbeluna*, id. The Mg. is composed of the same two words as the Ef.; for *uluna*, see **ata** (above), and for *veluna*, to live, see **mole** (below); and the meaning of the compound word is the same in each case. Fi. *tamata*, Sa. *taġata*, Tah. *taata*, id., belong here, and My. *oraġidup*.]

Atam̃ani, s., c. art. **natam̃ani,** male, lit. a male human being, from **ata** (above), and **manĭ,** q.v., male. [For New Hebrides forms of this compound word, see **ata** (above), Note 2. Fi. *taġane*, Sa. *tane*, id.]

Atatabu, or **at'tab,** s., c. art. **natatabu,** or **nat'tab,** lit. sacred spirits, sacred stones identified with such spirits, and objects of pagan worship: from **ata** (above), and **tabu,** q.v.

Atama, s., d. syn. c. **ore,** the pointed rubbing stick for producing fire by its friction with another stick: **a,** art., and **tama i,** q.v.

Atara. See **natara.**

Atāta, v. i., or a., a reduplicate, to have white spots or marks such as show where sores have healed. See next word.

Atāta, s., an albino. The radical meaning would therefore seem to be white. [Mg. *haṣaṭa*, white, pale, wan, sickly, Sa., Ma., *ata*, dawn, Ma. *ata-marama*, moonlight.] A. **waṣ'aḥ'**, white spot appearing on the head or feet of a horse, **waṣ'āḥ**, whitening spots of leprosy, **waṣ'iḥ'**, very white; from **waṣ'aḥa**, to be manifest, white (as milk), &c., shine as the dawn, moon, &c.

Ātĕ, c. art. **nātĕ na** (d. **nānte na**), the liver (of a shark), the spleen; in **arekabu** (for **atekabu**) it signifies the liver or principal viscus of the **kabu** (or **kobu**, q.v.), inside, and in **uateam**, q.v., the proper meaning seems to be the middle, the middle and more important part. [My. *ati*, the liver, then the mind, heart or inside, Mg. *ati*, the liver, the inside, Sa. *ate*, Ternati *hut*, the liver.] A. **kabd'**, **kabid'**, H. **kabed**, E. **kabdĕ**, the liver, Amh. **hodĕ**, the belly. A. **kabid'**, also denotes the belly with its parts, the middle and more important part (of a thing), the middle (of a thing). E. **kabdĕ**, viscus (nom. gen.), stomach, belly, inside, and particularly the liver, as the heaviest of the viscera. (See Ludolf's E. Lex.) H. **kabad**, E. **kabda**, to be heavy (primary meaning), &c. The verb is in Ef. dd. **kauota** (**kawota**), **kōt**, and **ēt**.

NOTE 1.—**Ārĕkabu**, q.v., c. art. **nārekabu**, dd. **tālekabu**, **nānekabu**, **tānekabu**, and **nānekama**, the liver, is composed of **āre** (for **ate**), the liver or principal viscus, and **kabu** (for which see **kobu**, the belly, the inside), and lit. denotes the viscus (or liver) of the inside; with **are** (for **ate**) corresponds Ml. U. **ere**, and New Guinea, Maclay Küste **arre**, the liver.

NOTE 2.—With Ludolf's statement (above), compare that in the Ha. Dict., where **ake** (for **ate**) is defined as 'the liver', and also 'a general name for several internal organs, qualified by different terms': thus **akeloa**, spleen (**loa**, long), and also **akeniau**; **akepaa**, the liver, as well as the simple **ake**: **akemama**, the lungs (see above, s.v. **amo**). In Sa. **atepili**, the spleen, **atevae**, the calf of the leg, Tah. **aterima**, the thick part of the arm. In Ef. **uateam'** (d. **uateau**), the kidneys (see above, s.v. **amo**), **ua-nate-natuo**, or **ua-nate-tuo**, the calf of the leg, in one dialect is denoted by **uateau natore**, lit. kidneys of the shin (i.e. the leg from the knee to the foot, see tore), and **uateau laso** denotes kidneys of the scrotum. **Ua-nate** has exactly the same meaning as **uate** (i.e. **ua-ate**), the only difference being that in the former ate c. art. is **nate**; **ua**, fruit, is used because the parts spoken of are round or fruit-shaped. In Ef. dd. the calf of the leg is **uateau natore, ua-nate tuo** (or **natuo**), and **nabela natore**, of which the last lit. denotes the belly of the leg (below the knee).

Atelaki na, or d. **telaki ana,** s., the owner of it, owner: from **a,** art., or **a,** prosthetic, and **telaki,** q.v.

Atena na (d. **atia na**), s., maternal grandmother; voc. **tata.** A. **gadat,** id.

(**Ati na**), s., **nati na,** child, d. **nani na,** q.v. [Ma., Tah., *ati*, offspring.] See s.v. **ani na.**

Atia na, s., paternal grandfather or grandmother: voc. **tia.** See **atena na, tata, tematete ta, tia, tematia ta,** and s.v. **atena.**

Ati(a), d. **uati(a),** v. t., d. for **ari a,** q.v.

Atoara, see **natoara.**

(**Atu na**), s., **natu na,** d. **nati na,** his, her child, offspring. See **ani na.**

Ātŭ, c. suf. **atu-ġi** (d. **uātŭ**), beat, smite, break off or divide off (as a piece of a plantation); **atu** (**namauri**), utter (an incantation), **at' usi,** utter rehearsing (see **us i**), **àtŭ saki,** plop up (of a turtle, also of the sound of the breath in the throat of a man recovering from a faint or dying); and **atu taku,** turn the back (to anyone on being addressed, as if not aware of it), **atu taluko,** turn oneself (from someone); **atu tuai,** break in pieces (a plantation) giving him (a portion); **fiàtu,** v. r., to be fighting, to be smiting each other: **nalaġi atu,** the wind beating, a hurricane; **atu nabau,** kill (by smiting the head); **atu ualubota,** rout the enemy (smite, break the enemy). With the ending and prep. **ki,** the word, **atu-maki,** means jerk, snap, as **atu-maki,** jerk (as the branch of a tree), **balusa atu-maki,** to paddle jerking (with a jerking motion of the paddle), **atu-maki nalō ra,** jerk their voices, or snap their voices. A. **hatā,** beat, smite, **hatiā,** be bent, stoop (a man), Nm. **heti,** declaim: cf. **hatta,** to break, to beat off (as leaves from trees), to utter (words).

Atuta (see **ta atuta ki**), s., set time, or place, as **i ta atuta ki nia,** he declares a set time to (one), i.e. to meet him on a certain day, or at a certain time (to do something), **ru tu natūta,** they kept the set time, **i risuġi natuta,** he changed the set time. See **ta atuta.**

Atu-maki, v. See **atu**.

Atu saki, at' saki, v. See **atu** and **saki**.

Atu taku, at' taku, v. See **atu** and **taku**.

Atu taluko, at' taluko, v. See **atu** and **taluko**.

Atu, see **banotu**.

Atua, s., God. Introduced word. In Meli. c. art. the word **tĕtua** (East Mai **rĕtua**, To. **hotua**, he **otua**, Sa. **le atua**), denotes among the heathen the same as **natamate**, that is, any spiritual being regarded as having supernatural qualities or powers, as a demon, good or bad, a ghost, a god: it is a general name. A human being on dying immediately becomes a **tĕtua** or **natamate**—that is, not only a spirit, but among the heathen, an object of superstitious regard. In Sa. **aitu, a spirit**, a god, seems to belong to the same stem, whence, with a. ending **a, aitua**, haunted. The word in Ha. (**akua**), To. (**otua**), Ma. and Sa. (**atua**), now denotes God in the Christian sense, and it has been introduced with this meaning into Aneityum, Tanna, Efate, Epi, &c. Der. uncertain; but cf. the A. word under Ef. **tuai, matua**, old. [Mg. *matua*, old, *matuatua*, ghost, spirit, *atua*, a song sung in honour of the sovereign, the idols.] If this is the origin of the word it accords with the ancestor worship of the islanders.

Atum-kol, s., echo, lit. offspring of the call or shout, and

Atuma, in pr. nn. **atumaneru**, offspring of war, &c. See **kola**, and for **atuma**, offspring, see **futum**.

Atuta. See p. 115.

Au, verb. pron. 1 pl. excl., we they, d. **pu**, d. **mu**, d. **u**: separate pron. **kinami**, we they; **au** is **a-u, a** for **na** in **na-mi, kinami**, and **u**, d. **u**, d. **pu**, or **mu** = **mi** in **nami**.

Äu, ad., yes, d. **äo**. **A**, dem. prefix, and **u**, or **o**, for which see **o**. H. **hahu'**, that (is it).

Au, v. i., to heal, get well, d. for **abu**, id., q.v.

Äu, s., a kind of lizard, d. for **käu**, id.

Au, v. i., to bark. See **ao**.

Āüa (**āwa**), s., veins, muscles, or **nāüa**: **i bi aua**, or **naua** (**a-**, or **na-**, art.), he is strenuous (veins, or muscles standing out). [Fi. and Sa. *ua*, Bu. *urök*, My. *urat*, Java, *wad* (through *uhat*, *uat*), Mg. *uzaṭa*, *huzaṭa*.] A. **'irḳ,'** &c., veins, &c., v. **'araḳa**.

Aüà (**awà**), ad., no, it is not: d. **eüo**, q.v.

Auaua, s. (**awawa**, a reduplicate), d. syn. **bau**, q.v., maternal uncle. [My. *uwa*, *wa*, *uwak*, an uncle or aunt.] A. **'amm'**, an uncle.

Aue, interj., surprise, commiseration. [Sa. *aue*, alas!

oh! of wonder.] A. awwi (&c.), alas! ah! oh!

Aui, interj., surprise, commiseration; **a**, dem., and **ui**, q.v.

Auis, interj., surprise, commiseration; **a**, dem., and **uis**, q.v.

Aul i, v. t., dd. **ul i, ol i, uil i.** See **ul i.**

Aum, s., c. art. **naum**, d. for **aime**, q.v.

Aure, s., a singer, bard, **a**, art., and **ure**, or **ore** (see **ore**). [Fut. *goro*, Ma. *whakaoriori*, Ha. *olo*, My. *uraura*, Mg. *hira*, to sing, &c.] E. **ḥalaya**, to sing.

Aüta, s., or ad., **auta**, ashore, on land, d. **euta**, q.v., **a**, prep., and **uta**, q.v.

Ba-, or **fa-**, caus. prefix, originally **ma.** [Mg. *ma-*, *fa-*, *mpa-*.] S. **ma-** (Maphel conj.), Mod. S. **ma-**, caus. prefix (St., pp. 110, 111): the Mafel or Maphel is simply the verbal noun of the ancient Aphel (H. Hiphil, A. 4). See Ch. IV.

Ḅa (**bwa**), and **ua** (**wa**), v. i., to rain = d. **boua** (**bowa**). [Epi *mboba*, *mbobo*, Ta. *ufu*, id.] A. **baʿa**, to rain continuously, **baʿaʿa**, rain, rain water.

Bà, or **fa** (**va**), v., to come, enter (a ship, &c.), tread (go upon), with suffix, **ba-si**, to tread, tread upon (go upon or in). (Fi. **va-t'a**, to tread upon.) This word in Ef. is found as **bai, bē**, to come, to possess, to be like, to abide, to be (before nouns), also in latter sense, d., **bi**, and d. **mi**; d. **mai**, to come, d **bē**, to come. [The form *mai* is common in Polynesian and Fi., and is the well-known 'directive', see Ch. III, 'Triliterals doubly weak.' Mg. *avi*, to come; Tah. *vai*, to abide, to be; Ma. *whai*, to possess.] H. **bo, ba**, E. **bawi**, come, enter, be like, A. **baa, faa**, be like, abide, possess, and **bawa, bawaa**, be like, abide.

Bā, v., to come from (from a place), as, **Ku bā se?** you come from where? **i bā nalia uan**, he comes from that place, dd. **bai, be, bāki** (where the prep. **ki** = from). [Mg. *avi aïza*? = *ba se*? = come from where? come whence? *avi*, to come.] See preceding word.

Bai, v., d., **bā**, q.v., to come from, as, **bai se?** come from where? See under **banotu.**

Bai, v., to be, d. **bi**, q.v.

Bai a, v. t., to gather together in order to carry home, as firewood, or fruit, &c., to put in, insert, **ba**, to enter, and prep. **i**, make enter a basket, **bai a nāla.**

Bà ki, v., c. prep., to go to (a place): **ba**, to go, and the prep. **ki**, to: **ba** is contracted for **ban, bano**, to go, q.v.

Ba, d. **mba**, final conj., that: used in the conjugation of the future and imperative and infinitive of verbs;

Ba, that thou, sign of 2 pers. sing. imperative; includes verbal pron. 2 pers. sing., a. [Motu *ba,* used in the same way in fut., inf., and imp., Fi. *me,* in imp. and inf., Ma. *me,* forming a kind of imperative future, Mg. *mba,* that, Ml. P. *ba, b',* that, used in conjugation of imp., inf., and future.] A. fa, that (final conj.), &c.

Bā, v., d. for **mā.** See **anī,** v.

Bāb, s., d. voc., father = **āb, bābu, abab,** id.

Ḅaḅa na, s., hollows, or channels; and

Ḅaḅa, s., c. art. **naḅaḅa,** a hollow, channel, or bed of a stream, dry except after heavy rains: it is an opening through the jungle;

Ḅaḅa, s., c. art. **naḅaḅa,** a board: [Sa., Tah. *papa,* My. *papan,* id.;] A. **baba-t',** facies, board, table, slab, **bib',** channel, **bab',** door, gate, hall, **baba,** to dig a hole, &c., H. **babah,** a gate.

Ḅaḅu na (d. **bamu na**), s., c. art. **naḅaḅu na,** the cheek. [My. *pipi,* Mg. *fifi,* id.] A. **faḳmu,** and **fa‘‘mu,** id.

Babaṭēġa, v. i., or a., variegated, versicoloured, as cloth: the formative prefix, **ba,** doubled; said to be denominative from **ṭôġa** (**toġa**), q.v., a versicoloured woven basket.

Bābu, s., d., voc., father: dd. **āfa, āb, abāb, bāb'.**

Ḅāfa, s., a small separate house used only by women dwelling apart from men during menstruation, and also at the time of parturition. From **afa,** to bear, carry, c. pref. **ḅa** (for **ma**). See **bäofa** (d.), which is from **ofa,** d. for **afa,** bear, carry: **bäofa,** though etymologically the same as **ḅafa,** has a different meaning, no such custom as is implied by the **ḅafa** obtaining among the speakers who say '**baofa.**' It denotes the act of menstruating, not the house for those menstruating.

NOTE.—In Ha. the house for menstruating women was called **hale pea.**

Bafanau, same as **fanau,** q.v.

Bafano, or **fafano,** v., to wash the hands. See **bano-li.** [Sa. *fafano,* wash the hands and mouth. Fi. *vuluvulu,* wash the hands. See *bulu-ni, bano-li, balo-ni,* &c., infra.]

Bafatu, or **fafatu,** v. t., to trust in, confide in, rely upon. See **fatu.**

Baġa, v. c. See **baġan i,** to feed, charge, fill;

Baġan i, v. c., to feed, lit. make to eat, **baġan ià sa,** lit. make him eat it; caus. prefix **ba,** and **kan,** to eat. With the n elided **baġa,** as **baġa nata,** feed anyone, **baġa sisi,** load a gun; **baġa,** absolute, as i **baġa** (of a pig or a fish), to wander about in search of food; **faġa** (of fire), **nakabu faġa**, a burning or devouring fire, **i faġa**, it burns, devours, or eats (of fire, and of an ulcer); **nafaġa**, a bribe, **nafaġafaġa**, a bait. [Fi. *vakani-a*, Sa. *fafaġa*, feed, cause to eat, Mg. *mamahana*, to feed, also load (a gun), caus. pref. *ma*, and *fahana*.] See **kan-i.**

Baġau-nabau, pr. n., c. art. **nabaġau-nabau:** the feeder of the oven with the slain; **baġa, ua, nabau.**

Baġa, s. See **baġo,** a hill, d. **maġo,** d. **beġa.**

Baġa, s., d. for **maġa,** the banyan tree.

Baġabaġa, v. i. See **baġobaġo.**

Baġarai, v. c., to dry, lit. make dry: from **ġara, kara,** dry. [My. *muġariġ kan*, id.] See **ġara, kara.**

Baġaranu a i, den. v. c.; from **ran,** c. art. **niran,** fresh water; to wash with fresh water after bathing in the sea: d. **bakanaru-mi,** id. (**naru,** transposed for **ranu**). [Sa. *faalanu*, to wash off salt water, ps. *faalanumia*; with *'i*, *faalanuma-'i*.] See **ran,** s.

Baġi, v., to mount, climb, ascend (a hill, ladder, tree, ship, &c.); may also have the prep. **ki** before the object, as **baġi nakasu,** or **baġi ki nakasu,** climb the tree, **baġi,** to go up, ascend, **baġi ki,** go up on. [Mg. *akaṭa*, *miakaṭa*, id., My. *miġ'ah*, id., Ma. *piki*, to climb, *pikitia*.] A. **'aka',** (4), to ascend.

Baġobaġo, v. i., or a., to be crooked. [Sa. *pi'o*, *pi'opi'o*, id., Ma. *piko*, bent, Mg. *vukuka*, crooked, My. *beġ'ok*, Ja. *beġ'oġ*, crooked.] H. **hafak,** S. **hpak,** A. **'apaka,** to turn, &c., H. **hapakpak,** crooked, twisted. Hence

Baġobaġoa, a., crooked, twisted: **-a,** a. ending; and

Baġobaġōra, a., id.: a. ending **-ra.**

Ḅaġo, v., to be behind, **i ḅaġo asa,** he is behind it, as **i ḅaġo nakoro,** he is behind the fence (of a man behind a fence put up about his house to shut out the public view), **i ḅaġo nafanua,** it is behind the land (of a ship taking shelter under the lee side of an island in a hurricane). The word **ḅaġo na,** s., denotes the heel; the lower part of the back (syn. **bisi na**); **ḅaġo nafanua,** west end of an island, is the opp. of **meta nafanua,** east end of an island (fore-end and heel-end); **ḅaġo na kelu,** or **ḅaġa na kelu,** is the after part of an army that (**kelu**) goes in a circuitous course to surprise the enemy—and in all these senses the word in one dialect is pronounced **m̈aġo na.** The hills behind the villages, or not far back from the shore, on which there is no jungle, are called **beġa, baġa,** d. **m̈aġo.** This word is much used in names of places, points or heels of the land: thus **Ḅaġona** is the name of west end of Deception Island, Havannah Harbour, and **Ḅaġo**, of the long point of land on the south of Fila harbour; **Selimbaġa**, a place on Tongoa, &c. The end of anything, as the land, a stick, &c., is called **meta-ḅaġo na**, lit. the eye or point of its end. [TaSa. *piġo na*, end or extremity.] H. **'aḳab**, A. **'aḳaba**, to be behind, to come from behind: cf. A. **ma'ḳob**: H. **'aḳeb**, the heel, A. **'aḳib'**, id., and the end of a thing: H. **'aḳeb**, also denotes the extreme rear of an army, and **'aḳob**, a hill, acclivity (A., E., id.).

Ḅaġo na, s., d. **ṁaġo na**, heel of foot; back part of body; hinder end (of an island) in opp. to **meta na**, fore end (i. e. east); hinder part of an army; an end (of anything); end of a house (the Efatese house has two ends), hence, inside of a house at the far ends, and then generally in one d. inside (of a house); end, i. e. bottom, of a hole or deep pit. See preceding word and **maġo**.

Baġote-fi, v. c., to buy it, purchase it, lit. to break, separate (from its former owner) a thing, d. **bakotufi**. See **koto**.

Baġokot, or **baġot**, v. reduplicate of foregoing.

Bā ġote-fi, v., to break a thing (as a stick) by treading (see **bà**) on it. See **koto**.

Bai, v., d. **bā**, to come from (a place): **ba** v., and prep. **i.**, d. **bā ki**, id., has prep. **ki**.

Bai, or **bei**, v. dd. **bi**, **mi**, to be, as, **i bai fatu**, it is a stone. See **bi**; and **bà**.

Baibai, or **baibaia**, v. i., or a., to be large, wide; said to be d. for **bebea**, q.v.

Bai na, s., d. for **bau na**, the head. See **ḅau na**.

Bai, s., d., c. art. **nabai na**, feathers or covering of a bird: d. **mau na**. [Ml. dd. *bai*, *moe*, id.] Same word as preceding: see **bau**.

Bai! baibai! interj., surprise and pleasure. [Mg. *baba*, id.] A. **baḥ'i baḥ'i**, id.

Baina, v., to go there (away from speaker): d. for **binēn'**: d. syn. **banotu**, q.v. **Baina**, is **ba ina**.

Baka, d. sometimes for **baki**, v., **ba**, to go, and prep. **ki** (rarely **ka**), to, as **i baki nalia uane**, he goes to that place.

Baka, or **faka**, caus. prefix. [Fi. *vaka*, Sa. *faa*, Ma. *whaka*, Mg. *aha*, *maha*, *faha*, *mpaha*.] vide Ch. IV.

Baka roa, v. i., to jerk over to the other side (a canoe sail): **boka-ti**, to strike, and **roa**, to turn round.

Ḅāka, s. a fence, a fence of stone or wood made for protection or fortification in war. [Ha. *pa*, a fence, Ma. *pa*, a stockade, fortified place, *pā*, to block up, obstruct.] H. ma'ākeh, a parapet (surrounding a flat roof) to hinder one from falling off, from 'aḳah, A. 'aḳa', to hold back (and 'āḳa), hinder, impede.

Baka-si, d. transposed for **kaba-si, koba-si**, to follow.

Bakabase, v. c., d. syn. c. **suer i**, to scold, vituperate: from **base**, id.

Bakabātĕ, or **bakafātĕ**, v. c., make the fourth time: from **bātĕ**, 4. [Mg. *fahefaṭa*, the fourth.]

Bakabulu-ti, v. c., nearly the same as the simple verb **bulu-ti**, q.v.

Bakabunuti, bakamānu, &c. See **bakaralima**.

Bakafakal i, v., to console, comfort: reduplicate from **bakal i**, id., q.v.

Bakafla, d. **bakafisa**, v., make how many times? make how often? See **bisa**.

Bakafiti, v., fold the arms across, hands on sides (**fiti na**): **baka** for **kafa, kafi-ti**, see **fakarog̃o**; lit., cover the sides.

I. **Bakal i**, v. c., to soothe, comfort, take tender care of (as of a child, or one in sorrow): see **kal**. A. 'agila, to soothe, comfort; E. 'egal, a child, Ef. **kal, fakal**, and d. **kekel**, id., usually vocative, and much used in proper names of children, as **kal nag̃usu**, child of the point (promontory), **kal**, or **fakal tamate**, child of peace, &c.

II. **Bakal i**, v. c., to sharpen (as a knife, axe, &c.) H. ḳalal, Pilpel, to sharpen; to move to and fro, A., E., id. See **makal**, sharpened, sharp, **kala**, little, &c. H. ḳalal, to be light, to be swift, fleet, to be diminished, little, so A. ḳalla, to be despised, H. ḳalon, shame, pudenda, Ef. **makal**. See Ch. III.

Bakalailai, v. c., nearly same as simple verb **lailai**, q.v., to be delighted.

Bakalarua, v. c., make the seventh time, or seven times. See **larua, kalarua**. [Mg. *fahafitu*, the seventh.]

Bakalatesa, v. c., make the sixth time, or six times. See **latesa, kalatesa**. [Epi *vaari*.]

Bakalatolu, v. c., make the eighth time. [Epi *vaarolu*.] See **latolu**.

Bakalifiti, v. c., make the ninth time. [Epi *vakoveri*.] See **lifiti**.

Bakàleba, v. c., make (himself) great, be proud: **leba, laba**.

Bakalima, v. c., make the fifth time, or five times. [Mg. *fahadimi*, the fifth.] See **lima**.

Bakamataku ki, v. c., to make afraid, to threaten, frighten: from **mataku**, to be afraid. [Mg. *mahatahuṭa*, My. *manakuti, manakut kan*, Sa. *faamata'u*.]

Bakamaturu ki, v. c., make to sleep, put to sleep: from **maturu**, to be asleep, to sleep. [My. *manidor kan*.]

Bakamauri, v. c., to make alive, save: from **mauri,** to be alive, live. [Sa. *faaola,* My. *maġidupi,* Mg. *mameluna.*]

Bakametà sa, v. c., to direct the eyes to, look at: **a bakametà gu is, i bakameta nà sa,** &c., seems to mean lit. I direct my eyes, make my eyes upon it, &c.: **meta,** or **mita,** q.v., v., and s. **Bakamita,** id.

Bakamirara. See **mirara.**

Bakanaru-mi, v. c., **naru,** transposed for **ranu**: d. for **baġaranu a i.**

Bakarairai, v. c. Nearly the same as the simple v. **rairai,** q.v.

Bakarau sa, v. c., divide it (among a number of persons), distribute it: from **rau,** q.v.

Bākàroġo, v. c., make (himself) hear or obey, be humble, quiet, meek; from **roġo,** q.v.

Bakāru. See **bukaru.**

Bakarua, v. c., make the second time, or two times. See **rua, karua.** [Mg. *faharua,* the second.]

Bakaralima, or **bakarualima,** v. c., make the tenth time, or ten times. [Epi *vaduñlimo.*] See **rualima,** or **ralima, karalima.**

NOTE. — The caus. prefix **baka** may be attached to the word or words denoting any number, as **bakabunuti** (**bunuti,** 100), **bakamānu** (**mānu,** 1000), make the hundredth, thousandth time, or one hundred, one thousand times, **bakaralima lima** (**ralima lima,** 50), **bakamanu ralima** (**manu ralima,** 10,000), make the fiftieth, ten thousandth time, or fifty or ten thousand times, &c.

Ḅakas, or **ḅokas,** s., c. art. **naḅakas,** flesh; then, a pig (not a sow or a boar) specially reared and esteemed for its flesh. [Epi *bukahi,* a pig (not boar or sow), Fut. *pakasi,* a pig (gen. name), Ero. *mpokas,* a pig (gen. name), An. *pigat′,* a pig (gen. name).] A. **manḥus′,** having much flesh, fleshy, from **naḥaṣ′a,** to denude a bone of flesh, to take the flesh from off a bone.

Bakasa, v. c., **bakasa ki,** or **bakasà i,** to paint (as the face), hence **nafakasa,** s., a festival (adornment); to clean, make clean (as a place), to clear, make clear. [Fi. *ai qisa,* paint for the face.] A. **nakas′a,** to paint, to colour; to clear, make clear (as a place): **bakasa,** dd. (trspd.) **bisaki, biski.**

Bakasau, v. c., dd. **bisakau i, bisaui, bisaku-ti,** to make or build up a fire, lit., make to join on to, i. e., one stick to another, to make a bigger fire. (By joining together the smouldering ends of two fire sticks and then joining on to them the ends of other sticks a fire is built up.) The initial **bĭ,** or **ba,** in this word is the causative prefix: the simple verb is **sĭku-ti,** q.v.

Bakaser i, v. c., to loosen or remove a **tabu** (as from a place), make common or non-tabu. See **ser i.**

Bakasere, v. c., to treat kindly carefully providing for, to entertain hospitably. See **sere,** ps. **masere.**

Bakasikai (d. **fakasikitika**), v. c., make the first time, or one time. [Mg. *faharaika*, the first.] See **sikai, kasikai.**

Bakasiki-ti, v. c., to tie or bind fast the edge of a mat where the plaiting ceases: see **siki-ti.**

Bakasoro-fi, v. c., make to burn: from **soro,** v. i., to burn, q.v.

Bakatabtabu ki, v. c., make **tabu,** or declare **tabu.** See **tabu.** [To. *fakatabu*, to interdict.]

Bakatar i, v. c. Nearly the same as the simple verb **tar i,** q.v.

Bakatau, v. c. Nearly the same as the simple v. **tau,** q.v.

Bakateba, v. c., caus. form, to watch, to look out or watch for, as **bakateba nabai saki ni aliati,** watch or look out for the rising flush of dawn. [Sa. *tepa*, *tetepa*, to look towards.] H. **ṣapah,** to look out, view, watch, look out for.

Bakatilas i, v. c., to suffice: from **tilas i,** q.v., and see also the simple v. **las i.**

Bakatoġo i, v. c., d. for

Bakatoko i, v. c., to make a show or feint of striking or pushing. See the simple v. **toġo-fi.**

Bakatolu, v. c., make the third time, or three times. [Mg. *fahatelu*, the third.]

Bakatuai, v. c., to prolong, put off, delay. [Sa. *fa'atuai*, id.] See **tuai.**

Bakau, or **bakauĕ,** v. c., to say or shout **auĕ! auĕ!** or **au! au!** to make a howling or barking noise in a well-known Efatese way expressive of joy, triumph, or derision: the howl or cooee repeated several times, ending in the loud jerking or barking utterance of **au! au! au!** H. **'avah,** to howl, cry out, A. **'aui,** to howl, as a dog, wolf, or jackal.

Bakauli, v. c., to make like, imitate, to be like to, resemble: the simple v. is **auli** (dd. **uli, oli**), or **uli,** q.v.

Bakauti, v. c., d. **buti,** q.v., make an end, finish. [Fi. *vakaoti*, To. *vakaochi*, Sa. *faaoti*, Ma. *whakaoti*.] H. **ḳaṣeh,** an end, **ḳaṣah,** A. **kaṣ'a',** 2, to finish: for **ḳ** to **'**, v. Ch. II.

Bake, d. **baku,** v., to search, to search for (as to search for insects in the head, or for fleas and such like in mats or cloth). S. **bḳa',** or **bḳo',** to search.

Baki, v., to go to (a place), **ba,** to go, and **ki,** prep. 'to': d. **be'** (nearly **beh**), id.

Baki, prep., to, unto. See Ch. V, Prepositions.

Bāki, v., d., to go or come from (a place), dd. **bā, bai: bā,** to come, and prep. **ki** (to), from. For **bā** see **bai, bā, bà.**

Bakē, d. for **baki se,** go where? **bakē** is for **baki ē,** go to where? **se,** d. **ē,** where? See Ch. II.

Bakilina, v., to go or come into the light, i. e., into view, to appear: **baki,** go or come to, and **lina,** light. See **lina,** d. **ali.**

Bakitakita, d. for **makitakita,** q.v.

Bako, s., shark, d. **ḇaké.** [Malo *bagio,* Epi *bekeu.*] Der. uncertain.

Bākor, v., d., to come in front of, to appear: **bā,** to come, and **koro,** q.v.

Bakotu-fi, v. t., d. for **baġote-fi,** q.v.

Baku, v., d. for **bake,** q.v.

Baku, v. t., to pluck out, **baku sa,** pluck it out, ps. **mafaku,** plucked out, **tafakaka,** d. **tafaġka,** (i.e., **tafak'ka**), v. i., to burst, explode. [Sa. *fa'i,* pluck, extract, *mafa'ifa'i,* extracted, Ma. *whakiwhaki,* and *kowhaki,* to pluck, My. *kopak,* to burst, break out, Mg. *vaki,* burst out, *mitifaka,* to burst, *mitefuka,* to sound (as the explosion of a gun).] A. **faḳa',** to burst, to pluck out, **ta-faḳḳa',** 5, to be burst.

I. **Ḇala,** v. i., to be smooth. [Sa. *molemole, lamolemole,* id., Tah. *moremore,* smooth, without branches, as a tree; even, without protuberances; also, hairless, *more,* v. i., to drop or fall, as *pia* leaves when ripe, Ma. *moremore,* v. t., to make bald or bare; strip of branches, &c.] A. **māra,** n. a. **maur',** to fall off (as wool or hair from the body, feathers from an arrow); to pluck out or off (as hair, wool).

Ḇāla, i bi ḇāla, it is smooth, level. See preceding word.

Ḇala-ġara, v. i., d., to be poor, lit. smooth (or bare) dry, bare and dry: **ġara,** or **kara,** dry, q.v.

II. **Ḇala,** v. i., often pronounced **ḇela,** d. **ḇola,** to incline to; be close to: **i ḇala nakasu,** inclines and keeps close to a tree (hiding), **ḇalà sa,** inclines and keeps close to it, **ḇala-afi nafanua,** hugs the land (*a ship*), (see **af i**); **ḇala** is close to (as a man to a tree, or one board to another), hence to be stuck and inclining from side to side to get through (as a man in the vines of the jungle, or in any confined place, as a narrow door; a bone in the throat, or the branches of a fallen tree in those of another); **ḇala-taġoto,** or **ḇala-ġoto,** incline across, hence cross, a., as **nakasu ḇalataġoto** (see **ġoto**), a cross beam, or cross stick, hence **fāla,** a ship's yards (because they are fixed across or on the mast), and sticks fastened across or on a tree for a ladder to climb it are called fāla, or **balafala**, and **ḅala-ġalu** (see **ġalu**), is the upper cross board at the end of a canoe; **fāla**, also denotes a litter, so called because the sticks forming it are fastened across or upon each other. [Sa. *pilia*, to be entangled (as one tree falling against another, &c.), *pilipili*, be near, *pipili*, a cripple, Ma. *piri*, to stick, come close, keep close, skulk, hide oneself, *pipiri*, come to close quarters, join battle, Ha. *pili*, to cleave to (as to a friend).] A. **māla**, n. a. **mayl'**, to incline, incline to, bend or lean to (something); to be close or near to; to have a part of the body (vitio naturae) inclined or bent to one side (used also of a building leaning to one side); 3, make a hostile incursion. Nm. **miel**, v. i., slant, deviate, incline (towards), **mail** (gerund), slope, inclination, propensity.

III. **Ḅala**, s., the belly, usually pronounced **ḅele**, q. v.; **ḅalau**, for **ḅala am'** (like **uateau** for d. **uateam'**), the inside of a man, or of anything (hollow or womb of the **am'**, abdomen), **ḅaloa** (ending a), a hollow, a valley, **ḅalua**, a hollow or hole in a rock, **falea**, a cave, **ḅalakutu na**, the hollow at the back of the head (lit. the hollow of his **kutu**, q.v.), **ḅaloleba**, the stomach (lit. the big hollow), **ḅile na**, or **ḅela na**, his mother (lit. his womb, the womb that bore him), **nafelak**, a family, tribe, **bela-ki**, to gird (oneself), to tie or fasten under one's girdle or belly, to take with one, to conceive (*a woman*), **ḅela**, source, **ḅelu**, **uelu**, to hide, be hidden, to be doubled up, **taḅelu**, doubled up, bent. [Ma. *wharua*, a., concave, s., valley, *whawharua*, s., mother, *whare*, a house, people of a house, *wharetaġata*, connection by marriage, Tah. *fare*, a house, *farefare*, a., hollow, as the stomach for want of food.] H. **beṭen**, the belly, the inside, the womb, mother, **baṭan**, properly to be empty, hollow, vain, i.q. **baṭal** (see **ḅalo** infra), A. **baṭn'**, belly, inside or middle of anything, pl. connections by marriage, a tribe (small), **baṭana**, to have the belly distended with food, to be intimate and familiar, to be hid, 4, to fasten the girth under the belly (of a beast of burden), to cover, hide, 5, to put a thing under one's belly, S. **bṭan**, to conceive, have in the womb, A. **baṭuna**, to have a great belly.

Ḅalāf i, v. t., incline to keeping near to: **ḅala** II., and **āf** i.

Ḅalaġote-fi, v. t., incline (or

bend) across it: **ḅala** II., and **ġoto**, or **koto**.

Ḅalafis i, v. t., hug (as a ship hugging the coast): **ḅala** II., and **afis i**.

Balaġa-ti, v. c., to lift up (as the cover from anything); and

Balaġa-saki, v. c., lift up, stripping off (as the husk of reeds): Hence

Ḅalaġa na, s., husk, scale, or similar thing that is or may be *lifted up from* what it covers or encloses: syn. **laġalaġa na**. See **laġa-ti**, **laġa**.

Balafalà sa, v., to be entangled (as one tree falling against another). [Sa. *pilia*, id.] The radical idea is seen in **ḅala** to be entangled or stuck in the throat (*a bone*); the bone *inclines to one side* and so sticks. See **ḅala** II.

Balafala, s. See **fala**, s.

Ḅalas, c. art. **naḅalas**, i. e., **naḅa** or **nabaḅa las**, big hollow; **nabua naḅalas**, the road of the big hollow or gorge behind Utaon.

Ḅalau na, s., the belly, inside; inside, middle of anything: **ḅala** III., and **au** for **amo**: **ḅalau** is, lit., the hollow or middle or inside of the belly.

Ḅalaus i, v. t., to go through or along a thing lengthwise, not to go across it (**ḅalaġotefi**): **ḅala** II., and **us i**, to follow, go through or along (as a road, &c.).

Ḅalea, s., d. for **ḅāloa**, valley: **ḅala** III., and a. ending **a**.

Ḅaleḅalea, and **ḅeleḅelea**, full of hollows, bellied, large: **ḅala** III., and a. ending **a**. [Ha. *pele*, to have a large belly; to be large.]

Bale-si, v. t., d., to husk, strip off (as the envelope of sugar cane); and

Bala-saki, v. t., id. A. **wafala**, to decorticate.

Balĭ, v. i., to fast;

Balĭ ki, v. t., to fast from (a thing);

Balĭfalĭ, v. i., to fast (*many people*). [Mg. *fadi*, id.] A. **'abala**, or **'abila**, to abstain; to be devoted to the worship of God, 2, to mourn (the dead).

Balĭkau i, v. t., to go or step over: **ba**, to go, and **lĭkau**, or **lakau**, q.v.

Ḅalo, v. i., a., ad., to be empty, vain, null and void, to no purpose or effect: **i ḅalo**, it is empty, **nasuma ḅalo**, an empty house, **lo** or **te ḅalo**, an empty, i. e., a worthless thing, a trifle, nothing, **i toko ḅalo**, he remains in vain, to no purpose, for nothing, idle; d. **mole**; hence **sera te ḅalo**, or **sera te mole**, to deem worthless, vain, to despise. [Fi. *wale*, uselessly, for nothing, idly, Ha. *wale*, Sa. *vale*.] A. **baṭala**, n. a. **buṭl'**, or **boṭl'**, to be vain, nothing, to no end or purpose, in vain, for nothing, idle, H. **baṭal**, to be empty, vacant, idle (cognate **baṭan**, **ḅala** III.), E. **baṭala**, to be empty, vain.

Bālo, prep. or ad., d., above,

up: see **(b')** prep., Ch. V, and **ulua**, v. [Malo *aulu* (*a*, prep. 'on'), (Fut. *weiluġa*, see *elaġ*, infra, Ha. *maluna*, above, up, *ma*, prep., and *luna*, Ef. *elaġ*).] Amh. **balai** above, and exactly as Ef. **bālo ki** (above to), **balai ka**, as *above* his house, or *above* anything: the prep. **ba**, E. **ba**, on, and **lai**, the upper part, high, A. **'alu**, **'alo**, upper part.

NOTE.—Compound preps. or ads. of this kind consist of a preposition prefixed to another word, which may be an ad., s., or **a.** used substantively (as English *above*, *aboard*, *around*, i. e., on-bove, on-board, on-round): thus Ef. **elaġ**, d. **bālo**, Sa. **iluġa**, Ha. **maluna**, Malo **aulu**, Amharic **balai**, above, on high, on the upper side or part, all consist of the preps. **e**, **i**, or **a**, q.v., or **ba**, **b'**, or **ma**, q.v., and words signifying high, up, or the upper part and side, for which see **ulua**, **elaġ**, **lu**, **laġa**, infra.

Balo-ni, v. t., dd. **balo-si**, or **bĭlo-si**, **bulo-si**, **bulu-ġi**, **bunu-li**, **bulu-ni**, **bano-li**, to wash (anything) to wash (by rubbing): **fafano**, or **bafano**, q.v., to wash the hands. [Sa. *fufulu* to rub, to wash, My. *basuh*, Mg. *uza*, to wash.] A. **maṣa**, n. a. **mauṣ'** to wash; to rub with the hand.

Ḅaloa, s., c. art. **naḅaloa**, a valley, lit. what is hollow or concave, **-a** being the a. ending. [Ma. *wharua*, a., concave, s., valley.] See **ḅala** III.

Ḅaloleba, s., the stomach: **ḅalo**, cavity. See **ḅala** III., and **leba**, **laba**, big.

Balōtu, v. i., d., to go there, or thither (away from the speaker), dd. **banōtu**, **bĭnōtĕ**, **bĭnāṣ**, **nēt**, to set out, go away (from the speaker), hence a common word of farewell to one departing is, **Ku balotu**, you are going away, to which the one departing replies, **Ku mato**, you remain. See **banotu**.

Ḅalua, s., a hole or hollow in a rock: see **ḅala** III.

Balu-saki, v. t., to paddle (a canoe), row (a boat);

Balu-sa, v., to paddle, row, **balusà sa**, paddle or row with it (a paddle or oar). [Epi dd. *mbeluo ka*, *mbahua kin*, v. t., An. *ahelet'*, to paddle, to row, to sail, Am. *fuloh*, to paddle, Fi. *ai vot'e*, an oar, *vot'e*, to paddle, to row, *vot'e-taka*, v. t. (= *balu-saki*), Pa. *palusa*, Ml. d. *masu*, Ml. A. *sua*, Malo *mo sua*, Ta. *asua*, Fut. *sua*, Mg. *vui*, act of rowing, *mivui*, to row, *vuizina*, rowed, *fivui*, an oar, My. *d'ayuġ*, an oar, *d'ayuġ*, *bārd'ayuġ*, to row.]

NOTE.—**Balu-saki** is the same as **vot'e-taka**. The verb 'to row' is **balu**, **vot'e**, **(m)-beluo**, **(m)bahua**, **vui**, **masu**, and without the preformative **b'** (**v'**, **m'**), **asua**, **sua**, **d'ayuġ**, and the l in **balu**, t′ in **vot′e**, h in **mbahua**, s in **sua**, d in **d·ayuġ**, all are variations of the same original consonant which is elided in **vui**. The word for 'oar', **ai vot′e, fivui**, is in Ef. **uose**, d. **uohe** (**wose**, **wohe**), Fut. **foi**. In Fut. the connection between **sua**, to paddle, and **foi**, an oar or paddle, is not so apparent as that between Ml. P. su, to paddle, and **bos**, a paddle, because in **foi**, as in **vui** (= Fi. **vot′e**) the s has been elided; and the connection between Ef. **balu**, to paddle, and **uose**, a paddle, is not so apparent as that between Epi **mbahua**, to paddle, and **voho**, a paddle, Epi d. **bahua**, to paddle, **boho**, a paddle. See **uose**, infra. A. **gaḍafa, ḳaḍafa**, (or **'at′afa**), Amharic **ḳazaf** (or **'azaf**), to propel with oars, to row, Mod. A. **ḳaddaf**, or **'addaf**, part. **mo'addif** (anc. **mo'aḍḍif**, or **mo'azzif**, cf. **vot′e**, **bose**, **uose**, **vui**, **foi**). **Sua** is without the preformative, cf. **'azafa, 'addaf**: **balu** seems to have the same prefix as Sa. **pale**, to row, without which is Sa. **ālo** (ps. **alofia**), and **alo-fa'i**, to paddle, row, and with another verb, Sa. **taualo**, to row, to keep on rowing. As to the prefix in **balu** compare that in **batok**, **batu**, q.v.

Balu na, or **ḅalu na**, s., relative, friend; a brother's brother. or sister's sister. A. **ma'lai**, helper, relative, friend, associate, **walai** to be closely related, to be a friend, helper.

Ḅalu-naki, v. t., to be a **balu** to a brother or to a sister.

Ḅalu ġor i, v. t., help, befriend, take the part of. See **ġor i**.

Ḅaluk, s., c. art. **naḅaluk**, an inlet or small bay, a cul de sac: **ḅa**, and **luku**: v. **ḅaḅa**, and **luku**.

Bamasokò sa, v. t., come upon, find: **ba**, go, and **masoko**, q.v.

Bamau-ri, v. t., d. **bamau sa**, come upon, find it; **ba**, go, and **mau** (**sa**), q.v.

Bamau, v., to reach to, or terminate at, as **i bamau nalia uane**, it reaches to, or stops or terminates at, that place; hence, absolute, **i bamau**, it terminates, stops, or ceases: **ba**, go, and **mau**, q.v.

Bamu na, s., the shoulder blade, shoulder, d. **bau na**. [Tah. *papa*, the shoulder blade.] See **ḅaḅa**, a board.

Bamu na, s., d. for **ḅaḅu na**, q.v.

Bān, v., d. for **mān**; **ānī**, q.v., c. preformative **m**.

Ban, v. i., for **bano**.

Ban, s., and **baniben**, s., armlet, worn between the elbow and the shoulder, and woven so that the outer surface consists of different coloured beads (carved out of shells) arranged in regular figures. [Malo *ban*, Epi *beni*.] See **ḅanu**, **ḅinu**, **ḅanaġa**.

Banĭ, v., to act violently, to be hot, angry, to oppress, as **ru banĭ kiena**, they violently destroy or take away a man's property (from his house or plantation), as in time of war, or as a punishment for crime; **baniban us i**, follow him, acting oppressively, persecute him. See **bani a**, infra.

Banako, v. t., dd. **binako**, **bunak**, to steal, **banakò sa**, and **banak ia**, d. **bunako n'**, steal it. [Ma. *whanako*, *whenako*, Fi. *butako*, Ero. *prok*, Ml. *fenake*, My. *cholog̀*, Ja. *ñolog̀*, Mg. *halaṭa*, c. pref. *mag̀alaṭa*, id.] **A. saraḳa**, n. a. **sarḳ'**, Mahri **heriq**, **ḥeliq**, and **desoq**, to steal.

Ḅanaġa, s., mats, d. **ḅanu**; so called because they are plaited, see **ḅinu**.

Banei, v. i., to come here (to the speaker); same as **banĭmai**, or **banŏ-mai**. [Ml. P. *vine*, id.]

Banei, s., d. **bane**, volcano: see **bani a**, v. t. [Pa. banei, id.]

Bani, or **ban i**, v. t., to burn; to roast, to cook by roasting on the fire; **bēn** or **fēn** cooked or roasted, dd. **beni a**, **banu sa**, **banu-s**. See **banei**; [Sa. *faafana*, to warm up food, *mafanafana*, to be warm, To. *mafana*, heat, warmth, Ma. *mahana*, warm, Ta. *mahana*, warm, the sun, a day, Ja. *panas*, hot, warm, *panaskan*, to heat, Mg. *fana*, *vuafana*, warm (applied to food cooked and warmed the second time), *mafana*, *mafanafana*, warm, *hafanana*, s., heat, *manafana*, and *mahafanafana*, v. t., to heat, *mihafana*, v. i., to be hot, grow hot.] **A. wamiha**, to be hot, n. a., **wamat**, **wamhat**.

Banĭmai, v. i., to come here (to the speaker), opp. to **banotu**, go there (away from the speaker): see **banŏmai**. [Epi *mbinime*.] See **bano**, and **mai**.

Bano-li, d. **bălo-si**, v. t., d. for **balo-ni**, q.v.

Bano, v. i., to go, go off, or away. [Malo *vano*, Epi *mbano*, *mbene*, Ma. *whano*, Meli *fano*, Fut. *fano*, Ta. *uven*, An. *apan*.] **H. panah**, to turn the back, turn to go. See Ch. III. *f*.

Banŏmai, **banămai**, or **banĭmai**, v. i., to come here or hither, dd. **ba bē**, **umai**, **mai**, **bē**: **bano mai**; with **ba**, for **bano**, corrupted to **u**, **umai**; and, without **bano** (or **ba**), **mai**, d., or **bē**, d., as a verb in the sense of the full expression, **bano-mai**, or **babe**. See **ba**, **bano**, supra; and under the following word. [Meli *fano mai*.] For **mai**, see **bà**, **bā**, to come, supra. **Mai** is for **bai**, **bā**, for which also is d. **bē**: d. **bā bē**= **bano mai**.

Banōtu, sometimes pronounced **balotu**, v. i., to go away (in a direction from the speaker), to go there or thither, dd. **bĭnōtĭ, bănāş, bĭnāş, binēn, baina,** and **nōtu, nēt.** [Ma. *whanatu, whano,* and *atu.*] **Bano,** and **atu.** See Ch. III. *f.*

NOTE 1. **Mai,** or **bē,** coming after a verb is an ad. or 'directive' signifying here, hither. [So in Fi., Sa., Ha., Tah., To., Ma.] Coming before a verb in Fi. it signifies to come, as **au sa mai kauta,** I have come to take; so in Ef. **a mai buati,** I have come to take: in two Ef. dd. **a mai, a bē,** I have come. So Mg. **avi** is also a verb signifying 'to come'. Before a noun or the ad. 'where', **mai** signifies 'from' in Fi., Sa., Ha., To. (**mei,** or **me**), Ef. (**bai, bā, be**), and Mg. (**avi**), thus Fi. **maivei?** Sa. **maifea?** Tah. **mai hea?** To. **meife?** or **mefe?** Ef. **bā se? bai se?** or **bē sabe?** Mg. **avi aiza?** from where? whence? The Mg. and Ef. are verbs—**i bā se? avi aiza izi?** he comes from where? In the other cases the **mai,** as in **mai hea?** is called a prep. Ef. **i bā,** or **bai se?** is, literally, he comes (from) where? and in one dialect the prep. **ki**=from, is expressed as, **i bā ki ē?** he comes here (or hither) from where? In Fi. **mai** is also a prep. signifying in, at.

NOTE 2.—**Nōtu,** or **nēt** (or **atu**), in two dialects is a verb (**nōtu, nēt**), with the same meaning as **banōtu,** for which it is used, as dd. **mai** and **bē** for **banomai, bābē.** For **notu,** or **nēt,** see Ch. III. *f.* In Ef. **atu,** is not used separate from **bano.**

Ḅānu, s., d. **ḅanaġa.** q.v.

Ḃanu sa, and **banus.** See **bani a,** to roast.

Bäo, v. i., d. for **mā, mān, bā, bān, bōn.** See **anĭ,** v. i.

Bäofa, s., d., menstruation, **i su baofa meamea** (said of a woman menstruating while still suckling a child): **ḅafa.**

Bara, v. i., to be burned (as food in cooking): see **būria,** d. **bouria,** or **bauria, taḅara.** [Ma. *wera,* burnt, hot, and *tawera, hawera,* s., heat, *pawera,* hot, S. *vevela,* to be hot, ps. *velasia, vela,* done, well cooked, My. *parik, marak,* to kindle, set on fire.] H. **ba'ar** (Ch. **bĕ'ar,** to burn, Pael, to kindle), to burn up, to kindle, to be burned.

Bara, v. i., or a., to be barren, d. **oro.** E. **'abara,** to be barren, **'ebur,** barren.

Barab, v. i., or a., long, high (as a hill). [Malo *barauo,* Fi. *balavu,* Ml. U. *periv,* long, also wide.] Ef. dd. **baraf, baram, barau, birerife** (see **laba, leba**), prop. extended, cf. Ml. U.

Baraf, d. **barab.**

Baraġai, d., transposed for **baġarai.**

Bara-ti, v. t., to beat. [Fi.

waro-t'a, My. *palu*, Ja. *pala*, Mg. *veli.*] A. **wabala,** to beat.

Bara-ti, v. t., to bind together. [My. *barot*, to gird, to bind round.] H. **ḥibar,** to connect, join together. See **faràtĭ,** infra, H. **ḥoberet,** a joining.

Ḅaraḅara, v. i., to cluck (of a hen): cf. **meromero.**

Baram, d. **barab.**

Bara-tuna, s., d. for **bura.**

Barau, d. **barab.**

Bārau, v. i., to reproach, speak loudly reproaching. See **rau.**

Barĕ, v. i., to be moved, move about, **bare ki,** v. t., to move, agitate, **barefare ki,** id. A. **farĕfara,** to move, agitate.

Bare, or **barea,** v. i., or a., d. **uorea,** or **orea,** to be blind (a man), to have a white speck (of an eye whose sight is lost), to be dirty looking, like a sightless eye (of half-raw food). [Ml. A. *bar*, U. *oror*, Epi *mbili.*] H. **'avar,** E. **'awir,** to be blind; and

Baretau, a., black and white spotted (as a pig), also a yam that has been peeled, or a tree that has been barked, **i bi baretau: tau,** white, and **bare,** for which see the following word; and

Barea, or **borea,** d., v. i., or a., black, dirty coloured. [My. *biru*, blue, TaSa. *berika*, black.]

Ḅaro, v. i., or a., to be heedless, **taliġa ḅaro,** deaf, d. **na ḅaro,** one deaf, **ḅaroḅaro,** to be heedless, indifferent, **taḅaro,** to be heedless, refractory, lawless, **bārua,** free from, as **i tumana bisa bārua ki nia,** he declares himself free from it (as a crime), **marua,** to cease, leave off, **lo bārua ki nia,** see the nakedness of someone, literally, or as to his poverty or being devoid of food, &c. See **baror, būra.** H. **para',** to loose, let go, make naked, **pāru'a,** lawless, unbridled, A. **fara''a,** to empty, leave off, be free from (as free from cares or labour, careless, idle), 5, **tafarra''a,** to be idle.

Ḅaro, c. art. **naḅaro,** s., one deaf.

Baro-si, or **baru-si,** v. t. This verb was used thus in the old days: to fell a big tree they burned round the base of it, then **ru baru-si,** or **baru lu, namalifera,** that is, smashed, broke, shaved, chipped, cut, or scraped off the charred wood; then burned the new exposed surface again, smashed or cut off (with the **karau tare**) charred parts again, and so on till the tree fell; to rub, grate, as one branch of a tree on another, or anything on anything. On E. Mai **barusi naniu** = Ef. **koi naniu** (see **koi**). **Tea farofaro,** that which cuts, shaves, rasps off, **barobaroa** (a. ending **-a**), fit for rasping off (as sandpaper or a grindstone). [Fi. *varo-ta*, to file, saw, or rasp, Sa. *valu*, scrape out nuts (=Ef. **koi**), to scrape (as *taro*), ps. *valua*, Ma. *waru*, to scrape, shave, cut (the hair), Ha. *walu*, to scratch, rub, rasp, polish, Tah. *varu*, to shave, to bark a tree, to scrape, My. *paras*, to shave, to pare close to the surface, Mg. *fara*, scrape, scratch, make smooth.] A. **faraka**, Nm. to rub, grate.

Baroaki, d. See **boroaki.**

Barobaroa, a. See under **baro-si.**

Baror, s., one careless, heedless, lawless, wicked, foolish. See **ḅaro.**

Ḅaroḅaro, v. i., or a. See under **ḅaro.**

Bārua, v. i., or a., made naked, devoid of, clear or free from. See **ḅaro.**

Barua, or **uarua,** v. i., or a., fat, big, large. [Mg. *baribari*, *bari*, large, full, well made, Fi. *vora*, to grow fat or stout.] H. **bara'**, to grow fat, **bari'**, fat, A. **wara'**, to be fat.

Barubaruta, a., fat; ending **-ta**: **barua.**

Barubarutena, a., fat; ending **-tena**: **barua.**

Ba-si, v., go upon, tread upon, **basi namatuna,** tread upon something: **ba,** to enter. [Fi. *va-t'a.*] E. ቢአት.

Basa, to speak. See **bisa.**

Ḅasĕ a, v. t., to break off (as a branch from a tree), to break off with a snap or jerk, **ḅasu,** id., **mafàsu,** d. **moàs** (**mowàs**), broken off, **ḅase-raki,** takes a different object, as **ḅase nara nakasu,** break off the branch of a tree, **ḅase-raki na-usu,** break off from a reed (the husk or covering, so as to make it bare), **ḅaseḅase-raki nia,** id., **ḅasu-li a,** to detach, break off, **taḅasuli,** detached, broken off, separated. [Fi. *basu-ka*, or *-raka*, to break, also to open one's eyes or mouth, *basi-a*, nearly syn. c. *basu-ka*. Sa. *fati*, to break off, ps. *fatia.*] A **faṣ'ṣ'a,** to break off, **faṣṣa,** detach, shiver off, H. **paṣah,** q.v., to distend, open (the lips), A. **faṣa',** to separate, detach (as flesh from a bone).

Basē, v. t., c. verb. suf., scold, vituperate, rail at, d. syn. **suer ia**: **bakabase,** id. A. **nabaza,** to reproach, blame, rail at.

Basīu, s., a bone piercer. See **siu.**

Baso i, v. t., to pierce. See **sui.** [Fi. *veso-ka* and *sua-ka.*]

Bastak, v., d. for **bātaka**: **basi, taka.**

Bastufi, v. t., d., to follow, to be like: **basi,** and **tufi.** A. **tabi'a,** to follow.

Ḅasu-li. See **ḅasĕ a.**

Bātaka na, v. t., to be like, equal to, sufficient for (**bastufi,** and **mautaka,** nearly syn.): **bā,** q.v., and **taka,** like, similar to.

Ḅatako na, or **batoko na,** s., the body, d. **mole na.** [Ta.

buti, My. *batağ*, Mg. *vatana.*] A. badano, the body.

Bāte, v., d. for **bātu**, q.v.

Bātĕ, num., four. [Mg. *efaṭa*, My. *ampat*, Sa. *fa.*] A. arba'aṭ', four.

Batĭ na, s., the teeth, a tooth, also a shoot (of banana or taro), a seed. [Fi. *bati.*] See Ch. II, 16. *b.* أَسْنَان, id.

Batĭ-ġāt, and d. **batĭ-ġaut**, s., a thorny plant, with *crooked*, grasping thorns, like teeth: for **ġaut**, see under **ġau**, **taġau.**

Batĭ-rik, s., mosquito: **batĭ**, and **rik**, q.v. Lit. small-tooth.

Bat i, or **bati**, v. t., to do, make, work at; **afiti**, q.v., slave. [My. *buat*, to do.] S. 'bad, to do, to work, work at, make, Ch. 'abad, slave.

Ḅātīk, d. **uārīk**, v. i., or a., few, to be few. See **tik**, or, **rik.**

Batīra, s., precipice, rugged declivity:

Batībatīra, a., rugged and precipitous: syn. **na tiroa.** See **tiro, tiroa.**

Bàtok, v. i., d., to remain: **toko**, q.v.

Bàtu, v. i., d., to remain: **tu**, q.v.

Ḅatu, s., **na ḅatu**, an adult, young man. A. fatiy', adult, fata', young man.

Bātu, v., d. **bate**, to close up the roof by *weaving* thatch on the ridge-pole: **na fātu**, the ridge-pole. [Epi *bofuġo*, v., id. Ma. *whatu*, to weave, Sa. Tah. *futu*, to plait, interweave.] H. 'abat, to interweave, 'abot, wreathen work.

Bàtua na, s., the knee: prob. **bau** (q.v.), the head, and **tua**, leg. [Ml. A. *lua*, leg, *mbulua*, knee, Ml. P. and Malo *bau*, knee.]

Bātua ki, v. t., to depart from (any thing or person): **bā**, to come, and **tua ki**, to place, lay down: lit. go laying down or leaving.

Bau na, s., d. for **bamu na**, q.v.

Bau, s., one slain, lit. head, skull.

Ḅau na, s., the head; a head or chief, specially, d. maternal uncle, that is, head of the family. [Malo *batu*, San Cristoval *bau*, head, Epi *baru*, Motu *ḅara*, Ml. *karu*, id.] Efate **bau**, v. t., to be above, over, surpass, **bau ġoro**, to be over, covering, **taḅau**, id., to surpass in dignity, also **mau**, feathers on birds, and head ornament of feathers, **ḅo** (for **bau**), **ḅo-fi**, **ḅoḅo-fi**, to be above, over, to conquer, and **ḅo ġoro.** A. fara'a, to ascend, surpass or excel in dignity, overcome, conquer, have the head covered with hair, n. a. far'u, summit, top, vertex, head or chief.

Bau lulu, s., a proud person, lit. high head: **lu.**

Baua, or **uaua** (**waua**), s., a pillow: preceding word and ending **-a**: also, v., to pillow one's head.

Bau-maso na, s., portion of the property of one deceased inherited by a member of the family: **bau**, and **maso**, q.v. For **bau**, see s. **bau-si**.

Bau, v. t., to be above, over, surpass, **i bau ġor ia**. See **taḅau**.

Bau-si, or **fau-si**, v. t., to fasten together; to plait (a mat); **bau rarua**, fasten together (the parts of) a canoe; **bau uaġo**, fasten a pig to the carrying pole: **ora naui i bau**, the yam vine fastens on or round the stake; redup. **bau-fau**; **bau-maso** (**maso** a portion) the portion collected or fastened or gathered together, **bau-teraġ ia**, fasten —to dry it (as wet cloth), i.e. fasten it on something in the sun or before a fire. [Sa. *fau* (Ma. *hou*), tie together, fasten by tying, ps. *fausia*, To. *fau*, fillet round the head, turban, Fut. *fausia*, to fasten, tie, Fi. *vau-t'a*, to bind together, Sa. *fau-la'i*, to be heaped up, to abound, Mg. *fehi*, *fehizana*, to tie, knot.] A. **ḥabaka**, to weave, bind, interweave, n. a. **ḥabīkat'**.

Bau ġor i, v. t., to be above, over: **taḅau sa**, to be above (as covering a thing), to be over, surpass him (in dignity or rank). See under **ḅau**.

Bäu or **fäu**, **bäo** or **fäo**, v. i., or a., new. [Malo *baro*, Ml. *mermer*, Motu *matamata*, My. *baharu*, Sa. *fou*, Fi. *vovou*, *vou*, Mg. *vau* (*havauzana*), new.] A. **maḥdut'**, part. of **ḥadat'a**, to be new, new. H. **ḥadas'**, S. **ḥdat'**, id., E. **ḥadas**, to renew.

Bauli, v. c., to buy by exchanging;

Baulu, or **faulu**, s., the thing given in exchange wherewith to purchase something, barter (wherewith to buy by exchanging). See **aul i**, **ul i**.

Bau-raġi, or **bau-teraġi**. See **bau-si**. **Teragi** is for **reraġi**.

Baus i, and **bausus i**, v. t., to ask him (or her), **bausus ià sa**, ask him it (or about it):

Bausu ki, to inquire about (a thing), **bausu baki**, to inquire at (a person), to ask, to question (a person). See **us ia**.

Bauria, d. for **būria**, q.v. See **bara**.

Ḅea (**kbe**, or **bwe**), s. See **naḅea**.

Be, d. **mai**, v., to come here, like **mai**, q.v.; also d. for **bā**, **bai**, to come or go from, as **i bē sāb?** he comes from where?

Bē è mia, v. t., to have it, **i bē nalo**, he has a thing, d. **i bi è nia**, he has it: **bi è nia**, **be è nia**. See **bà**.

Bē, or **bea**, dd. **bei**, **mia** (**tiamia**), v. i., or a., to precede, go before, be first, first. [Sa. *mua*, and *mua'i*, first, *muamua*, to go before, first, Lakon *mo*, Volow *mag*, Arag *moana*, first, Fi. *mada*, to precede.] A. **fuhat**, mouth, entrance (as of a river), hence the first or foremost part of anything, Amh. **pat**, or **fat**, fore-part, and c. a. ending **fataña**, first.

Be, d., a particle used after interrogatives, then, now, thus **uā be?** **sa be** (sāb)? where then? **takana aġa bat ia be?** how shall I do it then (or now). In other dialects it is not used. H. **'epo'**, then, now, as **ayeh 'epo'**, where then? cf. **'ēpoh** (**poh**, here), where? how?

Bĕ, **fĕ**, conj., if, should; **ku fĕ bano i fē uia**, should you go it were well, **i bĕ fano i bĕ uia**, should (or if) he go it were well. [Ta. *ip*, Fut. *pe*, if.] Amh. **ba**, **bĕ**, if, should (repeated in each clause as in Ef., Isenberg's *Amh. Gr.*, pp. 158–9).

Be a, or **fe a**, redup. **befe**, v. t., to read, also to count. A. **faha**, utter, pronounce, speak.

Be, or **bea**, redup. **bebea**, v. i., or a., to be great, wide extended. [Mg. *be*, great, large, Mota *poa*, Gao *bio*.] E. **'abya**, or **'abia**, to be great, wide, extended, **'abiy**, great, large.

Bebe, s., butterfly, H. **'up**, (Pilpel) **'ib'eb**, to flutter.

Beġa, d. **baġa**, q.v., a hill.

Bei ki, or **bai ki**, d. **bi ki**, v. t., to show: d. syn. **bisai ki**. [Tah. *fai*, divulge.] A. **baḥa**, to appear, be shown, manifest, show, divulge, indicate; hence

Beifei ki, make manifest, indicate.

Bei, v., **bei ki**, to watch for (as for an animal to take or kill it). [Ma. *whai*, search for, spy.] A. **ba''a** (**ba''ai**), to watch, observe, look at, look out for, rush upon (the prey) from an ambush, seek, &c.

Ḅei, or **ḅai**, a thing hidden, concealed, **i bi ḅei**, it is hidden. See **afa**: cg. to the word there given are A. **''abai**, H. **ḥaba'**, A. **ḥ'aba'**, to hide.

Bei, d. for **bē**, or **bea**, v. i., or a., to precede, first.

Bei, or **bai**, d. **ba**, prep. used mostly after verbs, connecting them with their object: **lo**, to look, **lo bei a**, look upon it, see it, **taruba**, to fall, **taruba bei a**, fall upon it, d. **ro**, to fall, **ro bei a**, to fall upon it; **an**, to be, to lie, **an bei a**, lie upon it; **toko**, sit, **toko bei a**, sit upon it; **ba**, to go, **ba ḅei a**, go or tread upon it (for instance, upon filth in the path, **ba bai intai**); the final **i** in **bei** or **bai** belongs to the pronoun of the third person. [Fi. *vei*, to, d. *va*.] E. **ba**, A. **fi**, **bi**, H. **b'**. See Ch. V.

Bei, s., **na bei saki ni aliati**, the ascending *rosy* cloud of dawn, the dim cloudy or misty appearance preceding daylight at dawn: d. **in tei saki**, the rising *rosy* cloud. See **tei.**

Ḅefe, or **fefe,** s., oven cover (made of leaves); a covering trap (for catching fowls). [Sa. *veve,* oven cover of leaves.] See (**ḅofi**), **ḅo.**

Beiġo, or **baiġo,** s., a trumpet (shell); d. a kind of flute (cocoanut shell). [Sa. *faġu-faġu,* a flute, To. *faġofaġo,* a flute blown by the nose.] A. **baḳa,** to blow a trumpet, **ba'ḳu,** or **ba'ḳo,** a trumpet.

Bela ki, v. t., to gird (oneself), **bela ki natali,** put on one's girdle or belt; to tie or fasten anything or carry anything between one's girdle and the lower part of the belly: hence, to take with one, to have with one or attached to one. See **ḅala** III. The s. is **nafelaki,** d. **nabŭlai,** or **ḅă-lai,** what is fastened, or girded round the loins, girdle.

Belaki, v. i., to be pregnant: **ḅala,** III.

Belaki, s., c. art. **nabelaki,** d. syn. **intamate,** great heathen feast or series of feasts periodically held at every village, at which there was *abundance of food,* singing, and dancing: prob. so called because of the *abundance of food,* and friendly feeling: **ḅala,** III.

Bĕla, or **fĕla,** if perhaps, if indeed, conj. **bĕ,** and ad. **la.**

Bela, v. i., to be smooth, level; **ḅala** I.

Ḅela, d. for **ḅala** II., q.v.

Bela-taġot. See **ḅala** II.

Bela-ġalu. See **ḅala** II.

Ḅēle, s., the dead body of a pig: said to be so called because its belly swells. **Ḅala** III. [Ha. *pele,* to swell out, have a large belly.]

Ḅele na, s., the belly (or **ḅălă na**); the womb; a mother (dd. syn. **eri na, raite na, susu na**); a source, as **ḅele ni toroġo,** the source or master of the **toroġo** (a species of divination), also **ḅele nai** (**naui**) **kanoa,** the beginning or feast of the first ripe yams: **ḅala** III.

Belbel, d. for **bile, bilebile,** q.v.

Beles, s., c. art. **nebeles,** a dance in which the two parties keep *meeting* each other. See **lasi, tilasi.**

Bēn, or **fēn,** a., cooked, broiled, roasted: **bani a.**

Beni a, d. for **bani a.**

Bēn, d. for **bān.** See **anĭ,** to be, abide.

Ḅelŭ ki, v. t., to fold, to double, **tàḅelŭ** (**takwelŭ**), folded, doubled;

Ḅēlu, v. i., to be doubled up, as it were folded together, hence to be hidden, to hide oneself, **ḅēlu ki,** to be hidden from, also **uēlu.**

Bèluuēlu, v. i., or a., folded, hence limp, doubled up, and **beluueluki,** a., doubled up, uneven, limp, limber, weak, flexible, **taḅelu.** [Ha. *pelu,* to double over, bend, or flex, as a joint, to fold, doubled, folded over, *pelupelu*, to double over and over, doubled over, Sa. *mapelu*, *mapelupelu*, to bend, stoop, Fi. *belu-ka*, to bend, curve, *kabelu*, bent, Mg. *valuna*, folded, doubled.] See **Ḅala**, III.

Bera, or **fera**, v. i., to crumble, fall to pieces, **bera-fēra**, and **taberafēra**, to crumble, fall to pieces, be scattered about in fragments;

Bēra ki, v. t., to scatter about, **tabēra ki**, to scatter about, make to fall to pieces, and **berafēraki**, v. t., and **tafera-fēra ki**, v. t. [Fi. *vuru-taka*, to crumble, *vuruvuru*, v. i., to crumble, and S., a crumb, Mg. *miveraberaka*, v. i., to crumble, *mahavera*, v. t., My. *âmbor*, scattered, *tabur*, to be scattered.] E. **farfur**, a crumb, Talmud, **parpor** from H. **pur**, **par**, to break, Pilpel **pirper**, to break in pieces.

Bera-gi, v. t., d. **bĭrĭġi**, q.v.

Berakati, d. **bera-ti**, **bera-tiki**, v. used as ad., fully, thoroughly, accurately; also thus, **tea berakati na**, a thing fully his, a thing his own. See **bura**, d. **biri**, to be full, full. **Berakati** is by transposition for **bera-taki**.

Beru, v. d., syn. **uma**, to clear for a plantation, to cut down trees, cut or clear the jungle. [Mg. *firala* (*fira*, cut, *ala*, wood, forest), *miferala*, cut down wood in order to make some use of the ground, clear the forest, Ja. *tipar*, felling and burning the forest for cultivation, Ma. *para*, to cut down bush, clear.] H. **bere'**, Piel of **bara'**, to cut down—'go into the wood and cut out room for thee there' Josh. xvii. 15.

Ḅēs, or **ḅēsŭ**, s., dry wood, hard dry wood used for fencing. A. **yabīs'**, dry (wood), Nm. **yabis**, dry (wood).

Ḅēs, d. **bēsŭ**, s., a young pig whose mother is dead and which is brought up as a pet and is therefore tame and gentle; also a motherless child, syn. **mitabusa**. So called from being deprived of the mother's milk, and, as it were, arid. See preceding word and **busa**: A. **yabisa**, to be dry.

Bĕtà, or **fĕtà**, s., a tribe, a crowd or lot of people, or of animals, accompanying each other, as **nabeta Toġoliu**, the tribe of Toġolius, the Toġoliu crowd, set, or lot; a shoal, **nabeta naika**, a shoal of fish. See **bita**, **bita-naki**, **ta**.

Beti, or **bati**, s., in proper names, as **Toġoliu beti**, **Metanibeti**, &c.: **beti** seems a form of the word **bati** (see s.v. **nabati na**), and prob. means chief of the family, or shoot.

Ḅeti, s., a kind of spear pronged with sharpened

human bones, and feathered: prob. so called because pronged or *toothed*. See **bati**.

Bi, v., d. for **umba ki**, q.v.

Bi, or **fi**, dd. **mi**, **bai**, v., to be, only used before substantives, or words used as substantives, as **i bi natamole, fatu, nakasu**, it is a man, stone, tree, **ru bi natamole uia**, they are good men. [Epi *mbe*, *ve*, to be, Ml. P. *fe*, A. *mbe*, *be*, U. *vi*.] See **bā**, supra.

Bi è nia (d. **bi è mia**, or **be e mia**), v. t., to have; **i bē nalo**, or **i bieni nalo**, he has something. [With *bieni*, we should perhaps compare My. *puñai*, to possess.] See **bà**, supra.

Bi ki, v. t., d. for **bei ki**, q.v., to show.

Bi, s., only in **meta-ni-bi**, small openings in the ends of a house through which light comes, and which are left uncovered in thatching. Of same stem as preceding word, whence is A. **buḥu**, a name of the sun, and **buḥ'**, the uncovered part of a house or tent.

Bīa, or **fīa**, d. **bīsa**, or **fīsa**. [Malo, Santo, &c., *visa*], v. i., or a., how many? as **ru bia?** they are how many? **natamole bia?** how many men? And, not interrogatively, **ru bia**, they are so many, few, **natamole bia**, so many men, i.e. a few men. [Sa. *fia*, ad., how many? Fi. *vit'a*, ad., how many? Mg., ad., *firi*, how many? *mifiri*, v. i., into how many parts does it divide?] The final part of **bia** or **bisa**, namely **a** or **sa**, is the interrogative pronoun. Compare as to the initial consonant, Tanna **keva**, d. **kuva**. See Ch. V. 5, and 4.

Bi, or **fi**, reflexive verb preformative (**ba**, or **baka**, **fa**, or **faka**, being the causative verb preformative), as **ru atu-ği**, v. t., they smite him, **ru fiatu**, v. r., they smite each other, they fight. **auli a**, v. t., exchange, replace, substitute for it, **bauli a**, or **fauli a**, v. c., nearly the same, make to take the place of, barter for it, **ru biauli**, v. r., they are bartering with each other, or they are replacing each other or taking each other's places (as men at the oar). [Sa. *fe*, 'the reciprocal particle', prefixed to verbs, Fi. *vei*, Mg. *i*, *mi*, reflexive verb preformative (Griffith's *Mg. Gr.*, p. 112). See Ch. IV.]

Bia, bibia, d. **biau**, or **beau**, d. **ia**, s., a child, youth, **bia kiki**, little children, **bia turiai**, young men; and in names of children as **bia-naru**, &c. [TaSa. *pipi*, infant, Ml. U. *bibi*, infant, Ml. A. *pepe*, infant, Mg. *afi*, *zafi*, My. *piyud*, *piyat*, *piat*, *piyu*, Ja. *bayi*, infant, child.] A. (**ḥafada**), **ḥafid**, **ḥafidat**, nepotes, offspring.

Biau, or **beau**, s., wave, waves. [Sa. *peau*, id., My. *ombak*, id.] E. **ababi**, A. **'ubāb'**, i.q. **'ūbab'**, flood, waves, from **'abba**, to have broken waves (*the sea*). Hence

Biafiau (for **biaufiau**), v. i., to be raised in waves, rough (as the sea). [Sa. *peaua*, rough (as the sea), lit. wavy, full of waves; *peau*, and the a. ending *a*.]

Biauli, v. r., d. **bioli**, barter or exchange with each other; take each other's places, as men at the oar or other work, spell each other. See **auli**.

Bialo, v. r., to wave (beckoning); reflexive of **alo-fi**, q.v.

Bib, s., d. for **ḅaḅa**, a board.

Bibisinu, v. i., to ring, sing (of the ears): **sinu**; **bibi**, is the preformative **bi** doubled.

Bibe, v. i., or a., for **bebea**.

Biḅila, v. i., or a., big, great: redup. of **ḅila**, q.v.

Bīfera ki, v. t., to show by a fera (or omen): **fera**.

Ḅiġo. See **buiġo**.

Ḅikutu ki, v. t., speak to each other (against someone in his absence); decide about (someone). See **kutu ki**.

Bila, v. i., shine, lighten, gleam, flash, appear; **bĭlafĭla**, redup., to do so repeatedly: **lo bilă ki**, glance at; **fila**, lightning; **bulĕ-meta**, eyeball (gleaming part of the eye). [Sa. *pula*, *pupula*, *pulapula*, to shine.] A. **baraḳ**, or **bara'**, shine, gleam, flash, glitter, appear; lighten (lightning), 2, open the eyes, glance at, **barḳ'**, lightning, pl. **buruḳ**, H. **baraḳ**, S. **barḳa**: hence **bila**, or **fila**, **bile**, or **file**, s., lightning: c. art. **nafila**.

Bila i, or **bilai**, v. t., pick up, gather up (anything, as fallen leaves, fruits, fish lying on the ground, &c.);

Bila ġuru ki, **bili lua**, **bili sai**, &c. See **ġuru**, **lua**, **sai**, **Bĭlai** has the pref. **b'**. [Fi. *vili-ka*, pick up, as fallen leaves or fruits.] E. **'araya**, gather (as fruits, herbs), glean (as after reapers): c. preformative.

Ḅila, also (dd. **mbula**, **bur**);

Biḅila, redup. (intensive), and

Ḅilena, **biḅilena**, v. i., or a. (**-na**, a. ending), big, large, great. [Mg. *bulubulu*, *mibulubulu*, a., thick, close, dense.] A. **'abula**, **'abila**, to be thick, big, **'abanbal'**, strong, great, large.

Bile, or **bila**, v. i., to be quick; hence sudden, confused, inaccurate, to err, make a mistake: redup. **bilebile** (d. **belbel**) quick, sudden, **bilieli**, sudden, quick, hence confused, erroneous: **tabile**, to be hasty, commit an error. Often used adverbially, as **ba bilebile**, go quickly, **si bile**, shoot missing (lit. hastily, erroneously, not hitting the mark), &c. H. **bahal**, **bahel**, prop. to tremble, be in trepidation, Piel to hasten, to hasten (as if to tremble) to do anything, Hi. id., Ch. (běhal) Ithpeal inf. hitbehalah, s., haste, speed, with prefixed bě, ad., quickly.

Bile, d. **bīlě**, v. i., to dispute, wrangle. [My. *babil*, to wrangle, squabble.] E. bě-hīl, (2) contradict, tabāhala, dispute, wrangle, bahl, dispute, altercation, wrangle.

Ḅili, v. t., **ḅili meta**, shut the eyes, redup. **biliuili**, id. (of many); hence

Ḅili, s., a blind person (with closed eyes); and

Bilil, s., a tree (whose leaves at a certain stage of their growth cleave together): d. **ḅilḅilo**, wink, close the eyes. See **uili**, **kuli**: **uili mita**, eyelids, and **i uili mita**, or **ḅili mita**, close the eyelids.

Ḅili, v. t., d. for **ḅelu ki**, q.v.

Ḅilàki, v. i., to be terrified, tremble (as it were) with fear. H. **balàh**, to be terrified, to fear, Piel **billeàh**, to terrify, and suffix **ki**.

Ḅīle na, s. See **ḅele na**, mother.

Ḅile-meta na, s., nephew or niece, child of a man's **ġore na**, that is, his full or uterine sister. Lit. mother, i. e., source, of the tribe or family, such nephew being a man's heir (and not his own son). D. syn. **fito na.**

Bilāġa, v. t., **bilàġà sa**, seek, search for it. See **lāġa**, **làġà sa**, id.

Bilele, v. i., r., to turn hither and thither, to go backwards and forwards, round and round: **lele.**

Bilele, v. i., r., d. for **bitoli**, q.v.

Bĭlĭāsa, ad., the morning (day-break) of the day after to-morrow: **bulo, āsa**; **bĭlĭ**, as in **bĭlĭ-boġ**, **bĭlĭ-mitamai.**

Bĭlĭboġ, ad. (d. **bulboġ**), morning: **bulo, boġ.**

Bilieli, v., see **bile**, **bilibile**, to be quick, &c.

Bilikit i, v. t., to peel (as a banana). [An. *milaġa*, to peel, Sa. *mile'i*, to husk, Fi. *loqa ta*, to peel.] E. **laḥaṣa**, to peel.

Bĭlĭmitamai, ad., the morning (day-break) of the morrow; **bĭlĭmitamai ki nia**, the morrow following it, **sera bĭlĭmitamai**, every recurring morrow: **bulo, mitamai.**

Ḅilis i, d. **ḅolis i**, **uolis i**, v. t., to spread out anything on the ground as a mat; hence to make a bed; hence **na uol**, s., that spread out, a bed, d. **na mäuol**; and from this latter is **mäuoli ki**, make a bed with (something), spread it out for a bed. [Mg. *velaṭa*, *mivelaṭa*, to spread, expand itself (be spread out), *mamilaṭa*, v. t., to spread.] A. **faras'a**, to spread out anything, as a mat on the ground, spread (a bed for anyone), hence **fars'**, a bed.

Ḅiliti, s., the fat in the belly of a pig: connected with **ḅele na**, the belly.

Bĭlĭsai, v., used as ad., together, as **i tili bĭlĭsai ki nia,** he told (two or more things) together: it is really a v. t., and **tili bĭlĭsai ki,** lit. he told gathering-together it: **bila i,** or **bilai,** and **sai** (see **saisai**).

Bilo, v. i., d. **bulo,** q.v., to awaken, to open the eyes; **bulo-ni,** d. **bulobulo i,** v. t., to awaken (from sleep), to cause to open the eyes. [Sa. *ala*, to awake, Ma. *ara*, v. i., wake up, *whakaara*, v. t., rouse, Fi. *yadra*, open the eyes, awake, *yadra-va*, watch for, *vakayadra-ta*, to awaken.] H. **'ur,** to awake, be awake, cause to awake, Hi. to arouse, awake (from sleep); to watch, followed by the prep. **'al,** to watch over anyone.

Bilo-si, v. t., d. **balo-ni,** wash.

Bilōra, for **bulōra,** q.v.

Bilu, or **biliu,** v. r., to go backwards and forwards between two places or parties: **liliu, liu.**

Bilu, uilu, uulu (wulu), q.v., to dance (*a woman* or *women*; men dancing are said to **sali**).

Bilulu, v. r., vie with each other, contend with each other for superiority. A. **'ala' ('alu),** 3, vie, compete, contend for superiority: see **lulu,** or **lu.**

Biluḅaki, v. r., to land cargo from a ship, or to land passengers (land each other): **luḅa-ki.**

Bimeta na, v. and s., to be his guide, lit. his eye: **bi,** to be, and **meta,** eye.

Binako, v. t., d. **banako,** q.v., to steal.

Binaka, s., mats, cloth: see **ḅinu.**

Bināta, and dd. **bunaṣ,** and

Binauta, v. i., to be numb, devoid of feeling, as one's limb from stoppage of circulation of the blood in it: **bi,** to be, **nāta,** a person (as if the limb belonged to some other person). See **ata.**

Binēn, v. i., d. syn. c. **banotu,** q. v., and **baina,** q.v.

Binàṣ, d. for **banōtu.**

Binoinoi, v. r., be confusedly together (as different kinds of things, people of different districts or languages), **tumara noinoi ra:**

Binofinoi, a., confused, perplexed, d. **bunofunoi: noi, nō.**

Binōtĕ, d. for **banōtu.**

Ḅinu na, s., as, **ḅinu nafanua,** head of the country (the chief and **natamole tabu** are said to be **ḅinu naf.**), **ḅinu naui,** head of a yam, syn. **bau naui, ḅinu namīt,** first half of a mat with long threads attached, from which the weaving or plaiting of the second half begins; hence

Ḅinu, v., as **ḅinu namit,** make a beginning of the second half of a mat, plaiting from the already finished half. See **ḅanu, ban, baniban, banaġa, binaka.** [My. *anam*, to weave.] E. 'anama, to weave, ma'nama.

Ḅinu, v. i., to whistle, dd. ḅin, bògĕ. [Am. *mofin*, Ml. P. and U., *puinpuin*, *winwin*, Mg. *enu*, *nenu*, *manenu*, to sound, crow, sing, ring, Sa. *vivini*, to crow.] A. ma'ānu, cantor, A. "aniya, sing, coo, "ina, cantus, H. 'anah, sing, &c.

Binunu, v., complete, **ba binunu ki**, to go throughout, complete (a piece of a fence): **nu, num.**

Bio-so, v. i., to call or cry out, shout, calling: **bio**, and **so**, q.v. The verb **bio**, or **fio** (see **rafioso**), means to cry out, shout. [Sa. *piapio*, an outcry, a shouting, Mg. *feu*, voice, sound, report.] H. pa'ah, to call, to cry out.

Bira-ġi, d.,

Biri-ġi, d. **firi-ġi**, v. t., to carry on the back, take, bring, lead. [Epi *mbario*, carry on the back.] A. ḥamala, to carry on the back, bring, send, impel to do something, S. ḥmal, collect, carry.

Biri-nāla, s., the plaited or braided (rope) handle of a carrying basket: see **āla**, and **bir i**, to plait.

Biri-ofa, s., the cloth in which a child is slung and carried on the back of its mother: **biriġi**, and **ofa** (i), d. **afa**, both of which verbs signify to carry on the back.

Ḅiràġoro, v., d. **ḅoraġoro**, q.v., to make, break into a noise near someone: see **ḅora i**, and **ġoro**.

Biraka, v. r., to give presents to guests at a **naleoüan** (feast after a death), lit. to give presents (or rewards) to each other: **raka-ti**;

Birakāna, s., the giving of such presents.

Biri-raki, v. t., to give presents to guests at a **naleoüan**: **biri a** (**biri naḅo ra**, i. e. make their hearts void of evil thoughts, i. e. pleased or good). See **biri**.

Birausi, v. r., to follow each other: **rausi**.

Bir i, or **biri**, v. t., to make void, bring to nought, as counsel, **bisa biri nalo na**: the radical notion is *break to pieces*, **biri na maietoa**, break to pieces or put an end to (one's) anger, appease, **biri naḅo na**, bring to an end the evil feelings of one's heart, appease. This verb is much used after other verbs, as **miṭoa, bisa**, &c., think void, i. e. despise, &c., and **bā biri nafanua**, means to go all through the land: **tale**, round, **tale-firi**, all round; reduplicated it is

Birifiri, nearly the same meaning as **biri i**. H. parar, to break in pieces, Hi. hefer, to break, as a covenant, make void, be void, bring to nought: cg. **para'**, and following word.

Biris i, and **boris ia**, v. t., to break down, destroy, **birisi**

nakoro, break down a wall: the notion of breaking in pieces, asunder, is implied in this word, which is cognate with the preceding. H. **paraṣ**, to break, break down, &c.

Ḅiri, v. i., to warble, whistle (birds). [Epi *faru, forfaru.*] A. **watta, watwata**, to twitter.

Bĭrĭ, d. for **bŭra**, to be full, q.v.

Bir i, v. t., to plait a string or rope. [Sa. *fili*, to plait; to be entangled, involved, Ma. *whiri*, twist, plait, Ha. *hili*, braid, plait, twist, fasten, Tah. *firi*, to plait, My. *pintal*, d. *pilin*, Bu. *pitoi*, Batavia *bilan*, twist.] A. **fatala**, n. a. **fatl'**, E. **fatlat**, twist, spin (**fetlat**). In H., A., Ch., Syr., and E.

Bir i, v. t., d., to stick, stab, pierce, as, **biri naui**, to stick a knife or fork into a yam while being boiled to know whether it is cooked. See **bur i**.

Birife, v. r., to seize, pull hither and thither (to take away a man's property as a punishment). A. **hadiba** id.

Biriġirigi, v. r., to be moaning, bemoaning oneself. See **riġi**.

Briġi, d., v. t., **bri** (i.e. **bĭri**), prob. for **meri**, q.v., to do. make: therefore it is **bri-ġi** (**bĭri-ġi**). See **meri**.

Biriġite na, s., d. for **bura na**, q.v.

Ḅirīki, s., a part, side. [Mg. *varaka*, to separate.] A. **fariḳ'**, a part, from **faraḳa**, to divide, separate, &c. Hence

Ḅirīki, s., a 'falling' star, a meteor: used also as a name of men.

Biri-sai, v. t., to pierce open, **birisai na ḅaġo āso**, pierce open the tunnel (or end of it) of the robber-crab, fig. to lay open some hidden wickedness: **biri**, to pierce, and **sai**, q. v.

Biroa, and **biroaroa**, v. r., to turn each other (in some work, causing it to be done in some other way), as, when one is doing some piece of work, to make him do it some other way is to **biroa**: see **roa**, to turn, to change.

Bisa, fisa, or **basa**, and **bisuraki**, v. i., to speak, **na fĭsān**, d. **nafsan**, the act of speaking, speech, a word; **tabisa**, to speak earnestly (**ta**, q.v., and **bisa**), **tafisafisa**, d. **tafisfis**, to speak earnestly; to pray (so used now in Christian sense); to utter inarticulate sounds (as those made by a cocoanut on the gravel which a rat is turning about trying to get at its kernel). [My. *bacha*, to read, recite, chant, Tag. *basa*, Fi. *vosa*, to speak, talk.] A. **nabasa**, and **nabaṣa**, to speak; to peep or chirp (*a bird*); **nabsat'**, a word.

Bisafisa, v. i., redup. of foregoing, to speak rapidly (as one in delirium).

Bīsa, or **fīsa,** d. **bīa,** q.v., to be how many? so many, a few; **bīsa-mau,** d. **bisi-ḅa,** to be only a few, few. See **mau.**

Bisàb, d. for **bisif,** v. i., or a., surpassing, excelling, as, **fonu bisab,** an excelling (big) turtle, **i uia bisif,** it is good, surpassing or excelling. See **safe.**

Bisai ki, v. t., to show, d. **bisā ki.** See **sai.**

Bisakaui, d. for **bisaku-ti,** q.v.

Bisàki (d. **biski**), d. transposed for **bakasa,** q.v.

Bisaka, or **busaki,** v. c., to raise up, to place above, fig. to appoint or make one a chief. See **saki.**

Bisaku-ti, v. t., d. **bakasau,** q.v. See **siku-ti.**

Ḅisalot (for **ḅosa-lot**), v. i., to clap the hands, lit. bring (the hands) together, sound, or crack: **ḅosa i,** and **lot.**

Bisau, v. i., dd. **futum, busuf,** or **busofu, bisobu,** to sprout forth, spring up. See **futum.**

Bisaui, d. for **bisaku-ti, bisakaui.**

Bisēka, v. i., d., to sit (as talking with a neighbour): **sēka.**

Bisela, v. r., to bear, bring forth, give birth to: **sela-ti.**

Bisera, biserasera, v. i., to be not of one size, to be different: **sera i.**

Biserĕ, v. r., to be near: **sere a.**

Ḅis i, or **uis i,** v. t., to take with the hand, grasp, take hold of, accept, receive. [Mg. *hazuna,* id.] H. 'aḥaz, A. 'aḥaḍ'a, Imp. ḥuḍ, Arm. 'ăhad, E. 'ahaza, n. a. 'ĕhazat, id.

Bisi na, or **bŭsi na,** s., the posteriors, the backside, the rump. Compare **busi,** d. for **muri,** q.v. [Mg. *vudi,* the posteriors, My. *buri,* the back, the rear, Ma. *muri,* hinder part, Sa. *muli,* the rump.]

Bis ia, or **bisi a,** v. t., to beget, procreate, make to be born, as a father his child; **mafis,** one begotten or born, **namafisien,** the being begotten or born;

Bisi, or **fisi,** v. t., to rub one stick on another to produce fire, **bisi nakabu,** produce fire by friction. The rubbing stick is pointed and rubs a groove into the other, the rubbed out dust at the end of which gradually is ignited. [Mg. *fusiṭa,* rubbed so as to produce fire by the friction, *mifusiṭa,* to produce fire by friction.] A. faṣa'a, 2, to rub (a thing), so that its soft and broken interior may be emitted.

Bis i, or **bisi,** v. t., to uncover or dig up anything buried under ground, to dig up, or uncover, by removing the covering earth, a dead and buried body, or any other thing buried in or covered with earth, as a yam, &c. A. **nabas'a,** to uncover what was covered or hid, as what lies hid under ground; to dig up again, or uncover by digging (*a corpse*).

Bīsībà, v. i., or a., d. for **bīsa-mau** (**bīsa-mau**). See **mau,** and **bīsa.**

Bisif, v. i., or a., d. for **bisab,** q.v.

Bisiġ, v. i., or a., to stink, be bad (mouldy, &c.), and of men, to be opposed, hostile: **siġi.**

Bisobu, v. i., to sprout forth, spring up. See **futum.**

Bisua, v. r., to meet together, to meet each other: **sua.**

Bisuaki, or **fisuaki,** v. r., or a., order or command (or send) each other; **i bisuaki,** he commands, that is, he commands some other person, or persons: **sua ki.**

Bisueri, v. r., scold or vituperate each other: **sueri.**

Bisuraki, or **bisureki,** i.e. **bisu-raki,** v., to speak, lit. to speak for, about; **nafisuraki,** speech, a word or utterance, **nafisuraki sa,** bad talk: **bisa.**

Bisuru, v. r., lie (deceive each other), **bisuru ki,** lie to (some one): **suru,** d. **sore-sore.**

Bitā, v. r., to be joined together, associated (of men); **bitā ki,** t., make to be joined together, or associated: **tā, bitā-naki.**

Bitaḅelu, and, d.,

Bitafetaḅelu, same as **taḅelu**: **ḅelu.**

Bitaġo, v. r., beg (from each other, or one from another), also **bitagò sa,** t., beg it, i.e. beg (for himself) it: **taġo-fi** (q.v.), beg of him. D. for **bitali,** q.v.

Bitaki, v.t., to place or fix the hot stones on the **nakoau** in the oven, d. **uataki a, bitaki nakeau**: **taki.**

Bital i, or **bitali,** d., v. t., beg, ask him (for something): preformative **bi,** and **talĭ.** [Sa. *fesili,* to question, ask, *sili,* ps. *silia,* to ask, inquire.] A. **sa'ala,** to question, 5, beg, 6, question, ask each other, n.a. **sa'lat,** H. **s'aal,** n.a. **s'ĕālah.**

Bitānaki nia, v. t., r., to accompany one, **bita-naki**: see **tā.**

Bitau sa, v. t., to invite, and

Bitautau (of many): **tau, tautau.**

Bitau-ri, v. t., to marry (her): **tau-ri.**

Bite, v. t., to cut; **bitēsu,** d. **bitēïu,** to cut reeds (see **usu**). [My. *potoġ,* to cut.] A. **batta** (and **baṭṭa**), to cut; hence

Bītĕ, s., an instrument for cutting, knife.

Bitè lua i. See **butè lua i.**

Bitefa, v. r., to arrange themselves opposite to each other for battle: **tefa.**

Bitei a, v. t., to paint, to smear with intei; **tei**, turmeric, a reddish powder (made from a plant) much used for smearing the body, or wounds, or the **nafona** (native cloth), and **tei**, d. **bei**, the rosy, reddish flush (of dawn). A. 'a'da'u, crocus, sanguis draconis, a red gum used for healing wounds, a plant with which cloth is coloured or tinged, **yadda'a**, to tinge or colour *a thing* with the thing called **'a'da'u**.

Bitelo, d. **butol**, **bitol**, v. i., to be hungry. [Fl. *vitolo*, to be hungry.] A. ṭalaḥa, to have an empty belly, ṭoliḥa, id.

Biteriki, s., an old woman, a matron, opp. to **māriki**, an old man, a senior; **mā-'riki**, **bite-'riki**, see **fiteriki**; **bite** means 'woman'. The common word for 'woman' in one dialect is **matu** [Ja. *wedo*], q.v.

Ḃitia, or **fitia**, v. i., to germinate, put forth shoots. See **ḃuti**, **ḃiti**. Dialect syn. **sulia**, from **suli na**.

Bīto, s., one lame, H. **pasaḥ**, to be lame, **pisseaḥ**, lame.

Bitoli, v. r., to pass (or go before) each other: **toli a**.

Bĭtò-si, v. t., to extend, spread out (as cloth, &c.), **i fito**, it is stretched out. H. **mataḥ**, S. **mtaḥ**, spread out, extend.

Bituà sa, v. r., give it, place it; hence **bituāna**, s., a giving, gift: **tua i**.

Bitua ki, v. t., place, lay down: **tua ki**.

Bituḃetuḃa, v. r., lit. to be touching each other (of things) in a series, then, to be continual, uninterruptedly, constantly; not redup. it is,

Bitub, to be touching or reaching to each other, as in **tālĕ bitub**, it is all round (the two ends of that which goes round), meeting or touching each other: **tuḃa ia**. [My. *tubitubi*, successively, uninterruptedly.] See **tuba i**.

Bituma ki, v. r., to point to with the finger: **tuma i**.

Bo, conj., particle connecting verbs thus, **i tulena bo lotu**, he arose and worshipped, **i tili a bo ban**, he said it and went away: the **bo** can sometimes be and sometimes is omitted as **i tulena lotu**: d. syn. **kai**. A. **fa**, Wr., *A. Gr.*, II. § 140, 'One finite verb may be put in apposition to another. In this case *a*) the first is the preparative act, introductory to the second,' as in the above Ef. examples: 'the older and more elegant form is to insert the conjunction **fa**,' its omission being a later construction. As to the **o** in **bo** it seems to be the third pers. pron., i.e. **bo** = 'and he' or 'and she', d. syn. **kai**.

Bō, d., other dd. **fō**, **mō**, **uō**, **ō**, a particle used after another particle to form the future tense, thus, **i ġa bo**

ban, dd. i ġa uo ban, i ġ'o ban, k'e fo ban, i ba mo ban (or, i mba mo ban), he will go away: without the bo (uo, o, mo, fo) as, i ġa fan, &c., the meaning is imperative, or permissive, let him go, he must go, should go, may go, lit. that he go, the particles ġa (or ka), and ba, being final conjunctions denoting ut, that, to (as in, I told him to go): see supra ba, conj., and infra ka (ġa), conj. In Ml. P., Motu, &c., this ba alone forms the future tense, and in Florida and Vaturanga this k' (ka, ġa) alone forms the future, thus k'e fan, i.e. ke fan, that he go, Ef., is in these two languages not only equivalent to this, but also equivalent to ke fo ban, he will go. It is therefore manifest that the particle bo does not by itself express the future idea, but, in Ef., &c., it is a final conjunction which does. See the following—

Bō, a particle used to form the present progressive or indefinite tense, as, **i bo ban**, he is going: **i ban**, denotes either he goes or he went. This is the same particle as is used in the future tense. It makes the verb to which it is prefixed a participle, thus, **iġa bo ban**, that he (be) going, **i bo ban**, he (is) going. See Ch. V. 10, *a*, *b*.

Ḅo na, redup. **ḅoḅo na**, or **bobo na**, s., the heart (i.e. the mind, the seat of the intellect and affections). The original meaning is seen in the phrase **nakasu naḅo na**, the cartilaginous substance on the front of the throat, lit. the stick, or tree, of the **ḅo** (pectus). [Mg. *fu*, the heart, mind.] A. **bahw'**, the cavity of the chest (pectus).

Ḅoa, v. i., to emit odour; **naḅo**, d. **tamo**, to emit odour, **ḅon**, odour. [Ha. *po*, *puia*, id., My. *bau*, Mg. *fufuna*, odour.] A. **fāḥa**, **fāḥ'a** (**fā'a**), to emit odour.

Bōb', d., father (voc.). See **āb**, **bābu**, &c.

Bobo. See **ḅo na**.

Bobo, v., as **bobo ki atelaġi**, to hail the new moon by making an exclamation or a series of sounds like bo! bo! bo! [Mg. *babababa*, cry, &c.] S. **yabeb**, clanxit, H. **yabab**, Pi. to exclaim, cry out.

Boboi, s., a mask, cover, or disguise; not only a mask for the face, but a cover of the whole body, made of **kaka naniu**, &c., and painted so as to appear terrific (to children); used at the **naleöuan** after the death of a chief when the **naḅea** was set up. Perhaps so called from concealing oneself with the mask or disguise. [To. *fufu*, hide, conceal, disguise.] See **ḅei**, supra.

Bobu, s., redup., d. **bua**, grandfather (voc.), mother's father. See **bua**, **tobu na**.

Bo-fi, and reduplicate

Bobo-fi, v. t., to cover, to be upon a thing, or above it, covering it: see **bau**.

Boġi, v. t., or **buġi**, to overshadow;

Boġor i, v. t., **boġi**, and **ġor i**, to be covering over—see **ġor i**, and **boġi**, infra;

Boġ-kor i, v. t., to be above, over, to overtop, overshadow, as a tree over a smaller plant, a higher chief over a lower (see **kor i**);

Boġi, or **boġ**, s., darkness, night, also 'day' in counting as 'third day', **boġ tolu**, or **moġ tolu**, &c., **te naboġ**, some day, some time, also **nauboġ**;

Boġien, s., darkness;

Boġ, s., a dark black powder, used in painting;

Boġ, a., black, dark. [Sa. *po*, night, ps. *poġia*, to be benighted, Ma. *po*, night season, Hades (from being dark), Ha. *po*, night, darkness, v. to be dark, become night, to be out of sight, hence slain, lost, to overshadow (as the foliage of trees), assemble thickly together, a. dark, dark coloured, ignorant, obscure, An. *piġ*, night, *apiġ*, black, *poïġ*, dark, Ja. *buġi*, night.] A. **faḥuma**, to be black, **fuḥum**, black, **faḥma-t**, night.

Bok, redup. **bokauok**, v. i., onomat., to blow, to pant. [Ma. *puka*, to pant.] H. **puaḥ**, to breathe, to blow, Hi. to pant.

Boka-ti, v. t., to strike, **bisa boka-ti**, to reprehend. [My. *pukul*, Mg. *puka*, strike.] A. **baka'a**, to strike with repeated blows; to cut up; 2, reprehend.

Bokas, s., Hades; **abokas**, c. prep. in Hades. See s. v. **bua**, بقعة.

Bokauoka, redup. of **boka-ti**.

Bokota, v. i., or a., dirty (as water): **ġota**.

Ḅolāf i, d. for **ḅalāf i**, q. v., d. **bolbolāf i**.

Ḅolà sa, d. for **ḅalà sa**, q.v.

Ḅolau ki, to steer (a canoe or ship): **boüolau**.

Bole, d. **buele**, v. i., to be lost, absent: **buele**.

Ḅolo, v. i., or a., to be empty (as a cocoanut): **ḅalo**.

Bōlo, s., a small basket. [Ma. *paro*, a small basket, To. *belu*, a cup.] H. **kpōr**, or **kĕpōr**, a cup, E. **kapar**, a basket.

Bolo, v., to do, redup. **bolofolo**, to do, to act, **nafolōn**, **nafolofolōn**, deeds (doing, acting), work, conduct;

Bolo, d., to behave deceitfully; and

Bolo-si, v. t., to do one, to treat him (as in quarrelling), to treat him, **bolo sā**, **bolo uia ki**, to behave ill, to behave well to. [Fi. *vala, valavala*, v. i., *vala-ta*, v. t., to make or do, *vala*, to fight, *valavala*, s., work, custom, habit.] H. **pa'al**, to make, to do, **po'al**, or **poöl**, deed, act, work, A. **fa'ala**, move oneself, act, do work, do (something to some one), 8, devise (deceit against some one), **fi'l'**, action, work, **fa'i-lat**, custom, n. a. **fa'lat**.

Ḅolïs i, d. for **ḅilis i**.

Ḃolboloa, or **bolŏboloa**, d. for **ḅaleḅalia**, large.

Ḅolōf i, d. for **ḅalāf i**, q.v.

Ḃoloġa, v. i., to turn itself about (as something sinking in water), **tafiloġa**, id. See **bulo ki**.

Bōlu, v. i., to be blunt (as an edged tool). A. **bohira**, to be blunt (as a sword).

Bon, bono, v. i., to be shut, closed, stopped, **bonò sa**, shut because of it, **bon, bonbon**, to crowd together, crowded together:

Bono-ti, or **bonu-ti** (and **mo-no-ti, bunu-ti, munu-ti**), v. t., to shut, close, plug, stop, block up, and

Bōn, a., and s., 1,000, d. **mānu**, 1,000; **bunuti, bunti**, 100. These words denote lit., a gathering, crowd. [Sa. *puni-puni*, shut in, close in, cover over, *punita'i*, to stop with, *tapuni*, to shut, *momono*, to plug, *monoti*, to cork, plug, *puipui*, to shut, Fi. *vuni*, *vuni-taka*, Mg. *afina*, My. *buni*, Fut. *buna*, Epi *mbin*, Ma. *pani*, *papani*, block up, *kopani*, shut to, close up, close in, Mg. *kumbuna*, or *humbuna*, shut, closed, *mikumbuna*, to shut, close, coalesce, Ha. *pani*, to close, shut, stop, Sa. *mano*, a myriad, a great number.] H. **baham, bahan**, A. **bah-hama**, 2, 4, 5, 10, to shut, cover, conceal, be mute.

Bono-ġor i, to crowd together (**ġor i**) about him or it;

Bonbon, d., a., redup. of **bon**, crowded together, **namer bon-bon**, people crowded together.

Boölau. See **boüolau**.

I. **Ḅora i**, or **ḅorai**, v. t., to rend, split open, split; **ḅorai nabati na**, part the teeth, i.e. open the mouth to speak, hence **ḅorai**, to make a noise, **ḅorai-ġoro**, make a noise (as children) about or near (one), **ḅorai-uora-ġoro**, id., dd. **ḅorà-ġoro**, **ḅira-ġoro**, id., **ḅorōrai**, v. t., redup., rend, split open, **elo ḅorōra**, the sun (rising) rending or splitting asunder or bursting through (the clouds), **taḅàre** (taḅàrre), v. r. (passive), to be split open, burst, hence to be open (as a door), **maora**, or **mauora**, redup. **maoräora**, v. i., to be rent, hence **uora**, a place, especially a landing-place for a canoe (perhaps from being an opening or split in the reef), and, therefore, often in names of places, a side (of an island), as, **uora n tan, uora n liġ**, lower, upper side (of Efate), **bora**, a basket woven out of the frond of a cocoanut palm whose stalk is *split asunder*, and the frond itself, **bora**, the sides of the head or face, the temples (which women used to cut and tear open with a sharp shell (**kai**) in mourning for the dead). A. **fara'**, to split, rend, slit, 5, **tafarra'**, to become slit, rent, burst, i.e. open, **faryat**, tumult, clamour.

Bora, s., the temples: ḅora I.

Bora, s., cocoanut leaf, or basket made of it, or plaited for thatching houses: ḅora I.

Borabora, s., cocoanut leaf basket: ḅora I.

II. **Ḅora**, v. i., to spring up, sprout, grow (of plants), be born (of men); **bakauora ki**, v. c., make to ḅora (men and plants), **nauora na, nauorauora na**, offshoot, offspring (of plants and men), **ōra naui**, the vine of the yam; **fara**, a cocoanut (fruit) that begins to shoot. [Motu *vara*, to grow, to be born, Oba *ḅiri*, to grow.] H. **paraḥ** (A. **fariḥ'a**, 2), to break out, burst forth (of the young as issuing from the womb), to sprout, to flourish (a plant), Hi. to cause to do so, sprout, shoot, H. **peraḥ**, sprout, shoot, A. **farḥ'ʼ**, offspring, shoot or sprout.

Ḅora-ḅau, v. and s., over-head, noon, only in the phrase **elo i ḅora-ḅau**, the sun is overhead, lit. splits-head: ḅora I., and ḅau.

Ḅora-ġoro, or **ḅorai-ġoro**, or **ḅorai-uora-ġoro**, to make a tumult, noise near (one): ḅora I.

Ḅorai, s., c. art., the sugar-cane;

Borairai, s., a reed like sugar-cane growing in streams. A. **bara'**, 4, to find sugar-cane.

Ḅora-kai, v. and s., to tear or rend the **kai** (a shell-fish, or its shell): ḅorai I. Men who were worthless and died poor, and had no pigs killed at their death and burial, **ḅora-kai**, in Hades, their jaws being torn and bleeding in doing so.

Ḅora-keso na, s., gills of fish; ḅora I., and **kesa** (dark coloured); dd. **morese na, kurumase na.**

Borau, v. i., to ride or be carried (on a canoe or ship, horse, vehicle, or other thing), to voyage. [Fi. *vodo*, embark, go on board, ride, Sa. *folau*, a voyage, the crew and vessel, To. *felau*, to navigate, make a voyage, a canoe, a fleet of canoes, a voyage, My. *prahu*, *prau*, a canoe, boat, ship, general name for any kind of vessel, *bārprau*, to travel by boat or ship.] A. **markab'**, E. **markab**, a ship, vessel, A. **rakib'**, navigating, voyaging, **rakiba**, to be carried, to ride (A. **markab'**, denotes a vehicle, carrying-beast, chariot, as well as a ship), H. **rakab**, to be carried (on a horse, chariot, the clouds, &c.—so Ef. **borau**).

NOTE.—A. **markab'**, is an infinitive, and therefore is

naturally in Ef. and Fi. a verb, My. and Sa. a substantive, and To. both a verb and a substantive.

Ḅorea, s., c. art. **naḅorea,** a dream, or vision (in sleep);

Ḅorea ki naḅorea, v., to dream a dream, or see a vision (in sleep). [Tah. *ria,* a vision in sleep, Santo *popori,* Lakon *boro,* id.] H. **mar'eh,** a vision (in sleep), A. **rōya,** sleep, what is seen in sleep, from **ra'a'** (H. **ra'ah**), to see, then to have a vision in sleep, E. id.

Bor i, or **bori,** v. t., to break, **bori nakasu,** break a stick, **mauori, mauoriuori,** to be broken, and

Bori-si, redup.

Boriuori-si, v. t., break to pieces. [Mg. *puriṭa,* Fi. *vorota.*] H. **pōr,** inf. of **parar,** to break, break to pieces (**pur,** to break), Hithpolel to be broken.

Ḅorroa, v. i., to grow crooked, for **ḅoraroa: ḅora** II., and **roa.**

Boro-silaia. See **buru masila.**

Boro-aki, v., also **bĭro-aki, bero-aki, baro-aki,** to bequeath to, or order to do (by will, when dying); to commission (one to do something), give orders to. [My. *pâsân,* to commission, enjoin, Sa. *poloa'i,* to leave commands (as on going a journey or dying), to command, Mg. *hafaṭa* (*hafarana*), a will or testament, order, bequeathed, ordered.] A. **waṣa',** 2, to bequeath by will, 4, id., and to give power to, or commission, by will; to command, to enjoin.

Borōri-si, contraction of **boriuori-si.**

Ḅosa i, v. t., to compress, **manu i tumana ḅosa ia,** a bird compresses itself (with its closed wings), **i ḅosai naniu,** he compresses a cocoanut (so as to break the shell), press together, squeeze (as a sponge), hence **ḅosa,** or **uosa,** v. i., to be compressed, i. e. narrow, and **taḅosa** (**sela uosa,** a narrow track, **natamole taḅosa,** a man thin as if pressed together), redup. **uosauosa; ḅosa naru na,** clap the hands, **ḅosa-lot,** clap the hands with a sound, d. **ḅosa ki,** i.q. **ḅosa i.** A. **hamaza,** to press with the fingers or hand, to compress, push, strike, bite, break.

Ḅosaḅosa, s., froth (coming from the mouth, as of one in sickness), sputum, d. **fut.** [Mg. *futafuta,* slaver, spittle, foam, *mifutafuta,* to slaver, to foam.] A. **bozāḳ', bosāḳ',** saliva, sputum.

Ḅosi, v. t., twist (a rope). [Sa. *fusi,* gird, My. *pusiġ,* twist, turn round.] A. **'afaṣa,** to twist.

Ḅota, v. i., and a., to be, or become, different, other, alien;

Ḅota i, v. t., to divide, part,

make one remove from the other, **ḅotauota** (or **ḅotōta**), redup.; **i toko ḅotauota**, he is in the middle or midst, exactly between two things, lit. he is parting or dividing (the two things), **māuota**, or **māota**, to be divided or parted, hence **na maota**, the midst or middle space between two things, i.e. the space by which they are parted, removed, or distant from each other. [My. *beda*, or *bida*, distinct, separate, different, *beda-kan*, to separate, to distinguish, to make a difference.] E. **b'ud**, other, alien, different, A. **ba'oda**, and **ba'ida**, to stand apart, be distant, remote, 2, 4, make to be so, 6, to be apart from each other, also to recede or go apart from some one, 3, make to be apart or distant, also to go apart or be distant, **bo'd'**, distance: cf. **banaḅota**, diverse, different. Hence

Ḅota, s., c. art., a person unmarried (apart);

Ḅotauota, and

Ḅotōta i, v. t., redup. of **ḅota i**.

Ḅotu, v. i., to swell (of a girl's breasts). A. **nabata**, (3) n. a. **nobōt'**, begin to swell (a girl's breasts); (1) to germinate.

Boua (bowa), v. i., to rain, d. for **ḅā**.

Boüa ki (bowa ki), v., d. **uā ki**, to fruit, to produce fruit. Ch. **pērā**, Syr. **pīra**, fruit, v. to bear fruit. See **ua**.

Boüolau ki, v. t., to steer (a canoe or ship), then, fig., to steer a country (**bouolau ki nafanua**), &c., that is, govern it, **bouolau ki emeromina**, govern the world (of God). [Ml. dd. *barau*, *baro*, *walu*, *foro*, Ef. *uolau* (*wolau*) in *bouolau-ki*.] E. **ḥadafa**, to steer (a vessel or ship), then, fig., to govern men, to steer, i.e. govern the world (said of Jesus Christ), **maḥdaf**, rudder, helm. See **uolau**, infra.

Note.—**Boüolau ki** is reduplicate, see **ḅolau ki** (d.), id., and **uolau ki**, and note the pref. **b'** (for m) in **ḅolau**.

Bu, d., verbal pron., 1 pl., excl., dual **moa**: d. **au**, dual **ara**.

Bua, d. **bobu** (q.v.), voc., maternal grandfather. [Fut. *bua*.]

Bu (nalo), v. t., to see (a thing). See **bunu**, **bunu-si**. [Santo d. *vai*, to see.] **Bu**, is for **bunu**. H. **bin**, to discern, perceive, see, n. a. **binah**, for **binat**.

Bu, s., c. art., a bundle. [Fi. *ai vau*.] See **bau-si**.

Bua, v., divide, as, **ta bua i**, cut, divide it (cut it open), **mafua**, and **tabua**, to be rent open, cracked, **ti bua i**, press, rend it (press, burst it open, as new wine old wine skins), and **fai** (or **fae**) in **maġafai**, a half, a division (of a thing), and **lao fai** (see **fai**). [Sa. *vaeġa*, a division, *vaevae*, to divide in parts, cut up, *mavae*, to be split, to be cracked open.] A. **fa'ā**, n. a., **fa'w'**, or **fa'y'**, 1, 4, to split, cleave, 7, to be open, to be separated, rent, cleft.

I. **Bua**, v. i., to be empty, vacant, having nothing (as an empty cocoanut), **tābu**, i.e. **tā bu**, men having nothing, or naked (name applied to the naked people of some neighbouring islands, i.e. people who use no waist cloth). A. **bahiya**, to be empty and bare (as a house).

II. **Bua**, and **bubu**, d. **mobu**, v. i., and a., to be deep (as the sea, or a pit), **i toko bua** (said of a yam down in the ground), **ebu** or **ebua**, in the deep part (of a thing), **i toko ebu**, or **ebua**, and **sofa ni ebu** is consumption or phthisis in the deep part (i.e. inside) of the body (deep-seated); **ebua** and **bokas**, **abokas**, the abyss, Hades, Malo **abua**, id., **buariri**, abyss, Hades (**riri**, to sink), and **buġi**, or **bubuġi**, to sink deep, d. **na tibu**, the deep. [Ma. *kopua*, deep, An. *ubo*, deep, Fi. *tobu*, d. *nubu*, deep.] A. **'amuḳa**, and **ma'uḳa**, 1, to be deep, also, to be distant, far off (**emai**, **ufea**), 4, make deep, 5, to be deep, H. **'amaḳ**, to be deep, **'ameḳ**, **'amīḳ**, deep, **'ămūkah**, A. **'amākat**, E. **'amaḳa**, to be deep, **'muḳ**, deep, **mā'mak**, any depth, a valley, the abyss (Hades).

III. **Bua** or **fua** (in **na fuaġoro**, d. **na mua-ġoro**, a spring on the shore covered by the flood-tide, (so called because the sea **mua ġor ia**, flows over it), and **mua**, v. i., to flow (the tide);

Buafua, v., **na tas i buafua**, or **naroa i buafua**, the sea or current flows or carries things floating on it;

Bua-ti, v. t., to take (make to go);

Buē a, v. t., make to flow upon (a thing), pour upon, moisten. [Ha. *puai*, to flow, as blood from a vein, or water from a fountain, to cast up; to boil up, as water from a spring, My. *buwaġ*, eject, expel, cast.] H. **naba'**, to bubble forth, gush out, Ch., S., A. **naba'**, **naba''**. Cf. A. **ba''a**, to gurgle out (as blood). The connection between the ideas of *going* or *flowing out* and *taking out* (making to go out) is seen in the cg. Ch. **nĕpaḳ**, to go out, caus. to take out, and also in H. **yabal**, to flow, caus. to bring, bear, carry.

Bubu, v. i., to gargle. [Sa. *pupu*, to gargle.] See under preceding word, and cf. A. **ba'ba'**, or **ba'ba'u**, gurgling sound of water flowing from a bottle or flask.

Bua na. See **buĭ na**.

Buġi, and

Bubuġi, v. t., to sink down, to dip (anything) [Ma. *poko-poko,* Ha. *poopoo*], put it down into the water; **uta buġi** rarua, load a canoe *deep*;

Bubu, v. i., to be deep: **bua** II.

Buele, d. **bole**, v. i., to be lost, missing. [My. *ilaġ,* to lose, be lost, missing, Fi. *yali,* Mg. *veri,* lost, missed.] H. **'abad**, Mendaite **awid**, to be lost, missing.

Buġafuġa, v. i., to be awake, to awake, **bugō-ni**, v. t., to awaken one. [Sa. *faġufaġu, fafaġu,* to waken, rouse from sleep, ps. *faġua,* Mg. *fuha, fuhafuha,* imp., awake, *mi-fuha,* v. i., to awake, *mamuha,* v. t., to awake, *fuhazina,* being awakened.] See **bulo, bilo.**

Buġo-ni, v. t., to awaken. See preceding word, and **bulo-ni**, Ch. II. 14. *b*.

Bui na, or **bua na**, s., c. art., backbone, tail, rump. [Fi. *bui,* tail, Fut. *bua,* back, To. *mui,* after, the hindermost end, tip, or extremity of anything, Sa. *muli,* the end, the rump, Mg. *vuhu,* the back.] See **muri.**

Buiġo, or **ḅigo**, v. i., to lose the way, be at a stand, perplexed, not knowing the way. [Compare Sa. *poġi,* to be benighted.] See **boġ.**

I. **Buka**, v. i., to be filled, swell out, as the belly when filled with food, or as a sail filled with wind; **namarita na i buka**, his belly is puffed up or swollen, or pants (with rage), **mafukafuka**, to be swollen or puffed up, **nafu-kāna**, the being swollen or puffed up. [Mg. *vuki,* satiated, filled, *mimuki,* v. i., *mamuki,* v. t., *vukisana, havu-kisana,* My. *bakat,* stuffed, filled, Ma. *puku,* to swell.] A. **nafaḥ'a**, to inflate, 8, to be inflated, to swell, **nafḥ'at'**, inflation of the belly, **man-fuḥ'**, ventrosus; obese;

Būka, s., a swell, as a ground swell. [My. *bakat,* id.] See **buka**;

Buk, s., as **nabuk natamole**, a band of men. [H. *puu,* a gathering or collection, sign of plural number, *he puu kanaka,* a gathering or band of men.] See **buka.**

NOTE.—This word is used in Ef. also for a gathering or collection of things, thus: **nabuk anena i onĭ au**, I am in his debt, but lit. his collection of things (which he has given me) remains on me (i.e. I have not yet repaid it).

II. **Buka-si**, or **bukĭ-si**, v. t., to open, as a roll of cloth, **buka ūa (ūwa)**, open the oven. [My. *buka,* to open, unclose, uncover, Mg. *vuha,* opened, *mimuha,* v. i., *ma-muha,* v. t., to open.] A. **fakka**, v. t., to open.

III. **Buka**, v. i., to bark (a dog), **buka ia**, bark at it,

bukai kusũe, bark at a rat, d. syn. **oro-maki**; also, **buka**, to cough. H. **nabaḥ**, A. **nabaḥa**, to bark (a dog). [Mg. *vuvu*.] Formed from the sound. A. **nabaḥa**, is followed by acc. with or without a prep.

IV. **Buka i**, v. t., to hit upon, meet, fall in with, find, as, **i ba bukai uaġo buele**, he hit upon, met, fell in with, or found a lost pig. H. **paga'**, id., as in Ex. xxiii. 4.

Bukāru, or **bakāru**, d. **fakāru**, v., to joke, jest, **bukāru ki**, v. t., mock, deride. [Motu *kiri*, to laugh, My. *gurau*, to joke, and *kara*, id., *bârgurau*, *mâġgurau*, joke, jest, *mâġgurau-kan*, v. t., mock, deride.] A. **kahara** (5) laugh, joke.

Buko na, s., c. art., protuberance or knob, as **nabuko naui**, protuberance or knob of a yam. [Ha. *puu*.] See **buka** I.

Bukoro, s., enclosure round a house at its base, name of a tree and its fruit (from its kernel being *enclosed*), a proper name (of men). [Ma. *pukoro*, sheath, case, halo, net.] See **koro**.

Bukota, v. i., or a., to be dark-coloured, dirty, blackish (as water with dust or earth in it): **ġota**.

Bukubukura, a., full of little swellings (pimples): **ra**, ending. [Ha. *puupuu*, id.; Sa. *po'u*, pimple, *po'upo'ua*, full of pimples.] See **buka** I.

Bukutu, s., a rise, hill. [Ha. *puu*, id., My. *bukit*, a hill.] See **buka** I.

Bul-meta na, s., eyeball, gleaming part of eye. See **bila**.

Bula, **mbula**, d. for **ḅila**, q.v., big, large.

Būlĕ, a., adult, **nafera būlĕ**, a lot of grown up men (adults). A. **bala''a**, to reach mature or full age, **bāli''**, adult; and

I. **Bule**, v. t., complete, used after other verbs adverbially, as, **i ba bule nafanua**, he went completely through the land, **le bule nagusu**, it (a canoe) completely rounded the point, **nafisan i soka bule nafanua**, the word shot (lit. leaped) through the whole land, from end to end, **noai i sera fule** (or **fulefule**) **nalia**, the water ran completely throughout the place. **Bule** is really a verb, in these instances, in apposition to the verb preceding it, as he went—completed (finished) the land, &c. [My. *bulah*, the whole, To. *fuli*, all.] A. **bala''a**, n. a. **bulū''**, to complete, go through to the end.

II. **Bule**, v. t., to strip off leaves, **ora naui i bule nakasu**, the yam vine strips off leaves from the tree, **mafule**, to be stripped of leaves (a tree). [My. *bulus*, stripped of leaves.] A. **'abala**, 1, 2, to strip off leaves, foliis nudavit *arborem.*

Būle, s., a shell, lit. gleaming, shining, glittering. See **bila.**

Bulĭboġ, d. for **bilĭboġ,** for **bulo boġ : bulo.**

Būlĭ, s., a corpulent person;

Bulia, a., swollen; and

Bulifulia, a., swollen here and there (the body), **a,** a. ending; and **mabulu,** q.v. [Sa. *fula,* stout, *fulafula,* swelling, *fulafula, fufula,* to be swollen.] H. **'afal,** prop. to swell up, be tumid, A. **'afila,** to have a tumour or hernia. See **telatela.**

Bulai, s., d. for **belaki,** and

Bulai, v. t., d. for **belaki,** to gird.

Bulo, d. **buil,** v. i., and s., dawn, break (of day): **iġa uo bulo (bo) mai,** he (or it) will come early, lit. will be early and come: **bulo-boġ,** dd. **buil-bog, bili-boġ,** morning, lit. break of night (day-break); and so **bulo asa, bulo metamai.** [My. *pagi, pagi ari,* morning, early, by times, presently.] H. **boḳer,** morning, dawn, day-break, presently, A. **bukra-t,** id., **bakara,** to be early.

Bulo, v. i., d. for **bilo;**

Bulò-ni, v. t., to awaken; **bulo nameta na,** open his eyes;

Bulobulo i, v. t., awaken him. See **bilo.**

Bulo ki, v. t., to turn, to twist, also **bulosi, bulusi, bulisi; tafolo,** to be turned, twisted, **tafulus,** to be turned, **bologa,** to turn itself (as a thing in sinking in water), **tafīloġa,** id., **bulora,** or **filora,** twisted, confused (as a lot of things turned or twisted about). [My. *pulâs,* Ja. *pulir,* to wring, twist, to turn aside (out of the way), to turn, turn round, Sa. *tafuli,* also, *fuli, fulisia,* turn round, *milo,* to twist, *mimilo, milomilo,* ps. *milosia, milosi,* to be twisted, to be perverse, *milomilosi,* Fi. *mulo-t'a,* to twist a single thread, Ma. *miro,* to spin, twist, Mg. *fuli, fulisina,* and *mamulisa,* id.] H. **palas** (Talmud **palek**), turn round, twist, spin, A. **falakat,** spindle.

Buloi, s., a mask, cover of the face. [Sa. *pulou,* a cover, disguise.] See **malöi.**

Buloki, v. i., or a., to be sticky, d. **bubulu.** See **bulu-ti.**

Bulōra, v. i., or a., to be twisted. See **bulo ki.**

Bulu-si, or **bulosi,** or **bilosi,** v. t., to wash. See **balo-ni.**

Bulusi, bulosi, or **bulisi,** v. t., to turn. See **bulo ki.**

Bulu-ti, v. t., to plaster, overspread with some sticky substance (as lime, oil, paint, pitch), to cover with a plaster or poultice, as a wound, **nabulu,** s., plaster, &c., **bubulu, bulubulut, buloki** (and **mabulu,** q.v.), to be sticky, as plaster; d. **fili,** q.v., hair. [Fi. *bulu-ta,* to bury or cover with earth, to apply an external remedy, *ai bulu*, an external application or thing that covers or buries, Sa. *puluti*, to glue, to pitch, *pulu*, glue, gum, resin, *pulupulu*, to cover the body with a cloth, *pupulu*, to interpose, to mediate, ps. *pulutia*, Fi. *bulu-ta*, to repair an injury, lit. to bury it, *ai bulubulu*, a peace offering, or thing offered as a reparation of an injury.] H. **kapar**, A. **"afara**, to cover, cover over: A. **"afara**, to cover, cover over; to cover (white hairs, with some dye or tincture, Ef. **bulu-ti**); to pardon (sin), 2, to cover with dust, H. **kapar**, to cover, overspread with anything, as with pitch, *to pitch*, Gen. vi. 14 (H. **koper**, pitch); to cover (i.e. pardon) sin, Pi. to make expiation for an offence; A. **"afiru**, hair, &c.

Bulu, bulufulu, and **fulufulu**: **bule** I.

Bulu, v. i., to fall down (as soft fruit from a tree, &c.), **mala bulu**, faint, fall down (a man): **i bulu natano.**

Bulu-aki, v. t., throw (as firewood on the fire, &c.), with a turning motion; and

Bulu-aki, d. for **bulo ki**, to turn, twist.

Bulum, or **buluma**, d. **bulim**, v. i., to be changed, lit. turned: **luma.**

Buma, v. i., d. for **fuġa**, to flower or blossom, **nabuma na**, s., its flower or blossom. [Ml. P. *puġ*, to blossom, *puġan*, its flower or blossom, Sa. *fuġa*, flowers, blossoms, My. *buġa*, flowers, blossoms, Mg. *vuni*, flower, *mamuni*, to blossom.] A. **fuḳaḥ**, flower.

Buna sum i, v. t., to cork, plug, hence

Bunaso, or **funaso**, s., c. art., a cork or plug: see **bono-ti**, or **bunu-ti**, and **sume-li.**

Bunàṣ, d. for **binata.**

Bunofunoi, d. **binofinoi**, v. r., to be confused, perplexed. See **binoinoi**: **noi, no i, nē.**

Būma, s., an insect that makes a shrill sound in the jungle in the evening, hence, **būma i ġai** (the **būma** makes its sound) is often used for 'it is getting dark', 'it is evening'.

Bunu, d. for **fanau**, q.v.

Bunu-li, v. t., d. for **balo-ni, bulu-ni.**

Bunu-si, v. t., to see (a thing). See s.v. **bu.**

Bunu, s., death, destruction, as, **ru sua bunu**;

Bunu e, v. t., to make an end of, to kill or destroy (fish, men, &c.), to extinguish or quench (a fire, or lamp), **ru sua bunu**, they met destruction (having fallen into the sea), **mafunufunu**, and **mafunei**, d. **fanei**, to be ended, to be finished. [My. *bunoh*, to kill, *mambunoh*, *mamunoh*, to kill, Mg. *vunu*, killed, *mamunu*, to kill.] Hence

Bunufunu, redup. of preceding word. See **nu**, to be ended.

Bunu-ti, v. t., same as **bono-ti**;

Bunutia, s., hundred, d. **bunti** (cf. **bon**); and

Bunuta (and **bunta**), v. i., or a., to be silent, lit. to be shut (the mouth), **ba funuta**, be silent, exactly equivalent to the vulgar English 'shut up', hence, **nafunuta**, s., a silent person, one that says little (a term of praise). See **bon**.

Bur, d. for **ḅila**, **bula**, to be big, large.

Būra, or **fūra**, v. i., or a., to be empty, to be devoid of, as, **i bi an fūra**, it is an empty shadow, **a būra ki nalo**, I am empty of the thing, devoid of it, A. fara‘‘a, 1, 2, to empty. See **ḅaro**. Hence

Bura, s., rubbish; **nabura naniu**, the husk of the cocoanut, **nabura na**, the husk or worthless part of a thing: hence the stalk of a fruit (as a worthless thing thrown away as rubbish) is called in different dialects **bura-tena**, **bura-ġitena**, **bara-tuna**, **biri-ġitena**, and **miri-ġitena**, i.e. the **bura** of it.

Bŭra, d. **bĭrĭ**, v. i., or a., to be full, **bakafura**, to fill. [Mg. *fenu*, full, *mamenu*, to fill, My. *pânoh*, full, *mâmâ-nohi*, to fill.] H. mala', to fill, to be full, Pi. · to fill; with another verb, to do anything *fully*, i.e. thoroughly, so Ef. **bera-ti**, d. **bera-kati** (**bera-kati**, d. by transposition for **bera-ti ki**), as **lo b.**, look fully or thoroughly at it, i.e. watch it, **roġo b.**, hear fully, i.e. obey, **i uia b.**, it is good fully, i.e. thoroughly good, and it can also be said **tea berakati na**, i.e. **tea anena berakati**, a thing fully or thoroughly his; A. mala', S. mla', same as H. Hence

Burafura, **furafura**, s., the jungle, forest, vegetation: so called because it fills the land. A place covered with any kind of weeds, &c., is called **nalia bura**, a full place.

Bura-ġitena, and

Bura-tena, see **bura**, s.

Burasa. See **marasa**.

Burau, or **burou**, s., the sky: H. **marom**, above, heaven.

Bure i, **fure i**, or **burē**, **burei ki**, **furei ki**, v. t., to wash, rub, as, **bure naui**, wash off the earth from a yam, **furei ki natuo na**, cleanse his feet, **furei ki lu nasoġa**; **bure biakik**, wash, cleanse a child, **bure nabau na ki naroro**, rub his hair with oil, oil his hair. [Fi. *bore-a*, to scrape, or wash the dirt off a thing, to brighten.] H. maraḳ, (rub), polish, cleanse by washing or anointing (cgg. maraḥ, &c.).

Bure i, or **bura i**, v. t., d., to leave, allow, forsake, abandon. A. **bara'**, 3, to leave, abandon. [My. *bir*, to permit, allow.]

Burei, d. **marağ ki**, v., to spit out, to spit, to spit on. E. **waraḳa**, to spit, **mĭrāḳ**, spittle.

Bur i, buri, v. t., to pierce, stick, **buri uaġo**, stick a pig: d. for **biri**. [Ma. *wero*, id.] E. **barara**, to stick, stab.

Buria, v. i., or a., to be swollen (of the body), to have the dropsy. [Ma. *kopurua*, dropsical, My. *buru*, elephantiasis, *burut*, hernia.] The **a** in **buria** is the a. ending. A. **nabara**, to raise up, heap up, 8, to swell, **nabrat**, a swelling on the body.

Būria (bauria, bouria), v., to kindle or make a fire (in the oven), **ru būria ua (uwa)**, and **ru būria**, they make a fire in the oven, or, simply, they make a fire, kindle up: this is done every evening about an hour before sunset. See **bara** (H. **ba'ar**).

Buroġ, v. i., or a., offensive, mouldy, filthy (as food). [Ma. *puru*, mouldy, and *kopuru*, *kopurupuru*, id.] A. **mara''a**, to be contaminated.

Buru masila, v. i., to roar (of thunder), **tifai i buru masila**, d. **boro silaia**, the thunder roars, or thunders sounding: for **masila** and **silaia**, see **sila**. [TaSa. *biri*, Mg. *varaṭa*, thunder, and to thunder, Ml. P. *omburumbur*, Ml. A. *amburambur*, to roar (of thunder), Ml. P. *berver*, thunder.] A. **barbara**, to roar.

Būru, burufūru, v. i., or a., to be short: d. **m̈īto**, q.v.

Buruma ki, or **bĕruma** (or **bĭruma**) **ki**, v., to be in the relation of son-in-law to parent-in-law, or of parent-in-law to son-in-law, syn. **monaki** (**monaki**);

Burumà, or **birumà**, c. art. **naburuma**, s., one in that relation, son-in-law, mother-in-law, father-in-law: see **m̈o na**. One greatly reverences his **buruma**, and holds him so that he will not approach him. For the derivation of this word, see Index for the word **m̈o**.

Busa, v. i., or a., redup. **busafusa**, to be young, springing up (of plants and animals), hence to be inexperienced, foolish, to be spotted (the skin, as with cold, &c.). [My. *mud'a*, young, immature, not deep in colour (light), foolish.] A. **wabis'a**, to be spotted (with white and black spots, as the nails or skin), 4, to germinate, or put forth plants (the soil).

Būsa, s., or a., dumb, mute. A. **yabisa**, to be arid (see **bēs**), 4, to be silent, mute.

Busa, a., orphaned, **meta busa**, orphan. A. **yabisa**, to be arid, dry. An orphan is called **meta busa**, because deprived of its mother's milk. See **bēs, bēsu**.

Busi, v., i.q. **ḅosi**, q.v.

Busĭ, v. i., to blow, spout (as a whale). [Sa. *pusa*, to send up a smoke (also applied to spray, dust, and heat), Tah. *puha*, to blow (as a whale), *puhepuhi*, to blow out of the mouth, blow, as with bellows, Ha. *puhi*, to blow or puff, breathe hard, blow a trumpet, &c., Mg. *fufuṭa*, blowing the bellows, *mifufuṭa*, to blow the bellows, My. *âmbus*, to blow, make a current of air, *âmbusan*, bellows, *âmbusi*, to blow, drive, a current of air.] A. **nafat'a**, i. q. **nafaḥ'a**, to blow with the mouth, blow out, puff, eject venom from the mouth (as a serpent), eject spittle (a man).

Busa, s., **nabusa**, a mist. See under preceding word.

Bus i, v. t., d., to lay down, leave, abandon ;

Busfus ki, d., redup., d. for **bure i**, or **bura i**, q.v.

Busi, or **fusi**, v. t., d. for **muri**, q.v. [Mg. *fudi*, returned, sent back.]

Busa i, or **fusa i**, v. t., break or smash to pieces, smash (as a yam), **mafusai**, ps. [Mg. *pușița*, and *pușika*.] H. **puș**, or **fuș**, to break in pieces.

Buta ki, d. for **milei**, q.v.

Buta, d., in **meta-buta**, blind, lit. eye dark. [Fi. *matabuto*, faint, *buto*, darkness, My. *buta*, blind.]

Buta, or **futa**, v. i., to spring up or out, as water from a spring ; to spring up or out, as smoke from a fire ; to spring out, as a musket ball from a wound—**i sī buta i**, he shot him, the bullet springing out from, or glancing off his body, wounding but not fatal ;

Butafuta, d. **futfut**, redup., to spring up or out, as water from a spring ;

Butu-raki, or **butĭ-raki**, d., v. i., to appear, come in sight. [Ma. *puta*, v. i., pass through, in or out, come in sight, My. *târbit*, to issue, come out, emanate, spring, arise, appear, escape.] A. **nabaṭa**, to spring up or out, as water from a spring, 4, ps. form, to appear, go or come forth, come in sight.

Butāki, dd. **mitāki**, **milāi**, q.v.

But, d. for **ḅota**, unmarried.

But i, or **buti**, or **futi**, v. t., to pluck, as a fowl, pluck out or up, as weeds, **mafuta**, to be plucked. [Fi. *vuti-a*, to pluck feathers, hairs off animals, hence, to pull up grass or weeds, Sa. *futi*, to pluck feathers or hairs, *fufuti*, ps. *futia*, My. *bantun*, to pluck, pull out.] A. **namaṣa**, 1, 2, to pluck out, as hairs.

Buti (for **ba-uti**), v., d. for **bakauti**, q.v. [Mg. *vita*, completed, finished, *mamita*, to finish.]

Bute (**lua i**), v. t., to praise. A. **madaḥa**, to praise.

Ḅuti na, **ḅiti na**, s., germ, knob or excrescence growing on a tree, a joint (from its bulging out). See **ḅotu**, and **buto**.

Butili, **bitili**, **fitili**, v. r., to

speak of each other, speak of one behind his back: **tili**.

Buto, v. i., to germinate, bud. A. **nabata**, germinate. Hence

Buto na, s., bud, d. **muto na**.

Buto na, s., navel, then middle; **malēbuto** (lit. the place of the middle), the middle (of the body, a land, anything), d. **but**, hence d. **tu-but**, rainbow, lit. stand in the middle (of the sky). [TaSa. *buto*, navel, *taġa nabute*, stomach, To. *bito*, Sa. *pute*, Tah. *pito*, navel, Tah. *pitopito*, a button, My. *pusat*, Mg. *fuiṭa*, the navel.] A. **bugrat** (or **bujrat**), the navel, a knob.

Butol, v. i., d. for **bitelo**, q.v.

Butua, v. t., d. for **bitua**, q.v., to place, lay down, give; **tā bituatua**, to speak (or pray) while giving (or laying down) an offering (to the **natemate**). Hence

Butut, s., a place where offerings to the **natemate** are put: now used for 'altar'.

NOTE.—The verb **butua** or **bitua** is the reflective of **tua**, q.v.: **bā butua ki**, go backwards and forwards between two things, to halt between two opinions.

Buturaki. See under **buta**, supra.

E, article, for **a**, sometimes **i**: **a, nĕ, na, in**.

E, dem., this, that, as **mal e** (for **mala uai**), that time, then: **e** is a contraction for **uai**: **raġ uai**, this time, now. See **i** (d.), dem. This **e**, or **i**, is used also as a tense particle—see **i**.

E, or **i**, prep., in, on; t. prep.: **na, nĭ, a, î**. [Sa. *i*, in, at, with, to, from, for, of, on, on account of, concerning, Ma. *i*, of, &c., and t. prep., My. *i*, t. prep., Fi. *e*, or *i*, in, with or by (instrumental).] A. **li**, H. **lĕ**, T. **nĕ**, Gurague **ya**, or **ia**.

Ē, inter. ad., where? See **sē**.

Ei, ad., yes. [Mg. *ei*, Sa. *e*, id.] A. **ey**, or **ei**, yes.

Ei à, or **ei ia**, ad., yes, that's it: preceding word, and dem.

Ei eri, ad., d. syn. **ei à**: **ei**, and **eri**, dem.

Ei, ad., here, d. **i**, q.v.

Ēï (ē-i), ad., no, it is not. [Er. *ēyi*, Mg. *ai*, id.] Neg. ad. **e**, and **i**, dem. H. **'i**, E. **'i**, not.

Eba, v. See **tali-eba, tali-ofa**.

Ebau, ad., at the head (of the island, i.e. the east), opp. to **etu**, at the foot (west); **e**, prep., and **bau**.

Eḅaġo, ad., in the end (of the house), inside: **e**, prep., and **ḅaġo**.

Ebua, or **ebu**, ad., in the deep: **e**, prep., and **bua** II. Also **ebua**, s., the abyss, Hades.

Ebut, d., in the middle; **e**, prep., and **but**, d. for **buto**, q.v.

Eġura, s., the stick used for spreading (scraping) out the heated stones of the oven : e, art., and ġura i.

Eis, ad., same as ais.

Eka na, s., a relative, family connection. See aka.

Ekatema, ad., on the outside of the house, outside: e, prep., and katema, q.v.

Eksakes, d. for kesakesa, q.v.

Eko, s. See neko.

Ekobu, ad., in the inside, in the house, inside: e, prep., and kobu.

Elà, d. for elau.

Elaġi, ad., and s., above, heaven: e, prep., and laġi, q.v.

Elalo, or elalu, ad., in front, before: e, prep., and lalo, or lalu, see alo, or alu na.

Elau, ad., on the sea, by the sea: e, prep., and lau.

Ēlo, s., d. ālo, the sun: āli.

Elo, or èl', v. i., to be sweet, pleasant, agreeable, redup. lolo. [Ha. *olu*, to be pleasant, agreeable.] A. ḥalā', ḥalw', id.

Elol, ad., d., in the belly, inside: e, prep.. and lol. [Ma. *roto*.] Ef. dd. rōăra, lōġa. A. rawṭ'o, رَوْضٌ garden, enclosure, lake, pool.

Emai (or emai), ad., in the distance, afar, far away; d. ufēa: e, prep., and mài. [Sa. *mao*, *mamao*, to be far off, distant, *mamao*, ad., far off, distant.] A. ma'oḳa, to be far off, distant, ma'ḳ', distance.

Emalebuto, ad., in the middle, inside: e, prep., and malebuto na.

Emate n, s., d. for namatiġo na, the grave: matĕ.

Enea, or inia, d., personal pron., 3 sing., he, she, it, dd. nai, niġā, kinini;

Enera, or inira, pl. of preceding word, they, dd. nāra, niġar, kiniara. See Ch. V.

En', vulgar pronunciation sometimes heard for nunu, to wipe, rub off.

Enĭ, v., d. for anĭ, contracted en, an, to abide, be.

Enu, pers. pron., 1 sing., I, dd. anu, kinau, kinu, keino.

Ère na, or èrĭ na, d., mother. See s.v. ani na, note.

Erai, dem., d., this: arai.

Eri, dem., this. See arai.

Erik, dem., this, here. See s. arai and ka.

Eru, dem., same as eri, d. nro, nra.

Ēru, s., c. art. nĭēru, arms, war: āru na.

Esān, ad., here, there, and

Esānien, id., and

Esās, id. : e, prep., and the demonstrative particles se, na, q.v. See ais (eis). [My. *sini*, *sika*. here, *sana*, *sanan*, *situ*, there, and with prep. *disini*, here, *disana*, *disitu*, there, Mg. *atu*, *etu*, *ati*, *eti*, here.]

Eseġa. See asaġa.

Esike, s., a forked stick, that which sike-ti, grasps, seizes: sike-ti, e, art.

Esai, or esei, s., the open, open space, d. esai leba, a road, lit. big open space: sai.

Ēso, or **ēsa**, d., ad., yes: **ei** (supra), and **so** or **sa**, dem.

Ēsu, d., ad., outside, away, **e**, prep. and **su**. [Cf. Fi. *esau* (*e sau*), on the outside, *sausau*, outskirts, *sausau kei vuravura*, ends or outsides of the earth.] H. **ḳĕṣu**, or **ḳṣu**, only pl. **ḳaswē**, **ḳiṣwoth**, ends or extremities (of the earth), A. **ḳaṣā'**, n. a. **ḳaṣw'**, **ḳaṣā'**, to stand apart, be afar off.

Esuma, ad., in the house, at home: **e**, prep., and **suma**.

Ēt, v. i., or a., d., to be many, dd. **kötĕ**, **kaüota**, to be great, plentiful. H. **kabad**, **kabed**, id.

Etaku, ad., at the back, behind. [Sa. **i tua**, **id.**] **E**, prep., and **taku na**.

Etan, ad., on the ground, down: **e**, prep., and **tano**, the ground.

Etu, ad., at the foot (of the island, i.e. the west, opp. to **ebau**): **e**, prep., and **tua na**, the foot.

Ēüo (**ēwo**), ad., no, it is not: **e**, as in **ēï**, and **uo**, dem.

Ëuta, ad., on shore, ashore, on land, opp. to **elau**: **e**, prep., and **uta**.

Fa (and **fĕ** or **fĭ**), inter. pron., in **safa**, **sefa**, what? also where? It is **ma** in **matuna**, q.v. A. **ma'**, H. **mah**, what? See Ch. V. 4.

Fäa na, s., d. **mao na**, the thigh: see **mao**.

Fa, or **ba**, q.v., to go.

Fafa-si, v. t., redup. of **ba-si**, q.v., to tread upon (of many).

Fā, d. for **mau**, in **mal fā nin** = **male mau ua** = this very time, now.

Fafan, for **bafano**, to wash the hands.

Fafaġa, redup. of **faġa**, q.v.

Fāfatu, v. r., to trust, confide, **fafātu isa**, to trust or confide in him, or in it. See under **fatu**.

Fafīne, s., d., a woman, and, a., female. See Ch. V. 17. *c*, for this word in the Oceanic dd., and in A.

Faġan i, v. c., same as **baġan i**, q.v. Hence

Faġafaġa, v., redup., and

Faġafaġa, s., a bait, and

Faġa, s., that which is given to eat, food; a present, a bribe.

Fai (**vai**), c. art. **nĭfai**, dd. **noai** (**n'uai**, i.e. **n'wai**), **nai** (**n'ai**), s., water. [An. *inwai*, Er. *nu*, Ml. *nue*, Epi *ue*, Sa., Fut. *vai*, Ma. *wai*, Bouru dd. *wai*, Ceram dd. *wai*, My. *ayer*, i.e. *ay* (*ai*), and *er*.] H. **ma'** unused in sing., pl. **maïm**, construct, **mē'**, water; Nm. **mâi**, E. **mai**, water. For My. **er**, v. Ef. **elo**, **èl'**.

Fai, v. t., d., divide or cleave, as **lao fai**, plunge into, cleaving (with a spear): **bua**, to divide, cleave, and see also **maġa-fai**.

Fai, s., a skate (fish). [Cf. My. *pari*, Tag. *pagi*, skate fish.] Der. unknown.

Fakal i, same as **bakal i** I. Hence

Fakal, a. (in active sense) **kano fakal**, a comforting person, comforter (in passive sense), **uaġo fakal**, domestic or tame animals, lit. pigs cared for, or taken care of.

Fakalo, or **fakal**, s., war. [My. *bârkalahi* (*kâlahi*), to fight, to quarrel, *kâlahi*, fight, quarrel.] (Mahri ghorat, war), H. **garah**, Hith., to make war (with any one).

Fakamatua, s., c. art., an ancient story: **matua, tuai.**

Fakamauri, i.q. **bakamauri**, q.v.

Fakaraġo, s., c. art., the rough prickly scab that covers a sore: **raġo. Faka-raġo**, d. **kafa-raġo**, for which it is transposed. For **kafa**, see **kafa i**, infra.

Fakaroġo, i.q. **bakaroġo.**

Fakaru, i.q. **bakaru**. See **bukaru.**

Fakaruku, s., the under part, as, **na fakaruku ki nakasu**, the under part of a tree (i. e. shade or shelter under its overhead foliage), **ki nauot**, (fig.) the shelter or protection of a chief: **rukua** (and the caus. prefix), q.v.

Fakasa, s., a festival: **bakasa.**

Fakataliġa, s., an ear pendant: caus. prefix, and **taliġa**, q.v.

Fakatokoi, or **fakatokei**, i.q. **bakatokoi.**

Fakau, or **fakaua**, s., d. **fikau, fikaua**, a messenger, ambassador, agent sent to do something for a chief or community; and

Fakau, or **fakaua**, s., a message such as the agent sent by a chief or a community carries to deliver, **i ofi nafakaua**, he carries the message (of state). See **kau, ġau**, grasp, take hold of, carry, &c. [Sa. *fe'au*, to send for (v. r.), *fe'au*, a message, To. *fekau*, to bid, command, order; a message, order; My. and Ja. *pâġgawa*, a grandee, a noble: In Java it is the title of the five chief councillors of state, and the word is derived from *gawa*, to bear or carry, convey, bring, Ef. *kau*, to carry (as a club), Fi. *kau-ta*, to carry, Sa. *'au*, to send, *'au mai*, to bring, *'au'auna*, a servant.]

Fāla, s. (see under **ḅala** II), a ship's yards.

Falafala, s., cross sticks fastened on a tree for a ladder to climb it: **ḅala** II.

Falea, s., a cave. [Tah. *farefare*, a., hollow, *fare*, a house, Ma. *whare*, Sa. *fale.*] See **ḅala** III.

Fām i, or **bām i**, v. t., to eat. [Tah. *amu*, to eat.] H. **pa'am**, A. **fa'ama**, to have the mouth full, to swallow down.

Fanau sa, v. t., d. **bunu**, to teach, to instruct: to preach. [Fi. *vunau-t'a*, to admonish, harangue, preach to.] H.

'anah, to harangue, proclaim, preach, admonish.

Fanauen, s., c. art., the teaching, i.e. either the act of teaching or the thing taught, law (as 'law' of Moses, recent use).

Fanei, v. i., d., to be extinguished, out (of a fire): see **bunu e, bunue.**

Fānu, s., d., darkness, shade, only in **kot-fānu**, evening, lit. time of shade, d. **raġ mēlu.** See **mēlu**, and under **ġota fanu**, infra.

Fanua, s., inhabited country, land, My. **bânua**, id. [Malo *vanua*, house, Santo d. *venua*, house, village.] H. **banah**, to build, as a house, ps. part. **banu'**, built, **binyaha**, building; A. **bana'**, S. **bna'**.

Note.—The Santo word has best preserved the primary meaning 'house', or 'building'; then a country, district, or land is called **bânua**, or **fanua**, because, like a house or village (or building), it is the dwelling-place of men, or place of buildings.

Fāra ki nameta na, v. t., to fix the eyes, stare with open and motionless eyes. Nm. **fagar**, 2, fix (the eyes), stare.

Fara, s., c. art., a cocoanut (fruit) that begins to shoot. [Cf. Fi. *vara*, a cocoanut ready to shoot.] Ḅora II.

Fara, s., a chafed place on the skin, especially on the thigh (from being rubbed or chafed in walking): **baro-si.**

Fara, or **fera**, s., a row, or rank, or band;

Farafara, or **ferafera**, s., a row, a lot, a band (as of sores on a limb), lit. a number of rows;

Bifara ki, or **bifera ki**, v. c., to put or arrange in rows. [My. *baris*, a line, row, rank, file, troops, *mâmbaris*, v., and *baris kan*, v., and *bârbaris*, v., *barisan*, parade, place where troops are exercised.] H. **ma'arakah** (and **ma'arot'** for **ma'arakot'**), disposing, ranging in order, a row or pile, battle set in array, army, or band; from **'arak**, to arrange in order, or in a row.

Fara-bule, s., c. art., a rank, row, or band, of adults or full-grown men: **fara**, rank, and **bule**, adult.

Fara-kāl, c. art., a row or band of men connected together by relationship, as of brothers: **fara**, and **kal**, see **bakal i.**

Faràti, s., c. art., sticks fastened above and upon the rafters of a house: a pr. name (the name of the chief of Sesake, the chief binding the people together as the **nafaràti** (lit. that which binds together) do a house). [My. *bâroti*, rafters, Fi. *vorati*, upper cross beams of a house.] From **bara-ti**, q.v. H. **ḥibar** (E. **aḥabara**, v. c.), to bind together, connect or join together, H. mĕḥabĭrot, couplings.

NOTE.—In d. rub (raf)=d. farati; and in d. rau (for raf) is rafter, which in another d. is tokai.

Fare, farefare. See **bare, barefare,** to move.

Farea, s., the public house of a village, d. **fare,** outside. [Mota *varea,* outside, Ml. P. *vere,* Ur. *vari,* outside, Mg. *ivelani,* outside (*i-velani*).] A. **barriyy',** outer, external (Ct. **barri**), Nm. **barrâni,** outer, exterior (and **barra,** out).

Farea, d. for **bi reko,** to be poor: **reko;** and **bi,** to be.

Farofaro, a., **tea farofaro,** a thing that rasps, &c.: **barosi.**

Fāsi, i.e. **fa-si,** v. t., tread upon, **fasi koro,** bind together the reeds of the **koro-**fence (which is done by treading upon them): **basi.**

Fasu (na meta na), s., d., eyebrows, **tafasi,** v. r., to make a sign with the eye. A. **ʿʿamaza,** to make a sign (with the eye, eyebrows), 6, make such signs to each other.

Fasu, fasua na, s., a part, portion; member (of the body). [Sa. *fasi,* a piece, a place, *fasifasi,* to split up in pieces, *fasi,* to split, beat.] H. **baṣaʿ,** cut in pieces, A. **baṣ'aʿa,** cut, cleave, **baṣ'ʿat,** part, a piece. (Cg. H. **badad,** to divide, **bad,** a part, pl. members of the body, A. **badda,** separate, disjoin, **budd',** portion, part (of anything), **badād',** part. See s. v. H. **badad.**)

Fātă, s., a bench, shelf, stand, platform, dd. **uēnr', uērĕ, uētĕ, kofeta.** [Sa. *fata,* raised house for storing yams in, a shelf, a bier, Tah. *fata,* altar, scaffold, piece of wood to hang baskets of food on, &c., Mg. *vaṭa* (and *vata*), box, shelf for keeping rice, &c.] H. **ʿomed,** platform, place, **ʿemdah,** a lodging (place). See **fatu.**

Fatok, same as **batok** and **matok: toko.**

Fatu, same as **batu** and **matu: tu.**

Fatu, hence **fafatu,** v., to trust in, rely upon, confide in; **fāta** (see ante); **ġ'ofita,** or **kofeta,** to be sticky, gluey, wet and sticky. [Sa. *faafatu-fatu,* to persevere indefatigably, *fatu* (*-amoa*), to have a swollen shoulder (from bearing burdens), Mg. *feta, fetaka, petaka,* sticky.] A. **ʿamada** 1, 2, 3, to sustain, prop up, make firm or stable, with a column, to be wet and sticky, 8, to rely upon, trust or confide in (**fāfàtu**); also, 1, to have the hump or the back contused with carrying (*a camel*), H. **ʿamad,** to stand (be firmly set), confide in, endure, persist, persevere, (cf. Sa.), A. **ʿimād,** higher structures, column, stake, **ʿamōd',** prop, column, stones put in the ground for supports for the foundation, column, prop of a family, chief, lord, the back, 'amīd', column and chief or prince (of a people), H. 'amūd, column, pillar, platform, scaffold. See **fāta** (ante).

Fatu, s., stone. [Mg. *vatu*, Ml. d. *var*, My. *batu*, Sa. *fatu*, id.] H. eben, E. ĕbān, stone.

Fatu, s., c. art. **nafatu**, the ridge of a house, ridge-pole: see **bātu**. [TaSa. *papatu*, id., Malo *uobatu*, id., Ml. U. *uobut*.] See **batu**, supra.

Fatuna, s., and ad., d. for **matuna**, q.v.

Fau, same as **bau**, q.v., a., new.

Faulu, s.. barter, i.q. **baulu**, q.v.

Faum, d. **fau**, new; **na faumuen**.

Faus i, same as **baus i**, ask, question; hence

Faus, pr. n. (Questioner), a spirit, officer of **Saritau** at the gates of Hades.

Fe, and **fefe**, same as **be**, **befe**; **nafeāna**, **nafefeana**, s., the act of reading, or counting.

Fĕ, conj., if, should, for **bĕ**.

Fe, d., conj., then, but. A. **fa**, id.

Fēa, same as **bē**, or **bēa**, to precede, first.

Fefe, same as **befe**.

Fēī, or **fē**, d., inter. pron., who? [Sa. *o ai*, Tah. *o vai*, id.] See Ch. V. 4. (2).

Feifei ki, same as **beifei ki**; **nafeifeien**, s., the act of indicating or showing, or the thing by which something is made manifest; a sign, token. See **bei ki**.

Feko, s., a cockroach, and similar insects.

Felak, s., c. art., d., a tribe, or family clan, dd. syn. **metarau**, **kainaġa**: **ḅala** III.

Felaki, s., c. art., girdle to which the **nafon**, or loin cloth, was attached: it is about six inches wide: **belaki**.

Fera, c. art., a row. See **fara**.

Fera-bule, **fera-kāl**. See **farabule**, **fara-kāl**.

Ferafera, rows. See **farafara**.

Fera, c. art., s., an omen, also **fefera**; the **natamole tabu**, having poured out some **namaluk** (**kava**) to the **natemate**, drinks off his own cup, and then looking into it sees some blood, or a human hair, or some other thing, which is called **fera**, an omen, or indication, good or bad, as the case may be: or he perceives the omen, good or bad, by '**lo namo**', which is another species of divination.

Fefera ki, or **fera ki**, and **bifera ki**, v., to show by a **fera**, as the **natemate** are supposed to do (see under the preceding word); to give an omen. [Mg. *fambara*, an omen, presage, My. *fāl*, omen (A.).] A. **fa'l'**, omen.

Fera, v. i., **fera ki**, v. t., **fera**-

fera, v. i., ferafera ki, v. t.: see **bera**.

Feroa, c. art., s., a crumb, food, H. **biryah,** food.

Fet, s., a bird's nest, made like a platform of woven twigs. [Sa. *fataniğa,* a nest.] See **fāta**.

Feta, c. art., s., a tribe: **beta**.

Fete, or **fite,** c. art. **nafete,** inter. pron., what? Nm. **maḍe,** what?

Fetta, s., soapstone, a soft stone that can easily be cut: **fatu,** stone, and **ta,** to cut.

Fi, v., to be: **bi**.

Fiàro ki, v., to go into the presence of some one, to be unabashed (opposite of **maliàre,** or **malière**). See **rairai**.

Fiatu, v. r., to smite each other, to fight, war: **atu**.

Fière, v. r., d., to speak, converse. A. **ḥāra,** 6, to converse, talk together.

Fifi, s., anything binding round, as a fillet or turban, &c., then a thing going round, as a ship round a cape or island, then hostile talk (with which one's adversary as it were binds him round);

Fifi ki, v. t., to go round, as a yam vine round a stake, a ship round an island: **fifi,** is for **fifisi,** redup. of **fisi,** q.v.

Fifis i, v. t., to bind round: redup. of **fisi**.

Fikit, or **fikat,** v. r., to be savage, given to biting, lit. to bite each other: **kat i.** [Fi. *veikata,* id.]

Fikoba, v. r., lit. to chase, or pursue, each other: **koba-si**.

Fili, s., d., hair, feathers, &c. [Po. *fulu, hulu, huru,* Mg. *vulu,* My. *bulu,* id.] See s.v. **bulu**.

Fĭlĭ, or **fĭlă,** c. art., same as **bĭla,** lightning: **bila.** [Sa. *uila,* My. *kilat,* Mg. *helaṭa,* id.]

Fĭlĭfĭlĭ, s., a gleaming or flashing shell worn as an ornament: **bila**.

Filora, same as **bulora,** and, redup.,

Filifilora. See **bulo ki**.

Fimeri, v. r., to be doing something to each other, usually in a hostile sense, to be fighting: **meri**.

Fimuri, v. r., to be returning each other, dismissing with presents, repaying: **muri**.

Finağa, c. art., s., food: **kan i.** [For other Oceanic forms of this word, see the lists of Codrington and Ray. Mg. *hinana,* id.]

Firā-ni, v. t., supplicate, or pray, him, and without object, **firā,** to supplicate, pray, also **bifirā, bifirā-ni.** [Tah. *pure,* to pray, *pupure,* to pray frequently.] H. **falal,** Hithp., to supplicate, pray.

Firaka, v. i., to delay. A. **'araka,** (5), to delay.

Fisa, v., **fisan,** c. art., s., to speak, word: **bisa**.

Fis i, or **fisi,** v. t., to bind round, to bind about, as a fillet, turban, or vine round the head, a string round a parcel, a bandage round a wounded limb; **fisi namanuk**, to bind up a wound; a yam vine binds round a stake (twines round it), and **fisi namē**, to twist a rope (bind round the one strand on the other—this is usually **bulo ki**); a whip or rod binds round the body to which it is applied, hence **tale fisi**, to flog (see **tale**, to go round), lit. to go round binding about, d. **mafisi**, to whip, flog: often the final **s** is elided, hence **fi-ġote-fi**, to flog him to pieces (for **fisi-ġote-fi**), lit. to flog—break him, and see **fifi** (supra), and **tafifi**; the word of an adversary is said to **fisi** the object of his anger, that is, bind him round; **fisi uaġo**, bind round a pig (in order to its being carried slung to a pole, so that it may not be hurt). [Sa. *fisi*, to entwine as a vine, To. *fi*, to twist, and *fihi*, entwine, twist, Ma. *whiwhi*, be entangled, *whakawhiwhi*, wind round, fasten, My. *pusig*, to turn round, twist.] H. **ḥabas'**, to bind, bind on, bind about, as a head band, turban, tiara, 'the seaweed is bound about (**fisi na bau ġu**) my head,' Jon. ii. 6; to bind up a wound, to bind fast, shut up; cf. (A. **'afaṣ**), **ḅosi**, q.v.

Fisi, a. used as s., **i bi fisi** (a boy that is circumcised, **ru tefe a i bi fisi**, they circumcise him, he is **fisi**). A. **'afṣa'u**, e praeputio apparentem habens glandem *puer*, **faṣa'a**, a glande *praeputium* reduxit puer.

Firi na, c. art., s., d. **fiti na**, q.v.

Firi, or **fir i**, v. t., same as **bir i**, q.v., to make void, bring to nought; hence

Firi, in **tale-firi**, round-bringing to nought, i. e. all round.

Firiġi, same as **biri-ġi**, to carry.

Fisau na, s., d., as **nafisau naui** = **ora naui**, the sprout, shoot, or vine of a yam: **bisau**.

Fisĭko na, s., flesh. H. **basar**, Ch. **bisra**, or **bisĭrā**, flesh. [TaSa. *vescko*, id.]

Fīso, c. art., s., an annual reed-like plant whose top is used for food. [Sa. *fiso*, a species of reed.] Der. unknown.

Fisuaki, same as **bisuaki**.

Fisueri, same as **bisueri**.

Fisuraki, c. art., s., talk, speech: **bisuraki**.

Fisurakien, c. art., s., the act of talking: **bisuraki**, q.v.

Fisurua, c. art., s., a lie, or lies; and

Fisuruen, c. art., s., lying: **bisuru**, q.v.

Fiti na, c. art., s., d. **firi na**, the rib, or ribs, side. [Er. *mperi*, Santo d. *porcra na*, Ma. *rara*, Mafoor *raar*, rib.] H. **ṣela'**, Ch. **'ala'**, rib, side, A. **ṣ'il'**, rib.

Fitaua, c. art., s., d. syn. with **fakaua** or **fikaua**: **tau**.

Fīt, v. i., d., to run. A. **fadda**, to run.

Fite, interr. See **nafete**.

Fitèriki, or **biteriki**, s., an old woman, matron, lady, as **màriki**, an old man, senior, sir: **māriki** is **mā'**, man, and **riki**, old, and **fitèriki** is **fite**, woman, and **riki**, old: for **fite**, see under **fafine** and **matu**; and for **riki**, old, what follows. [Ma. *ariki*, *first-born* male or female in a family of note, hence *chief*, *priest*, *leader*.] E. **lĕhĕḳa**, to advance in age; be the first-born, or eldest, in a family; be senior; **alhaḳa**, to grow old, **lhīḳ**, advanced in age, aged; contracted **liḳ**, chief.

Fitefa, same as **bitefa**.

Fitili, same as **butili**.

Fitia, same as **ḅitia**, q.v.

Fito na, s., d., syn. **ḅile-meta na**, q.v.: **buto**, v. i., and **buto**, s., bud.

Fo, d. for **bo**, q.v., particle used in the formation of the future tense.

Fōġa, s., d. **nāfo**, whetstone, grinding stone, and (because used as whetstone) pumice stone. [To. *fuaġa* (Ma. *hoaġa*, Sa. *foaġa*), a grindstone, a whetstone, *fuafuaġa*, pumice stone.] See **nāfo**.

Fōna, c. art., s., d. syn. **tofe**, the native cloth, or clothing, made from the bark of a tree. [E. Mai *funa*, id.] See **bono-ti**.

Fōnu, s., the turtle or tortoise. [Fi. *vonu*, My. *pãñu*. Mg. *fani*, Ha. *honu*, Sa. *volu*, To. *fonu*.] A. **'āwinat, 'ayinat**, the tortoise or turtle.

Fu, v. i., d. for **mu**, to hum, buzz, **laġo fu**, humming or buzzing fly (blow fly): **mu**.

Fua na, or **bua na**, s., **nafua n rarua**, the bottom (outside) of a canoe or ship, lit. the back, syn. **na matu n rarua**: **bua na, buĭ na**.

Fuaġoro, s. See **muaġoro**.

Fuata, v. i., or a., to have raised stripes on the skin (as from blows with a rod, or as are formed by the veins on the arm). See **bua** III, and **bua-ti**: the radical notion is *swelling out*.

Fua-ti, i.q. **bua-ti**.

Fuġa, d. **buma**, q.v.

Fuġaġa, v. i., to well up, spring, bubble up, welling over or spreading asunder (as a spring): **fua**, or **bua** III, and **ġaġa**, for which see **maġa**.

Fuġafuġa, v. i., or a., i. q. **buġafuġa**, q.v. [Sa. *faġu-faġu*.]

Fuġafuġa na, s., as, **fuġafuġa nabiau**, the whitened or breaking crest of a wave, lit. its blossom: **fuġa**.

Fule, and **fulefule**, or **bule-fule**. See **bule** I.

Fulu, and **fulufulu**: i.q. preceding word.

Fuluara, v. i., or a., to be bad, a rascal, ill-looking, horrid, malignant. A. **'afar**, عِفْرِيّ, &c., malignant, horrid, &c.

Fulus, v., to turn: **bulusi.**

Fumafuma na, s., d. for **fuġa-fuġa na**, q.v.

Funaso, c. art., s., stopper: **bunaso.**

Fura, same as **bura**, to be full.

Furei, s. See **futei.**

Furei ki, v. t. See **burei**: rub, cleanse; **furei ki natua na**, cleanse his feet, as by rubbing or scraping them on a scraper, &c.

Furei a, same as **burei**, or **bura i**, to leave.

Furiāna, c. art., s., the being swollen, or having the dropsy: **buria.**

Fus i, same as **bus i**, d. **mur i**, q.v.

Fusa i, same as **busa i.**

Fusfus ki, same as **busfus ki.**

Fut, c. art., s., d. for **ḅosa-ḅosa.**

Futei, dd. **furei, fuṭei, mitoi** or **mitei**, s., the white ant. See **rei, tei.** [Sa. *loi*, Tah. *ro*, ant, gen. name.]

Futfut, d. for **butafuta.**

Futum, v. i., dd. **bisau, busuf, busofu, bisobu**, to sprout forth, spring up, grow. [Fila, Meli, Aniwa, Fut. *somo*, id., Mg. *miṣemuka*, to germinate.] H. ṣamaḥ, Kal and Piel, to sprout forth, to grow (as plants, trees, the hair), and fig. used of the first beginnings of things which occur in the world, as Isa. xliii. 19, 'Behold I make a new thing; now it shall *spring forth*,' Hi. make to sprout forth or grow, and fig. make something spring up or exist, H. ṣemaḥ, offspring, Ef. **atuma**, id.

Ġ (pronounced **ng**).

Ġā, d., pers. pron., 3 sing., he, she, it (nom. suf. **n**, or **na**). [Ma. *ġā*, pl. art., Sa. *na*, he, she, this, that, these, those, Ha. *na*, pl. art., and sign of pl. number; Mg. *izi*, My. *iña* (*inya*), he, she, it, they.] See Ch. V. 2.

Ġa, conj., usually **ġo**, q.v., and: **ka**, in **kai**, conj.

Ġa, final conj., that, ut, d. **ka**, or **k'**, q.v.

Ġa, dem., this, here, there, always (in this form) suffixed as in **naġ, naġa**, q.v., **alaġa** (**alia ġa**), this place, or place here, i.e. here (d. **li ke**, see **ke**); but **alaġa** may be a contraction for **alia naġa**: **ka**, dem.

Ġaḅer, a., and s., grey-haired, aged, a grey-haired, i.e. aged person: **kaḅer.**

Ġāfa, s., a fathom (six feet). [Sa. *ġafa*, a fathom.] A. ḳāmat (Nm. ḳama), a fathom (six feet).

Ġafīkafī, s., a small basket; and

Ġafīkafī, v., to feel for or take hold of a thing in a basket with the fingers. A. ḳoffat, a basket, ḳaffa, to take stealthily between the fingers.

Ġaġa, v. i., to well out, or bubble up, as water from a spring, in **fuġaġa.** See **maġa.**

Ġai, or **ġei**, redup. **ġaiġai**, v. i., to cry, sing, &c.: **kai**, or **kei**.

Ġai (**ġa**, final conj., and **i**, tense particle of the fut.). See **i**, dem.

Ġaiġai, v. i., to pant, be out of breath. [Sa. *ga'ega'e*, to be out of breath, Ha. *nae*, *naenae*, to be out of breath, to pant.] S. **kaḥ**, to pant.

Ġai-taġoto, v. i., to scream (as in pain): **ġai**, and **taġoto**, for which see **koto**, to break.

Ġakalau i (**ġkalau i**), redup. of **ġalau i**.

Ġakarafi (**ġkarafi**). See **karafi**.

Ġakasi (**ġkasi**). See **kasi**.

Ġakat (**ġkatak**). See **kati**.

Ġakau sa, v. t., to grasp (as an oar, in pulling, or a branch of a tree): usually pronounced **ġkau**. See **ġau**, **kau**.

Ġakua, inter. ad., redup. of **kua**, or **ġua**, q.v.

Ġala, v. i., or a., small: **kala**.

Ġalakala, v. i., to laugh. [My. *gâlak*, to laugh loud continuously.] A. **ḳarḳara**, to laugh loud and long, **karkara**, to laugh, cf. **kalla**, 7, to laugh.

Ġalau i, v. t., d. **ġalau sa**, to cross over, d. (transposed) **lakau i**, q.v. E. **ḥalafa**, to cross over, **aḥlafa**, make to cross over.

Ġale-baġa, s., d., bowstring: **kale-baġa**.

Ġal i (**al i**, **kal i**), v. t., to stir round (as water or any liquid). [Ma. *garu*, a wave, *garue*, shake, move to and fro, Ha. *ale*, well up, *aleale*, make into waves, stir up, as water, *ale*, a wave, Sa. *galu*, a wave, *gagalu*, to be rippled, *galu*, to be rough, break heavily on the reef, &c., My. *alun*, Mg. *aluna*, a wave.] H. **galal**, to roll, hence **gal**, fountain, well, pl. waves, S. **galo'**, a wave.

Ġalu, c. art., s., husks, peel, &c. (for pig's food), better part of a thing; pudenda; d. the inner bark of trees: see **kalu-ti**. Cf. Ch. **gilla'**, S. **gelo'**, A. **gillu**, **gullu**, chaff, &c., a covering, better part of a thing.

Ġalu-ti, v. t., **ġaluti nāsu**, to put the bowstring on a bow, **naḅela ġalu**, covering board on end of a canoe; and

Ġalu, c. art., s., bowstring. See **kalu-ti**.

Ġaluġalua, v. i., or a., d. **saġaluġalu**, to be aged, experienced (of persons), to be mature, also to be worn out as with age (of anything), as if to be full of agedness, and mere husk or skin: it has the a. ending **a**; **naġalu matua**, an aged, full-grown, or full-bearded person, or one not immature. A. **galla**, 2, to become aged and expert or experienced.

Ġan i, **ġanikani**, v. t., to eat: **kan i**.

Ġara, v. i., to be dry: **kara**.

Ġaraġara, v. i., to be strong, vehement, and **ġarakarai**: **kara**, **karakarai**.

Ġarā sa, v., to meet (any person or thing), to come upon, hit, as, **ru ba ġára nata**, they went, met a person, **i ba ġarā sa**, it (as a calamity) came upon him, **i sī ġarā sa**, he shot (hit) it or him, **i bisa ġarā sa**, he spoke, met (or hit) it, i.e. he spoke to the point. H. **ḳarah**, and **ḳara'**, to meet.

Ġara ki, v. See **kara ki**.

Ġara, d., pers. pron., 3 pl., they: **ġa**, and **'ra.** [Ma. *ġārā*, they, them.] See Ch. V. 2.

Ġar i, v., and, redup.,

Ġarikari. See **kar i**.

Ġaro i, v. t. See **kar i**.

Ġaru-ti, and redup.,

Ġarukaru. See **karu-ti**.

Ġarei ki. See **karei ki**.

Ġaraf i, v. t. See **karaf i**.

Ġari, a., d. for **kasi**.

Ġasa, inter. ad. See **kasa**.

Ġas i, v. See **kas i**.

Ġasua, and **ġasukasua**, a. See **kasua**.

Ġāt. See **ġaut**.

Ġat i, v. See **kati**.

Ġat, v. See **kat**.

Ġatikati. See **kati**.

Ġati, d. for **kasi**.

Ġato na, d. **karo na**.

Ġau, v. t., to grasp: **kau**.

Ġaua, a., barbed (of a spear): **kau**, v. t., **taġau**. It has the a. ending **a**.

Ġaut, d. **ġāt**, in **bati-ġaut**, a plant with hook-like thorns, lit. grasping teeth: **kau**, v. t., **taġau**.

Ġel i, v. t., to clasp (in order to lift or carry), carry away;

Ġele-ti, v. t., id.; and

Ġelakela, v., used of many carrying away. See **kele-ti**, and **kalu-ti**.

Ġel i, for **ġal i**.

Ġema, d., verb suf., 1 pl., excl.: **ġami, nami**.

Ġemi, d. **ġami, nami**, nom. suf. 1 pl., excl.

Ġera-fi, for **kara-fi**.

Ġere na, s., in **mele-ġere na**, and **na ġaraġara na**, the part of the tail of a fish which when it is feeding near shore appears above water like a shark's fin. [Ml. P. *kare*, tail; My. *ekor*, *ikur*, tail.] H. **'aḥōr**, A. **'oḥ'or'**, hinder part, rear, end; Nm. **êkir**, end.

Ġesa, **ġesakesa**, for **kesa**, **kesakesa**.

Ġi, prep., and **ki**, q.v., to, belonging to, of.

Ġī, s., porpoise: perhaps so called because of the squeaking noise it makes on rising out of the water. See next word.

Ġi, **ġkī**, **ġiki**, v. i., creak, squeak, ping, moan. [Fi. *ġi*, to squeak, Sa. *'ī'i*, squeak.] A. **naḳḳa**, **naḳiḳ'**, creak, &c.

Ġie na, or **ġia na**, s., name, dd. **kiha na**, and **ġisa na**, q.v.

Ġiè sa, or **ġie ki**, v. (see preceding word), to have or acquire a name for or in connection with something.

Ġiki. See **kiki**, small.

Ġil i, or **kil i**, or **kili**, v. t., to dig. [Sa. *'eli*, My. *gali*, Mg. *hadi*, to dig.] A. **kara'**, n. a. **karw'**, to dig.

NOTE.—**Kili natano**, dig the

ground, kili ki nakasu natano, dig a stick into the ground.

Ġkiliki (i. e. ġikili ki), redup., intensive, as **ba ġkiliki natuoma**, dig thy feet (into the ground), i. e. stand firm, or simply, **ba ġkiliki**.

Ġkita, i. e. **ġikita**, v. redup. See **ġita, kita**.

Ġinit i, v., **ġini ġote-fi**. See **kinit i**.

Ġiriġiri, v. i., or a., to be bright, brilliant, shining, polished. [To. *ġiġila*, bright, brilliant, polished, My. *gilaġ*, and *gilau*, to shine, glitter, be bright, brilliant, dazzle.] A. gala', to be clear, shining, &c., galiyy', bright, shining, polished.

Note.—The A. word also denotes to be or appear uncovered: Ef. d. **karo**, to be unclothed, have the clothes removed, naked.

Ġis, or **ġisa**, ad., together, lit. as one, with numerals, as, **rua ruā ġis**, two, two together, in twos, and so with all the numerals. H. k'eḥad, as one, i. e. together, Ch. kaḥăda. See **ki**, as, and **sa**, s, one.

Ġisa. See **kisa**, or **kesa**.

Ġisa na, s., c. art., name, dd. **gia na, kiha na** (for **kisa na**). [TaSa. *kiṣa*, Ml. U. *se*, Malo *isa*, Epi (Ba.) *sia*, (Bi.) *kia*, Ta. dd. *riġe* (*nariġe*), *na'ġe* ('*ġe*), An. *t'a*, Fi. *yat'a*, Am. *sa*, Paama *isa*, Ta. d. *hġe* (*nahġe*).] A. 'ism' and sim', H. s'em, name.

Note.—The Ef. **ġisa** (**kiha, ġia**) has **k'** (or **ġ'**) prefixed, as Epi **kia**, and TaSa. **kiṣa**, for which see Ch. II. 11. *c*., not in Epi **sia**, Ml. **se**, Am. **sa**, Malo and Paama **isa**: in all these the final **m** of the original is elided, as it is in **ṭā** (q.v.), blood, and **nu** (for **num**); this final **m** appears as **ġ** in Ta.

Ġis i, v. t., to feel, touch, and **Ġiskis**, redup. See **kis i**.

Ġita i, v. t. See **kita i**.

Ġite ṭoa i, for **ġita ṭoa i**. See **kite ṭoa i**.

Ġo, conj., connecting substantives and sentences, and. [Ml. P. *ġa*, *ka*, Ml. U. *ko*, Fi. *ka*, and.] Amh. ka, and (with numerals).

Ġoba (**ġote-fi**), v. t., to cut, as a **nakoau**, with a knife. [Mg. *kapa*, cut, *mikapa*, v. t., to cut.] H. gub, A. gāba, to cut.

Ġoba-si, v. t. See **koba-si**.

Ġobera, or **ġobăra**, s., or **kobara**, side, as, **kobara kerua**, the other side. H. 'eber, Ch. 'abar, id.

Ġofu sa, v. t. See **kofu sa**.

Ġofkofua, a. See **kofkofua**.

Ġkofita (for **ġokofita**), a., sticky, gluey. [Mg. *feta*, *fetaka*, clay adhering, wet, sticking to.] A. 'amada, 2, 5, to be wet so as to stick (earth or clay).

Ġoġo, v. i., to wade, to wade half swimming;

Ġoġo, s., an aquatic bird. [An. *aġaġ*, to swim, Sa. *'a'au*, to swim, Fila *kaukau*, to bathe, Ma. *kau*, swim, wade, Ha. *au*, *auau*, swim, bathe, hasten, cf. Ja. *kumbah*, to wash.] A. **ḥamma**, 1, hasten, 4, bathe, or wash oneself in cold water, 10, bathe in hot water; and, general term, wash the body.

Ġoi, or **ġo i**, v. t., or **ko i**, as, **ġoi naniu**, to rub, scrape, or grind out by rubbing or scraping the kernel of the cocoanut, **suru-ġo i** (cover-drain out) to cover with one's mouth the aperture of a drinking vessel and drain out the contents, **koi**, a mark or boundary, also **koika nafanua**; redup.,

Ġoko i, v. t., to scrape (**nafona**); to mark, paint, or smear (**nafona**, i.e. native cloth), **koko**, the paint used for this, **ġokoi** (or **ġokai**, or **ġokei**) **nafona**. [Sa. *'o'ai*, to mark or paint native cloth.] H. **ḥakah**, i.q. **ḥakak**, cut into, *hack*, engrave, carve, draw, paint, delineate, **ḥok**, a defined limit, a bound, A. **hakka**, 3, grind by rubbing, 1, hack, cut, pierce, 7, drain out (as milk), **ḥakka**, scrape, rub; hence also

Ġko, or **ġoko**, v., to cut into, cut, hack, always followed by another verb, as, **ġko bora i**, **ġko ġote-fi** (used of cutting up the **nakoau**, or native pudding), **na kokoen**, s., the cutting up.

Ġokolau, see **ġakalau** (**ġkalau i**).

Ġōlĕ, s., a cripple, one lame. A. gayala, to be lame.

Ġkola (**ġokola**). See **kola**, **kokola**, to be dry.

Ġkola. See **kola**, shout.

Ġkolau. See **kolau**.

Ġolĭ na, c. art., s., bird's beak, lips, mouth. [Sa. *gutu*, mouth (of animals, wells, bottles), Ma. *ġutu*, lip, rim, *whakaġutuġutu*, grumble at, scold, Fi. *ġusu*, mouth, Fut. *raġutu*, beak.] A. **naḳara**, to peck with its beak (a bird); to scold, **naḳrāt**, foramen (*gulae*), **manḳar**, bird's beak.

Ġoloḅa, v. i., to be filthy, dirty. **Ḳarafa**, 3, to be defiled, 4, to be infected, contaminated, Nm., 4, to disgust.

Ġkolōfa. See **kolōfa**.

Ġolu-ti, v. t. See **kalu-ti**.

Ġon, v. i., to be firm, fast: **kon**.

Ġkon (**kokon**), redup. of preceding.

Ġkon (**gokon**), v. i., to be bitter: **kon**, **kokon**.

Ġonai, v. t. See **konai**.

Ġor i, or **kor i**, v. t., to enclose or surround with a fence (**nakoro**); then to enclose as with a fence a sick person (shutting out and prohibiting evil spirits or evil influences from him)—this is done by the 'Sacred Man' (**natamole tabu**)—hence **ġorokoro**, to divine, and **nekoro**, divination, or incantation, with its accompanying rites; redup., ġorokor i (native Christian prayer, **Atua O, ba ġorokoro ġami auga toko loġa namolien anaġo**—'O God, enclose us that we may abide in the loġa (enclosure) of Thy salvation)'; **ġorò sa,** to conceal it (as a crime with which one is charged); **ġor i,** to prohibit, as, **tuba ġor i,** prohibit, impede, obstruct, **bisa ġor i,** speak, impede, or obstruct him; **tu ġor i,** stand, obstruct; **ġkoro (ġokoro),** v., and **nakokoro,** s., a prohibition, also an obstruction or thing put to close up or obstruct the entrance to a house, a door. This verb is much used after other verbs as **bā ġor i,** to go obstructing, i.e. to meet, d. **bākor,** to meet, or rather to come or go before, i.e. appear before (any one), then to arise, come into sight (as a man, ship, &c.), and take place (as an event); **meri ġor i, bati ġor i,** like **ġor i,** simply mean to enclose or surround with a fence, **sera ġor i,** to enclose or encircle (the head) with a fillet, hence **seraġoro-bau,** a hat; **ġore na,** a brother's sister, or sister's brother, brother and sister being children of the same mother, or of the same **nakainaġa.** A. **ḥagara,** impede, prohibit, interdict, 2, to have a halo surrounding it (the moon), (see **koro**), 4, to conceal; **ḥigr', ḥogr',** a fence, a wall, what is prohibited, genitals of a man or a woman, kindredship, relationship, **ḥāgir',** a fence; H. **hagar,** to gird, **ḥagōr,** a girdle, clad. Nm., 2, to fence round, confine, forbid; E. **hagar,** town, village (Fi. **koro,** id.).

Ġore na, s., brother's sister, sister's brother. See under preceding word.

Ġoro, v. i., or **koro,** to snore. [Ma. *ġoġoro* (redup.), My. *ġorok,* Mg. *eruṭa,* id.] H. **naḥar,** A. (**ḥ'arra, ḥ'arḥ'ara**) **naḥ'ara,** S. **nḥar,** snort, breathe hard through the nose, E. **nehèra,** snore;

Ġore na, c. art., s., the nostrils, nose, dd. **usu, ġusu.** [Fi. *ut'u,* Sa. *isu,* Ma. *ihu,* My. *iduġ,* Ja. *iruġ,* Mg. *uruna,* nose.] H. **nḥīraim,** du., the nostrils, S. **nḥīro',** the nose, A. **noḥ'rat,** aperture of the nose.

Ġorot i, v. t., to cut round, as to cut round a stick in order to break it; hence

Ġoro ġote-fi, v. t., cut round, break it (as a stick). Nm. **ḥ'arat,** to shave off in turning, H. **ḥarat** (q.v.), S. **ḥrat,** cut in, engrave. See **karati.**

Ġota, redup. **ġoġota,** v. i., or a., black, dirty, **bukota,** dirty (as water with dust or earth in it). [Gilolo *kokotu, kitkudu,* black.] קָדַר, A. **ḳadara, n. a. ḳadru, kadara,** n. a. **kadra-t,** id.

Ġota fānu, s., or ad., evening, d. **kot' fān,** d. syn. **rāġ mēlu,** lit. time of dusk, or sunset:

ġota, or **kot'**, a time (see **kota**). A. **waḳata, 1, 2**, to fix a time, **waḳt'**, a time, a point or part of time: **fānu**. [Santo *punu*, to set (the sun), *puni*, dusk.] H. **pun** (perhaps i.q. A. **'afana** = **'afala**, cf. H. **'apal**, see **melu**), to set (as the sun), to be darkened.

Ġot, v., cut. See **koto-fi**.

Ġote-fi, v. t. See **koto-fi**.

Ġotokoto, v. i., to begin (break or cut, as it were, into the doing of something, 'break ground' in the matter), as **i ġotokoto bat i**, he began—did it: **koto-fi**.

Ġū, d. **mu**, nom. suf., your, 2 pl. (**ku**, verb. pron., 2 pl.): separate pron., 2 pl., **kumu**.

Ġū, dd. **mu**, **kama**, verb. suf., you. See preceding word, and fol.

Ġu, d. **k** (for **ku**), nom. suf., 1 sing., my, as, **narugu**, my hand. See Ch. V. 2.

Ġua, inter. ad., why? lit. that what? It is used with the verbal prons., as, **i kua**, it is for what? Indefinitely **i kua**, it that so (assent): **kua** and **ġua** are equally used. كَيْنَه, that what? why? See Ch. V. 5.

Ġua, v. i. See **kua**, Sa. **ġu**, to growl.

Ġūku, v. i., to stoop, be incurved, **maġuku**, to be incurved, **ġuku rumu ki m̄ō na**, to shrink or incurve the bosom to her son-in-law (of a mother-in-law bowing and covering her bosom and face so as not to be seen by her son-in-law), d. **kuku ruma**. [Mg. *huhuka*, bow down, cover.] E. **g'uḥḳa**, to be incurved, bent, specially from old age, hence **guḥuḳ'**, one aged, bent, and shrunk together.

Ġuku-taki, v. t., to make **ġuku**. See **ġuku**.

Ġulu-ti, v. t. See **kalu-ti**.

Ġulu, v. i. See **kulu**.

Ġum i, v. t., or **kum i**, to absorb in the mouth (as a lolly). H. **gama'**, to absorb, to drink up, to swallow, i.q. Ch.

Ġum i, v. t., dd. **um i**, **ġu i** (**ġw i**), **m̄ i** (**mw i**), to seize, grasp, catch, hold, with or in the hand. [Sa. *'u'u*, to take hold of, to grasp, ps. *'umia*, Fi. *qumi-a*, *ququ*, id., My. *gâmgam*, Ja. *gâgâm*, to clutch, to clench, the fist, the clenched hand, To. *kuku*, hold in the hand, or mouth, bite, ravenous, Ma. *kuku*, grate, Mangarwan *kuku*, wipe.] A. **ḳamḳama**, to collect, to seize or catch with the hand, to take, **ḳamma**, to sweep, voravit.

Ġunut i, v. t. See **kinit i**.

Ġura i, v. t., to scrape off, **ġura ua**, to scrape or rake off the heated stones from an oven, **maġir i**, v. t., scrape, **maġura**, v. i., or ps. a., diminished, lean, **iġura**, d. **iġiri**, the stick for scraping or raking the stones from an oven, **ġura biri ki** (d. syn., **sera biri ki**), to startle (one) (as by coming behind one and suddenly laying or sweeping the hand on him): **kar i, ġaru.** H. **gara'**, to scratch, to scrape, scrape off, then take away, withhold, to diminish, Ni. to be taken away, withheld. Note the Ef. **maġura**, denotes, lit. taken away from, i.e. diminished, lean, with the prep. **ki, maġura ki**, to withhold from (one), **meta maġura ki**, he eyes withholds (something) from (one), he is stingy; in one d. **i meta makur ki**, is said to denote he eyes withdraws from (one), he is covetous, lit. he eyes scrapes off (from some one).

Ġure-si, v. t., to gnaw: see **ġura i** and **kar i**. [Sa. *ġali*, gnaw, Fi. *quru*, v. i., *quru-ta*, v. t., to eat anything unripe, to scranch, eat ravenously, to gnaw, My. *greb*, to gnaw.] This word seems properly to denote, scranch, scrape off, absorb, H. **gara'**, scrape off, A. **gara'a**, to absorb, swallow.

Ġuru ki, v. t., to gather together, **ġuru-maki**, v. t., id., or **kuru ki, kuru-maki, ġkuruk** (**ġukuruk**), gather together (without object); and

Ġurua, s., c. art., a field (of battle, of yams), so called because men or things are gathered together in it; **kuru.** A. **kara** (mid. و), كَوْرٌ, كَوْرَةٌ, to gather together, **karkara**, cf. H. **gur**, (3), to be gathered, to gather together, **'agar**, collect, gather in.

Ġurui, and

Ġuruni, s., c. art. **naġuruni**, a woman, wife, female. See Ch. II. 17. *e*.

Ġusĭ, v. i., to be crooked, contorted, **maġusĭ**, crooked, contorted. A. **'akis'a**, to be crooked, contorted, 5, id.

Ġusu, v. i., to stoop. A. **nakasa**, to stoop.

Ġusu na, s., c. art., the nose: **ġore na**, q. v.

Ġusuġisu ki, v. den., from preceding word, to nose (a thing), i.e. smell it. [Mg. *uruka* (from *uruna*, the nose), *miuruka*, to kiss by touching noses.]

Ġusu, v. i. See **kusu, kosumi.**

Ġusu-mi, v. t. See **kosu-mi.**

Ġut i, v. t., and **ġukut i** (**ġkut i**). See **kut i.**

Ġutu ki, v. t. See **kutu ki.**

I, verb. pron., 3 sing., he, she, it, sometimes pronounced **e**; also dd. **i, e**, verb. suf., 3 sing., him, her, it. [Epi Ba. *o*, Epi Bi. *c*, him, her, it; Fut. *i*, Ml. P. *i*, TaSa. *i*, he, she, it.] Separate pron. **nai**, dd. **inia**, or **enea, ġa**, or **niġa**, he, she, it.

I, dem., d., this, here, d. **ei, raġ i**, this time, now.

I, or **e**, a tense particle used after **ka** (sign of past tense, as, **i ka fano**, he went), and **ġa**, and **ba** (final conjs.), thus, **i kai bano**, he had gone, **i ġai bano**, let him have gone, the notion expressed being that the action (as going) was done or is to be done *before* the doing of something else. Dialect syn. **ko**, **ba i bano** = **ba ko bano** = that thou have gone, lit. that thou *now* (before something else to follow) go. [Cf. *e* after verbs in Ha. and Tah.] Probably the dem. **e**, this or that (perhaps contraction of **uai**, this, now, that, then, thus, **iġai bano** = **iġa bano uai**, which is sometimes used, the expression denoting exactly the same, only the ad. being differently placed, as in English we might say, let him *now* go = let him go *now*), thus, **i kai** (or, **ka e**) **bano**, he went then (that time), **ba i bano**, go *now* (this time), d. **kui ban**, you now go (as bidding farewell).

I, dem., in **ēï**, not that, no: syn. **ēüo**, **e**, and **uo**, dem.

Ī, no, compare **e** in **ēï**. [This neg. ad. is seen in Sa. *i* (in *i'ai*, no), To. *i* (in *ikai*, no); for the *kai*, see *tika*.]

I, prep. (also **e**), contracted from **ni** (**li**), often t. prep. [Ma. *i*, id.]

Note.—The verb. suf., 3 sing., is often combined with this prep. **ia**, d. **i**, for **iia**, **ii**.

Ia, s., d. for **bia**, child.

Ia, verb. suf., 3 sing., dd. **i**, **e**, him, her, it.

Iak, s., d., mother (vocative). See **aka**, and **i**, art. [Mg. *kaki*, and *ikaki*, my father (voc.).]

Ibē! iebē! iboï! interj., exclamation of wonder, surprise, and pleasure, d. **bai**. See **bai**; **i**, as in **io**, **iore**.

Iġam, dd. **aġam**, **niġami**, **kiġami**, **kinami**, q.v., 1 pers. pron. exclusive.

Iġin, d., ad., here; **i**, prep., and **ġin** (or **kin**), q.v. [Sa. *i'inei*, Fut. *ikunei*, id.]

Iġira, d. for **iġita**, 1 pers. pron. inclusive.

Iġiri, s., and

Iġura, s., same as **eġura**.

Iġita, dd. **aġita**, **niġita**, **kiġita**, **nininta**: **ġita**, for **nita**, 1 pers. pron. inclusive.

Ika, s., c. art. **naika**, fish. [Sa. *ia*, My. *ikan*, Santo d. *ika*.] Cf. H. **dag**, pl. const. **dĕgē** and **dagah**, const. **dĕgath**, fish. It is possible that **ika** is the same by the elision of the **d**. See Ch. II.

Iki, a., small, little; in **kariki** (**kar' iki**), little children. See **kiki**. [To. *iki*, small, little.]

Ikin, or **kin**, s., c. art. **nikin**, a bird's nest. [Mg. *akani*.] H. **ḳen**, A. **wakn'**, **wukunat**, id.

Iliḅaġoen, s., a basket with closed bottom, a purse, or wallet: **ala** (basket), **ḅaġo**, **uon** (**ḅon**).

Ili-fiki, v., also **lele-**, or **lili-fiki**, d. syn. **kelu-faki**, as, **rarua i ili-fiki nağusu**, the canoe rounds the point, or cape. See lele, lili.

Ilisela, ad., throughout, for **lili-sela**, lit. all round (throughout) the way: **lele** (or **lili**), **sela**, q.v.

Imrum, d. **imrau**, ad., inside the house: **i**, prep., **moru**, hollow, **um**, house. See **katema**.

Īn, s., or **nīn**, the wind, the air: **laği**. [My. *ağin*, Mg. *anina*, the wind.]

In, dem., this, d. **na**. [Cf. Sa. *nei*, this, now, Mg. *ini*, that, this, My. *ini*, this.] Assy. **annu**, this.

Inia, **inea**, or **enea**, d., pers. pron., 3 sing., he, she, it.

Inin, here: **i**, prep., and **nin**, this.

Inini, d., s., c. art. **nainini**, spirit, soul. See **anu**.

Inira, **inera**, or **enera**, d., pers. pron., 3 pl., they.

Inira, or **nira**, or **nera**, d., verb. suf., 3 pl., them.

Inuma, s., d. for **isuma**, q.v.

Io, ad., yes. [Sa. *io*, Fi. *io*, or *ia*, yes, Ja. *iya*.] H. **'īhu'**, E. **'ewa**, yes.

Iorĕ, ad., d. **ōrĕ**, yes. [Fi. *iarai*, yes.] From **īo**, and **ri**, dem. See **eri**.

Ĭra, or **ĕra**, or **ra**, verb. pron., 3 dual, they two.

Ira (d. **ir**), or **ra**, verb. suf., 3 pl., them.

Ïru, or **eru**, or **ru**, verb. pron., 3 pl., they, d. **ĭu**, or **u**.

Īs, ad., or interj., no, not so. [Mg. *isi*, id.] **I**, neg. ad., and **s'**, dem. See **sĕ**.

Isi, s., c. art. **naïsi na**, basis, foundation; **naisi matua na**, its great foundation, **naisi matua nafisan**, the great foundation of the discourse or speech, its text, **naisi namal**, the foundation of the affair; and

Isuma, d. **inuma** (s to n), s., a clearing for a plantation, lit. the foundation of the clearing for cultivation. See **uma**. A. **'iss'**, &c., a foundation.

Ita, s., c. art. **naita**, d. for **nāta**, a human being, man. See **ata**.

Īta, interj. of exhortation, come! now then! come now! [Ta. *ita*, id.] A. **hī'ta**, adesdum, adeste.

Itaki, s., dd. **otaki**, **uataki**, a split stick for grasping and lifting hot oven stones, the native tongs: **i**, art., and **taki**.

Iu, or **ĕu**, verb. pron., 3 pl., d. for **īru**, or **ĕru**, they.

Ĭu, s., c. art. **naiu**, or **naiyu**, d. for **nausu**. See **usu**.

K, d., verb. suf., 2 sing., thee, d. **ko**. A. **ka**, thee.

Ka, **kĭ**, or **kĕ**, ad., as; **tera kĭ māla**, move (lit. fly) like a hawk (of the dancing of women who move with both arms stretched out like the wings of a hawk); usually prefixed to another particle, as, **kĭte**, as. A. **ka**, H. **kĕ**, as.

K, d. **ġu (ku)**, nom. suf., 1 sing., my, as, **naruk**, my hand. [My. *ku*, Mg. *hu*.]

Ka, k', tense particle, past indefinite, as, **a ka bano**, I went, **i ka bano**, he went. [Fi. *ka*, a sign of the past tense, sometimes of the present.] For this **ka**, see Ch. V. 10. *c.*

K', d. **ġa**, d. **ka**, final conj., that, in order that: prefixed to the verbal pron. it loses its vowel: in the d. in which this particle is pronounced **ġa**, the verb. pron. is put before it—**i ġa**, he that, i.e. that he, d. **ke** (**k'**, that, **e**, he), that he, **ka** (**k'**, that, **a**, I), that I, d. **a ġa**: the order seen in **ka**, that I, **ke**, that he, is the older and more correct: examples, **ka fan**, that I go, **ke fan**, that he go, let him go, and so with every verb in the language. This is not a tense but a mood, though the idea of futurity is implied: to make the future tense **fo** (see **bo, mo, uo**) is added, thus, **ka fo ban**, I shall go, I will go, **ke fo ban**, he will go (he shall go, is rather **ke ban**, i.e., he must go, but also, let him go, and, he may go, and, to go, or, that he go). As final conj. A. **ka'**, H. **ki**, that, in order that (with the future), Latin ut (with the subjunctive). It is not surprising that **k'** in some dialects denotes the future. Thus in Florida it denotes the future, as, **ke bosa*** (**k'**, this particle, and **e**, he), he will speak, compare Tigre Matt. xvi. 27 (when the Son of Man) *shall come* (**kimaṣe**), for the simple future in Ethiopic: this Tigre **ki** is **k'**, the particle in question (A. **ka'**), and **i**, verb. pron. or preformative, 3 sing. [Ef. d. *ġa*, d. *k'*, final conjunction, Ysabel *ġe*, *ġi*, Raratonga *ka*, usually *kia*, Ma. *kia* (the *a* is a dem. added), To. *ke*, Mg. *h'*: Raratonga *ka*, future, in some places past, Florida *k'*, future, Mg. *h'*, future.] See Ch. V. 8. 1.

Ka, d., dem. **ki**, or **ke**, this, there (near), as, **nauot ka**, this chief; **ke**, and **ġa** in **naġa**. See word after next below. [My. *iki*, *ika*, *iku*, this, that, TaSa. *aki*, or *ake*, this.] E. **ka**, dem., seen in **zĕku**, Amh. **yĕh**, or **ĭhĕ**, for **ĭkĕ**, this, Arm. **dek, dak, deka', dake'**, A. **ḍaka**. With the Semitic demonstrative **ka** (Dillmann, *Gr. Eth.*, §§ 62, 65), seen in these words (whence E. **kia**, prefixed to personal pronouns) compares probably Assy. **aga**, this (Sayce, *Assy. Gr.*).

NOTE.—This Semitic dem. **ka** is seen also in E. **'elku**,

* Ef. **ke bisa**, that he speak, he may, must, &c., speak, let him speak.

'elkĕtu, Ch. **'illek**, A. **'olaka**, &c., these, those.

Ka, prep., usually **ki**, rarely **ka** (see Ch. V. 11. 3), as, d. **i ba ka tafa** (commonly **i ba ki tafa**), he went *to* the hill: **ki**, or **ġi**, to, belonging to, of, for, from, and transitive prep. after verbs; prefixed to the nom. suf. it forms poss. prons., as **kaġu, kama, kana,** &c.; **kana**, his, for him, is syn. c. **kakana, kanana**; see Ch. V. 11. (6). [My. *ka*, to, unto, towards, after, according to, much used in composition in the formation of other preps. and ads., as in *kan* transitive prep. after verbs, and *akan*, to, &c., and particle of the future tense, Mg. *hu*, to, for, belonging to, and particle of the future tense, Ma. *ki*, to, towards, &c., and, after verbs, transitive prep.] Amh. **ka**, to, of, from, Himyaritic **ka** or **ki**, after verbs transitive prep.; H. **ki** is a conj., that; compare **'ad ki**, until (conj.), or until that, with E. and Amh. **'eska** (**'es**, for H. **'ad**), prep., to, unto. Thus the same particle which is a final conjunction (see above, under **k'** (**ġa, ka**), final conj.) in A. and H., is a prep. in Himyaritic and Amh.

Ka, or **ki**, dem., rel. pron., art. (same as word before the preceding, above), prefixed to pers. prons., nom., **kinau, kiġita**; see Ch. V. 1. *a*.

Kaba-si, d. See **koba-si**, to follow.

Kaḅe, s., a small basket. [Ma. *kakapu*, a small basket for cooked food, so called from being curved (*kapu*) like the hollow of the hand (*kapu*).] S. **kapo'**, poculum H. **kaf**, or **kap**, hollow of the hand, pl. a hollow vessel, pan, or bowl (H. **kafaf**, to bend, curve).

Kaḅĕ, s., a kind of crab.

Kābe, d. **kâfinī**, s., a pigeon, d. **kime**. [Ma. *kukupa*, Tah. *uupa*, Am. *um*, Epi *ama*, id.] A. **ḥama'**, pigeons.

Kabu, s., d. **koau**, the native 'pudding' (tied up in a bundle, and cooked in the oven); the main article of native food: see **kofu**. [Tah. *ohu*, a bundle of some food tied up and baked in the native oven, Sa. *'ofu'ofu*, to envelop in leaves (for cooking).] A. **kobbat, kabab'**, 'kibby,' the national dish of the Arabs, made of pounded or brayed wheat and fish or flesh, gathered into a round mass, and cooked in the oven. See the verb under the word **kofu**.

Kabu, s., fire; and

Kabu teraġi, v., to burn heating it (cold food), to warm or heat (cold food). [My. *api*, Sa. *afi*, Mg. *afu*, fire, Sa. *afia*, ps., to be burnt accidentally.] S. **ḥab**, to burn, A. **ḥobaḥib'**, (redup.) fire. See **teraġi**.

Kabu, s., in **talekabu na.** See **kobu.**

Kaḅer, v. i., or a., to be grey-haired, aged;

Kaḅer, d., s., a husband, lit. an aged man;

Kaḅera, d., s., a wife, an aged woman, d. **aḅera,** or **abura,** c. art. **nâḅera, nàbura** (k elided). A. **kabira,** to be advanced in age, **kabīr,** advanced in age and fully grown, E. **'eber,** old woman (**k** elided).

Kaf, v. i., to be bent (as with hunger). See also **kai.** [Ma. *kapu,* curly, *kapu,* the hollow of the hand.] H. **kafaf,** to be bent, **kaf,** hollow of the hand.

Kafa i, v. t., to cover (as a rotten wood board with another), A. **kaffa,** 1, 2, to cover, &c.

Kafa-raġo, s., see d. transposed **faka-raġo.**

Kafika, s., the rose apple. [Fut. *kafika,* Fi. *kavika,* Ml. P. *ḥaviḳ,* Malo *aviga,* TaSa. *kabika* (*khabika*), id.] H. **tapuaḥ,** an apple (so called from its scent, from **nafaḥ**), A. **toffāḥ',** an apple, not only the common one, but also the lemon, citron, &c.

Kafikafi, v., **ġafikafi,** q.v.

Kafinī, s., d. **kabe,** q.v.

Kafi-si, v. t., to uncover, open (eye, basket, &c.), A. **kafaḥa,** to uncover.

Kafu-ti, or **ġafu-ti,** v. t., to wrap up (a thing, as a stone, with cloth, so as to cover it all round), same as **kofu sa,** q.v., which is used of thus wrapping up food to be cooked; hence

Kafukafu na, s., pellicle, as of an egg or fruit (its wrapper or covering), d. **kamu.**

Kai, v. i., to be bent, for **kaf,** q.v.

Kai, conj., d. syn. **bo,** conj., q.v.: **ka** (see **ġa,** conj.) and **i,** he, she, it.

Kai, or **kae,** tense particle (compounded of **ka,** q.v., sign of past tense, and **i,** or **e**) of the pluperfect. See **i.**

Kai (or **kei**), **ġai,** v. i., to cry, sing (men, birds), sing out, sound, &c. [Ml. P. *keke,* to sing.] E. **naḳawa,** to sound, give forth a sound (of the human voice, songs of birds, &c.), A. **naka'a,** to cry out, sing out.

Kai, s., a sharp shell used for scraping: **ġoi.**

Kaimi-si, v. t., to make to exist, as (the heathen used to say of the sea, &c.), **i tumana kaimi-si,** it made itself to exist; and

Kaimis, s., c. art. **nakaimis,** one that does anything hiddenly and wonderfully, as destroying an enemy by changing one's form magically and deceiving, &c. H. **ḳum,** arise, exist, go forth, grow up, stand (be fixed), Hi. cause to arise, exist, A. **kāma,** 2, rightly appoint and dispose (a thing), 4, prepare (evil against a person), &c.

Kainaġa, s., c. art., a tribe or family clan. [(Sa. *'aiga*, a family, relations.) To. *kai-naga*, a meal, victuals.] See **kan i. kainaġa** is for **ka-ninaġa**, orig. **kanitana**.

Kaka, s., **kaka naniu.** See under **aka.**

Kakana (**kakaġu, kakama, kakaġita**, &c.), poss. pron., syn. **aġana**, &c., q.v. : **kaka** is **ka** prep. doubled. [Epi *gka, gkana*, his, &c.]

Kakat, s., a bite. See **kati** or **kat i.**

Kakei, s., c. art. **nakakei**, a story (traditional). A. **ḥa-ka'**, to narrate, Nm. **ḥucèya**, narrative, tale.

Kāl, s., a child. See under **bakal i** I.

Kala, v. i., or a., little, small. See under **bakal i** II. [Mg. *keli*, id.]

Kalai, d., s., a spider's web, and d. **nilau**, and

Kalau, d., id., lit. a woven thing. [My. *labalaba*, and *lawalawa*, a spider.] H. **'arab**, to weave. See **kolau.**

Kalau, ġkalau. See **ġalau i.**

Kale-baġa, s., d. **kalemaġa**, bowstring (made out of the **baġa** or **maġa** tree) : **kalu.**

Kālī, s., native spade, digging stick : **kil i.**

Kal i, or **ġal i**, q.v., and redup.,

Kalikal i,

Kalu, and **ġalu**, s., bowstring, **kalu nāsu** : **kale** in **kale baġa.** See **kalu-ti.**

Kalu, s., d. **kul**, cloth, clothing, lit. a covering ; and

Kalu-ti (same as **ġalu-ti**), d. **kulu-ti**, v. t., to cover, as with a mat or rug, **i kalu ki nakalu**, he covers (himself) with cloth or clothing, **i kalu**, d. **i kulu**, or **i ġulu**, middle sense, he covers (himself), as with bedclothes, i.e. mats or such like, also to put the bowstring on a bow (or **ġalu-ti**) and to clasp round with the arms (a violent man, to restrain him, or a pig, &c., stooping to lift it in order to carry it) : the vowels of this word are changed in **kalu, kulu, kele** (**ġalu, ġulu, ġele**), **ġolu.** See similar changes of vowels in the My. word under **kela**, infra. A. **galla**, 2, to cover, 5, to be covered, clothed, **gullu**, coverings, clothes, &c., as rugs : the idea of covering arises from that of wrapping round or rolling up—see the cg. H. **galal**, to roll, and its related words in *Ges. Dict.*, and see below, under **kela, kelu.**

Kalumi, s., the spider. See under **kalau.**

Kama, d. for **kabu**, in **ane-kama**, q.v.

Kama, d., verb. suf., 2 pl., you, d. **mu**, My. **mu.**

Kamam, d. for **kinami**, q.v.

Kami, d., pers. pron., 2 pl., you.

Kami, v. t., to seize, grip, take with the fingers, or with nippers, compress or squeeze between two things (like **alat i**); same as **kamut i**, q.v.

Kamu na, s., pellicle, d. for **kafukafu na**, q.v.

Kamut i, or **ġamut i**, v. t., to take, grasp with the fingers, nip, then (like **alat i**) to nip or cut with scissors, to cut the hair; hence

Kam, s., c. art. **nikam**, native tongs (a split stick for grasping hot oven stones, and lifting them), lit. that which (**kami**, or **kamut**) nips, seizes, grasps, d. **kau**, q.v., or **ġau** (**aġau**), and

Kamkam, s., scissors. [My. *cubit*, or *chubit*, Ja. *juwit*, to nip, pinch, My. *aġkub*=*aġau*, tongs, nippers, Ha. *umiki*, to pinch with the fingers, Fi. *qamuta*, to take hold of, or hold as with pincers, to shut (the mouth), *ai qamu*, anything to *qamuta* with (My. *aġkub*), as pincers, bullet mould, vice.] H. **ḳamaṣ**, to squeeze together, hence to take with the hand, **ḳamaṭ**, to hold fast with the hands, to seize firmly, **ḳafaṣ**, contract, shut (as the mouth), **ḳabaṣ**, to take, grasp with the hand, A. **ḳabaṣa**, to take with the tips of the fingers, **ḳabaṣ'a**, take, grasp with the hand.

Kana-, pref. to nom. suf., forming poss. pron., **kanaġu**, **kanama**, **kanana**, &c.: **kanana**, d. **kinin**, is syn. c. **kakana**, q.v. [Epi *kana-*, d. *kona-*, as, *kanaku*, my, &c.] **Kana-** is **ka**, prep., and **na**, prep. See Ch. V. 11. (6).

Kana, v. i., d. **kano**, to shrink from, to be unable; **i kana bat i**, he is unable to do it (shrinks from, or is afraid), **i sua bo kin**, or **bo ki**, he takes (acquires) a mind shrinking from, afraid, unable (to do something). A. **kana'a**, to shrink from, not daring, or being afraid.

Kan i, v. t., to eat, redup. **kanikani**: **tea kanien**, that which is for eating, **nakanien**, act of eating, the eating, food, **finaġa**, q.v., food, **baġan i**, to feed, make to eat, or **faġan i**, q.v., and **faġa**, **faġafaġa**, **nakabu faġa**, devouring (eating) fire, **nalaġi kanikani**, a strong wind, **kana**, a squall; **kainaġa**, a tribe, family clan (from eating together). [Fi. *kana*, to eat, *kani-a*, to eat, *vakani-a*, feed, cause to eat, used also of the *heat* of the sun, and *violence* of the wind, Sa. *ai*, My. *makan*, Mg. (*m* transposed) *humana*, *hanina*, to eat.] A. **'akala**, to eat, 3, eat together, 4, to feed, cause to eat, **'akīl'**, one who lives with one, messmate, familiar friend (cf. **kainaġa**, and A. 3), H. **'akal**, to eat; A. **'akala**, (2), to scratch (the head), **'akila**, to be itchy, Ef. **makinikini**. to be itchy.

Kana, s., a squall. See under preceding word.

Kanäu, or **kanäo**, s., d. **kanoa**, **kano**, child; **nasuma nĭ kanoa**, or **kano**, the womb, lit. house of the child (or fœtus). In E. Mai this is called **kiri fanau**, the cover (**kiri** = **kuli** = skin or covering), or skin of the child. This word is familiarly used by men to each other as a vocative, as **kanäo**, or **kano**, mate! (child!), pl. **kanŏ maġā**, you people, d. **nakanoa**, **kano ni Efate**, man of Efate, pl. **nakan Efate**, people of Efate, lit. children of Efate, d. **nati ni Efate** (see **ani**, **ati**, child): hence **kano** is sometimes equivalent to 'person', as **kano sa**, **kano uia**, a bad, a good person;

Kan, c. art. **nakan**, children (of a place);

Kano, or **kanoa**, s., see **kanäo**;

Kanoa, s., c. art. **nakanoa**, see **kanäo**. [My. *kanak*, child, *anak*, id., as Ef. **kanäo** and **ani**, q.v., child, so Mg. *zanaka* and *anaka*, Sa. *fanau*, Ef. **kanäo**.] A. walada, H. yalad, E. walada, to bring forth, bear (of a mother), to beget (of males), and used in E. also of the earth bringing forth its produce.

Kano, or **kanoa**, d. **kanau**, or

Kanoka, v. i., or a., to be produced (as it were born, of yams), **naui i kanoa** (d. **kanau**), the yam is produced, born, or growing (as if the **insat**, q.v., had brought it forth new born), **naui kano**, new or growing yams. See preceding word, and s. v. **ani**. For the change of the first radical of this Semitic word to **f**, **k**, and **z**, and **'**; of the second radical to **n**; and of the third radical to **k**, and **'**, see Ch. II.

Kara, or **ġara**, redup. **ġaraġara**, v. i., or a., strong, and d. **karakarai**, or **garakarai**, strong, **taġaraġara**, strong, vehement. [My. *kras*, hard, violent, strong, vehement, force, Mg. *heri*, power, strength, force, might, *miheri*, strong, powerful, mighty, *heri*, being forced to, compelled, constrained.] A. ḳahara, n. a., ḳahr', to be mighty, might, force, alḳahharo, omnipotent (God).

Kara, or **ġara**, redup. **ġaraġara**, v. i., or a., to be dry, **baġara i**, v. c., to make dry, to dry (a thing), **nakarān**, the being dry, also, the being (bare and dry) poor, poverty; **kara**, dry, then hard, strong, stiff, rigid (as dry wood). See also **kara**, s., and **makarakara**, v. i., infra. [My. *kriġ*, dry, *kriġ kan*, to dry (a thing), Mg. *haraka*, dried up, scorched, parched.] H. ḥarar, to burn, be hot (cf. A. ḥarra, E. ḥarara); the primary idea is that of 'the shrivelled roughness of things that are dried or scorched', Ges.; to be burned, to be dried up.

Kara, s., c. art. **nekara**, the nettle (so called from its burning; compare **makarakara**, to be burning, to be hot, as the mouth with pepper, or the skin stung by a nettle). See preceding word, and compare H. **ḥarul**, the nettle, so called from its burning, from the root **ḥaral=ḥarar.**

Kara ki, or **ġara ki**, v., to seize, grasp, and

Kar i, or **ġar i**, v. t., to scratch, scrape, shave, seize, redup. **ġarikar i**, also **karu-ti**, or **ġaru-ti**, v. t., to scratch, and **karo i**, or **ġaro i**, v. t., to scratch, scrape, redup. **ġarokaro**, and **karokaro**, **karokaroa**, or **ġarokaroa**, itchy, scratchy, scabby, and **ġaru**, and **taġaru**, v. t., to seize, grasp, **ġaru sera**, (grasp everything) be grasping, redup. **ġarukaru**, id., **karo**, to scrape, sweep, to swim (i.e. *sweep* with the arms—to swim without doing this is **āfa**, or **ofa**), **karati**, **karakarati**, scratched, marked, scored; **kārĭ**, s., a plane (from being moved with a sweeping or sawing motion, or shaving); **kare-si**, v. t., to scratch, scrape; **ġure-si**, v. t., to gnaw, scranch. [My. *garis*, Ja. *garit*, to scratch, score, *garu*, to rake, &c., *garut*, scratch, scrape, claw, *garok*, to scrape, *gârap*, grasp at, *gâraji*, a saw, *greb*, to gnaw, *karat*, *karot*, *kârot*, grind or gnash the teeth, make a grating noise, *karut*, to scratch, *kârok*, to rub, curry (a horse), *kikir*, to rasp, file, a rasp, file, avaricious, Mg. *haraṭa*, shaved, *manaraṭa*, to shave, *kuri*, gnaw, scrape, Fi. *kari*, or *karikari*, v. i., *kari-a*, *karitaka*, v. t., to scrape, *karokaro*, prickly heat, itch, Sa. *'ili*, a rasp, file, saw.] A. **garra**, to drag, snatch, sweep, seize, H. **garar**, to scrape, sweep, saw (primary meaning), to drag or snatch away, to saw (**mĕgerah**, a saw), to gargle, produce rough sounds in the throat (see Ef. **karo**, throat, infra), cognates S. **graʿ**, to shave, H. **garaʿ**, scratch, scrape (see Ef. **ġura i**, **maġir i**), &c.

Karab, s., dd. **karau**, **karaf**, **karam**, a cutting instrument. H. **ḥereb**, id.

Karafi, v. t., to scratch, scrape (the earth or ground); hence

Karafi, v. i., to creep on the ground (as it were scratching or scraping on the ground): see **kar i**. **Karafi** is **kara-fi.**

Karaka, v. i., to move tremulously (creep), as crabs and such like animals do; **karaka ki naburuma**, (a mother-in-law) creeps or shrinks away from her son-in-law (trembling and afraid): **kara-ka**, compare preceding word.

Karakarati, a., see **kar i.**

Karati, and redup.,

Kare-si, v. t., to scratch, scrape, and, from the idea of scraping together, being gathered together.

Karesi, or **karisi**, s., a cluster (as of cocoanuts), and

Karesibum, d. for **karesi-bunu** (see **bunu**), pr. n., of a person mentioned in a myth, one of the two sons of a woman who came down from heaven, lit. seize—kill. See **kar i**, and **bunu**.

Karei sa, d. **karei ki nia**, v. t., to dislike, be averse from, hate. [My. *iri*, to hate, Mg. *hala*, hated, detested, abhorred.] A. **kariha**, to dislike, abhor.

Karei, or **ġarei turi**, to dislike (the thing he is bidden or sent to do) abiding with (some one). See **turi**, and cf. **kita roā sa**.

Kārĭ, s., a plane. See **kar i**.

Kārĭ, v. i., to hasten, **takārĭ**, id. [Ma. *kari*, rush along violently.] A. **kāra**, 1, 8, to hasten.

Kari-iki (**kariki**), s., little child, little children, and

Kari-kiki (**karikiki**), s., id. (**kiki**, little), and

Kari-riki (**kaririki**), s., d., **riki**, little, and **kari**, boy, child. A. **‘‘ail’**, Mahri gairu, H. **‘ul**, S. **‘ula**, boy, child. See Index under غال.

Karo, **karoi**, **ġaroi**, v. i., to swim (sweeping with the arms): **kar i**.

Karokaro, and

Karokaroa, scabby, itchy: **kar i**.

Karo na, s., c. art., dd. **ġaṭo na** (**ġaro na**), **kanro na**, the throat, gullet. H. **garon**, the throat, from **garar** (see **kar i**), E. **g’ĕre**, the throat.

Karo, v. i., d., to be uncovered, have the clothes off, naked. H. **galah**, to be naked. See **ġiriġiri**.

Karu-ti, or **karut i**. See **kar i**.

Kasā, and **kasafa**, also **kasāna**, inter. ad., for what? why? d. **kua** : **ka**, final conj., and **sā**, or **safa**, q.v., what? See Ch. V. 5.

Kasāna, inter. ad., for what? **kasā**, with the dem. **na** suffixed.

Kasau, s., c. art., small branch, fruit stalk, **nakasau na**, its small branch, d. (transposed) **sakau**, id., and also a reef. See **sakau**. [My. *gusoġ*, a reef of rocks.] A. **ḳaṣ’ib’**, long and slender branch, H. **ḳiṣbe’**, pl. const., ‘the ends, i.e. the roots *of the mountains* (in the depth of the sea),’ Jon. ii. 7; perhaps, the branches *of the mountains* (running out into the sea).

Kas i, or **kasi**, **ġas i**, v. t., to rub, wipe. [My. *gosok*, *gosot*, *gosoki*, *gisik*, *kisil*, to rub, Mg. *kasuka*, rubbed, *mikasuka*, to rub.] A. **ḳas’s’a**, (3), to rub, **kas’a’** (**ḳas’w’**), to rub, wipe.

Kas-toru, s., handkerchief, lit. sweat-wiper: **kas i**, and **toru**, q.v.

Kasĭ, v. i., or a., to be sweet, redup. **ġkasi** (**ġakasi**), dd.

ġari, ġaṭ, kati. [Cf. Mg. *hanița*, fragrance, *manița*, sweet smelling, My. *manis*, sweet, luscious, mild, gentle.] A. naḳuṣa, to be sweet, naḳiṣ', sweet, fragrant with sweet odour.

NOTE.—The ḳ elided and initial n retained in My. and Mg.

Kāsu, s., an old man, a kind of priest or sacred man. [Fi. *qase*, an old man.] S. ḳas'is'o, an old man, a priest, from kas', to grow old (Freytag), A. kas's', a Christian Presbyter.

Kasu, or **kas**, d. **kau**, s., c. art. nakasu, tree, wood. [Epi dd. *yesi*, *lakai*, Ml. dd. *nige*, *nai*, TaSa. *tagai* (*taghai*), Fut. *rakau*, Sa. *laau*, My. *kayu*, Mg. *hazu*, tree, wood, Mg. *hazu*, hard.] H. ʿeṣ, tree, wood, Ch. ʾaʿ, from H. ʿaṣah, A. ʿaṣaʾ, to be hard, firm. See Index.

Kasua, or **ġasua**, d. **kasu**, v. i., or a., hard, strong, redup. kaskasua, id., nakasuāna, s., the being hard or strong, strength. [Ja. *kakas*, hard, firm, rigid, stiff, cf. *kuwasa*, strong.] H. ḳas'ah, A. ḳasaʾ, to be hard, stiff, H. ḳas'eh, hard, firm, fast, strong, powerful.

NOTE.—In Ef. naḅona i ġasua, his heart is hard, meri ġasua ki nia, treat him hardly, or with violence.

Kat, or **kati**, v. i., to thunder, tĭfai i kat, or i ġat, the thunder thunders. See following word.

Kat i, or **ġat i**, v. t., to bite, to make fast, as, nakasu i ġati natua na, the log makes fast his foot, i.e. jambs it and holds it firmly fixed against something; to compress between two things; to bite, redup. katikati, na kakat, s., a bite, fikit, to bite each other, savage; nalaġi i katikati, the wind becomes fixed (in a certain direction); i tua ġat ia sa, he gave him for it, i mate ġat ia, he died for it, as, for sin; i kati, or ġati, to thunder, is said to be the same word, tifai i ġat, and when a 'thunderbolt' rends a tree it is said, tifai i ġati ḅora ia, the thunder bites, rending it (ḅora I). The Efatese say that the thunder has teeth, and the idea in tifai i ġat is that the tifai is biting, i.e. grinding its teeth together, or rending with its teeth. [Ma. *kati*, block up, closed, *kakati*, a bundle, sheaf, and, v. t., tie up in bundles, *katikati*, v. i., champ, move the jaw as in eating, Fi. *kata* (*vei kata* = *fikit*), to bite, a., close together, as boards on a floor, My. *gigit*, to bite, *gigitan*, a bite, Mg. *hehița*, s., hold, grasp, seizure, clutch, bite, *kaikița*, a bite, bitten, *manaikița*, v. t., to bite, *kekerina*, being bitten.] S. nkat, to bite.

Katak, v. i., to coagulate. [My. *kantal*, *kandal*, id.] A. ḥ'atara, id.

Katau, s., a kind of crab. [Cf. My. *kâtam*, a crab; to nip, snip off.] Cf. A. ḳaṭama, to bite, cut off. See **koto**, a kind of crab, infra.

Kate, tense part., d., past, **a kate**, **ku kate**, **i kate**, **au kate**, &c.: **ka**, and **te**.

Kate, s., c. art. **nakate**, anything, a thing, lit. the that-that, d. **nete** (**ne te**, the that). See **ka**, and **te**. [Fi. *ka*, a thing.] Dem. **ka**, and dem. **te**.

Kate, s., **kate ni rarua**, the stick on the outside of the canoe superstruction on the side opp. to the **sama**.

Katema, ad., outside of the house. H. ḥuṣ, outside, and **ema**, house. See **imrum**, **suma**. In **ekatema**, q.v.

Kati, d. for **kasi**, sweet, redup. **kakati**.

Katoro, s., a basket. A. ḳa'-ṭarat, a basket.

Kau, s., a collection, bunch, herd, &c. A. gam', a collection, gama'a, v. See **umkau**, **makau**, **ko-fakal**. [Sa. *'au*, a troop, gang, bunch, cluster.]

Kau, or **ġau**, redup. **kaukau** (c. art. **aġau**, d. **ni kam**, tongs, forceps, nippers, for grasping), v. t., to grasp with the hand, **i kau naḅe**, he grasps a club (carried on his shoulder), then to carry anything on the shoulder, **i kau näuos**, he grasps the oar (in rowing), **i kaukau narā nakasu**, (the flying fox) grasps the branch of a tree (moving along it as it were hand over hand, till it finds a resting-place), hence, **ba kaukau**, (of men) go seeking a resting-place. See **kam**, **kamut i**. [My. *gawa*, Fi. *kauta*, to carry.]

Kau, d. **au**, a lizard, perhaps from grasping or clinging.

Kau, v. i., to bend (as with hunger), also **kai**, and **kaf**, q.v.

Kau, s., d. for **kasu**, tree, wood.

Kau, v. i., or a., d. for **kasua**, hard, strong.

Kaua, s., an open worked wicker basket or trap for catching fish: so called because

Kaukaua, a., full of openings or apertures, as if windowed, or apertured: the final **a** is the a. ending. A. **kaww'**, an opening in a wall, **kawwat**, a window (Nm. **couwa**, dormer window), Ch. **kaw**, a window, from **kawah**, or **kavah**.

Kaukau, s., c. art. **nakaukau**, the upper cross (i.e. above, and across the **kiat**) or binding sticks between a canoe and its outrigger (**sama**); from grasping or holding together, **kau**, v. t.

Käuota, v. i., or a., to be great, plentiful, dd. **kōte**, **ēt**, q.v.

Kĕ, or **kē** (cf. **kei**), dem., this. See **ka**, id., and **ko**, id.

Ke, d., that he, **k'**, final conj., and **e** (or i) verb. pron., 3 sing.: **ka**, **k**.

Kē, **keke**, interj. See **ake**! and **ako**! [Florida *ke! keke!*]

Ke, d., verb. pron., 2 sing., you, dd. **k**, **ma**, **ko**.

Keikei, s., c. art. **nakeikei**, tattoo marks or lines upon the skin. [Fi. *qia*, to tattoo.] See **ġoi** (or **koi**, or **kei**).

Kei naniu, for **koi naniu**. See **ġoi**.

Kei, d., dem., this, that (near), for **koi**, q.v.

Kekel, s., d. for **kal**, child, infant. See under **bakal i** I.

Kēl, redup. **ġkēl** (**kekel**), v. i., to sweep round or wheel in curves (of a bird in flight without moving its wings); and

Kēla, s., the curved beam or wall-plate that goes round the end of a native house; and

Kele-ti, v. t. (see **ġolu-ti**, **ġele-ti**, **ġel i**, **ġulu-ti**, **kaluti**), as, **keleti**, **kel**, or **ġolu nāsu**, put the bowstring on a bow, **nuana i laba i keleti narā nakasu**, its (a tree's) fruit plentiful *bends* the branch of the tree, **i keleti uaġo** (or other heavy thing to be carried), he stoops down and clasps the pig (or other heavy thing) to lift and carry it, hence, **kelakela**, or **ġelakela** (of a people carrying such things, as in going to a **naleöuan**); and

Kelu-faki, v. t., to round or double a cape (of a canoe or ship), cg. syn. **ili-fiki**; and

Kēlu, a., going round, as **baġana kēlu**, its (the army's) rear or hinder part (see **baġo**, **baġa**), going round, making a détour (to surprise the enemy). [My. *guliġ*, *goliġ*, *giliġ*, *guluġ*, to turn round, revolve, roll, roll up, *igal*, to whirl, curly, and *ikal*, to whirl, gyration, Mg. *kudia*, a wheel, rolled, *mikudia*, *mikudiadia*, to roll, and *mikudinkudina*, &c., also *kuriana*, twirled, *mikuriana*, to twirl, and *misiġerina*, *misiġeriġerina*, to turn, wind, roll, revolve, also *hudina*, &c.] E. **k'arar**, often red., A. **karra**, n. a. **karat'**, go round, revolve, **karkara**, to turn (a mill) round, 2, to revolve, wheel (as a bird in flight). See Ges. s. v. H. **karar**, for egg.

Ken, for **kana**, v. i.

Kerikeri, v. i., to be deep, as a pit, the sea. A. **ḳa'ara**, to be deep.

Kesa, **kesakesa**, **ġesa**, **ġesakesa**. See **kisa**.

Kētaku, or **kēĭtaku**, s., the hinder end of a canoe, ad. behind: for **ko itaku**. See **kobē**, and **ko**, face.

Ki, ad., see **ka**, ad., as: also in **kite**.

Ki, d., **k'**, dem., and **i**, verb. pron., 3 sing., syn. c. the simple **i**.

Kĭ, d., dem., this, or **kĕ**, id.: **ka**, dem.

Ki, v. i., to be fearful, faint-hearted, shrink from (for fear). H. **ka'ah**, A. **ka'a**, id.

Ki, prep. (the usual form), c. art., **aki**, the, that which to, or of, also **ġi**, **aġi**. See ka, prep.

Ki, same as **ka**, art.

Ki, redup. **kiki**, v. i. See **ġi**, **ġki** (**ġiki**), v. i., to squeak.

Ki, d., verb. pron., 2 pl., you, dual **kia** : **ku**.

Kia-, or **kie-**, pref. to the nom. suf. forming possessive pronouns **kiaġu**, **kiama**, **kiana**, **kiaġita**, **kiaġami**, **kiamu**, **kiara**, or **kiata** : **kiana**, his (country, plantation, house, vicinity). The use of **kakana** is different, his or its (as a weapon to kill him, a door for a house, oar for a boat, &c.) [Epi *kiaku*, *kiamo*, *kiano*, *kiandro*, *kiememi*, *kiemiu*, *kialo*, same as Ef. **kiaġu**, **kiama**, &c.] Ef. **kia-**, is in Ta. **kafa-**, Ef. **kiaġu** = Epi **kiaku** = Ta. **kafak**, 'my'. See Ch. V. 11. (3), (7).

Kia, d., verb. pron., 2 dual, you two, d. **ko ra**. [Epi *ko*, An. *ekau*, id.]

Kiaġ, d. for **kiama**, thy (vicinity) : **kia-**, and **ġ**, suf. pron., 2 sing.

Kiat, s., c. art. **nakiat**, the sticks which cross from the canoe to the outrigger (sama) joining them together. [Sa. Tah. *iato*, Ta. *nikiatu*, Fut. *akiato*, Ha. *iako*, id., Ma. *kiato*, thwart of a canoe.] A. **ḥ'āta**, to sew, to join together, **ḥ'iato**.

Kie, s., c. art. **nàkie**, the plant whose leaf is baked, dried, and split into thin threads to be woven into mats, &c. [Sa. *'ie*, a fine mat, cloth.] See under **neko**.

Kiġami, d. **kinami**, 1 pers. pron. exclusive.

Kiġita, d. syn. **niġita**, 1 pers. pron. inclusive.

Kīkĭ, v. i., or a., and **iki** in **kariki**, small. [To. *iki*, id.] For **riki**, q.v.

Kikita, or **ġkita**, redup. of **kita**.

Kilakila, a., knowing, sagacious, shy, **i meta kilakila** (of an animal). [Fi. *kila*, wild, suspicious, on the look-out, as an animal.] A. **'akala**, 1, 2, to be intelligent, prudent, sagacious, **'akil'**, a., id.

Kil i, or **kili**, v. t., to dig, hence **kāli**, s., a digging stick, and **nakīli**, s., a current (as in the sand, lit. that which digs). [Sa. *'eli*, to dig, *ma'eli*, to be dug, My. *gali*, to dig, Mg. *hadi*, ditch, trench, &c., dug, *mihadi*, to dig, Ma. *keri*, *kari*, to dig.] E. **karaya**, A. **kara'**, H. **karah**, Ch. **kera'**, to dig.

Kīli, s., c. art. **nakīli**, d., a current : **kili**.

Kilikili, v., redup. of **kili**, used of many digging : **ru kilikili**, they (as the people of a district and whose yams are ripe) dig.

Kĭlìti, s., a sow, a mother-pig. [An. *karite*, or *kerite*, an animal that has had young.] Kiliti, lit. that brings forth (young), or the bringer forth, i.e. mother. See **ani**, note, and **kano**.

Kin, s. See **ikin**, nest.

Kin, d., dem., this: **ki**, dem., and **in**, dem. [Assy. *agannu*, this, **aga**, dem., and **annu**, dem.]

Kinam, d. **kinami**,

Kinami, pers. pron., 1 pl., excl., we, they; **k'**, dem. **ina**, we, **'mi**, they.

Kinau, pers. pron., 1 sing., I, shortened **kinu**, dd. **keino**, **anu**, **enu**: **k'**, dem. prefix, and **'nau** (for **'naku**, hence nom. suf. **ġu**, d. **k**). [An. *aiñak*, Epi. *naġ'u*, TaSa. *enau*, Sa. *o a'u* (for *ko aku*), My. *aku*, Mg. *izahu*, *ahu*, I.] H. **'anoki**, shortened **'ăni**, Assy. **anaku**, Aram. **'ăna'**, **'eno'**, E. **'ana**, I.

Kinit i, also **ġinit i**, and **ġunut i**, v. t., nip with the fingers, **nakini na**, the fingers (nippers), **kini ġote-fi**, nip, breaking it (reeds for thatching), hence **nakini-ġot**, reeds for thatching. [Fi. *kinit'a*, nip, pinch between finger and thumb, Sa. *'ini*, to take hold of with the nails, pinch, ps. *'initia*, Ma. *kini*, Ha. *iniki*, My. *gântâs*, to break off, nip off, snap off.] A. **ḳaraṣa**, to nip (with the fingers), pinch, grasp with the points of the fingers or hand, snip off;

Kini na, s., c. art., the fingers, or toes, lit., the nippers, or graspers; also claws, talons;

Kini ġote-fi, v. t., and

Kiniġot, s., c. art., see **kinit i**.

Kintu, dem., that (near): **kin**, dem., and **tu**.

Kinu, I, see **kinau**.

Kiri, d., s., c. art. **nakiri**, d. syn. **ori**, rubbing stick for producing fire. [Sa. *'ili*, rasp, file, saw.] See **kar i**, **maġiri**.

Kirikiri, s., gravel, pebble. [Sa. *'ili'ili*, Ma. *kirikiri*, My. *krikil*, *kârikil*, *karikil*, gravel, pebble.] H. **garger**, A. **girgir'**, a berry, from H. **garar**, see **kar i**, cg. A. **garal'**, gravel.

Kirikiri, a., small, like pebbles, **bia kirikiri**, little children. See preceding word.

Kīs, s., a shell, used for cutting. A. **giz'at**, a shell, from **gaza'a**, to cut.

Kis, d., dem., this, here: **ki**, dem., and **sĕ**, dem.

Kisa, a., in **mita kisa**, blind (the eyes sunk into the head). A. **ḥaṣ'**, id. And

Kisa, or **ġisa**, v. i., or a., redup.,

Kisakisa, v. i., or a., to be putting forth leaves, hence to be green; hence

Kisa, s., c. art., **nakisa**, d. **takis**, a green stone or chalk (used only for painting himself by a chief), a chief's grave (in the bush, sacred). A. **ḥ'awiṣa**, to have the eyes sinking into the head, 4, to put forth leaves (a plant), to germinate.

Kihi na, d. **kui na**, q.v.: **kihi na**, i.e. **kisi na** (h being for s in that d.).

Kis i, or **kisi**, v. t., also **ġis i**, redup. **ġiskis**, to feel, touch, **lo ġiskis**, to look, exploring (as at a person's body partly uncovered). A. **gassa**, to feel, touch, to explore or grope with the hand or with the eyes, H. **gas′as′**, Pi., E. **gasasa**, to feel, touch, S. **gas′**, to feel, touch, to explore.

Kĭsau, v. i., d. **kĭsur**, to remove, get out, stand apart: **i kisau ki nabua**, he removes from, or stands out, or gets out of the road, **ba kisau**, get out (of the way), remove, stand away. A. **ḳaṣa'**, **ḳaṣww'**, **ḳuṣuww'**, **ḳaṣā'**, to stand apart, to be remote.

Kistu, dem., this here: **kis**, dem., and **tu**.

Kĭsur (**ksur**), d. for **kisau**. See (d.) **ēsu**.

Kĭta, a., little, small, **li kita**, small place (name of small boat entrance of Havannah Harbour) opp. to **li leba**, big place (name of large entrance to Havannah Harbour). [Sa. *iti, itiiti*, small, few, Ma. and Tah. *iti, itiiti*, small, little, My. *kate, kite*, Mg. *kitika*, diminutive.] H. **ḳaṭan**, to be small, little.

Kita (rare), or **kite**, ad., as, takes the verb. pron., as **i kite fatu**, it is as (or like) a stone, **kite**, or **kite uan**, as, as if, **i bisa i kite i maieto**, he speaks as if he were angry, **i marafi kite nifila**, it is quick as lightning. A. **kaḍa**, like, as this, as that. See **ki**, as, and **te**, **kite**, or **kita**, lit., as that, or like that: **te**, dem.

Kita, or **kite**, conj., or, d. **ko**: **rarua kite boat**, a canoe or boat; inter. particle at the end of sentences, d. **ko**, as **i bano kite?** has he gone? fully this is, **i bano kite i tika?** has he gone or not? For **kite**, disj. conj., see **ko**, conj., infra.

Kita, v., to divine, redup. **kikita**, **ġkita**, lit. to perceive or feel with the eye or the mind (cf. **roġo**, **roroġo**), **bati kita i**, or **ġita i**, to try (cf. **bati roġ i**), lit. make or do feeling or perceiving or knowing or finding out. [Ma. *kite*, to see, know, perceive, find out, discover, *matakite*, to divine, s. one who foresees an event, Mg. *hita, mahita.*] A. **wagada**, to find with the eye or the mind (*a thing sought*), to perceive by the feeling of the body (*a thing*), or by the mind, 4, make to find or to perceive.

Kità i, and **ġità i**, v. t., to hate, redup. **kitakita i**, to be envious of, to hate; and

Kita roà sa, or **kita roà i**, to hate turning after him (someone), as a boy sent a message meeting another boy and (hating to do the message)

turns after him to play. See roa. H. ḳuṭ, followed by prep. bĕ, to loathe, also ḳuṣ and naḳaṭ.

Kita, in **bakita** and **bakitakita**. See **makitakita**, id.

Kite. See **kita**, ad.

Ko, verb. suf., 2 sing., you, dd. **k, ke, ma, ġ**.

Ko, d., verb. pron., 2 sing., you, d. **ku**, d. **ke**.

Ko, sign of imperative, 2 pl. (sing. **ba**), lit. that you: **k'**, final conj., and **o**, fragment of pers. pron., 2 pl.

Ko, d., ad. of assent, d. syn. **na**, and redup.,

Koko, id., d. **ko**, interj. See **ako** and **kori**: **ko**, dem.

Ko, d. for **uo** (**wo**), as **i ko toko** (d. for **i uo toko**) he (is) remaining (has not yet gone). See **bo**, supra, (**k** for **b**).

Ko, dem. See **koi**, E. **ku**, dem.

Ko, d., disj. conj., or; inter. particle at the end of a sentence, as, **i bano ko?** has he gone? fully, **i bano ko i tika?** has he gone or not? D. syn., in both uses, **kite**, or **kita**. [An. *ka*, id., Er. *ku*, or.] H. A., S., **'aw**, or.

NOTE.—**Kite** has a dem. suffixed to **ki, te**, and therefore lit. denotes or—this.

Ko, s., c. art. **nàko na** (or **n ako**), the face, a part; **nakona**, his face (see **nako**, infra), **nakonako ki**, to face (someone), **nako nafakotoen**, a part of the price, **ba tu au nakon**, give me a part, **nakon ru bano nakon ru toko**, a part (of the whole number of men) go, a part remain; and, without the article, shortened to **ko**, as, **ko-bē ni rarua**, or **nakobe**, the forepart of a canoe, **keitaku ni rarua**, or **nako-itaku**, the after-part of a canoe; **ko-be**, the part before, the front, **i baki kobe**, he goes to the front, **kē-itaku**, the part behind, behind, **i baki kē-itaku**, he goes behind, or to the rear. A. **wagt'** (**wagṭo**), the face, a part or side, **wigāt**, a band, **wagaha**, 3, to face (someone).

Koa, a., fibrous, stringy, as a yam when cooked, **naui koa**: **aka, ako**, and **a**, a. ending.

Koakoa, redup. of **koa**, very stringy or fibrous.

Koau, s., c. art. **nakoau**, d. **kabu**, the native pudding. See **kofu sa**.

Koba-si, v. t., to follow, to drive away, to pursue: **i koba nabona**, he follows his own heart (does or strives to do what is in his mind); v. r., **fikoba**, to follow each other, or to drive away each other;

Koba-usi, v. t., i.e. **koba**, and **usi**, to track; to follow after. A. **kafā**, to follow, to drive away.

Kobara, s., see **ġobara**.

Kobu, d. See **kubu**.

Kofa, s., and redup.,

Kofakofa, s., an alcove, temporary house or shed, tent.

H. ḳubah, a tent, chamber (so called from its arched form, from ḳabab, to make gibbous and hollow, to arch, to vault). A. ḳubbaṭ, tent, vault, chamber, hence the word *alcove.*

Kofakal, s., a herd of pigs cared for, lit. herd cared for: **ko** for **kau,** q. v., a herd, and **fakal.**

Kofe na, s., **nakofena,** his skull, the skull. A. ḳiḥf', the skull.

Kofeta, d., s., **fata,** q.v., a bench, platform.

Kofu sa, v. t., to enclose (as fish in a net), wrap up or en-enclose (as a pudding in leaves, to be put in the oven). See **kabu,** d. **koau,** the native pudding ; and

Kofukofua, a., redup., and with a. ending **a,** bent up at the edges, as a shovel, or anything, as it were *rolled up* or turned over. The pudding, **koau,** is laid on a mass of leaves, very wide and long, which are rolled up or over it all round, completely enclosing it, and then tied up. [Fi. *kovuta, kokofu* blistered (small balls or pimples), *kovu,* banana leaf in which native puddings are done up, d., a coat, *kovuna,* to do up in a *kovu,* Sa. *'ofu,* a garment, *'o'ofu,* put on a garment, *'ofu'ofu,* to envelop in leaves (for cooking), *'ofulua,* twenty leaf dishes of native food ; Ma. *kohu, kokohu,* a., somewhat concave, bent or warped so as to become concave (cf. Ef. **kofukofua**), *kohu,* to cook in a native oven any article contained in a hollow vessel, To. *kofu,* to enclose or wrap up, to clothe, Ha. *ohu,* to roll up (as the sea that does not break) a roller, a swell, *ohua,* a crowd of people, *ohui,* to twist round, *ohuohu,* heavy, burdensome, a wreath worn round the neck, to dress in uniform, Tah. *ohu,* a bank or ridge of earth thrown up, a bundle of native food tied up and baked in the native oven, to bend downwards as the branch of a tree, to stoop, to twirl round as a wheel.] A. **kabba,** to roll up into a ball, to make into balls (food) for cooking, to invert, to stoop, to be heavy, A. **kobbat', kabāb',** (see under **kabu,** d. **koau,** supra): **kobbat** also denotes a mob of horses, crowd or mass of men, herd of camels, a ball of threads rolled up together, a heavy ponderous thing, a hill, **kabkaba,** 2, to be wrapped up, enveloped, to wrap up or envelop oneself in one's garment).

Koĭ, d., dem., this, d. **kei** : **ko** dem., and **i,** dem.

Koia (ko-ia, ko-ya), same as preceding.

Koi, s., and

Koika, s., a boundary, from

Koi, or **ko i,** v. t. See **ġoi.**

Koko, s., c. art. **nekoko,** reddish juice or paint for **nafona,** made from a plant (also called **nekoko**): **ġoko i.** [To. *koka*, Sa. *'o'a*, id.]

Kokoro, s. See under **ġor i.**

Kokoti, s., a net for catching fish: **koto.**

Kola, d., and redup.,

Kokola, v. i., to be bent, d. **kolo, kola ki na buruma,** (a mother-in-law) bends or stoops to the son-in-law. H. **kara'**, id., transposed. A. **raka,** see **lako,** infra.

Kola, v. i., and redup.,

Kokola, v. i., or **ġkola,** to be arid, dry; hence

Kōla, s., a dry stick or log. A. **ḳahala, ḳohol',** to be arid, dry.

Kola, v. i., and **ġola,** and redup. **ġkola (kokola),** to call out, cry out, to speak loud; hence

Kola oli, s., echo, lit. calling out like. See **oli.** [Fi. *kaila*, to shout, Mg. *akura*, s., shouting.] H. **ḳara',** to cry out, call out.

Kolau, redup. **ġkolau.** See **ġalau i.**

Kolau, s. See **kalau,** spider's web, dd. **kalai, nilau; namera kolau,** web of fat on the inwards of a pig. [An. *nilva* = **kolau,** *nilvanilva* = **namera-kolau.**]

Kolau (see preceding word), pr. n., prob. originally given to a warrior full of stratagems. See also the verb under **kalau,** to weave, to lie in wait, watch in ambush (as in war). A. **'aruba,** to be wily or cunning.

Kolobu na, s., its joint (of a bamboo or reed), applied also to the knobs or rivets on a tank. A. **karibu,** joint of a bamboo or reed.

Kolōfa, v. c., to be bent, as with hunger or famine, redup. **ġkolōfa.** See **lofa i, lōfa.** [Fi. *kalove*, bent, from *love-t'a*, to bend.]

Komam, dd. **kinami, kimam.**

Kon, v. i., or a. (with ending **n**), and redup.,

Kokon, ġkon, to be bitter (of anything), **kona ki,** to be bitter towards (someone), **namarita na i ġkon,** his belly is bitter (he is angry). [Sa. *'ona*, *'o'ona*, bitter, sour. *'ona*, bitter, poisonous, *'onā*, to be poisoned, *'o'ona*, *'onasia*.] A. **ḥoma-t,** E. **ḥama-t,** H. **ḥamah,** bitter, heat, gall, poison.

Konai na, s., c. art. **nakonai na,** his gall or bile: **kon,** bitter.

Kona, v. i., **ġona,** to stand firm, to be fixed, firm, then, to have the mind fixed upon, to be occupied with, **kona ki.** H. **kun,** prop. to stand upright, Hi. to set up, found, then to apply one's mind to, Ni. to stand firm, fixed, steady, firm, constant;

Kona ġor i, v., to stand firm protecting him (as in war). See **ġor i.**

Konā i, or **konai,** v. t., and **ġonai,** to pierce (as a board with an instrument like an awl). E. **ḳanawa,** to pierce.

Konai sai, v., to pierce through. See **sai.**

Kore na, s., see **ġore na**, brother's sister, sister's brother, children of the same mother (actually), or, if not, members of the same **nakainaġa.**

Kor i. See **ġor i.**

Korò sa, v. t., conceal it (as misconduct of which one is accused): **ġor i.**

Koro, s., c. art. **nakoro**, a fence, a wall, d. **àra**, c. art. **nàra**: **ġor i.**

Kōro, s., a fish fence, enclosure for catching fish; a ring (or halo) round the moon: **ġor i.**

Koro, s., c. art. **nekoro**, incantation or rites of divination; and

Koro, v., to divine: **ġor i.**

Koroatĕlaġi, d., or **nakoroatĕlaġi**, the sky, dd. **koroinlaġi, rikitĕlaġi**, lit. the fence, or that which surrounds or encloses the **atĕlaġi**, q.v.

Koroinlaġi, s., d., the sky, lit. the fence, or that which encloses heaven. See **laġi, elaġi.**

Koroki, v., to insist (as in argument), provoke, irritate. S. **gareg** (Pael), to provoke.

Kori, or **koria**, also **kuri**, or **kuria**, s., a dog, a warrior, a brave, cognate **oro**, to bark. [Sa. *uli*, id., Ma. *kuri*, a dog, any quadruped, To. *kuli*, a dog, Fut. *kuli*, Ta. *kuri*, Epi *kuli, kuliu*, TaSa. *vuriu*, Malo *vuria*, Ml. *kuri*, id.] A. **gorw'**, a young dog, **gariyy'**, brave.

Kori, interj., also in **akori, kori la!** this now indeed! here, or there indeed! **ko**, dem., **ri**, dem.

Koro, v. i., to snore. See **ġoro.**

Kọroi, d. **kurüi**, a woman; and

Koruni, kuruni, q.v. See Ch. II. 17. *e*.

Kos i, kus i, v. t., to cut or shear off (as the end of the outer covering of a young cocoanut fit for drinking); and

Kosu-mi, v. t., to husk a cocoanut, also **kusu-mi, ġusu-mi; i ġusu**, v. i., said of a ripe cocoanut which separates itself and falls from the tree, **kusu-mi**, or **ġusu-mi**, v. t., to gather cocoanuts from the tree, **kusu**, or **ġusu**, v. i., to be ripe, soft, **makusukusu**, to be ripe, soft, **kusue na**, s., the soft place on the top of a child's head, the last to close up, **makus**, q.v., s., cutter or knife. A. **gazza**, to cut off, shear; to cut (grass, &c.) in order to gather provender, to cut off the clusters of dates from the tree; to begin to ripen (dates), 4, to have (sheep) ready for shearing, or ripe grain, to be ready to be gathered from the tree (dates), to be ripe or ready for gathering (fruit of the palm tree), for reaping (grain), for shearing (sheep); **migazz'**, a cutting instrument.

Kosu, s., a cutting instrument

made of bone: preceding word.

Kosoāfa, s., c. art. **nakosoafa,** dd. **nasoāfa, soāfa,** a plant used in ceremonial or ritual purifications: it is swept down the limbs to carry away the uncleanness; lit. the tree that carries (away); **kosu** (see **kasu**), and **afa i.**

Kota, s., a time, in, **i ta kota ki** (a person), he appoints a time to or for (someone); and in

Kotfān, d. for **ġotafānu, ġota fānu,** q.v., evening.

Kōte, d. for **käuota,** and **ēt,** q.v.

Koto bolo, s., a basket (see **bolo**). [Ml. *gat,* Malo *gete,* To. *kato,* Sa. *'ato,* a basket.] A. **ka'ṭat,** a basket (for carrying dates).

Koto, s., a kind of crab: so called from nipping. See following word.

Koto-fi, v. t., **kote-fi, kotu-fi, ġote-fi,** redup. **kotokote-fi, ġotokote-fi** (intensive), to cut, to cut off, break off; **eni ġote-fi,** to lie across it, **bala taġoto,** inclined across, across, **ba ġote-fi,** go across it, **soka ġote-fi,** leap across it; **sai ġote-fi, tuba ġote-fi,** pronounce judgement against him, condemn him to death, **i ġotokoto bat i,** he made a beginning, first did it (*broke* ground in the doing of it), **makoto,** broken (a stick, or anything), ceases (as war), **a makoto ki,** I cease from (a thing, as a thing I have sold), have no further connection with, separate from, cease from (a thing or person), **kuti nakoau,** cut up the pudding (cooked), **ġkuti (ġukuti),** to make a stealthy invasion or inroad, **i ġai taġoto,** or **makotokoto,** he screams abruptly, cries out in sharp, sudden, broken screams; **kokoti,** a net (cutting off the fish); **baġote-fi,** to buy it (make it separate from its former owner); **i kote-flau isa,** he breaks me off from it (a thing I possessed); **bikutu,** v. r., decide about (someone), **bikutu ki nia,** decide about him, **sera makoto,** to be startled, surprised, **makot,** a place. [Sa. *'oti,* to cut (as the hair), *'o'oti, 'oti'oti,* Fi. *koti-va,* to clip, or shear, *ai koti,* scissors or shears (originally a shell or shark's tooth).] A. **ḳaṭa'a,** cut, cut off, separate, cross (a river); cease; decide about (a thing); to snap (as a rope), break; to break off, cease from (a journey, &c. = **makoto ki**); to invade, or make an inroad, stealthily, &c.; **maḳṭa',** a place.

Ku, verb. pron., 2 sing., and pl., you.

Ku, dem., this, as, **nai ku na,** d. **ġā kin,** this (is) he, or it, **nai ua naġa, nai ua, nai naġa, nai kis.** [My. *iku,* that.] E. **ku,** id. See **ko, ka, ki',** dem.

Ku, d., **kua**, or **ġua**, v. i., to cry out, vociferate, cry or call out, low (an ox). H. **ga'ah**, S. **g'o'**, cry out, vociferate, low (an ox).

Kua, **ġua**, preceding word.

Kua, ad., inter., and indef.: **ġua**, q.v.

Kuba na, s., c. art. **nakuba na**, its or his day; d. for **uba na**, or **ube na**, q.v.

Kubeġa, s., d., a net (for catching fish), d. **kuḅena**, id. [Sa. *upeġa*, Tah. *upea*, Ma. *kupeġa*, id.] A. **kiffat**, a net, from **kaffa**, to wrap round, &c.

Kubu, s., inside, the belly, also **kobu**, and **kabu**, d. **kama** (in **arekabu**, q. v., **ānekama**), then, inside (a house), and with the prep. **e**, **ekubu**, **ekobu**, in the inside, inside: then, **ekobu**, in one d. denotes also a house. [Mg. *kibu*, the belly, *kubani*, its centre or middle, *kubuni*, the inside, inner part, entrails.] A. **ga'fu**, the belly, interior cavity of a thing, inside (of a house), from **gāfa**, to be hollow.

Kufaġufa, d., v. i., to fly, to flap the wings, flutter. [To. *kapakapa*, to flap the wings, My. *kapak*, to fly, flapping the wings, not gliding.] A. **ḥ'afaḳa**, 1, 4, to fly, to flap with the wings.

Kui na, d., s., c. art. **nakui na**, d. **kihi na** (i. e. **kisi na**, in that d. h is for s), the back, rump, tail: **kui na** d. **bui na**, and **kihi na** (i. e. **kisa na**) d. **bisi na**, by the change of **b** and **k**.

Kuku, v. i. See **ġuku**.

Kuli na (d. **uili na**), s., the skin, bark. [Ha. *ili*, Ma. *kiri*, skin, bark, My. *kulit*, skin, hide, pelt, leather, bark, rind, husk, shell, Mg. *hudiṭa*, skin, bark.] A. **gilid**, id.

Kulu, v. i., to wrap oneself up, to cover oneself up (as in bed);

Kulu-ti, v. t., same as **kalu-ti**;

Kulu, s., c. art. **nakulu**, cloth, covering, that which covers;

Kulekule, or **kulukulu**, d., id.: **kalu**, q.v.

Kuma na, s., or **ġuma na**, c. art. **na kumana**, inner bark, pellicle, or cover, as of an egg, orange, &c.: d. for **kamu na**.

Kum i, v. t. (see **ġum i**), to absorb, redup. **kukumi**.

Kumu, d., pers. pron., 2 pl., you, dd. **akam** and **akamus**, **kami**, **nikam**, **nimu**, **nēm**, or **nēŏm**, **ēgū**. [My. *kamu*, Tag. *kamo*, Ml. P. *hamdi*, Epi *kamiu*, Ta. *ituma*, id.]

Kunuti na, s., c. art. **nakunuti na**, food, fruits, as the almond; also new yams. See **kan i**. A. **'ukīlat**, whatever is eaten, as fruits, &c.

Kūra, s., c. art. **nakūra**, a plant; so called from its bitterness. Of a stingy man who withholds food from a visitor it is said, **nalo anena**

i **bi nakūra.** See under **ġura i.**

Kuraf, d. for **karafl**, q.v.

Kuri, or **kurīa**, s., same as **kori, korīa,** dog.

Kūru, or **kūra**, a., shrivelled, dried, **nāli kuru,** shrivelled dried leaves (as banana leaves when withered and dry are). See **kara**, or **ġara.**

Kuru ki, v. t., to gather together; and

Kuru-maki, v. t., to gather together; and

Kuruk; and

Kukuruk (**ġkuruk**), v. i., or mid., to gather itself, or to be gathered together: see **ġuru ki**; belonging to this stem are also **takāra,** crowd (of men), and **makara,** to be gathered together, d. (transposed) **maraka,** or **meraka.** See **ġuru.**

Kuruku na, s., **kuruku natua na,** the ankle: **kuruk.** The ankle is so called because the leg *gathers itself*, as it were, into the knob of the joint.

Kurumase na, s., d. (transposed) for **borakese na,** q.v.

Kuruni, s., a woman. See Ch. II. 17. *e.* And

Kurui, s., a., id.

Kus, d., v. i., to be hidden; d. **ġusu** (i.e. **kusu**), q.v., to stoop. As to connection of these two meanings, see **ḅelu**: a man *stoops* to avoid being seen, or to be hidden.

Kus i, or **kusi**, v. t., to go in the track of, follow, usually **usi,** q.v. (the **k** being elided), **rafe kus i,** to go through following it (as a pig going through a hole in the fence of a garden following another pig(, hence the proverb, **uaġo iskai i ḅora bua nakoro, uaġo laba i rafe kus i,**"one pig bursts open the fence, many pigs go through the opening following (or after) it: in **takus i, rukus i (nrukus i)** the **k** also is not elided. See **usi.**

Kusu na, d., s., dd. **kui na, kihi na, bui na,** q.v.

Kusu, v. i., and

Kusue na, s. See **kosu-mi.**

Kusue, or **kusuüe** (pronounced **kusuwe**), d. **kusu**, s., rat (or mouse). [Ta. *yasuk*, Ml. dd. *khasup*, *akasu*, Pa. *asua*, Santo dd. *karibi*, *keriu*, Ma. *kiore*, Sa. *iore*, My. *tikus*, Mysol *kelof*, Gilolo *luf*, *lupu*, id.] A. ḳuṭrub', rat.

Kut i, v. t., to cut, and

Kukut i (**ġkut i**), redup.: **i ġkuti ban,** he goes to make an inroad stealthily (as in time of war); also **sī kut i** (**sī**, to shoot) to shoot not killing, but only *cutting* or wounding; and

Kutu ki, bikutu ki, to decide about (someone). See **koto-fi.**

Kutu, s., louse. [Sa. *'utu*, louse, an insect which eats the skin of the hands and feet, My. *kutu*, louse, To., Fut., *kutu*, Ta. *kiget*, An. *get*, Ml. P. *gut*, Malo *utu*, louse.] A. ḳurdu', &c., id.

NOTE.—There is no other

word for flea in Ef., but to distinguish a flea from a louse the former is called **kutu n koria**, the **kutu** of the dog, so Fut. **kutu kuli**, My. **kutu anjiġ** (**anjiġ**, dog), TaSa. **utu vuriu**, but Malo **utu** (simply). The Efatese say there were no fleas in the island before Europeans brought them. In Sa. flea is **'utufiti**, and in Fi. **kutu ni manumanu.**

La, d. **le**, ad., indeed, certainly, surely, particle of emphasis, as **uisĭ la**, yes indeed, **i la masĭkina**, he indeed is one, or one only, **i le sa**, he is indeed bad, **i ġa fano la**, let him go indeed. [Sa. *la*, My. *lah*, id.] A. **la**, certainly, surely, indeed.

La i, or **lai**, v. t., to put out, or eject from, the mouth, as food, froth, the tongue (see **lē**) : **lua.**

Lāba, v. i., to be much, many ; **laba** or **leba**, **labalaba** or **lebaleba**, to be or become big, grow up, d. **lafulafu**, to be or become (grow) big, **lalaba**, or **leleba**, big, great, **leba**, elder ; **tea laba** or **leba**, plenty, enough (no more), it is enough, **milāba**, last, **nameliġu milāba i en lu ua**, my last footprint is in this place, i.e. I will come no more here, **tea milāba**, the last (person or thing), **i libi milābā sa**, he looked upon it for the last time, d. **leb**, indeed, very ; **barab** (**barau**, &c.) long. [Sa. *lava*, to be enough, indeed, very, *loa*, long (and *leva*, long, of time), Mg. *lava*, long, tall, continuing long (=Ef. *barab*, *baraf*), My. *luwas*, *luas*, wide, extensive, large, ample, Fi. *levu*, great, or large ; in great numbers, all, as, *era sa lako levu*, they are all, or many, gone (= Ef. *ru lāba bano*), *vakalevu-taka*, to increase ; cause to be great or many, *balavu*, long.] H. **rabab**, to become much or many, to be increased, to be much or many, inf. **rob**, a being much or many, abundance, multitude ; poetically multitude is almost used for 'all' (so in Fi. and Ef. **levu**, **lāba**), a being great (of might), a being *long* (of a way), **rab**, much, many ; enough (it is) enough (no more, cease, leave off, so Ef.) ; big (great, large, vast), applied to a *wide* space, to a *long* way, and to things generally in the sense of great, big ; elder. The cognate and supplementary verb is **rabah**, to be multiplied, increased, often to be many ; to become great, to grow up, to be great. See Index.

Labalaba, or **lebaleba**, v. i., and a., redup. of **laba**, or **leba**, v. i., and a., to be great, big, as, **natasi leba**, the great sea. See **lāba.**

Labo, s. See **leba** : **leba boa.**

Laf i, or **lafi**, v. t., to take,

take up, carry (a thing), take up (a song). [Ha. *lawe* (ps. *lawea*) to take, carry.] A. rafaʻa, to take up, carry.

Lāfi na, s., c. art., the cover, sheath, or envelope of the flowers or buds of the cocoa-nut palm; the hard substance (of same shape) of the cuttle-fish (d. **namaġi rofa-rofa** = little canoe of the cuttle-fish). A. "ʻilāf', a cover, sheath, or envelope, H. ʻalaf, to cover, to wrap up, A. "ʻalafa, to enclose in a sheath or vessel.

Lafuis, dd. **rĭfālu, libuis, lifāru**, q.v.

Lafulafu, d., v. i., and a., to grow up, big: **lāba**.

Lāġa, v. t., to seek, search for, **lāgā sa**, seek it, **bilāġā sa**, id., and redup.,

Làġălāġā sa, v. t., id. (frequentative). A. **rāma**, to seek, search for, n. a. **marām'**.

Laga-ti, v. t., to raise, lift up (as a thing from the ground), and

Lāġa, s., that which raises: **lāġa laġa-ti** (the planks of a boat);

Laġa i, or **laġai**, v. t., to raise, lift up (as the wind raises thatch from a roof); then to raise (a thing, so as to make it conspicuous), as, **i mirama laġa-ti**, it (the moon, &c.) shines raising it (into view, making it conspicuous); hence

Laġa (without object) to shine (to raise into view, make conspicuous), **bisa laġa-ti**, to speak raising it (into view), **laġa-ti**, to speak with a loud voice, **laġa**, v. i., to sing, and

Laġalaġa, v., redup. (in all these senses): **nalaġalaġa na**, s., a thing raised from or off something (as a scale from the eyes, husk from grain, &c.): **malaġa, malaġalaġa**, to be raised (so as to be conspicuous, as a ship on the sea); **balaġa-ti**, v. c., to make raised (a thing), **balaġa-saki nia**, v. c., **ḅalaġa na** (see under these words), **taḅa-laġa**, v. r., to raise itself, be raised (from above, or off, anything);

Laġi, s., with prep. **elaġi**, ad. (used also as a prep.) and s., the sky, heaven, above. [Sa. *laga*, to rise up, to raise up, redup. *lagalaga*, s., a stick for raising up flat coral, v., to raise up (as a heavy weight), *lagalagaola*, to raise the finger nails from the flesh, *lagi*, the sky, heaven, v., to call out with a loud voice, to sing, Ha. *lana*, to float (on water), float (i. e. be lifted up, raised) in the air, *lani*, sky, heaven, *luna*, the upper side of any thing, the upper, the above, a., upper, higher, above, and, with a prep., ad., or prep., above, Sa. *iluga*, id., My. *lagit*, sky, firmament, *lalagit*, the palate, an awning, canopy, Mg. *lanitra*, sky, heaven.] H.

rum, ram, v. to be high, to raise (anything, voice, &c.), lift up (take up, away), rim, **ramut, marom** (barou), **ramah,** E. **rama** (for **ramat**), the third heaven, **aryam,** heaven, **aryamat,** the heavens, Mod.S. **mirem,** &c., to raise up.

Laġāraf, v. i., or mid., to mourn (as for the dead): **laġa-ti,** to raise, and **teraf i,** to scratch, from raising the hands and tearing or scratching the cheeks in mourning (see **ḅora** I., **bora na,** the temples).

Laġāfaru na, v. and s. compounded, to raise its wings (a bird): **laġa-ti,** and **afaru na.**

Laġafasu ki, v., make a sign to: **laġa-ti,** and **fasu na.**

Laġilaġi, v. i., to be proud, uplifted. [Ha. *lanilani,* to be high-minded, proud, show haughtiness.] See **laġa-ti.**

Laġa ki, v. t., to have, to possess. See **laka.**

Laġi, s., c. art. **nalaġi,** the wind: other forms of this word are **īn,** and redup. **àġièġi,** with article **nīn, nàġièġi,** the air, the breeze. [Ml. *nien,* Paama *laġ,* Am. *liġ, yiġ,* Fi. *t'aġi,* My. *aġin,* Mg. *anina,* Bu. *löma,* the wind, Sa. *mataġi,* to blow, be windy, ps. *mataġia,* s., the wind, Ma. *mataġi,* the wind, *koteġiteġi,* gentle wind, *koheġi,* or *koheġiheġi,* wind.] A. **nasama,** to blow gently (the wind), **nasam',** a light wind, **na'sam,** and **nasim',** a light wind, breeze, air.

Laġo, s., fly; **laġo fū,** buzzing fly, blow-fly. [Sa. *laġo,* a fly, My. *laġau,* a large fly, a blue-bottle.] A. **lakka'u,** a fly, from **laka'a,** prehendit extremo rostro *rem.*

Lāgo, v., to prop, s., the wooden pins whose sharpened ends are driven into the sama (outrigger), and whose upper ends (crossed) hold and bear up the **nakiat,** of a canoe. [Sa. *laġo,* Santo *lako,* props of a canoe.] A. **rakaḥa,** to prop, see **laka.**

Laġor, or **laġora,** or **laġoro,** ad., d. **lakor,** q.v.

Lai. See **la i:** redup.,

Lailai, v. t., frequentative or intensive.

Lai, or **lei,** contracted to **le, li,** s., woman, as, **le kiki,** little woman (in addressing a female child or girl), **le,** or **li meroan,** women, ladies (in addressing an assembly of women): this word is used before names of females, as **ma,** q.v., is before names of males, as, **lei, le,** or **li, māko,** madam, mistress, miss, or lady, **mako.** [Fi. *adi,* contracted *di,* id., Bali *luh,* Mota *iro, ro,* id.] H. **'is's'ah,** Ch. **'ita,** S. **'atto',** A. **'untha,** woman, Ch. emph. **'itta', 'intta',** id. But see Ch. II. 17. *f, e.*

Lai, s., c. art. **nalai,** or **inlai,** or **nilai,** sail (of a canoe or ship). [Sa. *la*, Ma. *ra*, Mg. *lai*, My. *layar*, N. Guinea *rer*, id.; My. *layar*, to sail, to navigate, also *bârlayar*, and *malayar*.] See **tiri, riri**, to fly, &c. **Lai** is what makes the canoe fly, its *wings*. Ma. *rei-a* (from **rere**, to fly), to be sailed over. Cf. **lea**, infra.

Lailai, v. i., to be delighted, rejoice. [Mg. *laulau*, play, playthings, *milaulau*, to play.] A. **laha'**, n. a. **lahw'**, to play; to be delighted.

Lai, or **lei**, or **la i**, v. t., to pluck, to gather (fruit), **lai nua nakasu**, to pluck or gather the fruits of trees. See **bila i**, or **bilai**. [My. *lâli*, to pluck, to gather.] E. **'araya**, H. **'arah**, to pluck, to gather (as fruits).

Lai, or **lei**, v. t., to tie up, as **lei namanuk**, to tie up a wound. A. **'ara'**, to tie up; fasten.

Lak, d. for **lako**, q.v.

Laka, s., **laka leo**, foundation or cause of a matter or affair; and

Laka, or **lake**, c. art. **nalake na**, its foundation, then, its cause, as, **nalake na tafa**, the foundation of the hill or mountain, **Atua i bi nalakeġita**, God is our foundation, i.e. our upholder, **te uane i bi nalake nafakal**, that is the cause of the war, then **nalakena**, because, lit. its cause; and

Lake, or **laki**, v. i., to marry (of a woman): **lake ki nanoi**, marry a husband, lit. betake herself to a husband; and **lake kiena**, betake herself to his house, and then generally of anyone, **i lake**, he betakes himself (to dwell somewhere), **i lake en lu ua**, he has betaken himself to dwell here; **laġa ki**, v. t., to have, to possess, d. **lakea ki**, **telakie na**, its possessor, or **telake na**, **atelakie na**, **atelakea na**, or **atelake na**, id., **Atua i bi atelakea ġita**, God is our possessor, possesses us. [Ma. *taketake*, a., well founded, *take*, s., root, stump, post of a *pa*, cause, *putake*, s., base, root, reason, cause.] A. **rakaḥa**, to lean upon (something); to betake oneself (to someone); to place upon, found, as to found (his house upon a rock), 4, to support (prop up), 5, to abide (in some place; to use free power (in a matter); **rukaḥ'**, the firm side of a mountain, by which it is upheld, **'arkaḥ'**, a foundation.

NOTE.—The expression **tulake**, is composed of **tu**, to give (or **tua**), and **lake**, and means to give in trust to (to give relying upon or trusting in)—**i tulake is**, he gave in trust it, **i tulak irà sa**, he gave in trust to them it (as a present or money to be taken charge of and conveyed by them to the person for whom it is intended).

Lakau, v. t., d. (transposed)

for ġalau i, q.v., to cross over. [Sa. *la'a*, to step, to pass over, ps. *la'asia*, redup. *lala'a*, *la'ala'a*; *la'ai*, to pass over, break over (as a wave over a canoe from one side over to the other), *la'aġa*, *la'asaġa*, a step, a stepping over.] Hence

Lakau, s., a crossing place in a fence; a stile.

Lako, s., d. **lak,** a small enclosure (like a hole, for putting or confining a pig in). See following word.

Lako, v. i., dd. **laku, loku, loko, roko, nrok,** to stoop, be curved, then stoop or crouch, concealing herself (as a mother-in-law from her son-in-law), to be concealed (as one stoops in order to be concealed, see **ḅelu, kusu**), redup. **lakolako,** c. prep. **ki, lakolako ki,** to be crouching and stooping and concealed from (someone), **toko lōku,** to abide concealed or in concealment, **luku,** id., **lukutaki nia,** or **loko-taki nia,** to place him in concealment (as a wounded warrior for surgical treatment), **ba lakosaki nia,** to creep upon it stealthily (as a hunter upon a bird), hence **ba lako,** to hunt (birds), lit. to go concealed, **luku,** or **luk,** a hole or pit, **luku noai,** a well, **lako,** or **lak** (see preceding word), **ḅaluku** (i. e. **ḅa luku**), a curved **ḅa** (concavity). [Fi. *roko*, a bowing form or posture, a., bent like a bow, ad., *sa lako roko*, goes stooping or bowing, *ai roko*, bowstring, *roko-ta*, bend a bow, *roko-va*, bow to, pay respect to, *rokoroko*, reverence, respect, *vakaroko*, bow down with weakness, or go stooping, Sa. *lolo'u*, to bend, bend down, bend round.] A. **raka'a,** n. a. **roko',** or **ruku',** to stoop, to be curved or bent, to bow or be bent down (as in prayer), **rak'at,** bowing, stooping (as in prayer), **ruk'at,** a hole, pit.

Lakolako ki, redup. of preceding word; and

Lako-saki, the same.

Lakor, ad., i. e. **la-kor,** indeed now: **lakor** is sometimes practically syn. with **la** as, **i fe la mai matol,** or **i fe lakor mai matol,** he may indeed come to-morrow, or the latter may be rendered, he may indeed now come to-morrow. This is the lit. translation, but it might be expressed, he may perhaps, or possibly, come to-morrow, hence, **i lakor sa ko mākĭ,** it indeed now is bad, or don't-know, and simply, **i lakor sa,** expresses that the thing very probably is bad in the speaker's opinion, who, however, does not state, as a positive, ascertained fact that it is so: **la,** ad., and the dem. particles **ko** and **r'** (**ra, ri, ro, ru**).

Lākōrĕ, s., a kind of flute. A. **nāḳōr',** cornu, tuba, Nm. **naqour,** clarion, A. **naḳara,**

3, to make hollow, hollow out (as wood), A. **naḳur'**.

Lala, s., an idiot, one demented, a fool. [Fi. *lialia*, s., an idiot, a., foolish, out of one's mind, Mg. *adala*, s., an idiot, one destitute of reason, a lunatic, a fool, a., foolish, infatuated.] See **alialia**.

Lālā ġor i, v. t., to conceal, deny: **ġor i**, and **lālā**, for **laulau**, redup. of **lau**.

Lalo na, or **lalu na**, s., c. art. **inlalo na**, the belly, then the front (see **elalo**), and the under side (as of cloth): **alo na**, q.v.

Lam i, d., v. t., to eat, hence

Lamien, s., c. art. **nalamien**, act of eating, food. H. **laḥam**, to eat.

Lao. See **lau**.

Larua, num. 7, **la**, for **lima**, 5, and **rua**, 2.

Lāsa, or **lās**, s., a bowl (as a kava bowl), a dish, a cup. [Ml. P. *ras*, Malo *lasa*, Santo *las*, id.] A. **ṭās'**, vasculum, Ct. **tāss**, a bowl, Nm. saucer, flat cup.

Laso na, s., c. art. **inlaso na**, the testicles. [Pa. *àsï*, Am. *luho*, Ml. dd. *lisi*, *erasi*, Fut. *raso*, id., Sa. *laso*, scrotum.] A. **ḥ'iṣy'**, and **ḥ'uṣy'**, and **ḥ'uṣyat**, **ḥ'uṣa'**, the testicles.

Lasoa, v. i., or a., to have swollen testicles: preceding word and a. ending **a**.

Las, or **lasi**, v. i., or a., big, large, great, sufficient; and redup.,

Lasilasi, id.; and

Las i, or **lasi**, v. t., to meet, i.e. to suffice, be sufficient for, as **nafinaġa i lasiġita**, the food is sufficient for (meets) us and you, **tilasi**, id., also to meet, come upon, come across (a person) **i tilasinami nabua**, he met us—them on the way, **bakatilasi**, to suffice, redup. **tilatilasi**, id. A. **'araṣ'a**, to meet, **'aruṣ'a**, to be wide, large, 5, **ta'arraṣ'a**, for which is used also **ta'arraṣ'a**, to meet, 2, to make wide, large.

Latesa, num. 6, **la**, for **lima**, 5, and **tesa**, 1.

Latolu, num. 8, **la**, for **lima**, 5, and **tolu**, 3.

Lau, s., the sea; usually with the prep. **e**, **elau**, or **a**, **alau**, q.v.

Lau, s., c. art. **nilau**, dd. **kalau**, **kolau**, q.v. [Bisaya *lawa*, a spider's web, Fi. *lawa*, a net; an ambush; to lie in ambush.]

Lau i, v. t., to plant (a yam or other plant); to plant anything upright, as a post or stake; to plant (a spear in anyone); **laulau i**, to plant, (words in anyone), putting him out, or exposing him in his true colours; **lau suru e**, to plant (words, in anyone) tempting him; and

Lau, v. i., to stand upright (to be planted), **lau tu**, lit. to stand planted, i.e. to stand upright; to fall down (planting itself), as rain, &c.; and

Lau ġor i, v. t., to plant, surrounding or concealing him or it; redup. **lālā ġor i** (for **laulau ġor i**), id., intensive; and

Lau fai i, v. t., d. **lau bua i,** to plant (as a spear, in anyone) piercing him. See **fai, bua.** [Sa. *to*, to plant, to build, to fall (as rain), &c., To. *tau*, to implant, to plant, to drop, to fall, &c.] H. **naṭa'**, fut. **iṭa'**, inf. **ntoa'**, to set (anything) upright, to plant (any plant); to plant (anything, as a people); to fix, fasten in; set up (as a tent, an image), n. a. **ṭa'at.**

Launa, s., c. art. **nalauna,** redup. **nalalauna,** a community, as the people of a village or district. Lit., the people *planted*, born in the country: see preceding word.

Lausa. See **lousa.**

Lausu na, s., the nose, d. for **naġusu na; la,** art. (usually **na**), and **usu,** for **ġusu,** q.v., nose.

Le, s. See **lai,** woman.

Lē, v. t., for **lai,** or **la i**: **i lē mina,** he puts out the tongue: **lua.**

Le, ad., d. for **la.**

Le, also **leo,** and **lo,** v., to see, as **lo nasān,** see evil, **lo nafanua,** see the land, to look, **lĕbi,** or **lĭbi,** look upon, **libi-si** (d. **lim-si**), look upon him, **libi nata,** look upon, see a person, d. **leḅa nata,** look upon a person, **leḅa i,** look upon him, see him, d. **lekă nata,** look at a person, **lekā,** look at him, see him;

Lele is, redup., to look for it, d. **leoleō sa, rai,** q.v., aspect, look, forehead, **rairai,** to be in countenance, unabashed, unashamed, **leo,** or **lo,** to watch, i.e., to look, **ba lo,** behold. [Sa. *leo*, to watch, redup. *leleo*; *leoleoġa*, a watching, *leoleosa'i*, to watch, My. *liat*, to see, to look, *liati*, *liatkan*, &c., Mg. *hiraṭa*, sight, seeing, Fi. *rai*, a., seeing, *rai*, *rairai*, to look, *rai-t'a*, to look at, *rairai*, a prophet (a seer), *vakarai-taka*, to show.] H. **ra'ah,** to see, **ra'ah bĕ,** look upon, see, **ra'ah 'et',** look at, Hi. to show, **ro'eh,** a prophet, seer, A. **ra'a',** to see, 4, show, E. **re'ya,** to see. See also **borea, naborea.**

Le, leo, lu (in **lu rik,** d.), **lo,** s., c. art. **nale na, naleo na, nalo na,** his voice, speech, word, **roġi nalō na,** hear his voice, i.e. obey him, or **roġi berakati nalōna,** or **nalēona,** d. **nalēn**; without the nom. suf. and with or without the art. it signifies a thing, something, as, **nalo sikai,** one thing, **nalo lāba,** many things; **nalo naġiena,** on account of, for the sake of, his name, lit. the thing of his name; **lo-soko,** true, lit. true thing, **lē-soko, lo ḅalo,** empty, worthless thing, **lo sa,** bad thing, **lo uia,** good thing, d. **lo amau,** true, lit. true thing, hence the expressions **sera-loamau**, or **sera-lēsoko**, to believe, **sera-loḅalo**, to deem worthless, despise. [Sa. *leo*, the voice, a sound, *leoleoā*, a., loud talking, To. *lea*, speech, voice, language.] A. **la‘‘a’**, to speak, n. a. **la‘‘w’**, sound, voice, **lo‘‘at**, word, language, dialect (see **misleo**, infra).

Lea ki, v. t., to toss away, throw down (anything), to sweep, drive away (as the wind trees), and redup.,

Leleaki, v. t., intensive. [Sa. *lele*, to fly, *lelea*, to be driven by the wind (as if made to fly), To. id. and *le*, to drive.] See **tiri**, **riri**.

Leana, v. i., or a., d. **lēna**, d. **lēġ**, to be straight (not crooked), then to be right, upright, righteous, **bisa lēna**, speak straight, i.e. right, **natamole lēna**, a straight, i.e. upright or righteous man; **tu lena**, to stand straight, stand up. [Fi. *donu*, straight, then righteous, *vakadodonu-taka*, to make straight. Sa. *tonu*, a., right, straight, correct, To. *tonu*, straight, direct, clear, *faka-tonu*, to make evident, manifest, *tonuia*, righteous, *tu tonu*, (stand) upright.] H. **taḳan**, to be or become straight, Pi. to make straight, to dispose rightly (proverbs).

Lēḅa i, **leba i**, or **lebe i**, d., v. t., d. syn. **lēka**, to look upon it: **le**, to look, see.

Leba, redup. **leleba**, **lebaleba** (intensive), v. i., or a., to be or become big, great: **nale-balebān**, greatness, the being great: **laba**.

Leba, s., c. art. **naleba**, s., a species of earth, clay, mud, dirt, **lebalebara**, a., dirty, soiled (a. ending **ra**), d. **leba-lebā**, a., id. (a. ending **a**), d. **laḅo** (i.e. **leba ḅo**, or **ḅoa**) stinking **leba**, slush, mud. [Ha. *lepo*, to be dirty, defiled, soiled, s., dirt, ground, clay, *lepolepo*, dirty (intensive).] A. **ṭabi‘a**, to be dirty, **ṭabe‘**, **ṭaba‘**, dirt, mud, **ṭaba‘a**, to impress or seal, (4) to make a water vessel from clay, **ṭub‘an**, clay.

Lebaleba, v. i., or a. See **leba**, **laba**.

Lebalebā, a. See **leba**, s.

Lebalebara, a. See **leba**, s.

Lebule, v., i.e. **le** (**lele**), to go round, and **bule**, q.v., to complete, to go completely round (of a canoe, as round a point or headland): **lele**, **ili-fiki**.

Lēġ, v. i., or a., d. for **lēna**, **leana**.

Lei. See **lai**, s., woman.

Lēka, v. t., **lēkā**, look at him, **lēkă nata**, look at, see a person: d. **leḅa**. See **leo**.

Lele, or **lili** (**lle**, or **le**, **lli**, or **ili**, **l’**), to wind, to go round, turn, curve, as, **raru i sefa**, **soko**, or **bā lele ki nafanua**, the ship runs, moves swiftly, or goes curving round the land (island), **nafisan i soka**

lele nafanua, the word moves swiftly round (i.e. all through) the land, le-bule, q.v., le, or li-taku na, or lele taku na, to turn behind his back, lele takunà sa, to turn behind one's back with it (i.e. to do, say something, concealing it from someone), ili-fiki, or lili-fiki naġusu, to round the point or cape (a canoe), ilisela, or lili-sela, as, i surata ilisela, he walked all the way, lit. round the way (see sela), i talele (or talle or tàle), he turned aside, i talele ki, he turned or turns aside from (a person or thing), malele, to be bent or curved (as a branch of a tree heavy with fruit), bilele, v. r., to turn hither and thither, lūsi, or lŭlūsi (i.e. lele usi), lit. to go round following or tracking it, as, lulusi noai sera, he follows the stream, walking in the water, lusi nakasu, goes along a stick, lili maroa, lit. to go round turning itself. [Fi. *lele-t'a*, to bend.] A. **lawa** (لَوَى), to wind, bend, turn, &c., E. ለወለ (cg.) for ለወለወ, H. לוה.

Note.—See the cognate liu, liliu.

Lele, s., tortoiseshell, the cover of the turtle; a tortoiseshell bracelet. The shell of the turtle is called lele from its round or curved form. See preceding word. [Mg. *rerc*, the largest kind of tortoise.]

Lēmina: lē, v. t., to put out, and mina, s., the tongue, to put out the tongue, syn. lua mina. See lē, lua, v. t.

Lēna, d. leana, q.v.

Leo, to look, see le; le or leo ġoro ġita, to watch, look for, expect, look after us.

Leo, s., c. art. naleo, thing, affair; hence

Leöuān, s., c. art. naleöuān (i.e. naleo uān, that thing, or affair), a feast (in heathenism), or heathen gathering, in which offerings or sacrifices are made to the natemate, and presents given to the guests.

Lēr, v. i., d. for liliu, q.v., to return, go or come back, also, i mer lēr briġi, he did it again, lit. 'he mer (q.v.) returned did it.'

Les, s., c. art. nales, a plant with thick dark leaf; and

Lès, a., dark or dusky, as in fal'lès (fale les), dark or dusky cave (name of a big cave at the entrance of Havannah Harbour); ra lès, Dark-rā or Dusky-rā, a name of Hades. See rā. A. la'isa, n. a. la'as', to become dark, or blackish, 'al'asu, of a dark colour, dusky; multus et densus, *de planta*.

Lēs, s., coral rock, or stone. Cf. A. radat, a rock in water; radat, rocky, stony, a place like a rugged hill.

Lesilesi, for lasilasi.

Let, v. i., or a., to be stiff, rigid; redup.,

Lelet, id., intensive; and

Lēt, s., spasm, rigidity, as in tetanus. See **leti, alati.**

Let i, for **alat i**;

Leti bati ore, same as **alaterabati**;

Leti lua i, v. t., to grasp, or seize, taking it away, **leti lua i kiana**, grasp it away from him;

Letileti, a.: **natamole letileti**, a grasping man: **alati.**

Letilet, or

Letilot, v. i., to crackle, as the bubbles of boiling water; and

Letilot, s., c. art. **naletilot**, d. **naltelta**, froth, i. e. lit., bursting bubbles. See **lita.**

Li, s., place: for **alia.**

Li, s. See **lai**, woman.

Lī, v., d. See **lulu.**

Lia, s. Same as **li**, or **alia**, a place.

Līḅa, s., an arrow with a broad point (about the size of a shilling) for shooting birds, or the arrow head of such an arrow; and

Liḅa i, v. t., to shoot birds with the **liḅa** (which does not *pierce* them, but kills them by a violent blow or shock). A. **lagafa**, to strike violently; **lagīf'**, an arrow with a broad head.

Libi-si, d. **leḅa i**, or **leba i**, v. t., look upon him, see him: see **leo.**

NOTE.—In two other dd. this word occurs (the **b** changed to **m**) as **lim-si** or **limĭ-si**, and **lumi**, see **him.**

Libo, v. i., hide, to vanish, disappear, be hidden, **talibo**, id.; hence **lībo**, s., a vanishing demon, a demon that assumes the aspect of someone to deceive, and appears to one in the forest, and then vanishes after the evil deed is committed, leaving the victim to return home to die; **liboki**, c. art. **naliboki**, a name of Hades (the invisible world, or hidden refuge or home of the dead);

Libo, s., an evil demon. See **libo**, v. i.,

Liboki, s., c. art. **nalibòki**, the invisible world, or hiding place where departed souls dwell, Hades. [Sa. *lafi*, to hide oneself, *lalafi* (of many), *lafita'i*, to conceal, *lafitaga*, a hiding place, Mg. *levina*, buried, interred.] A. **ṣ'aba'**, n. a. **ṣ'ab'a** and **ṣ'ubu'**, to hide (in the earth), 8, to hide, be hidden (hide oneself), cf. **ṣ'āba**, to lie hid in wait for the enemy, **maṣ'ba'**, hiding place.

Libu, v. i., to be covered or dirty with ashes, ash-coloured;

Libu, s., an oven stone, the stones that are heated red hot for cooking in the oven (so called because covered with ashes, or ash coloured); hence

Lilibu ki, v., to put the libu

on the oven fire to be heated. See **abuabu.**

Libu, or **lebu,** s., d., the middle of the lower part of the body at the upper part of the back of the pelvis. [Ml. Ur. *livu,* TaSa. *libuka,* the middle.] H. **leb,** the middle, heart, **lubbu,** cor et medulla *rei,* &c.

Lĭbuis, d. **lĭfāru,** q.v.

Lifa i, v. t., to bend, and redup.,

Lifalifa i, id., intensive; **malibai,** to be bent, see also **lofa, malofa,** and **lufa.** [Sa. *lavalava,* wrapper round the loins, *lavasi,* to tie round and round, entwine (as a serpent), *lavelave, lave,* to entangle, be intertwined, intricate, My. *lipat* (*lampis, lapis, lâmpit, lâpit*), Ja. *lâpit,* to fold, lap, lay in plaits, Mg. *lefiṭa,* folded, bent, plaited.] A. **laffa,** to be intricate, involved, intertwined; to wrap up, wrap round, to fold: Nm. wrap up, roll up, **loffa,** coil of turban, winding of road, **lifafa,** wrapper, envelope, bandage, 8, to be wrapt, &c.

Lifalifa, v. i., to blaze, **nakabu i sor lifalifa,** the fire burns blazing, or putting forth flames. [Ha. *lalafa, lafalafa,* to blaze (of a fire), Mg. *lelufa,* My. *malapu.*] A. **lahiba,** n. a. **lahb',** to blaze, put forth flames.

Lĭfăru, s., and a., dd. **lĭbuis, răfālu, rĭfālu,** a part, some, as **natamole lĭfāru,** some men, **lĭfāru ru bano, lifaru ru toko,** some went, some remained. [Fut. *efaru,* some, many, Niue (Savage Island) *falu,* some.] A. **ba'ṣ'u,** a part, some, and pl. dem. **li** (**ri, ra**). See Ch. V. 1.

Li-fiki, for **ili-fiki,** q.v.

Lifu, s., d. for **rifu,** q.v.

Lifu, v. i., and redup.,

Lifulifu, v. i. (intensive), to be covered, dirty, with ashes, as in mourning, d. for **libu,** id.

Liġa, s., d. **taliġa,** ear, the ears: **taliġa,** q.v.

Liga, v. i., to sing, and redup.,

Liġaliġa, id. (of many), and

Liġana, s., c. art. **naliġana,** a song, d. **nalaġ**: **laġa,** q.v.

Liġĭ-si, v. t., to pour out, **maliġi,** or **maliġsi,** to spill, be poured down. [Sa. *liġi, liliġi, liġiliġi,* to pour, *maliġi,* to spill, to be poured down, *maliġi,* s., a pouring (of rain), Ma. *riġi, ririġi,* to pour out, An. *aijaġjiġ,* to pour out.] A. **raḳa** (mid. y) 1, 4, to pour out.

Liġliġ, v. i., to be proud: **laġilaġi,** q.v.

Lĭkau, for **lakau,** v. t.

Liko-ti, v. t., to tie, fasten (with a rope, as a boat to a ship, an animal to a stake, &c.), and

Liko, v. i., to be fastened to, affixed to, adhere to: **i likò sa,** it is fastened to, as a leech to the body, &c.;

Liko, s., c. art. **naliko,** a rope for fastening or suspending;

Likoliko, redup. of **liko-ti** (used of fastening or suspending the yams to a horizontal pole). [My. *lăkat*, to adhere, *lâkatkan*, to fasten, Ja. *rakât*, to adhere, Mg. *raikiṭa*, stuck, adhered to, *miraikiṭa*, to adhere, *rekiṭa*, id., *mandrekiṭa*, to fasten.] A. **'aliḳa**, to adhere, be affixed, be fastened to, 2, to suspend, 4, make to adhere, fasten, **'alaḳo**, a rope.

Lilia, d. for **liliu**, q.v.

Lili-maroa, v. i., to go round turning itself: **lele**, or **lili**, and **maroa**.

Liliu, v. i., to return, go or come back: **liu**.

Līma, num., five; d. c. art. **nalima na**, his hand; **bakalīma**, q.v. [Sa. *lima*, five, the hand, My. *lima*, Mg. *dimi*, five, Epi *jimo* (and *limo*), five, *juma*, hand; d. *lima*, *yima*, or *sima*, hand; d. *lima*, five, *ma*, hand; An. *nijman*, or *nikman* (=Ef. **nalimana**) his hand, five.] A. **ḥ'amsat**, **ḥ'ams'**, five, **alḥ'ams**, digiti: Mahri **khomo**, Sokotra **khemah**, five.

Lim-si, d. for **libi-si**, q.v.

Līna, s., the light. [Mota *dina*, My. *dina*, Er. *dan*, day.] As, **i en līna**, it is in the light (not concealed), d. **i en ali**: **aliati**, **ali**.

Lira, redup. **liralira**, dd. **nrirnrir** (i.e. **tirtir**), **liṭaliṭa**, **litalita**, v. i., or a., to be bright, shining, gleaming, brilliant. A. **naṣ'ara** (2), and (*b*), **naṣ'ira**, 4, to be bright, shining, gleaming, brilliant.

Lirea, v. i., or a., for **litea**, q.v.

Lisi, v. t., to lay down, put down, and

Lisaki, v. t., to throw down, throw away, E. **rasaya**, to lay down.

Lisoa, v. i., dd. **tiso**, **toto**: **toto**.

Lita, v. i., and **liti**, to crackle, to burst, explode, as wood, or a stone in the fire, see **letelot**, also **lot**, to crackle (as a fire), explode (as a gun), to sound (as a crack or explosion), and **melita**, to crack or crackle (as wood in the fire, &c.), and then **nağiena i melita**, his name resounds, he is famous; and

Lità i, or **litai**, or **litai i**, v. t., **līta i lita i**, a spark, or fragment of something, bursting or crackling or exploding in the fire, leaps or explodes on to him; also, a wasp stings him;

Līta, s., a spark, fully **līta nakabu** (see preceding word); also a red wasp (because it is red like a spark, or because its sting burns like fire): d. (transposed) **tīla**. [Fi. *lidi*: *lidilidi*, to burst, or explode, s., report of an explosion, as of thunder, or a stone in a heated oven, *lidi-ka*, to strike in flying off, *lidi ni buka*, a spark, *lidi-ka*, to crack between the finger and thumb nails, as a louse, My.

lâtok, to crackle, to decrepitate, *lâtup*, and *lâtub*, id., *lâtum*, to boom, or give out a booming noise.] See lot.

Lita-kuruma na, v., to have the breast (**kuruma**, see **ruma**), thrust forward or out (bulging or swollen out), in a spasm (the opisthotonic) of tetanus, then, to be bulging or swollen stiffly out (of the face of a log or board that should be level): see **lōt**, spasm, or rigidity, as in tetanus; **let, lelet**, to be stiff, rigid (of anything, as of a dead body, &c.).

Litea, a., or v. i., dirty, to be dirty, d. **lirea**: used of anything, as cloth, &c. Also, as in English we speak of a 'dirty-looking' sky or night, so, **tokalau meta lirea**, dirty-looking **tokalau** (**tokalau** is an easterly wind). [My. *lâtah*, Ja. *latup*, turbid, foul, muddy, Mg. *lutu*, dirtiness, filth, dirty, soiled, *malutu*, dirty, filthy, foul.] A. **lataḥ'a**, n. a. **latḥ'**, to be dirty.

Liu sa, v. t., to pass by (lit. to put him behind, make him go back, by passing him), to surpass, d. **tōli a**, d. **toliu sa**;

Liu-uaki (**waki**), or **liu-àki** (see also **lu-aki**), v. t., to turn, as to turn a stick end for end, d. **lia ki**, and **lilia ki**;

Liliu, d. **lilia**, d. **lēr**, v. i., redup., to turn back, return, go or come back: **biliu**, q.v. [Sa. *liu*, to turn, to turn over, to turn into, to change, redup. *liliu*, *liuliu*, *faaliliu* to turn round, *maliuliu* to be able to turn, To. *liliu*, to return, Ma. *ririu*, to pass by.] لَوَّى, to return, turn back, i. q. وَلَّى, 2, 5, n. a. تَوَلٍّ, **tawalli**=Ef. **tōli**.

Lo, s., d. **li**, **alia**, as, **lo koi**, or **koia**, d. **li ke**, this place, here.

Lo, s., thing, and c. art. **nalo**: **le**.

Loamau (**lo**, thing, and **amau**, true), s., a true thing, truth, a., true, d. syn. **losoko**, or **lesoko** (**lo**, or **le**, thing, and **soko**, true), d. **lo-ua** (**uwa**).

Lo, v. i. and t., to look, to see: **leo**, **le**, id.

Loa, s., c. art. **naloa**, dirt (on anything);

Loa, redup., **loaloa**, a., and v. i., to be black, to be blackish. See also **malolo**, or **milo**, **milolo**. [Fi. *loa*, a black cloud, black paint for the face, *loaloa*, a., black, *loanimata*, the black part of the eye which surrounds the pupil, Ml. P. *roro*, dirty.] A. **loʿwat**, **lawlaʿ**, blackness.

Loa i, v. t., to rub, smear; and

Lo-fi, v. t., same as **alo-fi**, q.v., to rub on, to smear; also

Loa-si, d. **loa-ri**, v. t., and redup.,

Loloa-si, d. **loloa-ri**, v. t., to rub, also to flatter; hence

Lolo, s., paint (for the face). [My. *lulut*, and *lulur*, to cleanse the skin by friction and cosmetics, to rub the skin with cosmetics, to smear.] H. **ḥala'**, to rub, strip, A. **ḥala'**, to rub and to smear the eyes with collyrium, **ḥalō'**, oil or paint (used by women for their faces), H. **ḥala'** (A. **ḥala'**, see **èlo**, **lolo**, sweet, pleasant), Piel, to stroke, to soothe anyone, from the primary idea of the roots **ḥala'**, **ḥalah**, i.e. that of rubbing, hence to stroke anyone's face, i.e. to soothe, flatter.

Lobu, s., bamboo (the plant); also, bamboo water vessel and bamboo knife. [Santo *lumuo*, Ml. *nambu*, New Guinea dd. *bau*, *ifa*, *inba*, *kem*, Sa. *'ofe*, To. *kofe*, bamboo, Ha. *ohe*, bamboo, a reed generally, bamboo knife, a kind of flute.] H. **'ebeh**, a reed, A. **'aba'at'**, a reed, and **'abau**.

Lofa na, s., c. art. **nalofa na**, his track (so called because his track is marked by *bent* grass, &c.): **lofa**, **lifa i**.

Lofa i, v. t., to bend; same as **lifa i**. [Sa. *lofa*, to cower down, crouch, Fi. *love-t'a*, to bend, *kalove*, bent.]

Lōfa, s., hunger or famine (because it bends one); a sword (because it is flexible): **lōfa lofa i**, hunger or famine bends him: **lofa i**.

Lo-fi, redup. **lolo-fi**. See **loa i**, **loa-si**.

Lōg̃a, s., an enclosure, garden, the inside of an enclosure; given as d. for **elol** (in the sense of enclosure, that is, the inside of an enclosure). See **elol**.

Lokoloko ki, same as **lakolako ki**; **lako**, v. i.

Loko-taki, v. t., same as **lukutaki**: **lako**, v. i.

Loku, a., concealed, **i toko loku**, he remains concealed: **lako**, v. i.

Lokuloku ki, same as **lokoloko ki**.

Lolo, s., voc., uncle, redup. of **alo ana**, q.v.

Lolo, s., c. art. **nalolo**, thread: the native thread was made by *rubbing* the fibre between the hand and the thigh: **loloa-si**.

Lolo, a., or v. i., redup. of **èlo**, q.v., sweet, pleasant.

Lolo-fi, redup. of **lo-fi**, and

Loloa-si, or

Loloa-ri, redup. of **loa-ri**, q.v.

Lolofa, a., or v. i., d. **lulum**, **lumu**, to be wet, moistened: see **tiu**, d. **luma**. [Fi. *luvu*, to sink in the water, *luma*, to kill by putting the head under water, Ma. *rumaki*, to dip in water, Mg. *rubuka*, plunged, dipped, soaked.] Ch. **ṣeba'**, to dip into (H., A., id.), Ithpael **'iṣṭaba'**, to be wet, moistened.

Lolo-mina, a., **lolo**, sweet, pleasant, and **mina**, q.v., sweet and pleasant.

Lor, s., d. **roro**, the oily milk expressed from the grated kernel of the cocoanut for puddings. See **ror, roro i.**

os, or **loso**, redup. **lolos**, or **loloso**, v. i., or mid., to bathe, to wash (oneself). [TaSa. *lalos*, Ml. *roso*, Malo *loloso*, id., Ml. *roso-vi*, to wash (clothes, &c.).] A. **raḥaṣ'a**, n. a. **rahṣ'**, to wash (clothes, the body), H. **raḥaṣ**, to wash (the body), to wash oneself, E. **raḥsa**, to be wet.

Losia, v. i. See **lusia.**

Lot, v. i., to crackle, as a fire; explode, as a gun, &c.;

Lotelot, v. i., redup., to crackle frequently and rapidly, as the bubbles in a boiling pot;

Lotelot, s., c. art. **nalotelot**, same as **naletilot**, froth; also,

Lot, s., c. art. **nalot**, froth (i. e. a mass of bursting or crackling bubbles). A. **la''aṭa**, n. a. **la''ṭ**, **li''aṭ**, to crackle, &c. (as water boiling, &c.).

Lousa, redup. **lolousa**, v. i., to be wet, or **losa, lolosa.** See **lūsa.**

Louua, d. for **loamau** (**lo**, a thing, and **uua**, i.e. **uwa**, for **amau**, true).

Lu, s., d. for **lo**, a thing, in **lurik**, a thing, lit., little thing.

Lu, s., a place, for **li, alia**, as **lu ua**, this place, here, **lu uān**, that place, there.

Lu, v. i., to rise up, as, **intano i lu**, the ground rises up (as when the swelling yams below heave it up), redup. **lulu, nabiau i lulu**, the waves rise up; **lulu**, to be uplifted, proud, **bau lulu**, a proud person (lit. high head), also **lulu**, d. **lĭ**, to vie with, contend for superiority, **bilulu**, v. r., to vie or contend with each other for superiority, **bilulu ki**, vie or contend with each other for superiority about (something); **ulua**, to grow up, **ulĭ, ālĭ**, and **ula**, a leaf, and **lulu**, the hair (of the head, face, or other part of the body), redup. **uluulua**, q.v., to be growing up, putting forth leaves, also to be hairy, to be woolly (as a sheep), to be covered with down (a plant). [Ha. *ulu*, *uluulu*, to grow up, lift up, &c.] A. **'alu**, H. **'alah**, A. **'ala'**, n. a. **'uluw'**, to ascend, go up, be above it, over it, overlay it, become supernatant upon it; overcome, become superior; exalt (himself); recoil (from), remove, or go away (from), 2, to take up or off, 3, to vie, contend, or compete for superiority, 4, take up, take out, &c. H. **'alah**, to go up: inanimate things are also said to go up, as smoke, a rising ground, a plant which sprouts forth and grows, whence the participle **'oleh** (a plant) sprouting forth (Ef. **ulua, ulu**), and **'aleh**, a leaf (Ef. **ulĭ, alĭ**);

used also of things which are *taken up*, carried away, Hi. (causative) to take out or up (as out of a pit), to take up, or away, to put up (*the cud*, from the stomach into the mouth, of ruminating animals), generally, to make to go up (out or away), E. redup. **la'ala, 'al'ala,** to make to go up, lift up, take up, **le'lena,** height, highness, &c.

Lua, v. t., **lua i, lua ki,** to vomit, to put out (as the tongue, anything), to flow out, **lu ē a,** flow out on or into it, **lua ki,** to put out (anything, as words, to utter), hence **luaki,** an utterance, proverb; also **lē,** and **lai.** This verb is much used after other verbs, as, **sela lua i,** bear or carry (taking) out, or away, **bā lua i,** &c.; **miroa lua i,** think (taking or putting) out or up (discover it by thought), &c. [Fi, *lua, luara, lua-raka,* to vomit, Sa. *luai,* to spit out, Ha. *luai,* to vomit, *lualuai,* to ruminate, chew the cud, to raise the food again from the stomach to the mouth, as ruminating animals, Ma. *ruaki,* Tah. *ruai,* to vomit, My. *luwat,* or *luat,* to vomit, *luwar,* or *luar,* out, away, *luwari,* and *luwarkan,* to put out, expel, Mg. *lua,* s., vomit, *mandua,* to vomit, *luaṭa,* ad., over and above, *luaṭa,* taken up, put out, *manduaṭa,* to take out or up, *luarana,* being taken up.] قاء, to flow, n. a. **t'a't,** vomit, and **ta'a,** n. a. **tai'at,** and **t'a'a,** n. a. **t'a'at,** to vomit, &c.

Lualua, v. t., redup. of preceding. See **lua.**

Lua, s., c. art. **nalua,** a landslip: **lua.**

Luàki, s., an allegorical utterance, a proverb or parable;

Luaki, v. t., **i luaki nafisan,** he utters speech, **i tili luaki lau erā sa,** he says a proverb (parable, or allegory) planting it on them (lit. planting, piercing, or fixing them with it). See **lua ki.**

Lualua, s., c. art. **nalualua,** an old plantation (*out* of which the yams have been taken); the hair or grass-like growth on rocks under the sea: **lua.**

Luḇa ki, v. t., to pour out (as water, grain, &c.), **luḇa,** mid., to pour (itself) as rain; also used of pouring out anything (as men) from a ship, **luḇa ki ra,** pour them out, or land them, hence **biluḇaki,** v. r., to pour each other out, to land (men); **maluḇaki,** to be spilt, poured out (water or fluid), **taluḇaki,** to be spilt or poured out (as water or fluid). [My. *tumpah,* to spill, shed, pour out, *mânumpah,* id., Fi. *livi-a,* to pour gently, or in a small stream, *talivi,* to be poured out, spilt.] A. **ṣabba,** to pour out (of all things, and of things dry); to pour, be poured out, 5, 7,

8, to be poured out, and ṣāba, n. a. ṣa'b', to pour out.

Lūfa, s., loin wrapper, *girdle* round the loins. See **lifa i.**

Luġ i, v. t., to bend, make curved, and redup.,

Luġluġ i, id., d. **nuġnuġ i**; hence

Luġ, s., c. art. **naluġ**, d., the native pudding (see **nakoau, kabu**), so called because wrapped in leaves which are bent or curved round it. [My. *leg'ok*, bent, crooked.] A. lāga, n. a. la'g', 2, to make curved, to bend.

Luk, or **luku**, s., a hole or pit, a well: **luku noai**, well (pit or hole) of water: **lako.**

Luku, a., same as **loku.**

Luku-taki, v. t., same as **loko-taki.** See **lako, v. i.**

Luko, v. i., same as **liko**, v. i.

Luku-ti, v. t., same as **liko-ti.**

Luko, s., c. art. **naluko**, same as **liko**, s.; takes the nom. suf. **nalukona**, or **nalikona**, its rope, i.e. the rope for tying or fastening it.

Lukuluku, same as **likoliko.**

Lukoluko, and

Lukuluku ki, same as **loko-loko ki**: **lako.**

Lulia, and

Luluia, v. i., for **ululia**: **ali-alia**, q.v.

Lulu, v. i., redup.; and

Lulu, v. t., l'lu, d. lī, vie, contend with for superiority, dispute with: **lu**, and see **bau lulu, and bilulu.**

Lulu, s., c. art. **nalulu**, as **nalulu nabau na**, the hair of his head, **nalulu na**, his hair: **lu**, and see **uluulua.**

Lulu, v. i., to roll: **i lulu ban**, it rolls away;

Lulu ki, v. t., to roll up (as cloth into a bale); hence

Lulu, s., c. art. **nalulu**, a roll, a bale; and **talulu**, and **talu**, or **tal'lu**, s., a roll (of cloth), a crowd (of men), a herd (of pigs), a heap (of stones): see also **malilu**, to roll. See **lele.**

Lulu, v. i., to sink, d. **tutu**, q.v.

Luluk, s., a thing rolled up (as cloth). See **lulu ki (lulu-ki).**

Luma, or **lum**, v. i., and redup.,

Lumlum, to be wet. See **lolofa**, d.;

Lūma, s., the wet, as **luma iġa luma**, the wet is about to wet, or will wet ('it will rain', or 'is going to rain');

Lume a, v. t., **lume nafanua**, to wash (immerse) or cleanse the land by a religious service or ceremony performed by the **natamole tabu**, or priest: so if a man has been poisoned, **natamole tabu i lume a ki**, the poison, cleanses or washes him from the poison by a religious service or ceremony. When the land is suffering from drought, **natamole tabu i lume**, or

lumi a, and the hard-baked and therefore barren earth becomes soft and moist (**lum, lulum**), clothed with verdure, and fruitful, yielding abundance of food; redup.,

Lulume a, id. The radical meaning of the word is to dip, to immerse (see under **lolofa**). [Fi. *lomo-t'a*, to dip, to dye, *luvu*, to sink in water, to be flooded (as the land).] H. **ṣaba'**, A. **ṣab''a**, to dip into, to immerse, then to dye, to tinge, S. **ṣba'**, to tinge, **ṣaba'**, to wash, E. **ṭam'a**, to tinge, to immerse (in water). See also **riu, tiu, tutu, tuma.**

Lumĕ-si, v. t., to turn, d. **lume**, to wrap up, **buluma**, or **bulima**, to be turned, to be changed (in form or appearance). [Tah. *rumi*, to wring, turn over, upset, Ha. *limu*, to turn, to change, to have various appearances, *limulimu*, twisting, turning.] E. **ṭawim**, to roll up, fold up.

Lum̊i, v. i., to swell up, d. **lug̊i**. A. **wārama**, to swell (cg. H. **'aram, rum**).

Lumi a, to look upon it, see it: d. for **libi-si**, d. **lim-si**, d. **leba i**. See **le, leo, lo.**

Lūsa, v. i., to be wet, also **lousa, lolousa**. E. **reḥsa**, to be wet.

Lusi, redup. **lulusi**. See **lele** (and **usi**).

Lusia, v. i., to be dirty, faded, **i bi namau lusia** (of a lazy, languid husband). [My. *lāsu*, languid, feeble, Mg. *lazu*, fading, withering, faded.] A. **lāt'a**, to dirty, to be slow, 5, to be dirty, **lūt'at**, languor, laziness, **'alwat'u**, languid, faded, withered. See **milesu.**

M' (**ma, mĭ, mĕ**), a formative prefix or preformative particle: the **m'** is sometimes changed to **b**, and **f**, as **toko**, or **to, mato, bato**, or **fato**; in the causative prefix it is **b'**, or **f'**, being the initial consonant of **baka**, or **faka**, rarely **ba**, or **fa**; in the reflexive prefix it is **b'**, or **f'**, being the initial consonant of **bi**, or **fi**. In **bi**, or **fi**, q.v., the **i** is a fragment of the ancient reflexive prefix, as the **a** in **ba**, or **fa**, q.v., is the ancient causative prefix. In many cases **ma-** (often **mi-**) is found prefixed to verbs having a passive sense, the same verbs being without the **ma-**, active: in these cases we may regard the word as representing the ancient ps. part., or the ancient n. a. (active, or passive). The preformative **m** (originally **ma**) in H. and Arm. **mĕ**, or **m'**, A. **mo**, or **mu**, E. **ma**, Amh. **ma**, was attached to infinitives and participles (active and passive). Sometimes **ma-** in Ef., or **m'** (**b', f'**) is to be regarded as originally prefixed to the simplest form of the verb. See **borau** (A. **markab,** an infinitive), &c.

M, ad., contraction of **mo,** q.v.

Ma, s., day; in **mās, maisa, mes, masus (nanum, nanu, nanofa, nanoasa, nāsa, uāsa, āsa)** to-day, lit. this day. H. **yom,** A. **ya'm',** S. **yom,** Ch. emphatic **yoma',** and **sa,** dem.

Ma, prep., for, contraction of **maġi,** or of **manĕ** (d. **mini**), as **i manai** (or **maġinai**) **bat i,** d. **i manena bat i,** d. **i māsa bat i.** See **maġi.** [Ma., Fut., &c., *ma,* id.]

Ma, s., contraction for **maġa,** in names of places. [Ma. *ma,* id.] **Maġa,** q.v.

Ma, d. **me,** prep., with (of accompaniment), and. [Ha. *me,* Ma. *me,* with, and, Mg. *amana,* with, and, Mota *ma, me.*] H. **ʿim,** A. **maʿ,** with, together with: may, like **me,** sometimes be translated by 'and'.

Mā, v. i., for **mānĭ**: **anĭ,** v., q.v., c. preformative **m'.**

Māni, v. t., to rub, grind, or grate (as yams);

Mā, s., c. art. **nimā,** a fern tree; the rough bark of it (used as a grater): **nimā,** that which **mā,** i.e. grates. [Ma. *wani,* scrape, rub.] A. **maḥana,** n. a. **maḥn',** to rub, scrape.

Mā, s., a man, a male, opp. to **lai (lei, le, li),** a female, a woman; used also before names of men, as **lai,** before names of women; as **ma tuele,** Mr. **tuele; mā-riki,** lit. old man, senior, sir, often used also before names of men, like **mā**: **mā** is a contraction of **mare,** q.v. [Ysabel (Gao) *mae,* male, and used also before masculine names.]

NOTE.—This **ma** (contraction of **mare**) occurs also in d. **ma'anĭ, manĭ** (sometimes pronounced **mwanĕ,** or **moan**), and denotes male, thus **nata-manĭ,** or **ta-manĭ,** a male, male, lit. a male human being, and in another d. the initial **m** is elided, and for **manĭ,** we have **ānoĭ,** q.v., a male, male. Ch. II. 17.

Ma'anĭ, or **maanĭ,** or **manĭ** (or **mwanĭ,** or **moan**), a., male, d. **ānoi,** s. and a., male: see preceding word. [Malo *muera,* Oba *amera,* Celebes *burani* (husband, Wallace), Ambrym *miliġ,* Bali *muwani,* Epi d. *man,* and Ef. *ta-,* or *ata-mane,* Epi dd. *sumano, atamani* (*sumano, ata-mani*), Ta. *yeruman,* TaSa. *la-mani,* Fi. *taġane,* To. *ta-ane,* Fut. and Sa. *tane* (*ta-ane*), id.] Ch. II. 17.

Maḅe, s., c. art. **namaḅe,** the chestnut tree and its fruit. [Tah. *mape,* id.; also the kidneys of any animal; An. *mop(o),* the chestnut, also the inside (i.e. belly) of a box, inside (i.e. belly) of an animal, the pluck, the heart, liver, and lungs, Malo *mabue,* chestnut.] See under **amo**, **amoamo**.

Maḅelu, maḅelubelu, v. i., d.; refl. of **ḅelu**; to be bent, doubled, folded: **ḅelu**.

Maḅor, d. **mäuora**, q.v.

Mabulu, v. i., or a., d. **mafulu**, fat: **bulia**.

Mabulu, s., a large kind of pigeon.

Mabulu, v. i., or a., sticky; waxy, as a yam when cooked: **bubulu, bulu-ti**. See **mofa**.

Mafa, a., swollen, in **las mafa**, d. **las mäu**, swollen testicles (**mäu** for **mafu**). H. **bua'**, **ba'ah**, A. **ba''a'**, to swell. See **fuata, bua** III.

Mâfa, v. i., as, **i maf ban**, he goes hiddenly or unobserved = **i bi ḅei ban**;

Màfa na, s., his being hid or unseen (in going): see **ḅei**, and **afa**.

Māfa, d., v. i., or a., to be broken, cracked, d. **mafua**, q.v. [To. **mafā**, crack, rent, split.]

Mafa i, or **mafai**, v. t., to cover: see s., **ḅei**.

Mafaifai, v. i., or a., to be smashed to pieces: **fai**. See **bua**, to divide, cleave.

Mafaku, v. i., to be plucked up, or out: **baku sa**.

Mafasu, v. i., to be broken off, snapt off. [To. *mafachi*, id.] **Base**.

Mafirifiri, v. i., to be loosed, to be made void: **bir i**, v. t.

Mafis, s., a knife, d. for **makus**, q.v.

Mafisĭ, s., a child, one begotten or born, and

Mafisĭ, v. i., or a., to be begotten, born, brought forth;

Mafisien, s., c. art. **namafisien**, the being born or brought forth: **bis i**, v. t., to beget.

Mafisi, v. t., to beat: **fisi**.

Mafu, s., c. art. **namafu** (d. **namam**), a mist; ceremonial uncleanness: **abu, abuabu**.

Mafua, v. i., to be split, cracked: **bua**, to divide, cleave. [Sa. *mavae*, to be split, cracked.]

Mafukafuka, v. i., to be swollen out, puffed up: **buka** I.

Mafule, v. i., to be stripped of leaves: **bule**.

Mafunai, or **mafunei**, v. i., to be consumed, annihilated, as wood in the fire; and

Mafunufunu, v. i., to be brought to an end, to be ended, finished: annihilated: **bunu e**.

Mafusai, v. i., to be smashed to pieces, as a yam: **busa i**.

Mafuti, v. i., to be plucked: **but i**.

Maġa, v. i., to gape (see **maka, ġaġa, fuġaġa**), open out, then to wonder, then to gape or open the mouth (to speak), to speak, **maġa asi**, is to speak about it, lit. to open the jaws, part asunder the jaws (**asi**), **maġa lua i**, speak it up or out, lit. gape outing it, **maġa lo saki**, d. **maka lo saki**, to gape looking up; hence

Maġa, s., a small canoe: **na-maġa**; and

Maġa, s., c. art. **namaġa,** d. **nabaġa,** the banyan; and

Māġān, s., c. art. **namāġān,** the act of gaping, wonder: and

Maġamaġa, v. i., redup., to gape often and rapidly, to pant; and

Maġa-fai, s., a division, a part (see **fai, bua**); and

Maġa, s., the first part in names of places, as gorges or valleys, and especially of places in the depths of the abyss of Hades: sometimes, but rarely, contracted to **mā,** as **maġa-tika,** or **ma-tika,** the lowest abyss in Hades. [Ma. *maga,* brook, water-course, ditch, and contracted *mā,* in names of streams, Sa. *faamaga,* to open the mouth, to gape (To. *fakamaga*); *maga,* a branch (as of a tree, road, or stream, or anything having a branch, or forked), Tah. *maa,* cloven, divided, My. *gaga,* to gape, *magu,* wonder, amazement, *magah,* to pant, palpitate, *mâga,* open.] E. **naḳaʿa,** to gape, to yawn, to be rent, parted or sundered, and of water gushing forth (see **fuġaġa**), A. **manḳaʿ,** a place where water remains (i.e. a hollow, fissure in the earth, or valley), **naḳaʿa,** to rend asunder, E. **nḳaʿat,** an opening, gap, fissure;

Maġa, s., see above, in names of the following places in Hades, signifies chasm, yawning chasm, gulf, or abyss, of which there are several, some say six, one below the other, viz.—

Maġa-ḅoaḅoa, evil-smelling abyss—see **ḅoa**;

Maġa-bua, profound abyss—see **bua**;

Maġaliu, s., name of a place in Efate, lit. the turning gap. See **liu.**

Maġàli, v. i., to be turned round: **elo i maġàli,** the sun is turned round (it is late in the afternoon). See **kelu.**

Maġa-lulululu, sinking sinking abyss: **lulu**;

Maġa-naḅonaḅo, evil-smelling abyss: **naḅo**;

Maġa-seasea, abyss of oblivion: **seasea**;

Maġāsi, v. i., to speak about, lit. to open or part the jaws: **maġa, asi.**

Maġa-tika, or **ma-tika,** abyss of annihilation (this is the lowest abyss): **tika**:

Maġa-tiro, sinking abyss. See **tiro.**

NOTE.—**Maġatiro** in one dialect is **maġalulululu** in another: and **maġaḅoaḅoa** and **maġanaḅonaḅo,** denote the same. Thus there are five abysses yawning one below the other in succession. All these are below **bokas,** which is the uppermost, and the first to which departed souls go, and also the general name of Hades.

Màġa, prep. and pron. of 3

person, denoting, with-them, thus—(1) **kihe māġa?** who they? d. **se màni?** d. **se mai?** d. **fei mānaġ?** (2) John **māġa,** d. John **mānaġ,** d. John **mera uan** (or **meroan**), John and his companions; (3) **natamole māġa,** d. **mānaġ,** d. **mera uan,** a man with them (i.e. a man with those beside him), some men, indefinite plural. The literal meaning of **māġa** in (1), (2), (3), is with-them there: **kihe māġa?** who he with-them there (beside him), or together with them there (beside him); John **māġa,** John together with them there beside him; **natamole māġa,** the man together with them there (beside him). It is probable that **māġa** is a contraction of which **mānaġ** is the fuller form; and the **-ġa** (for **naġa**) is the dem. 'there' (see **ġa,** dem.) This **mānaġ** = with them there: in addressing a number the speaker says **tāgu māġa,** or **mānaġ,** or **mera uan,** my friends, lit. my friend with them there (beside you); so, **tai mānaġ,** &c., brother with them there (beside you), brothers. The expression **mera uan** is **me,** with, together with, **ra,** them or those, and **uan,** dem. (that) there, and **mānaġ** and **māġa** differ in having the **r** elided (as it is in **öu, u,** for **eru, ru,** they, verb, pron.) and the suffixed dem. **naġ** or **naġa,** q.v., instead of **uan,** q.v. **Mani** (and **mai**) are not used as in (2) and (3), but only as in (1) in the above example. [Ma. *ma,* Ha. *ma,* Fut. *ma,* Ta. *min,* d. *mi* (*mèh*) pl., *mī,* dual.]

Maġasaġa, v. t., to make a **saġa** (crotch, fork): **maġa,** and **saġa.**

Maġau, pr. n., c. art. **namaġau,** for **nabaġau.** See **baġau.**

Maġi (d. syn. **mini**), comp. prep., for, contracted **ma,** q.v.: **maġi** is **ġi,** q.v., and **ma,** on account of, in, to, and thus **aġinai** = his, **maġinai,** on his (account), in his (interest), i.e. for him; in one d. the genitive prep. **niġ,** q.v., of, denotes also 'for', **niġā**=his, and also= for him. Both **maġi** and **niġ,** when = for, are placed between the verbal pronoun and its verb, thus, **i maġinai,** or, **i niġā mate,** he for him died. [Mota *mun,* for, An. *imi,* to, for, Ma. *ma,* for, &c.] See Ch. V. 11. (8).

Maġie na, prep. and s., for his name, **i maġiena bat i,** he for his name did it, **tuġa maġieġita bat i,** let us for our names (i.e. for each of us) do it, &c.: **ma,** i.e. **maġi,** for, and **ġie,** name.

Maġiri, v. t., to scratch, scrape: **ġiri,** see **ġura.**

Maġo na, s., c. art. **namaġo na: baġo na,** q.v. for meaning and origin, is the same word.

Maġoaġo (m' prep.), d., ad., dawn, early morning, lit. at dawn. [Cf. Arag. **vaigogo**, to-morrow.] E. **goḥa**, to dawn, **goḥ**, dawn.

Màġoro, s. See **muaġoro**.

Maġura ki, v., to withhold from, d. **makur ki** : **ġura i**.

Maġura, v. i., or a., to be lean, d. **makur** : **ġura i**.

Màġura, s., c. art. **namàġora**, contraction of **muaġoro**.

Maġuku, v. i., to be bent, &c. : **ġuku**. [An. *meyuy*, old, wrinkled, *makaka*, bent, crooked.]

Maġusi, v. i., to be crooked, contorted, cross-grained, as wood; also, **nabona i maġusi**, his heart is crooked. See **ġusĭ**.

Mai, ad., here, as **bano-mai**, to come here, **lo mai**, look here, &c., and v. i., to come here. See **bai**, **bē**, **bā**, to come.

Mai, s., c. art. **namai**, a rope, a string. See d. **mē**.

Mai, or **ma i**, v. t., to chew (softening food for an infant). [Sa. *mama*, to chew, ps. *maia*.] A. **ma"ma"a**, to chew (meat), but not wholly.

Mai, d. for **màni**, as **sei**? who (is) he? **se mai**? who (are) they? See **māġa**.

Maia, s., a species of banana.

Mai, distance, only in **emai**, ad., q.v.

Maieta, or **maita**, d., and

Maieto, or **maito**, d., v. i., or a., to be black, black. [My. *itam*, Mg. *mainti*, Bisaya *maitum*, Tagala *itim*, black.] A. **'adhamo'** (**aḥtamo**, **'atḥamo**, &c., id.) black, **'idhamma**, and **'itḥamma** (i.e. **dahama**, **taḥama**, 9), to be black.

Maieto, **maito**, v. i., to be angry, **maitō sa**, to be angry on account or because of it, **maito ki nia**, to be angry at him, **maito ki nià sa**, to be angry at him on account of it. A. **ma'iṭ'a**, to be angry, **ma'iṭ'o**, and **mā'iṭ'o**, angry.

Maietoa, and

Maietoan, s., c. art. **namaietoa**, anger, **namaietoan**, the being angry, anger.

Mailoa (ma-, prep.), s., ad., d., dawn, early morning, lit. at dawn. [An. *imraiġ*, to-morrow, Mg. *maraina*, morning.] See **aliati**.

Mailua. See **malua**.

Mailum, **mailumlum**. See **malum**.

Maimai, v. i., to be in a tumult (of haste or passion), **namarite na i maimai**, his inside (heart, feelings) is in a tumult. [Mg. *maika*, and *maimai*, a., hasty, in a hurry.] A. **ma'ma'a**, to do a thing hastily, to be in a tumult, **ma'ma'at**, crackling (of burning reeds or such like).

Mairĭ, v. i., to live: dd. **maurĭ**, **mōlĭ**.

Maisa, ad., to-day, dd. **mās**,

mēs, masusa. See ma, day, and s, dem.

Mak, v. i., d., to fall, become mild, gentle, die away, as the wind: cg. mäo. S. mak, to be cast down, prostrated, humble, mild.

Maka. See mako.

Maka, v. i., or maġa, q.v., to gape, to wonder, to be amazed, i makā sa, or maġā sa, he is amazed or gapes at (because of) it; and maka lo saki, or maġa lo saki, he gapes looking upwards. See maġa.

Makaka, v. i., or a., to be ragged or fissured, as cloth. See aka.

Makāl, s., an ant (so called from its smallness, or quick and light movements): kala, and bakal i II.

Makāl, s., shame, pudenda. See under bakal i II.

Makàl, v. i., or a., and redup.,

Makalkal, to be sharp: bakal i II. [To. *machìla*, sharp.]

Makalakala, v. i., or a., to be itchy: connected with makal, ant, thus, makal i makamakala ki nau, an ant moves about on (is creeping or running on) me, and therefore, a makalakala, I am itchy: bakal i II.

Makamakala ki, v., to move about or creep on (one), of an ant (makāl), hence makalakala, itchy.

Makara, v. i., to be assembled, to be a crowd or many together, dd. maraka (transposed), and merā, or marā (k elided): kuru, ġuru.

Makarakara, v. i., or a., to be burning, as the throat from eating curry with too much pepper: kara.

Makas i, v. t., to pluck out or off, as a scab or anything from the skin, loose bark from a tree, husk from a cocoanut. A. naḳas'a, (3), to pluck out. See bakasa ki.

Māki, v. t., to be ignorant of, not to know; redup.,

Makimaki, as, i makimaki isa, he is ignorant of, does not know, it;

Māki, don't know (in answer to a question);

Māki, pr. n. of a demon or spirit, one of the officers of Saritau at the gate or entrance of Hades. When the spirit of a deceased person presents himself after death for admission to Hades, Faus (another spirit) asks 'Who is it?' If Māki says, 'Māki' (i.e. don't know), a dreadful punishment is inflicted by Saritau; if he says 'He is one of our people' admission without punishment is given. [My. *mukir*, Ja. *maġkir* (*muġkir*), to deny, disavow.] A. nakira, 1, 4, 6, 10, to be ignorant of, not to know, 4, to deny, to disavow, Munkar', name of the angel who together with Nakir is said to have the office of examining deceased persons in the grave: see Koran.

Mākinikini, v. i., to be itchy: **kan i.** [Sa. *ma'ini, ma'ini'ini*, to tingle, to smart.]

Makit i, v. t., to seize or take with the **uatàki** (native tongs) the hot oven stones, **ru sela uataki makiti fatu isa**, or **maki fatu isa**. H. ḥatah, to take, take hold of, seize. It is once applied to a man, elsewhere always to fire or burning coals.

Makita, redup. **makitakita**, v. i., or a., to be bent, curved, only in the expression **lo makita**, to look bent, i. e. to look round or back, **lo makitakita**, id., d. **bakita, bakitakita**. A. ka'aṭ'a, to bend, to curve, mak'uṭ'', bent, curved.

Mako, and **maka**, s., offspring; in pr. names, as, **maka fōlu, lai**, or **li mako**, &c.: **aka** (**ako**). [TaSa. *maka pi*, grandchild (offspring, or offshoot, of grandfather, *pi*), Fi. *makubu*, or *mokubu*, grandchild.]

Makota, or **makoto**, v. i., to be broken, and redup.,

Makotakota, to be much broken; and

Makota ki, to be broken from, i. e. to cease from (some person or thing); and

Makota, s., a part (of a plantation), a place, **makot i milate**, the place is cold, i. e. there is no one about the place (on calling at a house and finding no one at home), **makota ua**, this place, lit. this part: **koto-fi.**

Makus, s., a wooden knife (used for cutting up puddings), d. **mafis.**

Makuskus, or

Makusukusu, v. i., to be soft (ripe): **kosu-mi.**

I. **Mala bulu**, v. i., to faint, falling down (of men), to become soft and falling down (of breadfruit) — see **bulu**; and

Māla, s., faint, as, **mate ki māla**, to faint, lit. to die in a faint; a species of hawk (of a faded colour);

Malamala, v. i., to be foolish (My. *bâbal*, silly, doltish), c. art. **namalamala**, a fool, one foolish; and

Mala, s., c. art. **namala**, a fool, one stupid, foolish, senseless; and

Mala nono, v. i., to abide senseless, deprived of sense or motion (as by terror): **no**, to abide. H. **nabal**, to be or become faded (used of leaves and flowers falling off from being faded), to fall down, to faint, to lose one's strength (of men); and to be foolish (the mind faded), flaccid, devoid of vigour, stupid, **nabal**, foolish, senseless.

II. **Malamala**, v. i., or a., to be naked, naked; and

Mala, s., or **malala** (intensive), the *cleared* place at each village, in the midst of which the **naḅeas** are set up, and in which are performed the sacrifices, singing, and dancing of the **intamate**; often in the names of places (because cleared or bare, because having a mala, or cleared place). [Ma. *marae*, enclosed space in front of a house, yard, Tah. *marae*, a., cleared, as a garden, or a place of worship, s., the sacred place formerly used for worship, where stones were piled up, altars erected, sacrifices offered, prayers made, and sometimes the dead deposited, Sa. *malae*, the open space where public meetings are held.] And also

Mala, s. (also **malo**), a place or part (as of a garden), a part of time, and

Malmal, s., a small place, or part. See under **ali**, or **alia**.

III. **Mala**, v. i., or a., d. **malala**, to be loose, and redup. **malamala**, id. A. **ḥalla**, to loosen, **maḥlul'**, loosened, loose, Ct. **mahlūl**, loose.

Malamala i, or **malamalai**, d., redup. of (**malai**) **mĭlai**, or **mĭlei**, q.v.

Malāfiāfi, v. i., or a., to be thin. [Ha. *lahi, lahilahi*, thin, My. *rampiŋ*, thin.] A. **raffa**, n. a. **rafaf'**, to be thin.

Malārĭ, d. for **mĭlātĭ**, q.v.

Malasilus, redup. of **milesu**, q.v.

Malat, s. See **melat**.

Malatiga, d. **malandigi**, ad., and prep., near, **malatiga ki**, near to: **mala**, place, and **tiga**, **tigi**.

Malau, v. i., to be bad tasted (as stale food), to be corrupt, loathsome (as bilge water). [Tah. *marau*, old, worn out, fading, My. *lamu*, loathsome, fat, corpulent.] A. **ṭahhama**, to loathe, fat, corpulent.

Malei, or **male i**, v. t., to divorce. [Sa. *alei*, to divorce.] A. **ḥala'a**, to divorce.

Malebuto, ad. and s., middle part; inside, heart: **mal** (**mala**), place, part, **e**, prep., and **buto**, the middle.

Malele, v. i., or a., to be bent, curved: **lele**.

Maleoleo, d. **malolo**, v. i., to become tame, gentle (i.e. intelligent), as an animal does when domesticated. A. **ra'a'**, 4, **'ar'ā'**, n. a. **'irā'**, to become prudent, intelligent.

Malĕr, d. **malĕru**, or **malĭru**, v. i., to be transparent, shining (as smooth water or glass reflecting the light): **lira**.

Malēra, v. i., to be thin, running, of a fluid, as paint. See **lōr**, **roro**, **ro i**, **roro i**.

Maletiletĭ, v. i., to be stiff (as the back, in some disease): **let**, **lĕt**.

Malĭ, and redup. **malĭmalĭ**, v. i., to be drooping, as the countenance in shame; and

Malĭ, s., c. art. **namalĭ**, a plant (which when eaten is said to make one so); and

Malĭèrĭ, i.e. **malĭ-eri**, v. i., to be ashamed, lit. to be drooping or abashed in the face or countenance: see **rai**, face, forehead. [My. *malu*, to be ashamed, abashed, *malumalu*, bashfully, Mg. *malu*, *malumalu*, bashfulness, *mimalu*, *mimalumalu*, bashful, meek-eyed, shamefaced.] H. 'amal, 'amel, to languish, to droop, prop. to hang down the head.

Maliblib, v. i., weak, limber, d. **maliflif**: **lifa i.** A. **laflafa**, weak.

Malibu, s., widow (also widower), i.e. one mourning, lit. covered with ashes: **libu**.

Maliflif, d. **maliblib**, q.v.

Malifus, dd. **malus**, **mäus**, v. i., or a., bent: **lifa i.**

Maliġo, v. i., to be dark; and redup.,

Maliġoliġo, id., intensive; and

Maliġo, s., c. art. **namaliġo**, darkness, d. **malik**, q.v.

Malik, v. i., redup. **maliko-liko**; **namalik**, s., to be dark, darkness, d. **maliġo**. [Epi *mikoleko*, Vanua Lava *maleġleġ*, *meliġliġ*, black.] A. **ḥalika**, to be very black (**ḥolakliko**, very black), part. **maḥluk'**.

Malilu, v. i., to roll away, to roll, **malilu ki**, v. t., to make to roll, to roll (a thing) away: **lele**.

Malilua, v. i. See **malua**.

Malio ki, v. t., to forget (a thing): **lailai**. [My. *lalai*, Ja. *lali*, to forget.] A. **laha**, n. a. **lohiyy'**, being diverted to forget (a thing).

Malis, d. for **malūs**: **malifus**.

Malitiġa, dd. **mariríġi**, **mul-tiġ**: **malatiġa**.

Malo, s., a place, part; a part of time; **mal**, or **malo taġeli**, a crooked part (either a place difficult of access, or crooked conduct): c. art. **na malo na**, the trunk (of a tree or the body): **mala**. See **ali**, **alia**.

Malo, s., a kind of rock in the sea. [Santo *malo*, a rock.] Cf. A. **marw'**, very hard stones.

Malo, v. i., to be weary, unwilling, averse; **malo ki**, v. t., to dislike (a thing). [My. *malâs*, averse, &c.] A. **malla**, to dislike, to be tired, weary; **mallo**, disgusted, wearied.

Malöĭ, s., a mask. [To. *bulo*, to mask, to veil, *buloa*, and *bulobulo*, a mask; veil for the head. Ha. *pulou*, to cover the head, veil the eyes, s., a veil.] A. **barḳa'a**, to cover the face, to veil, 2, to be covered with a veil, veiled, **burḳa'o**, a veil, **burḳū'**, id.

Malöĭlöĭ, v. i., to be feeble, tottering from weakness. [Ha. *loeloe*, *maloeloe*, feeble.] A. **la'la'a**, 2, to be twisted and moved (from hunger), to be infirm and weak from disease or languor.

Malolo. See **maleoleo**.

Malosu, d. **milesu**, q.v.

Mal-taġeli. See **malo**, s., and **taġeli**.

Malu, v. i., or a., to be bare, cleared; redup.,

Malumalu, id. See **ali**, **alia**, **mala**.

Malua, and **mailua**, v. i., to do anything gently and quietly, not to be in a hurry, to do after a time, by-and-by, d. **mailua**, **malilua**, d. **ma-**

lulu. [Fi. *malua*, go gently, not to hurry, by-and-by, *vakamalua*, gently.] See **malum**.

Malubaki, v. i., to be spilt: **luba ki**.

Malum, and **mailum**, v. i., to be weak, faint, soft; to do anything weakly, i.e. gently, not in a hurry.

Malumlum, redup., also **mailum**, **mailumlum**. [Fi. *malumu*, *malumulumu*, weak, faint, sick, My. *lâmah*, Ja. *lâmas*, soft, flexible, weak, feeble, faint, Mg. *lemi*, softness, meekness, gentleness, *malemi*, soft, meek, gentle, TaSa. *nalum*, Ml. *malum*, id.] A. **ḥaluma**, **ḥalīm'**, to be gentle, weak, &c. See Index.

Malūs, d. for **malifus**.

Mam, v. i., or a., to be soft (as ripe fruit), ripe. A. **ma'w'**, ripe or ripening dates, **mā'a**, to have such dates (a palm), **mā'**, soft, mild (of food).

Mam, s., c. art. **namam**, d. for **mafu**, q.v.

Māma, s., voc., father, dd. **āb**, **abāb**.

Mamau, redup. of **mau**, q.v.

Manamana, s., c. art. **namanamana**, a pudding mixed with pig's fat wrapped up (**munu-ti**) in leaves to be cooked in the oven; a captive taken in war (because such were cooked in the oven and eaten). See **munu-ti**, **bunu-ti**, &c.

Mānaġ, d. **māġa**, q.v.: **mānaġ**, i.e. **mā**, with them or those, **naġ** (dem.), there.

Manàki, v. i., to stay for the night, to rest, as a guest;

Manaki, s., c. art. **namanàki**, one who does so, a guest. [My. *mânâġ*, to rest.] Mod. S. **maneḥ**, to rest, Mafel, i.e. the causative with the preformative **m**; H. **nuaḥ**, to rest, A. **naḥ'a**, to kneel down, as a camel, **monaḥ'**, a place where camels lie down (to rest or sleep).

Mānĭ, v. i., or **mān**, contracted **mā**, to abide, to be: **anĭ**.

Mandu, d. for **maṭu**.

Maneinei, v. i., to be weak. A. **na'na'a**, to be weak.

Màni, as, sei, who (is) he? se **mànĭ**, who (are) they? d. **kihe māġa**? See **māgā**.

Mani, d. **mini**, prep., for. See **maġi**, and Ch. V. 11. (9).

Manifenife, v. i., or a., to be thin. [Sa. *manifi*, *manifinifi*, My. *mimpis*, *mipis*, *nipis*, *tipis*, Mg. *manifi*, thin, *hanifisina*, being made thin.] A. **naḥifa** and **naḥufa**, n. a. **naḥafat**, **naḥif'**, **manḥuf'**, thin, slender. Ct. **nahif**, thin, **nahafat**, thinness.

Manru, d. for **maṭu**.

Mānu, s., a multitude; d. a thousand (d. **bon**, a thousand), **mānumānu** (d. **bonbon**), a very great number, or multitude; see **bon**, **bonoti**, **bunu-ti**, **munu-ti**. [Sa. *mano*, a great number, *manomano*, innumerable.]

Manu, s., a bird, birds. [Ja. *manuk*, Ta. *manug*, Er. *menok*, Vanua Lava *mon*, My. *buruġ*,

Mg. *vuruna*, Sa. *manu*, id.] H. paraḥ, S. părah̤, to fly, parohto, bird (gen. name), A. farḥu, H. efroaḥ, young of birds;

Manumanu, s., a streamer or flag of a native canoe sail: preceding word. [Fi. *manumanu*, id., also a bird.]

Manu na, s., the palate and upper part of the throat. A. ḥanaku, the palate and lower part of the mouth answering to it (cg. **nanoa na**, q.v.), A. ḥanaka, to rub food with the palate, 2, to rub the palate.

Manua, v. i., to be finished, ended; and

Manunu, id., d. **manubu**. See **nu**.

Manubu, v. i., to be finished, ended; and

Manubunubu, id., redup.: **nubu**, **num**, **nu**.

Manubunubu, d. **matumutumu**, to be soft, sleek, as the skin of a newly born pig, or of an infant. See **nubu**, **tumu**, **noba**. [Ha. *nopunopu*, to spring or swell up, a., soft, spongy, thoroughly cooked, plump, fat, swelled out, *nopue*, plump, round, as a well fed, fat hog.]

Manuġnuġ, d., v. i., to be bent: **luġluġ i**.

Manuka, s., c. art. **namanuk**, wound. [Sa. *manu'a*, to be wounded, s., a wound, *manu'aga*, party wounded, Mota *maniga*, wound, *manigata*, wounded.] A. naka', to wound, H. nakah, E. nakaya.

Mao, and redup.,

Maomao, v. i., to be gentle, mild. A. mahiha, to be mild, cg. **mak**.

Mäole, or **mäuolĕ**, s., c. art. **namäole**, a bed; hence

Mäolĕ ki, v., to make a bed with (something): d. **uol**, see **bilis i** (**bolis i**, and **uolis i**).

Maon, s., d., c. art. **namaon**, sweat: der. uncertain. Cf. s. **bani**.

Mao na, s., d. **faa**, thigh. [My. *päah*, id., also the limbs or quarters of a slaughtered animal, Mg. *fe*, the thigh: Santo *wado*, id.] A. faḥdo, or faḥd', id.

Maonĭ, v. i., d. **mānĭ**: **anĭ**, v. i.

Mäora, v. i., to be rent, redup. **maoraora** (intensive): **bora i**.

Mäosa, d. **taos**, v. i., to be fatigued, tired. [Fi. *ot'a*, weary, tired.] A. fat'a', 4, to be fatigued, weary, 'aft'a', fatigued, worn out.

Mäota, or **mäuota** (**mawota**), v. i., to be parted asunder; redup.,

Mäotäota, id., and

Mäota na, s., c. art. **namäota**, interval: **ḅota i**.

Mara uoka, a., having the hands chapped with hard work, as with digging with the **kālĭ**, or with using an axe, **naruna i bi mara uoka**: **maras**, and **boka-ti** (or **uoka-ti**).

Mara, v. i., to rest, stop, **mara tu**, stand still;

Mara bakarogo, v. i., or a., to be quiet, rest quiet, peaceable: **mara**, i.e. **maro**, q.v., and **bakarogo**.

Marafi, v. i., to hasten, be quick; redupl.,

Marafirafi, id. See **sarafi**. S. **rhab**, whence **sarhab**, Pael, to hasten, **mĕsarhiba**, sudden, **mĕsarhibat**, hastily, quickly. Uhlemann (Syr. Gr., § 25, A, b) gives **sarheb** (Saphel, similar to Aphel), to permit to hasten, and to hasten = **arheb** (H. **rahab**, to urge on, press, &c.).

Marag ki, v. t., d., to spit out, to loathe. See **burei**.

Maraka, v. i., or a., to be willing, desirous;

Marakaraka, id., redup. See **raka**.

Maraka, or **meraka**, v. i., d. for **makara**, q.v.

Marasĕ, v. i., to be softened or excoriated (as the hands with work), to be peeled off, excoriated, **tamaras**, peeled off (of the skin of a body softened or macerated in water). A. **maras'a, marat'a**, to macerate in water, rub, scratch with the nails; and

Marasĕrasĕ, redup., to be peeled or excoriated here and there, as the skin. Compare **maratĕ**.

Marasa, or **murasa**, d. **burasa**, v. i., used as an ad., gently, slowly, by-and-by, as, **ba marasa mer ia**, do it gently, not in a hurry, slowly, or by-and-by. A. **rat'a**, to delay, to be slow, 2, soften; be fatigued, **murayyat'**, slow.

Marate, v. i., or **mareti**, to be excoriated, peeled, as the hand with hard work. See **marasĕ**. H. **maraṭ**, to make smooth; to polish; to make bald, pluck out the hair; **maruṭ**, to be peeled (as the shoulder with carrying burdens). Ch. to pluck (wings), to be plucked, A. **maraṭa**, to pluck from the body (hairs), 3, pluck out hair and wound with the nails.

Maràtĕ, or **marètĕ**, a., in **fatu maretĕ**, oven stones (hard, *smooth* or *bare* stones, worn smooth by the sea): preceding word.

Mare, v. i., to be turned, **lo mare**, to look turned (round), look back. See **roa, rea**.

Mare, s., a man (male, not female), as pr. n., **mare uota**, man of **Uota**: see **ma, maani**, or **mani**, and **mariki**. [Tah. *maroa*, a boy, a male (*tamaroa*, boy, *tamahine*, girl), Motu *mero*, a boy (not a girl), Malo *muera*, i.e. *mera*, Oba *amera*, a male, vir.] Ch. **mare'**, lord, S. **mar'**; A. **mar'** (also homo, see, infra, **mera**), **mor'**, **mir'**, vir., **mara'a**, (2) to be virile, masculine, and brave, as becomes a man.

Mareserisu, v. i., to shift,

subside (as a swelling). See risu.

Mārikĭ, s., lit. senior, sir, old man, Mr., opposite to fite **rikĭ**, matron, old woman, Mrs.: **mā**, for **mare**, and **riki**. See **fiteriki**.

Marita na, or **marite na**, s., the belly, bowels, also a rope or string; hence

Maritausa, v. i., to be angry, or **marita sa**, or **marita na i sa**: and **marita uia**, to be well or kindly disposed. See **sa**, **uia**. A. **muryiṭa'**, the belly. See the verb under **marate**.

Maritau, v. i., to wither, be withered. A. **ṣāḥa**, 2, v. t., to wither or dry plants (as the sun, wind), 5, **taṣawwaḥa**, to be withered.

Maro, v. i., to breathe, to rest, be quiet, to be glad, restful, contented, satisfied; **maro ki**, v. t., to perceive the odour of (to breathe or inhale the odour of), to smell; redup.,

Maromaro, v. i., to breathe; to rest; hence

Maromaroan, s., c. art., the act of breathing or resting, rest; and

Maro na, s., c. art., breath. A. **rāḥa**, n. p. **maroḥ**, to rest (i.e. respire); to be glad; to perceive the odour of; to blow (wind), 2, to be quiet, to rest, 4, to breathe, H. **ruaḥ**, to breathe, blow, Hi. to smell; to be pleased, glad (smell with pleasure).

Maroa, v. i., to turn round: **roa**.

Maroḅaroḅa, v. i., to fall down, be level, as the smoke of a fire signal. [Mg. *ravuna*, level.] See **roa** (**rowa**).

Marou, and **marourou**, s., d. (transposed) for **rūma**, q.v.

Māru, v. i., or a., d. **mēru**, to be limpid, clear, pure (of water). A. **namiru**, **namīru**, id.

Maru, d. for **maṭu**, q.v.

Maru sa, v. t., to rub; masturbate; to joke. A. **maraḥ'a**, n. a. **marḥ'u**, to joke, to anoint, to soften (the body with oil), H. **maraḥ**, to rub;

Maruen, s., c. art. **namaruen**, joking, &c.

Mārua, v. i., to cease, leave off, **marua ki**, to cease from; and

Maruāna, s., c. art., cessation: **baro**, v. i., **bārua**, q.v.

Mas, s. See **maso**.

Mās, ad., d. for **maisa**, **mēsa**, **masusa**.

Mas, and **sam**, ad., alone, only: **ma** for **mau** (as in **sikei mau**), and **'s**, **sa**, one.

Masa, d., v. i., to go, to walk. A. **mas'a**, id;

Masāna, s., c. art. **namasāna**, the going, walking.

Masa i, v. t., to rub, rub off, **masa ia nāfo**, rub it on the **nāfo** (to rub the rust off it);

Masamasa ki, redup., rub (as the rust off a needle, on a stone); and

Masamasoa ki, v. t., end. **'a**,

to stroke, smooth, flatter; and

Masa, v. i., at ease (as wild animals in their lair, as if smoothed into gentleness);

Masaki. See **misaki.**

Masamasa(n)ta, d., v. i., or a., end. **ta**, smooth, as a board: dd. **musi ki, mus i**, to stroke, smooth, rub. H. **mas'aḥ**, to stroke, anoint, A. **masaḥa**, to stroke, to flatter, wipe off, **ma'aṣa**, to rub strongly, **ma''as'a**, to rub gently, **masīḥ'**, smooth, S. **ms'aḥ**, to anoint; to measure; A. **masaḥa**, to measure (land), H. **mis'ḥah, mas'ḥah**, a part, a portion (Ef. **mas, maso, mis**, id.).

Mas, s., also **maso, masĕ**, and **mis**, a part, a portion, a place (part of the land), as, **baumaso na**, q.v., **masleo**, a portion of speech or words, as of a song, **masleo naliġana**, a portion of human speech, dialect (see **leo**), **maso ua**, this part, or place. See preceding word.

Mas', or **masu**, v. i., d., to come; hence

Masuen, s., c. art. **namasuen**, the act of coming. E. **maṣ'a**, to come (H. **maṣa'**, means to come to, i.e. to attain to, to arrive at, anything).

Mas i, v. t., to shave, as **masi nasina**, to shave the chin or part of the face covered with the beard: **masi noai**, shave off the surface of water, bail, or bale, out: hence, redup.,

Masimasi, v., to bail out (a canoe, or boat), and

Māsi, s., a knife, and

Masimasi, s., id., d. **mismis.** A. **māsa**, to shave, **mūsa'**, **mawasi**, a knife.

Masei, s. See **masoi.**

Masere, s., c. art. See **miseri.**

Masere, v. i., to be treated kindly; **sere, bakasere**; **te masere**, one treated kindly, as a beloved child.

Masere, v. i., to be torn: **sere.** [Fi. *kasere*, broken, loosed.]

Masiḅa, v. i., to be broken, done into fragments; and redup.,

Masiḅasiḅa, id., intensive: **siḅa i.**

Masi-ḅalo, s., wilderness, lit. empty part (of land). See **mas, maso**, and **ḅalo.**

Masīka, v., in **sera masīkā sa**, to desire, covet (a person or thing). A. **s'aḳa**, 5, to be desirous of.

Masiki na, d. **mihi** (for **misi**), v. i., taking the nom. suf. agreeing in number and person with its subject as, **a masikiġu**, I alone, **ku masikima**, thou alone, **i masikina**, or **masikinia**, he alone: **siki**, and pref. **ma.**

Masila, or **masilĭ**, v. i., to be thin; and

Masilasila, d., redup.; and

Masila na, s., c. art. **namasila na**, chip, shaving. See **sila i.**

Masila, in **buru-masila**, q.v. See **sila.**

Masirsir, d., v. i., to sob (as after crying). A. **zaḥara**, to utter the voice, to give forth a sound, to pant or gasp with vehemence and groaning.

Mas-leo, s. See **mas**, s., part or portion, and **leo**, voice, speech.

Maso, s. See **mas**, s., a part, portion, place.

Māso, v. i., or a., to be cooked, done, d. **mahi**. [My. *masak*, Mg. *masaka*, Ma. *maoa*, and *maoka*, and *maoġa*, cooked, also ripe, Bugis *motasok*, ripe, Tah. *maoa*, cooked, ripe, Fut. *moa*, Santo, d., *mäa*, cooked, To. *momoho*, ripe.] A. **naṣ'iga**, 1, 2, 4, to be ripe, cooked.

Masoi, masoei, or **masei**, s., star, stars, d. **mohoi**, c. art. **namohoi**. [Epi d. *mohoei*, Fila *masoi*, Fut. *fetu*, Sa. *fetū*, Santo dd. *vitu*, *maṣoi*, *vitui*, *vitiu*, My. *bintaġ*, *wintaġ*, and *lintaġ*, Mg. *kintana* and *vasiana*, Tag. *bitoin*, Sumbawa *bintoiġ*, Sulu *bitohon*, Menado *bituy*, Sanguir *bituin*, id.] See Ch. II. 13. a., and c (at end).

Masoi, or **masei**, star, is used in pr. n., as **Masei, Mare Masei**, &c.

Masok, v. i., to be violently agitated or enraged, as, **namaritana i masok**, lit. his belly or his bowels leaped up: **soka**, to leap.

Masoko, a., true, exact, to the point, as **nafisan masoko**, a word or speech true, exact, or to the point; as an adverb, **bisa masoko**, to speak truly, exactly, or to the point, **bā masoko**, to go exactly, **ba masokō sa**, go exactly upon it, &c.: **soko**.

Masol, v. i., to turn aside, decline. A. **zāla**, n. a. **zuwul'**, to decline (as the sun); cease to be in place, remove; start on a journey and change one's mind.

Masu, s., c. art. **namasu**, the time of harvest, or of plenty of food, opposite to **sukei**, q.v., lit. the coming, **namasu nafinaġa**, the coming of food, as yams, taro, bread-fruit, &c.: **mas'** (or **masu**), v. i., to come.

Masua na, s., c. art. **namasua na**, the top, crown, or summit (of anything): **sua, su**.

Masua, v. i., or a., to be bald. A. **nazi'a**, to be bald about the temples, **manzu'**.

NOTE.—Sa. **tula**, My. **sulah**, Mg. **sula**, bald, A. **ṣali'a**, to be bald on the forepart of the head, **ṣul'at**, place of baldness.

Masukuta ki. See **musukuta ki**.

Masula ki, v. t., to scorch (as the skin of a pig in order to its being scraped and prepared for cooking): **sulu**.

Masusa, ad., for **mas, maisa**, to-day.

Māt', v. i., to ebb; to be low water; hence

Māt', s., c. art., **namāt**, the ebb; low water; the shore left bare at low water. [Sa. *masa*, to be low tide; to be sour; to have an offensive smell; To. *maha, namaha*, to ebb, Fi. *māti*, to ebb, and s., *namati*, the ebb.] A. māt'a, to macerate and dissolve (a thing in water), H. masas, cg., to melt, flow down, to waste away.

Māta (or mwāta), a snake. [Sa., Fut., Fi. *gata*, id., Malo *moata*, Santo dd. *mata, maura*, My. *ular*, id. (Ma. *gata*, snail, slug, leech).] A. 'it'at', 'at'ā', a snake: 'at't'a, v., tinea *erosit lanam*, serpens *momordit*, 'ut'at, tinea, &c. See ula, My. ulat, worm, maggot.

Mata, s., the eyes, usually pronounced mita, or meta, q.v.

Mataisau, s., a carpenter. [Sa. mataisau, id.];

Matakseu, d., id. Mataisau is lit. the eye (or director or master) of cutting. See (mata), meta, and sau.

Mataku. See mitaku.

Mataloa, s., a pig with crooked tusks, one on each side, that is, a mature, full-grown pig. A. sala''a, and ṣala''a, to have or acquire a tooth or tusk on each side.

Matātā, s., a phosphorescent worm (which *gleams* brilliantly), phosphorescence of the sea. [Fi. *matata*, to clear up, as the weather, the sky.] A. ṣ'ā'a, to shine; Nm. moṣ'ui, phosphorescent.

Matau, s., d. na mitau, an anchor: tau.

Matautau, v. i., to utter sounds as one in sickness or pain, to groan, moan. A. hatafa, to moan, &c.

Matĕ, v. i., to die; and redup.,

Matĕmatĕ, v. i., to be quiet, soft, gentle; and

Matian, s., c. art. namatian, act of dying, death:

Matiġo na, s., c. art., the grave, d. emate n; tamate, v. i., to become calm (wind, wave), s., peace, a calm; also a series of feasts or festivals held every fifth day (see d. syn. belaki). [Sa. *mate*, My. *mati*, to die, Mg. *mati*, a., dead, *matimati*, lukewarm.] A. māta, to die; to become calm (the wind), 4, to soften by cooking. This word occurs in all the Semitic languages.

Matiratira, v. i., or a., to be shining, bright (as any polished surface). See tare.

Matiu, d., v. i., to sink. See tiu sa.

Mato, and

Matoko, v. i., to remain, abide, to sit: to, toko. [Mg. *mituaṭa, mitueṭa, mituiṭa, mitumueṭa*, to reside, dwell, abide, sit, rest.] See toko.

Matōl, ad., to-morrow: tola.

Matoltol. See matultul.

Matu, v. i., to abide, to abide standing: tu.

Matu, s., c. art. namatu, d., woman. See Ch. II. 17. c. [Ja. *wedo*, Sula *nifata*. Tidore *foya*, id.]

Matu ki, v. t., to strengthen or support with posts (a

fence), **matu ki nakoro**; and

Matu na, s., c. art. **namatu na**, post or stake (of a fence); the backbone, vertebral column, the back. A. **ma-tuna**, H. **matan**, to be strong, firm, A. **matěnu**, back, vertebral column.

Maṭu, v. i., to be thirsty, to thirst, dd. **manru, mandu, maru.** [Ml. P. *meruh*, Epi *mereu*, TaSa. *maroku*, Malo *madoge*, Bugis *madoka*, Santo (Pelia) *marara*, Marshall Islands *maru*, New Caledonia *malu*, to thirst.] S. **ọho**, to thirst, **ṣahyo**, thirst, H. **ṣiyah.**

Matua, v. i., or a., to be old, mature, elder, then (full-grown) large, great; also wise, opposite to **busa**, as, **meta matua**, wise, lit. old or mature, i.e. experienced eye, **bo matua**, wise, lit. old, mature, i.e. experienced heart; **te matua**, the aged, or the ancients; **meta matua ki**, to withhold from (a person, something);

Matuatua, redup. of preceding word, very old;

Matua, s., or ad., the right hand, or side: **tuai**, q.v. [Sa. *matua*, aged, elder, mature (*matuatua*, dim.), a parent, Fi. *matua*, mature, My. *mântuwah*, a father or mother-in-law, Mg. *matua*, eldest son or daughter, *ma-tuatua*, a ghost, apparition, Malo *matua*, right hand.]

Matũki, a. used as s., one trusted in, confident, brave, as a warrior: **tuki.** [Mg. *matuki*, confident, brave, trusting.]

Matulu, v. i., or a., to be swollen, thick; and redup.,

Matultul, id.: **telatela, tela-telana.**

Matumutumu, d. **manubu-nubu**, q.v.

Matuna, s., and ad., c. art. **namatuna**, d. **fatuna**, something, anything, somewhere, anywhere, somehow; also a ghost or apparition, lit. something: **ma**, or **fa** (the inter. pron. used indefinitely), q.v., and **tuna**, dem., **te** (or **tu**) with the dem. **na** added to it. See **safa**, or **sefa**. H. **mah**, anything, something, whatever, Ch. **mah di**, whatever, what that, that which, A. **ma'**, that which, whatever. See Ch. V. 4. d.

Maturu, d. **matur**, v. i., to sleep, **bakamaturu ki**, to put or make to sleep. [My. *tidor*, Ja. *turu*, to sleep, Mg. *turi*, s., sleep, *mituri*, to sleep, Bugis *matinro*, to sleep, Ml. P. *metur*, Malo *maturu*, TaSa. *tsuruve*, Santo dd. *chinaru* (*tshinaru*), *chinaro*, *chiranu*, *noro*, *rontui*, An. *umjeģ*, Fi. *mot'e*, Sa. *moe*, ps. *moea*, to sleep.] H. **yas'en**, A. **wa-sina**, to sleep, **sinat'**, H. **s'enat'**, and **s'enah**, sleep.

Mau, v. i., to recover from sickness, be well: **abu.**

Mau, v. i., a., and **maui**, and

ad., to be whole, all together (as a number of men), to be whole (of a thing), redup. mamau, id.; nai mau, it wholly, or only (of a substance), nara mau, they wholly or only (of a number of persons). [Epi *momou*, the whole, Ha. *pau*, a., all, ad., wholly, Mg. *abi*, all, every one, the whole.] A. wafā, to be whole, &c., n. a. وَفِيٌّ. Mau, maui, is of Form 25, see Ch. III, as مَوْفِيٌّ, maufi, maui, or mauwi.

Mau na, s., c. art. namau na, d. nabai na, covering of it (a bird), i.e. its feathers; na mau, the bunch of feathers worn as an ornament on the top of the head; na mau nasuma (d. na bau nasuma), nakasu, the top of the house, of a tree; mau naliati (d. bau naliati), midday; see bau.

Mau, or amau, a., true, lo-amau, or lo-mau, a true thing, d. maurĭ, or mōrĭ. [Tah. *mau*, true, Fut. *mari*, To. *mooni*, Ma. *pono*, Sa. *moni*, true]; and

Mau, a., used as s., one firm, intrepid, brave, i.e. warrior of such a character, also, in Mautukituki, pr. n. of a mythological hero. [Sa. *mau*, to be firm, to be decided, unwavering]; and

Mau sa, v. t., to come upon, obtain, find, bamau-ri, reach to. See bamau. [Sa. *maua*, to obtain, reach to, Tah. *mau*, to seize, take hold of]; and

Mau āsa, d. mau is, v. t. (to trust in), to desire, tea mau-mauan, a thing trusted in, or desired, te namauana, id. [Ma. *popono*, to covet]; and

Sera lo-amau āsa, v. t., to believe on or in (him or it). [Ma. *whakapono*, Fi. *vakabau*]; and

Mau, ad., very, indeed, continually, as, bisa mau, to speak continually, toko mau, abide continually, constantly, &c. [Ha. *mau*, continually]; elaġi mau, above indeed, in the highest place, toġa mau, very far away, malitiġa mau, very near, etaku mau, or maumau (intensive), behind indeed, the last (as the last *day*), malĕ mau ua naġa, this very time, d. mal fā nin (fā for mau), bīsa mau, few indeed, very few, d. bisiba (ba for mau), sikei mau, one only. [Fi. *dua bau*, Sa. *tasi pe*, one only]; mas (for mau sa, only one), and sam (for sa mau, one only), are like sikei mau; ti bano mau, did not go indeed [Aniwa, Fut., *sĭ fano ma, sĭ fano mana*, id.]; this mau after a verb preceded by the negative is very commonly used, but may be omitted, and ti bano, ti bano mau, are both used, though the latter is the more common. H. 'aman, to prop, stay, sustain, support; to carry (sustain) a child; **'amen**, to be firm, unshaken, faithful, A. **'amuna**, to be faithful, **'amana**, to confide in, trust, **'amina**, to trust, be secure; H. Niphal, to bear in the arms, to be firm, to be of long continuance, continual; to be sure, certain; Hi. to lean upon, trust, confide in, believe; stand firm, still, A. **'amana**, generally the same; S. **'eman**, to persevere, be constant, and, contrarily, to cease, Aph. to believe, **'amen**, &c., verily, truly, certainly, E. **'aman**, id., also truly, and **'amanawi**, id., **'amana**, to believe; both the m and the n of this word are sometimes elided in the ancient languages, as H. ĕmet′, Amh. äun. See Ef. **amau**, **una**, **amori**, **uua**, in **louua**; and

Mau-ti, v. t., to save, to protect: **mū-ti**. Hence **nauota maumau**, or **mūmū**, a chief saving, or protecting, a saviour.

Maua ki, v. t., to give food to (people, as to those who have been doing something for one); and

Maua, s., c. art. **namaua**, food, or provisions. A. **māna**, to give food, **mawunat**, provisions.

Mäu, d. for **mafa**, swollen.

Maüaüa (**mawawa**), v. i., to be separated. See **mafa**, **bua**.

Maüori (**mauori**), v. i., to be broken, and redup.,

Maüoriüori, intensive: **bori**.

Mäuosa (**mawosa**), v. i., compressed: **ḅosa**.

Mauri, s., as **mauri nalaği**, the place where the wind ends at, to leeward; the left hand or side, opposite to **matua**. [Sa. *muli mataği*, To. *mui mataği*, the place where the wind ends at, Ma. *maui*, Malo *marao*, Ta. *maul*, Epi dd. *mali*, *mau*, left, on the left hand.] See **muri**. Mahri **manghūra**, behind.

Mauri, v. i., to live, dd. **mairi**, **mōle**; **bakamauri**, make to live;

Maurian, s., c. art. **namaurian**, life. [Fi. *bula*, Sa. *ola*, Fut. *mauri*, My. *idup*, Ja. *urip*, Ta. *murif*, Mg. *veluna*, to live, Epi d. *mcouli*, *mauli*.] A. **'ās'a**, n. a. **'ais''**, **ma'as''**, **ma'īs''**, **ma'is'at**, to live, 4, make to live.

Mauri, a., true, **tili mauri**, speak true;

Mauri, s., c. art. **namauri**, a prayer or incantation, lit. what is true: **mau**, true.

Mäus (**mawus**), d. for **malus** (**malifus**).

Mauta, d. **mautu**, s., a rising ground; one's native land: so called because (**i tu mau tu**) it remains *firm* or *continuing*. See **mau**. [Sa. *mauğa*, a hill; a residing at a place (from *mau*).]

Mbā, v. i., for **bā**, or **mā**, v. i.: a mere euphonic change.

Mbàt, s., d. **nāḅe**, a club. [To. *mata*, a kind of club.] Nm.

nabboud, a club; also nabbout, a staff, club.

Me, prep., d. **ma**, q.v.

Mē, or **mēa**, v. i., to make water; also, redup.,

Memē, id., and

Mē, s., urine, **me-rikĭ**, dysuria, lit. small or scanty me; and

Mē, or **mēa**, v. i., to flow, wet, **us i mea**, the rain pours out, **i me nakoau**, it (a fluid, as water) flows upon or moistens the pudding; **nai me**, a flood or freshet, lit. flowing water, d. **naum**, a stream, lit. flowing water; **na bisi me**, semen genitale. [Mg. *mamani*, to urine, *amani*, urine, Ha. *mi*, *mia*, *mimi*, to make water.] A. **māha**, to have water (a well), leak (a ship), 2, to pour water; to wet with water; emit water (the ground), **mā'**, juice (of anything), semen genitale (H. me), H. me (of the feet), euphemism for urine. See Ges., Dict., s.v. **ma'**, who gives a root **mo'**, to flow. Hence

Mē, s., c. art. **namē**, d. **namai**, a rope, or string. [Sa. *maea*, To. *maia*, id.] And

Mē, and

Mēamēa, long; as, **tali me tuturu** (see **tuturu**), a rope long, hanging down, **i barau meamea**, it is long, like a long streak of water running down a tree, or the face of a cliff. See **mē**, **mēa**, to flow.

Meṁi, d., v. i., to be gentle, tame: **mäo**, **maomäo**.

Mela, **melamela**, for **mala**, **malamala**, fool, foolish.

Melat, s., c. art. **namelat**, or **malat**, flower (of a plant), then flower (of anything), that is, crown or most excellent part, as, **namelat natamole**, the flower of men, the most excellent of men. A. **warada**, 2, to flower, **ward'**, a flower.

Mele na, s., c. art. **namele na**, the hollow; as, **namelēru na**, the hollow (palm) of the hand, d. **nal'nāru na** (see **alo**, **aru**, belly, hand), **namele natuo na**, the hollow (sole) of the foot or feet, **namele ġere na**, the hollow of the tail of a fish. [Mg. *faladia*, i.e. *fala dia*, sole of the feet.] A form of the word **ḅele na**, belly, hollow.

Melesia, d. **melesira**. See **milesia**.

Meliboi, or **melibai**, v. i., to be bent, as grass by the wind, &c.: **lifa i**.

Mēliki, d., v. i., for **mēlu**, q.v., to be dilatory, slow.

Melita, v. i., to crackle, resound (as one's name): (lot) **lita**.

Mēlu, v. i., d. **meliki**. A. **mahala**, n. a., **mahlu**, to do anything gently and quietly, not in a hurry.

Mēlu, s., shade, **raġ mēlu**, time of shade, evening, **melu na**, its shade, or his shade (protection);

Melu, v. i., to be shady (as the day), and redup.,

Melumelu, id. [Sa. *malu*, to

be shaded, to be protected, *malumalu*, to be overcast, cloudy, Mg. *malumaluka*, shady, cool, gloomy.] H. **'afel**, obscure, dark (of the day), **'afal**, to be obscure, dark: cg. **'amal**, or **'amel**. See **mali**.

Mēlu, s., that which, or what **ṁilu**, departs or removes (from), separates (from): **ṁilu**.

Men, a. See **mina**, a.

Mena na, s., the tongue (of animal); of fire (flame); of knife (blade or edge); of breaker (edge of the wave); to be the **namena**, or tongue, of any one is to be his spokesman; hence

Mena i, or

Menamena i, v. t., to lick it with the tongue, tongue it. [Epi *mena*, TaSa. *me*, Santo (P.) *meme*, Guebe *mamalo*, the tongue, Mg. *menumenuna*, or *menimenina*, loquacity.] A. **manmul'**, the tongue, from **namala**, to be a detractor.

Mer, ad., d. **mero**, q.v.

Mera (for **mara**), s., c. art. **namera**, man in general, people, as, **namera ni Efate**, the people of Efate: **mera** is contracted to **fa** in **fa-fīne**, q.v. A. **mar'**, **mir'**, a male, or, in general, man, Ct. **mir'a**, man in general.

Merai, a., used as s., pertaining to a male, the male organs of generation, virilia: **merai ġara** (**ġara**, bare), addressed to young boys not yet wearing a waist cloth, or naked; a man is sometimes jocularly or disrespectfully spoken of as **merai tamana**, the **merai** of his father: **mare**, q.v., with the a. end. **i**. A. **ma-r'ayy'**, virilis, pertaining to a male.

Mera, s., d. **mara**, a rippling (of water): **meromero**.

Mera, conj., lit. with them, or with those: **me**, with, and **'ra**, them or those, as John **mera** Peter, John and Peter; this can also be expressed John **me** Peter, and John **nara** Peter (John they Peter); with dem. **uan**,

Mera uan, dd. syn. **manaġ**, **māġa**, as John **mera uan**, John and his companions, lit. John with those there (beside him); **mera uan**, can also be used of inanimate things, as, **fatu mera uan**, a stone with those (stones) there (beside it), stones.

Merā, d. contraction for **meraka**, **maraka**, for **makara**, q.v.

Merā, ad., again, d. for **mero**, q.v.

Merafālu, some, as, **korīa merafālu**, some dogs: **me**, with, and **rafālu**, see **lifāru**.

Merafālu, s., c. art. **namerafalu**, contraction of **namera rafālu**, some people.

Merà ġi, d. for

Merà ki, v. t., to go before, leading, to lead;

Merakian, s., c. art. **namerakian**, act of leading, also

meramera, redup., leading, and **nameramera n**, s., act of leading or ruling, kingdom, that led or ruled, **natamole meraki**, or **meramera**, leading or ruling men. E. **marḫa**, to lead; to go before.

Merakolau, s., web-like fat on the intestines (of a pig): **mera**, fat (see **merei**), and **kolau**, q.v., a web (spider's). In An. this is called **nilvanilva** (redup. of **nilva**, spider's web).

Meràroa, v. i., to turn round: **roa i**.

Merei, s., marrow; eel; caterpillar; medulla of banana fruit. H. **merī'**, fat.

Mer i, v. t., to do, to make to work, act, **namerian**, s., act of doing, what is done, conduct; **fimeri**, v. r., to be doing something to each other, fighting;

Merimeri, v., to keep on doing. A. **'amila**, to work, Nm. to work, act, be active, practise, 4, cause to work.

Mero, ad., again, dd. **merā**, **mer**, **moro**, **mrō**, **ro**, and **mo**, **m**, contraction of **mero**, as, **i mero bano**, he again went, lit. he turned went, d. **i mer lēr ban**, he again went, lit. he turned returned went: **roa i**. See Ch. V. 9.

Mērōmēro, v. i., hoarse, gruff, as, **i bisa meromero**, he speaks hoarse, gruff; and cf. **ḅaraḅara**, supra, to cluck. [Mg. *barabara*, hoarse, having a rough voice, *bara-feo*, a coarse, gruff voice, *farina*, hoarse.] A. **''ar''ara**, 1, 2, to make rough sounds in the throat (whether with the voice, or liquor, or the breath), **''ar''arat**, hoarse sound; sound of boiling water.

Emeromina, ad., and s., in the world, the world, lit. in the light, opposite to **abokas**, in the under-world, Hades (which is dark and gloomy): **e**, prep., and **meromina**, s., formed from **mirama**, or **merama**, to shine.

Mōru, v. i., d. for **māru**, q.v.

Mēs, ad., d. for **maisa**, **to-day**.

Mĕsa, ad., perhaps, expletive used at the beginning of a clause. E. **'emsa**, but if, quodsi.

Mesau na, v. t., to desire, and redup. (dd. **mūri**, **mōri**),

Mesausau, desire much, be lustful;

Mesauan, s., c. art., desire, will, what one wills: **sau**.

Meta, v. i., or a., to be raw, then, unripe, crude, green. [Sa. *mata*, raw, unripe, Mg. *manta*, raw, unripe, crude, green, My. *mantah*, raw, unripe.] A. **'anuṭ'a**, to be raw.

Meta, s., the eye, the eyes: **mita**.

Metita, v. i., or a., to be rotten, to be falling to pieces from rottenness. A. **t'a'iṭa**, to be rotten; to be falling to pieces from rottenness.

Mi, v., to be, d. for **bi**, q.v.

Ṁi, redup. **ṁiṁi**: for **ġumi**, q.v.

Miel, v. i., or a., to be red, and redup.,

Mimiel, id. [Sa. *melomelo*, *memelo*, red, Mg. *mena*, red, My. *merah*, red; the ruby; bay colour in a horse.] A. **ma‘‘ir’**, reddish, **’am‘‘aru**, of the colour of red clay.

Mihi, d., **masiki**, q.v.

Mikit i, v. t., d. for **makit i**, q.v.

Mila, v. i., or a., to be shy, skittish, to be wild, opposite to **malolo**. [My. *liyar*, wild, untamed, shy.] A. **hali‘a**, to be uneasy, timid, impatient, shy. Hence

Mīla, s., a wild animal; a warrior sleeping out in the bush and watching to cut off stragglers.

Milāba. See **laba**.

Mĭlaġ, s., a part, or half, c. art. **namĭlaġ**. Ch. **pelag**, a half, A. **filag’**, a part, a half.

Milaġo, v. i., d., to be sick, to be ill, have a disease. A. **ṣ’aniya**, (2), n. a. **ṣ’ana’**, to be ill, to be sick with a latent disease, Nm. **moṣ’na’**, faint, languid, moribund;

Milaġoan, s., c. art., the being ill, disease.

Milàkesa, or **milàkisa**, v. i., or a., to be darkish green: **milo, kisa**.

M’lame, d., s., c. art. **nam’-lame**, dew: **mala**, clear (rainless), and **mēa**.

Mĭlātĕ, dd. **malārĕ**, **mĭlānr**, v. i., or a., to be cold, cold. [Sa. *maalili*, Tah. *mâriri*, Ma. *makariri*, Fut. *makiligi*, id.] A. **maḳrur’**, cold, from **ḳarra**, to be cold.

Milāte, s., c. art. **namilātĕ**, cold, the being cold, also **namilatea**; and redup.,

Milamilati, v., to be coldish: **milāte**. [New Hebrides, TaSa. *makariri*, Ml. U. *milas*, Malo *magariri*, Ml. P. *mereus*, Epi *meneni*, cold.]

Milau, for **malau**, q.v.

Mile na, s., place, its place, d. for **alia na**, q.v., and see **malo**, a place.

Mile ki, **mile-raki**, v. t., to seek for (as for a pig in the bush), **milemile ki**, id., also **mole ki**, **mole-raki**, **mole-mole ki**. A. **‘āla**, (2), to go through a place, 4, to seek for; to desire eagerly.

Mile, or **milei**, v. i., or a., to be good, good, as, **noa milei**, tell good (well) it, **bati milei a**, make good (well) it, syn. **noa uia ki**, **bati uia ki** (**uia**, good), dd. **mitā ki**, **butā ki**, as, **noa mitā ki nia**, **bati butā ki nia**, id. [Raratonga *meitaki*, Tah. *maitai*, Niue *mitaki*, Fila, Meli, Ma. *marie*, Ha. *maikai*, to be handsome, good.] A. **malīḥ’**, beautiful, good, Nm. **melieh**, elegant, good.

Milès, v. i., or a., to be faded, drooping, withered: **lusia**. [Mg. *malazu*, withered.]

Miles, s., c. art. **namiles**, the

forest, the jungle, the bush. [My. *alas*, a forest, *alasan*, a forest country; a foundation, *alas-kaki*, footstool, Mg. *ala*, a forest, a wood, Bugis *alok*, id., Fi. *ra*, below.] A. 'araṣ'a, and 'aruṣ'a, to abound in grasses and herbs (of the land); 'arṣ'', the earth, soil, region, whatever is below, H. 'ereṣ, the earth, land, country, region, soil, Ch. 'ăra', earth; below.

Miles, s., a plant with dark leaves: **les**.

Milèsia, v. i., or a., d., and

Milèsira, id., to be faded, dirty, mouldy: endings **a** and **ra**; and

Ṁīlo, v. i., a., to be unclean, unclean. [Ml. Maskelynes *bīgal*, id.] H. **pigul**, E. **faḥala**, id.

Milo, or **miloa**, redup. **milolo**, or **miloaloa**, d. **malolo**, v. i., or a., to be dirty, to be darkish, of a dark, dirty colour: **loa**.[1]

Ṁilu, or **ṁilua**, v. i., to depart, go away (from), remove, **naṁiluan**, s., the removing, departure. See **lua**.

Ṁim, or **mam**, q.v.

Mīmi, s., voc., aunt (paternal). See **simam**. [Fut. *moma*, id.]

Mimita, s., a sign, a showing of something. See **mita**, **mimita**, v.

Mina, a., pleasant, nice. [Tah. *mona*, *monamona*, *momona*.] A. **'aniḳ'**, pleasant, nice.

Mina, tongue. See **mena**.

Mini-ġi, d. **minu-ġi**, **munu-ġi**, d. **mununa (munu-ma)**, v. t., to drink, also **minu**, **munu**; hence **namunuan** and **namunuġian**, s., drinking, drink. [Fi. *gunuva*, *unuma*, Ml. *min*, Malo *inu*, Epi *muni*, Sa. *inu*, ps. *inumia*, s., *inumaġa*, Santo *o'o-mia*, *ulu-mia*, My. *minum*, Mg. *minuna*.] See Ch. II. 13. *b*., 14. *e*., and 15, for the phonology of this word. Ch. **s't'a'**, **'is't'o'**, S. **s't'o**, H. **s'at'a**, E. **sataya**; and with the t' changed to **ḳ**, H. **s'aḳah**, A. **saḳa'**, E. **saḳaya**, to drink.

Minranin, d., ad., now; **mi nra nin**, **mi**, time, **nra nin**, this here; as to **mi** compare **ma**, day. E. **yom**, to-day, now, this time.

Mirà-ġi, d. for **mera-ki**.

Mirama, v. i., to be light, to shine; **namirama**, s., light; **emeromina**, in the light, the world;

Mirama-ni a, to shine upon or on it, or him. [Sa. *malama*, to be light, *malamalama*, v., to be light, s., light, *malama*, s., the moon, a lamp, torch, Ha. *lama*, a torch.] A. **lama'a**, to shine, &c.

Mirārā, v. i., or a., to be light (not heavy), slender, small. A. **raḳḳa**, to be thin, slender, slight, **raḳaraḳa**, to pour out not much (water or other thing).

Mirati, redup. **miratirati**, d. **minrat**, **minratinrat**, v. i., or a., to be loosed, untied: **rat i**, q.v. [Ma. *matara*, Sa. *matala*, *matalatala*, Tah. *matara*, *mataratara*, to be untied.]

Misa, or **ṁisa**, v. i., to be stinking, rotten, decayed, wasted away; and redup.,

Misimisi, v. i., to be wasted away (of a very old man). Ch. **mĕsa**, S. **msa**, to be decayed, putrefy.

Misafe, **misafesafe**, v. i., to be separated (as a cocoanut from its branch): **safe**.

Misaki, d. **masaki**, v. i., to be sick, to have fever, to be ill. [My. *sakit*, Sa. *ma'i*, Fut. *maki*, Ml. P. *mesek*, Epi dd. *msaki*, *miei*, id.] And

Misaki, or **misakia**, s., c. art., sickness. [Fut. *makiga*, sickness.] A. **s'aka'**, (2), to afflict (some one, a disease), **s'akat**, disease, **mas'kuww'**, afflicted with a disease.

Misal, v. i., or a., to be removed, separate (from others). A. **'azala**, to remove (one), 5, 6, 7, 8, to be removed, 8, separate (from others), **manzul'**, separated, removed.

Misal, **misalsal**, or **misalĭ**, **mĭsalĭsalĭ**, v. i., or a., to be light (not heavy). See **salĭ**.

Misaru, v. i., to hang down, prostrated: **saru**.

Misei, or **misai**, **miseisei**, v. i., or a., to be open, cracked: **sai**.

Misera, v. i., or a., to be parted, disjoined (as joints), separated: **sera**.

Misèrĭ, s., c. art., part of a woman's dress, consisting of a little mat, terminating in a bulky fringe, attached to the waist cincture and hanging down like an apron. See **seri**. A. **'azzara**, to cover the body with the covering or garment called **'izār'**, **mizar'**, a garment, covering, Nm. an apron.

Miseroà sa, v. t., to desire, covet: **soroà sa**.

Miseroana, s., c. art., coveting, covetousness.

Misimis, s., d. **masimasi**.

Misimis, v., d. **masimasi**.

Ṁīt, s., c. art. **naṁīt**, a mat; so called because plaited—see **bātu**, Ml. *vij*, Epi *mbie*, to plait (a mat). [Ml. *devij*, Epi *yembi*, a mat.]

Mita, v. t. (also **meta**), to look at, watch, observe, view, as, **i mita natai-inlaġi**, he watches or observes the cloud (to see if it will rain), **mitā sa**, or **mimitā sa**, look at, watch it (anything); and **mita ġita**, or **bakamita ġita** = **leo ġoro ġita** (see **leo**), watch, look for, look out for (expecting) us: **bakamita**, v. t., same as **mita**. [Sa. *mata*, to look at, *matamata*, to look, to view, *mamata*, id. (of many), Ha. *makai*, *makaikai*, to look at closely, inspect, search out, spy, act the part of a spy, to look on, look at, to examine secretly for evil purposes, To.

mamata, to look, look at, behold, discern.] A. ʻāna, 1, to emanate (water), to be a spy, 2, to flourish, produce flowers (a plant), to show, make conspicuous, 3, to see, look at or on, 5, to look at malevolently, to look at well, accurately, to be manifest, conspicuous, 8, to look at malevolently, to become a spy, to view or watch, to look out for.

NOTE.—For the phonology of this word, see Ch. II. 11. *c*, and 13. *b*.

Mita na, s., c. art. **namita na**, the eye, that which sees, looks at, watches, or observes; **mita noai**, a fountain; **mita**, the beginning; **mita**, bud, shoot, 'eye' (as of a potato), bud, germ, offshoot (of men); **mita nalaġi**, eye of the wind; **mita ḅaġona**, eye of its end, point of its end, end; **mita**, a window, door, or other opening, as the eye (of a needle); **i bi mita na**, to be the eye (i.e. guide) of some one; **namita nalo**, the eye (price) of something; **mita kita**, a spy (in war), see **kita**; **mita ni elo**, (d. **al**), the sun (eye of light, or of day, or fountain or source of light). [My. *mata*, Mg. *masu*, Sa. *mata*, the eye, &c., Fi. *mata*, eye, source, opening, point.] See **mita**, v.

Mitā, v. i., to bleed, **mitā nia**, bleeds on it, as **i tumana mitā nia**, redup. **mitāmitā nia**, he bleeds on himself (covers himself with blood), used also of rust—it rusts (covers itself with rust): **ṭā**, blood. [My. *bārdarah*, Bu. *madara*, to bleed.]

Mita-ḅaġo na, s., end, lit. point of its end: **mita**, s.

Mita-busa, s., orphan child: **mita**, s. (bud, shoot), and **busa**, q.v.

Mitaġa, and **mitaġataġa**, v. i., to be heavy: d. **miten**, q.v.

Mitailau (**mita-i-lau**), s., d. syn. **bilē-mita**, q.v., lit. germ or source of the tribe or community. See **launa**.

Mitāki, v. i., to be inclined to one side: **taki**, **tā**.

Mitaki, i.e. **mita ki**, d. **milei**, q.v.

Mitakisa, s., blind, the eyes receding into the head: **mita**, eye, and **kisa**.

Mitakitïk, d. **matakitakï**, a., last or first of a row (as of men); from closing up, or, as it were, binding together the series: **taki**.

Mitaku, or **mataku**, v. i., to fear, be afraid; **mitaku**, or **mataku ki**, usually contr. to **mitau ki**, or **matau ki**, v. t., to be afraid of, to fear; **bakamataku ki**, to frighten (one); hence

Mitakua, s., c. art. fear; and

Mitakuan, s., c. art., act of fearing, fear. [Sa. *mataʻu*, ps. *mataʻutia*, My. *takut*, Mg. *tahuṭa*, s., fear, *matahuṭa*, v. i., to be afraid, to fear.] A. **taḳa'**, v. t., to fear (derived from **waḳa'**, 8), **taḳiyyat**, fear, caution, taking heed, takwa, fear of God, takiyy', fearing God. See infra, mitataku.

Mitamai, or **matamai**, or **mitimai**, ad., to-morrow. [Mota *matava*, morning, Sa. *tafa*, to dawn.] A. ṣabaḥa, 4, to be morning, to be early, to dawn, E. ṣabḥa, to become light, or day, to dawn, A. ṣabāḥ', morning, maṣbaḥ', and muṣbaḥ', morning, dawn.

Mitanielo, s., the sun, lit. eye of day: **mita ni elo**. [My. *mata-ari*, Mg. *masuandru*.]

Mitäo, d., v. i., d. **mitefe**, q.v.: **tao, roa**.

Mitarau, s., c. art. tribe, lit. the bud, or germ, spreading out into many branches: **mita**, s., and **rau**.

Mitariki, s., the seven stars, Pleiades: **mita**, s., and **riki**. [Sa. *matalii*, Ma. *matariki*, id.]

Mitariki, s., as, **lo mitariki**, to look with little (i. e. contracted) eyes. Same word as preceding.

Mitaru, v. i., to sink down: **tiro**.

Mitasabo, s., a stranger, lit. eye not knowing: **mita, sabo**.

Mitataku, v. t., as, **i tumana mitataku na**, he heedfully watches himself, he being afraid watches himself: **mita**, v. t., and see **mitaku**.

Mitau, or **matau**, v. i., to abide, continue: **tau**.

Mitau ki, v. t., to fear: contraction for **mitaku ki**.

Mitaukian, a., dreadful, to be feared.

Mitausi a, v. t., to look after: **mita**, v. t., and **usi**, v. t.

Mitefe, d., v. i., to fall down, as a portion of a precipice. See **rŏua, roa**.

Mitefe-risu, v. i., to fall down (see preceding word), rushing or slipping to a distance: **risu**.

Miteftef, v. i., and

Mitefŭtefŭ, id., to twitter, chirp, peep (of a bird or fowl), to make a whispering noise (of men). H. ṣifṣaf, to twitter, peep, chirp (of birds), to make a whispering, peeping sound (of the voice of a wizard).

Mitei, or **muṭei**, s., c. art., breadfruit cheese (salt and sour), that is, breadfruit fermented and preserved. [Sa. *masi*, id., My. *masin*, salt (as water), Mg. *masimasina*, saltish, *ranu-masina*, the sea (salt water).] A. māṣiʿ, salt (of water).

Mitela, v. i., or a., to be broken (as crockery, or pottery). A. t'alaʿa, to break (the head), mut'allaʿ, broken. And

Mitela, s., c. art. **namitela**, a fragment, lit. that which is broken, the broken.

Mitèn, v. i., d. **mitàġa**, to be heavy, to be burdened: **tien**, or **tiana**, q.v., as also **taġo, taġie**. [Mg. *entana*, s., burden, *vua entana*, lifted up, *mientana*, to set out, *taiġina*, placed upon (a horse), *tuġua*, placed upon, My. *tuġ"aġ*, to ride, be conveyed by any vehicle, *tağ''uğ*, to bear, carry.] S. ṭ'an, to carry, Aph. to burden, load, ṭa'no', a burden, H. ṭa'an, Ch. ṭĕ'en, to be laden, A. ṭ'a'ana, 8, to sit on a camel, H. ṣa'an, to move tents, go forward (as a nomadic tribe), A. ṭ'a'ana, id., E. ṣa'na, ṣa'ana, to put on a horse, &c., and consequently of other things where one sits, is placed, upon another, ṣĕun, burden.

Miti, v. i., to move rapidly, to strive, quarrel, to jump backwards and forwards excitedly in a quarrel or a rage, to land or remove from a canoe; **miti ġoto**, depart or go rapidly across (as an arm of the sea); and redup.,

Mitimiti, v. i., to throb, flutter (as the pulse). A. **mata**, and **maṭa**, to move quickly.

Mitiri, v. t., to write, to carve, cut or make figures;

Mitimitiri, a., figured, as cloth ('print');

Mitiri, d. **manṣiri**, s., c. art., writing, figures; and

Mitirian, s., c. art., act of writing, what is written. [Santo d. *turi*, Epi *siri*, My. *tulis*, to draw, delineate, paint, picture, figure, write, Mg. *suraṭa*, colour, writing, written, *misuraṭa*, to be spotted, printed, of different colours, and *suriṭa*, *misuriṭa*, to mark, engrave.] (E. sa'ala, to paint, figure), A. ṣāra, 2, to figure, paint, 5, to be formed, muṣawwir, sculptor, painter, Nm. 2, to form, draw, trace, paint. The radical idea is that of cutting.

Mitiri, s., a kind of locust or grasshopper (so called from its mode of moving);

Mitiri, v. i., to leap flying (as a grasshopper): **tiri**.

Miṭoa, v., to think, **miṭoa ki**, v. t., to think of or about, dd. **miroa**, **mitoa**, **mintoa**, **minroa**; redup.,

Mitiṭoa, d. **minintoa**, v. i., to be thoughtful, sensible;

Miṭoān, s., c. art., act of thinking, thought: **ro**, **roro**, **ṭoṭo**, **rara**, or **ṭara**. [Mg. *eriṭa*, *eriṭariṭa*, cogitation, *mieriṭa*, *mieriṭeriṭa*, Fut. *mentua*, To. *manatu* (Sa. *manatu*), to think.] S. 'etra'i, to think, Ethpa. of r'o', Ch. rĕ'ah, to think, H. ra'ah, (3), to delight in, rea', a friend, lover, one loved, thought, will, Ch. ra'yon, thought.

Mīto (**mwīto**), v. i. or a., to be short, redup.,

Mitemīto, id., d. **būru**, **burufūru**. [Tah. *mure*, *muremure*, Ma. *poto*.] A. ma'don, short, or **mawdon** (n. p. of **wadana**).

Miu, v. i., to be wet: cg. **mea**. A. mai', fluid, ma'a, to flow gently on the surface, 4, to be dissolved in liquid.

Miura, s., c. art., dew: **miu**, and **ura**, q.v.

Mo, ad., contraction of **mero**.

Mo, d. **bo**, dd. **fo**, **uo**, **o**. See **bo**.

Ṁō na, s., father or mother-in-law, son-in-law: hence,

Ṁo-naki, v. t., to be related to (one) in this relationship. E. **ḥam,** father-in-law, son-in-law, A. **ḥam', ḥamō, ham'o,** &c., father-in-law or kinsman of the husband or the wife, Nm. **ḥamou,** father-in-law, **ḥamaya,** mother-in-law, H. **ḥam,** Assy. **emu,** father-in-law, Samaritan, a son-in-law, also, one espoused. 'The proper signification of the word lies in the idea of affinity.'

NOTE.—E. **Mai ma** = Ef. **mo,** Fila **ma,** brother-in-law, **vuġōna** (nearly pronounced like **vumōna**)=(in meaning) Ef. **buruma:** in Tah. **momoa** is to espouse, to contract marriage.

Moa, d., verbal pron., 1 dual, excl., pl. **bu, mu.**

Moàs, d. for **mafàsu.**

Mobu, d. **m'bua,** v. i., to sink: **bua** II.

Mofa, s., or **mafa,** when the blood of men or animals has been shed, and forms a pool on the ground, one feeling the smell of it, or of any similar thing, says **i naḅo mofa,** it smells **mofa; taumofa (tau mafa),** to make a sacrifice or offering to the natemate. See **taumafa.** A. **ma'habat,** a small pool, **wahaba,** to give, make an offering.

Mok, s., water flowing from the eye;

Mokemok, v. i., to flow from the eye (of water), to water (of the eye): cg. **miu, mou.** H. **mug,** to flow, flow down, dissolve.

Mokot, d., s., tongs: **mikit** i.

Ṁola, v. i., to yawn. [Ma. *kowhera,* to open, gape.] H. **pa'ar,** to open the mouth with a wide gape, S. **f'ar,** A. **fa''ara.**

Mole, d. for **ḅalo,** v. i., q.v.

Mole, or mole ki, molemole ki, d. **mile, mile ki,** q.v.

Moli na, s., d. for **batoko na,** q.v.

Moli, v. i., d., **mauri,** to live;

Molian, s., c. art., d. **maurian,** life.

Momoà, or **momo,** d., v. i., to yawn. [Tah. *mama,* to open the mouth, Sa. *mavava,* Fut. *mava,* to yawn, Mg. *vava,* the mouth, *vava,* opened, *mivava,* v. i., *mavava,* v. t., to open.] H. **peh,** mouth, A. **fah',** mouth, **faha,** to speak, **fawiha,** to have a wide mouth.

Momoa, v. i., d. for **amoamo, amo'mo.**

Monam, d. **monau,** s., c. art., grass (of any kind). A. **nama',** to grow, **namāya,** vegetation, **manma',** place of (a tree's) growth. The word 'grass' is connected with 'grow'.

Monamona, v. i., or a., to be yellow. [Ma. *pugapuga,* yellow colour, Mg. *vuni,* s., yellow, Amboyna *poko,* d. *apoo,* Ceram *poko,* yellow, id.] A. faḳa'a, n. a. fuḳu', to be yellow.

Mono-ti. See **munu-ti.**

Mori, d., a., true, **tili mori,** speak true: **mori,** true, used like **loamau, lesoko,** also **amori**: **mauri, mau,** true.

Mōri a, d., for **mesau na,** for which also is d. **mūri n.**

Morese na, s., d. **borakese na,** q.v.

Moro, ad., d. **mero,** q.v.

Moru, v. i., to sink, or be covered with water, as a canoe in the waves;

Moru-aki, v. t., to sink, overwhelm (a canoe), as, **nabeau i sera moru-aki rarua,** the waves rush, sinking, or covering, or overwhelming the canoe;

Morua, s., c. art., the deep, i.e. the deep sea;

Mōru, s., any deep place, as a hole, pit, grave; hence **imrum** (d. **imrau**), inside of a house, i.e. **moru nasuma,** or **moru uma,** the hole, i.e. the inside, of a house. A. **"amara,** to cover (a thing with water), **"amar',** much water, deep (of the sea), Nm. to overwhelm, drown, **"amra,** deep water, abyss.

Mos i, for **amos i,** q.v.

Mōso, s., the entrance to a harbour; a space or tract of country, as that between two mountains; pr. n. of the village and district on the northern end of Deception Island, at the boat entrance to Havannah Harbour, and in Ro-Moso, name of an inland village and district. H. **mahōz,** a seaport, coast, Ch. id., also a region, A. **ha'z',** border, side, region, hence also a port.

Mot, s. See **mut,** s.

Mot, or **motŭ,** s., c. art. **namot,** as, **nataku namot,** back of the land, or island; lit. what is broken off, hence a district or place. [Sa. *motu,* islet, district, *motu,* to be broken off, ps. *motusia,* v. t. *motusi,* s. *motusaga,* v. i. *motumotu,* s. *motumotuga,* My. *putus,* to break, Mg. *maitu,* broken asunder, snapped, *maituitu,* broken in pieces, *utusana,* being cut, broken, snapped.] A. **maḳṭa',** a place. See the verb under **koto-fi.**

Ṁota, s., c. art., and redup.,

Motaṁota, id., rubbish, refuse, as leaves of trees fallen on the ground, &c. [Sa. *ota,* rubbish, Ma., Tah. *ota,* Ha. *oka.*] And

Ṁota, v. i., or a., to be covered with rubbish, dirty. [Sa. *otaotā,* full of rubbish: a. ending *a.*] A. **"otā',** rubbish, refuse, husks, leaves, and scum mixed together, **"ata',** to have rubbish mixed with scum (as a river).

Mot i. See **mut i.**

Mou, moumou. Same as **miu,** q.v.

Mu, verbal suf. pron., 2 pl., you, d. **kama.**

Mu, v. i., to coo (as a dove), to hum—see **fu**. [Tah. *mu*, a buzz, *mumu*, to make a confused noise, as of a multitude of persons talking together, Ha. *mumu*, id., Sa. *muimui*, to murmur, Fut. *mu*, to buzz, Mg. *muimui*, hum, murmur.] H. **hamah**, coo, hum (as a multitude), A. **hamhamah**, to murmur, &c., Nm. to whoop, drone, sing lullaby.

Mū-ni, v. t., to take out (a thing, as out of a basket). [Mg. *vuaka*, *mivuaka*, to go out, *mamuaka*, to drive out, take out.] See under **bua** III.

Mua, v. i., to flow out, flow (of the tide); hence

Muāna, s., c. art., the flood tide, as opposite to the ebb; and

Mua-ġoro, s., c. art., dd. **fua-ġoro**, **màġoro**, a spring of fresh water on the shore that is covered (**ġoro**) by the sea at high water: **bua** III.

Mubu. See **mobu**.

Muku-ti, v. t., to cover or enclose in leaves (as bananas, to ripen them); to rub, wipe off; and

Mukumukuen, s., c. art., the doing so. [Fi. *moko-ta*, to embrace, to clasp round with the arms, Ma. *mukumuku*, *muku*, and *uku*, to wipe, rub.] A. **ḥaḳa** (mid. و), n. a. **ḥuḳ'**, to sweep, cleanse by sweeping; to rub; to surround, embrace, enclose.

Ṁuli (mwuli), v. t., to work into a round mass, as dough or clay; to gather rubbish into a heap; to clasp a pig (or man) round with the arms; and

Mulĭmul, v. i., or a., round. [TaSa. *molmol*, Ml. P. *moromor*, My. *bulat*, Mg. *buriburi*, round.] H. **fol**, E. **falfal**, round, roll.

Mulusi, v. t., to strip off the skin, and

Mulu, v. i., and **tamulu**, to cast the skin (as a snake, a crab, a scab, men in myths), redup. **mulumulu**; and

Mulu na, s., c. art., the skin which is cast; then, the lower rank which a chief casts off on his being promoted to a higher. [Fi. *kuli*, skin, *kulut'aka*, to strip off the skin, Mg. *hudiṭa*, skin, *manudiṭa*, to strip off the skin, *hudirana*, being flayed, skinned, Ef. *kuli*, d. *uili* (*wili*) and *uli*, skin, *mulusi*, to skin, *mulu*, also *tamulu*, to cast the skin, i.e. to be skinned, or to skin oneself or itself.] A. **gild'**, skin, **galada**, 1, 2, to skin, to strip off the skin. مَجْلُود, **mulu**, **mulusi**; and

Muluan, s., c. art., act of casting the skin; **namulusian**, s., the act of stripping off the skin.

Mulua, s., a grove or clump of trees: **ulua**.

Mūmū, a., saving, protecting, preserving: **mū-ti**, or **mau-ti**.

Munu-ġi. See **minu-ġi**.

Munu-ma, d. **munu-ġi.**

Munu-ti, v. t., to close up (as a wound, a hole in cloth, &c.); hence

Munuai, or **munue**, s., a sacred man (**natamole tab**) who by his **natabuan**, or magical power, closes up, or heals, wounds received by men in battle: **bunu-ti.**

Murasa, d. **marasa.**

Mūrĭ n, v. t., d. for **mesau na**;

Mūrĭan, s., c. art., d. for **mesauan.**

Muri, v. t. (d. **busi**), to return (as a thing borrowed), to repay, recompense, requite (for work done), to return (an injury), repay (a person, for an injury), redup. **murimuri**; hence

Murian, s., c. art., the act of returning, repaying, pay, requital, recompense, retribution. And

Muri na, s., c. art., the after part of a thing (as of a stream, that is, the place to which it flows and where it ends), opposite to **namita na**, the forepart of a thing (eye), beginning, source. [Fi. *muri-a*, to follow, also to imitate, Ma. *muri*, rear, hinder part, Sa. *muli*, end, back, or hinder part, rump, *mulimuli*, to follow after, To. *muli*, *mui*, Ja. *buri*, the back, rear, behind, after, My. *burit*, the fundament, Mg. *vudi*, the posteriors, stern (of a ship), *vuhu*, the back, *fudi*, returned, sent back, *mamudi*, to return the thing bought, *verina*, returned, sent back, *mamerina*, to return, send back.] See also **mauri, busi, bisi na, bui na, kui na, kusu na, kihi na, fua na, bua na, ġere na, urĭ na.** A. **'aḥ'ḥ'-ara**, to be behind, after, Nm. **mo'weḥ'ḥ'ar**, placed at the end, **mouḥ'ir**, stern, hinder part, **'eḥ'ir**, end, **'uḥ'ur'**, behind, after part, H. **'aḥar**, to be after, behind, **'aḥar**, after, behind, hinder part, extremity, **'aḥōr**, hinder part, rear, **meaḥōr**, from behind, behind; also in Arm. and E.

Muru, v. i., to laugh, **muru ki**, to laugh at (one). [Ta. *maliali*, My. *ilai*, Mota *marae*, to laugh.] A. **harharaṭ**, laughter (**harhara**), **ḳarḳara**, laugh repeatedly (**ḳarra**).

Murubua, s., a bat: **moru, bua**; from its dwelling in deep holes.

Musa-ġi, v. t., to take on board a canoe or ship (men or things); redup.,

Musamusa; and

Musagian, s., c. art., and

Musamusoan, s., c. art., the act of doing so; and

Musĭ a, v. t., to put or drag immersed in the water (a thing, as a log); and

Musu, v. i., to dive (as a man), to set (the sun); **elo i musu**, the sun sets, or has set. A. **"amasa**, dip, submerge, to set (as a star), and **ḳamasa**, dip, plunge, dive, and **maḳasa**, immerse in water.

Musi a, v. t., to remove a child (from the breast), wean it; and

Mus (**ki susu**), v. i., to be removed (from the breast). H. **mus'**, remove, take away.

Mus i, v. t., rub, smooth, flatter;

Musamus i, id., redup.: **mos i.**

Musuku-taki, v. t., to abhor: **siki-naki.**

Mut, v. i., to slip or fall out, as a rope out of a block. A. **ma'aṭa**, to take a sword out (of its sheath), 8, **'amma'ṭa**, id., also, to fall out (as hairs).

Mū-ti, v. t., d. for **mau ti**, to save, keep, preserve, protect. A. **'amana**, 4, render secure, protect, give security to (some one). Hence

Mūtian, s., c. art., act of saving, salvation.

Mut i, and **mot i**, v. t., to bind; and

Mut, s., c. art., a bond, rope. A. **maḳaṭa**, (6), bind, **muḳṭ'**, bond, rope.

Mutui, v. i., to sneeze. [Sa. *mafatua*, to sneeze.] A. **nafaṭa** (cf. **'afaṭa**, 2), to sneeze.

Na, ad. of assent, and interj., d. syn. **ko**: dem. **na**. H. **na**, indeed, &c.

Na, d., dem., this, as, **mal na**, this time: **in.**

Na, sometimes **a**, also **ĭn**, **nĭ**, **n**, **la** (in **lausu**), the article. [Mg. *ni*, Epi *na*, Fi. *na*, *a*, Sa. *le*, the article.] A. **al**, **hal**, H. **ha**, A. **a** (the **l** being assimilated to certain letters). In Mod. A. **al** is pronounced **al** or **el**, and **l'**. In South Arabia **am** was (and even still is) used for **al**. A. **al** (and H. **ha**) is sometimes used as a relative pronoun; so in Efate: see **niġ**, **aġi**.

N', a particle expressive of past time, in **nanum**, **nāsa**, **nanoasa**. [Mg. *n'*, Sa. *na*, sign of past tense.] See Ch. V. 10. *c*.

Na, d. **n**, and **na**, or **nia** (**sikina**, or **sikinia**), nom. suf. pron., 3 sing., his, her, its. [Sam. *na*, sing., Mg. *ni*, pl. and sing., My. *nia* or *ña*, pl. and sing.] See **nai**, note.

Na, d. **n**, verbal suf., pron., 3 sing., him, her, it. See **nia**, and **nai**, note.

Nabatĭ na, s., is **bati**, q.v., c. art., tooth, teeth; seed, also the shoots from the roots of a banana, and the shoots or roots of taro. [Ml. *ribo*, Epi *livo*, Sa. *nifo* (whence *nifoa*), Fut. *nifo*, Mg. *nifi*, teeth. This is another word for tooth, teeth. A. *nāb'*, pl. *nubūb'*, &c., tooth, teeth, *nāba*, 2, 4, to put forth roots (a plant).]

Naḅe, s., d. **mbat**, club. Nm. **nabboud** and **nabbout**, id.

Nāḅe, or **nāḅea** (**nakbe**, or **nakbea**), d. **nakima**, s., a hollowed log, set up in the middle of the **malala** or **mala**, used as a drum or musical instrument in the dances of the **intamate**, and on which the face of **Uota**, and symbols of the **natemato** (the deceased) are carved. [Sa. *nafa*, To.

naffa, Fut. *kafa*, a drum, Ml. U. *nambwi*, id.] H. nekeb, a hollowed thing, that which is hollowed, used as a musical instrument (Ezekiel xxviii. 13), English Version, 'pipes': 'thy tabrets and thy pipes'; from nakab, to hollow out.

Nabis, s., end, the last, d. **nakis**: **bisi na.**

Nabo, or **naboa**, d. **tamo**, v. i., to smell; and

Nabo n, s., its smell. [Sa. *namu*, to have a bad smell, To. *namu*, odour, either good or bad, Fut. *namu*.] See **boa**. A. **fāha**, 6, to emit odour.

Nabua, s., a road, path. A. **nabiyy'** and **nabiy'**, id.

Nafete (d. syn. **sefete**), d. **nefeha**, d. **(te)uase (wase)**, inter. pron., what? which? M.S. **mudi**, A. **mada**, Nm. **made**, what? **Nafete** is **na**, art., and **fete**, and **sefete**, **sefa**, q.v., and **te**.

Nāfo, s., dd. **āfo**, **foġa**, whetstone, pumice stone. A. **nasfa-t**, id.

Naġa, or **naġ**, dem., this, that: **na**, dem., and **ka**, dem., changed to **ġa**.

Nàġ, or **nàġa**, s., dd. **lāg**, **rāg**, **nrāk**, **rān**, time. A. **'ān**, time.

Naġasa, inter. ad., when? i. e. **naġa sa?** lit. what time? also indefinitely, when, whatever time. Ml. U. **seve-liġ** = Ef. d. **sefe-naġ** = what time? **naġa-sa?**

Naġo, pers. pron., 2 sing., you, dd. **ago**, **ag**, **niġo**, **keiġa**, **keina**, **nēġo**.

Naġore na, s., nostrils, nose. See **ġore na**.

Nai n, d. for **nani n**, child. See **nei n** and **ani**.

Nai, pers. pron., 3 sing., he, she, dd. **ĕnĕa**, or **ĭnĭa**, **ġā**, **niġa**, **kinini**. [My. *inya*, or *iña* (Ef. **inĭa**, or **iña**, sing.), pl. and sing., they, he, she.] See Ch. V. 2.

Nai, s., water, d. for **noai**, **nifai**.

Nai, s., side board of a canoe to keep the waves out, a protector or defence of a place (a warrior who keeps out the enemy); d. a fence. [Sa. *āi*, a fence, a railing, *āi*, to fence in, To. a fence.] A. **nawa'**, **naa'**, to guard, protect.

Naita natuo, s., d. for **uanate-natuo**, the calf of the leg, hence **nalake naita natuo n**, the ankle, lit. the base of the calf of the leg.

Nakate, s., d. syn. **nete**, q.v., lit. the that that.

Nakima, s., d. **nabea**.

Nakis, s., d. **nabis**: **kusu na**, **kihi** (or **kisi**) **na**.

Nakis, or **nakisa**, or **nakes**, s., green or blue paint: **kesakesa**.

Nàko na, s., the face. See **ko**, s.; **n**, art., and **ako**; hence

Nakonakoa ki, v. (formed by ending **a**, from preceding word) to assume the face, or appearance of (**ki**) some one;

Nakonako ki, v., to face (some one), i. e. front (him). A.

wagaha, 5, id., to front or face each other.

Nālu, or **nālua**, an arrow. A. **nabl'**, arrow.

Namu, s., d., mosquito, d. **na mamamami** (d. **batirik** = small tooth). [Sa. *mamu*, Tah. *namu*, *ramu*, Fut. *namo*, My. *ñamok*, Bu. *namok*, Mg. *muka*, Ml. U. *num*, TaSa. *moke*, Malo *mohe*, Ta. *kumug*, An. *inyum*, Motu *namo*, id.] A. **namus**, mosquito.

Nanoa na, s., the neck, i. e. **n'**, art., and **anoa**, neck, cg. **manu na**, q.v. [Santo d. *alo*, d. *ralo*, Bu. *oloġ*.] A. **'unḳ'**, **'unuḳ'**, **'anīḳ'**, neck.

Nanofa, ad., d., yesterday, and

Nanoasa, ad., d. **nāsa**, the day before yesterday, and

Nanu, ad., d. **nanofa**, and

Nanum, ad., d. **nanu**, yesterday. [Fi. *e na noa*, Santo *nonovi* (*pwanovi*, to-morrow), Epi *niobo* (*bani*=*maisa*=today).] **Nan-ofa**, **nan-u**, **nanum**, consist of **ofa**, **u**, **um**, day (see **ma**, s., day), and (Fi. **e na noa**, **e**, in or on, **na**, the; **noa**, past day = **nu**, **num**, **nofa**), **nan'**, i. e. **na**, the art., and **n'**, q.v., particle expressive of past time, as in **nāsa**, infra. **Nanōasa** (for **nanofasa**) has **sa** (for **rua**, sometimes **ra**, 2): hence **na nofa**, lit. the past day, and **na noasa**, the second past day. **Nanoasa**, **nāsa**. [Epi *nua*, d. *niaha*, Ta. d. *neis*, id.]

Nānua, s., necklace, beads, i.e. **n'**, art., and **anua**. H. **'anaḳ**, necklace.

Näo, s., d. **noa**, q.v.

Naob, s., lime, d. **noba**, q.v.

Nāra, pers. pron., 3 pl., they (for **nai 'ra**), d. **ġara**, or **niġara** (**ġa 'ra**), d. **inira** (**inia**, and **'ra**). See **ra**, and **nai**.

Naro, d. for **nalo**. See **lo**, a thing.

Naroa, s., **na**, art., a current (of water, especially in the sea): so called because **i roa**, turns (itself). See **roa**.

Nāsa, ad., the day before yesterday, d. **nanoasa**: **nāsa** is without the article and for **noasa** (in **nanoasa**).

Nasafa, inter. pron., also **nasefa**, and **nesefa**; **na**, art., and **safa**, or **sefa**, q.v.

Nasaġa, s., **na**, art., a stretch of sea between two places. See **saġa**.

Nasu na, **na**, art., s., juice, what flows out, or exudes. [Sa. *su*, to be wet, *sua*, juice.] A. **nazza**, to exude, **nizu**, flow, water.

Nāta, a person. See **ata**. **Nāta na**, or **nāte na**, soul, spirit;

Natamole, a living person,

Natamate, or **natemate**, a dead person, a ghost, a demon, an object of worship. See **ata**, **moli**, **mate**, **atamole**, **atamate**.

Natara, s., **n**, art., and **atara**, a., a virgin, young woman; **naġuruni atara**, a young woman. [My. *dara*, Ja. *rara*, a maid, virgin.] A. 'aḍara, to be a virgin ('aḍera', a virgin).

Nātĕ, or **nāṣĕ**, s., the banana, or plantain, plant and fruit: **n**, art., and **ātĕ**, or **āṣĕ**. [Ml. P. *nevij*, Ml. U. *navits*, Ero. *nobos*, Epi *vihi*, Am. *nohos*, Ml. dd. *navis*, *abus*, Paama *uhisi*, Fi. *vudi*, Ulawa *huti*, Fut. *vuji*, Fila *butsh'*, Aniwa *hutshĭ*, Niue *futi*, My. *pisaṅ*, Ceram *fudi*, *phitim*, Sanguir *busa*, Mg. *unṣi*, d. *huṣi*, id.] A. **muz'**, Amh. **muz**, id.

Nātĕ-kuru, s., dried, withered banana leaves. See **kuru**, a.

Natemate, for **natamate**. See **atamate**.

Natoara, s., **n**, art., a kind of grass (sword grass). H. **ḥaṣir**, grass, A. **ḥ'aṣ'ira**, to be green.

Naturiai, s. See **turiai**, a., young man.

Näu, s., reeds; Pan's pipes; for **nausu**: **na**, art., and **usu**, q.v.

Nau, v. i., usually **nu**, q.v.

Nau i, v. t., to rub, wipe off. See **nu e**.

Nāüa (**nāwa**), **na**, art., and **üa** (**wa**), q.v.

Nē, for **noi**, v., to dwell, or be beside (some one): the verb **no** is intransitive, and **i** is the t. prep. [Fi. *no*, to lie (of things, not persons), Sa. *nofo*, to sit, dwell, remain, Ma., Tah., Ha. *noho*.] H. **navah**, and **naah**, to sit down, to rest, to dwell.

Ne, dem., here, there, this, that, **uane**, **kine**, **netu**. See **in**, **na**. [Sa. *nei*, this.]

Nēgo, pers. pron., d. for **nago**, q.v.

Nei n, or **nai n**, s., his child, d. for **nani n**. The **n** of **ani**, q.v., is elided: **nai** for **nani**.

Neinei, v., as **boka neinei a**, beat it soft, beat making it soft (or weak). See **maneinei**.

Nēko (for **naiko**), s., **n**, art., and **eko**, the wooden mallet for beating native cloth (in making it). [Sa. *i'e*, To. *iki*, id., Ha. *ku*, *kuku*, to beat native cloth.] A. **waḳa'a**, to beat, (7), to sharpen, make thin a knife, (8), make slender, &c., **waki'**, sharp, thin, slender. (For To. **iki** meaning 'small', see Ef. **iki**, **kiki**, id.). **kie** also belongs here, the leaf being rubbed and split into slender threads.

Nēru, **nāru**, and **nieru**, war, lit. arms: art., and **aru**, q.v.

Nēt, d. for **binēt**, **banotu**, q. v.

Neta ki, v. t., to throw, **net i**, to throw upon, hit with a thing thrown. A. **nada'**, to throw, H. **nadah**, Pi., to cast out.

Nete, s., a thing, anything, something, d. syn. **nakate**: art., and **te**, dem., lit. the that. **Nete ra**, their thing, also **āra te**, id., **āgu te**, my thing, **āma te**, thy thing.

Netu, dem., this, that: **ne**, dem., and **tu**, v., lit. this or that standing out or up.

Netua, d. **nerua**, s., twins, art. and **tua**, or **rua**, 2, lit. the two. [Fi. *drua*, id.; also double, a., as a double canoe, a double fruit.]

Ni, prep., of (genitive), to, belonging to, also **i**, in, on, at (with art. **ani**, q.v.), t. prep. after verbs, as **mesau ni au**, desire me (also **mesau au**, d.), **i**, as, **soka-ri**, join on to, **no i**, &c. [Fi. *ni*, *i*, or *e*, of, in, and t. prep., Ma. *i*, of, belonging to, &c., and t. prep., Battak *ni*, Bu. *ri*, Holontalo *li*, Tag. *ni*, Mg. *ni*, *n'*, *ani*, of, belonging to, My. *i*, t. prep.] A. **li**, H., Arm. **lĕ**, E. **la**, T. **nĕ**, id. See Ch. V. 11. 1.

Nĭ, art., also **na**, in, n. [Mg. *ni*, id.]

Nĭ, same as **na**, ad., and interj.;

Ni, verb. suf., 3 sing., d. **nia**, q.v.

Nia, verb. suf., 3 sing., same as **na**, q.v., once (in **sikinia**, and **sikina**, his one, he alone) nom. suf. (which usually is **na**). See **nai**, **inia**.

Niba ki, v. t., to throw away, make to go away. A. **nafa'**, drive away, expel, hurl away (as a torrent, rubbish, the wind, dust).

Nifai, s., water, dd. **nai**, **noai**: **ni**, art., and **fai**, water.

Nife ni, a., v. t., to fan, t. prep. **ni**, lit. to wave, or brandish, on or to;

Nifenife, v. i., to fan, to wave, or brandish, as the branches of a tree in the wind;

Nīfe, s., a fan. H. **nuf**, to wave up and down, Hi. **henīf**, to wave, to shake.

Niġ, d., prep., of (gen.) for (dative), **ni**, art., and **ġ** (for **ġi**, i.e. **ki**, q.v.), dd. **naġ**, **naġi**, **naġki**, and, art. without its **n**, **aġi**, d. **aġki** (**ġk** for **ġ**).

Niġa, d., pers. pron., 3 sing.: **ni**, **n'**, dem., and **ġa**, or **iġa**.

Niġara, d., pers. pron., 3 pl.: **niġa**, and **ra**, pl. dem.

Niġita, pers. pron., 1 pl., incl.: **ninita**.

Nikenika, v. i., to be silent, quiet, or noiseless, or stealthy; also to move quickly along a sharp ridge (of a mountain), or along a log across a stream. [Ha. *nihi*, to walk very softly and quietly, as on tiptoe, to do a thing quietly or secretly, *nihinihi*, standing up on edge, narrow ridged, or edged, Ma. *ninihi*, to move stealthily.] A. **naga'**, to hasten; communicate a secret, 3, act, or speak, secretly (with some one), **naga'**, branch of a tree, higher part of land, **nagwat**, higher part of land, a secret.

Niko na, s., the spine (ridge) of a cocoanut leaf. See preceding word.

Nin, dem., d., this: **n**, art., and **in**, dem. [My. *nun*, that.]

Ninita, or **nininta**, d., obsolete, see **niġita**, **niġinta**, pers. pron., 1 pl., incl., we (and) thou, dd. **keiġita**, **iġira**, **akit**, **nikit**: **ninita**, nini, we, and **ta**, thou. [An. *inta*, verb. pron., id., Santo d. *niti*, and *inti*, separate pron., id., Ml. d. *ante*, id., My. *kita*, Mg. *isika*, Sa. *'o i ta* (*tou*), id.]

Nis, dem.; also, **nistu**, this; art. **ni**, and **se**, dem. [S. Cris. *nasi*, that.]

Niti, or **nit i**, v. t., to plane, shave (wood). A. **naḥata**, n. a. **naḥt'**, id.

Niu, s., c. art. **naniu**, the cocoanut palm. [Fi. *niu*, Er. *noki*, An. *neaig̃*, My. *nior*, Ceram *niula*, Ml. *kula*, Mg. *nihu*, Sa. *niu*, id.; *niu piu*, fan palm (therefore *niu* is a general name for a palm); *niui*, to sprinkle with the juice of the cocoanut, Ha. *niu*, to whirl about.] A. **naḥ'lu**, palm (gen. name), **naḥ'īlu** (coll. name), **naḥ'ala**, to sift, to pour out or sprinkle (snow, as the clouds), Nm., 7, to drizzle.

No i, or **noi**, d. **nē**, **noi**, d. **ne**: hence redup. **noinoi**, and v. r., **binoinoi**, d. **binofinoi**. See **nē**, for **noi**;

Nono, v. i., **no** (in **no i**), redup., to abide, as, **mala nono**, abide senseless. See also **binoinoi**, to abide with each other, and **binofinoi**, or **bunofunoi**.

Noa, s. (for **na ua**), d. **näo**, a swell, or wave. See **ua'a**.

Noa ki, v. t., tell, lit. say to, dd. **ni ki**, **ti ki**, **nofa i**, q.v.; **noa i**, v. t., say or tell it; **binoa**, to speak about each other, v. r.

Noai, s., d. **nifai**, water; for **na uai**.

Noḅa, s., c. art. **nanoḅa**, d. **naob**, lime (ashes of coral); and

Noḅanoḅa, v. i., or a., to be dusty, become dust, fly in the air (dust). [Sa. *navu*, lime.] and

Noba-ni, v. t., to wrap in leaves with hot stones and cook, to cook, d. **tuma-ni**; and

Noḅanoḅa, v. i., to be cooked, soft. See also **manubunubu**, and d. tomo or **tumu**, **tumutumua**, **matumutumu**. [Ha. *nopu*, thoroughly cooked, soft, plump, fat, swelled out, and *nopunopu*, spring or swell up (in the mind), swell, be large, round, spring up.] A. **ṭabaḥa**, n. a. **ṭabḥ'**, to cook, roast, to ripen, 2, to grow up, 7, 8, to be cooked, **ṭubbaḥ'**, **ṭābiḥ'**, fatness, **ṭabīḥ'**, cooked.

Nōbu, s., flood, d. **tōbu**. A. **ṭāf**, to flood (Ct.), **ṭawwafu**, a flood.

Nof, d. for **num**, v. i., q.v.

Nofa i, v. t., d. **noa i**, q.v., to tell. A. **nabā'**, (6), 2, show, declare, announce, tell.

Nono. See ante, **no**, **nono**.

Notĭnotĭ, v. i., or a., to be spotted (as an animal). H. **naḳod**, spotted (as an animal), Nm. **noḳṭa**, a spot, **monaḳḳaṭ**, spotted, H. **naḳad**,

A. **naḳaṭa**, to mark with points.

Nōtu, d., see under **banotu**, Note 2.

Nu, v. i., d. **num**, q.v., hence **manua**, **manunu**.

Nu ē a, v. t., to wipe, rub off; redup.,

Nunu ēa, id., and

Nūnu, s., a wiper, rubber, and

Nunu-tafe, s., the wrist, lit. snot-wiper. [Sa. *nunu*, to grate down, *nuaġa*, a grating down.] A. **t'amma**, (4), to sweep (a house, or place), (5), to rub, wipe off. (Cf. A. **tamma**, Ef. **num**, **nu**, for **t** to **n**.)

Nua na, s., **n**, art., and **ua**, q.v., fruit.

Nuanua, v. i., to wave about, or to and fro (as the branches of a tree); **nuanua ki**, v. t., to wave, make to wave, or shake (anything). H. **nuʿa**, to move to and fro, wave to and fro, Hi. move to and fro, shake.

Nub, s., d. rub, q.v.

Nubu na, d. **tumu na**, s., c. art., the soft swelling protuberance of anything (as of a yam) growing. See **noḅanoḅa**.

Nubu, v. i., d. **num**, and

Nuf, v. i., d. **num**, q.v.

Nuġnuġ, v. i., to be careless, heedless, **maturu nuġnuġ**, to sleep and be devoid of all care or thought, be utterly heedless. A. **nūmat**, heedless, careless, **nāma**, to sleep, doze, be quiet, tranquil, 2, deaden (as pain).

Nuġnuġ i, v. t., d. **luġluġ i**, q.v.: hence **manuġnuġ**, q.v.

Num, v. i., to be finished, completed, dd. **nu**, **nau**, **nubu**, **nuf**, **nof**; **ru nau**, **nu**, **num**, **nuf ban**, they *all* have gone, **a bat ia i nu**, I have done it, it is finished. See **bunu**, **manunu**, **binunu**, **manubu**, **manubunubu**. A. **tamma**, n. a. **tum'**, &c., to be all, whole, finished, completed, at an end, and, transitive, to complete, &c.

Numnum ia, v. t., d. for **nuġnuġ i**.

Nūra, s., syn. **miura**, q.v., is for **ne ūra**: **ura**.

O, sign of vocative, interj., as, **temanami o**, O our father. [Ml., Santo, Malo **o**, id.] E. **o**, id.

O, dem., **io**, **äo**, **ore**, or **iore**, q.v. [Fi. *o*, in *oqo*, Tah. *o*, Mare *o*, Motu *o*, dem.] The Semitic pers. pron. 3 sing. used as a dem., and as a verb substantive.

O, verbal suf., 1 sing., me, d. for **au**.

O, v. i., contr. for **onĭ**, q.v.; also in **bäo**.

Ob, s., d., c. art. **naob**, d. **nanōḅa**, lime (ashes of coral): **noḅa**.

Ōf, s., dd. **um**, **ubu**, **ūa**, cooking oven. A. **mifa**, oven.

Ofa, in **taliofa**, dd. **taliaba**, **talieba**. See **tali**. **Ofa**, to whirl round. [Tah. *ohu* (also =*kofu*, q.v., supra), to whirl round, Ma. *koumuumu*, My.

ubâģ, mubâģ.] E. **kabab,** to whirl round.

Ọfa, i. q. **afa,** to swim, be above, float on; and

Ofa i, i. q. **afa i,** q.v.

Ofa ki, v. t., i. q. **afa ki**; **nalia ofakian,** a place of burial, to be buried in, **naofakian,** act of burying, burial.

Ofa, a., high, tall, as a tree. [Mg. *avu,* high, lofty, eminent, proud.] H. **gabah,** to be high, as a tree, **gobah,** height (as of trees), pride, **gaboah,** high, lofty, proud.

Ōf i, or **ōfi,** v. t., to be near to, alongside of, d. **āfi**;

Ofiofi, v., a., near to. [To. *ofi,* near to, at hand.] A. **wahafa,** n. a. **wahf',** to draw near to, approach near.

Ola, s., a spear. [Ulawa *ilula,* New Ireland *lelu,* Maklay Küste (N. G.) *iur,* id.] A. **'allat',** pl. **'alal', 'ell'**, id.

Oli, d. **uli,** q.v.

On, s., sand, d. **aran,** q.v.

Onĭ, contr. **o,** d. **anĭ,** q.v., to abide, be.

Or, d., s., c. art. **naor,** or **na uor.** See **uora.**

Ora na, s., sprout, shoot, or vine (as of a yam);

Oraora na, id.: **bora, uora.**

Orān, and **orain,** d. **oraone,** s., sand: **arān.**

Oraora, s., dazzling (variegated) rays of the (morning) sun, **oraora ni elo**; and

Oraorana, a., **na,** a. ending, variegated. [Tah. *purepure,* spotted, chequered, of diverse colours.] E. **ḥubur,** variegated, of various colours, Ch. **ḥabarbar,** spotted.

Ore, i. q. **aure,** q.v.

Ōrĕ, d. **ōr,** ad., yes, that's it: **o,** dem., and **re,** or **ri,** dem., cf. **iore.**

Ori a, v. t., to rub, grate, **ori,** v. i., to make a creaking, grating noise (as the branches of trees rubbing against each other);

Ōri, s., the rubbing stick in producing fire by the friction of two sticks. [Tah. *oro,* Sa. *olo,* to rub, *olo,* a plane, My. *urut,* to rub, Mg. *uṭa,* rubbed, *urina,* being rubbed.] A. **'arata, 'arat'a,** to rub.

Oro, v. i., to grunt (a pig), to growl, snarl (a dog), and with transitive prep. **ki, oro-maki,** to bark at (a person or thing), **bioro,** v. r., to make a confused murmuring noise (as a crowd of men all speaking at once); and

Orooro, id., redup., cf. **uru, uruuru.** [Ma. *ġuru,* to sigh, grunt, rumble, *ġeġere,* to growl, *ġeri,* to chant (in launching a canoe, &c.), *ġeġeri,* to grunt, My. *kurkur,* to grunt (a pig), Mg. *eruṭa,* to snore, *eruna, mieruna,* to growl, snarl, roar.] A. **naḥ'ara,** Nm. to grunt, **ḥ'ara,** to low, **ḥ'arḥ'ara,** snort, snore, **harra,** to growl, snarl (a dog), to creak, **harharat,** murmur or sound of copiously flowing water.

Oro, d., v. i., or a., to be barren: d. for **bara,** q.v.

Oroa, v. i., or a. Same as **oraorana**, to be coloured, variegated: a. ending a, d. contr. **oro**; hence

Oroa, d. **oro**, s., a species of grasshopper, so called from its colours.

Otaki, d. **uataki**, s., native tongs: **taki**.

Oti, i. q. **uti**, q.v.

Ra, d. **nra**, dem., this, that. See **arai**.

Rā, s., a depressed place, damp or watery: **ruku**.

Rā, verbal pron., 3 dual, they two; pl. **ru**, they. See Ch. V. 2.

Rā na, s., branch. [Sa. *la*, Ma. *ra*, My. *daan*, Mg. *rahana*, *rahaka*.] A. **s'agnat, s'agan'**, id.

Rā, or **ṭā**, dd. **tā**, **nrā**, s., blood, **mitā**, to bleed. [Er. *de*, TaSa. *rai*, Malo *dai*, Motu *rara*, Sa. *toto* (redup.), Ja. *ra*, My. *darah*, Mg. *ra*, blood.] H., E. **dam**, S. **dem**, A. **dam'**, blood; **damiya**, to bleed.

Ra, v. i., vociferate, in **rasoso**, **rafioso**. [My. *ruwah*, id.] H. **ru'a**, Hi. vociferate.

Ra, verb. and nom. suf., 3 pl.: **nara**, they.

Ra, num., two: **rua**.

Ra tan i, **rara tan i**, **ṭara tan i**, **tara tan i**, v. t., to forget, lit. to think burying or covering it. See **miṭoa** and **tun i**.

Rabà na, s., side (of a river or valley). A. **ṣ'affat'**, id.

Rabaraba, v. i., to flap the wings. A. **rafrafa**, id.

Rabaraba kaf (or **kai**), v. i., to be bent with hunger or famine; and

Rāba, s., hunger or famine, in **li rāba**, goddess, or she demon of hunger (a 'sacred stone'). H. **ra'eb**, E. **rĕḥaba**, to hunger, H. **ra'ab**, hunger, famine.

Rabaġ, see **tabaġ**.

Rafālu, d. **lifāru**, q.v.

Raf i, v. t., to scratch, dig, scrape. A. **ṣaḥafa, ṣaḥf'**, id.

Rafē, v. t., to weave a reed fence; hence

Rafēna, s., a reed (woven) fence, d. **rofe**; and

Rafean, s., c. art., the act of weaving a reed fence. H. **'arab**, to weave, intertwine, A. **'araba**, a knot, H. **'arubaḥ**, interwoven work, or network.

Raf, s., d. **rau**, binding cross-sticks in framing a roof. Preceding word.

Rafe, v. t., to go through (as through a hole in a fence, the eye of a needle); and

Rafe-aki, v. t., to make to go through, as, **rafeaki nausu**, make a reed to go *through* among the others in weaving, a **rafēna**. See **rafe**.

Rafioso, v. i., to call out as when in terror or danger: **ra**, v. i., and **bioso**.

Rafite na, s., wall or side of a house. E. **arafete**, partition, wall.

Raġa-ēlo, d., v. i., to warm or dry oneself in the sun (ēlo): **raġa** is transposed for **ġara**, as **baraġai** for **baġarai**, q.v.

Rāġ, s., time, c. nom. suf. **raġi na**, its time: d. **rān, rāni na**, dd. **laġ, naġ**. A. 'ān', time.

Raġo, s., c. art., thicket, roughness. See **fakaraġo**;

Raġoa, and **raġoroġoa**, v. i., or a., to be full of **raġo**, as a reef full of jagged, sharp rocks. [Mg. *rukuruku*, roughness, rough.] H. **raga'**, (2) to be corrugated, rough.

Rāġo, s., rollers on which a canoe or boat is hauled up. [Ma. *raġo*, id.] See **lāġo**.

Rai, d. **re**, s., forehead, aspect, face. [To. *lae*, My. *dai*, Ja. *rai*, id.] E. **rey**, sight, aspect;

Rairai, d. **tairai**, v. i., to be in good countenance. See **bakarairai**, and **lo, leo**.

Raite na, or **reite na**, d., s., mother. See under **ani na**.

Raka, v. i., to be willing, and **maraka**; also, redup.,

Rakaraka, id., and **marakaraka**, id.; also,

Rakana, s., the willingness, readiness, **tuġa fat ia rakana sikaimau**, let us do it, the readiness or willingness for it one only, i.e. with one mind or will. S. **rĕgag**, to desire, to will, Ethpael id., **rega**, desire, will.

Rakaf i, and **rakof i**, v. t., to cleave to. and

Rarako, d. **tarako**, as, **toa i rarako**, sits on, cleaves close to (her eggs). S. **nḳaf, etnaḳaf**, to cleave to, cg. E. **lakaf.**

Raka i, v. t., to lift, raise up, and

Raka-ti, id. A. **raḳiya**, 2, raise up, make to go up.

Rakei, v. t., to adorn, dress; **tumana rakei**, adorn or dress himself. [Sa. *la'ei*];

Rakei, d. **rakī**, s., c. art., dress, adornment. E. **laḥaya**, to adorn, dress.

Raku sa, v. t., redup. **raraku sa**, and **taraku sa**, and d. **taku-ti**, to bind up, to remove anyone's things, as in a flitting; **i raraku**, he is doing so, or is removing to another district, or flitting, to remove, carry away (anything). [Sa. *la'u*, Ma. *raku*, Marq. *naku*, scratch, carry away, Mg. *raġuṭa*, to scratch.] A. **raka** (final ؏), to dig, to bind up.

Rakua, and, dd.,

Rakum, rakoma, s., a crab. [Epi *lakum*, Fi. *qumuqumu*.] A. **ḥ'umḥ'um'**, a crab.

Rāles, a place in Hades, lit. dark pit, swamp, or depressed place: **ra**, and **les**.

Rāna, dem. and num., those two: **ra**, 2, and **na**, dem.

Rāna, and redup. **rarāna**, v. i., or a., to branch out: **rā**, and a. ending **na**.

Rān, rāni na. See **rāġ, raġi na**.

Ran, d., s., water. [Fi. *drano*,

Sa. *lanu*, My. *danu*, J. *ranu*, Carolina *ralo*, Mg. *ranu.*] A. rahalu, water (of a kind).

Rarua, d. **raru**, s., a canoe, boat, or ship: v. Note. [My. *prahu*, Ml. *ndrav*, Segaar *rai*, Ta. *laou* (*laau*), An. *elgau*, Er. *lo.*] A. **markab.** See **borau**, supra.

NOTE.—The Ef. **raru** corresponds to the *rahu* in My. *prahu*, both the *r* and the *h* of the final syllables *ru*, *hu* being for the original *k*, and **raru**, through *ratu*, Ta. d. *tata*, for *raku*, My. (*p*)*rahu*, Motu *laka*(-*toi*), Mg. *lakana*, An. *elgau* (for *elegau*), Ta. d. *laou* (*laau*), Er. *lo*: in the two latter the original *k* is dropped as in My. (*p*)*rau*, Segaar *rai*, Er. d. *lai*. In all of these the final radical b (or v) is elided, Ef. **raru** is for **raraw** (for **raraf**). In Meli, and Fila, Fut. *vaka* (Santo *aka*), the *v*, like the My. *p* (in *prahu*) is for the original servile m (in **markab**), and the first radical r as well as the final (as in **raru**, &c.) elided. The m was pronounced v, then w, then only the vowel was retained, *elgau*, *aka*, then the vowel was dropped, *laou*, *lo*, *tata*, **raru**, Mg. d. *laka*.

Rās, d. **nras**, dem. and num., these two: **ra**, 2, and **s**, dem.

Ras i, v. t., d. **tas i**, to shave (the beard or chin), shave (or strip) off (as fruit from a tree, shave or strip the tree). E. **laṣ′aya**, to shave.

Ras, or **res**, d. **tas**, redup. **reres**, or **teres**, v. i., to rustle, crash (as the foliage of plants, or waves of the sea, moved by the wind, or men in a tumult). H. **ra‘as′**, the primary notion lies in noise and crashing: used of the rustling of grain moved by the wind, **ra‘as′**, noise, tumult.

Rasoso, v. i., see **rafloso**; **rasoso**, to vociferate, calling (for help): **ra**, and **soso**.

Rat i, v. t., d. **tat i**, d. **nrat**, to loose, untie. See **mirati.** [Sa. *tala*, *tatala*, Tah., Ma. *tara.*] H. **nat′ar**, Hi. **hitīr**, to loose.

Rau’, and **ndau’**, v. i., d., to go. Ct. **rawāh**, to go.

Rau, redup. **rarau**, v., to grope for with the hand, seize, snatch out or away. [Ma. *harau*, grope for with the hand, Ha. *lalau*, extend out as the hand, Ma. *rau*, catch, lay hold of, gather, Ha. *lau*, seize, take out of a place, To. *lau*, nip, pinch, An. *rap*, grope for, and *raprap*, My. *raba*, to feel for, grope.] A. **lamaa**, to feel for, grope, take away.

Rau, s., leaves (for food to be cooked, and for putting food on, as on a plate, when cooked). [Mg. *ravina*, My. *dawun*, Sa., Ma. *lau*, *rau*, Fi. *drau*]; and

Rau, s., as, **rau nasuma**, *eaves*

of a house, **rau mita,** lashes of the eyes, eyelashes ; a tribe, group, **bi rau,** in parties, **rau,** a fruit that grows in *clusters* ; and

Rau, in **bakarau,** to divide, distribute ; and

Raua, rauraua, a., hairy, as a rope, **nakasu rauraua,** a tree full of branches. [Mg. *ravi-ravi,* hanging over, suspended] ; and

Rau, in **bārau,** i. e. **bā,** to go, and **rau,** speak violently and reproachfully, to 'carp'. [Sa. *lau,* speak, abuse indecently.] A. **hadiba, hadaba,** to pluck, to have long eyelashes, to have long branches, **hadab',** branches, leaves, see **rifu, birife.**

Rēa, s., d. for **rēko, bisa ki rea ki nau,** speak as a pauper to me: **reko.**

Reaki, v. t., to strain, and, s., a vessel for straining, a strainer, colander. [Lakon *reak,* id.] A. **rāḳa,** 2, **raw-waḳa,** to strain, and **rāwaḳ'** (and **rawuḳ'**), a vessel for straining, a strainer, colander.

Rei a,. roi a, rei, rerei, or **terei,** d. **roroi,** to moisten the pudding (**nakoau**) with **lor** (the rich oily juice of grated cocoanut). A. **rā'a,** 2, to moisten bread with fat, **rā''a,** 2, id., 1, to bend, turn, 3, wrestle, 5, roll itself (an animal), 6, wrestle.

Rei, s., c. art. **nerei,** a band of men ; a clump of trees. A. **rā'a,** to grow, luxuriate, 2, be congregated, **rī'at',** a band, a crowd.

Rei, d. **rea,** d. **reko,** q.v.

Rei, d. **tei,** v., **rei natano,** burrow, or cover itself with earth, as the white ant (**futei, furei**) does. A. **damma,** (2), to cover its hole with earth, **dimmat',** ant.

Rēko (see **rei, rea, farea**), s., a pauper, poor. H. **rēḳ,** empty, vain, impoverished, poor.

Reluko (or **raluko**). See **taluko.**

Rere, rerea, v. i., to break rushing upon the sand or shore (of waves), also **tarere.** Ch. **rĕ'a',** to break in pieces, H. **ra'a',** id. S. **etra're',** id.

Res, reres, teres. See **ras.**

Ri, d., verb. pron., 3 pl., dd. **ru, eu, u.**

Rī. See **tī.**

Rĭ, or **rĕ,** dem., **eri,** &c.: **arai.**

Ria, d., verb. pron., 3 dual, d. **rā.**

Ribu, riribu, to sound (with a trumpet), **ribu-aki baiġo,** sound a trumpet, **taribu,** to sound trumpets alternately (of two men). See **rubua.**

Rifālu, d. **lifāru,** q.v.

Rifu, d. **rife,** d. **lifu mita,** d. **rau mita,** s., eyelashes, and see **birife** or **birifu,** to snatch, pluck away, plunder. [My. *rambiya, rambu, rambut,* Mg. *rumbu, rumbuṭa, rumbiṭa, rumbaka,* My. *rampas, rabat.*] See **rau.**

Riġi, ririġi, or **tiriġi,** v. i., to make a tremulous groaning noise in suffering pain, biriġi-riġi. A. ranna, vociferate, utter the voice with weeping, make a noise, twang, tinkle.

Riki, a., small, kari-riki, uarik, batik;

Riki, s., c. art. neriki, child, little one. [Ha. *lii*, Tah. *rii*, Ma. *riki*.] E. dawik, to be small.

Riki, old, see under the word fiteriki.

Riki, s., ṭiki, nriki (d.), pud. mul. A. rika', id.

Rikit, v. i., to be small: riki.

Rikitelaġ, d. for koroatelaġi: koro, atelaġi.

Riri, in buariri (Hades), for tiro, to sink.

Riri, v. i., to fly, d. for tiri.

Riri, s., a spark: tiri.

Riri-mita, s., tears; turu, tu-turu. [To. *tulu he mata*.]

Risu, v. i., to move, shift: rosa.

Riu sa, d. tuma i, to point out. See tiu.

Riu sa, riuriu sa, also tiu, or tū sa, q.v.

Ro, d., v. i., to fall, c. prep. ro bei a, fall upon it: roa.

Ro, ad., again, d. mero;

Roa i, v. t., to turn. See mero, ro, meraroa; and

Roa-leo, and roaroa-leo, s., echo; roa, rowa, d. doa, dowa (see also maroa, mare, biroaroa, taroaroa). H. s'ub, Arm. tub (A. t'aba), to turn, S. t'ub, again: for the Ef. expression for 'again', see Ch. V. 9.

Roa, or roua (rowa), or ṭoua, v. i., to fall, dd. ro, röuo, töuo, tiḅe (ndiḅe), täo, mi-täo, mitefe, lubu. [An. *erop*, My. *rubuh*, *mârubuh*, *râbah*, *mârâbah*, *ribah*, *mâ-ribah*.] H. rafah, S. rĕfo', etrafi, to cast down, to sink, or fall down.

Roḅa, s., affluence; and

Roḅa-leba, s., great affluence, a rich man. A. raf'', afflu-ence.

Roba-ġi. See toba-ġi.

Roba, roroba, or toroba, d. nrob, v. i., or a., to be insane, senseless. A. rāba, (2), to be insane, stupefied.

Ro-bei, d. oro-bei, v. t., to snarl, snap, bark at: ro, for oro, and t. prep., bei.

Rōfa, s., a red or purple dye or colour. A. ṣohbat, a red or reddish colour.

Rofarofa, or tofarofa, and tofe, v. mid., to cover oneself with cloth, clothe oneself, be clothed, tofe, cloth, cloth-ing. H. 'aṭaf, to cover, be covered, be clothed. S. 'ṭaf, id.

Rofe, s., d. for rafēna.

Roġo, roġ i, v. t., d. toġi (doġi), d. nroġ, also ṭoġ i, to hear, obey, to feel, know (as grief or pleasure), roġo na-ḅon, to perceive or feel or smell the odour (of anything), roroġo, or toroġo, v. i., to be still, s., a species of divina-tion (in order to know what is to be done) by a certain movement in the muscles of the arms or legs, roġoroġo ki, to make heard, report, roġoan, roġoroġoan, s., c. art., report, tāki roġo-saki, bend or incline oneself hearing (a person); bakaroġo, q.v.; maroġo, or maṭoġo, or manroġ, v. i., to be idle, amuse oneself, maroġo ki, to amuse oneself at the expense of (someone). [Sa. *loĝo*, My. *dâĝâr*, Mg. *reni*, and *rea*.] A. 'aḍina, to hear, to know, to feel the smell of, 2, cause to hear, make known, proclaim, H. 'azan, Hi. he'zin, to hear, listen, to obey.

Rogo, ṭoġo, in **sera-ṭoġo**, s., anything: **roġo** is A. **hano**, a thing. [Santo *sonu*, TaSa. *kinao*, Ml. *nanu*, a thing, Florida *hanu*, Oba *heno*, Ja. *ano*, Mg. *anu*.] A. **hanu**, a thing.

Roko, v. i., d. **lako**, q.v., d. **nrok**, to stoop.

Romi, **roromi**, v. t., to compassionate, to love. See **rumi**.

Rō na, **roro na**, s., thought, mind, also **ṭoṭo na**, and d. **nro n**; v. **mitoa**; and

Roro, or **ṭoṭo**, v., to think, **rara**, &c. (**tan i**), d. **totu**.

Ror, s., oil, also same as **lor**, q.v., the oily or fatty expressed juice of grated cocoanut used to moisten or fatten puddings: **ro i**, **roro i**, **rei**.

Roro na. See **ro na**.

Roro i. See **ro i**, **rei**.

Roroa, v. i. See **toroa**.

Roro-fi. See **toro-fi**.

Rosa-ġi, v. t., to drag, haul, make to move, shift; and

Rosa, v. i., to move, shift, **ṭosa**, dd. **nros**, **nrus**, **tosa**, also **rusa**, **risu**; and

Ros, s., c. art., a breaker or wave that sweeps up upon the sand of the shore. [Sa. *toso*, *tosotoso*, to drag.] A. **ra'aṣa**, to move, shake, drag, 4, id.

Rot i, or **ṭot i**, v. i., to embrace clasping to the breast, to embrace or encircle, bind round. Hence

Rot, s., anything going round another as a band or girdle (as an ulcer round one's leg, &c.); and

Rot i, as, **ta rot i**, **ta rotirot i**, or **rutirut i**, cut a band or girdle round (as in barking a tree). A. **rabaṭa**, **rabṭ'**, to bind.

Röuo (**rowo**), i. q. **rau'**, to go.

Ru, verb. pron., 3 pl., they: d. **ri**.

Rū sa. See **riu sa**, **tū sa**, **tiu sa**.

Rua, num., two. See also **tua**, **ra** (and **sa**, in **uasa**), d. **nru**. [Sa. *lua*, My. *dua*, Ja. *roro*, Mg. *rua*.] H. **s'ne**, &c., Mahri **tharo**, Soc. **tarawah**, M.S. **tirā**, Assy. **sina**.

Rub, s., d. **roba**, d. **nub**, d. **raba**, s., q. v.

Ruḅa, s., additional wife taken by a man already married. [TaSa. *narau*, a wife, Mg. *rafi*, one of two or more wives of the same husband; adversary, opponent; *rafiṭa*, joining together, contention, strife.] A. rafā', to join, sew together, make peace, 2, to utter a formula of blessing or prayer to a new spouse, rafa', 2, id. ('Mayest thou live with concord and with children').

Ruḅaki, s., a big flat nakoau. A. ra"if', round thin cake baked on the hearth.

Rubua, d. **rufua**, s., clamour; noise, tumult (as of mourners in wailing). S. **rhab**, make a noise, uproar, tumult, utter lamentations (Mark v. 38, 39), cg. H. **ra'am**, v., to make a noise, thunder, s., uproar, clamour, tumult.

Ruku, s., a hole, cf. **rā**; edible clay found in holes, syn. **tano rā**; a bribe secretly given, or given *underhand* to procure the death of one hated, **nafa-karuku**, hollow or hole under anything, as a cellar under a house, **sī ruku**, to go under (through the hole or hollow under) anything; and

Rukua, d., s., a hole, pit, a hole or hollow with water in it, cf. **rā**. A. **raka'**, to dig (the ground); to revile (someone). **rakiyyat**, a pit, **rika'**, pud. mul.

Ruma na, s., c. art. **nàruma na**; **n**, art., and **ruma**, or **aruma**, and **kuruma** (in **lita-kuruma**, q. v., the breast, bosom.) [Sa., Ha. *uma*, Motu *geme*, id.] A. **ḥa'zūm'**, the breast, bosom.

Ruma, dd. **bara**, **oro**, v. i., or a., to be barren. H. **'arab**, E. (tr.) **'abara**.

Rūma, and **tūma**, s., a pool of water, d. transposed **marou**. A. **'arīm'**, a hole, trench, or hollow in which water is collected.

Rumi, **rurumi**, v. t., same as **romi**, to compassionate, love. A. **raḥuma**, **ruḥm'**, id.;

Rumian, s., c. art., and **rurumian**, compassion, love.

Rūmo, d. **rūma**, pool.

Rūrū, redup. of **rū**, **riu sa**. See **tiu**, **tū sa**.

Ruru, v. i., to tremble;

Ruru, s., c. art., an earthquake. [Tah. *ruru*, to tremble.] S. **r'el**, to tremble.

Ruru, s., a cluster. [Tah. *ruru*, to congregate.] See **rei**.

Rusa, see **rosa**; **rusa-ġi**, see **rosa-ġi**;

Rusarusa-ġi, redup., d. **nrus**, **nrusa-ġi**.

Rutirut i. See **rot i**.

Sā, interrogative pron., contr. of **safa**, **sefa**.

Să, or **se**, or **s**, dem., this, here. H. **zeh**, E. **zĕ**.

Sa, d. for **ta**, neg. ad., only in prohibitive clauses.

Sa, **sĭ**, s. num., one, in **ġis** (or **ġisa**), **sam**, **mas**.

Sa, **s'**, verbal suf., 3 sing., d. **a**, as, **ti ki nià sa**, say to him it, d. **ti ki nià a**, id.

Sa, s., d. **ta**, d. **sëàt**, q.v.

Sa, caus. pref. See **sarafi**, **saġaluġalu**, **siġiri**. [My. *sa*, Tah. *ta*.] H. **s'a**, Arm. **sa** (Shaphel, Saphel).

Sā, v. i., or a., to be bad, evil,

sāsā, intensive. [Fut. *sa*, My. *jahat*, Fi. *t'a*, Malo *sat*, Ta. *ra*, Mg. *raṣi*.] A. **sā'**, to be bad, evil, **sawat**. Hence

Sān, s., c. art., the being evil; also the being ill, sickness, misfortune, misery; and

Sāsānă, v. i., or a., to be ill, have a disease: redup.

Sābĕ, inter. ad., where? **sa**, and **be**, q.v.

Sabe-li, v. t., to bind, tie, d. **tami-si**. [My. *simpul*, v., and s., knot.] H. **ṣamam**, cg. A. **zamma**, &c., to bind.

Sabe-li, v. t., to beat, slap. [My. *tampar*, Ja. *tampel*, Fi. *saba-laka*.] A. **ṣafa'a**, to beat, slap.

Saberi ki, v. t., to scatter, break asunder or to pieces, scattering, d. **sabura ki**.

Saberik, v. i., to be broken to pieces, fallen or parted asunder. [My. *sibarkan*, *sābar*.] See **tasabsabu**. H. **s'abar**, Ch. **tebar**, A. **tabara**, break in pieces.

Saḅo, v. i., or a., ignorant, to be ignorant, **sasaḅo**, to be ignorant, to not know (his way), **sabo-naki**, v. t., to be ignorant of or about, dd. **subnĕki**, **sbu-nĭ**; see also **tasabo**; **nàsàḅo** (for **naṭa saḅo**), a stranger (not knowing the place), **meta-saḅo**, id. A. **safoha**, to be ignorant, 6, id.

Săfa, **sefa**, or **sofa**, v. i., to pant, redup. **sofasofa**, to hasten, to run;

Sōfa, s., consumption, hard breathing. [Mg. *sefusefu*, *sevusevu*, *sevuka*, in haste, bustling, to hasten.] H. **s'a'af**, to breathe hard, pant; to hasten.

Safa, **sefa**, **sefe**, inter. pron., what? c. art. **insefa**, **nasafa**, what? Without the art. it is used adjectively as **sefe nakasu**, what tree or wood? With the art. it is used substantively, as, **i tili nasafa**, what does he say? See Ch. V. 4. *c.*, *cc.*

Safaki, pr. n. **Ma safaki**, name given to a man who had buried a relative; a sea animal, so called from burying itself in the sand: **afa ki**.

Safana, c. art. **nasafana**, what that, what (is) there? **safa**, and **na**, dem.: contr. **sāna**. [My. *apa*, Epi *ava-kai*, Malo *sava*, *savana*.]

Saf i, or **safi**, v. t., to pluck or gather fruit; to scrape, **safisafi natano** (with a hoe), **safisafi-raki**, scrape, pluck off the husk from (reeds), **safi nauot**, to excel the chief; **safisafi**, big, so **bisab**; **bisif**, excelling; **misafe**, to be separated (as fruit from a tree). See also **sifa**, **sifĭ**. [Fi. *sivi-a*, *uasivi*, excel.] H. **'asaf**, gather (as fruits), assemble, draw back, take, take away (as breath); radical meaning, to scrape, **yasaf**, to add, to increase, to surpass, excel.

Saġa, or **seġa**, s., a crotch, fork (as made by two branches). [Fi. **saga**]; and see *nasaġu*;

Saġa-fi, v. t., to take hold of

with a crotch or forked stick. [Fi. *saġa-va*, take hold of with tongs.] See **seġa**. A. **s'aḳḳa**, 2, 5, to be sundered, split (wood), **s'iḳḳat**, half of a thing, part, distance.

Sāġ, ad., d., there. [My. *sana.*] **Sa**, and **ġ**, dem.

Saġaluġalu, d. syn. **ġaluġalua**: **sa-**, c. prefix.

Saġarà sa, v. t., to rub, grate, ground on, as a canoe or ship on a reef. [Ha. *ili.*] **Gar i**, and **sa-**.

Saġo, s., a trumpet (conch). H. **t'aḳa'**, E. **ṭaḳwa**, to blow a trumpet.

Sai, v. i., to come forth, go forth into the open (as men), **saisai**, to assemble, **sai**, to shoot forth (of a plant), **buka sai** (of a blossom expanding into a flower), **sesai**, shoot forth (as a serpent), **misai**, to be opened, cracked;

Sai ki, v. t., make to go forth or out (as the tongue, hand, anything);

Sai a, v. t., to cleave, split, open it (as a secret, &c.), **tili sai a**, tell it out, &c.;

Saisai, v. i., assemble (come forth of many); also to be associated together, or have in common, **ru saisai isa**; **saisai ki**, make to assemble; **so** or **soă** [Sa. *soa*, Ma. *hoa*], a follower, companion, associate; **sī**, to blow (with the breath), to shoot (with a gun), **sī**, to blow (the wind); d. **sui**, or **sī**, to rest, or spell (one), to help; **esei**, in the open, an open space; **bisai ki**, to put forth, to show;

Sai, s., c. art. **nesai**, a scented, white-leaved plant. A. **s'ā'a** (y), to become open, be divulged; c. prep. **bi**, to make open, divulge; to leave undivided; to follow, 2, to roast; to blow (with the breath), 3, follow each other; to aid, 4, make open, **s'ai'**, associate, follower, **s'aya'**, common (to many, see **saisai**), **s'āi'**, common (to many), not distributed; made open, open; **s'ī'at**, a band, assembly, **s'ayu'**, a firestick.

Saka-fē, s., first ripe fruits or yams. See **taka-fe**, d.

Sakau, s., a reef; d. a branch. See **kasau**. [Fi. *t'akau*, Sa. *aau.*]

Sakĭ, v. i., to ascend, go up, **bisaki**, v. c., to put up, to appoint (raise up) a chief; **sakesake**, to be up, to sit upon, **tasaki**, id., **sakei ki**, to shout a person's name, attributing something (to him). [Sa. *a'i*, Ha. *ae*, My. *daki*, To. *hake*, Ma. *eke*, *whakaeke.*] H. **nasaḳ**, Arm. **nsaḳ**, imp., **saḳ**, id.

Sala, s. See **sela**.

Sali, v. i., to move lightly, easily, to dance, to float, drift; **sali-aki**, v. t., to send afloat (a canoe, or anything), to send adrift, **misal**, **misalsal**, d. **salsal**, light (not heavy), moving easily, lightly. H. **'azal**, to go quickly (spin along), A. **'azala**.

Sali a, v. t., to weave. [My. *sâriġ*.] H. 'azal, S. 'zal, A. ''azala, to spin, weave.

Sali, v. t., to deceive; and redup.,

Salisali, to deceive. H. s'alah, Hi. to deceive.

Salube, d. **saluke**, v. i., to be ignorant, not to know. A. sarafa, (3), to be ignorant, not to know.

Sam, a., or ad., one alone, only: **sa**, 1, and **m** for **mau**.

Sama i, v. t., to rasp, scranch (sugar-cane, in sucking its juice). [Ml. U. *tsumwi*, Ml. P. *jimuc*, Malo *samai*]; hence

Sama na, s., chips, dregs, shreds (as of sugar-cane with the juice extracted), sawdust, &c.; hence

Samā, v. i., or a., dreggy, shreddy: **-a** ending. A. safana, to rub, or shave off the skin, or bark, adze, chip, safin, safinat, H. sefinah, a ship. See **seme**, or **sama**, infra; and see **sema**, **sesema**.

Samben, d., ad., there: **sān** (sāġ), and **bēn**, v. i.

Samit i, also **samat i**, d. **sumat i**, v. t., to beat, chastise. [Fi. *samu-ta*, My. *chamiti*, *chamati*, a whip or scourge.] H. s'amaṣ, to thrust, *to hasten* (see infra, **sumati**), s'amat, to smite, strike, A. s'amaṣa, to impel, thrust, s'amiṣa, to hasten, speak hastily, s'amaṭ, Nm., to whip.

Samura, s., a thing or word of no consequence, that falls to pieces, as it were, for **sabura**: **saberi-ki**.

Sān, ad., there, here, **esān**, also **esanien**. [My. *sana*.] **Esanien** is **esan**, there or here, and **i en**, it is. See **anī**, v. i.

Sante, s., d. **sëàte na**, q.v.

Sào-fi, v. t., to look upon, see, d. **sā-fi**, **sao kiana**, look about (in) his place or plantation. H. s'a'ah, and s'a'ah, to look, to look about.

Sar i, or **sari**, v. t., to saw, also **seri**, to cut with a sawing motion, **sāra**, a saw. [Malo *sarosaro*, to saw, *isaro*, a saw, Fut. *seria*, to saw.] H. nas'-ar, Arm. nsar, to saw, A. nas'ara, was'ara', as'ara, E. was'ar, wasar, H. sur, to saw, rub, sweep, &c. Hence

Sara ġote-fi, to saw asunder.

Sarafi, used as ad.; **bat sarafi a**, did it hastily, i. e. badly, confusedly, incompletely. See **marafi**, and cf. **tere-ti**, **sumati**. **Sarafi** is Safal form.

Saria, v. i., to look around; **saria kiana**, look about, or go about, (in) his plantation. [Fi. *sarasara*, v. i., to survey, *sara-va*, v. t.] H. s'ur, (2), to look around or about, (1), to go about.

Saru, v. i., to hang down prostrated (as the broken branch of a tree, or a broken arm), **misaru**, id. A. ṣara'a, to prostrate, sarī', prostrated.

Saru, v. i., to be loud, noisy, speak aloud, **saru ġoro**, speak aloud or be noisy, drowning the voice (of someone); and

Saruru, v. i., to roar, resound (as the sea, or a waterfall). [My. *dâru*, Ja. *sâru*, *sru*.] A. **ṣarra, ṣarīr'**, to make a noise; to sound, to cry out vehemently, make a great clamour.

Sās, esās, ad., here: **sa**, dem.

Sasāna. See **sa**.

Sati na, s., the shrivelled and worthless seed yam when the new yam has sucked all the substance out of it: **sa**.

Sau-fi, v. t., to scoop, or shave, the surface off water; to cut or shave off the surface of wood, **sau-baba**, an adze, lit. plank shaver or cutter—see **mataisau**, a master cutter, carpenter; to strip off, peel off (as clothes), **sau lua i**. [Mg. *sauka*, *saufina*, to scoop out (water), to draw water, Ef. **sau noai**.] H. **s'a'ab**, to draw water. The primary idea lies in *taking off the surface*, cg. **saḥaf**, to sweep, scrape off, **ḥasaf**, to strip off, A. **saḥafa**, to scrape, peel, or rub off, to shave.

Sau, v. i., to blow (wind);

Sau, s., c. art. **insau**, gentle breeze, cold air, as in the morning and evening. H. **nas'af**, to blow, **nes'ef**, the evening twilight, when a colder gale blows; the morning twilight.

Sau, s., dew. [Ma., Tah., Ha. *hau*, Sa. *sau*, Mg. *andu*, dew.] A. **nada'**, for **nadau**, dew.

Sau, v., to desire, **mesau na**, v. t., desire, **insau**, a gift, **sautoġa**, id., a free gift, hence, as ad., 'for nothing'; **sau uia** [Fi. *sau vinaka*], liberal in giving, **sau sa** [Fi. *sau t'a*], stingy; **sau mitaki**, d., syn. **sau uia**; **sau sera**, greedy (desiring everything). A. **s'aha'**, to desire, 2, to say 'I will give what you desire', 3, to be like (someone), 4, to give to one what he desires, 5, 8, to desire (a thing).

Sāua i, v. t., to fix (as upon a shelf, in a fork of a tree, &c.). See **soa ki** (for **saua ki**);

Sāuā ia, v. t., to shoot with an arrow called **saua**;

Sāua (**sawa**), s., a pronged arrow (which adheres tenaciously). A. **nas'aba**, to stick, inhere, be fixed tenaciously, 2, make a thing be so, 4, id., **nos's'ābat**, an arrow, Nm. **nas'ab**, 2, to shoot, squirt, *fie*, into.

Sau ki, v. t., as, **i tumana sau ki nia**, he admires himself, **sau roa i**, to mock such a one by pretending to join with him in such admiring, to mock. A. **s'aa** (mid. و), to admire.

Sauro-aki, v. t., to place (their voices) with accuracy together, as giving a shout altogether: for **saruru-aki**, see **saruru**, supra.

Sau-taki, v. t., to place upon, as food upon food already in the oven, or as a speech upon a speech by another previously spoken, lit. to make like to: sau, A. 3.

Sautoġa, s. See preceding word.

Se, who? some, any; it takes the nominal suf., as **seġamu**, who of you? **seġara**, and **seara**, who of them? or some, any of them, one or more of them. **Se** (Ch. V. 4. *d.*), and nom. suf. **Segamu** (se-ġamu), interrogatively, is, Who (or which) of you? indefinitely, some, or any of you;

Sei, d. **fei**, inter. pron., sing., who? pl. **se mai**, d. **se mani**, d. **kihe** (for **kise**) **māġa**. [Sa. *'o ai*, Tah. *o vai*, Ma. *a wai* (pl. *a wai ma*), To. *ko hai*, *a hai*, Epi *sie*, Malo *isei*, Mg. *iza.*] See Ch. V. 4. *a.*, and *aa.*

Sĕ, or **s**, dem., this, here. See **sa**. **Sĕ** is the common form.

Sō, inter. ad., where? See **sā**, **safa**.

Sē. See **so i**.

Sea, **sesea**, or **seasea** (redup.), v., to forget, be forgetful, **sesea ġor i**, forget him. See **maġaseasea**. A. **saha**, to forget, be forgetful.

Seara, d., some, a few. See under **seġara**.

Sëàtĕ, s., a firestick (by which the fire can be rekindled), dd. **santĕ**, **tā**, **sa**. See **sai**.

Sefa, **sefe**, or **sĭfĭ**. See **safa**, what? This inter. is sometimes used indefinitely in the sense of whatever, however, as, **a belake namanuka sifi naġa**, I have received, or I carry, a wound however now (or here), **fatu sefa**, a stone however, or whatsoever. A. **ma**, qualiscunque.

Seġa, s., or **saġa**, q.v., a crotch, fork.

Sēka, v. i., to sit; **sēka ki**, to sit about, or on (someone, or thing, consult about it or him); **biseka**, v. r., to sit with someone, or with each other. H. **s'akan** (A. **sakana**, H. **sakan**), **s'aken**, to set oneself down, to lie down, to rest, to abide, dwell.

Sĕkē, **skē**, v. t., to raise up, set upright: **saki**.

Sĕke-mau, v. i., to swear, **sĕke**, and **mau**, true: a man who swore, as in denying a charge, often tore off his loin cloth, and imprecated all kinds of calamities upon himself if he were not speaking the truth. A. **saḥaga**, to peel, scratch, comb the hair, **saḥug'**, frequently and rapidly swearing.

Sekof i, v. t., to catch rapidly with the hand (a thing thrown). A. **zaḳafa**, to take rapidly, snatch, 8, to take with the hand, snatch quickly.

Sela-ti, v. t., to bear, carry; d. **sola-ti**; **selasela** (of many); **sela**, bear (a child), **bisela**, v. r., to bear, bring forth, **nafiselan**, child-bearing, childbirth, d. **bisol**. [Fi. *t'ola-ta.*] E. **ṣawar**, to bear, carry.

Sela ġisa na, v. t., to call his name (so and so); **selà ki**, v. t., attribute to (one, something); **sela**, go, as, **sela tera ki**, go after (one), **sela butuaki**, go between two points, be of two minds;

Sela, s., road, path; landing-place of canoe; a portion of time (cf. **mal**, place, time). [My. *salekan*, to call, *saleh*, proceed, *saleh*, a road.] A. **s'ala'**, to proceed, 4, to call.

Sel i, v. t., to bind. [Fi. *soli-a*.] H. **'asar**, to bind, S. **'sar**.

Sel sa, to be unable, **selu ḅia**, be able, **sele atai naḅo na**, be able to know his mind, d. for **sili atai naḅo na**, lit. to know (how) to enter his mind, i. e. to understand his secret views: **sili**, q.v.

Seloa, s., a flat wooden dish. [Mg. *suliaka*, flat, as a dish.] H. **ṣelaḥa**, pans, such as were flat and broad, not deep, A. **zuluḥ'**, large pans, E. **ṣaḥl**, platter.

Sema, **sesema**, v. i., to be bare, sticking out (as one's bones), or as the point of an auger or piercing instrument: **sama i**.

Semasema, v. i., to rejoice. H. **samaḥ**, to rejoice.

Semam, s., paternal aunt, **ana semam**, his aunt: **susu**, **mam**.

Sema-ni, v. t., to praise, glorify. S. **s'abaḥ**, Pa., to praise, glorify;

Semanian, s., c. art., praise, glory, also act of praising.

Semani, s., the rudder, or steering oar of a canoe, d. **uose-mān**. [Paama *seman*, TaSa. *lamani*.] **Se**, in **semani**, is contr. for **uose**, q.v., oar, and **mani** is **manu**, a bird, a figure of which (a bird) was carved on the stern of the canoe where the steering oar is held firmly in steering: hence the rudder was called **uose-man**, the oar of the bird.

Semasemana, or **samasamana**, v. i., or a., disgusting: **-na**, a. ending. A. **s'aḥama**, to be corrupt (as food).

Seme, or **sama**, s., the outrigger of a canoe, or, more accurately, the part of the outrigger, shaped exactly like a canoe, which floats in the water. [An. *jmaiġ*, i. e. *jimaiġ*, Ta. *timen*, TaSa. *ṣama*, Fi. *t'ama*, *t'ama kau*, a canoe whose outrigger is only a stick (*kau*), in distinction from a double canoe; To. *hama*, the smaller canoe of a double canoe, My. *sampan*, a small boat, Mg. *sambu*, a ship.] A. **safīnat**, **safīn'**, H., S. **sefīna**, ship, vessel.

Note.—The Tongan *hama* suggests that the *seme*, or *sama*, was originally not a mere log fashioned into the shape of a canoe, but a real canoe, and that the outrigger canoe of Oceania is a degenerate form of the 'double canoe'.

Sera i, v. t., to bind, fasten on, as the handle of a basket on a hook, **serā ki**, id., **sera**-

ġorobau, a hat, lit. fasten upon the head. H. s'arar, to twist, be firm; S. s'rar, to be firm, s'arar, to make firm, stable, Aph. 'as'ar, to firmly believe. Hence

Sera loamau, seralesoko, believe true;

Sera lobalo, sera teamole, believe worthless, despise;

Sera tea sa, sera tea uia, believe bad, believe good;

Sera masīka, make firm desire;

Sera soġ, make firm **soġ,** q.v.;

Sera ġor i, make firm upon, or covering.

Sera, v. i., to run, flow (water, stream). A. **sāla,** id.

Sera i, v. t., to sweep (as a house), **tea sesera,** a sweeper, broom [Mg. *suruka*, sweep];

Sera ġuru-maki, v. t., sweep, gathering together; and

Sera kuruk, v. mid., id.; and

Sera taua ki, v. t., sweep into heaps; and

Sera lo tua, v. t., sweep things giving (them) to (someone), used of men telling an evil doer of his misconduct and its consequences. Hence

Seralotu, v. mid., to repent; and

Sera tua, v. t., to sweep (together things) giving (them) to (someone), as a peace offering; and

Sera biri ki, syn. **ġura biri ki,** to startle; and

Sera makoto ki, id. A. **safara, safr',** to sweep (as a house).

Sera ġisa na, d. for **sela ġisa na;**

Sera usi, v. t., to call (pronounce) after (one, as in learning to read): **sela,** and **usi.**

Sera i, v. t., to rend asunder, as the two branches of a forked stick; **misera,** rent asunder. A. **ṣāra,** (3), wrench asunder.

Sera, or **sere i,** or **serei,** v. t., to importune, entreat. A. **nazara,** to ask importunately, to entreat pressingly.

Sera lua, v. t., to remove (clothing, &c., from one; also ceremonial uncleanness, **sera lua namam**), make to go out, or away. A. **sāra,** 2, remove, make to go; **sār',** and **sāir',** the whole, every, part, some, any. Hence

Sera, any, some; **sera-roġo, sera nalo,** something, anything; every, **sera natamole,** every man; the whole, all (with nom. suf.) **sera ra, serasera ra,** the whole, all, of them, every of them, **sera bakauti era,** every of them all; every (kind), **sau-sera,** greedy, **bā sera,** going every (where), a vagabond; also, d., **i nuf sera,** it is finished all [Fi. *sara*, ad.]; **bisera, biserasera,** of every kind (**i bisera,** i.e. **i bi sera,** it is (in) every (kind, or sort).

Serab, v. i., to flow out (as of a vessel, run over). A. **sariba**, to flow (of water), **sarab'**, flowing out.

Sera mimi, d., syn. **sera bakauti**; and

Serume (sera 'me): **sera**, and **me**, or **mimi**, contr. of **mau**, **mamau**.

Sere, as, **nakasu i tuba sere nakalu**, the stick thrust tearing the cloth, **masere**, torn, rent. A. **nasara**, to tear, to rend.

Sere ra, v. t., dwell among, near them, **bisere**, to be among, near, **bakasere**, and **masere**, q.v. A. **'aṣara**, 3, to be near, 6, to be near to each other, **'iṣr'**, love, &c.

Sereserea, or **seriseria**, v. i., or a., to be hairy, hirsute; a. ending **a**. A. **s'a'ira**, to be hairy.

Seri, v., to be unable to do a thing (from old age and infirmity); **seri nalo**, forsake, leave, abandon a thing, **bakaseri**, to loose (a prohibition, or **tabu**). [Fi. *sere-ka*, untie, unloose.] H. **s'arah**, Ch. **sera**, to loose, Pi. **s'ereh**, to loose, to desert, leave.

Seri, v. t., to speak of, decide, consult about; make a sign, show. A. **s'āra**, 2, 3, &c., make a sign, show, consult.

Seri, v. t., to strain; **sāri is**, strain with it, **nakalu sāri**, straining cloth. S. **ṣlal** (**ṣal**), to strain.

Seri, v. t., to hollow out (as a canoe). H. **sur**, to hollow out.

Seri, v., as, **seri taku-ra**, to cover their back, **seri namaseri**, or **namiseri**, put on the **miseri**, q.v.

Seri, **seri ġoto**, to cut;

Seritau, s., the cutter-up of a human body for the oven, **Seritau**, or **Saritau**, or **Sāra**, pr. n. of a demon who is lord over the entrance to Hades, and whose helpers are **Maseasi**, **Faus**, and **Māki**. A. **ṣara**, (5), to cut; and **tau**, q.v., to cook.

Seru e, v. t., rub, wash (clothes, &c.), **seseru**, rub (as oil on the head). Same as **sesere**, **sesera**. So also,

Sēru, s., a comb. [Fi. *seru*, Sa. *selu*, My. *sisir*, syn. *garu*.]

Sès, d., to be small: **sos**.

Sesere, d., rub, grate. Same as **sesera**, **sera**, to sweep.

Si, v. See **su**, **sua**, finished off.

Si, d. **soi**, v. t., scrape, cut (**si nabora na**, scrape the cheeks with a shell removing the skin); **sisi**, redup. A. **saḥa'**, n. a. **sahy'**, scrape off, with the notion of cutting. Nm. also to harrow (the ground).

Sī, **sīsī**, to blow (wind, breath); **sī**, v. t., to blow (a thing, as the fire), to shoot (with a gun); **sī-ruku**: **sai**, q.v.

Sī, d. **sui**, to help: **sai**, q.v.

Siba i, d. **suba i**, v. t., to break (as a yam), redup. **sisiba**, and **sibasiba i**; **masiba**, **masibasiba**, to be broken, **na**

masiba, a fragment. [Fi. *sove, kasove*, Mg. *sumba, simba.*] Ch. **s'ibeb**, to break in pieces, **s'iba**, a fragment.

Sibu na, s., feathers (short) on a bird's back. A. **ziffu**, small feathers (of a bird).

Sieġ, v. i., to hang on the waist cloth (of a woman); and

Sieġ, s., c. art. **nasieġ**, a woman's waist cloth. A. **was's'aḥa**, v., id., **wus'aḥ'**, s., id.

Siel, a., red. [My. *serah.*] A. **s'ahila**, to be of a dark reddish (&c.) colour.

Sifa, v. i., to depart, withdraw, **namaron i sif**, his breath departs, i.e. he dies; **sifa ki**, v. t., make to depart, toss, throw away, **sifesife**, redup.; **sifa**, v. i., to assemble. See **safi**.

Sīfanua, s., a cannon, lit. shoot the land: **sī fanua**.

Sifili, and **sifili ki**, d., transposed for **sili-fi, sili-fiki**, q.v.

Sifiri, s., parrot. A. **ṣafara**, to sibilate.

Siġi, v., redup. **siġsiġ**, v., to be hostile, disobedient; **siġsiġleo** (**leo**, thing, or voice), to be disobedient, to sin, **siġsiġleo ki**, to be disobedient to (one), **nasiġsiġleoan**, disobedience, sin, **bisiġ**, q.v., v. r., to stink, to be disobedient, opposed to someone or to each other. A. **zahuma**, **zahm'**, **zahuma**, to stink, to be alienated from, hostile to, someone, and therefore disobedient.

Siġsiġi, v. t., to kindle. H. **nasaḳ**, **hisīḳ**, Ch. **asiḳ**, id.

Siġir i, v. t., or c., to strengthen: **ġara**, and caus. pref. **si**. [Cf. syn. My. *maġkras kan*, My. *mampaheri.*]

Sikara, v. i., or a., prickly, spiny, and of hair standing on end: ending **-ra**. A. **s'āka**, 2, to be spiny, hirsute, **s'ākat'**, spiny.

Sikai, or **sikei**, num., one, d. **sikitika** (redup.): **tesa** (in **la-tesa**, q.v., d. **la-teha**), also in **masiki**, d. **mihi**, also in **ġisa, mas, sam**; and

Siki, with nom. suf. (translated in this case as nominative, as in H. and A.), as **sikīna** (his one), he alone, **sikīra** (their one), they alone, &c. In **i sikīna uia** (and similar expressions) the meaning is, he alone is good, i.e. he is incomparably good; and

Sikiskei, one (by) one; **sikiski ġisa**, one by one together, and see **bakasikei**. H. **'aḥad**, Mod. S. **ḥda**, &c.

NOTE.—[Mg. *isa, irai*, also *isaka, iraika*, My. *asa, sa*, Sa. *tasi.*] See Ch. II, on this and the other numerals.

Sik ē, v. t., d. **siko e**, to avenge: **soka-ri**.

Sik ē, or **sek e**, to raise: **saki**; hence

Sike-rau, d. **sī-rau ki**, or **sīĕ-rau ki**, to raise or lift up a leaf (**rau**), presenting cooked food to one to be eaten.

Sīke, to be swearing, and

Sike-mau (see **sĕke-mau**), to swear true; and

Sike, v. t., to comb (the hair): **sĕke-mau.**

Sike-ti, v. t., redup. **sikesike**, to grasp with tongs, or with a forked stick; hence

Esike, s., tongs, syn. **uataki**, H. **ḥazaḳ**, to hold fast, stick fast (A. **ḥazaḳa**), Hi. to take hold of, seize.

Siki-naki, v. t., to abhor, loathe, abominate, d. **masuku-taki**, or **musuku-taki.** A. **zahaḳ**, Nm., to take disgust for, loathe.

Sikitau, s., only child: **sikai, sikei, totau.**

Siko e, v. t., to avenge, d. **sik ē**: **soka-ri.**

Siko sa, v. t., to gaze at: **siko mau isa**, to gaze continually (see **mau**) at, redup. **siko-siko**: hence

Sīko, s., kingfisher, lit. gazer (because it sits *gazing* into the water for fish). H. **sakah**, Ch. **seka'**, to look at, to contemplate.

Siko-ti, or **siku-ti**, v. t., to adhere to (someone), continue or dwell with. A. **'as'iḳa**, to adhere to (someone).

Sila i, v. t., as **ta sila i**, chop, peeling or shaving off, chop or cut a thin shaving off; hence

Masilă na, s., a shaving, chip; and **masila, masilasila**, to be thin. [Mg. *silaka*, and *silaṭa*, to peel, bark, skin, chip off.] A. **saḥala**, to peel, bark, shave, or scale off, **masḥul'**, small.

Sila, v., to crack, as thunder, **boro silai, buru masila**, id., **silasila**, redup., **ta silasila**, id. [Sa. *faitilitili*, Ma. *whatiri*, Ha. *hekili.*] A. **ṣalla, ṣalṣala**, to sound, to crack (thunder), **muṣalṣil'**, braying (an ass).

Sila i, v. t., to help, aid, support, strengthen, **tasila** (dd. **tasiġa, ahika**) helper, supporter, **sīl**, wall plate (*supporter* of roof), **tua-sīl**, givers of support (to a chief, as giving food or other aid when he is making a feast, &c.). A. **'azara**, 2, to aid, help, strengthen, support, make firm, H. **'azar**, to help, aid. Hence

Sīl, s., wall plate (supporter) of a house, help (**tua sīl**, give aid or help).

Sila i, or **sela i**, d. **sol i, sila-sila i**, v. t., to rub, as to rub (oneself with oil, &c.) [Fi. *sola-ta*, rub, Sa. *soloi*, wipe, Ma. *horoi*, wash, Ha. *holoi*, wash, wipe, brush.] A. **"asala, "usul'**, to wash.

Sili, v. t., to enter, **sili isa**, enter it (a house), enter him, that is enter under his protection; **sili-fi a**, enter into him (as a spirit or demon into a man); **sili-faki**, or **sili-fiki**, make to enter into, also thrust or throw into (anything into anything). [Sa. *sulu*, thrust into, take refuge, *sulu-fa'i*, and *sulu-ma'i*, My. *julok*, thrust into, Mg. *juluka*, enter, Fi. *t'uru, t'urut'uru, t'u-ru-ma, t'uru-maka*, enter, push, or thrust into.] A. **daḥala**, n.

a. **duḥ′ul’**, to enter (a house); take refuge with, 2, make to enter, 4, make to enter, thrust, &c., in. This word is used much to denote among other things the *entering into* a man of a spirit or demon. See **alialia.**

Sili ki, or **sila ki,** v. t., make to shake (anything; if water, to sprinkle), **silisili ki,** id., to pour out, shake out, throw away, throw down, **ru sili ki fisera,** they flee in different directions (those overcome in battle), lit. they throw (themselves, shake out, or scatter themselves) in different (or every, or all) directions. H. **zalal,** to shake, make tremble, pour out, shake out, A. **zalzala,** to shake, make to tremble.

Simbolo, s., d., a basket. A. **zibbil’, zimbil’,** id.

Simi-ki-leo, or **sima-leo,** d. **suma-ki-leo,** s., echo, lit. sound of the voice. A. **zāmat,** vehement sound, and **leo.**

Sina, or **sinĕ,** v. i., to shine, be clear, **us i sine,** the rain clears up, Fi. ut′a sa siga. [Fi. *siga*, sun, day, My. *siyag*, day, clear.] A. **ṣaḥa’**, E. **saḥawa,** H. **ṣaḥaḥ,** to shine, be clear; sun, day, in derivatives. See Ch. II. 17 *g*.

Sīnu, sisīnu, v. i., to be hot, burn (of the grass on the hills, yearly), to be inflamed (of one's face) **nako na i sīnu,** his face is inflamed (with passion); hence

Sīnu, s., c. art., the burning of the grass on the hills; a place on which the grass has been burned: see also **tunu, bitunu,** d. **biṣīn.** [Sa. *sunu.*] A. **saḥ′ana,** n. a. **ṣuḥ′un’**, to be hot, **saḥ′una,** and **sah′ina,** to be hot, 2, to heat, **suḥ′n’**, and **ṣuḥ′n’**, hot, H. **s′aḥan,** S. **s′ḥen,** to be hot, inflamed (sore), heat oneself at the fire.

Siora, s., a pipe for drawing off water from one place and pouring it out at another; said to be for **sie rau** (for **sike rau,** lit. lift up, distribute).

Sīrak, a., used as s., for **sītaki,** i. e., **sī tāki,** blow, heeling over (a canoe), a squall or high wind: **sī,** to blow, and **tāki,** to incline over.

Si-rau, or **sīerau,** contr. of **sikerau.**

Siri ki, v. t., to scatter, sprinkle, of seeds, water, **siri kīa ki,** i. e., **siri ki uia ki,** scatter or sow well (seeds); and

Sirisir i a, v. t., to scatter (or sprinkle) on him (as water or blood spurting on one);

Siri, v. i., to sprout, shoot (of a plant); and

Siria, d., v. i. (**-a,** ending), to sprout, shoot; and

Siri na, s., c. art., a shoot, sprout; and used of men, offspring; hence in proper names of children and men, **siri,** (seed, offspring) as, **siri fakal,** &c. H. **zara‘**, scatter, disperse, especially to scatter seed, sow, bear seed (of a plant), **zere'**, seed, offspring, A. **zara'a**, scatter seed, to produce plants.

Sisi, si, redup.; hence

Sīs, s., a shell used for scraping.

Sīsī, v. i., redup. of **sī**, to blow; hence

Sīsī, s., a gun; **sī fanua**, a cannon.

Sito, v. i., cacavit, A. **s'aḥaṭa**, (8), cacavit.

Sïu, s., a pricker, or awl (a sharpened bone). [To. *hui*, needle or pin (of bone).] A. **s'i'a'**, a prick, spike. See **sui**.

Siua (**siwa**), v. i., to hunt for fish, or shellfish (on the reef), **siuē** (**siua i**) v. t., hunt (fish, or shellfish, on the reef). A. **sāfa** to examine or explore the ground by the smell, hence to hunt.

Siua, or **sua**, d. **siuo** (**siwo**), (**suwa**), v. i., to descend. [Sa. *ifo*, To. *hifo*, An. *asuol* (*asuwol*.)] A. **safala, suful', sifl'**, to be low, to descend.

Siuer (**siwer**). dd. **suara, suuara, surata**, v. i., to walk, proceed, go away, **sisiuer**, redup., walk about. [Sa. *savali, savalivali, savaliġa*.] A. **safara**, 3, n. a. **sifār'**, &c., to make a journey, go away. See Ch. III. *h*, and pp. 70–1.

Soa, s., c. art. **asoa na**, companion, follower, or **neso** (art. **ne**), especially of the opposite sex, hence, **tauso**, q. v.: **sai**. [Fi. *sa*.]

So e, d. **sē** (for **so i**), v. t., to call (one);

Soso, v. t., redup., to call, **sos i** (for **soso i**) call (him): also in **bioso, rasoso, rafloso**. E. **ṣaw'a** to call, H. **s'ua'**, Pi.

Soa ki, soüa ki. See **sāua ki**.

Soà-ni, or **soè-ni**, v. t., to mock. A. **haza'**, to mock.

Soàr i, or **souar i**, v. t., to abrade, scrape, scratch, as **raġo i souari rarua**, the roller scrapes, scratches, or tears by scraping, or abrades (the bottom of) the canoe, **souasouar i**, redup., and **soàra**, or **souara**, v. i., to split open (as a ripe seed, pod, or banana), i. e., to be abraded, or uncover or abrade itself. S. **safar** to shave, to abrade, H. **safar** (to scratch, polish), to write, A. **safara**, to sweep, uncover the face (a woman), to shine (the dawn), H. **s'afar** (scratch, polish), be bright, beautiful, Ch. **s'ĕfarpara**, S. **s'afra**, the dawn.

Soata, v. i., to slip. A. **dahaṣ'a**, to slip. E. **dĕhaṣ'a**.

Sobē na, s., c. art., the nape, or back of the neck. E. **zaban**, id., A. **zabbunat**, neck.

Sobu, v. i., d. syn., **bēa**, to precede, be first. A. **sabaḳa, sabḳu**, to precede, be first.

Sofa, sofasofa, v. i., **sōfa**, s. See **sefa**.

Soġa, s., c. art., d. **nasok**, dust, rubbish, a lot of things (belonging to one);

Soġasoġa, id.; hence

Soġa-leba, s., a rich man, lit. big lot of things; and, d.,

Soġoa, v. i., or a. (ending, a), rich;

Sok, d. **soġa,** s. ;
Soksok, d. **soġasoġa,** s. ;
Sok-leb, d., **soġa-leba** ; also
Sok, s., d., c. art., a cloud. H. s'aḥaḳ, dust, a cloud, A. saḥ'ḳ' ; the verb signifies to rub, hence dust (from being rubbed small).

Note.—**Soġoa,** lit. signifies full of dust, dusty, dust being taken in the sense which is given it in the vulgar English phrase 'to come down with the dust'.

Soġ i, or **soġi,** v. t., d. **suġ i.**

Soġo-ni, v. t., to press upon, compress (one, as by crowding upon him), to straiten, **soġosoġo-ni,** redup. ;

Sōġ, or **sōġī,** s., what straitens, compulsion, force. constraint, &c., as, **i meri soġī au,** makes or uses constraint or force upon me (to compel me to do something), **i tili sōġ soko i,** he declares force or compulsion upon him (to make him pay a fine, or to suffer death, as the case may be). [My. *sâsak,* straitened, *sâsakkan,* to straiten.] H. ṣuḳ, Hi. (A. ṣ'aḳa, 2), to straiten, compress, press, urge upon, force, compel, H. ṣōḳ, distress.

Soi, d., v. t. See **sī,** to scrape. [Fi. *so-ya, soi.*] Hence

Soi, or **soia,** s., the hole scraped out for the yam to be planted in.

Sōk, s., c. art., what stops or blocks, as a dam : **suk i,** q.v.

Soka, v. i., to leap, jump, go swiftly ; to be violently excited, inflamed with anger (of the belly) ; **soka i,** v. t., to spear ; inivit mulierem ; **soka-ba,** v. i., to go swiftly away, hence, s., what goes swiftly away, a worthless or lost thing or person ; **soka-ba ki,** v. t., throw away, make to be **soka-ba** ; **soka ki,** v. t., make to **soka,** throw. A. zaḥ'ḥ'a, (4), leap, (2), inivit mulierem, (5), go with vehemence, (6), to be angry, burn with rage.

Soka-ri, v. t., to join on to (one thing on to another), then to repay (one thing by another, the one thing being regarded as joining on to, or touching, the other), to avenge (one slain, by slaying another, also **sīkē,** d. **sīko**) ; **soka-soka-ri,** redup. ;

Sokarian, s., c. art., a joining, as a splice ; repayment, retribution, vengeance ;

Soka-taki, v. t., to join on to, to meet, **tumara soka-taki ra,** meet together. H. nas'aḳ (A. nasaḳa), to join, 2), kiss (join mouth to mouth), join on to each other, meet (of two things), Hi. to join on to (one thing on to another).

Soko, v. i., or a., to be true, true, as **naleona i sokō sa** his voice (prediction) is true as to or about it (thing predicted, as is known when it takes place as foretold), **le-** or **losoko,** a true thing, truth, **tili lesoko,** to speak truth, d.

syn. **tili mori**, speak true, d. **tili loamau**, speak truth. See also **masoko**. [Sa. *sa'o*, straight, correct, right, My. *suğ'uh*, true.] A. **ṣadaḳa**, n. a. **ṣadḳ'**, to be true, H. **ṣadaḳ**, to be straight, right, just.

Soli, v. t., rub. See **sila i**, id.

Sōlĭ, sosolĭ, v. i., to creep (i. e., to rub or scrape along the ground, cf. **karafi**);

Asolat, s., a worm: **a**, art. [Sa. *tololo*, ps. *tolofia*, Fut. *toro*, Ha. *kolo*, TaSa. *tari*, Malo *nsalansala*, to creep, *sulati*, a worm.] H. **zahal**, to creep, crawl.

Sore, v. i., to lie, be untruthful, d. **bisuru**;

Soresore, id. H. **zur**, to turn aside, A. **zāra**, tell lies.

Sor i, or **sori**, v. t., to give (a thing). [Fi. *soli-a*, give, My. *sârah*, and *srah*, to submit, *sârah kan*, to give.] A. **ṣ'ara'a**, 1, to submit, 4, to give.

Soro, v. i., to burn, flame, **soro-fi**, v. t., send a flame on to, also to treat with violence, to rush violently and with savage rage upon (as a wild pig charging a man), **baka-sorosoro-fi**, v. c., make the fire to burn up. [Mg. *doro*, Sa. *tolo*, *matoro*.] A. **sa'ara**, to kindle (a fire, war), 2, to rage (of a camel), 3, to treat with cruelty and rage, **so'r'**, blaze of fire, rage, insanity, **sa'ir'** flame of fire, fire bursting into flame.

Soroà sa, v. t., to covet, desire;

Sōro, a. used as s., a covetous person, and see **miseroa**. A. **s'ariha**, to covet.

Soroa, d., v. i., to be sick, syn. **sasāna**. A. **s'arro**, fever, and **a** ending, from **s'arra**, to be bad, as **sasāna**, from **sa**.

Soroa, s., c. art., d. **tiroa**.

Sore, v. t., to saw (one, of the breakers sawing one on the reef); and

Soro-aki, v. t., to make a man's body saw on the reef (of the waves or breakers): **sar i**.

Soo, v. i., to be small (syn. **mito**), d. **sēs**, small, little. E. **heṣoṣ**, id.

Su, sua, v. i., to rise up (**tobu i tubu sua**, swells up) as ground in which the growing yams are swelling (cf. **lua**); another form of this word is **tu**, to stand up;

Su raka-ti, v. t. (to take up, lift up), to startle;

Sua i, v. t., to take up, lift up. then to take, receive, obtain, acquire, as, **i su naleo**, he obtained something; and to bear, as, **i su nafolofolon sa anena**, he bore his sin, i. e., he received its punishment; and to meet, as, **i sua nata**, he met a person, **bisua**, v. r.; **su-naki**, to carry on the head (of women), **su-ni**, to put on (clothes), hence **susu**, clothed (having clothes upon or carried or borne by one); to meet or take up the (odour of a thing) **su roği naḅon**.

The notion of *meeting* is in that of lifting oneself or rising up against (one); and a swelling in the skin is said to sua, i. e., raise itself up, it rises up; **su** (**nasuma**), s., the upper part (ridge-pole) of a house, and **masua**, s., the highest part or top of anything. **Su** or **sua** is also used in proper names of children, as **Sua raġoa**, &c. H. **nasa'**, to take up, lift up, E. **nasa'**, take, receive, A. **nas'a'**, be exalted, grow, to bear, carry, to bear one's sin, that is, to receive its punishment. H. **si'**, **sĕ'et'**, height, a raising or lifting up, a *rising up* in the skin, A. **nas'a'**, to grow up, to be raised, high, 4, to produce, 10, perceive or feel the odour (of a thing), **nasā'**, sprout or shoot (of a plant)—**sua** (in pr. names), young people.

Su, sua, d. **si,** v., finished off, as, **i nu su,** it is ended or completed, finished off, **i bati su ē a,** he has finished off doing it; **i bano su,** he has gone, he has finished off going, completed going. The word thus forms with any other verb a completed tense denoting that what is expressed by the first verb is *finished off*. A. **sawa,** 2, 8, to finish, be finished.

Su na, s., c. art., highest part (as ridge of a house, or top of the head), cf. **masua na,** top (of anything): **su,** or **sua.**

Sū na, s., c. art. **nasū na,** q.v., juice.

Sua, for **suua** (**suwa**), **siua, siuo.**

Sua, s., brother. See **tai.**

Suasua, v. i., to be willing; and

Sua ki, v. t., to impel, order, send. See **bisuaki,** A. **s'ayiya,** 1, to be willing, to will, 2, to impel.

Suara, or **suuara** (**suwara**), **susuara,** d. **siuer,** q.v.

Suāra, v. t., to meet (as a head wind, any obstruction in one's way): **sua,** and **ara,** v. t.

Suer, v. i., d. **suerai.**

Suerai, v. i., to put out **rai,** i. e. **tai,** q.v., dung, cacavit: **sui,** see **sai,** v. t., and **tai.**

Suër i, v. t., to vituperate, d. **sur.** S. **ṣe'ar,** to vituperate.

Suba i. See **siba i.**

Suḅe, v. t., to place, determine, appoint, constitute, syn. **tōnaki,** as, **i suḅe biri a,** he appoints it over again (and differently), syn. **tōnaki biri a,** as to appoint a day of meeting, &c., and afterwards to alter the day, appointing another; **i suḅe roa au,** he appoints me, changing, changes or alters (**roa,** to turn round, to alter) the appointment he made with me, as having first appointed me a certain day, he afterwards changes the appointment to another day; hence

Suḅe, s., what is placed, fixed, redup. **susuḅe,** as upright stones firmly planted in the ground, **nafera susuḅe,** a row of such stones, **suḅe,** such a stone, a statue, an idol or sacred stone; a thing fixed firmly, as a plank firmly nailed, a stone firmly fixed, a wind continuing firmly in one quarter, **nalaġi i bi suḅe** the wind is firmly fixed (in some quarter); also, custom, as a thing fixed, **suḅe nafanua,** custom of the country, **suḅe na,** its or his custom, also the fixed nature, custom, or disposition, **suḅe niġ Atua i lēġ,** the nature, custom, or disposition, or fixed character of God is righteous: **suḅe i tōnaki nafanua,** the fixer, or constitutor, or establisher—fixed, established, or constituted the country. In this last sense it is a general term used to denote either the first or early or ancient inhabitants of a place (the original settlers of a district), or, which is the same thing in another form, the persons who figure in Efatese myths, or the spirits of such, now being **natemate**; or the deity who constituted the world. In the same active sense *suḅe* in Epi denotes chief, or headman, dd. *tumbo, sumba,* Malo *suḅe,* id. H. **niṣṣab,** officer, director. In the Shepherd Islands it is now used for **Atua,** q. v. [Ma. *tupu,* firmly fixed, Sa. *tupua,* a stone supposed to have been a man petrified, an image, Fi. *tovo,* habit, nature, practice.] H. **naṣab,** i. q. **yaṣab,** to set, put, place, Hi. **hiṣṣib,** to make to stand, place, erect, set up (as a column), fix, establish (as bounds), Ho. to be fixed, planted, **yaṣṣib,** firm; A. **naṣaba,** to place, fix, set up, declare, appoint, constitute; **naṣb',** a thing set up, a statue, what is worshipped besides God, i.e. an idol; **naṣīb,** erecting, setting up; **naṣibat,** stones placed or fixed round a waterhole.

Sub-neki. See **sabo-naki.**

Subu. See **sobu,** v. i., and d., s., child, offspring.

Su-bua, v. t., to lift up, or ascend, bursting or breaking through (the ground, hence **subua (natano),** a demon or demons who do so), syn. **suḅora i,** and **sua-sai: su** or **sua,** to rise, or lift up, and **bua.**

Suġ i, v. t., to kiss, d. **sum i.**

Suġ i, v. t., to block up, d. **suk i,** q. v.

Sui, v. t., d. **sī,** q.v., to help; to blow upon; also (see **sai**), to make holes in (as a moth in cloth); also to burn with heat, as **elo i sui a,** the sun burns him; and redup., **elo i tera suisui,** the sun shines burning (hot); and

Sui, s., heat; **sui ni elo,** heat of the sun. See **sai.**

Suk i, v. t., d. **suġ i**, to block up, obstruct. **A. s'akka,** (2), (3), block up, obstruct;

Suk i, v. **t.**, to cause to stoop, **suki lifa ia** (a burden) makes him stoop, bending him; to still, as **suki namaritana,** still the commotion (of passion) within him, **suki namaieto,** stills the anger; and

Suki, v. i., to be patient, firm, quiet, still, sink (subside). H. **s'akak,** to stoop (A. s'akka), subside, be appeased, Hi. to still;

Suki, v. t., make fast, firm, **seli suki a, bisa, tili** (&c.) **suki a,** tie firm, speak making it firm and sure, **meri suki-suki,** make firm, **turi suki,** nail firm. A. **s'akka,** (3), adhere, cohere firmly;

Suki, v. t., to stick, stab. A. **s'akka,** (7), transfix (with a spear).

Suka, v. i., to draw back, recede, **sukasuk,** redup.; hence

Sukei, or **sukai,** s., c. art., the receding (of food), the annual time of scarcity of food, opp. to **namasu.** [Fi. *suka,* cf. *t'uqa.*] H. **nasag, sug,** to draw back, retreat.

Suku-ti. See **siko-ti.**

Suku-ti. See **sike-ti.**

Sula, v. i., to rise up (as a rising ground);

Sūla, s., a rising ground. H. **salal,** to lift up, cast up a bank.

Suli na, s., shoot (as of a banana), offspring (of man); hence

Sulia, v. i., to have shoots (as a banana). [Sa. *suli,* a young banana, son of a chief.] H. **neṣer,** a sprout, shoot; offspring.

Su-lua i, v. t., to bring up (a child): **su,** or **sua,** and **lua.**

Sulu ē, v. t., to scorch with flame, illuminate with a torch (**ne sulu**), and see **masula ki**; hence

Sulu, s., c. art. **nasulu,** a torch. [Sa. *sulu,* v. and s., Ja. *suluh.*] A. **s'a'ala,** 1, 2, 4, to kindle (a fire), 8, be kindled, 10, light or kindle (a torch), **s'u'ulu,** flame of fire, **mas''al',** a torch.

Suma, s., c. art. **nasuma,** house, d. **uma,** d. **hiṁa,** see also **katema, imrum:** [My. *rumah,* Ja. *umah,* Ml. *im,* TaSa. *ima,* Motu *ruma.*] A. **ḥ'a'mat, ḥ'im'** &c., house.

Sumat i, v. t., to beat, d. **samit i**; d. **sumanr i,** to beat, also used as an ad., hastily, confusedly, ineffectively, as, **lo sumanr i, briġ sumanr i,** &c., see, do hastily, confusedly, ineffectively (cf. **sarafi, tere-ti**). See **samit i.**

Sum i, v. t., to kiss, dd. **suġ i, soġ i.** [An. *aijumnyi,* to kiss, Sa. *soġi,* rub noses, salute, *soġisoġi,* to smell, My. *chyum,* to smell, to kiss.] A. **s'amma,** to smell. There is no trace of this meaning in **sum i.** In E. **sa'ama** is to kiss.

Sum i, v. t., to suck, as fat. [My. *isap,* An. *at'moi,* to kiss, lick, suck, as fat.] A. **saḥab,** Nm., suck in (liquid or air).

Sume-li, v. t., to make a sucking noise to (to attract one's attention). See preceding word.

Sumi-li, v. t., d. **sumo-li,** to shut, close (as a door), to patch up, repair (as a hole in a mat); hence

Sumili, s., a thing like india-rubber in a clam shell which, when touched, causes the shell to close; an ornament (shell) which stops up a hole pierced in the septum of the nose. A. **samma,** (4), to stop (as a bottle), (6), to patch up, repair (a thing).

Sur, v. i., to go (of a departed spirit going to Hades); siuer. See Ch. III. *h*.

Sur i, v. t., d. **suer i,** q.v.

Sura i, v. t., to root up, extirpate (as the things growing in one's plantation). E. **sarawa,** to root up, extirpate.

Surata, sursurata, v. i., d. for **suara,** to walk, go on a journey. See Ch. III. *h*.

Suru ki, v. t., make to **suru,** i.e. to be covered, as by inserting an arrow head into the (reed) shaft; and

Suru-faki, v. t., make to be covered, as by thrusting a thing into the dust or earth; and

Suru ġoi, v. t., to cover, drain out (as the milk of a cocoanut) by covering the aperture of the nut with the mouth and draining out the contents. For **ġoi** see **ġo i. Tasuru ki,** to conceal, **suruoli,** dd. **suruili, suru-auli** (see **uli, auli**), to take the place, or assume the form of, hiddenly or stealthily, and, s., a demon, or demons, who do this to destroy men. [My. *suruk,* to conceal, Mg. *saruna,* to cover.] E. **sawara,** to cover, **tasawara,** to be hidden, secret, to hide.

Su-rua, s., upper of the two ridge-poles of a house: su na, and **rua,** two.

Suru ē, v. t., to allure, tempt (deceiving), lit. to deceive;

Surusuru ē, id., redup. See **sore, bisuru.**

Suruk, i.e. **su-ruk,** also **si-ruk,** and **sai-ruk** (see **sai,** and **ruku**), to go into the **ruku** (of anything).

Surut i, v. t., to scarify, make fissures on the surface of anything. A. **s'arata,** to scarify.

Susu, s., the breast or breasts; a calabash (round like a breast): **susu na,** d. his mother, lit. his breast, or mamma; hence

Susu, v., to suck the breast, **bakasusu,** to suckle. [Sa. *susu,* the breast, to suck the breast, Fi. *sut'u,* the breasts, to suck the breast, My. *susu,* Mg. *nunu,* the breasts.] H.

s'od, A. t'idy', pl. t'udiyy', breast, breasts.

Ta, passive or reflexive passive prefix to many verbs. [Fi., Sa., My., Ja., Mg., id.] A., E., **ta**, reflexive or reflexive passive prefix to verbs.

Ta, and **ṭa**, nom. and verb. suf., 3 pl. (very common), for **ra**.

Ta, s., for **ata**, man, person.

Ta, neg. ad., not, dd. **ti**, **tu**, and see **sa**. [Sa. *le*, My. *ta*, Mg. *ṣi*.] H. **lo**, **le**, **li**, Ch. **la**, A. **la**.

Ta i, v. t., to chop, cut, also to speak or utter (as it were making a chopping noise), redup. **tata**. [Fi. *ta-ya*, My. *tatah*, Sa. *ta*, Mg. *tatana*.] A. **haḍḍa**, to cut quickly; utter speech quickly.

T', conj., that (because), **ta**, that I, **te**, that he, **tĕ ku**, that you: **tĕ**.

Ta, ad., now, dd. syn. **uo**, **ko**, **i**, as, **i ta toko**, **i uo toko**, **i ko toko**, he yet (now) remains: **ta**, dem.

Ta, verb. pron., 1 dual incl. [An. *intau*, Sa. *ta*, *taua*.] The **ta** of **niġita**, or **ninita**, and **-a**. See Ch. V. 2.

Ṭā, or **rā**, d. **nrā**, q.v., blood. Originally **tā**, as in **mitā**, to bleed.

Ta, s., d. **sa**, d. **sëàtĕ**, q.v.

Tā na, s., friend, companion. [Cf. Fi. *tau*, *to*, Ma. *ta*.] A. **ṣāḥi**, contraction of **ṣaḥib'**, friend, companion, **ya ṣaḥi**, (cf. Ma. **e ta**!) O friend, comrade! **ṣaḥaba**, to be a friend or companion, to take with one as a companion, 3, to accompany (someone), 8, to be companions to each other. Hence **bitā**, and **bitā-naki**, q.v.

Ta-atuta, v. and s.: **ta**, cut, speak, utter, and **atuta**, s., a fixed or appointed time; **ta-atuta ki**, appoint a time and place (of meeting) to (someone). H. **'adad**, A. **'adda**, to number, especially days, time, hence S. **'ad'da**, same as H. **mo'ad**, a set time, appointed time, cg. H. **ya'ad**, A. **wa'ada**, 3, to appoint a time and place (of meeting).

Ta-bau, s., syn. **taġoto-bau**, a cap, or hat, lit. cut-head.

Ta, v., to bend, bow, incline, extend, as, **ta bau**, bend the head, bow, **ta tuba**, strike. turning aside, deflecting (a spear, &c.), **ta ġor i**, extend over it (of time, so many days), **ta ġor i**, extend over (or cover) it (the day in the past named). H. **naṭah**, fut. **yiṭṭeh**, to extend, to incline, to bow, to turn.

Tab, d. **tiba**, dd. **tama**, **tam**, neg. ad., not: **ta**, not, and **ba**, for **ma**, as in Assy. **aama**, not, i.e. H. **mah**, A. **ma**, used indefinitely.

Taḅa na, d. **tauba na**, s., side, or shore (as a side). [Ma. *tapa*.] A. **ṭaff'**, side, shore.

Taba i, d. **tama i**, q.v.

Taba, v. t., to be like, **tabale**, to be like that thing (**taba le**), so, also **tabalai**, **tabalān**, **tabalas**, **tabalo uai** (**taba lo**, or **l'** (thing), and **uai**, **n**, **s**, **i**, dem.) to be like that or this thing, **tabalo uanaġa**, id.; also **tabale sā**? **tabale safa**? to be like what thing? to be how? [My. *damakiyan* so, Mg. *mituvi*.] H. **damah**, to be like.

Tāba, s., property given away in payment of a fine for misconduct: **tā**, to cut, and **ba** (away) as in **soka-ba**.

Taḅa, v. i., to turn, bend, **taḅa lo sua**, or **lo saki**, bend looking down, or up, **taḅa kai**, bend contracting the stomach (as to avoid a spear), **bitelo taḅaḅa**, to be bent with hunger, also **tama**, as **tamà-lu**, d. **tumalu**, to bend rising (in setting forth or out), **taḅa soka**, to bend, leaping (as in climbing a tree), d. **tama**, or **tuma soka**, also, to leap aside. A. **dafa'**, 6, to turn hither and thither, **dafa'**, bending, **'adfa'**, bent, curved (of men).

Tabaraba, for **rabaraba**.

Tabaġ, v. t., to slap. [My. *tapuk*, Ja. *tabuk*.] E. **ṭafaḥa**, to clap with the hand, Ch. **tepaḥ**, the palm of the hand, My. **tapak**, id.

Tabalaġa, v. r. (see **balaġa-ti**), to raise itself off, as a scab, &c. Reflexive causative.

Tabalās', or **tabalāsoa**, v. i., **tabale**, and **aso**, to burn, to peel itself off after a burn (of the skin): **tabal'**, is the reflexive of **bale-si**, or **bala-si**; and

Tabales, v. i., reflexive of **bale-si**, to peel itself off, as the skin of one's lips; and

Tabales, s., husk (as of cocoanut, chestnut), finger nails.

Tabara, v. i., to be burned.

Tabara ki, v. t., to burn: **bara**.

Tabare, **tabarebare**, v. i., reflexive of **ḅora i**, to be split, split open, to be open.

Taḅàre, s., a male animal. Compare E. **tabā't**, mas, a male.

Taḅaro, **taḅaroḅaro**, v. i., to be heedless, careless, disobedient: reflexive of **ḅaro**; and

Taḅaro, d., s., senselessness, sin.

Taḅasuli, v. i., to be detached, broken off: reflexive of **basuli**.

Taḅau sa, v. t., to cover, to be over (surpass, be above another): **taḅau-ġoro**, lid, cover: **bau**.

Tāḅelu, v. i., reflexive of **ḅelu**, q.v.

Tab e, v. t., to take. [Fi. *tabe-a*, Mg. *taba*.] S. **nsab**, to take.

Tabe, s., c. art. **natabe**, a freshet; see **tafe**.

Tabe, v., to lean or incline, **tabe to osa**, lean abiding on it, **tabe ki**, lean upon, trust in (a thing);

Tabĭtab, s., a thing leaned upon, or trusted in. [Fi. *ravi*, My. *arapi*.] A. **ṣ'āfa**, 4, to make to lean or incline (a thing towards a thing), 1, be the guest of someone.

Tabei, v. t., to desire or purpose setting the mind on. A. **bayya**, 5, id.

Tabēra ki, v. t., to make to be **tabera**, scattered, **taberafera**, or **taferafera**, to be scattered, **taberafera ki**, make to be so: **bera, berafera**.

Taḅēs, s., axe: **ta**, to cut, and **ḅēs**.

Taḅetĭ, v. i., to adorn oneself. S. **ṣabet**, to adorn, Ethpa. adorn oneself.

Tabilakiġon, d. **tabilaġon**, v. i., to stumble, d. **tabila kon**, id. lit. to strike, or knock (the foot) by mistake (hastily) fast (that is, the foot caught fast): **ta, bila**, or **bile, ġon**, or **kon**.

Tabisa, v. i., to speak;

Tafisafisa, v. i., to pray: **bisa**.

Tāḅora i, v. t., to cut, splitting (a thing);

Tāḅorai na, s., c. art., the body where it forks off or is divided into the two legs: **ta, ḅora i**.

Taḅos, v. i., compressed, narrow: **ḅosa**.

Taḅotai, v. t., to divide; **ta**, cut, and **ḅota**.

Tābu, s., naked people, people of other islands of the New Hebrides, so called by the Efatese: **ta**, men, and **bua** I.

Tabu, tab, v. i., or a., to be forbidden, prohibited; to be sacred;

Tabua, s., c. art., sacredness; and

Tabuan, s., id. A. **dabba**, n. a. **dabbu**, to prohibit.

Tabua, v. i., to be split open, cracked, also **mafua**: **ta**, and **bua**.

Tāfa, s., c. art. **natāfa**, a hill, lit. that which goes up or is high; and

Tāfa (d.), ad., high, above. [Fi. *t'abe*.] T. **dayaba**, to go up. E. **diba**, above.

Tafagka, tafakăka. See **baku**.

Tāfakarua ki, i. e., **tā**, utter, and **bakarua**; to repeat a thing, as a slanderer's words to the person slandered.

Tafar. See **taiār**.

Tafasi, v. See **fasu**, eyebrows.

Tafe, v. i., to flow out, go out. [Sa. *tafe*, Fi. *dave*, id.];

Tafe, s., c. art., d. **tabe**, freshet. [Sa. *tafiġa*, id.] H. **zub**, Arm. **dub**, to flow out.

Tafea, d. for **tofe**, q.v.

Tafera, s., c. art., breaker, breakers; and

Taferafera, v. i., to break, as waves. See **bera**.

Tafi, v. t., to be near. A. **ṭaffa**, to be near.

Tafi na, s., and c. art. **a, atafi**, follower, successor of a chief (next in rank), that is, his present helper and right hand man, and who is his recognized successor. A. **tabi'**, follower, helper.

Tafifi, v. i., to be involved, entwisted: **fifi, fisi**.

Tafilo, tafolo, taifolo, and **Tafulus.** See **bulo ki, bulusi.**

Tafiloġa. See **bulo ki,** and **boloġa.**

Tafirofiro, to be twisted (crooked): **biri.**

Taġa, s., basket, d. **toġa,** q.v.; d. stomach. [Sa. *taġa, taġa 'ai.*]

Taġāl, s., a hook for hanging things on: **taġeli.**

Taġaraġara, v. i., or a., strong: **ġara, ġaraġara.**

Taġaru, v. t., to grasp: **kar i.**

Taġataġ, s., a mist, or mass of clouds: **taġotaġo.**

Taġau, s., a hook, so called from seizing;

Taġau, taġauġau, v., to grasp, seize;

Taġau lua, select, lit. grasp or seize, lifting up or out: **ġau, kau.**

Taġelĭ, taġelĭġelĭ. See **takel.**

Taġi, v. i., to wail, cry, ring, sing, clank, hum, &c. (as a drum, &c.); **taġi-si,** v. t., to bewail, **taġitaġi,** redup., **nataġian,** wailing, sounding (in various ways). [Sa. *taġi,* My. *taġis,* Mg. *tani,* a cry, *tumani, mitumani,* to cry.] A. **ṭanna,** to tinkle, &c., Nm. to clank, ring, hum, **tanien,** din, **tantun,** to tinkle, jingle.

Tàġia, v., d. **tine (ndine),** to hoist the sail on a canoe, **taġi-aki rarua.** See under **miten,** and **taġo.**

NOTE.—The idea is that of making the sail mount on the canoe as a horseman mounts a horse, or a burden mounts, or is placed upon, the back.

Tàġièġi, v. i., to be slow, dilatory. A. **'āka,** 5, to be averse, to delay.

Taġotaġo, v., to be placed one thing above or upon another, as the stories of a house, banks of clouds (see **taġataġ**), generations of men; and

Taġo na, s., such a thing, or things, as the story of a house, a generation of men, leaves of a book (which lie one upon the other). See under **miten** (and cf. **tiana, taġi-aki, mitaġa**).

Taġo-fi, v. t., to beg, ask (a person for a thing), **tataġo sa,** beg, ask for (a thing); **bitaġo,** v. r., to be asking, begging, earnestly (from others). [My. *taña, tañai,* id.] See **bitali.**

Taġōto, s., tomahawk, axe: **ta, ġoto;** and

Taġote-fi, v. t., to cut with an axe.

Taġura, s., a heap (of stones): **ġuru, kuru.**

Tai or **tae,** v. t., d. for **ata i,** or **atai,** to know. H. **yada',** to know.

Tai, s., excrement, filth. [Sa. *tae,* My. *tai,* Mg. *tai.*] H. **ṣeah,** excrement, filth, from **yaṣa',** to go out.

Tai na, s., d. **ke sua,** brother's brother, or sister's sister. [Fi. *tat'i,* Malo *tasi,* Ml. *tesi,* Bauro *asi,* Epi *tahi,* Motu *tadi,* My. *ad·ik,* Bu. *anri,* Mg. *zandri.*] A. **raṣī',** brother, properly collactaneous, from **raṣiʻa**, to suck.

Taiār, a., d. **tafar**; **fatu taiar**, or **tafar**, crumbling stone: **bera, taferafera.**

Taifolo, d. **tafolo.**

Tairai, d. **rairai.**

Taka, a., such as, like, such like: S. **da'k**, id. (**'ak**, and **d'**), talis;

Takanĭ (**takan uan, takana uai**, &c., putting any dem. after it) like this, that, &c.; so, in this way, in that way, thus, &c.; also, interrogatively, how? S. **da'k hana** (for **da'k**, see preceding word), such as this, like this. This S. word is composed of **d'** (dem. or relative pron.), **a'**, or **ai** (inter.), **k'**, as, like (ad.), and **hana**, or **'na**, this; without the **d'**, S. **'akana**, how?

Taka, is also used thus, **bi taka sikei**, are as one, alike, **sera tāka**, every what-like, or kind, **taka leba**, first-born of children, **taka-fē**, d. **saka-fē**, first ripe (yams), **taka riki**, youngest of children.

Taka-ni, v. t., to thrust on, or into (a thing), to thrust (a thing), **taka sila ki**, thrust making to shake or fall. H. **daḥah**, A. **daḥa**, &c., to thrust.

Takal i, or **tikal i**, d., v. t., to carry. S. **s'ḳal** to carry.

Tak'amo, or **takaamo**, to carry on a stick across the shoulder: **taki**, and **amo.**

Takāra, s., the crowd, lit. men (**ta**) gathered together (**kāra**): **ta, kuru, ġuru.**

Takara, s., c. art. **natakara**, that which seizes, or grasps, or lays hold (of one), as the consequence of some act, &c. See **kar i, taġaru.**

Takāri, v. i., to hasten, go swiftly, sail swiftly (as a canoe): **kāri.**

Takel, takelkel, v. i., or a., to be crooked, then unrighteous, d. **taġelĭ, taġelĭġelĭ.** H. **ʻaḳal, ʻaḳalḳal**, A. **ʻaḳila**, 5, &c., id.

Takes, d. for **nakes**, or **nakisa**: **kisa.**

Tak i, or **taki**, v. t., to fasten (as thatch on a roof, a rope on a log, anything on anything), and see **mitakitaki**; to fasten the tongs on an oven stone (to lift it), **bitaki, uataki, otaki**; and **matuki**, trusted in, confident, brave. [My. *taguh.*] A. **wat'iḳa**, to trust in, be firm, steadfast, confident, resolute, 4, to fasten, to bind.

Tāki, v. t., to incline, to pour out (anything by inclining a vessel); **taki**, to incline (oneself), **taki mita**, incline watch, **taki toroġo-saki**, incline, hearken to, **lo tāki**, look inclined, look round or back, **mitaki**, to be inclined, lean over (as if ready to fall); see **sī-rāk**, i. e. **sī-taki**, a squall, lit. blow, incline (a canoe, or cause it to heel over on its side). H. **ṣaʻah** (A. **ṣaʻʻa'**), to incline (as a vessel which is to be emptied); to be inclined, bent, stoop.

Taku, v. i., to be after, behind, d. **nruk**; or **itaku, inruk**;

Taku na, s., the back; **etaku,** or **itaku,** at the back, behind (d. **inruk**), also outside (the village), also the (time) behind, or after (as opposite to the time before, the past), as **te naliati etaku,** some day after, as he died, **sela itaku ru afa ki nia,** some time after they buried him, generally **tau itaku, naliati itaku,** the years, or days after (i. e., hereafter), **naliati itaku mau,** the last day, day of judgment. [Sa. *tua,* Malo *tura,* Epi *taka,* Motu *dolu,* the back.] A. ṭ'ahr', the back, E. **daḥr,** posterior part, **daḥari,** the last, **dĕḥara,** after, behind, **daḥara,** to be after, behind.

Takutaku, v. i., to speak [Sa. *ta'u,* tell, Ma. *taku,* Fi. *tukuna.*] A. **naṭaḳa,** to speak.

Taku, s., brothers-in-law, sisters-in-law, syn. **tauīen.** [Mg. *zauṭa, zau,* My. *tiri,* family relations.] A. ṭ'ahara, ṭ'ahr', and ṣihr', to aid, befriend, socius, tribe, family, &c.

Takuer, or **takuwer,** s., a big man, a strong man: **ta,** man, and **kuwer.** A. **kabura,** to be great, of big body.

Takus i, or **takusi,** v. t., to be like, similar to, also, with **k** elided, **tausi,** id., and to follow, also **rausi** (t to r), v. t., to follow, from **usi,** v. t., to follow, and also (in **rafe-kusi**) **kusi,** id. See **usi** and **bausi,** A. **ḳaṣṣa,** to follow; to narrate, and 5, 8, to follow; 1, to be near, 10, to ask.

Taku-ti, d. **raku sa,** q.v.

Talakolako, v. i., to whisper, i. e., to conceal what is being said (from someone): **ta,** utter speech, and **lakolako.**

Tàle is, v. t., d. **tèle is,** to search for. [Mg. *tadi.*] A. **dāra,** 2, Nm., to rummage (vulgar), lit. to turn over (things, in search of something);

Tale, s., c. art., a belt, also a rope, string; and

Tale ki, v. t., to make to go round (as a yam vine round a stake), **tale is,** to coil round something (as a snake), **tale ki māro** (see **roa**), to whirl round (as the eyes in dizziness), **tali ki,** to twist round one (crooked dealing, to injure), **tālo,** round, around, **taltāl,** round. [Mg. *tadi, mitadi,* to twist, *tadi,* a rope, My. *tali,* a rope, string, bandage, &c.] A. **dāra,** to go round, whirl, turn; be dizzy, 2, make round, 4, turn round, **da'ro,** orb, around, **dairo,** round; circuit, &c.

Tale, s., c. art., the taro (so called because round). [Sa. *talo,* My. *talās,* id.] See preceding word.

Taleàba, and **taltaleàba,** v. i., to whirl round (as a wheel), **taleaba ki,** v. t., to make to whirl round, to turn round (as a grindstone): **tale**, and **àba**.

Talebaġa, s., d. syn. **kalebaġa**, bow-string: **tale**, and **baġa**, s. (the tree from which the string is made).

Talefa, s., a side region, circuit: and

Talefan, s., the circuit of the horizon: **tale**.

Tale-firi, a., all round (as round an island, &c.): **tale**, and **firi** or **biri**.

Talekabu na, d. **arekabu**, q.v.

Talemāt, s., plantation, enclosed and cultivated field. Cf. H. s'ĕdemōt', and s'ĕremōt', id.

Taleuor, s., a side, circuit: **tale**, and **uor**, or **uora**. See **bora i**.

Taliāli, v. i., to be slow, delay: **aliāli**. [Sa. *tali, tatali.*]

Talibo (see **libo**), to hide, be hid, hide oneself.

Tàlĭga na, s., c. art. **nataliġa na**, d. **liġa na**, and **nàlĭga na**, the ear or ears. [Ml. P. *ririġa*, Epi dd. *tiline, seliġo*, An. *tikġa*, Motu *taia*, Sa. *taliġa*, Fut. *tariġa*, My. *taliġa*, Mg. *tadini.*] H. **'ozen**, du., used also as pl., **'azĕnaim**, **'azĕne**, S. **'adna**, Ch. **'uden**, **'udĕna**, A. **'uḏn'**, pl. **'aḏān'**, and **'uḏun'**. For the verb, see **roġo, toġo**.

Tali-si, v. t., to prize up, wrench up (as the side of a flat stone). See **tila i**, or **til ē**.

Talle, or **tal'le**, v. i., to turn aside (as from a path); and

Talele, id., **talele ki**, to turn aside or away from (a person or thing.) See **lele**.

Tālo, taloālo. See **alo-fi**.

Tālo, a., round, and ad., round about: **tale**.

Talokuloku ki. See **taluko**.

Taltal, a., round: **tale**.

Taltalūra, s., a sea snake covered with round strips or bands.

Tàlu, or **talŭlu**, s., a crowd, herd: **lulu**.

Taluḅaki, v. i., to be spilt, poured out, to pour itself out: **lubaki**.

Taluko, or **taluku**, and **talukoluko ki**, v., to conceal oneself from; **atu taluko baki nia**, turn away from, or conceal oneself from: **lako**.

Taluġ i, d., and

Talum i, d. See **tulum i**.

Tam i, v. t., to add to, dd. **tàm i, täum i**. [Mg. *tuvana*, and *tuvuna.*] A. **ṣ'amma**, to add.

Tama i, d. **taba i**, v. t., to cover (as fruit, &c., covering the ground, being abundant), to rub, and see **atama**, that which rubs, syn. **ore**. A. **ṭamma**, to cover with abundance (Nm. smother, overwhelm), (2), to scrape or shave.

Tama na. See **tema na**.

Tama, dd. **tab**, (**tiba**), q.v.

Tama, for **taḅa**, q.v.

Tamaliām', v. i., to delay. A. **mahala**, 5, to delay, and H.

mahah, to delay, linger (prop. to refuse, turn back).

Tamàlu, v. i., to bend, rise (to set out), to go or come forth, set out: **taḅa, lu, lua.**

Tamaras, reflexive of **maras**, q.v.

Tamate, v. i., to fall calm, be calm (as the sea, the wind), hence

Tamate, s., c. art., peace (opposite to war), a calm, silence; also, the festivals in honour and worship of the dead, at which the people of different villages assembled: **mate.**

Tamisal, or **tamusal**, s., an unmarried person: **ta**, a person, and **misal.**

Tami-si, d. **sabe-li**, q.v., to tie.

Tamo, v. i., d. **naḅo**, to smell, see **naḅo.**

Tamole, s., man: **ta**, man, and **mole**, to live, living. [Fi. *tamata*, Sa. *taġata*, My. *oraġ-idup*, Mg. *ulumbeluna*, id.]

Tamon, s., smell, d. **naḅon.**

Tamtam, a., dusky; **raġi tamtam** (syn. **raġ meḷu**), evening, lit. time dusky, or of dusk. A. **'atama**, to be evening, dusky, **'atamat**, dusk of evening.

Tamulu, v. i., syn. c. **mulu**, q.v.

Tanekabu, s., d. **arekabu.**

Tan i, v. t., to earth it, to cover with earth, then with anything (**tun i**);

Tanu-mi, v. t., to cover with earth, put into the ground; and

Tanu-maki, id.; hence

Tano, s., d. **tan**, earth of any kind, soil, clay, ground, and **etan**, ad. and prep., on the ground, below. [Sa. *tanu*, ps. *tanua*, and *tanumia*, My. *tanām*, *tanamkan*, *tanuman*, *tani*, Sa. *tanuma'i*, *tanuġa*, *tanumaġa*.] A. **ṭāna**, to cover with clay; to cover, **ṭino**, dialect **ṭāno**, earth, clay.

Tanoabu, d. **tanoafu**, d. **tanoau**, s., ashes: **tano, abu;**

Tanonōn, or **tanoonōn**, s., level ground, d. **tēn**: **tano**, and **onĕ**, reduplicated.

Tanotanoa, a., soiled with earth: **tano**, and ending **a.**

Tanu e, tanua, v., to spit, dd. **tani, taniu**; and

Tanua, d. **taniu**, s., c. art., spittle. [Sa. *anu*, ps. *anusia*, Motu *kanudi*, ps. *kanudia*, Fi. *kanusi*: My. *ludah*, Ml. *rut*, Malo *lito*.] A. **rawwala**, n. a. **tarwilu** (**taniu**, Ef.), id.

Täo, v. i., to fall, d. for **roa** (**röuo, töuo**).

Tao, s., d., v. t., to lay down, leave, permit, &c. [Mg. *läu*, *mandäu*.] A. **wada'a**, not used in perfect, fut. **yada'o**, imp. **da'**, to lay down, leave, permit. So A. **waṣ'a'a.**

Tàos, v. i., d. **maosa**, q.v.

Taosi, d. **tausi.** See **takusi.**

Täoti na, s., bone, bones, weapons made of dead men's bones. [My. *tulaġ*, Mg. *taulana*.] A. **'aṭm'**, Mahri (m elided) **'aṭaiṭ** (Von Maltzan), **at'āt'** (Carter), H. **'eṣem**, pl. **'ăṣāmōt'**, id., often of bones of the dead.

Tara, taratara. See **tera**, to be quick.

Tārĕ, v. i., or a., to be pure, clean, white, **tartāre,** whitish, **matiratira,** polished, bright, shining. A. **ṭahara,** to be clean, pure, H. **ṭaher,** to shine, be bright, clean, pure.

Tare, v. i., to cry, call out (of men); to call out, i.e. crow (cock). A. **ṣaraḥa** and **ṣarā',** to cry, call out, **ṣarīh',** a crying or calling out, a cock.

Tarere, v. i., to break on the shore with noise (of breakers): **rere.**

Tari, or **tar i,** v. t., to drag, draw along. [Mg. *tarika,* My. *tarik,* Ma. *tari.*] A. **na-tara,** id.

Taroa, s., a pigeon. [My. *dara.*] A. **ṭair',** id.

Taru-si, or **taro-si,** v. t., to pray to (the **natemate**), **taro-taro,** redup. [Sa. *talalo, talotalo,* ps. *talosia,* Ha. *kalo-kalo,* Tah. *tarotaro.*] A. **ṣala',** E. **ṣalaya,** Ch. **ṣela,** to pray.

Taruḅa, v. i., to fall; **taruḅa bei,** to fall upon; **taruḅa ki,** v. t., throw down, make to fall, d. **tarubik,** v. i., and

Taruḅa, s., c. art., sticks thrown on or laid across the rafters of a house. E. **ṣadefa** (A. **ṣadafa,** to decline), to fall.

Tas, tasi, s., c. art., the sea. [My. *tasik,* To. *tahi,* Sa. *tai.*] A. **ta's',** the sea.

Tas i, or **tasi,** v. t., to shave: **ras i.**

Tas, v. i., for **ras, teres.**

Tasaḅo, v. i. See **saḅo.**

Tasabsabu, s., shattered to pieces: see **sabe-riki.**

Tasiġa, s., d. for **tasila.**

Tasike, v. i., to lift, raise (the head): **saki.**

Tasila, s., helper, assistant: **sila i.**

Tasilasila, v. i., to make a clear startling sound (of men), to crack (of thunder): **ta,** chop, &c., and **silasila.** See **sila.**

Tasmen, s., salt: **tas,** the sea or salt, and **men,** or **mina,** q.v. pleasant (so called because it makes food pleasant tasted).

Tasuki, v. i., to bow: **suki.**

Tasuru ki, v. t., to conceal: **suru.**

Tata, v., voc., maternal grandmother. [TaSa., Ml., *tata,* father, Ml. and Malo *tata,* paternal uncle.] See under **atena na.**

Tata, redup. of **ta,** to chop, cut.

Tatā-ġasi, v. t., **tatā,** same as **tatau** (in preceding word), redup. of **tau,** and **ġasi,** to (wipe) stroke, smooth, flatter.

Tatalai, talai, also **tilai, titilai,** v. i., to warm oneself (at the fire). [Fi. *tatalai,* Mg. *mitulu* (buhu).] A. **ṣala, ṣalyy',** &c., to warm (one, oneself, at the fire), be warmed at the fire.

Tatamares, tamares, with **ta-** doubled.

Tatau-fi, v. t., as, **bisa tatau-fi,** to speak, deceive: **tau.**

Tati, d. **rati,** q.v. [Sa. *tala,* Tah. *tara.*]

Tatok, or **atatok** (or **natatok,** s.), a., resident, native: **ta,** man, and **toko.**

Tatu, s. (see **tui**), a stake, post (of a fence), then **tatu nafanua,** lord or chief of the land. A. **watada,** to fix, stake, make firm, **watadu,** stake, post, H. **yated,** pin, nail, then 'prince'.

Tau, tautau, v. i., or a., to be pure, clean, white. [Ma. *tea.*] A. **naṣa'a,** to be pure, white.

Tau, v. i., also **mitau,** to abide, as, **i tau suma,** he abides (in) the house, **i tau narā nakasu,** it abides (on) the branch of the tree (as a bird or fruit), **naḃona i tau isa,** his heart is fixed, abides on (the person or thing), **i tau isa,** it abides (as fruit) on it (the branch), **i tau ki nuana,** makes to **tau,** as a tree makes fruit to **tau,** yields (fruit), **nakasu i tau,** the tree yields (fruit), **tau nata,** take a person to one's house (as a guest), **tau ē a; mamitau, matau,** d., an anchor. A. **t'awa',** to abide, remain, (2), take for a guest, (4), make to stay, detain.

Tau asa, and **toü-ġi,** and **toü-ni,** v. t., to measure, to weigh; **tau,** also **to, toto,** s., a measure; and **to-naki** (for **tau-naki**), d. **towa-naki, tawa-naki,** to place, set, fix firmly, establish, appoint, determine, ordain, also to compare; **tau,** redup. **tautau,** to commission (one to do something), command, hence **fitaua,** c. art. **nafitaua,** one commissioned, a messenger, also a commission or message (syn. **fakaua,** q.v.). [Fi. *tatau-naka,* My. *titah,* to command, order, decree.] H. **ṣawah,** to set up, place (S. **ṣo'**), to constitute, appoint, decree, charge, command, commission, cg. H. **s'awah,** to be like, resemble.

Tau, tatau-fi, tātā ġasi, tautau, v. t., to deceive, mislead. S. **t'a', ta'uta**; also in H. and A.; to err, deceive, mislead.

Tau, bitau, bitautau, v. i., and t., to invite (as to a feast); **tau,** in **tau-mafa,** to invoke, ask, pray; **taumafa,** is **mafa,** to give a gift, to sacrifice, to (a deity, or **natemate**), and **tau,** to invoke, pray, thus **taumafa,** to invoke or pray (while) sacrificing, or giving an offering. A. **da'a,** to call with a loud voice; to invite; to invoke, pray.

Tau, s., a season, time, year. [Mg. *tauna,* My. *taun* (*tawun*), Sa. *tau.*] A. **zaman,** S. **zĭban,** Mod. S. **zōna,** id.

Taua, s., a heap, a crowd, a herd; **taua ki,** to heap, pile. [My. *tâmbun, timbun, tumpuk,* id., Mg. *tauna.*] H. **ṣabar,** A. **ṣ'abara,** id.

Tau, tautau, v. t., to commission. [Fi. *tatau-naka,* id., My. *titah,* to command, order, decree (**to-naki**, infra.)] See **tau.**

Tau-ġi, v. t., to grasp firmly with the hand, to pluck off with the hand (as fruit), **tau isa**, hold it firmly in the hand. [Sa., Ma. *tau*, to pluck fruit with the hand, Mg. *sambuṭa*, My. *sambut*, to lay hold of, Fi. *taura*, take hold of.] H. **ṣabaṭ**, A. **ṣ'abaṭa**, (1), (5), (7), to grasp, lay hold of firmly, pluck, also **ṣ'abaṭ'a**, (1), (8), hold (a thing) in the hand, seize, grasp.

Tau-ri, v. t., to bind, be bound firmly to, to marry (*a woman*), to tie firmly to (as a boat to a ship to be towed), **taura ki, tau lua i**, to be fixed or bound firmly (to one), bringing out one (as from bondage, or from her relations), to redeem; to marry; **bitauri**, v. r., to be bound, or tied, or attached, firmly to each other, to be married. [Sa. *taula 'i*, hang on to, *taula*, an anchor.] A. **ṣabara, ṣabr'**, to bind, be bound to, &c.

Tāü-ni, or **tāö-ni**, v. t., to cook, to bake (in the oven). [Sa. *tao*, ps. *taoa, taoina; taona'i*, to bake food the day before giving it; To., Ma., *tao.*] A. **taha**, n. a. **tahw'**, to cook. Hence

Tāö, s., c. art., leaves for cooking which are put into the oven along with the food to be cooked. [To. *tau*, the cooking leaves, Tah. *tao*, leaves and stones put into the inside of a pig to be cooked.]

Tauēru isa, v. t., to haul, drag, **tau** and **eru**, i.e. **aru**, the hand, lit. fix the hand on (to drag), as to drag a man to punishment.

Tauī, v. t., to twist, wring (as to wring clothes after washing them), to milk (as a goat), squeeze, or wring (the milk out). A. **ṭawa'**, (E. **ṭawiy**, H. **ṭawah**), to wring, twist.

Tauīen, or **tawien**, s., a sister's husband, a wife's brother, that is, brother-in-law; but, d., a general name for reliable friend, brother, or sister, and in another d. the word is applied to father-in-law and son-in-law. [Fut. *safe*, Aniwa *nosafe*, Ta *yafuni*, d., c. art. *nevun.*] A. **ṣafiyy'**, a friend of a pure and sincere mind, i.e. a real friend, **ṣafa'**, 3, to be of sincere and pure affection (towards someone), 4, to show sincere love, 6, to live in mutual sincerity of friendship.

Taubora, s., an ornament that abides on the side of the head: **tau, bora.**

Taulalo, v. or s., to hang, or be fixed or what hangs or abides in front of the belly, **nasieġ i taulalo: tau, lalo.**

Taumafa, d. **taumofa**, v. i., to invoke giving an offering (to the **natemate**), **taumafà**

sa, give an offering of or with it (something), **taumafa ki nia**, offer it (something), **taumafa tua i**, make an offering, giving to him (a **natemate**). [Ml. P. *tomav*, Ha. *kaumaha*, to offer in sacrifice, to offer a gift upon an altar, s., a sacrifice, Tah. *taumaha*, a portion of food offered to the gods or spirits of the dead.] **Tau** (to pray, invoke), and **mafa**, or **mofa** (q.v.), giving or offering. A. **ma'habat**, a gift, H. **habhabim** (Hos. viii. 13), offerings (to God), A. **wahaba**, H. **yahab**, to give.

Taumako, s., the wild (edible) yam that grows or abides on the hills: **tau**, and **mako**, for which see **aka**, **ako**.

Taumi. See **tami**.

Taunako, s., a thing (like the peak of a cap) worn over the forehead. [Cf. syn. Sa. *taumata*]: **tau**, and **nako**.

Tauruuru, v. i., to grumble, murmur, mutter: **ta**, and **uruuru**.

Tausi, v. t. See **takusi**.

Tauso, or **tausoa**, v. i., to commit adultery or fornication (of either sex): **tau**, and **so**, or **soa**. [Fi. *daut'a*.]

Te, dem., rel. pron., conj., as **aġute**, mine this, **ana te**, his this or that; **te uia**, what (is) good, that which is good, or he or she who is good, **te sa**, that which is bad, or he or she who is bad; in this sense d. **tea**, as **tea uia**, **tea sa**; **te nata**, what, or whatever person, any person, someone; **te**, redup. **tete**, may be used substantively, as, **te ru ban**, or **tete ru ban**, some went; **te**, dem., is found in **fite** (**nafite**, **sefete**, what this, that, or it? or simply, what?) also in **matuna**; with art., **nete**, s., the that, anything, something, and d. with dem. **ka** prefixed, **nakate**, id.; **te** is also found with **ka**, dem. prefixed in one d. as a tense particle (see **kate**, tense particle, supra); **te**, or **t'**, is also used as a conj. and before the verbal pron. of the 1st person sing., **a**, and of the 3rd sing., **i** or **e**, loses its vowel, as **ta ban**, that I go, or be gone, **tē ban**, that he has gone, or because he has gone. In one dialect for **i kate**, **ku kate**, **a kate ban**, he, you, I went, there is **ka te ban**, **ku te ban**, **ki te ban**, I went, you went, he went. A. **ḍa**, dem., **ḍu**, rel., S. **d'**, Ch. **di**, rel. and conj., that, because.

Tea. See **te**.

Teḅa, or **taḅa**, v. i., to dry up (of liquid or moisture), to become dry; and **mun teḅa ki**, to drink, making it dry (liquid). E. **naṣefa**, to become dry (as a river); to dry up (as a spring), **nĕṣuf**, dry, dried up.

Teël, s., shellfish, &c., got on the reef, lit. **te el'**, that which is pleasant, sweet, or tasty: **te elo.**

Tefa, tetefa, v. i., to draw up in order of battle; and

Tefa ki, v. t., to put in a series, to range (troops, in order of battle); **bitefa,** range themselves in order of battle, face to face; **tefa-ġi,** d. **tefa-ni,** v. t., to put things in a series, either one before or one above another. [Fi. *tuva,* v. i., *tuvā,* v. t., to place in regular order, to range in close compact, or place one upon another, *tuvai nai valu, tuvai valu,* to put in the attitude of war, put in battle array, *tuva na lawa ni valu,* arrange or put in ranks the *lawa ni valu.*] A. **ṣaffa,** 1, 2, 6, 8, to set or place in order in a series; to arrange the line of battle, draw up in order of battle; Nm. to arrange (troops), 2, id., to range themselves mutually face to face.

Tef i, or **tefi,** redup. **tetefi,** v. t., to cut; **tefi,** to circumcise. [Fi. *teve, tava,* Sa. *tefe,* To. *tefe,* Sa., To. *tafa,* Mg. *tapaka.*] A. **'aṣ'aba,** to cut.

Tefarafara, v. i., to break (of the sea); and

Tefara, s., c. art., breakers: **tafera, taferafera.**

Tefarere (i. e. **tefarrere**), v. i., to break rushing up on the shore (of the breakers): **tefara,** and **rere.**

Tei, s., c. art. **intei,** a reddish powder made from a plant, turmeric: **bitei.**

Tei. See **rei.**

Ṭei a, for **toitoi.**

Telake na, d. **telakea na,** s., lord, owner, possessor: **lake.**

Telatela, v. i., or a., to be large, wide; and

Telatelana, id., c. ending **-na.** and see **matulu, matultul, matoltol,** swollen, large. [Epi *toru,* large, Sa. *tetele, telatela, latele, vatele,* Ma. *tetere,* large, swollen.] H. **'adīr,** large, great, **'adar,** to be wide, A. **'adira,** to have hernia (to swell out).

Tēle, v. t. See **tāle is,** to search for.

Telei, or **talai,** s., the ancient axe, or adze-like axe (a shell). [Sa. *talai,* to adze, Ma., Tah. *tarai,* chop with an adze, Ha. *kalai,* to chop, hew, pare, carve.] A. **s'araḥa,** to cut, slice, carve, dissect.

Teluko. See **taluko.**

Tema na, or **tama na,** s., father: see Ch. II. 11. *c.* [Sa. *tamā,* My. *rama,* id.]

Temaḅalu, s., brothers, lit. **te** (he who), **ma** (with), **ḅalu,** (brother): **ḅalu;** and

Temabalu ta, for **temabalu ra,** who (or those who) with their brother, i. e. brothers. So **tema** in the following words is, lit., he or she who or those who, or that (person) or those (persons) with.

Temabau ra, s., d., uncle and nephew: **bau.**

Temaḅele ta, s., mother and child: **ḅele na.**

Temagore ta, s., brother and sister: **ġore na**; d. **mera ġore na.** See **mera.**

Temaloa ta, s., d. syn. **temabau ra**: **alo ana.**

Temam̃ō ta, s., mother-in-law and son-in-law: **m̃ō na.**

Temaratauīen, s., i. e. **te māra tauīen**, that with (his) **tauīen**, d. syn. **temataku ta**: **tauien.**

Temarauota, s., i. e. **te māra uota**, that with (her) **uota** (husband), wife and husband: **uota**, d. **me nimariki.**

Temasere, s., a beloved one, especially a child much cared for; **te**, that, **masere**, loved, cared for. See also **sere, bakasere.**

Temaṭāfa, for **temarāfa**, s., father and child, lit. that (i. e. the child) with the father. See **afa.**

Temataku ta, s., a man and his brother-in-law (his wife's **ġore na**): **taku na.**

Tematema ta, s., father and child: **tema na.**

Tematete ta, s., maternal grandmother, and her grandchild: **atena na.**

Tĕmatĭ, i. q., **ma**, with, and, only with numerals. H. לְעֻמַּת, see עֻמָּה.

Tematia ta, s., paternal grandfather (&c.) and his grandchild: **atia na.**

Tematobu ta, s. maternal grandfather and his grandchild: **tobu na.**

Tematua ta, s., paternal grandmother and her grandchild: **tua na.**

T'te na, s., juice: **toto.**

Tēn, d. for **tanonon.**

Tena na, s. See **atena na**; d. **atia**, or, **tia na.**

Tēr, v. i., to be slow, tardy. A. **'aḥ'ḥ'ara**, 5, to be slow, tardy.

Terā sa, v. t., be ignorant of, forget, not to know (it), d. **rere**, d. **tenr.** A. **ṣ'alla**, to not know, be ignorant of; forget.

Tera, v. i., to shine (of the sun), **tera i**, v. t., shine upon it (of the sun). [My. *târaġ, târaġ kan*, Fi. *t'ila*, Malo *sarasara.*] H. **ṣahar** (cf. **zahar**, &c.), to shine.

Tera i, tetera i, v. t., to go after, to do anything after (or in the track of) another, **bakatera i**, to answer (make one's word to go after another's), **bā**, and **sela tera i**, go after, **ġua tera i**, shout after, **bisa tera i**, speak after; also to rehearse, recount, **tera usi**, to recount following, **tera uti na**, to go after close to. [My. *turut*, follow, go after.] A. **'at'ar'**, track, **'at'ara**, 4, make something follow another, 5, 8, follow the track of someone, go after, 1, recount, rehearse.

Tera, v. i., to be quick, swift, **tera ki māla**, wheel, swoop, shoot, or glide swiftly like a hawk, **tera ġulu-ti**, swoop (upon one) clasping (him, as in war), **tera tukituki**, run rapidly beating the ground with one's feet, **tera belbel**, to be exceedingly swift or quick, **tera mau**, to be quick indeed or truly, to be instant, do instantly, **tera bile**, to be very quick, **teratera**, redup.; **tera lo saki**, to turn quickly, looking up, **tera tabo** (d.), to turn quickly bending the head down, **torutoru**, to sweat. [Ma. *tere*, Sa. *teletele.*] A. **darra**, (10), to run vehemently, or swiftly, 4, to turn or whirl a spindle very swiftly, H. **darar**, (also) to fly in a circle, wheel in flight; and like A. **darra**, to spout, to pour out (as rain, &c.), to sweat, Ef. **toru**, **torutoru**. Hence

Ter e, v. t., to pour into; and

Tera, s., c. art., a pouring out; **natera ni us**, a rain squall, an outpouring of rain.

Terā, a., having (lit. that has) branches, as **tera rua**, **tolu**, &c., having two, three, &c., branches (of a tree): **te**, and **rā**.

Terafi, v. t., for **rerafi**, to scratch (as the ground). See **rafi**.

Terági, v. t., in **kabu teragi**, to heat cooked food over again, **terági** is for **reragi**, as in **bauragi**, **bau-terag i** (see **bau-si**, **baraga i**, **raga-elo**).

Teratār, v. i., to stagger, totter (as a man drunk). A. **tartara**, to stagger (as a man drunk).

Teratera, v. i., to be delirious, insane; A. **hatara**, 1, 4, to make, or to be delirious, insane; also **torotoro**.

Tere, **teretere**, v. t., to feast, to entertain (especially visitors at a festival), also to make a feast or banquet for a friend who visits one. The radical idea lies in that of gathering folks together for a festival, or enclosing them as it were in one's house and hospitality. H. **'aṣarah**, an assembly of people for keeping a festival, **'aṣar** (primary idea is that of surrounding, enclosing), Ni., (3), to be gathered together, especially for a festival, A. **a'aṣīr**, breakfast and dinner, or supper.

Tere, s., c. art., the mast (of a canoe or ship), calf (column) of the leg. A. **ṣariyat**, Nm. **ṣari**, the mast (of a ship), a column.

Tere, s., and **teretere**, s., the comb (of a cock); the eaves of a house. [Sa. *tala*, Tah., Ma. *tara*, H. *kala.*] Nm. **torra**, crest, comb of bird, A. **ṭorrat**, extremity, side of anything, forelock, pointed, from **ṭarra**, to cut, to sharpen, to snatch, to shoot (as plants), to propel vehemently, irritate, stir up.

Terei, v. t., for **rerei**, for **roroia**: **rei**.

Terina, s., enclosure. H. **ṭur**, fence, enclosure.

Teres, for **reres**: **res**.

Tere-ti, v., used as ad., as, **boka tere-ti**, to smite or strike hastily (and therefore ineffectively, confusedly), syn. **sarafi**, and **sumati**, and **bilo**, or **bilebile**: **tera**, to be quick.

Tete, s., voc., mother. See under **ani na**.

Tete, and **tetea**. See **te**.

Ti, and d. **ṣi**, neg. ad., not: d. **ta**. [Sa. *lē*, Ma. *te*, Fut. *si*, My. *tu*, Mg. *ṣi*.]

Ti, v. t., to say; **ti ki nia**, say to him, tell him, **ti ki nià sa**, tell him it: dd. **ni**, **noa**, **nofa**, q.v.

Tī, s., chief, as, **ti Tongoa**, chief of Tongoa: for **tui**, q.v.

Tī, and **rī**, v. t., to push, thrust, propel, or drive. A. **ḍaya**, to propel, thrust.

T'tie na, or **t'tia na**, s., saliva, water of the mouth, **nat'tia na i serà sa**, his mouth waters because of it, lit. the water (of his mouth) runs at it: **titia**.

Tiamia, v. i. or a., to be first, d. **bea** or **tobea** (for **toko bea**): **tia**, to abide or be, and **mia**, d. **bea**, q.v. [Oba *tomua*, Sa. *mua*, and *tomua*.]

Tia na, or **tie na**, s. See **atia na**.

Tiana, v. i., to be with child. See **mitēn**. S. **ṭ'yina**, laden, gravid.

Tiba, neg. ad., not. See d. **tab**: **ti**, ad., and **ba** for **ma**, as in Assy. **aama**, not.

Tib ē, or **tuba i**, v. t., to shoot with an arrow;

Tiba, or **tuba**, s., c. art., an arrow, i.e. what is cast: **tuba**. [Mg. *ṣipika*.] E. **nadafa**, (2) to shoot with an arrow, (1) to strike, (3), to prick, H. **nadaf**, to drive away. The radical idea is thrusting, pushing.

Tība, s., the post in a house that supports the ridge-pole: Compare A. **dī'mat**, column, pillar, from **da'ama**, v.

Tibi-li, v. t., to burn, to sear. A. **ṣ'ahaba**, to roast, to broil.

Tibu (pronounced **timbu**), d., s., c. art. **natimbu**, the deep (sea): **bua**.

Tiele, v. i., to finish a laugh with shrill cries, in a whinnying manner (of women). H. **ṣahal**, to utter shrill cries; to neigh (of a horse), A. **ṣahala**, n. a. **ṣahil'**, to whinny.

Tifai, s., thunder: **ti**, art., and **fai**. [Sa. *fai-tilitili*, Fila *tefachiri*, Aniwa *tefachiri*.] A. **baḥḥ'** (used of thunder), hoarse, cf. Sa. **fā**, hoarse.

Tikal i. See **takal i**.

Tiġi na, or **tiki na**, s., side, edge;

Tiġi elo, v., to bask in the sun, warm oneself in the sun. A. **ṣ'aḥa**, to bask or warm oneself in the sun, **ṣ'aḥiyat**, side, outside or edge. Hence

Tiġi (side) in **malitiġi**, **maliriġi**, &c., place at the side, that is, beside, near: and

Tiġitiġi na, s., d., edge (outside or exposed edge or side of a thing), and

Tiki na, and

Tikitiki na, id.; and

Tiki nrā nin, d., this point (of time), now.

Tīka, a strong negative, it is not, no, by no means;

Tiki (or **tikă**), neg. ad., not; **i tiki ban,** he did not go; and

Tika, and **tiki,** the same, used, with the **verb.** pron., as a verb, to be not, to exist not, dd. **ṣika, nika,** rika, **tika**: neg. ad. **ti,** and **ka.** It is thus construed: **i tikā sa,** it is not in it or him, or he has it not, **i tika ki nia,** it is not to or in him, or he has it not, thus, **namuruen i tika ki nia,** there is no laughing in him, **i tika ki namuruen,** he has not laughing. For **ti** see **ti,** neg. ad., supra; **ka** is to be compared with the E. **ko,** in **'eko,** not, **ko** being a contraction of **kona** (A. **kana**), to be; and **tika** with the Talmudic and Mandaite **lika,** not, is not (Nöldeke, *Mand. Grammatik*). [Fut. *jikai,* My. *tak,* Mg. *ṣia,* and *diahue,* To. *ikai,* Sa. *ʻai,* no, not, not so.]

Tiki-amo, d. **takāmo,** q.v.

Tiki, v. i., to be soft (of the skin), syn. **busa,** as, **nauili na i tiki,** or, **i busa,** his skin is soft (his skin is bad, or has an uncomfortable feeling, as on hearing some dreadful story, or witnessing some fearful thing). See **busa.** A. **'atiḳa,** (*b*), (3), to become soft and tender (of the skin).

Tiki na, and **ṭiki na,** s., for **riki na.**

Tiko, s., a staff, a walking stick, a pole by which a canoe is poled forward in shallow water. [Sa. *toʻo,* a canoe pole, a stick in which is fixed the perch of a pigeon, *toʻonaʻi,* to lean on a staff, to lean on anything for support, *tootoo,* a staff, walking stick, *totoʻo,* to lean upon a staff, To. *toko,* a post used to make fast canoes to, *tokotoko,* a staff, My. *tâkân,* Mg. *tehina,* a staff, *mitchina,* to walk with a staff, to walk leaning on a person.] A. **toka'at,** a staff, a support, he who leans much on his side, and props himself up. Hence, Nm., **taka,** 8, **itteci,** to lean upon. Hence

Tiko ki, v. t., to pole (a canoe). This is done by leaning upon the **tiko,** and so throwing one's weight upon it.

Tila i, d. **til ē** (and **tali-si**), v. t., to wrench, prize (with a lever), to struggle, wriggle, wrestle (as through a narrow place); **tilā ki,** v. t., to wrench, sprain, twist (as one's foot by stepping into a hole); **tilatila,** v. t., wrench up with a lever roots and rocks in making a hole in which to plant a yam; hence

Tīla, s., a lever, crowbar. [Mg. *tuluna,* *mituluna,* to struggle together, to wrestle.] A. **'atala,** to violently drag and wrench away, 3, to wrestle with, **atalat,** Nm. **'atela,** crowbar, lever, hod.

Tila i, tīla, d. for **lita i : līta.**

Tilasi, and redup. **tilatilasi : lasi.**

Tilai, titilai. See **talai, tatalai.**

Tili, v. t., to tell, relate (a thing). [Sa. *tala,* v. and s., tell, relate, tale, narration, *tala'i, talatala'i,* To. *tala.*] A. **tala',** to follow, to relate (a narrative), read, recite.

Tili mar, v. i., d. for **lele maroa,** to revolve or roll turning round : **lele, maroa.**

Tinom i, d. for **tulum i.**

Tirāgi (riraġi), v., to look at (as at a spectacle). A. **rāna,** to look at.

Tirā sa, d. **rirā sa.** See **terā sa.**

Tiri, v. i., to fly (of birds), d. **riri ;** also to fly into a rage, to be transported with rage, flying and jumping about excitedly ; **i tiri,** syn. **i miti,** as, **i tiri ƀas i,** or **i miti ƀas i,** he (transported with rage) flies snatching him (the object of his passion, as if to tear out his eyes). Hence **rīri,** a spark, and **mitiri,** a grasshopper (from leaping and flying), and **taroa,** a pigeon. [Sa. *lele,* Ma. *rere.*] A. **ṭāra,** to fly ; to be swift, move quick.

Tiriġi, for **ririġi, riġi.**

Tirikit, v. i., to begin to drop or sputter (of rain). [Fi. *tiri,* to drop.] For **tiri,** see **tuturu,** and for **kit, kita,** small, little.

Tiro, v. i., to sink, roll down (as in the sea, or down a precipice, or into a pit) ; hence

Tiroa, s., c. art., a precipice, or deep, steep place. [Fi. *tiro, siro, sisiro,* My. *turun, turunkan.*] A. **ḥadara, ḥudur',** to descend, put down. See **mitaru, toroaki ;** also

Tiro e, d., v. t., to swallow, send down, make to sink down (into the stomach) ; and

Tiro-aki, v. t., make to sink down (as an anchor,) to anchor, d. **toro-aki, tirotiro,** redup.

Tiso, v. i., to exude, d. **lisoa, tisē,** exude on to (a thing) : **toto.**

Titi, v., to tread, **titia ki nakasu,** tread on a log (as on a log thrown across a stream). [My. *titi.*] A. **waṭiya,** to tread.

Titia, v. i., to slaver, dribble (as an infant), to have saliva flowing, to have the mouth watering, **nat'tia na,** saliva, water of the mouth. [Mg. *rura,* saliva.] H. **rir,** saliva, A. **rāla,** to slaver, dribble (of an infant), **riyal',** saliva, cf. My. **liyor,** slaver, dribble.

Titiro, v. i., to gaze into the sea looking for fish or shellfish ; to look at one's image in water or a looking-glass.

[Fi. *tiro*, *tiro-va*, to look at oneself in the water, peep at, Sa. *tilotilo*, ps. *tilofia*, to peep, spy, Mg. *tarața*, *tarafina*, Ma. *tiro*, *tirotiro*, *titiro*, look, gaze, Ha. *kilo*, to look hard, earnestly, to star-gaze, prognosticate, act as a sorcerer.] A. **naț'ara,** to gaze, look for, consider, spy, to prognosticate, divine.

Tiū sa, d., v. t., to sink, dip, **matiu,** v. i., to sink, d. redup. **tutu,** d. **lulu,** v. i., to sink, d. **riū sa,** v. t., to point out with the finger, d. **tuma i,** v. t., to point out with the finger, d. **tiū sa, tū sa,** d. **tū-ni a,** or **riū sa,** or **rū sa,** or redup. **tiutiū sa, tūtū sa, riūriū sa,** or **rūrū sa,** v. t., to smear, tinge, colour, or paint **nafōna** (native cloth). See also **lolofa, lum, luma, lulum.** [Ma. *totohu*, to sink, *tohu*, mark, sign, *toi*, finger, also toe, Tah. *tohu*, to point at with the finger, make a sign, To. *tuhu*, v., to point with the finger, s., the forefinger, Sa. *tusi*, to mark (native cloth), to write, to point out, *tusitusi*, striped, Fi. *luvu*, to sink, Mg. *tsubuka*, soaked, drenched, dipped, My. *tud'iġ*, to point at with the finger, to indicate. See also under **lolofa, luma.**] H. **ṭaba',** to sink, cg. **ṣaba',** A. **ṣaba'a,** to dip into, immerse, E. **tam'a,** id., to be dipped, plunged, H. **ṣaba',** to dip in, immerse, to dye, tinge, **ṣeba',** something dyed, a versicoloured garment, Ch. (see **lolofa**) **ṣĕba',** A. **ṣaba'a,** to point out or at with the finger, **'aṣbi', 'aṣbu',** &c., the finger, H. **'aṣba',** finger, also toe, A. **ṣaba''a,** to dye or colour (cloth), to make a sign, indicate.

To, v. i., contr. for **toko,** or **tok,** dd. **ti, te,** to rest, sit down, dwell, remain, be. [Malo *ate*, Ml. d. *at*, Mg. *tueța*, *tuața*, *tuița*.] See **toko.**

Tō, redup. **toto,** d. **touo,** d. **tau,** s., a measure, equal. [Fi. *rau*.] And

Tō-naki, v. t., to compare; to place, fix; to appoint, determine, establish. See **tau.**

Tō (and see **tofi**), v. t., to push, press upon. A. **da''a,** to push, propel.

Tōa (**towa**). or **tō',** s., a (domestic) fowl, also a bird (= **manu**). [Fi. *toa*, My. *ayam*, Ceram dd. *tofi*, *towim*, Bouru dd. *tehui*, *teput*, *teputi*, Cocos Island *ufa*, bird, Tag. *ibon*.] H. **'ōf,** bird (gen. name), A. **'a'f',** gallus.

NOTE.—For Ef. **toa,** see Index under ר.

Toa i. See **roa i.**

Tōb, d., v. i., or a., to be large, great. [Epi *sombi*, Mg. *dube*.] A. **'aț'oma,** to be great.

Tob, s., c. art. **natob,** spittle. H. **tof,** E. **tafe',** to spit.

Tobaġ i. See **tabaġ i.**

Tobaroba. See **rabaraba.**

Toḅet, s., rubbish heap. Cf. H. tofet, spittle. See **tob**.

Tobu, s., a tumour, swelling. See **tubu**.

Tobu na, s., grandfather, ancestor. [Malo *tubu*, Ta. *tupu*, Po. *tupuna*.] See **tubu**.

Tobu, s., d., a **natemate**, spirit, familiar spirit, demon, d. **tobua**. [Ma. *taepo*.] A. **taifo**, vulg. A. **taif**, id.

Tōbu, d. **nōbu**, q.v.

Tofe na, s., native cloth, clothing. [To. *tapa*, H. *kapa*];

Tofe, v. i., d., to put on the **tofe**, to dress. See under **rofarofa**.

Tofi, v. t., to push. A. **da'aba**, to push.

Toġa, d. **roġ**, d. **taġa**, s., a basket. H. **ṭene'**, id.

Toġa, s., far away, also, **natoġa**, a distant place or country. H. **raḥoḳ**, S. **ruḥḳa**, E. **rĕḥuḳ**, far off, away.

Ṭoġa, for **toġa**, basket.

Toġo i, d. **toko i**, v. t., to push, thrust, and see **bakatoko i**. H. **daḥaḳ**, A. **daḥaḳa**, to push, thrust.

Ṭoġo, d. **nroġo**, for **roġo**, to hear.

Toitoi, v. t., also **teitei** (and **ṭei**), to hate. A. **'ada'**, (2), n. a. **'adw'**, (b), **'adiya**, to hate.

Tokei, or **tokai**, s., c. art., a prop, or rafter (which reaches from the ground to the ridgepole in an Efatese house); then **natokai nafanua**, the prop, i.e. chief, of the land. [Mg. *tuhana*, prop, support.] See **tiko**. A. **'atka'ā**, to prop up.

Toki, tokitoki, v. t., to gather up one's things, or pack up, preparatory to flitting. See **raku, taku-ti**. [Fi. *toki-a*.]

Toko, d. **tok**, v. i., to rest, sit down, dwell, remain, be, contr. **to**, q.v., sometimes pronounced **tuk**. [My. and Ja. *duduk*, *dodok*, Mg. *tuaṭa*, (see **to**), Fi. *tiko*, *toka*.] H. **takah**, Pu. **tukah** (Deut. xxxiii. 3), A. **waka'a**, 8, **'ttaka'a**, cf. 5, to sit (Luke xiv. 8), to remain. Hence

Tokōn, s., c. art., a village, remaining or dwelling place.

Tōki, s., an axe; and

Tōk, s., violence, force. A. **takka**, to cut, H. **tōk**, violence.

Tokalau, s., easterly wind: **tok**, remain, **alau**, on the sea.

Toko i. See **toġo i**.

Toko-naki, v. t., to strike on (as one's foot on a stone, the wind on a mountain). [Ma. *tutuki*, To. *tukia*.] See **tuki**.

Tokora, s., a place. [Mota *togara*, behaviour, *togava*, a station.] See **toko**.

Tokotoko na, s., a shark's fin: **toko i**.

Toko-ni, v. t., to kindle, set fire to, redup. **tokotoko**. A. **ḍaka'**, to kindle.

Tol, s., violence, force. See **tila**, to wrench.

Tola, v. i., to be early dawn, **toa i tola**, the cock crows, lit. crows at early dawn ;

Tola, s., the dim early dawn ; the dim distance in the sky ; and

Tolarola, id., redup. ; and, d. **tolau**, id. Hence **matōl**, d., to-morrow. H. **s'aḥar**, A. **saḥara**, to be far remote, **saḥira**, to do, or to set out at early dawn, 8, the cock crew at early dawn, H. **mis'ḥar**, the morning.

Tolĕ na, s., c. art., egg (of a bird), d. **atol mita na**, eyeball. [My. *tâlor*, Mg. *atudi*, and *antudi*, Oba *toligi*, Sulu *iklug*, Nias *ajuloh*, Poggi *agoloh*.] Mahri **ḥali**, Amh. **'ank'ilal**: the radical meaning is 'round'.

Toli a, v. t., to surpass, to go past, before, **bitoli**, v. r., d. **bilele**; to pass or go before each other, d. **tōliu sa**. See liu.

Ṭōm, or **tōm**, s., turmeric, a reddish curry powder. [Fi. *damudamu*, red, Mg. *tamutamu*, turmeric, *tumamutamu*, yellow, of an orange, saffron colour.] A. **'adoma**, to be red, H. **'adamdom**, reddish.

Tomo na, s., **tumu na**.

Tomotomoa, v. i., **tumutumua**.

Tōnako, for **taunako**.

Tontonō sa, v. i., to be perplexed, in pain or distress on account of (something): **tunu**.

Tore, or **tere** (**natuona**), s., the leg below the knee. See **tere**, mast (of ship), column.

Toro, v. i., to leak (as a canoe). A. **ta''ara**, to boil, emit water (as clouds), to leak (as a vein or vessel).

Toro, v. t., to lay down, abandon, let down, permit, **tor ea**, lay it down, &c. ;

Torò sa, lit. lays down or abandons on account of it, i. e., gives up his old mind or opinion in consequence of the evil it has brought upon him, rues ; **tor ea**, put into (as liquid into a vessel), **totor ea**, id., syn. **tutua ki**;

Toroa, v. i., to be rich, **toro** (lay down, store up, and ending a): **matoro-toro**, let down, slackened, slack (as a rope) ;

Toro-aki, for **tiro-aki**. See **tiro**.

Toro na, s., his impulse, onset, power, might. [Ma. *tara*, courage, mettle.] This same word occurs as **tere na** (comb of cock, &c.), where see the verb. A. **ṭarra** to propel vehemently, &c., Nm. **ṭarr**, free will, arbitrary power ;

Torotoro na, id., redup.

Torotoro, for **teratera**.

Torotoro, v. i., to sweat.

Torutoru, id., and

Tōru, s., sweat. See **tera**.

Tōs, d., v. i., to creep, d. for **rosa**.

Ṭot i. See **rot i**.

Totau, dd. **tatau**, **titau**, **titu**, s., a child, infant. [Mg. *zaza*.] E. **ṣa'ṣ'āe**, H. **ṣe'ĕṣa'em**, offspring.

Ṭoṭo, v., to think; and

Ṭoṭo na, s., thought, mind. See **miṭoa**.

Toto, dd. **tiso, lisoa**, v. i., to exude (as gum, juice, from plants). [Fi. *titi, titi-va*, My. *titik*, Mg. *mitete, mitate, tetevana*.] A. **naṣ'ṣ'a**, n. a. **naṣ'īṣ'**, to exude. Hence

Toto, s., a plant abounding in a milky juice, and its juice.

Totofa, d., v. i., to swell: d. **tubu**, q.v.

Toü-ġi, d. **toü-ni**, v. t., to measure, to weigh. See **tau**, d. **tau asa**, to measure.

Touo, d. for **roua**. See **roa**.

Tu, verb. pron., 1 pl. incl.; dual **tā**. See **niġita, ninita**.

Tu, v. i., to stand, dd. **ṣu, ru**, and see **su**; also to abide, dwell, be; **tu lena**, stand up straight, used also of rising up, to rise up; **tu-ri** also occurs, to stand, or abide to (or with) a person, and **tu-raki**, to stand or abide for (a person or thing). [Fi. *tu, tu-ra, turaġa*, TaSa. *turu*, Ml. P. *tu, tutu* (=My. *diri*), Sa. *tu, tutu, faatu, tula 'i, tulaġa*, Ma. *tu, tutu, turaġa*, Ha. *ku* (1, rise up, 2, to stand), My. *diri*, Mg. *juru*.] H. **nasa', so', s'et**, imp. **sa'**, cf. Hithp., E. **nasa'a**, A. **nas'a'**. See **su**, supra.

Note.—This word also occurs as **matu, batu, fatu**; and, like **toko, matoko**, and also **anĭ**, it is put after demonstratives, as **uane tu, uane matu, nin batu, nistu**, &c., lit. this or that standing or being (there or here).

Tua, v. t., to place, put down; also to give, **tua i**, give him; **tua ki**, place, put down; used also of liquids, **tua ki nia las**, put or place it in the vessel (cf. **tor ea**), make it to fall into the vessel, redup. **tutua ki, bitua ki nia**, or **bitūa sa**, to put down, also to give (a thing); with some verbs it is like 'from' as **bā tua ki nia**, go or come from, lit. go or come leaving, or putting it down, or placing it, hence **bā bituaki**, to halt between two opinions (in which the reflexive force of **bitua**, v. r., comes out), **ba bituaki**, lit. being, to go leaving it over and over again. H. **natan, ten, tet, tĕnak, matanah**, Ch. **matĕna**, H. **matat**, to give, a gift; also, to set, place.

Tua na, s., name of various relatives, as brother's wife, husband's mother, paternal grandmother, and her grandchildren, husband's sister. See under the following word. [Ml. U. *tuan*, elder brother, My. *mântuwah*, father-in-law or mother-in-law.]

Tuai, or **tuei**, a., old, ancient, and ad. long ago, also a long time hereafter. See **bakatuai**, to make long (of time), **matua**, old, mature, &c. [Sa. *tuai, faatuai, matua*, My. *tuwah*, Ja. *tuwa, bârtuwah, bâtuwah, mântuwah*, Bu. *matua*,

Mg. *antiṭa, anti* (*panahi*), *antu* (*andru*), *matua, matuṭa.*] A. **'adiyy'**, old, ancient (has the a. ending), and **'a'd'**, from **'ada,** to confer a benefit on one, to favour, &c. (see preceding word), **mo'id'**, powerful, experienced, accustomed. See **matua.** A. **'adiyy'**, **'adiyyat'**, old, ancient, Mg. *antiṭa, antu-andru* (= Ef. aliati **matua**), **tuai,** My. *tuwah,* id. Then My. *bartuwah, batuwah, mantuwah,* Ef. Mg. Po. **matua,** Ef. **matuatua,** very old, Mg. *matuatua,* a ghost (spirit of the departed, *ancestral* spirit), seem to be from this (i. e. **tuwah, tuai**), as also Ef. **tua,** and probably the Po. **atua** (**aitu**), q.v. supra.

Tua, d. **tue,** s., c.art., twins: **rua.**

Tua, v. i., to go, redup. **tutua.** Hence

Tua na, or **tuo na,** s., legs, feet. [An. *t'uo,* Ta. *su,* legs.] H. **s'uḳ**, to run, whence **s'oḳ**, Ch. **s'aḳ**, A. **saḳ'**, **suḳ'**, the legs.

Tuasil, s., giver of help: **tua,** place, give, **sila.**

Tui, pronounced also **tī,** s., as **tui Tongoa,** chief of Tongoa. [Fi. *tui.*] A. **waddu,** for **watadu.** See **tatu,** supra.

Tuba i (see **tiba i, tibè,** which is the same word), to thrust, impel, hence **tuba ki,** to send, and **natuba,** s., an arrow, also a prick, sting, or thorn; **tuba ġote-fi** (to thrust breaking) to condemn, or adjudge to die, **tuba ġori** (thrust over or in front of) to forbid, **tuba ġasi** (thrust wiping), to wipe, and redup. **tubatuba i,** to impel, propel, send off: from the idea of thrusting comes that of reaching to, touching, hence **bitub, bitubetuba,** v. r., to be touching (thrusting, lit.) each other, i. e., throughout, wholly, continually, as, **tale firi bitub,** all round wholly, **tafisafisa bitubetuba,** pray continually (one prayer touching another as in a series), and, **i mate tuba nasefa?** he died on account of what? lit. touching what; **ru tumara tuba ra,** they touch each other (as of any two things, also of one thing done in retaliation for another). See **tiba i.**

Tubara. See **tabara.**

Tubatua, v. i., to kneel, lit. to stand on the knees: **tu, batua.**

Tubu, or **tub,** d. **totofa,** or **totoba,** v. i., to swell. [Oba *tutumbu,* Ml. *timb.*] Arm. **ṣĕba,** H. **ṣabah,** to swell, **ṣabeh,** a swelling. See **tobu,** supra. This word also means to will, as Arm. **sĕba,** to will, to wish, properly to be inclined, prone, so H. **ṣabah**; hence in Efatese (cf. S., John iii. 27, and 8) **tuma,** d. **tumbu** (**ndumbu**), with the nom. suf. denotes will, **sua sponte,** as, **i tuma-na,** he of his own will or accord, as 'Who told him to do this?' **i tumana**

bat ia 'He of his own will or accord did it', Meli tubu, id.; Po. **tupu**, Mg. **tumbu**, My. **tumbuh**, see Ch. III. *d*, where also see A. **ṣaba'a**, **ṣubu**, &c., to grow.

Tubut, d., s., rainbow: lit. stand in the middle (i.e. of the sky): **tu**, **buto** (middle).

Tuġo-fi, d. for **toko i**, **toġo i**.

Tuk i, or **tuki**, v. t., to strike, beat, pound, redup. **tukituki**; and, **uru tukituki**, run quickly, lit. run beating (the ground with the feet). [Fi. *tuki-a*, To. *tuki*, Ma. *tuki*, *tukituki*.] H. **duk**, **daḳak**, A. **dakka**, **daḳḳa**, &c., beat, pound, Nm. **daqdaqa**, sound of horses' feet beating (the ground).

Tuki, in **matuki**, s., q.v., and **Mau-tukituki**, or **Mau-tikitiki**, name of a mythical person, one of the first men. [Mg. *tuki*, *matuki*. See *matūki*, supra.] See under **taki**, supra, and see **mau**.

Tu-ki-roa ki, v. t., to give in commission: **roa**, as in **boroa ki**, and **tua**, or **tu**, to give.

Tuku, v. i., to go down, sink down, also v. t., **tuku nalai**, lower the sail (of a canoe), **tuku bia kiki**, put a child in a cloth basket to be carried on the back. [Ma. *tuku*, To. *tuku*, Sa. *tuu*, Ha. *kuu*, Fi. *tuku-t'a*.] H. **s'uaḥ**, A. **saḥ'a**, **ṣaḥ'a** (**t'aḥ'a**, **taḥ'a**), to sink down, H. **s'uḥah**, **s'iḥah**, a pit, **s'aḥat**, pit, cistern, the grave. Hence

Tuk, s., a hole, enclosure like a hole or pit; and

Tukituki, s., the seven stars (because like an enclosure); and

Tūk, s., **uora tūk**, place of the pit, i.e. Hades; and

Tukituki, or **tukutuku**, s., name of a place on the western side of Efate, where is the entrance to Hades; and

Tuku, s., a fence, stake, or post (because sunk in the ground and firm).

Tukunua, s., d., a story, tradition, d. syn. **kakai**. See **takutaku**.

Tula, s., wax of the ear. [Fi. *tule*, id., *daliġatula*, deaf, Sa. *tuli*, deaf, My. *tuli*, deaf.] A. **ṣalaḥ**, deafness.

Tu-lake, v. t., to give in commission: **tua**, give, and **lake**, q.v.

Tuletule, v. i., to swing; and

Tule-aki, v. t., to swing; and

Tula, s., d. a swing, v. i., to swing. H. **dalal**, **dalah**, **talal**, A. **daldala**, and **taltala**, to swing.

Tuli for **tili**, to tell, relate.

Tuluku, for **taluko**.

Talūm i, or

Tulūm i, v. t., to swallow down, dd. **tuluġ i**, **tinom i**, **tunuġ i**, **taluġ i**. [An. *atleg*, My. *tâlân*, cf. *pârlân*, *târlân*, Mg. *telina*.] A. **lahima**, n. a., **lahm'**, 5, 8, Nm., 5, **telehhem**, to swallow down.

NOTE.—Sa. and To. 'to swallow' is **folo**, A. **bali'a**, id.

Tuma, d. **tumbu** (see under **tubu**). S. **ṣĕbu**, will.

Tuma, or **tama sok**, for **taḅa soka**: **taḅa**.

Tūma, d. **rūma**, q.v.

Tuma i, v. t., to point out with the finger, **bituma**, v. r.; d. **riū sa**. See **tiū sa**.

Tuma i, v. t., to knock (as a door), as a sign to open it. And

Tumatuma i, id., redup. [Sa. *tumu*, cf. My. *antam*.] For **tuba i**.

Tumàlu, for **tamàlu**: **taḅa, lua**.

Tuma-ni, v. t., d., to cook (in a particular way), redup. **tutuma**; and

Tumu na, d. **nubu na**, q.v., also **tomo na**;

Tumutumua, v. i., or a., formed from **tumu** by a. ending **a**. See **noba-ni**, and **noḅanoḅa**, and **matumutumu**, and **manubunubu**.

Tumana, s., a parcel: **taum i, tam i**.

Tumi, or **tomi**, v. t., to suck. [Motu *toboa*.] E. **ṭabawa**, to suck.

Ṭumi. See **rumi**.

Tu na, s., bones (of fish), and

Tutu, a., bony. [Fi. *sui*, d. *dua*, bone, *suisuia*, lean, bare of flesh, bony, rough, sharp.] A. **s'a'a**, 4, to become spiky, to be rayed.

Tuni, v. t., to heat, **tuni fatu**, to heat red hot the oven stones. [Fi. *tunu*, *tunutunu*, *vakatunu-na*.] And

Tunu, v. t., to heat, to oppress or make to suffer (as heat does); **bitunu**, to be hot, painful, dd. **bitin**, **biṣin** (see also **sinu**, **sisinu**, and **tontono**); **tutun**, to light up (torches, the evening cooking fires); and

Tunu, s., heat (of fire, or of the sun). See **sīnu**.

Tuni. See **tani**.

Tunika, s., place where the watchers at a **koro** (fish-trap) noiselessly remain: **tu**, to stand, and see **nikenika**.

Turà sa, v. t., to lengthen (as by splicing); **tutur ki**, to delay for (as for a sick man unable to walk quickly), d. **tutura ki**, **bakatura ki**, id. A. **ṭāla**, 1, 2, 4, make long, lengthen, to delay.

Turausi. See **tera usi**.

Tu-ri, see **tu**, to stand up.

Tur i, d. **turu sa**, v. t., to sew; also to nail; to go through an opening (as a ship through the entrance of a harbour);

Turi, and **turituri**, s., needle, also nail. See **turu ki**.

Turiai, or **turiei**, s., offspring, youth, children. young man, young men. A. **ḍuriyyat'** (vulg. A. pronounced **doriya**), children, offspring, progeny, from **ḍarra**, v.

Turua (a. ending **a**), full of holes (as a rock of holes through which rain percolates);

Tuturu, v. i., to drip (as eaves), leak (roof);

Tuturu, s., a drop, dripping, c. art.; and

Turu ki, drip or leak through. See also **tiri-kit.** [Sa. *tulu'i, tulutulu, faatulutulu,* To. *tulu, tului,* To. *tulu he mata* = **riri mita** (tears), Fi. *tiri, turu. titiri, tuturu, tiri-va, turu-va.*] A. **s'alla,** (3), to sew, (2), shed tears, **s'als'ala,** to drip, fall in drops, **was'ala,** to drip, drop, leak out.

Turubi-si, or d. **torobi-si** to lay down, leave, permit (d. **turuk,** permit), E. **tarafa,** A. **taraka.** See Ch. II. 14. *c.*

Turuk, d., v., to permit. A. **taraka,** id., E. **tarafa.**

Tū sa (see **tiu sa**), d. **tū-ni,** to tinge, mark, colour native cloth.

Tūsi, s., book, writing, Sa. word. See **tiū sa, tū sa,** for its origin.

Tutu, v. i., to sink: **tiū sa.**

Tutua ki, redup. of **tua ki,** to place.

Tutua, redup. of **tua,** to go.

Tutuma, redup. of **tuma-ni,** to cook.

Tutun (redup. of **tunu,** q.v., to heat), to light up (torches and cooking fires, as in the evening).

Tuuti, v. t., to tie: hence

Tuut, s., a knot. [Tah. *toti,* My. *tambat.*] E. **ṣ'abaṭa,** Arm. **ṣĕbat** and **ṣĕwat,** id.

U, verb. pron., 1 pl., excl. (contraction for **au**), d. **bu, mu** (dual **moa**). we (and) they. Mahri **hem,** or **habu,** they (Ef. **bu** = **habu** = **'mi** in **kinami, nami**).

U, s., in **näu,** d. for **usu;** also in **bitëu,** for **bitesu.**

U, verb. pron., 3 pl., they: d. for **ru** (for **nu, mu**).

U, v., d. for **ba,** q.v.; in **umai,** to come here.

Ua (**wa**), dd. **ua** (**wa**), **ui** (**wi**), interj., ad., yes: **ua,** dem.

Ua (**u-a,** and **u-wa**), s., oven, dd. **um, ubu,** of (ov).

Ua (**wà**), d. **uè** q.v., inter. ad.

Uā, s., c. art. **naua** (**nawa**), and **aua,** veins, or muscles. [Fi. *ua,* Sa. *ua.*] See **aua.**

Uā, v. i., d. for **ḅa,** and **böua,** to rain: **ḅa.**

Uā ki, v. t., d. **böuā ki,** to yield fruit; and

Uā, s., c. art. **näuā** (**nawā**), or **nuā na,** its fruit. [Ta. v., *auwa,* s., *nowa,* Oba, v., *mo ai,* Sa., v. and s., *fua,* My., s., *buwah,* Ja. *uwoh, woh,* My., v., *barbuwah,* Mg., s., *vua,* v., *mamua,* Ef. d. **ueti na** (**weti na**), Malo *vira,* Ml. P. *fana,* Er. d. *mil,* fruit, Ml. P. *mi uan,* Malo *mo vira,* to bear fruit.] See under **böua.** Arm. **fēra, fīra,** &c., H. **pĕri,** fruit; **para,** to bear fruit, E. **faraya,** id.

Ua, yes, that's it: **ua,** dem.

Ua, dem., this: with other demonstratives suffixed, either this or that, **uāna, uane, ua naġa, uai, uase, uai na, uai naġa,** and with **tu, uane tu,** dd. **uo uose, uintu.** Connected with this word are ua, uua, ui, uisa, uiko, uila, uanà. H. po, fo, this. See Ch. V. 1.

Ua'a, s., a swelling, rise, i bi ua'a (of, e. g., an island seen from a distance swelling up or rising out of the sea). See **fuata**, and **bua** III.

Uābĕ, inter. ad., d. syn. **sābĕ**, where now? where then? See **bĕ**, and **ue** (d. **ua**).

Uāġo, s., d. **uàk**, pig, swine. [Ta. *puka*, Fi. *vuaka*, Sa. *pua'a*, Malo *boi*, Epi *buc*, Bouru *babuc*, My. *babi*, Mysol *boh*.] This name seems lit. to denote 'grunter', Ta. *puka*, to grunt, *puka*, s., a pig. Compare supra **buka**, to bark, to cough (also d. **buku**). A. **fāḳa**, **fuāk'**, or **fuwak'**, to emit hoarse guttural sounds, **faḳfaḳa**, to bark.

Uai, dem., this, that; and

Uaia, id., also **uai na**, **uai naġa**, **uai ntu**, id. Compare English, this here, this 'ere, for this.

Uaka na, s., d. for **aka na**: **aka**.

Uako, interj., a mere exclamation: **ua** and **ko**, dems.

Uālu, for **ḅalu**, friend; and

Uāluḅota, s., enemy, lit. alien friend.

Uan, inter. ad., d., where? See **uē**. [Santo *veai* and *even*, id.] See Ch. V. 4. *b.*, *bb.*

Uāna, dem., that: **ua**, dem., and **na**, dem. suffixed to it.

Uànà, interj., an exclamation, see! look out! Dems. **ua**, and **na**.

Ua-nate natua na, s., d., calf of the leg, lit. fruit of the belly (liver) of the leg.

Uane, dem., this: **ua**, **ne**.

Uārīk, d. for **ḅātīk**, q.v.

Uāsa, ad., d. **āsa**, the day after to-morrow. [An. *vil'*, Epi *vĕūa*, Ml. *vis*, *wisa*, Am. *buġirua*, Santo *poġirua*, Lo *weria*, Mota *arisa*.] The word **uāsa** is **ua** (for which see **ma**), day, and **sa** (for **ra**, or **rua**, 2), 2 or 2nd: in **poġi-rua**, **poġi** is another word for day, and, in **arisa**, **ari** is still another, Ef. **ali**.

Uase, interrog. See **nafete**, **fete**, d. **feha**.

Uase, dem., this: **ua**, **se**.

Uasi, v., d. for **asi**.

Uata, s., a portion: **ḅota i**.

Uataki, v., d. for **bitaki**; and

Uataki, s., dd. **otaki**, **itaki**.

Uateaf, and d.,

Uateam, and d.,

Uateau, s., kidneys: **ua**, fruit, **ate**, liver (&c.), and **amo**, belly, lit. fruit of the liver (or inside) of the belly; and

Uateau-laso, s., testicles, lit. kidneys of the scrotum.

Uati, v., d. **ati**.

Uatu, v., d. for **atu**.

Uaua (**waua**), v. and s., for **baua**, q.v.

Uba na, or **ube na**, s., his day, d. **kuba na**. H. &c., **yom**, &c., id.

Uboġ, s., day. See **boġ**.

Ubu, s., dd. **um**, **ua**, and **of**, q.v.

Uè, inter. ad., where? dd. **ua**,

(uan, uabĕ), uai, bai, mbè. [Fi. *vei*, Sa. *fea.*] See Ch. V. 4. *b.*, *bb.* Ef. uābe, is uā be, where then? See be.

Uei, interj., an exclamation: uai.

Uēlu, v., for ḅēlu, and

Uēlu, s., a heathen function in which the men pass days in the bush, *hidden* from the women, under the direction of the natamole tabu, in order to ascertain from the natamate, in dreams, what their future fortune is to be.

Uen, s., c. art., sand: aran.

Uēnr, d. for

Uēre, d. for

Uēte, d. for fāta, q.v.

Ufea, ad., afar, far away, at a distance: d. emai, q.v.

Ui, interj., and ad., yes (that's it): ua, or uai, dem.

Ui, uia, also ḅia (pwia), v. i., or a., good, well, beautiful, &c. [Mota *wia*, Am. *wi*, Ml. *bu*, Santo *va*, Ma. *pai* (*whakapaipai*, to adorn), Sula *pia*, Ceram *fia*, My. *baik.*] H. yapah, to be fair, beautiful, Pi. to adorn (cf. Ma. supra), yapeh, fair, beautiful, good, excellent.

Uiko, interj., exclamation: ui, interj., and kọ, dem.

Uila, interj., exclamation: ui, interj., and la, ad.

Uili na, s., d. for kuli na, the skin.

Uiroa, s., a crooked kind of yam: biri, tafirofiro.

Uis, or uisa, interj., and ad. yes: ui, and sa, dem.

Uisi, v., for ḅisi, to take with the hand.

Uisi, uisiuisi (wisiwisi) d. ḅisiuisi, d. ḅisi, d. ḅusiwusi, v., to make, to work, ḅisi ekobu, make a house, uisiuisi ki, work at, nauisian, work, or act of working. [Sa. *osi*, Ja. *yasa*, Mg. *asa.*] H. ʻasah, n. a. maʻăseh (work), to make, produce by labour.

Uisiki na, s., elbow, or anything, as a corner, like an elbow, uisiki aru na (or, naru na), rump of the arm, d. maġo naru na, heel of the arm; uisi, for bisi, s., q.v., and prep. ki.

Ula, s., a maggot. [Sa. *ilo*, My. *ulat*, Mg. *uliṭa.*] E. ʻeṣ'e, vermis, ʻaṣ'ya, vermes producere (Ex. xvi. 23 (4), Acts xii. 23): A. ʻut'aṭ: see ṁata.

Uli, for uili, kuli, skin. Mahri gotl. See kuli na.

Uli, or ul i, v. t., dd. oli, auli, uili, to take the place of, to substitute for, to barter for, buy. See biauli, d. bioli, v. r., and bauli, faulu; also, c. art., naulu, s., barter, and redup.,

Uliul, id., and especially in the phrase uliul nako, substitute the appearance (or face) of some other person for his own to deceive (demons were supposed to do this). [Mg. *vidi*, *mividi*, to buy, Fi. *voli-a*, id., *volivoli*, to trade or barter,

Santo *uliul*, give for, buy; Ha. *ouli.*] A. ʿāṣʹa, to do or give something for another thing, 2, 3, id., 4, id., 5, accept one thing for another, 8, substitute one for another; ʿawiṣʹ, one (person or thing) in place of another, in place of, maʿuṣʹat, what is given for another thing (i. e. one thing given for another thing, Ef. faulu, id.).

Uli na, s., leaf, leaves, also ulu; and

Ulua, v. i., or a., to put forth leaves, to grow up (of plants and hair), and redup.,

Uluulua, id., also to be full of leaves, to be hairy, hence lulu na (for uluulu na), hair. [Ha. *ulu*, *uluulu.*] See lu lulu, &c. A. ʿala, n. a. ʿaluwʾ, H. ʿalah, to go up, whence A. ʿilawat, the head, H. ʿaleh, leaf, leaves, ʿōleh, sprouting forth, growing up.

Ululuia, ululia, and lulia. See alialia.

Uluma, s., a pillow for the head. [Ha. *uluna*, To. *uluga* (*ulu*, the head), Tah. *urua* (*uru*, the head), Ma. *uruga* (*uru*, the head), id.] See Ch. II. 16. *b*, for this word for 'head', and Index under letter ר for the Semitic forms of it, and of the word for 'pillow'.

Um, s., oven, dd. ubu, &c. See of.

Uma, v., to clear for a plantation, cut down the jungle for this purpose, d. syn. beru. [My. *uma.*] And

Uma, s., a clearing for cultivation, in isuma, q.v. [My. *uma.*] A. ḥʹamma, to cut; to sweep out, to clean, ḥʹimmʾ, a garden vacant of trees and fruits.

Umai, d. See banomai, bābē. [Sa. *o mai.*]

Umba i, v. t., to cast on it, umbaki, v. t., to cast a thing, d. ḅi. E. haypa, to cast.

Umkau, d. makau, or mukau, a cluster, gathering, hence d., many, all: kau.

Un, s., a fish scale. [Sa. *una*, id., Ma. *unahi*, Ha. *unahi*, to scale a fish, fish-scale, My. *unus*, to pull out.] H. ḥalaṣ, A. ḥʹalaʿa, to pull out, pull off.

Una, v., to cover or bury itself in the sand or mud (of a snake, and an eel-like fish which does so);

Una ki, v. t., to make to bury itself in the ground (a post or fence stake);

Una, s., an eel-like fish that burrows or buries itself in the sand;

Una, s., a post, or fence stake. H. ʾomnah, column, post, stake (because supporting).

Unu, s., ghost. See anu.

Uo, dem., d. for ua.

Uo, for bo, mo. See mo, bo.

Uokati, v., for boka-ti; hence

Uoka, chapped, sore (of the hands, as from striking or chopping with an axe, &c.).

Uoki, s., an axe. A. **waḳiʻ**, a sharp cutting instrument.
Uol, s., c. art., a bed; and
Uolis i, v. See **ḅolis i, mauol**, &c.
Uol. See **ḅol, ḅolo.**
Uolau. See **ḅolau, böuolau.**
Uolo, interj., exclamation. [Fi. *uala.*] See **uoro.**
Uon, dem., d. for **uane.**
Uon, v. for **ḅon.**
Uonda, s., d. **uete.**
Uontu, dem., **uon, tu**: d. for **uanetu.**
Uora, v., and
Uora na, redup. **uorauora na**, s., and
Uoratan, s. (**uora**, sprout, **tano**, of the ground), a plant that springs up of its own accord (without being planted or sown); fig. a person without friends or connexions to avenge him, **i bi uoratan ba faku sa**, he is a person without friends, pluck him up (i.e. uproot, or kill him). See **ḅora** II.
Uora, or era, s. See **ḅora** i.
Uorausi, d. for **uru usi.**
Uori, uoriuori, mauori. See **bori.**
Uoro, and **auoro**, interj., exclamation (d. **uolo**): **uo**, dem., and **ro**, dem., and **a**, as in **ako, ake**, interj.
Uosa, uosauosa, uosaġoro. See **ḅosa, ḅosauosa, ḅosaġoro.**
Uose, or **uos**, d. **uohe**, s., oar, paddle. See **balu-sa.** [Ml. *bos*, Epi. Bi. *voho*, Fi. *vot'e*, Ta. *vea*, Fut. *foi*, Sa. *foe*, My. *dayuġ*, Mg. *fi-vui*, Bisaya *bugsai.*] A. **miḳdafʼ, migḍafʼ, miḥdafʼ, miḳḍafʼ**, Amh. **maḳzaf**, A. **ʻʻadufʼ**, oar.
Uose, dem., d. for **uase.**
Uota, or **uot**, s., c. art., **nauota**, or **nauot**, a chief, lord, husband; the chief idol of the Efatese. [Mg. *vali*, or *vadi*, husband or wife, one of a pair, Fi. *wati*, husband, or wife, Tah. *fatu*, Ha. *haku*, chief, lord, Ml. P. *mar*, Santo *mul*, chief, lord.] A. **baʻala**, to become a husband, or wife, **baʻlʼ**, husband, or wife; in South Arabia, lord, also name of an idol; H. **baʻal**, lord, husband, Arm. **baʻal, bĕʻel**, E. **baʻalĕ**; **bel (Bel)**, chief idol or god of the Babylonians; Baal, c. art., lord, an idol of the Phoenicians, their chief deity, **Baal** also occurs in pr. nn. as מְתוּבַעַל, 'man of **baal**', cf. Ef. **Mari uota** which probably means 'man of **uota**'.

NOTE. Among the Efatese a face was cut or carved usually upon the arm near the shoulder-joint, but sometimes on the chest of many of the people, called **uota**, or **narai nauota** 'the face of uota', and the same was also carved upon the **naḅeas** erected in every village in the public worship ground. Another form of this word in Efatese is **fatu**, thus **Mare uota**, pr. n., is also in one village **Mare fatu.** The great conical rock (about which there is a myth) in the sea fourteen miles north of Efate is called **Uota.** It has the shape of the ancient Semitic Baal pillars, and the Efatese in passing it used to lower their heads or veil their faces. It is also called **Uota-n-mānu,** or **Fatu-n-mānu. Mānu,** multitude, denotes also 'abundance', 'wealth,' and **Uota-n-mānu** seems to mean **Uota** of wealth, or plenty, i. e. who gives wealth, or plenty to his worshippers. **Uota** is said to have a wife: a natural cave on the coast of Efate opposite to the idol is called the wife of **Uota.**

Uota, uotauota: for **ḅota, ḅotauota.**

Uoti, d. for **uti, oti.** See **uti.**

Uotu, s., a mark; hence

Uotuuotu, a., having marks. A. **nabat'u,** mark.

Ura, v., in, **masi ura ki,** to scoop up water, sprinkling (someone); and

Ura, s., c. art. **niura,** dew, or rain water on the foliage of plants (from its sprinkling and wetting people). H. **yarah,** sprinkle, to water, hence **yoreh,** rain, lit. sprinkling.

Ura, s., lobster, prawn. [Sa., Ha. *ula,* Ma. *koura,* My. *ud·aġ,* Ja. *uraġ,* Mg. *urana* (*uranurana,* eating greedily).] H. **ḥawar,** to be white, become pale, A. **ḥara,** to be bleached, &c., 4, to eat greedily, **ḥawar',** Nm. **ḥaur,** red leather.

Note.—Ef. **ura** seems to be so called because of the *red* colour which the lobster assumes immediately on being put on the fire to be cooked: hence the proverb, **i ti bi ura iġa miel marafi,** it is not the lobster to become red immediately (said of wickedness whose punishment does not follow at once, but will come, however slowly).

Uri na, s., the latter or after part, i.q. **muri na,** s.

Uru, v. i., to run. A. **"āra** H. **'ir),** to run.

Uru, uruuru, v. i., to growl, grumble, mutter, murmur. See **oro, orooro.**

Us, d. for **su,** v. t., to take up.

Usi (for **kusi**), v. t., follow in the track of, investigate, ask, question; and redup.

Usūsi, v. t., investigate, ask. See **takusi.** [My. *usir, maġusir, tarusir.*]

Usĭ, v. i., to hasten, **usŭ-naki,** v. t., hasten about, or as to. H. **ḥus'** (and **'us'**), A. **ḥās'a,** to hasten.

Usiraki, or **usereki,** i. e. **usiraki** (**usi** q. v. to follow), v., to follow through, hence, as ad., throughout.

Ūsŭ, s., c. art. **nausu,** d. **iu,** or **u,** a reed. [Ml. *ui,* Epi *yi,* Sa. *u,* Fut. *ġasau,* To. *kaho.*] E. **ḥasĕ,** H. **ḥes,** reed, arrow.

Uta, s., land, **euta**, **e**, prep. ashore, on land, by land. [Sa. *uta*, My. *utan* (*hutan*).] A. "uṭat', land planted with trees; and

Uta i, or **uta ki**, v. t., to load (make sink, immerse) a canoe. [Ma. *uta*, Mg. *undrana*.] And

Uta, s., c. art. **nauta**, a canoe load, cargo. [Sa. *uta*, Ma. *utaġa*.] And

Utu, **ut ī**, v. t., to fill (by immersing) a water vessel. [Sa. *utu*, *utu-fia*, Ha. *uku-ki*.] A. "āṭa ("a'ṭu), 4, to immerse.

Uta na, v. t., and **uta i**, v. t., to pay for, repay, give in payment for (pay for work done, &c.), **i utai.a**. [Ma. *utu*, s. payment, equivalent, *whakautu*, to pay for.] A. 'ada', 2, to pay for, repay.

Uti, v. t., to tie, bind; and prep., near, by, beside, as **toko utina**, stay by or beside him. H. **'anad**, id., A. **'inda**, rarely **'unda**, prep., near, by, beside.

Uti na, s., membrum virile. [Motu *use*, Astrolabe Bay (N. G.) *uti*, Ma. *ure*, To. *ule*, id.] A. 'uss', id.

Uua, (**ua**, or **uwa**), d. for **amau**, 'true', **lo-ua**, for **lo-amau**, q.v.

Uui (**uwi**, and **u-i**), s., c. art. **naui** (**nau-i**, or **nau-wi**), the yam. See **afa ki**.

Uulu, v. i., also **uilu** (**wulu**, **wilu**), for **ḅilu**, q.v., to dance. [Ml. U. *velu*, Malo *velu*, Motu *mavaru*, Ha. *mele*.] H. **maḥol**, and **mholah**, dance, dancing, from **ḥul**, or **ḥil**, to go round, also to dance (in a circle).

Uusike, and **uisiki**, q.v., elbow.

INDEX OF SEMITIC WORDS

PRELIMINARY NOTE

It is very possible that some words may have been omitted inadvertently from the following Index. And it is to be observed that it has not been attempted to give a word as a rule in more than one Semitic language, though it may occur in all. Nor are the Semitic verbal noun-forms given with the verb, except occasionally: for these the reader may consult Ch. III, and the Dictionaries under the words given. Also as a rule only the Efatese words are given: by looking up these in the Dictionary the words in other Oceanic dialects can be sufficiently found. The Semitic words, in the Index in their native dress, are given transliterated into the Roman character in the Dictionary.

In the Dictionary the servile ending **t** (for which see Chs. II, IV) is usually represented thus, **liko-ti**, **luku-taki** (the finals **i** and **ki** being the transitive particles as explained in Ch. IV): but in the Index the hyphen is omitted. The Dictionary would have been greatly enlarged had all the Efatese words derived from verbs and adjectives by the formative ending **an** (in one dialect pronounced **en**) been inserted, as a derivative is regularly formed from every verb and adjective in the language, as explained in Ch. IV.

א

אוֹ, אַו, أَوْ, ܐܘ; **ko, ki-te.**

ኦ; **O.**

أَبٌ, אָב, אַבָּא; **ābŭ, āfa, tama,** Mahri *hab, haīb, ḥeib.*

אוד, אָבַד; **buele, bole;** Mandaitic אויד.

אָבָה, أَبَاءَةٌ, أَبَاءٌ; **lobu.**

אבן, አብን ; እብን; **fat, fatu.**

אֵבֶר, אֶבְרָה; **afaru, ofari.**

እጓል (v. عَجِل).

أَدٌ, or يَدٌ; **aru, faru** (hand).

أَدَى, أَدِيٌّ, **uta ia, uta na.**

أَذَنَ : أُذُنٌ, إِذْنٌ, n.a. أَذَانٌ, أَذَانَةٌ, (pl. آذَانٌ), אוֹדֶן, אוּנְה, ܐܕܢܐ, እዝን, אֹזֶן, אָזְנֵי; toġo, doġo, roġo; liġa, talĭġa.

אֲדַמְדָּם, أُدْم; tom, ṭom.

إِدِر, אָדַר, אַדִּיר; telatela, ma-tulu.

אָוָה (v. عَوَى); ao, au, bakau, bakauĕ.

آوِنَة; fonu.

אֱוִל, אֱוִל, غَزَلَ, ܚܠܐ, غَزَلَ; sali, sali a.

أَزْر, مِئْزَر; seri, miseri.

ܣܡܐ, ܣܡ; ܣܡܐ, ܣܡ;

حَدّ (Vulg. for أَحَد), (sikai=חדא, حَدَّة);

אֶחָד, አሐዴ, وَاحِد, חַד, חדא, Amh. *ande*, Tig. *ade*; iti, sa; Mg. My. *isa, asa*;

وَاحِدَة, חדא, Amh. *andit*; sike, tika, tesa, teha, sikai; Mg., Sumatra *isaka, sara, sadah*, &c. Cf. אחת (ד elided), for אַחֶדֶת, አሐቲ for አሐዴቲ, m. አሐዱ.

אָחַז, أَخَذَ [تَأَخَّذَ], Imp. خُذْ; ḥisi, Mg. *hazuna*, and *tazuna*; Arm. אֶחָד, አኀዘ, አኀዝት (n. a.).

אָחַר, أَخَرَ (the ' quiescent in Aramaic); ġere, kusu, kihi, kisi, kui, bui, muri, busi, uri, mauri, nabis, nakis, tēr.

أَيّ, אֵי, interrogative; sei, he, fei, ē, sē (and see safa); with nom. suf. pronoun, se-ġamu, se-ġara, or seara, interrogative, which or who of you, or of them? and indefinitely, some or any of you, or of them; and see كَأَيِّ; and taka, وَمَن (وَ, and مَن, ai, interrogative, and k 'as').

إِي; ei (ei a, ei eri).

אִי, ኢ; ī (ëi, ewo, īs).

אִיהוּ, אִי הוּא; io (io re), ia.

أَيْمُ, Mod. A. *ama*; safa, sefa.

أَكَلَ, 1, 3, 4, أَكَّلَ, אָכַל; kani, kana, baġani, faġani, baġa, faġa, finaġa, kainaġa, kani-ana, kunuti.

آلْ (el, a, or l-), הַ, Phoen. *a*, article; na, a, la, in, ni, ra, ta.

أَلّد, see وَلَدَ.

أُلَى, إِلَّا (yla, ila), &c., אֵל, אֵלֶּה, እሉ, እላ, Amh. እለ, እነ; era, ra, la, li, nara, inira, niġara, Mg. *izareu*: libuis, see بَعْض.

אֵרוּ, אֲרֵי, אִלּוּ, ܗܐ, הֲרֵי, ܗܐ ܟܠ, Assy. *ullu*; eri, ero, eru, ra, ri, ro, ru, arai, aroġ, erik.

أَنْفٌ; **meta, manta.**

آنِق; **mina.**

እንቍላል, Mahri *ḥali*; **natole, atol** (Poggi *agoloh*).

إِنْسَانٌ, إِيسَانٌ, אִישׁ, أُنَاسٌ, אֱנוֹשׁ, אֲנָשָׁא, نَاسٌ, نَاتٌ; **nata, ata, ita, nata-mole,** &c.

אָסַף, יָסַף; **safe, sifa, misafe, bisif, bisab.**

אָסַר, ܐܣܰܪ; **sel i.**

אֵפָה, مِيفَى; **ubu, of, um, ua** (**uwa**).

אֵפוֹ, פֹּא, פֹּה; **ua, uo, be.**

אָפֵל, אֹפֶל, أَفَلَ, أَفِنَ, and cf. H. פּוּן; **melu, fanu.**

أَصْرٌ, 3, 6; **sere, bisere, bakasere, masere.**

אָרַב, אֲרֻבָּה; **rafe, rafe-aki, rafēna, rafeana, rofe, raf,** d. **rau, kalau, kolau** (d. **nalau**), **kalum̄i.**

אָרַג; **taraġ**, Maori *raġa*.

إِرَى, אָרָה, ሐረየ; **lai a, bila i, bila.**

أَرَكَ, 5; **firaka.**

ሐረፍት; **rafite.**

أَرَضٌ, أَرْضٌ, אֶרֶץ, אֲרַע; **miles.**

إِسٌّ; **isi, is.**

(אֵשֶׁת) אִשָּׁה, אִתָּא, Emph. אִתְּתָא; **lai, lei, le, li**; Bali *luh*, Mota *iro*. See Ch. II, § 17.

أَنْتَ, أَنْتُمْ, אַתָּה, (אַבָּה), אַתֶּם, (אַכֶם), &c.; **aġo, akam,** &c., **ta,** in **niġi-ta**; Mandaitic אנאת, **naġo**: pl. (*m.* elided) أَنْتُوا, d. **kumu,** Mod. S., أَنْكُوا, *entu*, *enku*, for *an-* or *entun*, *enkum*, d. **eġū.**

2 p. pron. sing.: nominal suffix (thy), and verbal suffix (thee): كَ, **ka, k**; Ef. **k, ko, ġo, m̄a, ma,** 'thee'; **m̄a, ma,** 'thy,' Er. *ka*, *ma*, Ta. *k*, *m*, Aurora *ġa*, Pentecost *m̄a*, Lakon *ġ*[1]: verbal pronoun suffix (nom.) as preceding, E., and Himy. *ka*, but in H., Arm., A., and Assy. *ta*,[2] (as E., and Himy. *kemu*, pl.) My. *kau*, Mg. *nau* (the last two pl. for sing.); verbal pron. prefix (nom.), A., &c., *ta*, *te*, *ti*, *tu*,[3] Ef. (not *written* prefixed) **ku, ko,** Epi *ka*, *ko*, *ku*, Ml. *ke*, Pa. *ki*.

Pl.: nominal suffix ('your'), and verbal suffix ('you', acc.), A. *kumu*, *kum*, E. *kemu*, H. *kem*, Assy. *kunu*, *kun*, Arm. *kom*, *kun*, *kon*; My. *mu*, Ef. **mu** (and v. s., in one d. **kama,** 'you,' acc., in another **kem,**

[1] *ML.*, p. 125. [2] *C. G. S. L.*, p. 171. [3] Id., p. 185.

[1] Id., pp. 173–4.

in Ch. II there cited), **bu** (**mu**), **u**, **-mi** (in **kina-mi**), **u** (in **au**).

3 p. pron. pl. (used also now in Oceanic as often in Mod. S. and Amh. for sing. as well as pl.), A. *humu*, *hum*, (*himu*, *himi*), *human*, H. *hem*, *hemah*, Arm. *himo*, *himon*, *inun* (for in-*hun*), *henun*, *enun* (for en-*hun*), Mod. S. *ani* (an-*i*, for ha-en-*i*), Talm. in-*ho*, Mahri *hem*, *habu*; Ta. *in*, Ef. **ĭnĭa**, or **ĕnĕa**, **n-ĭgā**, na-**i** (for na-ia), Epi *naiu*, My. *iña*, and *īya*, Sa. *ia*, and *na*, Er. *iyi*, Mg. *izi*: Ef. d. k-**inini**, Epi n-*iga-na*, Mare n-*ubone*, *bone*[1], Ef. *k-ina*-**mi**, Santo ana-*m*, Mg. ana-*i*.

Nom. suffix (poss.), A. as above, H. *hem*, *am*, and *amo*, Arm. (*hom*), *hon*, *hum*, E. *homu*, *omu*, Mod. S. *i*; Ef. **ana**, **n**, **na**, and **nĭa**, **ña** (the vowel before the **n** merges in the final vowel of the noun), Sa. *na*, My. *ña*, Mg. *ni*, Mota *n*, *na*, Ysabel *ña*, and *a*, Dayak of South Borneo *e*[2], Epi *no*, and *na*.

Verbal suffix (acc.), A., &c., as above; Ef. **n**, **na** (and sometimes **nia**, i.e. **ña**), **a** (for **na**), **ia** (for **ina**), **s**, **sa** (for *n*, *na*), My. *ña*, Mg. *ni*, *zi*, Ysabel *ña*, *za*, Santo *na*, *nia*, *a*, *ia* (see Ef.).

Verbal pron. suffix (nom.): it is disputed as to whether the A. *-una* (3 p. pl. preterite) is the plural ending of nouns in this pronoun suffix, *C.G.S.L.*, pp. 168–70; in Mg. *ni*, My. *ña*, it is the pronoun.

Verbal pron. prefixed (nom.): *C. G. S. L.*, pp. 181–4, **ya**, **yĕ**, **yi**, **i**, **nĕ** (Syriac), of which different explanations are given: Ef. **ĭ**, or **ĕ** (not *written* prefixed but always before and with the verb), Ta.[3] *r-*, d. *t-* (written prefixed and both for *n*), Ml. *ni*, and *ti*, Am. *ĭ*, Pa. *ĕ*; these are short forms of the 3 p. pron., as Ef. **ru** (pl.), **ra** (dual), for **nu**, **na**.

To indicate when this pron. is used in the plural sense, either a different phonetic form of it is used, or there is combined with it the plural demonstrative for which see أُولَى.

[1] See *M. L.*, pp. 112–16, for the pers. prons. in a long list of Oceanic dialects.

[2] See *M. L.*, p. 125, for this suffix pron. in a long list of Oceanic languages.

[3] *S. S. S.*, pp. 140, and fol.

הָמָה, هَمْهَمَ ; mu, fu, mamamami.

هَمَزَ ; ḅosa, uosa, taḅosa, ḅosa (-lot).

هَنَ ; sera-roġo, roġo, or ṭoġo.

הָפַךְ, هكو, أَفَكَ, הֲפַכְפַּךְ, הֲפֵכָה ; baġobaġo, baġobaġōa, baġobaġōra (Po. *piko, fo'i, hoki*), v. Ch. V, § 9.

هَرَ, &c. ; oro, bioro, oroma ki.

هَرْهَرَةٌ (قَرْقَرَ, to laugh) ; muru, murumuru ; Ta. *maliali*.

هَتَاءٌ, هَتِيَ (هَتْ) ; atu, atuġ i, atuma ki.

هَتَفَ ; matautau.

هَتَرَ ; teratera, torotoro.

הֲרִי, v. أَلِي.

ו

وَبَلَ ; barat i.

وَبَشَ ; busa.

وَجَدَ ; kita, ġita.

وَجَّهَ, 5, 6, وُجْهَةٌ ; nako, nakonakoa ki.

وَدَعَ, fut. يَدَعُ, and cf. وَضَعَ ; täo.

وَدَّ, see وَتَدَ.

وَهَبَ, יָהַב, مَوْهِبَةٌ (הַבְהָבִים) ; mofa, mafa (Sa. *mafat*), in taumafa, *taumafatia*.

وَهَفَ ; ōf i, āf i.

وَطِئَ ; titi, titia ki.

وَطْوَطَ, وَطَ ; ḅiri, ḅiriḅiri.

وَكَا, تُكَأَةٌ, tokai, tiko, اتَّكَا, toko (תכה, q.v.).

وَكْنَ, כֵּן ; iki(na) ; Mg. *akani*.

وَلَدَ, وُلْدٌ, ወልድ, ወደ, יָלִיד, وَالِد, أَلَد, وَالِدَةٌ, יֶלֶד, ወለደ ; in this word (*a*) the first radical is dropped, e.g. in ሊደ, לֵדָה ; (*b*) the third in לֵת, for לֶדֶת, and ወለት, for ወለደት (cf. the similar elision of **d** in the numeral word for 'one'). Both elisions (*a*) and (*b*) are exemplified in Mg. *rai*, ወላዲ, 'father'; Ef. raita, Celebes *leyto*, Mg. *reni* (for *raini* ?), An. and Ml. *risi*, Pa. *lati*, Fila *leta*, ወላዲት, 'mother': nati, nani, natu (N. G. dialects, Kiriwina *latu*, Sariba *natu*), reita, ere ; kan, kanäu, kanoka, kunuti, kiliti : Ml. *anatu*, My. *anak*, *kanak* ; Mg. *anaka*, *zanaka*.

وَلِيَ, مَوْلًى ; ualu, ḅalu, balu, ḅaluna ki, ualu ; liu, tōli (Arabic 5).

وَمَسَ ; amos i, mos i, mus i.

وَمِئَ, وَمْأَةٌ ; bani, banus.

وَنَلَ ; bales i, balasa ki, tabala, tabales.

חלץ, خَلَعَ; una.

خَمَّ, 1, 4; ġoġo.

חָם, ሐመ, حَمُو, Assy. *emu*; ṁō, mona ki. Hence ተሐመወ, ታሐማ, Ef. buruma, i. e. buruma (bu- for mu-; and r for t, see Ch. II, § 13 *b*, T, r).

[Compare (?) A. حَمَا, defend, look after, guard, protect, 5, be prohibited, refrain, 6, fear, reverence, avoid, keep away from, مُتَحَامَاةٌ, inaccessus, vetitus.]

حُمَّةٌ; kona, kokona, konai(na).

حَمَى; kabe, kafini, kime, (حَمَامٌ).

حَنَكٌ; manu (cognate عنق).

حفد حَفِيدٌ (حَفِيدَةٌ); bia, ia (d.), biau; Mg. *afi*, *zafi*, My. *piyu*, *piat*, *piyud*, *piyat*.

ሐጸጸ, ሐጸ, ሐጸጽ; sos, sēsī.

חָצִיר, حَضِيرٌ; Mahri *ḥadauer*, *ḥadauwer*; atoara, natoara.

חָקָה, חָקַק (حَكَّ, هَكَّ); koi, kei, kokai, koko, keikei, ġoko, koi, koika.

חָרַר; kara, ġara, baġara i, makarakara.

חָרָב, 'a cutting instrument, axe,' &c.; karab, karam, karaf, karau, id.

حَرٌّ; on, wen, oraone (reduplicated) orain, ārān; Po. *one*, *oneone*.

حَسَّ; ara, ara i.

חָתָה; makit i, mikit, mokot.

خ

خَدٌّ, خَدَّ; àsi, asi(na).

خَالَ (mid. و), خَالٌ; alo, lolo.

خَوِصَ, 1, 4, خَوْصٌ; kisa, ġisa, kisakisa, ġisakisa, nakisa, takis, mila-kisa.

خَاطَ, خِيَاطٌ; kiato.

خَالَ (mid. ي), خَالٌ; (see s.v. aloara, aloaloara); Sa. *ila*.

خَيَّمَ, خَيْمَةٌ, خِيَمٌ; d. hiṁa, suma; ema, and um (in katema, imrum).

خَلَعَ; malei (مُخْلِعٌ); Sa. *alei*.

خُضْخُمٌ; ra-kum, ra-koma, rakua.

خَمَسَ, خَمْسَةٌ; Mahri *ḥomo*, Soc. *ḥema*; lima, Epi *sima*, *yima*, Ceram *hima*.

خَفَقَ; kufaġufa.

خَصْيٌ, خُصْيَةٌ; laso, lasoa.

خَرَطَ, חָרַט, ܚܪܛ; ġorot i.

خَتَرَ, خَتَارَةٌ; katak, My. *kantal*.

ط, ט

ጠበሠ; tumi, tomi.

طَبَعَ, طَبْعٌ; tomo, tumu, tuman i, matumutumu, noba (d. ob), nubu, nobanoba, noban i, manubunubu, tutuma, tumutumua.

طَبِيعٌ, طَبَعٌ; leba, lebalebā, lebalebara, طَبْعَانٌ.

طَهَا, طَهْوٌ; tāö, tāön i, tāün i.

طَعْمٌ; malau, My. *lamu.*

طَهُرَ, טָהֵר; tāre, taretare, matiratira.

ظَهَرَ, ظَهْرٌ, ደኀረ; taku, Po. *tua.*

طَوَى, טָוָה, ጠወየ; taui.

طَالَ (mid. و), 1, 4, 5; tura, tutura, bakatura.

ጠፈሠ; lume, lumes i, buluma, bulima.

طَوَافٌ; tōbu, d. nōbu; vulgar طَافٌ.

طَارَ (mid. ي), طَيْرٌ, طَائِرٌ, طَيَّارٌ flying, طَيَّارَةٌ navigii genus; tiri, riri, rīri, lai (N. G., Motu *lara*, Galoma *lola*, Sinaugoro *laia*), mitiri, taroa, teroa, lea ki, lelea ki.

Note on the word lai, sail, Mg. *lai*, N. G. *rer*, *lara*, *laia*, Po. *la*, *ra*, My. *layar.* My. *layar* is both v. and s., a sail, and to sail, Mg. *milai*, to sail. Ma. *rere*, to fly, *reia*, or *rereġia*, to be sailed over: *reia*, i.e. *re-i-a*, and *rereġia*, i.e. *rere-ġ-i-a.* So My. *layaġ*, to fly, is *laya-ġ*, and *layar* is *laya-r*, the original radical *r* having become *y* (as in the word *tiyaġ*, Ef. tere, mast), and the original servile *-t*, *-ġ* (as in Ma. *rere-ġ*), and *-r*: see Chs. II and IV for this, and for the Ma. *-ia.* In Ef. and Mg. *lai*, Ma. *reia*, the radical *r*, in My. *y*, has disappeared, as also in To. *le*, Ef. lea, q.v. in Dict.

طَاسَ (mid. ي), طَاسٌ; lāsa.

طَانَ, طَانٌ (mid. ي); tan i, tano, tanu, tun i, tanotanoa, tanum i, tanuma ki.

طَافَ (mid. ي), طَيْفٌ; tobu, Ma. *taepo*, vulgar A. *taif*, an apparition, a spectre.

طَيْسٌ; tas, tasi.

طَنَّ; taġi, taġis i.

طَمَّ; tama i, taba i, atama.

ጠዐመ, טָעַן, טְעֵן, طَعَنَ, 1, 8, ጸሐለ, ጸዐለ; taġi, tine, tiena, taġo, mitaġa, taġotaġo, mitaġataġa, taġia ki, miten.

طَفَّ, طَفٌّ; taḅa, tauba, taf i.

dd. are, ale, ane, Sariba (N.G.) *kate*.

كَبُر, كَبِير, ከቡር; kabuer, ġabuer, kabuera, abura, abuera, takuwer.

كَذَا; kita, kite.

كَهُر; bakāru, fakāru.

כָּוָה, כַּו; kaua, kaukaua.

كَوْكَب, כּוֹכָב, ܟܘܟܒܐ, Mahri *kabkob*, &c.; ṁasöi or masöi, &c. See Ch. II, § 14 (*a*), and (*c*) (at end). N.G., Galavi *gwamegwame*, Dobu *kuadima*.

כּוּן; kona, ġona.

كَارَ (mid. و), 1, 8; kārī, takārī.

كَارَ (mid. و), 2, גּוּר; kuru, ġuru, ġurua, kuruma ki, makara, ta-kāra, taġura.

ܟܣ; ġaiġai.

كَيْ, כִּי; ka, ġa, k-, (T. *k*-).

ܟܣ, interrogative particle; ka, ko.

كَأَيِّ (ex كَ et أَيّ), quot? tot, how many? so many, literally 'as what?' (= כַּמָּה, Ta. *keva*, *kuva*); Guadalcanar *ġisa*, Mahaga *ġiha*, Rotuma *his*, An. *ehet'*, Po. *hia*, *fia*, Ef. bisa, fisa, bia, Mg. *firi*, Java *pira*.

كَيْفَة, that what? for what purpose? for what? why? kua (kuwa), ġua? d. syn. kasafa, kasā? ka, and sefa, or safa, what?

ከመ, כְּמוֹ, كَمْ; kama, kumu, kamu, mu, kem.

كَنَعَ; kana, kano.

כָּפַף, כַּף; kaf, kai.

كَفَّ, 1, 2, kafa i, kafa-raġo, d. transposed faka-raġo.

كُبَّة, كُفَّة; kubeġa; To. *kubeġa*, Ma. *kupeġa*, Sa. *'upeġa*, Ha. *upena*, Marq. *upeka*, Tah. *upea*.

ܟܦܐ, כַּף; kabě.

كَفَا, transposed كَفَا; kaba, kabās i, kobās i, transposed bakās i.

كَرِهَ; karei, ġarei.

כָּרַע, A. (transposed) رَكَعَ, q.v.; kola, kolo.

كَفَحَ; kafis i.

كَرَا, كَرْو, ክርየ; kili, ġili, kāli; Fi. *kali-a*, *kali-va ka*.

كَرْكَرَ, cf. كَلَّ, 7; ġalakala.

כְּפוֹר; bōlo.

كَرَّ, كَرْكَرَ, ከለለ, &c., kelu, kelet, kelekelet, &c.; Mg. *hudina* (*herina*), My. *ġuliġ*, &c.

ל

لِسْنٌ, لِسَانٌ, pl. لُسْنٌ, أَلْسُنٌ, أَلْسِنَةٌ, לָשׁוֹן, לְשֹׁן, ልሳን, كحم, Mahri *lesa*; Mg. *lela*, My. *lidah*, Fut. *rero*, Sa. *alelo*. For Ef. **mena**, v. نَمَل.

מ

مَا, מָה, Himyaritic *ba*, *va*, neut. interrog. pron.; **ba, fa, ma.**

מ־; **m-**, in all Semitic languages, prefixed to verbal nouns; **b-, f-, m-** (**bo, mo, fo, uo, o**); and in all Oceanic dialects, in like manner.

مَاذَا, vulgar A. maḍe; **fite, feha, uase (wase).**

مَاةٌ, مَاءٌ, מוֹא, מֵי; **mē, mēa.**

مِائَةٌ, Catafogo *ma'at* (مائة), ምእት, Amh. *mato*; Tambora *mari*, N. Brit., and D. of Y. *mara*, Santo *vel*, Bouru *bot*, *utun*, Amboyna *hutun*, Malekula *ġut*, Savu *natun*, My. *ratus*, Ja. *atus*, Mg. *zatu*, Carolines *puku*, *fok* = 100, hundred.

Note the **nunation**, and see Ch. II, § 13.

مَدَحَ, مَدَةٌ; **bute (lua i).**

مَهَهٌ, מָהָה, مَهَهٌ, مَةٌ; **mäomäo.**

مَهَلَ, مَهْلٌ; **mēlu, meliki.**

מוג, **mok, mokemok.**

مَوْدُون (وَدَنَ); **mïto, d. būru.**

مُوزٌ, ሙዝ; **ātě, aṣě.**

مَانَ, مَؤُونَةٌ; **maua.**

مَاصَ, مَوْصٌ, مَوْصَةٌ; (My. *basuh*, Mg. *uza*), **fafano, banol i, balos i, &c.**

مَارَ, مَوْرٌ; **ḅala.**

مَاسَ, مُوسَى, pl. مَوَاسِي; **mas i, māsĭ.**

מוּשׁ; **mus i, mus ki.**

مَاثَ (מָסַס); **māt.**

مَاتَ, مَوْتٌ; **màtě, tamàtě.**

ማይ, מֵי, מַיִם, مَاءٌ; **fai, ai, wai.**

مِيقَى; **of, ubu, um, ua.**

مَخو; **mak.**

مَالَ, مَيْلٌ; **ḅāla, fāla, ḅole, balafala.**

مَاعَ, 1, 4, مَايِعٌ; **miu, mou, miu-ura.**

مَلَّ, مَلٌّ; **malo.**

مَحَنَ, مَحْنٌ; **mān i, mā.**

مَطَا, 1, 2, 8; see s. مَتَا.

מָלֵא, مَلَأَ; **bura, burafura, biri, berat i, bakafura.**

مَلِيحٌ; **mile i, mala i, mitā ki, butā ki.**

مَنْحُوضٌ (v. نَحَضَ); **ḅakas.**

מְסָא, ܡܣܐ; misa.

מְסַס, (מָס), مَاثَ; māt'.

مَعْ, see עִם; ma, me.

مَعًا, مَعَى; mam, mim.

מְעִי, مَعْيٌ, pl. أَمْعَاءٌ; amo, maḃĕ.

مَعَطَ; m̃ut.

مَعِضَ, مَاعِضَ; maito, maieto, maietoa.

مَعْمَعَ; maimai.

مَغْمَغَ; mai a (Sa. *mama*).

مَعُقَ, 5; timbu: see عَمُقَ.

مَعَرَ, مَعِيرِ, مَغَرَ; miöl.

مَقَطَ, مَقْطٌ; mut, mot.

መርሕ; merak i, meraġ, meramera.

مَرُوٌّ, and امرءٌ, מְרֵא; mare, vir, mā, vir, mera, homo, m̃ane, 'male,' ano(w)ai, ano(w)i, for (m)ano(w)a(n)i, Ceram *manowai*, Ml. *banman* (redupl.), 'male, husband,' Oba *mera*, Malo *m̃era*, Santo, &c. *man(i)*;

مَرْءَةٌ, إِمْرَأَةٌ; màtu, bite, fafine; *but*, *fid*, *baine*, &c., kuruni, *yale-wa*, *yare-vin*, &c.: see Ch. II, § 17.

מְרִיא; mera (kolau).

مَرْئِيٌّ; merai.

مَاصِعٌ; mitei.

መጸጸ; mas, masu.

مُرَيْطَاءُ; marita.

مَرَخَ, מָרַח; maru.

מָרַט; maratĕ, marĕtĕrĕtĕ.

مَرْكَبٌ, መርከብ; borau, rarua.

מַעֲרָכָה, מַעֲרָכוֹת, מַעֲרוֹת, (עָרַךְ); fara, farafara, bifara ki.

መረቀ; maraġ, bure i.

מָרַק; burē.

مَرَسَ; marasa, maresĕresĕ.

מָשַׁח, مَسَحَ, מָשְׁחָה, (مَعَسَ, مَعَشَ, مَغَشَ); masa, masamasoa ki, masamasanta, mas, maso, masi.

مَشَى; masa.

מָתַח, ܡܬܚ, مَدَّ; bito, bitos i.

مَتَا, and مَطَا (final و), 1, 2, 8; miti, mitimiti.

מָתַן, مَتُنَ; matu ki;

מָתְנַיִן, مَتْنَانِ, مَتْنٌ, 'the back'; na matu na: matu ki, den. v. as in ūna ki (fr. אָמְנָה).

ነ, נ, ن

נָא; na, nī.

נָאָה, נָוֶה; no, nono, binoĭnoĭ, binofinoĭ; Sa. *nofo*.

نَانَا; neinei, maneinei.

עֶפֶל, عَفِلَ ; **buli, bulia, mabulu, mafulu.**

عَضَبَ ; **tef i, tetefi.**

עֶצֶר, עֲצָרָה, أَعَاصِيرُ ; **tere, teretere.**

عَفَصَ, عَفَسَ, 1, 8, (cf. חבש, **fis i**) ; **ḅos i, ḅus i, fis i, fifi, tafifi.**

عَفَرَ, عِفْرِيّ, &c. ; **fuluara.**

עֵץ, אָע, ዕፀ, ዕፀው, أَعْضَاء, عَصًا, عَصَاة ; عَصًا, عَضْوٌ, עֵצָה ; **kàsu, kàs, kau.**

عَقَّ, عَقْعَقَ ; **akò, aka, koa, aka, eka, uaka (waka), makå, makaka, kaka.**

عَقَبَ, עָקֵב ; **baġo, bako, maġo, baġa.**

עָקָה, מַעֲקֶה, عَقِيّ ; **ḅāka.**

عَقَلَ, 1, 2, 5, עָקַל, עֲקַלְקַל ; **kilakila, takel, takelkel, taġelī, taġeliġeli.**

عَرِيَ, עָרָה, عَرًا, מַעַר, מַעֲרָה, مُعْرًى, مُعْرًى ; **alia, li, lo, mala, malo, malmal, malamala, malu,** &c.

عَرِيمٌ ; **rūmå, tūma,** (transposed) **marou.**

עָרַךְ, מַעֲרָךְ, מַעֲרָכָה, מַעֲרֶכֶת ; **fara, bifara ki,** My. *baris.*

عَرَفَ, عَرَّافٌ, 'diviner' ; **arīfōn,** 'diviner,' عَرْفَان, 'sciens.'

عَرَضَ, عَرُضَ, تَعَرَّضَ, and تَأَرَّضَ ; **las i, lasilasi, tilas i, bakatilasi, beles.**

عَرَتَ, عَرَّتَ ; **ori,** My. *urut.*

עָשָׂה, מַעֲשֶׂה ; **uisi (wisi, wisiwis), ḅisi, ḅusiwusi.**

عُشٌّ ; **uti.**

عَشِقَ ; **sikot, sikut i.**

عَشَرَ, עֶשֶׂר, ܥܣܪ, ܥܣܪ̈ܐ, &c. ; Tah. *ahuru,* Rotti *hulu,* Sa. *fulu,* Ma. *ġahuru,* Vila and Meli *ġafuru, nofuru,* Santo *ḥbulu, nafuru,* &c., Mg. *fulu,* My. *puluh.*

عَتَّ, عُتَّةٌ ; **ula** ; عَتَاء, **ṁāta** (ṁ for ġ, Fut. *ġata,* Fi. *ġata,* Ma. *ġāta*).

عَتَلَ, 1, 3 ; عَتَلَةٌ, **tila, tilas i.**

عَتَمَ, عَتَمَةٌ ; **tamtam.**

عَتَقَ, *b*, 3 ; **tiki.**

עָשָׁן, عَثَنَ ; עשן, عَثَّنَ ; **asu, àsua.**

عِرْقٌ (v. عَرَقَ) ; **āüa,** (a-, art., and ua), **ua,** Bu. *urök.*

غ

غَبَى, see חָבָא.

غَبَنَ ; **afina, afila, afin i, afit i, afis i.**

غذف (v. قذف, and جذف).

قَاحَ, 6, (قَاعَ), mid. و ; ḅoa, tamo, nabo.

فَاخَ, &c., פּוּחַ ; bok, bokauok.

פוּץ ; busa i, fusa i, mafusai.

פִּן ; fānu, fān (d. mēlu, see אֲפֵל).

פּוֹר, inf. of פָּרַר, (cg. פּוּר) ; bori, mauori, boriuoris i, bororis i, boris i.

فَخْذ, thigh ; cf. Santo *wado*, Ef. mäo, d. fäa, My. *päah*, Mg. *fe*, thigh.

فَحَمَ, فُحُم, فَحْمَة ; boġ, boġi, boġian, ṁoġ, Kiviri (N. G.) *pom*.

פָּלַל, Hithp. ; fira, firan i, bifira.

פּוֹל, ፈለፈለ, ܦܠܦܠ ; ṁul i, mulimul.

פָּלַשׁ (cf. פָּלַךְ, فَلْكَة, Talm. פִּלֵךְ): bulus i, fulus i, bulo, tafolo, tafulus, filora, bulora, bologa, tafiloġa ; Sa. *fulisi, tafuli, milosi* ; My. *pulȃs. pulir*, Mg. *fuli, fulesina, mamulisa*.

פָּנָה ; bano, ban, (contracted) bā.

פָּלַג, فَلَجَ ; milaġ.

פָּעָה ; bio-so, ra-fio-so.

פָּעַל, فَعَلَ, فَعْلَة ; bolo, bolofolo, bolos i.

פָּעַר, ܦܥܪ, فَغَرَ ; ṁola.

פִּסֵּחַ ; bito.

فَضَّ, قَصَّ, قَصَى ; basu, base, ḅasul i, basera ki, mafasu, moȧs, taḅasuli.

فَقَعَ, 2, 3, bisi, 3, fisi (cf. اِفْقَعَ).

فُوق ; buka, bukas i.

فَقَأَ, 1, 5 ; baku, mafaku, tafakka, tafaġka, (tafakka), 5, تَفَقَّأَ.

فَقَحَ, فُقَّاح ; buġa, fuġa, buma, fuma.

فَقْم (فَغْم) ; bamu, babu.

فَقَعَ, فُقُوع ; monamona.

פָּרָה, פְּרָא, ፈረየ, ፋረየት ; 'to fruit, bear fruit'; Arm. ܦܐܪܐ, פֵּירָא, H. פְּרִי, ፍሬ, 'fruit'; boüa, ua (wa), d. weti, Malo *vira*, Sa. *fua*, Mg. *vua*, My. *buwah*.

فَرْخ (אֶפְרוֹחַ), ܦܪܘܓܐ ; manu, wose-man, se-mani, My. *buruġ*, Mg. *vuruna*, Ja. *manuk*.

פָּרַח ; ḅora, fara, ōra, uora, bakauora ki.

فَرَى, تَفَرَّى; ḅora i, ḅorai, borōra, bora, uora (ora, era), tabare, mauora, maora, maoräora, tabarebare.

פּוּר, פִּרְפֵּר, ፈርፈረ, פַּרְפּוּר; bera, fera, tabera ki, taberafera, berafera, tafar (taiar).

فَرَقَ; baros i, farofaro, barobaroa.

פָּרַע, فَرَعَ; baro, bārua, marua, būra, barorŏ.

فَرَعَ, فَرْعٌ; bau (Epi *baru*, Malo *batu*), baua, uau-a (uaua), bai, mau, taḅau, ḅau, bo, ḅo-fi, ḅefe.

פָּרַץ; biris i.

فَرَقَ, فَرِيق; ḅirikĭ.

فَرْقَرَ; bare, barefare.

פָּרַר, הֵפֵר; biri, birifiri, tabiri, mafirifiri.

فَرَشَ, فَرْش; bilis i, bolis i, uolis i, uol, mauolĭ, maolĭ.

فَتَاة, 4, أَفْتَى; maosa (mawosa), taosa (tawosa).

فَتِيّ, فَتًا, فَتًى, فَتَاء; ḅatu.

فَتَلَ, فَتْل, ፈተለ, ፋትል, ፍትሎ, ፍትለት; biri, tafirofiro; Sa. *fili, filo,* Maori *whiro,* Tah. *firi, taviri,* Bugis *bitoi,* My. dd. *pintal, bilan, pilin.*

פְּתִיל, ፈትል; mīlo, Ml. Mask. *ḅigal.*

צ, ܨ

ጸእጻእ, צֶאֱצָאִים; titu, titau, tatau, totau.

צָבָא, צָבָה; tubu, tub, tōbu, tuma, d. tumbu.

صَبَّ, 1, 5, 7, 8, and صَابَ (mid. و); luba, luba ki, maluba ki, talubaki; My. *tumpuh.*

صَبَّحَ, ጸብሐ, مصبح; mitămai, مُصْبِح.

ፀበጠ, צָבַת, צָוַת, צוות; tuut i, tuut.

צָבַע, צֶבַע, אֶצְבַּע, ጠመዐ, טָבַע; صَبَعَ, صَبَغَ, أُصْبُع; tuma, tumatuma, tiū, riū, rū, tiutiū, tutū, tutu, lulu, matiu.

צְבַע, אֶצְטַבַּע, Ch. (A., H. id.); lolofa, lum, luma, lulum, lume.

صَبَرَ, صَبْر; tau, taur i, taura ki.

צָבַר, صَبَرَ; taua.

ܨܒܬ; tabètĭ.

ጸደፈ, صَدَفَ; taruḅa, taruḅa ki, in taruḅa, taruḅa suk.

צָדַק, صَدَقَ, صَدْق, ܨܕܩ; soko, masoko, le-soko.

רָעָה, רְעָה, ܪܥܐ; ܐܬܪܥܝ; miroa, miṭoa, mintoa, minroa, mitiṭoa, ro, roro, rara (tan i), ṭara (tan i), ṭoṭo, toto.

רָעַם, see ܪܥܡ; rufua, &c.

ܪܥܠ, רָעַל, רָעַד; ruru.

رَعَصَ, 1, 4; risu, rusa, ros, nrus, risuġ i, rosaġ i, ṭosa.

רָעַשׁ, רַעַשׁ; ras, tas, res, reres, teres.

رَفَّ, رَفْرَفَ; malaflafi.

رَفَا, رَفَاءٌ; ruḃa.

رَفْغٌ; roḃa.

رَغِيفٌ; rubaki.

رَفَعَ; laf i.

רָפָה (cg. רָמָה), ܪܦܐ; roua (rowa, rowo), roa, towo, täo, tiḃe, mitäo, ro, mitefe, d. lubu, (Aneit. *erop*(*se*)), maroḃaroḃa.

رَفْرَفَ; rabaraba.

رَضِيعٌ; tasi, &c., tai na.

رَقَّ, رَقٌّ; mirārā, bakamirārā.

رَقَى, 2; raka i, rakat i.

ש, שׂ

شَجْنَةٌ, شَجَنٌ; rā, rārān, terā (te rā).

שָׁאַב, סָחָה, &c.; sau, sauf i.

سَالَ, سَأْلَةٌ, سَآلَةٌ, שָׁאַל, שְׁאֵלָה; bitali, d. bitaġo, taġo-fi.

שָׁאַף; safa, sefa, sōfa, sofa, sofasofa.

شَبَّ, شُبٌّ; subu, subua, sibi (in pr. nn.).

שָׁבַב, שְׁבָא; siba, sisiba, masiba, sibasiba.

سَبْعَةٌ, Assy. *sibit*, Mahri *ibet*; Mg. *fitu*, Santo *bitu*, 'seven,' J. *pitu*, Sa. *fitu*.

سَبَقَ, سَبْقٌ; sobu (= d. bea, precede, be first).

سَحَفَ, see סָחַף.

שְׁדֵמוֹת, שַׁרְמוֹת; tălemāt, tŭlemāt.

شَهَا, شَهْوَةٌ; sau, mesau (d. mūri), sauta ki, sautoġa.

سَاءَ (mid. و); sā, sāsāna.

شَاءَ (mid. و); sau, tumana sau ki.

سَهَا; sea, sesea, (Maġa) sesea.

شُهِلَ; siel.

ܫܡܫ; semàn i.

שָׁוָה, v. צָוָה (tau), to, towo, tōna ki, tōun i.

שׁוּחַ, שׁוּחָה, صَاخَ, &c.; tuku, tuk, tūk, tukituki.